Forensic CBT

Forensic CBT

A Handbook for Clinical Practice

Edited by

Raymond Chip Tafrate
and Damon Mitchell

WILEY Blackwell

Registered Office
John Wiley & Sons, Ltd, The Atrium, Southern Gate, Chichester, West Sussex, PO19 8SQ, UK

Editorial Offices
350 Main Street, Malden, MA 02148-5020, USA
9600 Garsington Road, Oxford, OX4 2DQ, UK
The Atrium, Southern Gate, Chichester, West Sussex, PO19 8SQ, UK

For details of our global editorial offices, for customer services, and for information about how to apply for
permission to reuse the copyright material in this book please see our website at www.wiley.com/wiley-blackwell.

Library of Congress Cataloging-in-Publication Data

Forensic CBT : a handbook for clinical practice / edited by Raymond Chip Tafrate & Damon Mitchell.
   pages   cm
  Includes bibliographical references and index.
  ISBN 978-1-119-95329-6 (cloth) – ISBN 978-1-119-95328-9 (pbk.)   1. Forensic sciences.
2. Cognitive therapy.   3. Criminal psychology.   I. Tafrate, Raymond Chip.   II. Mitchell, Damon.
  HV8073.F559467 2013
  365'.6672–dc23

                                2013014730

A catalogue record for this book is available from the British Library.

Cover image: © Andrea Zanchi / iStockphoto; Man in raincoat © Cavan Images / Getty
Cover design by Cyan Design

Set in 10/12.5pt Galliard by SPi Publisher Services, Pondicherry, India
Printed in Malaysia by Ho Printing (M) Sdn Bhd

1   2014

...for it had ever been my opinion, that no man was past the hour of amendment, every heart lying open to the shafts of reproof, if the archer could but take a proper aim.
Oliver Goldsmith, *The Vicar of Wakefield, 1766*

This book is dedicated to those practitioners who routinely work with some of society's most marginalized members. All too often, their efforts to alleviate human suffering and enhance safety in the communities in which we all live go unacknowledged.

Contents

Contributors

Jai Amrod, PhD
Algoa Correctional Center, Jefferson City,
Missouri, USA

Arnoud Arntz, PhD
Department of Clinical Psychological
Science, University of Maastricht,
Maastricht, The Netherlands
Maastricht Community Mental Health
Center, Maastricht, The Netherlands

David P. Bernstein, PhD
Forensic Psychiatric Centre "de Rooyse
Wissel," Venray, The Netherlands
Department of Clinical Psychological
Science, University of Maastricht,
Maastricht, The Netherlands
Expertise Centre Forensic Psychiatry (EFP),
Utrecht, The Netherlands

F. Michler Bishop, PhD, CAS
Department of Psychology, SUNY College
at Old Westbury, Old Westbury, New York,
USA
Alcohol and Substance Abuse Services,
Albert Ellis Institute, New York, New York,
USA

James Bonta, PhD
Public Safety Canada, Ottawa, Ontario,
Canada

Alison M. Byers, PsyD
Diversified Search, Inc., Philadelphia,
Pennsylvania, USA

Christmas Covell, PhD
Private Practice, Tacoma, Washington,
USA

Cory A. Crane, PhD
Research Institute on Addictions, University
at Buffalo, Buffalo, New York, USA

Andrew Day, MSc, DClinPsy
The Forensic Psychology Centre, Deakin
University, Victoria, Australia

Raymond DiGiuseppe, PhD
Department of Psychology, St John's
University, Queens, New York, USA
Albert Ellis Institute, New York, New York,
USA

Christopher I. Eckhardt, PhD
Department of Psychological Sciences,
Purdue University, West Lafayette, Indiana,
USA

Eva Feindler, PhD
Department of Psychology, Long Island
University, Brookville, New York, USA

Clare-Ann Fortune, PhD, PGDipClinPsyc
School of Psychology, Victoria University of
Wellington, Wellington, New Zealand

Arthur (Art) Freeman, PhD
Department of Psychology, Midwestern
University, Downers Grove, Illinois,
USA

Frank L. Gardner, PhD, ABPP
Department of Advanced Studies in
Psychology, Kean University, Union,
New Jersey, USA

Steven C. Hayes, PhD
Department of Psychology, University of
Nevada, Reno, Nevada, USA

Krista M. Holman, MA
Department of Psychology, Central Michigan
University, Mt Pleasant, Michigan, USA

Howard Kassinove, PhD, ABPP
Department of Psychology, Institute for
the Study and Treatment of Anger and
Aggression, Hofstra University, Hempstead,
New York, USA

Marije Keulen-de Vos, MSc
Forensic Psychiatric Centre "de Rooyse
Wissel," Venray, The Netherlands
Department of Clinical Psychological
Science, University of Maastricht,
Maastricht, The Netherlands

Erica King, MSW
Orbis Partners, Inc., Ottawa, Ontario,
Canada
Muskie School of Public Service, University
of Southern Maine, Portland, Maine, USA

Daryl G. Kroner, PhD
Department of Criminology and Criminal
Justice, Southern Illinois University,
Carbondale, Illinois, USA

Jennifer D. Luther, BS
Center for Criminal Justice Research,
Corrections Institute, University of
Cincinnati, Cincinnati, Ohio, USA

William L. Marshall, OC, FRSC, PhD
Department of Psychology, Queen's
University, Kingston, Ontario, Canada
Rockwood Psychological Services, Kingston,
Ontario, Canada

Kimberly Maurelli, MA
Department of Psychology, Central Michigan
University, Mt Pleasant, Michigan, USA

Harvey B. Milkman, PhD
Department of Psychology, Metropolitan
State University of Denver, Denver,
Colorado, USA

Damon Mitchell, PhD
Department of Criminology and Criminal
Justice, Central Connecticut State
University, New Britain, Connecticut, USA

Zella E. Moore, PsyD
Department of Psychology, Manhattan
College, Bronx, New York, USA

Robert D. Morgan, PhD
Department of Psychology, Texas Tech University, Lubbock, Texas, USA

Raymond W. Novaco, PhD.
Department of Psychology and Social
Behavior, University of California, Irvine,
Irvine, California, USA

Matt D. O'Brien, MSc, MA, C Psych Assoc
Rockwood Psychological Services, Kingston,
Ontario, Canada

George F. Ronan, PhD, ABPP
University of St. Francis, Joliet, Illinois, USA
Contract Psychologist, Kane County
Diagnostic Center, Batavia, Illinois, USA
Dixon Correctional Center, Dixon, Illinois,
USA

Tanya Rugge, PhD
Public Safety Canada Ottawa, Ontario,
Canada

Lori Seeler, PsyD
University of St. Francis, Joliet, Illinois, USA
Contract Psychologist, Kane County
Diagnostic Center, Batavia, Illinois, USA
Dixon Correctional Center, Dixon, Illinois,
USA

David J. Simourd, PhD
Algonquin Correctional Evaluation Services,
Kingston, Ontario, Canada

Joel G. Sprunger, BA
Department of Psychological Sciences, Purdue
University, West Lafayette, Indiana, USA

Key Sun, PhD, MSW
Department of Law and Justice, Central
Washington University, Ellensburg,
Washington, USA

Raymond Chip Tafrate, PhD
Department of Criminology and Criminal
Justice, Central Connecticut State
University, New Britain, Connecticut, USA

Michael J. Toohey, MA
Department of Criminology and Criminal
Justice, Central Connecticut State
University, New Britain, Connecticut,
USA
Department of Psychology, Hofstra
University, Hempstead, New York, USA

Marilyn Van Dieten, PhD
Orbis Partners Inc., Ottawa, Ontario,
Canada

Glenn D. Walters, PhD
Department of Criminal Justice, Kutztown
University, Kutztown, Pennsylvania, USA

Kenneth W. Wanberg, ThD, PhD
Center for Addictions Research and
Evaluation (CARE),
Arvada, Colorado, USA

Tony Ward, PhD, PGDipClinPsyc
School of Psychology, Victoria University
of Wellington, Wellington, New Zealand

Jennifer Wheeler, PhD
Pacific Evaluation, Consultation, and
Treatment Services, PLLC, Seattle,
Washington, USA

About the Editors and Contributors

Jai Amrod, PhD, is a licensed psychologist who, for more than 25 years, has provided therapy for inmates incarcerated by the Missouri Department of Corrections. His therapeutic work has involved functional contextual and compassion interventions, with a primary focus on Acceptance and Commitment Therapy. His current writing interests include barriers that professionals face that stymie therapeutic change, and critical cinema and ambiguity.

Arnoud Arntz, PhD, is professor of Clinical Psychology and Experimental Psychopathology at the University of Maastricht, The Netherlands. His main research interests lie in the fields of anxiety and personality disorders, both applied and fundamental. Professor Arntz is scientific director of the Research Center of Experimental Psychopathology of Maastricht University and of the Dutch-Flemish Graduate Research School for PhD training. He also practices as a psychotherapist at the Community Mental Health Center of Maastricht, where he mainly treats patients with personality disorders. Together with Marcel van den Hout, he is editor of the *Journal of Behavior Therapy and Experimental Psychiatry*.

David P. Bernstein, PhD, is Professor of Forensic Psychotherapy, an endowed chair sponsored by Maastricht University and Forensic Psychiatric Center "de Rooyse Wissel." He received his doctoral degree in Clinical Psychology from New York University in 1990, and joined the faculty of Maastricht University in 2004, where he serves as Chair of the Forensic Psychology Section. His main research areas are personality disorders, psychological trauma, and forensic issues. He is an internationally known expert on Schema Therapy, an integrative therapy for personality disorders. His current research focuses on developing more effective treatments for forensic patients with personality disorders.

F. Michler Bishop, PhD, CAS, is Director of Alcohol and Substance Abuse Services at the Albert Ellis Institute in New York City, and author of *Managing Addictions: Cognitive, Emotive and Behavioral Techniques*. He advocates for an integrative, goal-focused approach to the treatment of addictions, incorporating a variety of evidence-based treatment options. As one of the founders of SMART Recovery®, he was instrumental in the development of its Four-Point Program. He has conducted numerous workshops on CBT, REBT and SMART Recovery in the United States and internationally.

James Bonta, PhD, received his PhD in Clinical Psychology in 1979 and began his career as a psychologist at a maximum security remand centre. In 1990, he joined Public Safety Canada, where he is currently Director of Corrections Research. He is a Fellow of the Canadian Psychological Association and recipient of the Criminal Justice Section's Career Contribution Award for 2009. His interests are in the areas of risk assessment and offender rehabilitation. He coauthored with the late D. A. Andrews *The Psychology of Criminal Conduct* (now in its 5th edition). He is also a coauthor of the various Level of Service risk/need instruments that have been translated into six languages and used by correctional systems throughout the world.

Alison M. Byers, PsyD, received her BA from Georgetown University, a Master's Degree in Criminology from Cambridge University, England, and her doctorate in Clinical Psychology from Long Island University's CW Post. Alison trained as a family therapist at Philadelphia Child Guidance Center. She is a consultant with Diversified Search, Inc., in Philadelphia. Her areas of expertise include juvenile rehabilitation, family violence, and trauma.

Christmas Covell, PhD, received her doctorate in clinical psychology from the University of Nebraska-Lincoln, specializing in forensic psychology. Her work has focused on performance of psycho-legal evaluations, as well as treatment of individuals with sexual behavior problems across a variety of institutional and community settings. Dr Covell is a licensed psychologist in private practice, and presently provides forensic evaluation, clinical consultation, and treatment services in the state of Washington.

Cory A. Crane, PhD, completed graduate training in clinical psychology at Purdue University and a predoctoral internship in clinical psychology at the Yale University School of Medicine in the Forensic Drug Diversion program, a branch of the Division of Substance Abuse. He is currently an NIAAA postdoctoral fellow with the Research Institute on Addictions, University at Buffalo, SUNY. His primary research interests focus on the influence of cognitive moderators on the relationship between acute alcohol intoxication and event-level occurrences of interpersonal violence.

Andrew Day, MSc, DClinPsy, is Professor in Forensic Psychology and Director of the Forensic Psychology Centre at Deakin University. He has a clinical background, previously working as a clinical and forensic psychologist in both the United Kingdom and Australia and is particularly interested in the application of psychological thought and practice to the correctional setting. Professor Day is a member of the Australian Psychological Society's Colleges of Clinical and Forensic Psychology. His current research interests center around the development of therapeutic regimes within prison settings, effective practice with offenders from Aboriginal and Torres Strait Islander cultural backgrounds in Australia, and the role that anger plays in aggressive and violent behavior.

Raymond DiGiuseppe, PhD, is a Professor and Chair of the Psychology Department at St John's University in New York City and Director of Professional Training at the Albert Ellis Institute. He is past-president (2006–07) of the Association for Behavioral and Cognitive Therapies, and President-Elect of the Division of Psychotherapy of the American Psychological Association. He serves as Co-Editor of the *Journal of Rational-Emotive & Cognitive Behavior Therapies*. Dr DiGiuseppe has contributed to the scientific literature with six books, more than 120 chapters and articles, and hundreds of conference presentations. He has studied anger problems and coauthored the *Anger Disorders Scale* and the *Anger Regulation and Expression Scale*.

Christopher I. Eckhardt, PhD, is an associate professor of psychological sciences at Purdue University, West Lafayette, Indiana. He completed his BA at the University of Michigan and received his PhD in Clinical Psychology from Hofstra University. His research program is supported by federal and foundation funding and examines the affective and social information-processing correlates of interpersonal violence, the effects of alcohol use on these processes, and how risk factor research using I³ theory may inform cognitive-behavioral interventions for partner abusive men.

Eva Feindler, PhD, is a professor and the Director of the Long Island University doctoral program in Clinical Psychology. She received her undergraduate degree from Mount Holyoke College and her graduate degrees from West Virginia University. She has authored books (*Adolescent Anger Control: Cognitive-Behavioral Strategies; Handbook of Adolescent Behavior Therapy; Assessment of Family Violence; Comparative Treatments of Anger Disorders*), numerous articles on parent and child anger, its assessment and treatment, and has conducted professional workshops in the United States and internationally. She is featured on a training video (Research Press) which presents the components of *Aggression Replacement Training*. She was recently appointed as the co-chair of the Board of Directors for the International Center for Aggression Replacement Training.

Clare-Ann Fortune, PhD, PGDipClinPsyc, is a lecturer in Clinical Forensic Psychology in the School of Psychology, Victoria University of Wellington, New Zealand. Dr Fortune teaches in the Forensic Psychology and Clinical Psychology programs at Victoria University. Dr Fortune's research interests focus on treatment access and outcomes for youth offenders. She has published papers on rehabilitation and young people who have engaged in sexually abusive behaviors. Dr Fortune has also worked as a Clinical Psychologist specializing in youth forensic mental health, substance use, risk and rehabilitation.

Arthur (Art) Freeman, PhD, is Professor of Psychology and Executive Program Director of the Clinical Psychology programs in the Department of Behavioral Medicine at Midwestern University, Downers Grove, Illinois, and Glendale, Arizona. He is a Diplomate and Distinguished Founding Fellow of the Academy of Cognitive Therapy, and was, for 13 years, the Founding Chair of the Department of Psychology at the Philadelphia College of Osteopathic Medicine. In addition to 100 plus book chapters, reviews, and journal articles, he has published over 75 professional books and serves on the editorial boards of several US and international journals. Dr Freeman is a past president of both the Association for Behavioral and Cognitive Therapies and the International Association for Cognitive Psychotherapy.

Frank L. Gardner, PhD, ABPP, is Professor and Director of the PsyD Program in School and Clinical Psychology at Kean University in Union, New Jersey. He earned his PhD in Clinical and School Psychology from Hofstra University, and is board certified in clinical psychology by the American Board of Professional Psychology. With over 30 years of experience as a practicing clinical psychologist, Frank's specialties include the evidence-based psychological treatment of anger and violence, mood disorders, anxiety disorders, and interventions for performance enhancement. In addition, he is co-developer of the Mindfulness-Acceptance-Commitment (MAC) approach to performance enhancement, and is the founding Editor-in-Chief of the *Journal of Clinical Sport Psychology*.

Steven C. Hayes, PhD, is Nevada Foundation Professor at the Department of Psychology at the University of Nevada. An author of 35 books and over 500 scientific articles, his career has focused on an analysis of the nature of human language and cognition and the application of this to the understanding and alleviation of human suffering. Dr Hayes has been President of several scientific and professional societies, including the Association for Behavioral and Cognitive Therapies and the Association for Contextual Behavioral Science. His work has been recognized by awards such as the Lifetime Achievement Award from the Association for Behavioral and Cognitive Therapies.

Krista M. Holman, MA, is a doctoral candidate in clinical psychology at Central Michigan University. Her clinical and research interests focus on work with forensic and veteran populations, with an emphasis on violence reduction and substance abuse treatment.

Howard Kassinove, PhD, ABPP, is director of the Hofstra University Institute for the Study and Treatment of Anger and Aggression. He is a Fellow of the American Psychological Association and the Association for Psychological Science. Board certified in Clinical Psychology, and Cognitive and Behavioral Psychology, he has more than 75 publications and 125 presentations to his credit. Professor Kassinove frequently lectures on anger disorders around the world. In addition to editing *Anger Disorders: Definition, Diagnosis and Treatment*, he coauthored *Anger Management: The Complete Treatment Guidebook for Practitioners* and *Anger Management for Everyone: Seven Proven Ways to Control Anger and Live a Happier Life*.

Marije Keulen-de Vos, PhD, is a researcher at Forensic Psychiatric Centre "de Rooyse Wissel." She completed her master's degree in mental health science in 2005 at the University of Maastricht (The Netherlands) and is currently finishing up her PhD research, which she started in 2008. Her research focuses on forensic treatment, especially on schema therapy, schema modes, and personality disorders. Since 2008, she also has an honorary appointment at Maastricht University's Faculty of Psychology and Neuroscience.

Erica King, MSW, works with jurisdictions in the United States and Canada to evaluate correctional programs and policies, deliver training and technical assistance, and design organizational and workforce development strategies around the implementation of evidence-based practices and gender-responsive principles. Ms King is a Policy Associate of the University of Southern Maine's Muskie School of Public Service, and a Senior Associate with Orbis Partners, Inc. She is the coauthor of the chapter "Connecting to the community: A case study in women's resettlement needs and experiences" in the book *Working with Women Offenders in the Community*.

Daryl G. Kroner, PhD (Carleton University), joined the Department of Criminology and Criminal Justice at Southern Illinois University Carbondale in 2008. Prior to this appointment, he was employed as a correctional psychologist from 1986 to 2008. Current research interests include risk assessment, measurement of intervention outcomes, interventions among offenders with mental illness, and criminal desistance.

Jennifer D. Luther, BS, is a Research Associate with the University of Cincinnati Corrections Institute. As a developer, author, and trainer of evidence-based curricula, she works to implement these approaches in jurisdictions across the country. Having served in the field of corrections for 20 years, she has facilitated a variety of cognitive-behavioral therapeutic groups throughout the continuum of criminal justice programming. Ms Luther was trained through the Motivational Interviewing Network of Trainers (MINT) and inducted as a network member. She is passionate about evidence-based programming, and our individual and collective ability to effect positive change.

William L. Marshall, OC, FRSC, PhD, is Director of Rockwood Psychological Services and Emeritus Professor at Queen's University. He has been engaged in treatment and research with sexual offenders for 44 years and has over 380 publications including 20 books. Bill has been, or still is, on the editorial boards of 17 international journals. In 2006 Bill was made an Officer of the Order of Canada, the highest honor a Canadian citizen can receive.

Kimberly Maurelli, MA, is a doctoral candidate in clinical psychology at Central Michigan University. She is completing her predoctoral internship at the Federal Correctional Institution in Fort Worth, Texas. Her research and clinical interests include problem-solving, substance abuse, and anger control treatments for correctional populations.

Harvey B. Milkman, PhD, is Professor, Department of Psychology, Metropolitan State University of Denver. He received his baccalaureate from City College of New York and his doctorate from Michigan State University. In 1985–86 he was recipient of a Fulbright-Hays Lectureship award at the National University of Malaysia. From September 1992 to June 2002 he was Director of Project Self-Discovery: Artistic Alternatives for At-Risk Youth, a national demonstration model funded by The Center for Substance Abuse Prevention. He has authored numerous articles, chapters, and books on causes, consequences, prevention and treatment choices for substance abuse, behavioral addictions, and criminal conduct.

Damon Mitchell, PhD, is a licensed psychologist and Professor in the Department of Criminology and Criminal Justice at Central Connecticut State University. His research interests are in the areas of criminal thinking, sexual aggression, and substance abuse. He frequently consults with state criminal justice organizations and engages in the evaluation of criminal justice programs.

Zella E. Moore, PsyD, is an Associate Professor of Psychology at Manhattan College in New York. She received her PsyD in Clinical Psychology from La Salle University. From a clinical perspective, Zella has worked extensively with individuals with depressive disorders, anxiety disorders, and schizoaffective disorder, yet specializes in the treatment of anger dyscontrol and its behavioral manifestations. Zella is also co-developer of the Mindfulness-Acceptance-Commitment (MAC) approach for enhancing human performance, and is the founding Senior Associate Editor of the *Journal of Clinical Sport Psychology*. Finally, Zella is most dedicated to teaching and mentoring undergraduate psychology students at Manhattan College.

Robert D. Morgan, PhD, is the John G. Skelton, Jr. Regents Endowed Professor in Psychology at Texas Tech University. His research interests are in correctional mental health treatment, forensic mental health assessment, and professional development and training issues.

Raymond W. Novaco, PhD, is Professor of Psychology and Social Behavior at the University of California, Irvine. He has extensive expertise on the assessment and treatment of anger with a variety of clinical populations, including those with a history of violence. He received the Best Contribution Award in 1978 from the International Society for Research on Aggression for his book, *Anger Control: The Development and Evaluation of an Experimental Treatment*, the Distinguished Contributions to Psychology Award in 2000 from the California Psychological Association, and, in 2009, the Academic Award from the Division of Forensic Psychology of the British Psychological Society.

Matt D. O'Brien, MSc, MA, C Psych Assoc, is the Clinical Director of the prison-based Rockwood Programs and Clinical Advisor to St Lawrence Youth Association, which provides treatment for juvenile offenders. Matt previously worked for Her Majesty's Prison Service for 10 years and has been at Rockwood for 7 years. He has written a number of book chapters and journal articles and is a coauthor of a book describing Rockwood's programs.

George F. Ronan, PhD, ABPP, is a professor in the department of psychology at Central Michigan University. His research interests focus on problem-solving, scoring story narratives, and the application of clinical psychology within criminal justice settings.

Tanya Rugge, PhD, is a Senior Research Advisor in the Corrections and Criminal Justice Research Unit at Public Safety Canada. Over the years she has interviewed numerous offenders and victims, conducted risk assessments, worked clinically with female offenders and conducted research on recidivism, high-risk offenders, young offenders, Aboriginal corrections, and evaluated several restorative justice programs as well as community supervision practices. She has been involved with the Strategic Training Initiative in Community Supervision since its inception in 2006.

Lori Seeler, PsyD, received her doctorate in clinical psychology from Midwestern University in Downers Grove, Illinois. She is an adjunct professor at the University of St. Francis, and conducts forensic evaluations for the Kane County Diagnostic Center. She recently accepted a position at the Dixon Correctional Center in Dixon, Illinois.

David J. Simourd, PhD, obtained his PhD in Psychology with a specialization in correctional/forensic psychology from Carleton University in Ottawa Canada in 1992. Since then he has provided psychological assessment and treatment services to justice-involved clients in prison, mental health, and community settings. In addition to clinical interests, Dr Simourd has engaged in scientific research on the topic of offender assessment and treatment and has shared his clinical and research knowledge by way of publishing articles and book chapters and consulting to a variety of correctional organizations throughout North America, Asia, and the Caribbean.

Joel G. Sprunger, BA, is a graduate student in the doctoral program in clinical psychology at Purdue University, West Lafayette, Indiana. He received his BA from Purdue University at the Indiana University-Purdue University Fort Wayne campus. His current research interests include the examination of risk factors for interpersonal violence (IPV), particularly the impel-ling and disinhibiting processes through which these factors impact IPV likelihood, as well as how these variables may inform treatment/prevention efforts.

Key Sun, PhD, MSW, is a Professor of Law and Justice at Central Washington University. His academic training and research experience involve three interrelated areas: psychology, criminal justice, and social work. His publications have appeared in psychological and criminal justice journals and textbooks.

Raymond Chip Tafrate, PhD, is a licensed psychologist and Professor and Chairperson of the Criminology and Criminal Justice Department at Central Connecticut State University. He frequently consults with state criminal justice organizations in the development of cogni-tive-behavioral programs for adolescents and adults with difficult-to-change problems such as alcohol and drug dependence, intimate partner violence, anger, and persistent criminal behavior. He is also a member of the Motivational Interviewing Network of Trainers, a Fellow and Supervisor of the Albert Ellis Institute, and the co-chairperson of the criminal justice spe-cial interest group of the Association for Behavioral and Cognitive Therapies. His most recent books are *Anger Management for Everyone, Understanding Anger Disorders*, and the *Anger Regulation and Expression Scale*.

Michael J. Toohey, MA, is an Instructor of Criminology and Criminal Justice at Central Connecticut State University, and a PhD candidate in Clinical Psychology at Hofstra University. Specializing in anger management, he has coauthored several publications and lectured on techniques of cognitive-behavior therapy in the United States and Romania. Michael is an approved supervisor in Rational Emotive Behavior Therapy at the Albert Ellis Institute in New York.

Marilyn Van Dieten, PhD, is a senior partner with Orbis Partners Inc. and has devoted her career toward the implementation of evidence-based programs with criminal justice, homeless, and healthcare clients. She received the Maud Booth Award from the Volunteers of America at the American Correctional Association in 2003, and the Brian Riley Award from the International Community Corrections Association in 2006. Dr Van Dieten has authored or coauthored the following programs: *CALM (Controlling Anger and Learning to Manage It)*, *Counter-Point, Community Transition*, and *Moving On*. She is currently working with the National Institute of Corrections and the National Resource Center on Justice Involved Women to enhance outcomes with women in corrections.

Glenn D. Walters, PhD, is an associate professor in the Department of Criminal Justice at Kutztown University in Pennsylvania. His research interests include the creation of a psychological theory of criminal behavior, assessment and intervention with criminal thought processes, and developmental patterns leading to crime. He has published more than 200 articles and book chapters and is the author of 17 books, including *The Criminal Lifestyle, Crime in a Psychological Context: From Career Criminals to Criminal Careers*, and *Drugs, Crime, and their Relationships: Theory, Research, Practice, and Policy*.

Kenneth W. Wanberg, ThD, PhD, is a licensed psychologist, director of the Center for Addictions Research and Evaluation, in Arvada, Colorado, and a consultant and trainer with numerous criminal justice agencies. He has been doing research for over 45 years in the areas of criminal conduct and substance abuse focusing on multivariate studies identifying different patterns and dimensions of substance use and addictive behaviors in adolescent and adult clinical and offender populations. He and his associates have developed reliable and valid instruments measuring multiple problem dimensions and conditions related to substance use and abuse. Dr Wanberg is author and coauthor of numerous research articles and 13 books addressing the treatment of juvenile and adult substance abusing offenders.

Tony Ward, PhD, DipClinPsyc, is Professor of Clinical Psychology and Clinical Director at Victoria University of Wellington, New Zealand. He has published over 325 chapters, articles, and books, mostly on forensic and correctional psychology. His most recent book, coauthored with Richard Laws, is *Desistance from Sex Offending: Alternatives to Throwing Away the Keys*. Professor Ward's research interests include offender rehabilitation, ethical issues in forensic and correctional practice, evolutionary approaches to crime, and cognition in offenders.

Jennifer Wheeler, PhD, maintains a private practice in clinical and forensic psychology in Seattle, Washington. She received her doctorate in Clinical Psychology from the University of Washington, where she specialized in human sexuality and forensic psychology, including the evaluation and treatment of sexual offense behavior. She has worked in a variety of institution-based programs in Washington State, including prison-based, civil commitment, and psychiatric facilities for adult and juvenile populations. She has published numerous articles and chapters on a variety of psychology topics, including forensic psychology, sexual behavior, and couples therapy.

Preface

The origins of this book began with a simple observation from our work as consultants to criminal justice agencies and programs: *Among practitioners there existed a high level of interest in cognitive-behavioral therapy (CBT), but a relative scarcity of CBT resources in the forensic arena.* We wondered why we were unable to find an authoritative and comprehensive source of expert guidance, clinical wisdom, and inspiration for practitioners working with one of the most complex and challenging clinical populations. Where was the manual outlining the cognitive targets? Where was the handbook containing user-friendly forms and worksheets to be used with justice-involved clients? How does CBT in prisons or community corrections differ from interventions typically delivered in mental health settings? What does forensic CBT actually look like?

We hypothesized that one of the reasons for this scarcity of practical resources was an unfortunate disconnection between the psychology and criminology literatures that has developed over the last half century. For example, a rich empirical literature on offender attitudes exists that primarily focuses on thinking patterns as variables that predict program behaviors and recidivism, with much less attention dedicated to treatment issues. In contrast, a plethora of CBT programs from psychology emphasize methods and strategies for altering thinking and behavior but tend to highlight patterns central to anxiety and depression rather than antisocial patterns. It is interesting to note that the cognitive revolution in criminology predates the Ellis and Beck models but has never fully bloomed into a broad array of empirically supported treatment programs.

In an effort to bridge the gap between those psychologists working from traditional CBT mental health backgrounds and those from criminology, we organized a panel titled *CBT for Criminal Justice Populations: Lessons Learned from the United States and Canada* for the 2010 World Congress of Behavioral and Cognitive Therapies, in which the presenters discussed their application of one or more of the existing CBT models to the problems of forensic clients. Over coffee later, we informally discussed the need for a forensic CBT handbook, and through an act of serendipity, were approached by an editor from Wiley later that day who had noticed our panel in the catalogue and asked if we might be interested in putting such a volume together.

As the book began to take shape, scholarly presentations and informal discussions about how to apply CBT to justice-involved clients continued at professional meetings of the Association for Behavioral and Cognitive Therapies and Canadian Psychological Association.

The ideas and treatment models presented at those meetings comprise some of the chapters of this volume. In addition, we reached out to leading forensic researchers and treatment experts from around the world and were pleasantly surprised at their overwhelmingly positive response and willingness to contribute to this book.

Our primary goal in assembling this text is to create an authoritative and comprehensive resource on the use of CBT for a wide variety of justice-involved clients. The development of the content was guided by two objectives. The first was to present a diverse array of models within the CBT umbrella rather than a single CBT approach. For example, how might forensic treatment look from a traditional CBT perspective as compared with an acceptance-based or schema-focused approach? In order to accomplish this first objective, contributions were solicited from leading experts in the major schools of CBT. The second goal was to present the material in a manner that would be useful to practitioners. Toward this end, contributors were provided with an outline of specific practical clinical concerns to discuss and reviews of research were generally relegated to brief subsections of chapters. The inclusion of worksheets, exercises, and other clinical materials was encouraged.

Organization of the Present Volume

This book is divided into five parts. The first presents six approaches to the treatment of antisocial patterns. Such a considerable portion of the book is devoted to this single clinical construct because it is a day-to-day pressing concern for practitioners who work in forensic settings, but one about which practical information to guide treatment is lacking. Practitioners working in more traditional environments will also encounter individuals with antisocial patterns and will find the material in this part of the book useful for conceptualizing and treating such cases. Although the authors in Part I are considering antisocial patterns from their unique approaches, all were asked to discuss a core set of topics: (i) setting the treatment agenda and enhancing motivation; (ii) identifying and conceptualizing relevant thinking targets and/or core beliefs; (iii) strategies for disputing, challenging, accepting, and/or defusing problematic thoughts or beliefs; and (iv) strategies for reinforcing new thinking and behavior patterns with exposure, in session activities and/or homework. Chapter 2 tackles the antisocial pattern from a traditional CBT perspective, conceptualizing treatment from the point of view of cognitive therapy (CT) and rational emotive behavior therapy (REBT). Chapter 3 presents an acceptance and commitment therapy (ACT) group intervention developed for use with incarcerated populations. In contrast, Chapter 4 describes conceptualization and individual treatment from a schema-focused model. Chapters 5, 6, and 7 discuss treatment from the perspective of criminal thinking models, which are informed by the Risk-Need-Responsivity (RNR) model as well as traditional cognitive and social learning principles. The approaches in Chapters 5 and 6 are both based on the use of empirically supported criminal thinking instruments as a means of identifying treatment targets. The training of probation officers in the use of CBT techniques, detailed in the Chapter 7, underscores the interest of criminal justice agencies in CBT and the dissemination of CBT into forensic case management practices.

Part II concerns the treatment of four problem areas that are commonly targeted by the courts for mandated treatment and for which clients rarely seek help voluntarily: (i) anger, (ii) interpersonal violence (IPV), (iii) addictions, and (iv) sexual aggression. The goal in constructing this section was to obtain two unique CBT approaches for each problem area. Contributors were asked to include discussion of the same core set of topics mentioned earlier (e.g., setting the agenda, identifying relevant thinking targets). Chapters 8 and 9 present two approaches to the treatment of pathological anger. The anger episode model presented in Chapter 8 is rooted in traditional CBT, while the contextual anger regulation model presented in Chapter 9 is aligned with an acceptance-based approach. Chapters 10 and 11 offer two alternatives to the Duluth model, which has dominated IPV treatment. A new theory of IPV, Instigating-Impelling-Inhibiting (I^3), and an accompanying treatment model, are the subject of Chapter 10, while Chapter 11 presents the violence reduction program, which is a couples-based approach rooted in the General Aggression Model. Two approaches to the treatment of substance abuse are the focus of Chapters 12 and 13. A six-pronged REBT-based approach is provided in Chapter 12, while an eclectic approach that incorporates treatment of criminal behavior and problem substance use with an emphasis on building empathy and social responsibility is described in Chapter 13. Chapters 14 and 15 both concern CBT for sex offenders but with different emphases. The Rockwood model presented in Chapter 14 integrates a strengths-based perspective into sex offender treatment, while the Recidivism Risk Reduction Therapy (3RT) presented in Chapter 15 integrates the RNR model.

Part III is devoted to the use of modified CBT strategies for female, juvenile, and culturally diverse forensic populations. Chapter 16 highlights the differential needs of justice-involved women and discusses how to conduct gender-responsive treatment. Chapter 17 provides an overview of an array of evidence-based CBT programs for juvenile offenders and at-risk youths, including programs that emphasize family involvement. Chapter 18 considers the impact of cultural differences on treatment delivery and responsivity. The treatment of offenders who identify from Indigenous cultural backgrounds in Australia is used to highlight the importance of integrating cultural perspectives into CBT practice.

The chapters in Part IV are intended to highlight potentially useful but underdeveloped areas of practice and emerging trends. Chapter 19 presents an efficient and clinically practical method for conducting ongoing assessment and documenting treatment progress. Chapters 20 and 21 provide overviews of two treatment models that have permeated forensic practice over the past 10 years: motivational interviewing (Chapter 20) and the good lives model, a strengths-based approach (Chapter 21). Both chapters emphasize strategies for integrating their respective models into CBT. Treating prisoners suffering from depression and post-traumatic stress disorder using a new schema-based model, centered on schemas related to interactions with others, as opposed to the self, is presented in Chapter 22. Part V consists of the final chapter, which presents five recommendations for applying CBT to justice-involved clients that were distilled from the rich clinical chapters preceding it, and also discusses directions for the evolution of forensic CBT.

Labels and Language

There are many terms used to describe individuals who receive services in criminal justice settings: *offender, probationer, parolee, prisoner, justice-involved client, court mandated client, inmate,* and *patient* to name just a few. Similarly, many terms are used to describe professionals who deliver those services: *counselor, therapist, clinician, practitioner, case manager,* etc. Often the setting where treatment is delivered or the preference of the provider will dictate the terminology that emerges. Readers will find an array of terms used throughout this book. Authors were asked to be consistent through their chapters in the terminology they chose, but were free to use the terms they thought fit best with their own work and settings.

In Gratitude

Bringing together the various authors and perspectives presented in this volume was a large undertaking. Our burden was eased by the willingness of a great many talented psychologists, researchers, and professionals from around the world who shared their clinical expertise. We are thankful for the considerable time and effort they spent preparing their chapters and their cooperation and responsiveness to our editorial feedback. Through this experience we have gained many new colleagues and our understanding of forensic practice has been vastly enriched.

We would also like to express our gratitude to Andrew Peart, our acquisitions editor at Wiley, for getting this book off the ground. He achieved a wonderful balance of being on top of the details while also being easy-going and flexible. We appreciated his enthusiasm and support throughout this project. We would also like to thank Olivia Evans, Robert Hine, Mahabunnisa Mohamed, Gnanambigai Jayakumar and the rest of the production team at Wiley for helping to shape this book into its final form.

Much thanks to Nicole Grimaldi, our graduate assistant, for her invaluable assistance in handling many of the details required to bring a project like this to completion. Additionally, Karolina Waldzinska, our undergraduate assistant, provided her expertise in formatting many of the figures in this volume. We would also like to acknowledge the support from our colleagues in the Department of Criminology and Criminal Justice at Central Connecticut State University (CCSU). We are especially appreciative of the support of Dean Susan Pease for fostering an atmosphere at CCSU where scholarly work such as this can be conducted.

Both of us would like to thank our families for their support and patience throughout the years of development of this book. Many late nights and weekends were devoted to this project and we are grateful for their encouragement along the way.

Finally, we would like to thank our colleagues at the following agencies and programs: the State of Connecticut Court Support Services Division, the State of Connecticut Department of Correction, Community Solutions Inc., the Connection, Inc., and Wheeler Clinic. Our consulting experiences with these agencies and programs have shaped our thinking and spurred our interest in developing this book. Our hope is that the following chapters will be useful to forensic practitioners, and by extension, of benefit to their clients and the safety of the public.

Raymond Chip Tafrate
Damon Mitchell
July 2013

1

Introduction

Critical Issues and Challenges Facing Forensic CBT Practitioners

Damon Mitchell, David J. Simourd, and Raymond Chip Tafrate

Although the scientific conundrums of one generation are often made obsolete by the technological advances of the next, the area of forensic treatment may be an exception. The problem is not a lack of knowledge regarding the components of effective treatment: Instead, the problem is one of their dissemination into practice. Scholars have noted that quackery marks the correctional treatment landscape (Gendreau, Smith, & Theriault, 2009; Latessa, Cullen, & Gendreau, 2002) with nonscientific and "commonsense" theories of criminal behavior (e.g., offenders lack discipline; offenders need to get back to nature) leading to subsequent programs (e.g., boot camps; wilderness adventure) that do not reduce recidivism. Perhaps worse, a variety of bizarre forensic "interventions" that escape scientific evaluation altogether pop up (e.g., dog sled racing; aura focus therapy; see Gendreau et al., 2009, for a list) and make forensic treatment appear similar to the patent medicines of the nineteenth century that claimed to cure a variety of ills but were often no more than opium dissolved in alcohol.

What makes correctional quackery a serious matter of concern rather than a source of comic relief is the sheer size of the criminal justice population and the scope of the financial and human costs. In the United States alone, there are over 2 million people in jail or prison, and an additional 4.8 million on probation or parole (Bureau of Justice Statistics, 2012) at an annual cost of approximately $70 billion (Pew Center on the States, 2009), and incalculable human suffering on the part of victims. In order to make an impact on such a large and significant social problem, there is a correspondingly large need for competent forensic professionals utilizing sound assessment and treatment practices.

The Complexities of Clinical Work in Forensic Contexts

Effecting change through clinical intervention is not an easy endeavor in the best of settings. There are at least two specific aspects of clinical work with justice-involved clients that make it particularly challenging. The first is the behavior of the clients themselves. By definition, a forensic client is a person who has committed a criminal act and this, by extension, means they have caused harm to someone else. This makes forensic clinical work a perpetrator-based enterprise. It is a normal human condition to have personal reactions to human tragedy, and forensic practitioners are no different. The degree to which this occurs depends on the practitioner and can range from negligible to extreme. At the low end of the reaction continuum, practitioners can remain relatively unaffected regarding a client's character or behavior and can be clear-headed in formulating a clinical opinion. At the other end of the continuum, clinicians can have excessively negative reactions to the nature or behavior of the client and possibly fall prey to such clinical events as compassion fatigue (Joinson, 1992), which can significantly compromise clinical judgment.

A second professional challenge in working with justice-involved clients relates to the goals of treatment and the consequences of treatment failure. In general psychotherapy, the clinical goal is often symptom relief. For example, depressed clients seek relief from low mood in order to have better and more enjoyable life functioning. The consequences of failing to effect change may be disappointing to such clients and clinicians, but less than optimal outcomes result in relatively limited harm to others. In contrast, clinical tasks with justice-involved clients may not be geared toward symptom relief but rather to a broad class of rule-violating behaviors (Bonta, 2002). Practitioners identify and attempt to therapeutically modify the factors responsible for antisociality such that risk potential for future rule violation behavior is reduced. Practitioners working with justice-involved clients often have a realization, typically based on historical behavior, that clients have the potential to commit future antisocial acts. It may be determined, for example, that criminality is linked to criminal thinking. Thus, the goal is to modify antisocial thoughts with the understanding that future criminal conduct is less likely to occur. Unlike in general psychotherapy, suboptimal treatment performance with forensic populations can result in an unchanged criminal risk profile, the consequences of which are future criminality and victimization. The fact that justice-involved clients are notorious for being resistant to treatment and chronically fail to complete interventions offered to them (Olver, Stockdale, & Wormith, 2011; Wormith & Olver, 2002) only adds to the professional challenges.

Effective forensic practitioners are not born – they develop certain competencies that set them apart from less capable practitioners. There is no clear information articulating the essential features of a good forensic practitioner; however, information exists on generic clinicians that can serve as a guide for forensic clinical work. Welfel (1998) identifies three areas of competence linked to the degree of clinical effectiveness with clients:

1. *Knowledge* – expertise in understanding the theory, research, and application of information in the field of practice.
2. *Skill* – understanding of therapeutic procedures and the application of those procedures to clients.
3. *Diligence* – attentiveness to the clients' needs.

The knowledge competency may be unique in that it will shift from clinical specialty to specialty (e.g., the specific knowledge base for effective forensic practice will be different from that of health or neuropsychology) while the skill and diligence competencies are more likely to cut across clinical specialties. Below we focus on the unique knowledge competencies that are relevant to forensic practice.

Knowledge in three specific areas may serve as the foundation for effective clinical practice with forensic clients. The three areas concern an awareness of: (i) criminal risk variables; (ii) the Risk-Need-Responsivity (RNR) model of offender assessment and rehabilitation; and (iii) the offender treatment effectiveness literature. Practitioners fluent in these areas will be better equipped to provide effective treatment to justice-involved clients, which hopefully translate to better clinical outcomes.

Criminal risk variables

The first core forensic knowledge area relates to the primary factors responsible for anti-social conduct, often referred to as criminal risk variables. Justice-involved clients have multiple problem areas and it can be difficult to determine what problem assumes clinical priority. Information on the relative importance of certain risk factors can assist in the treatment planning process. Although there is extensive literature available on general criminal risk factors, research evidence from meta-analytic literature reviews exists on the predictors of criminal behavior among adult male (Gendreau, Little, & Goggin, 1996), juvenile male (Cottle, Lee, & Heilbrun, 2001), juvenile female (Simourd & Andrews, 1994), adult sex (Hanson & Bussiere, 1998), and mentally-disordered (Bonta, Law, & Hanson, 1998) offenders. Andrews, Bonta, and Wormith (2006) have identified those risk factors most closely linked to recidivism, and have referred to them as the *Central Eight* (see Box 1.1).

The Risk-Need-Responsivity (RNR) model

The second area of core knowledge concerns the RNR model of offender assessment and rehabilitation developed by Andrews, Bonta, and Hoge (1990). While the RNR model may be unfamiliar to practitioners who come from traditional mental health backgrounds, it has come to be important in the practice and research literature around correctional assessment and treatment. We recommend that practitioners unfamiliar with the model start with Andrews and Bonta's *The Psychology of Criminal Conduct* (2010) before jumping into the large base of conceptual and empirical work on RNR that appears in scholarly journals. Each component of the model is briefly described below.

Box 1.1 The 'Central Eight' Criminal Risk Variables

1. History of antisocial behavior (early and continuing involvement in antisocial acts).
2. Antisocial personality (adventurous, pleasure seeking, poor self-control).
3. Antisocial cognition (attitudes, values, beliefs supportive of crime).
4. Antisocial associates (close association with criminal peers and relative isolation from prosocial others).
5. Family/marital (lack of nurturing relationship; poor monitoring of behavior).
6. School/work (low levels of performance and satisfaction in school or work).
7. Leisure/recreation (low levels of involvement and satisfaction in prosocial pursuits).
8. Substance abuse (abuse of alcohol or drugs).

The Risk component concerns the dosage of clinical services and contends that services be titrated to the degree of presenting problem; with the presenting problem defined as risk to reoffend. Specifically, higher risk cases should receive proportionally more services than lower risk cases. The Need component relates to the targets of clinical services and suggests that clinical attention be placed on the specific factors giving rise to the client's antisocial behavior. Moreover, the Need component distinguishes between criminogenic (those more strongly related to criminality – attitudes, companions, etc.) and noncriminogenic (those weakly related to criminality – self-esteem, social status, etc.) and suggests clinical attention focus on criminogenic needs. The Responsivity component relates to providing clinical services that are tailored as best as possible to the unique learning styles of the client. Research on the RNR model has revealed that adherence to RNR principles is linked to better clinical outcomes for justice-involved clients in terms of lower recidivism (Andrews & Bonta, 2010; Andrews & Dowden, 2005; Latessa, 2004).

Mental health symptoms are classified *less criminogenic* in the RNR model. They are related to recidivism, but not as strongly as the Central Eight. Therefore, practitioners must not assume that addressing their client's depression, anxiety, or low self-esteem will have an appreciable impact on the client's likelihood to recidivate. In fact, a recent study found that for forensic clients with both significant mental health symptoms and criminogenic risks/needs, focusing solely on the mental health components produced limited effects on recidivism (Guzzo, Cadeau, Hogg, & Brown, 2012). Forensic clients high on both mental health problems and criminogenic risks/needs will require good mental health treatment and interventions that directly address criminal risk factors. This suggests that like co-occurring mental health and substance use disorders, treatment for mentally disordered justice-involved clients should target both problem areas. In cases in which the mental health symptoms are particularly severe, alleviating psychological distress is important so that justice-involved clients can later work on criminogenic needs, but alleviating distress does not replace the importance of intervention around criminogenic needs.

Treatment effectiveness with offenders

Familiarity with the "what works" literature on forensic treatment is the third area of core knowledge. Energetic debates about the effectiveness of offender treatment have raged for years in the forensic literature. The lightening rod of interest in this area can be attributed to Robert Martinson (1974), who after reviewing the correctional treatment literature concluded "nothing works." As was pointed out previously, the clinical outcomes of interest in forensic settings are most often focused on rule-breaking conduct and thus the determination of treatment benefit is focused on a very specific criterion, namely future criminality (i.e., recidivism).

After Martinson's (1974) report, the field of forensic rehabilitation saw the development of a generation of manualized cognitive-behavioral therapy (CBT)-based programs as well as the first meta-analyses of offender rehabilitation programs. Both of these developments supported the potential for CBT to be effective with justice-involved clients. In a little over a decade after the Martinson report several manualized group treatments based on CBT principles were introduced, including: Aggression Replacement Training (Goldstein, Glick, & Gibbs, 1998), Moral Reconation Therapy (Little & Robinson, 1986), and Reasoning and Rehabilitation (Ross, Fabiano, & Ross, 1986). The three programs have different foci but were all specifically developed for offenders, can be delivered by trained facilitators rather than psychologists, and have been found to reduce recidivism (Milkman & Wanberg, 2007; Wilson, Bouffard, & MacKenzie, 2005). The first meta-analysis of offender rehabilitation programs found a moderate effect on reducing recidivism – e.g., well-run treatment programs decreased reoffending by 30%, while simple custody (in the absence of treatment) results in an increase of recidivism by 7% (Andrews, Zinger, Hoge, Bonta, Gendreau, & Cullen, 1990). Subsequent meta-analytic reviews of the offender treatment literature have occurred over the years, confirming the main findings of the Andrews et al. study, and suggesting an average reduction in recidivism of 10% (McGuire, 2002). As in the general psychotherapy literature, attention has focused on the types of treatment related to the best change outcomes among offenders, and CBT has been found to be the therapeutic modality of choice (Landenberger & Lipsey, 2005; Lipsey, Chapman, & Landenberger, 2001).

The growing literature on the relative effectiveness of CBT with justice-involved clients has not gone unnoticed by criminal justice agencies. In the National Institute of Corrections (NIC) and Crime and Justice Institute's (CJI) *Implementing Evidence-Based Practice in Community Corrections: The Principles of Effective Intervention*, CBT is specifically highlighted in Principle 4: "Provide evidence-based programming that emphasizes cognitive behavioral strategies and is delivered by well trained staff" (NIC & CJI, 2004, p. 5). Interest in using CBT-based interventions with offenders has more recently been extended into the field of probation and parole with efforts made to train supervision officers to use CBT skills in their sessions with offenders (see Rugge and Bonta, Chapter 7).

CBT, Criminology, and Offender Thinking Targets

Cognitive-behavioral therapy is well established in several human services disciplines but it has been surprisingly slow to be used in forensic practice. Indeed, the correctional quackery movement (lack of utilization of empirically supported treatments for offenders) suggests that it may be an uphill battle for CBT to become more commonplace amongst practitioners. While the relative effectiveness of CBT with justice-involved clients has been established, a practitioner may wonder how CBT in forensic settings is different from CBT in traditional settings. For example, what are the most important cognitive targets for intervention and are they the same as those found with traditional mental health clients? Unfortunately, confusion exists in that two literatures have emerged regarding the specific thinking patterns proposed as essential in guiding problematic behaviors. One, for CBT and mental health problems, is based on the models of Ellis (1957, 1962) and A. T. Beck (1963, 1967); the other, which came out of criminology, is connected to the work of Sykes and Matza (1957).

Ellis's rational emotive behavior therapy (REBT) is firmly rooted in stoic philosophy and is often encapsulated by the quote from Epictetus "men are not disturbed by things but the views that they take of them" (Gill, 1995). The goal is to teach clients to become less reactive to life's daily hassles and inconveniences through a philosophical shift. In terms of relevant cognitive targets, Ellis hypothesized that *demandingness* (insisting that other people or the world conform to one's own terms), *awfulizing* (exaggerating the consequences or level of hardship associated with difficult or challenging situations), *low frustration tolerance* (the tendency to underestimate one's ability to deal with discomfort or adversity), and *self or other rating* (blaming or condemning other people or oneself "in total" for limited and specific things that they do), as the major culprits leading to disturbed functioning (Walen, DiGiuseppe, & Dryden, 1992).

Beck's Cognitive Therapy (CT) is connected to philosophical work on how humans construct and experience reality. This model includes several levels of cognitive processes. At the most basic level are core beliefs and schemas, which tend to be global and overgeneralized conceptions about the self, other people, and the world. These beliefs are formed in early childhood and often remain below the level of conscious awareness. Core beliefs influence the next level of thinking, which consists of attitudes, rules, and assumptions, and form the basis for how an individual thinks, feels, and behaves across different situations. Lastly, automatic thoughts are quick evaluative thoughts that spring up in response to different stimuli and form the stream of consciousness that humans can learn to identify with minimal effort. In the early stages of treatment, the emphasis is on modifying automatic thoughts by testing them against observable data from the real world (J. S. Beck, 1995). Traditionally, Beck and colleagues have proposed specific categories of cognitive distortions to be modified in treatment (J. S. Beck, 1995; Leahy & Holland, 2000). Some examples include *fortune telling* (predicting the future negatively), *mental filter* (focusing on the negatives instead of seeing the whole picture), *all or nothing thinking* (situations are viewed in only two categories instead of a continuum), *over-generalization* (making sweeping negative conclusions that go beyond a specific situation), and *personalizing* (attributing a disproportionate amount of blame to oneself rather than considering other factors).

In both the traditional CT and REBT models, how people think about events is proposed to exert a powerful influence over feelings and actions. Over time, patterns of thought develop and with years of repetition these thoughts become automatic and inflexible. The first step in treatment is to develop an awareness of the thinking patterns associated with excessive emotions and problematic behaviors. Distorted and irrational thoughts are then challenged, based on logic or evidence, and new thinking that will bring about emotional and behavioral change is developed and practiced in day-to-day life (Leahy & Holland, 2000; Walen et al., 1992).

While many of the interventions that have emerged from the CT and REBT traditions have established themselves as some of our most empirically supported treatments for a wide variety of disorders (for a meta-analytic review see Butler, Chapman, Forman, & Beck, 2006), the extent to which the belief patterns targeted by these traditional CBT models underlie criminal behavior has not been well established. For example, a curious finding emerged from a doctoral dissertation that focused on irrational beliefs and convicted felons. On two separate self-report paper-and-pencil tests that measured irrational beliefs, the felon group (at pretest) reported fewer thinking errors than other populations, including college students who had previously taken the same instruments (Swanston, 1987). Were the offenders to be considered the standard for rational and healthy thinking? Was the felon group dishonest in completing the questionnaires? Or, are the existing cognitive models derived primarily from work with prosocial anxious and depressed patients missing the mark when it comes to justice-involved clients?

Surely, most chronic offenders do not harshly criticize or blame themselves when they receive negative feedback, as CT would suggest is the pattern for depressives? Similarly, many offenders may be unlikely to make the error of awfulizing or overestimating danger in ambiguous situations, as REBT proposes is common for those suffering from anxiety. In fact, offender thinking may be just the opposite; showing a lack of concern for how one's actions affect others and a tendency to underestimate danger and risk in favor of overly optimistic predictions regarding likely outcomes (Yochelson & Samenow, 1976).

In the field of criminology, at around the same time as the development of CBT, a model of dysfunctional thinking tailored specifically for offenders, which has come to be known as neutralization theory, emerged from Sykes and Matza's (1957) work with juvenile delinquents. They proposed that five cognitive techniques allow offenders to neutralize (minimize self-blame and disapproval from others) their actions. Neutralizations such as *denial of responsibility* (delinquent acts are due to outside forces), *denial of injury* (minimizing harm caused by one's actions), *denial of the victim* (victim is seen as the wrongdoer deserving retaliation or punishment), *condemnation of condemners* (cynicism directed at those responsible for upholding society's norms), and *appeal to higher loyalties* (loyalties to smaller antisocial groups take precedence over larger society), provide justifications following a criminal act and also set the stage for continued criminal activity. The authors acknowledged that these patterns exist to some degree across society but suggest that they are stronger and more prevalent among justice-involved clients. The theory has since been expanded to include a variety of adult offenders as well (see Maruna & Copes, 2005, for a review).

Several other cognitive conceptualizations from the criminology literature have been applied to offender thinking. Mylonas and Reckless (1963) identified *self-justification, loyalty, belief in luck*, and a *tendency to exaggerate society's shortcomings* as important attitudes possessed by justice-involved clients. Expanding upon the work of Sykes and Matza (1957), Scott and Lyman (1968) proposed their theory of accounts, which describes and classifies people's descriptions of their misconduct. They distinguish between *excuses* (in which a person acknowledges engaging in misconduct but denies responsibility for it) and *justifications* (in which a person accepts responsibility for the behavior but denies that it was wrong). A common theme running through the criminology literature on offender thinking is the importance of excuse making – to minimize responsibility for criminal conduct – as the leading cognitive treatment target. Indeed, intervention programs with offender populations seem to place special emphasis on challenging thinking that minimizes accountability. Having offenders take personal responsibility for their actions seems to be a cognitive focal point (Maruna & Mann, 2006). Thus, rationalizing, minimizing, justifying, blaming others, and seeing oneself as a victim are all viewed as important cognitive targets. In several recent reviews it has been suggested that an overemphasis on excuse making in the offender treatment literature, has resulted in too little attention being paid to other, perhaps more important, cognitive patterns that contribute to offending behavior (Henning & Holdford, 2006; Maruna & Copes, 2005; Maruna & Mann, 2006; Mitchell, Tafrate, Hogan, & Olver, 2013).

Although both CBT and neutralization theory and its offshoots developed around the same time and emphasized the role of thinking patterns, almost two distinct literatures have emerged – each rarely referencing the other (Maruna & Copes, 2005). This may partially explain why neither seems to adequately address the cognitive patterns that facilitate criminality. As noted earlier, antisocial cognitions are a major risk factor for criminal behavior. However, practitioners with mental health backgrounds may find that attempts to restructure client thinking around the traditional cognitive targets of CT and REBT are a poor fit with chronic offenders. On the other hand, criminal justice practitioners influenced by the criminology literature may place too much emphasis on offender responsibility and favor confrontation over collaboration in attempts to alter thinking patterns. Neglected in both approaches, and in clinical practice, is the *empirical criminal thinking literature*, which identifies and measures the thinking patterns that facilitate the antisocial and self-destructive conduct observed in justice-involved clients. Drawing from sources in criminology and psychology, including traditional CBT, neutralization theory, psychopathy, and differential association theory, existing criminal thinking instruments assess multiple thinking patterns, varying from as few as three to as many as eight (the instruments developed in this area are discussed in more detail by Kroner and Morgan in Chapter 5, and by Walters in Chapter 6. Although there are several criminal thinking instruments available, and despite the importance of criminal thinking in the RNR model described above, criminal thinking "has been largely overlooked in the mainstream assessment and treatment of offenders" (Simourd & Olver, 2002, p. 429).

We believe it is time for greater integration of the CBT, criminological, and psychological literatures that are geared toward forensic practice. This book reflects an attempt to better connect these disparate bodies of knowledge. Such integration holds promise for finding better solutions for addressing a broad range of antisocial behaviors that lead to a staggering amount of human suffering worldwide. We hope that in the chapters that follow, forensic practitioners find a rich foundation of clinical wisdom to guide their work and avoid the quackery noted earlier. As readers will find, there is reason to be optimistic that a future generation of forensic practitioners can conquer the conundrums that have historically overshadowed quality forensic clinical work.

References

Andrews, D. A., & Bonta, J. (2010). *The psychology of criminal conduct* (5th ed.). New Providence, NJ: LexisNexis Matthew Bender.

Andrews, D. A., Bonta, J., & Hoge, R.D. (1990). Classification for effective rehabilitation: Rediscovering psychology. *Criminal Justice and Behavior, 17*, 19–52.

Andrews, D. A., Bonta, J., & Wormith, J. S. (2006). The recent past and near future of risk and/or need assessment. *Crime & Delinquency, 52*, 7–27.

Andrews, D. A., & Dowden, C. (2005). Managing correctional treatment for reduced recidivism: A meta-analytic review of program integrity. *Legal and Criminological Psychology, 10*, 173–187.

Andrews, D. A., Zinger, I., Hoge, R. D., Bonta, J., Gendreau, P., & Cullen, F. T. (1990). Does correctional treatment work? A psychologically informed meta-analysis. *Criminology, 28*, 419–429.

Beck, A. T. (1963). Thinking and depression: I. Idiosyncratic content and cognitive distortions. *Archives of General Psychiatry, 9*, 324–444.

Beck, A. T. (1967). *Depression: Causes and treatment.* Philadelphia, PA: University of Pennsylvania Press.

Beck, J. S. (1995). *Cognitive therapy: Basics and beyond.* New York: Guilford Press.

Bonta, J. (2002). Offender risk assessment: Guidelines for selection and use. *Criminal Justice and Behavior, 29*, 355–379.

Bonta, J., Law, M., & Hanson, R. K. (1998). The prediction of criminal and violent recidivism among mentally disordered offenders: A meta-analysis. *Psychological Bulletin, 123*, 123–142.

Bureau of Justice Statistics. (2012, November 29). One in 34 U.S. adults under correctional supervision in 2011, lowest rates since 2000 [on-line]. Available: http://bjs.gov/content/pub/press/cpus11ppus11pr.cfm

Butler, A., Chapman, J. M., Forman E. M., & Beck, A. T. (2006). The empirical status of cognitive-behavioral therapy: A review of meta-analyses. *Clinical Psychology Review, 26*, 17–31.

Cottle, C. C., Lee, R. J., & Heilbrun, K. (2001). The prediction of criminal recidivism in juveniles: A meta-analysis. *Criminal Justice and Behavior, 28*, 367–394.

Ellis, A. (1957). Rational psychotherapy and individual psychology. *Journal of Individual Psychology, 13*, 38–44.

Ellis, A. (1962). *Reason and emotion in psychotherapy.* New York: Lyle Stuart.

Gendreau, P., Little, T., & Goggin, C. (1996). A meta-analysis of predictors of adult recidivism: What works! *Criminology, 34*, 401–433.

Gendreau, P., Smith, P., & Theriault, Y. L. (2009). Chaos theory and correctional treatment: Common sense, correctional quackery, and the law of fartcatchers. *Journal of Contemporary Criminal Justice, 25*, 384–396.

Gill, C. (1995). *The discourses of Epictetus.* London, UK: Orion Publishing Group.

Goldstein, A. P., Glick, B., & Gibbs, J. C. (1998). *Aggression Replacement Training*, Rev. ed. Champaign, IL: Research Press.

Guzzo, L., Cadeau, N. D., Hogg, S. M., & Brown, G. (2012, June). *Mental health, criminogenic needs, and recidivism: An in depth look into the relationship between mental health and recidivism.* Paper presented at the 73rd annual convention of Canadian Psychological Association, Halifax, Nova Scotia.

Hanson, R. K., & Bussiere, M. T. (1998). Predicting relapse: A meta-analysis of sexual offender recidivism studies. *Journal of Consulting and Clinical Psychology, 66*, 348–362.

Henning, K., & Holdford, R. (2006). Minimization, denial, and victim blaming by batterers: How much does the truth matter? *Criminal Justice and Behavior, 33*, 110–130.

Joinson, C. (1992). Coping with compassion fatigue. *Nursing, 22*, 116–122.

Landenberger, N. A., & Lipsey, M. W. (2005). The positive effects of cognitive behavioral programs for offenders: A meta-analysis of factors associated with effective treatment. *Journal of Experimental Criminology, 1*, 451–476.

Latessa, E. J. (2004). The challenge of change: Correctional programs and evidence-based practices. *Criminology and Public Policy, 3*, 547–559.

Latessa, E. J., Cullen, F. T., & Gendreau, P. (2002). Beyond correctional quackery: Professionalism and the possibility of effective treatment. *Federal Probation, 66*, 43–49.

Leahy, R. L., & Holland, S. J. (2000). *Treatment plans and interventions for depression and anxiety disorders.* New York: Guilford Press.

Lipsey, M. W., Chapman, G. L., & Landenberger, N. A. (2001). Cognitive-behavioral programs for offenders. *Annals of the American Academy of Political and Social Science, 578*, 144–147.

Little, G., & Robinson, K. (1986). *How to escape your prison: A Moral Reconation Therapy workbook.* Memphis: Eagle Wing Books.

Martinson, R. (1974). What works? – Questions and answers about prison reform. *The Public Interest, 35*, 22–54.

Maruna S., & Copes, H. (2005). What have we learned in five decades of neutralization research? *Crime and Justice: A Review of Research, 32*, 221–320.

Maruna, S., & Mann, R. E. (2006). A fundamental attribution error? Rethinking cognitive distortions. *Legal and Criminological Psychology, 11*, 155–177.

McGuire, J. (2002, November). *Evidence-based programming today.* Paper presented at the International Community Corrections Association Annual Conference, Boston, MA.

Milkman, H. B., & Wanberg, K. W. (2007). *Cognitive-behavioral treatment: A review and discussion for corrections professionals.* Washington, DC: National Institute of Corrections.

Mitchell, D., Tafrate. R. C., Hogan, T., & Olver, M. E. (2013). An exploration of the association between criminal thinking and community program attrition. *Journal of Criminal Justice, 41*, 81–89.

Mylonas, A. D., & Reckless, W. C. (1963). Prisoners' attitudes towards the law and legal institutions. *Journal of Criminal Law, Criminology, and Police Science, 54*, 479–484.

National Institute of Corrections (NIC) & Crime and Justice Institute (CJI). (2004). *Implementing evidence-based practice in community corrections: The principles of effective intervention* [on-line]. Available: http://nicic.gov/Library/019342

Olver, M. E., Stockdale, K. C., & Wormith, J. S. (2011). A meta-analysis of predictors of offender treatment attrition and its relationship to recidivism. *Journal of Consulting and Clinical Psychology, 79*, 6–21.

Pew Center on the States. (2009). *One in 31: The long reach of American corrections.* Washington, DC: Pew Charitable Trusts.

Ross, R. R., Fabiano, E. A., & Ross, R. D. (1986). *Reasoning and rehabilitation: A handbook for teaching cognitive skills.* Ottawa, Ontario: T3 Associates.

Scott, M. B., & Lyman, S. M. (1968). Accounts. *American Sociological Review, 33*, 46–62.

Simourd, L., & Andrews, D.A. (1994). Correlates of delinquency: A look at gender differences. *Forum on Corrections Research, 6,* 26–31.

Simourd, D. J., & Olver, M. E. (2002). The future of criminal attitudes research and practice. *Criminal Justice and Behavior, 29,* 427–446.

Swanston, M.C. (1987). Effects of rational-emotive imagery on self-reported affect and behavioral infractions in prisoners. *Dissertation Abstracts International: Section B. Sciences and Engineering, 49* (01), AAT 8800465.

Sykes, G. M., & Matza, D. (1957). Techniques of neutralization: A theory of delinquency. *American Sociological Review, 22,* 664–673.

Walen, S., DiGiuseppe, R., & Dryden, W. (1992). *A practitioners guide to rational emotive therapy* (2nd ed.). New York: Oxford University Press.

Welfel, E.R. (1998). *Ethics in counseling and psychotherapy: Standards, research, and emerging issues.* Pacific Grove, CA: Brooks/Cole Publishing.

Wilson, D. B., Bouffard, L. A., & MacKenzie, D. L. (2005). A quantitative review of structured, group-oriented, cognitive-behavioral programs for offenders. *Criminal Justice and Behavior, 32,* 172–204.

Wormith, J. S. & Olver, M. E. (2002). Offender treatment attrition and its relationship with risk, responsivity, and recidivism. *Criminal Justice and Behavior, 29,* 447–471.

Yochelson, S., & Samenow, S. E. (1976). *The criminal personality, Volume 1: A profile for change.* New York: Jason Aronson.

Suggestions for Further Learning

Book

Andrews, D. A., & Bonta, J. (2010) *The psychology of criminal conduct* (5th ed.). New Providence, NJ: Matthew Bender and Company.

Journal articles

Latessa, E., Cullen, F., & Gendreau, P. (2002), Beyond correctional quackery – professionalism and the possibility of effective treatment. *Federal Probation, 66,* 43–50.

Simourd, D. J., & Olver, M. E. (2002). The future of criminal attitudes research and practice. *Criminal Justice and Behavior, 29,* 427–446.

Part I
Criminal Behavior and Antisocial Patterns
Conceptualizing Treatment from Different CBT Perspectives

Section 1
Traditional and Next Generation CBT Models

2

Traditional Cognitive-Behavioral Therapy Models for Antisocial Patterns

Lori Seeler, Arthur Freeman,
Raymond DiGiuseppe, and Damon Mitchell

There is growing optimism that cognitive-behavioral therapy (CBT) is emerging as an effective method of treatment for individuals with antisocial patterns (Andrews & Bonta, 2010; Kuntz et al., 2004; Rodrigo, Rajapakse, & Jayananda, 2010; Salekin, 2002). However, therapeutic treatment with this population provides serious challenges and often patients themselves do not initiate therapy. Faced with a patient with antisocial patterns, a therapist can presume certain therapeutic challenges will arise, including obstacles in establishing a therapeutic alliance and a scarcity of intrinsic motivation to change. The patient may focus on changing "enough" to pacify the intervening party (i.e., judge, probation officer) as they were either ordered to participate in therapy or therapeutic intervention was "strongly suggested." The biggest therapeutic challenge arises from motivating the patient to *want* to change. Individuals with antisocial patterns come in all shapes and sizes, and for genuinely curious therapists, getting down to the underlying schema and engaging in reality testing with this population can be very rewarding.

CBT has become a large umbrella of interventions and techniques, many of which can be adapted for treating forensic patients. A perusal of the CBT literature and review of well-known training institutes' websites reveals that an agreed upon definition of CBT does not currently exist. Although an assortment of approaches are described in this volume, the hallmarks of the traditional CBT models are summarized in Box 2.1. Following a discussion of the changes in terminology and labels used to describe antisocial patterns, this chapter provides an overview of how the traditional CBT approaches of Beck (A. T. Beck, 1963; J. S. Beck, 2011) and Ellis (1994; DiGiuseppe, Doyle, Dryden, & Backx, 2013) can be applied to forensic treatment.

Antisocial Patterns: Changes in Terminology and Diagnosis

Although the diagnostic term Antisocial Personality Disorder (ASPD) is relatively new, descriptions of individuals who chronically violate rules and demonstrate a disregard for others can be traced back hundreds of years. Mental health professionals have adopted a number of different

Forensic CBT: A Handbook for Clinical Practice, First Edition.
Edited by Raymond Chip Tafrate and Damon Mitchell.
© 2014 John Wiley & Sons, Ltd. Published 2014 by John Wiley & Sons, Ltd.

Box 2.1   Hallmarks of CBT

Active: The patient is involved in the treatment generation, structuring, and implementation of therapy, not merely along for the ride.

Culturally relevant: Therapy takes into account the patient's social and cultural experience and milieu.

Empirically supported: The selected interventions have empirical support of their efficacy.

Motivational: The therapist and the therapy must be designed to increase the patient's motivation for change.

Directive: The therapist must be able to direct and, at times, choreograph the therapy sessions and the overall therapeutic work.

Here-and-now: The focus of the therapy is to work in the present to help the patient change their patterned behaviors, not to review and decide what caused current problems.

Collaborative: The therapist must be able to estimate how much of the collaboration the patient can offer, and then the therapist must supply the balance. Therapy is rarely 50/50.

Cognitively appropriate: The therapy must be developed and progressed in terms of the patient's ability to understand the constructs and goals of the therapy.

Problem-focused: The emphasis in therapy is on problems, not complaints, whether the complaints are the patient's ("*I get no respect*"), or the complaints of others ("*He needs to stop doing what he is doing*"). The complaints are turned into a problem list that is agreed upon and workable.

Solution-oriented: Insight is useful, but not, in and of itself, adequate to bring about change. The patient and therapist seek solutions for the identified problems.

Single-session: Each session is viewed as a separate entity. While the series of sessions are obviously contiguous, each therapy session needs to have an identified agenda, beginning, middle, and end. In the event that the patient does not return for the next session (or, for that matter, for the next several scheduled sessions), there is an endpoint and concluding statement for each session.

Integrative: The therapy must include and integrate cognitive, behavioral, affective, systemic, biological, motivational, and social dimensions.

Dynamic: The dynamic core of CBT are the schema. These must be identified, explicated, and modified.

Time-limited: Therapy that is time-limited does not necessarily demand a set number of sessions. Rather, it implies that the therapist plans how the therapy sessions will be allocated and used from the initial session to termination.

Psychoeducational: The therapy will require the acquisition and building of basic skills that are designed for improved functioning and adaptation.

Structured: The therapy must be carefully structured both overall and for each specific session. The use of agenda setting will assist both therapist and patient at being more successful in the therapy work.

Comprehensive: The therapy must attempt to be inclusive, thorough, and broad.

Systemic: The therapy addresses the multiple systems and the overlap of those systems in the patient's life, e.g. social system, criminal justice system, educational system, family system, or cultural system.

labels to identify antisocial symptom clusters in an attempt to categorize such individuals. The first incarnation of antisocial patterns in the *Diagnostic and Statistical Manual of Mental Disorders* (DSM) was the diagnosis of *Sociopathic Personality Disturbance* in DSM-I (American Psychiatric Association [APA], 1952). Individuals with this condition were described as, "ill in terms of society and conformity with the prevailing social milieu" (APA, 1952, p. 38). A sub-type, *Antisocial Reaction*, referred to "individuals who are always in trouble, profiting neither from experience nor punishment, and maintaining no real loyalties to any person, group, or code. They are frequently callous and hedonistic, showing marked emotional immaturity, with lack of sense of responsibility, lack of judgment, and an ability to rationalize their behavior so that it appears warranted, reasonable and justified" (p. 38).

The disorder was reformulated as *Antisocial Personality* in the DSM-II (APA, 1968). Individuals suffering from this syndrome were portrayed as possessing behavior patterns that brought them into repeated conflict with society. They were described as "incapable of significant loyalty to individuals, groups, or social values. They are grossly selfish, callous, irresponsible, impulsive, and unable to feel guilt or learn from experience and punishment. Frustration tolerance is low. They tend to blame others or offer plausible rationalizations for their behavior. A mere history of repeated legal or social offences is not sufficient to justify this diagnosis" (APA, 1968, p. 43). These emotional and interpersonal problems were noted to persist even if flagrant antisocial activity declined later in adulthood.

The DSM-III (APA, 1980) added "lying, stealing, fighting, truancy, and resisting authority…" and "unusually early or aggressive sexual behavior, excessive drinking, and the use of illicit drugs" (APA, 1980, p. 318) to the description of the disorder. With the publication of DSM-III-R (APA, 1987), the description of the disorder was again expanded, this time to include physical cruelty, vandalism, and running away from home. It was in this iteration that the requirement for the diagnosis included evidence of Conduct Disorder from childhood or adolescence.

Antisocial Personality Disorder in DSM-IV-TR (2000) became the principal diagnostic category for behavioral difficulties (i.e., deceitfulness, impulsivity, irresponsibility, etc.) related to criminality. Overall, ASPD is portrayed as a perplexing and socially relevant problem inas-much as the disorder is "a pattern of disregard for, and violation of, the rights of others" (APA, 2000, p. 685). By definition, these individuals create problems for the broader society as this disorder incorporates criminal acts that may threaten or injure people and property. However, the diagnosis of ASPD is not simply a matter of the individual having engaged in a single criminal behavior. As stated previously, the criminal history of ASPD individuals begins with problematic behaviors in childhood or early adolescence (e.g., truancy, running away, fighting, lying, and theft) suggesting a pattern of long duration. Although significant changes in the diagnostic criteria of ASPD, and personality disorders overall, were initially proposed for DSM-V, these were ultimately found to be in need of further study, and ASPD criteria remain unchanged with the publication of the DSM-V (APA, 2013).

Psychopathy, a construct related to ASPD, appears to be the first personality disorder recog-nized in psychiatry (Millon, Simonson, Birket-Smith, & Davis, 1998). This syndrome is char-acterized by egocentricity, lack of empathy and remorse, a parasitic and exploitive orientation toward others, thrill seeking, and irresponsibility (Hare, 1996). Modern conceptualizations of psychopathy are based on Cleckley's (1964) book *The Mask of Sanity* and Hare's (2003) operationalization of the construct with the Psychopathy Checklist-Revised (PCL-R). In Hare's model, psychopathy is comprised of two correlated factors. Factor 1 encompasses traits such as egocentricity, remorselessness, and manipulativeness, which mark the psychopath's interpersonal and affective style; while Factor 2 includes antisocial, impulsive, and unstable lifestyle attributes (Harpur, Hare, & Hakstian, 1989). Other researchers (Cooke & Michie, 2001; Cooke, Michie, Hart, & Clark, 2004) define psychopathy as being comprised of three dimensions: *an arrogant, deceitful interpersonal style* (i.e., self-centered, manipulative, superficially charming); *deficient affective experience* (i.e., callousness, low remorse, low guilt, lack of empathy); and an *impulsive or irresponsible behavioral style* (i.e., excitement-seeking, a lack of long-term goals, impulsiveness). While there is overlap in the symptoms of psychopathy and ASPD, psychopathy is the more severe condition. Thus, individuals with psychopathy would be expected to also meet criteria for ASPD, but not everyone with ASPD will have psychopathy (Hare, 1996).

A pessimistic theme runs through the psychopathy literature, noting that the condition is resistant to current therapies (Thornton & Blud, 2007) and a predictor of recidivism (Wormith, Olver, Stevenson, & Girard, 2007), violence (Campbell, French, & Gendreau, 2009), and institutional misconduct (Edens, Poythress, Lilienfeld, & Patrick, 2008). Nonetheless, a number of key controversies, such as symptom stability, the potential treatability of individuals who meet the criteria for the syndrome (Edens, 2006), and whether psychopathy represents an extreme variant of normal behavior or a discrete class of people (Wright, 2009), remain unresolved.

These two different conceptualizations of antisocial patterns – ASPD and psychopathy – create a conundrum in that many practitioners will mistakenly equate the two disorders and use the terms interchangeably. Surprisingly, and perhaps because of the changing criteria across the various editions of the DSM, relatively little is known about the nature and course of ASPD. In contrast, a vibrant research base has accumulated over the past three decades in the area of psychopathy using the PCL-R. These two different conceptualizations of antisocial patterns produce sharply different prevalence rates in criminal justice populations. For example, estimates of ASPD among prison inmates range from 50% to 80%, while estimates of psychopathy in the prison population are in the 15–20% range (Hare, 2003). In comparing the actual symptom lists of both disorders, ASPD overlaps more with the behavioral and impulsive elements of psychopathy than with the affective and interpersonal deficits that are foundational to the psychopathy construct. As the disorders emphasize somewhat different symptom clusters, and as psychopathy represents a more severe end of the antisocial continuum, conclusions about research findings on psychopathy should not automatically be assumed to extend to patients diagnosed with ASPD (Ogloff, 2006).

As a group, patients with antisocial or psychopathic features may present in a variety of treatment settings, depending upon their particular mixture of criminal behavior and clinical psychopathology. They may be inmates in a prison or correctional institution, inpatients in a psychiatric hospital, or outpatients in a clinic or private practice. Whether inmate, inpatient, or outpatient, the motivation for these individuals to come and then actively participate in treatment usually results from an external source (or force) pressuring the individual to "change." Family members, significant others, employers, teachers, or, more frequently, the criminal justice system, may insist that the person who engages in antisocial behavior seek treatment because of performance problems, strained interpersonal relations, or legal involvements as a result of a court order subsequent to some criminal justice action. Often, therapeutic recommendations are ultimata for seeking treatment or else losing a job, going to (or returning to) prison, or being expelled from school. Courts may often offer offenders a choice – go to therapy or go to jail. In community corrections, successful probation is often contingent upon attendance in treatment programs. While motivation varies, many individuals choose to attend treatment.

Setting the Stage for Treatment

A reasonable question is whether individuals with antisocial patterns are treatable using CBT or any other psychosocial intervention. Often clinicians dismiss treatment entirely by labeling these individuals as unable to profit from treatment. In exploring the etiology of this perspective, three points emerge. The first stems from the psychoanalytic idea that involvement in psychotherapy requires a superego: Antisocial individuals are untreatable by virtue of their lack of empathy and lack of acceptance of community rules and norms (superego). The second source of the untreatability myth stems from the coerced nature of treatment: Because the patients have been brought into therapy against their will they lack the necessary intrinsic motivation to change. A third factor is the prevailing view that antisocial individuals are homogenous in terms of treatment need, when in fact they may be quite heterogeneous in areas such as cognition, affectivity, interpersonal functioning, and impulse control.

Tailoring treatment to the patient

Society has certain moral rules; therefore, case conceptualization with antisocial patients should begin with the clinician gaining insight into the patient's cognitions regarding social rules and conventions. Identifying current thoughts that contribute to the patient's problematic behaviors (which resulted in referral for therapeutic intervention) will provide the foundation for improving moral and social behavior. Major theories regarding moral (Gilligan, 1982; Kohlberg, 1984) and psychosocial development (Erikson, 1950) have provided a foundation to improve cognitive functioning. For example, Kagan (1986) suggested fostering a transition from simplistic, egocentric thoughts toward more formal cognitive operations of abstract thinking and societal consideration. CBT can be designed to take several courses of action, depending on the level of cognitive development of the individual, the patient's motivation to change, and the therapist's motivation and therapeutic skills. For one subset of patients with antisocial patterns, therapy would be designed to help make a transition from thinking in mostly concrete, immediate terms, to consider a broader spectrum of possibilities and alternative beliefs. For others, CBT might focus on developing concrete rules for behavior that best avoid punishment and get more of what the patient wants without harmful consequences.

Assessment and information gathering

One of the initial tasks of therapy is gathering a complete historical account of the patient's life and experiences. Information gathered will provide the clinician with foundational information in which to conceptualize treatment, including family history, interpersonal relationships, and academic, vocational, legal, medical, substance use, and mental health histories. Although antisocial patients may be hesitant to provide consent, the therapist should attempt to ascertain additional collateral sources of data beyond self-report. Collateral information is useful, especially if the patient denies experiencing problems. This topic can be broached by asking, "What would your spouse/significant other/family member say is challenging for you?" If the patient has a significant person in their lives, including them in a therapy session will lead to another perspective of the patient's functioning. Anyone the patient identifies as important in their life can be invited into a therapy session (e.g., parent, sibling, significant other, friends), subsequent to obtaining verbal and written consent. Discussing collateral involvement in therapy can also enhance the therapeutic relationship. The clinician should ask the patient if there is any topic in particular they would like to discuss in the identified collateral's presence, as well as topics the patient does not want to discuss in their presence. This information will help tease out areas of difficulty the patient may not initially feel comfortable discussing. If a collaborative session is permitted, the clinician and patient should meet alone prior to the beginning of the collaborative session to ensure understanding of off-limit topics as well as including concerns the patient has had since the previous session. Depending on the nature of the referral for treatment, collateral information may also be gathered from outside sources (e.g., probation or parole officer, police records, legal history, treatment records).

While gathering historical data and collateral information, it is also important to be attentive to nonverbal behaviors. Emotional reactions, tone of voice, body language, the patient's frustration tolerance, and ability to focus are significant indicators that the clinician should recognize and process with the patient. Subsequent to gathering historical data and collateral information, it is important to collaboratively discuss conceptualization and proposed treatment plans with the patient. This discussion will allow for clarification of difficulties, lead to a more accurate conceptualization of treatment, and strengthen the collaborative nature of therapy.

Raising concerns and developing a treatment agenda

Based on the assessment, a treatment contract is usually formulated within the first several sessions. In formulating a treatment contract, the clinician is explicit in informing the patient about his or her antisocial symptoms and characteristics. Reviewing with the patient the current ASPD criteria have been recommended by Beck, Freeman, Davis, and Associates (2004). One strategy is to ask the patient to consider which of the symptoms appear applicable to his or her life. It may also be useful to frame the problem as a *"lifestyle disorder"* that develops over time and has its roots in childhood or early adolescence. Adults suffering from this syndrome are often unaware of their own symptoms until they experience significant losses or serious negative consequences (Beck, Freeman, & Associates, 1990). The patient can be reminded that this is a serious disorder affecting judgment and behavior, and that it tends to have very negative long-term consequences for the afflicted individual (such as alienation of friends and family, physical harm from others, or extended incarceration). Thus, the patient may wish to use therapy for evaluating potential changes before these consequences develop further. Thus, this discussion and immediate structuring help to set specific goals and provide direction for the course of treatment. An additional advantage of directly discussing ASPD criteria is that it allows patients to view, possibly for the first time, a variety of disparate symptoms as being part of a unified disorder. For example, a patient may acknowledge that chronic lying, irritability, and failure to sustain consistent employment have been disruptive patterns in his life, but has never viewed these patterns as being part of the same problem constellation. Even offender patients who do not precisely meet criteria for ASPD may benefit from examination of the similarity between their characteristics and those of ASPD. Wanberg and Milkman (see Chapter 13) make a similar recommendation about reviewing symptoms of ASPD and psychopathy with clients.

Clearly, the more specific the goals are the more specific the treatment can be. It also helps the therapist in setting clear limits for the therapy, inasmuch as it details the therapist's role and involvement in treatment. Without this clarity of focus, function, and purpose, the antisocial patient is not likely to see any reason or meaning in starting and continuing psychotherapy, and may blame the therapist for delving into areas the patient finds it difficult to tolerate. Inasmuch as the patient with antisocial patterns often sees their problems as other people's inability to accept them as they are, or blames societal attempts to limit their freedom, the patient's involvement in therapy may be minimal.

Building the therapeutic relationship

As noted earlier, antisocial patients are usually not in therapy by choice, and may complain of disjointedness in the therapy session, make critical comments about the therapist taking notes, challenge them regarding explanations of the CBT model, and blame them for a lack of progress or unsuccessful treatment. The clinician must be able to respond to these challenges confidently in order to establish rapport and potentially conduct additional sessions. Subsequent sessions will require the clinician to maintain control, foster motivation and collaboration, and integrate cognitions, behaviors, and biological and social constructs within the highly structured therapy session. In this regard, it seems that the CBT approach was specifically designed for antisocial individuals.

The bidirectional nature of the therapeutic relationship in terms of transference and countertransference must be made explicit, inasmuch as previous experiences and expectations of the patient and therapist affect their perceptions of one another and their reactions to the events of therapy. The establishment of an effective therapeutic relationship will be extremely difficult, if not impossible, if the special challenges of patients with antisocial patterns are not recognized and addressed early and often in the therapy. The therapeutic interaction will be a microcosm of the patient's responses to other people and situations in his or her environment. The patient's maladaptive, inflexible behaviors are sure to surface in the therapeutic relationship as in any other relationship; when they do, the alert therapist can point them out explicitly and use them as "grist for the therapeutic mill."

At the same time, the therapist must remember that such patients are especially susceptible to making false attributions of hostile or aggressive thoughts, actions, attitudes, and emotions about the therapist, due to inflexible ways of thinking and relating. The therapist must monitor his or her own automatic, and often negative, emotional responses to the patient. For example, the therapist may feel manipulated by a patient who repeatedly misses sessions with questionable or even ludicrous excuses, or may have strong feelings regarding a patient's criminal actions. Additionally, because of the challenges of forming a strong therapeutic alliance, the collaborative nature of the therapy must constantly be a focus. Therapists must keep in mind that collaboration with many patients with antisocial patterns may be 80-20, or 90-10, with the therapist carrying the greater burden. Unfortunately, this imbalance of effort often brings with it a high level of therapist stress and burnout (Freeman, Pretzer, Fleming, & Simon, 1990). It is essential that clinicians working with this population have colleagues with whom they can discuss these difficult challenges in order to deter fatigue and burnout. Setting mutually acceptable goals for therapy that are reasonable, sequential, realistic, meaningful, proximal, and within the patient's repertoire have the greatest likelihood of success.

Antisocial patterns are generally chronic and egosyntonic (patients see their behaviors as consistent with who they are), leaving the patients themselves often baffled by the responses of others, and unable to understand how present circumstances arose. For example, an antisocial patient may be astounded when a therapist questions physically aggressive responses to minor provocation. It is common for antisocial patients to view their behavior as externally caused, and see themselves as victims of unfair, prejudiced, hostile, and "stupid" laws.

It is impossible for the therapist to begin the therapeutic relationship "in the middle," that is, to assume that there are implicit, universal rules and styles of relating that both therapist and patient already know, practice, and agree upon. The therapist should not necessarily expect the patient to be able to generalize adaptive interpersonal behaviors from previous therapy or from previous relationships and interactions and extend them into the present therapeutic work.

As a general guideline in CBT, therapists are advised to continue treatment only when it is reasonably clear that the patient is benefitting from it. In attempting to identify and discuss real-world problems, the therapist is once again likely to encounter the patient's denial of problems, which may lead to frustration on the therapist's part. For example, a therapist may become frustrated in attempting to coerce the patient into admitting that he or she does have problems. This, however, will probably damage rapport and cause treatment avoidance, dropout, or ongoing power struggles. Incorporating techniques from motivational interviewing, such as *agreeing with a twist* (reflect emotion and then reframe) and *emphasizing personal choice and control* (provide reassurance that change is his/her choice; however, eliciting from patients the consequences of not changing), is often eye-opening and will go a long way in maintaining congruence and increasing participation in treatment (Miller & Rollnick, 2002). See Tafrate and Luther (Chapter 20) for a detailed discussion of integrating motivational interviewing into offender CBT programs. Additional treatment options to be considered might include a 2-week trial period for slow starters, referral for alternative services such as family therapy, an intensive inpatient treatment program, a partial hospitalization program, or referral back to a probation officer.

Applying Traditional CBT Models to Antisocial Patients

Beck's Cognitive Therapy

Although Beck's Cognitive Therapy was not originally developed to treat antisocial patterns, the cognitive life of antisocial patients can be understood within this framework, which conceptualizes psychopathology across three levels of belief: (i) schemas and core beliefs; (ii) intermediate beliefs; and (iii) automatic thoughts (J. S. Beck, 2011; Beck et al., 1990, 2004). For the therapist accustomed to working primarily with depression and anxiety, the cognitive targets of antisocial patients may be unfamiliar at first but upon closer examination, they can be seen in many respects as the inverse of those commonly found in depressed and anxious patients. For example, chronic offenders do not seem prone to harshly criticize or blame themselves when they receive negative feedback, as might be commonly seen with depressed patients. Nor is their problem that of awfulizing or overestimating negative outcomes, as is common for those suffering from anxiety. Antisocial thinking patterns may be just the opposite, showing a tendency to minimize responsibility for negative outcomes and to underestimate danger and risk in favor of overly optimistic and self-serving predictions (Maruna & Mann, 2006). A conceptualization of the cognitive life of antisocial patients across the three levels of belief is described below.

Schemas and core beliefs   The most fundamental conceptualizations of self are schemas, which can be likened to a pair of eyeglasses; they are the lenses that color perceptions of the world. Schemas are developed in one's family of origin, and go on to influence perception, motivation, affect, cognition, and behavior throughout life. They are made up of core beliefs, which are central to understanding how a patient thinks, acts, feels, and responds, but may not be consciously articulated by the patient. While core beliefs can be negative or positive, it has been theorized that typical negative core beliefs for mental health patients fall into three categories: helplessness, unlovability, and worthlessness (J. S. Beck, 2011). Additional schemas, such as Predator and Paranoid Overcontroller, have been proposed as central for patients with antisocial patterns (see Keulen-de Vos et al., Chapter 4).

Schemas and core beliefs are difficult to modify because they were learned very early in life, were modeled by significant others, strongly reinforced, and acquired from a credible source. They are global in nature, rather than specific to a situation. They do not reflect the dimensional nature of characteristics and abilities and instead contain polarized judgments. Thus, pathological core beliefs provide a definition of "self" that predisposes an individual to maladaptive thoughts, feelings, and behavior.

The difficulty of schematic change depends on the degree of integration of the schema into the personhood of the patient. Table 2.1 describes degrees of schema entrenchment and malleability. At the most static end of the continuum, a schema is *Ossified*, metaphorically cast in granite: the core beliefs are fixed and inflexible, and change is unlikely. A step down on the continuum, *Dogmatic*, is marked by schematic rigidity, where the schema may change only at great cost and with great difficulty. At a midpoint, *Steady*, there is a stability and predictability to the schema. As the continuum shifts away from stability, a schema may be *Creative*, allowing the patient to make productive changes in their core beliefs. At the furthest point from Ossified, schemas may be *Chaotic*, and marked by actions and thoughts that unpredictably shift in ways that are confusing to the therapist and patient. Schema-focused interventions specifically for offenders are presented in detail in Chapters 4 (Keulen-de Vos et al.) and 22 (Sun).

Intermediate beliefs   At a more easily accessible level of awareness (and modification) are the often unspoken intermediate beliefs and assumptions that people have about themselves, others, and the world. Intermediate beliefs have their origins in core beliefs. Therefore, among the unfortunate consequences of antisocial core beliefs are intermediate beliefs that tend to be maladaptive and potentially self-destructive and/or harmful to others. For example, an offender with a core belief "*I'm in control*" may have their interpersonal behavior driven by the intermediate belief "*Things have to be done my way*" and balk at their probation officer's review of the conditions of probation. As with schemas and core beliefs, conceptualizations of intermediate beliefs around antisocial personality patterns may be different from those commonly found in depression and anxiety.

Although there is no consensus regarding the primary intermediate beliefs associated with antisocial patterns, we propose that one source for identifying such a list lies in the burgeoning

Table 2.1 Schematic type and malleability.

Schematic type	Characterized by	Potential to shift
Ossified	Schematic paralysis	Nothing likely to bring about change
Dogmatic	Schematic rigidity	Change may come, but with difficulty
Steady	Schematic stability	Internal rules are clear and predictable
Creative	Schematic flexibility	Rules can be bent or changed, as needed
Chaotic	Schematic instability	Rules shift and change without warning

literature around the assessment of criminal thinking patterns. No fewer than six instruments measuring criminal thinking patterns have been developed or revised since the mid-1990s:

- Psychological Inventory of Criminal Thinking Styles (PICTS; Walters, 1995);
- Criminal Sentiments Scale-Modified (CSS-M; Simourd, 1997);
- Measure of Criminal Attitudes and Associates (MCAA; Mills, Kroner, & Forth, 2002);
- Texas Christian University Criminal Thinking Scales (TCU CTS; Knight, Garner, Simpson, Morey, & Flynn, 2006);
- Measure of Offender Thinking Styles (MOTS; Mandracchia, Morgan, Garos, & Garland, 2007);
- Criminogenic Thinking Profile (CTP; Mitchell & Tafrate, 2012).

Each instrument measures multiple thinking patterns, which are represented as subscales. Although the above instruments have a combined 32 subscales, taking content overlap into account reduces the number of distinct thinking patterns to 13 (Mitchell & Tafrate, 2010). These patterns represent types of beliefs that are neither as fixed and global as core beliefs, nor as situation specific as automatic thoughts (discussed later), but can be conceptualized as occupying a middle level of thinking processes. Table 2.2 presents 13 types of intermediate beliefs derived from the empirical criminal thinking literature.

Antisocial intermediate beliefs cluster around three areas, which include: (i) the patient's perception of themselves or others (e.g., Criminal Associates, Disregard, Emotionally Disengaged, Hostility Toward Criminal Justice Personnel, Overconfident, Power and Control); (ii) interaction with their environment (e.g., Excitement Seeking, Exploit, Hostility Toward Law and Order, Justifying); and (iii) problem-solving and decision-making (e.g., Cognitive Shortcut, Inability to Cope, Poor Judgment). Antisocial intermediate beliefs are not just reflected in criminal behavior. They influence a broad swath of a patient's life including their relationships with family and friends, choice of friends and activities, and attitudes and behavior at work/school. Such thinking themes facilitate a great deal of self-destructive behavior as well as behavior that is harmful and hurtful to others.

The case of Michael, an offender referred to a day reporting center for an employment program, provides an example of how intermediate beliefs may be reflected in criminality as well as a variety of non-criminal problem behaviors. Michael's instant offense (he had several prior offenses which will not be discussed) began when he saw an unattended purse at a mall. Instead of turning the purse over to security, he saw it as a legitimate opportunity for personal gain (Exploit). The woman who left the purse was perceived as careless, stupid, and deserved to have it taken (Disregard). Michael spent the cash and was arrested trying to sell the woman's driver's license. He was sentenced to probation, where he complained that he was being treated unfairly because he was being punished so severely while individuals who have committed far worse crimes get lighter sentences (Justifying). In fact, rather than perceiving probation as a break and an opportunity to avoid prison, he saw himself as the victim of an unfair criminal justice system (Hostility Toward Law and Order). Aside from contributing to, and coloring his perception of his offenses, Michael's intermediate beliefs were also reflected in a variety of other difficulties. His beliefs in the areas of Exploit and Disregard had significantly strained his family relationships: He had been kicked out of his mother's home a year earlier for refusing to work or contribute financially to the upkeep of the house, and more recently had been asked to leave his grandmother's house for similar reasons. He had ceased speaking with his mother and grandmother, angered when they had kicked him out, and in fact had only

Table 2.2 Antisocial intermediate beliefs derived from the criminal thinking literature.

Type	Characterized by	Sample beliefs
Beliefs related to perceptions of the self or others		
Criminal Associates	One can relate best to antisocial peers	My current criminal friends look out for me
	Developing relationships with prosocial peers is unproductive	I don't have anything in common with people who live a straight life
Disregard	Callousness; lack of concern, empathy and remorse	There's no point worrying about people you hurt
	Assume others are weak, gullible, to be taken advantage of	If people are victimized, then they deserve it
Emotionally Disengaged	Avoidance of expressions of intimacy and vulnerability to others	Don't show emotions that make you look weak
	Assume others will take advantage of vulnerability	If I open up to someone, they will take advantage of me
Hostility Toward CJ Personnel	Adversarial and suspicious attitude toward police, lawyers, judges, probation officers, etc.	The police are the real criminals
		Lawyers and judges are just out for themselves
Overconfident	Inflated view about oneself	I am a superior person
	Assume the actions of others are related to oneself	All women want me
Power and Control	Entitlement	Nobody can tell me what to do
	Need for domination over others	Other people have to listen to me
	Control over situations and the environment	
Beliefs related to interactions with the environment		
Excitement Seeking	Thrill seeking	I can't sit home at night, I need action
	Lack of tolerance for boredom	There is no better feeling than the rush I get when stealing
Exploit	General intent to engage in antisocial behavior when given the opportunity	If something isn't nailed down, you should take it
		If you can get on a government program to take care of things, you should do it
Hostility Toward Law and Order	Distrust and pessimism regarding laws and regulations	Laws are there to hurt you, not help you
		You can't get justice from the legal system
Justifying	Justification, rationalization, and minimization of antisocial behavior	Other people do a lot worse things than me
		If nobody gets hurt, there's no problem

(Continued)

Table 2.2 (*Continued*)

Type	Characterized by	Sample beliefs
Beliefs related to problem-solving and decision-making		
Cognitive Shortcut	Decision-making that favors a lack of discipline A lazy "path of least resistance" approach to problem-solving Extreme judging Overgeneralization	*Everything will take care of itself* *Just don't think about it, and it'll be okay*
Inability to Cope	Giving up in the face of adversity Easily overwhelmed	*Life has more problems than I can deal with* *I will never be able to change*
Poor Judgment	A tendency to overlook the likelihood of self-evident consequences from risky behaviors Assume decision-making skills are solid	*No one will ever catch up to me* *Drug use causes addiction in other people, not me*

Categories of intermediate beliefs are derived from the empirical criminal thinking literature referenced in the text.

contacted them to see if they would post bail for the instant offense. From his perspective, employment was a waste of time if it was possible for him to be supported without working. He was also reluctant to work because he would then have to pay child support, which he resented as the mother of his child was now living with another man who had a high income. He had no interest in seeing his son, as he had never wanted to have a child.

Although a patient's intermediate beliefs may be associated with a wide array of psychosocial as well as legal difficulties, the patient may not consider these thinking themes to be problematic. Instead, they are viewed as an accurate reflection of reality. While this means that adopting more prosocial alternative beliefs will be a challenging process, it also means that patients are unlikely to deny or minimize such beliefs. In fact, therapists are often shocked when patients verbalize such attitudes, and are astounded at the tenacity with which patients cling to their way of thinking in spite of negative consequences.

Intermediate beliefs may be spontaneously verbalized by clients, reflected in automatic thoughts (described later), inferred from multiple client statements and actions, or directly assessed with one, or several, of the validated criminal thinking instruments mentioned earlier. Once identified by the therapist, a belief pattern can be addressed in session using the Intermediate Beliefs Worksheet (see Appendix 2.A). In the first column, the patient and therapist collaboratively discuss a relevant belief target that has repeatedly led to poor decisions, damaged relationships, or criminal behavior. In the second column, the patient provides his or her recollection of one specific occasion where the belief influenced a decision. In the third column, the patient tries to sum up his or her thinking on that occasion, trying to capture as accurately as possible, their perspective at the time. The fourth column provides an opportunity for the patient to formulate an alternative perspective (Counter Response), which may have led to a different outcome. In the final column, the patient reviews the original choices (which reflected the influence of the intermediate belief) and then contrasts them with the choices that might have followed if the alternative belief was adopted. Kroner and Morgan (Chapter 5) and Walters (Chapter 6) provide additional suggestions for addressing specific criminal thinking patterns using criminal thinking assessment instruments.

Automatic thoughts   Emerging from intermediate beliefs are automatic thoughts. These are the unrehearsed, spontaneous words that immediately enter consciousness when responding to situations and circumstances that have triggered intermediate beliefs. Unlike core beliefs and intermediate beliefs, automatic thoughts are frequently articulated or can be easily brought into awareness. Automatic thoughts directly affect how people feel and behave. If an individual's intermediate beliefs are maladaptive and antisocial, the automatic thoughts that spring from them are likely to be distorted, criminally oriented, lead to self-destructive behavior, or actions that are harmful to others. For example, a probationer and former drug seller (whose intermediate beliefs reflect Excitement Seeking) expressed his frustration with an employment program and his desire to continue selling drugs with the automatic thought "*I can't live without the rush of excitement of having to look over my shoulder.*" A list of sample automatic thoughts – emerging from each of the intermediate belief categories proposed above – can be found in Table 2.3.

One of the hallmarks of the Beck approach to cognitive therapy is to help patients identify distortions in thinking, and to replace those distortions with more accurate and realistic perceptions and appraisals. The Modifying Automatic Thoughts Worksheet has been developed for addressing automatic thoughts related to risky decisions and criminal behavior (see Appendix 2.B). This worksheet may be utilized during the therapy session or given to the client as a homework assignment.

As an example of using this worksheet, a therapist noticed that magazines were disappearing from his waiting room. He suspected that Stephen, a patient with ASPD referred by the judicial system, was taking them. The therapist checked that the magazines were there prior to Stephen's session, and found that after Stephen's session, they were gone. When the therapist questioned Stephen about the missing magazines, Stephen was genuinely astounded that the therapist made such a "big deal" about a "stupid" magazine. Stephen initially vigorously denied taking the magazines and became verbally insulting: "*You people think that just because I have gotten into trouble in the past that I am to blame for anything and everything going wrong.*" When the therapist gently persisted, Stephen quickly switched his position that he must have inadvertently taken them: "*I was reading the magazine and must have accidently*

Table 2.3   Sample automatic thoughts emerging from intermediate beliefs.

Type	*Sample thoughts*
Beliefs related to perceptions of the self or others	
Criminal Associates	*You people in this program can't relate to me, me and my friends are from the streets*
	My boys would never snitch on me
Disregard	*If they want to mess up their lives by buying from me that's their problem*
	They said I raped her. How do you rape a prostitute? She got what she deserved
Emotionally	*Why should I open up to you? My case will be transferred to someone else anyway*
Disengaged	*You can't trust people because they take kindness for weakness*
Hostility Toward CJ	*The cops in my town have it in for me. If you had done the same thing as me,*
Personnel	*you wouldn't have been arrested*
	My probation officer does not like me. She's been waiting for me to mess up
Overconfident	*I'm smarter than this therapist*
	I watch Law & Order every night. I know how to outsmart the police
Power and Control	*She needs to listen to what I say*
	Those guys need to respect me
Beliefs related to interactions with the environment	
Excitement Seeking	*I can't take all the downtime in treatment. Especially at night. It's boring*
	I don't want to be a working stiff. I love the street. Rippin' and runnin'
Exploit	*How many times can I skip a session before I get kicked out of the program?*
	I'll look for a job when my unemployment checks run out
Hostility Toward Law	*Sending me to this program was just an attempt by the system to make sure*
and Order	*I go back to jail*
	I can beat the system
Justifying	*Our fighting doesn't affect the children. They have school problems because they don't behave*
	I only sniff cocaine and heroin. I'm not an addict – I never use needles
Beliefs related to problem-solving and decision-making	
Cognitive Shortcut	*I attended a program in the past. They're all the same, all a waste of time.*
	The GED is stupid, I don't need to learn to read and do math
Inability to Cope	*Looking at all these problems I have and thinking about changing them is too hard. I can't take it*
	I can't deal with all the pressure at work, I'll quit
Poor Judgment	*I've been clean for a week. I don't need to go to treatment*
	I'll never get caught selling. I know all my clients

stuck it in my coat pocket." He then reasoned, "*But aren't the magazines there for the patients? As a patient, I was then justified in taking the magazine home to read.*" Using the Modifying Automatic Thoughts Worksheet in-session helped to clarify some of the distorted thinking behind this incident. The therapist worked with Stephen to complete the form by writing out the Situation (being asked about taking magazines from the waiting room) and then in the first column listed each of the three automatic thoughts it generated. After discussion, evidence against each of the thoughts, and alternative beliefs likely to promote more positive future outcomes were identified. A completed worksheet for this example is provided in Appendix 2.C. Completing worksheets such as this can be useful in helping patients question some of their automatic thoughts, and open the door to more cognitive flexibility, and potentially more adaptive thinking.

Therapists may also wish to use a structured format for reviewing different problem areas and evaluating the "risk-benefit ratio" of various patient choices. A Choice Review Worksheet has been developed for this purpose (see Appendix 2.D). The worksheet may be adapted for homework, or may be modified to meet patients' specified needs. This format allows for a wide variety of scenarios for the patient to identify as problematic, assists them in considering possible actions, and to rate the advantages and disadvantages of each course of action. The first column lists specific difficulties the patient has verbalized, including facts regarding the situation. Some examples might include a problematic relationship, difficulties finding employment, or current physical health concerns. In the case of Stephen noted above, he may identify "taking things when he thinks it is not a big deal" as one of his problems.

Next, as many choices as possible are listed in the second column, the "Choice" column. The Choice column would typically include a mixture of current maladaptive behavior, as well as presumably more adaptive and socially acceptable alternatives. Options in the Choice column incorporate the patient's immediate, "automatic" reactions, as well as prosocial choices resulting from discussions between the patient and therapist. Stephen's Choice column may consist of: "*Take the magazine*" "*Ask the secretary to make a copy of the article*" and "*Write down the article and author and look it up on the Internet later.*"

The two adjacent columns consist of advantages and disadvantages of each choice listed. The therapist may assist the patient in identifying disadvantages to maladaptive behavior the patient may not have considered. Stephen's "Advantages" column, next to "*Take the magazine*" may include, "*I get what I want in the moment,*" while his "Disadvantages" column would state, "*Therapist will lose trust in me.*" Next to his choice of "*Ask the secretary to make a copy of the article*" his Advantages column may state, "*I get to finish the article later and do not damage a relationship,*" while his Disadvantages column would state, "*She might say 'No' and I do not get the article.*" Next to the choice of "*Write down the article and author and look it up on the Internet later*" his Advantages column may state "*Can look it up later and will not cause any trouble for anyone,*" whereas his Disadvantages column might state "*Might not find it on the Internet and then will not have it.*" After listing the disadvantages and advantages of choices, the patient rates the effectiveness of each choice on his or her life, using the 0–100 scale (zero being most ineffective and 100 being most effective).

Subsequent therapeutic sessions should include ongoing reviews of the behavioral choices listed, along with an evaluation of their effectiveness. Repeated ineffective choices could indicate a need to review and/or revise the previously identified advantages and disadvantages, or identify specific skill deficits that need to be addressed. Alternatively, the patient may need to process his or her continued ineffective choices, as they may result from unrecognized dysfunctional beliefs.

Rational-emotive behavior therapy

An alternative approach in CBT is Ellis's rational-emotive behavior therapy (REBT: DiGiuseppe et al., 2013; Ellis, 1994; Ellis & Dryden, 1997; Ellis, & MacLaren, 2005). REBT, like Beck's cognitive therapy, was designed as an intervention for internalized emotional disturbance such as anxiety and depression. The adoption of this model for treating criminal justice patients would also involve initial interventions that would increase motivation for change. REBT theory posits that irrational beliefs lead to dysfunctional emotions and behaviors, while rational beliefs lead to functional emotions and behaviors. Along with disturbed negative emotions, Ellis (1994) stressed that impulsive behaviors could be targeted with REBT; and he stressed the importance of long-term hedonism and delay of gratification as a characteristic of adaptive psychological functioning and as a goal of therapy (Ellis, 1994). Giving in to short-term desires to satisfy immediate urges, as is often the case in criminal justice patients, can be self-defeating. Pointing out any self-defeating emotions and behaviors would be the first step in REBT.

REBT states that irrational beliefs lead to dysfunctional emotions such as depression, anxiety, shame, guilt, disturbed anger, and long-term dysfunctional behaviors such as stealing, assaulting others, or substance use. Corresponding rational beliefs lead to sadness, disappointment, concern, apprehension, regret, and functional anger, and adaptive behaviors related to long-term satisfaction.

REBT identifies irrational beliefs as irrational schemas or imperative beliefs. Irrational beliefs are *tacit, unconscious*, broad-based schemas that operate on many levels. Irrational schemas consist of sets of expectations about the way the world is, ought to be, and what is good or bad about what is and ought to be. Irrational beliefs have the same characteristics as rigid, inaccurate schemas (David, Freeman, & DiGiuseppe, 2009; DiGiuseppe, 1996). Schemas help people organize their world by influencing many aspects of thought such as: (i) the information to which a person attends; (ii) the perceptions the person is likely to draw from sensory data; (iii) the inferences or automatic thoughts the person is likely to conclude from the data he or she perceives; (iv) the belief one has in one's ability to complete tasks; (v) the evaluations a person makes of the actual or perceived world; and (vi) the solutions that a person is likely to conceive to solve problems. Irrational beliefs/schemas influence other hypothetical cognitive constructs mentioned in other forms of CBT, such as perceptions, inferences, or negative automatic thoughts, and global, internal attributions of cause. Figure 2.1 represents how irrational beliefs relate to other cognitive constructs and emotional/behavioral disturbance. The REBT model suggests that interventions aimed at the level of irrational beliefs/schemas will change other types of cognitions and the emotional/behavioral disturbance; and that interventions aimed at other cognitive processes could, but not necessarily, influence the irrational schema.

Ellis (1994) defined three criteria for beliefs to be considered irrational. Irrational beliefs are either (i) illogical, (ii) inconsistent with empirical reality, or (iii) inconsistent with accomplishing one's long-term goals. These criteria are similar to those that Kuhn (1996), the historian of science, proposed that scientists use to evaluate theories. Scientists give up theories because they are logically inconsistent, fail to make empirical predictions, or lack heuristic or functional value (i.e., they fail to solve problems).

An activating event or trigger could generate up to five possible irrational beliefs. REBT theory maintains that "demandingness," or absolutist, rigid adherence to an idea, is the core of emotional disturbance and that the other types of irrational beliefs are less central and are psychologically deduced from, or created from, demandingness. The irrational beliefs and explanations concerning what makes them irrational appear below.

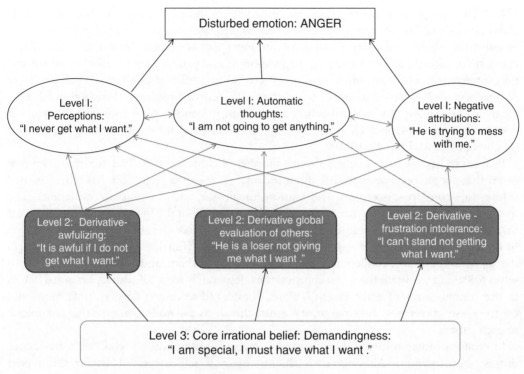

Figure 2.1   The relationship between irrational beliefs/schema, levels of cognitions, and emotions.

1. *Demandingness* is an unrealistic and absolute expectation of events or individuals being the way a person desires them to be (e.g., "*Everyone must show me respect*").
2. *Awfulizing* is an exaggeration of the negative consequences of a situation to an extreme degree, so that an unfortunate occurrence becomes "terrible" (e.g., "*It is awful that my ex got a protective order against me*").
3. *Frustration intolerance* (FI) stems from demands for ease and comfort, and reflects an intolerance of discomfort (e.g., "*I can't deal with having to come to this program every week*").
4. *Global evaluations of human worth*, either of the self or (**5**) others, imply that human beings can be rated, and that some people are worthless, or at least less valuable than others (e.g., "*Because I lost another job, I am a total loser*" "*Because my probation officer wants to see me every week, she is a real bitch*").

Ellis (1994; Ellis & Dryden, 1997) proposed the centrality of the MUSTs (demandingness) in causing other irrational beliefs and psychological disturbance. REBT defines irrational MUSTs, SHOULDs, and OUGHTs as the cognitive expression of the unwillingness to accept an unwanted outcome of reality related to one's striving to achieve something positive or to block something negative (DiGiuseppe et al., 2013). Such irrational beliefs are demands on reality that attempt to take away a negative undesirable outcome. In contrast, a rational belief is the cognitive expression of the basic willingness to accept an unwanted outcome of reality related to one's striving to achieve or to block something, independent of how much it deviates from what one wants and independent from how strong one's desire is.

REBT has proposed some hypotheses about which irrational beliefs are involved in specific disorders. Global human rating about the self could play a major role in depression, while global other rating could play a major role in anger and contempt. Irrational beliefs about comfort are thought to be prominent in agoraphobia and panic (Burgess, 1990), and frustration intolerance beliefs are often considered crucial in addictive behaviors (DiGiuseppe & McInerney, 1990), procrastination and other self-control problems (Harrington, 2005). Demands for comfort and control beliefs are thought to contribute to antisocial behaviors in criminal justice populations (Kopec, 1995; Nauth, 1995) and substance-abusing populations (DiGiuseppe & McInerney, 1990).

People can have irrational beliefs about a number of content issues. The five most common issues that people become irrational about include: (i) approval/rejection, (ii) achievement/failure, (iii) comfort/discomfort, (iv) fairness/unfairness, and (v) control/restrictions. The five types of irrational beliefs may be manifested in any of all of the five common content areas for a given patient. For example, in the first content area, the distress of some patients is driven by their demandingness for the approval of others, FI and awfulizing when they do not obtain the approval they want, condemnation of those who reject them, and condemnation of themselves for failing to obtain the social approval they desperately seek. Of course, irrational beliefs in the content areas of achievement/failure, comfort/discomfort, fairness/unfairness, and control/restrictions may also emerge, and astute therapists will notice patterns that are unique to each patient.

In criminal justice settings, therapists will often encounter patients who don't experience distress about anything. Although such patients engage in self-defeating behavior, they report no emotional disturbance or discomfort. This is often the case with alcohol and substance abuse problems, procrastination, and self-control problems. REBT proposes that such self-defeating behavior can serve as avoidance behavior that functions as an escape from disturbed, negative emotion. Such behavior is maintained by the avoidance of negative stimuli. Often the negative stimuli that patients are avoiding are their hidden emotions. Thus, a patient's criminal or substance-abusing behaviors effectively prevent them from experiencing unhealthy, negative emotion. A possible solution to this lack of awareness is to ask patients to imagine that they cease engaging in their criminal or substance-abusing behaviors. The therapist asks how would they feel and what would they think after they ceased doing these behaviors. For example, a therapist might ask a patient with an addiction to imagine that they are sitting in front of the alcohol, drugs, or some object or cash they want, but not take them and thereby deny themselves these pleasures. Patients usually report a very uncomfortable feeling akin to intense agitation, heightened arousal, muscle tension, or jitteriness. Ellis (1979) referred to this as discomfort anxiety. This emotion could be a result of an irrational belief that they *need* to have what they desire, and this idea might have remained out of their awareness because the patients were so successful at avoiding the unpleasant feeling by quickly doing or consuming whatever they want. Such an imagery exercise often reveals the disturbed emotion and irrational belief (DiGiuseppe et al., 2013).

Identifying the activating events, irrational beliefs, and emotional and behavioral consequences of those beliefs is a crucial step in therapy. REBT postulates that insight into what one is thinking, and its relationship to our disturbance is not sufficient for change. The next step is to teach patients that their beliefs influence their emotions and behavior and, therefore, the patient has power to change. Next, the therapist helps the patient examine and challenge their irrational beliefs. This process can include cognitive, imaginal, emotive/evocative, and behavioral techniques. An important component of the process is teaching new rational alternative beliefs that the patient can think when next confronted by the activating event.

Therapists can use three basic strategies to examine the patients' irrational beliefs (DiGiuseppe et al., 2013). First, they can conduct a brief ABC assessment (Activating event – Belief – Consequence) and then proceed to examine the irrational belief that was identified as occurring with the disturbed emotion and behavior (see Bishop, Chapter 12, for more discussion of this type of assessment). Then the therapist challenges the belief and helps the client construct a new rational alternative belief. The second strategy involves the therapist teaching the client the distinction between rational and irrational beliefs first, and then challenging the client's irrational beliefs while reinforcing alternative rational beliefs. A third strategy involves teaching clients the distinction between irrational and rational beliefs and then having the client rehearse and adopt the new alternative rational beliefs when they confront their triggers outside of the treatment sessions. No research yet exists to support which of these strategies is the most effective.

Debidin and Dryden (2011) reviewed the literature on REBT with criminal justice samples. They uncovered 36 studies that either referred to the use of REBT, addressed the relationship between emotional disturbance and offending, combined methods from CBT and REBT that drew specifically on the philosophy and methods of REBT, or were known by the authors to use REBT methods. They concluded that the evidence shows (i) a moderate relationship between negative emotional states such as anger, shame, and guilt, and criminal behavior, supporting the need for an intervention such as REBT that targets these emotional problems; and (ii) programs that included REBT as a component of the treatment provided reduced criminal behavior. However, it was not possible to determine the specific contribution made by REBT to positive treatment outcomes as considerable methodological flaws existed in the designs of the studies.

Not included in the Debidin and Dryden (2011) review were data on one of the most widely used REBT interventions with a criminal justice population, the CALM – anger intervention program (Winogron, Van Dieten, Gauzas, & Grisim, 1995). This program was used through the Canadian Federal Prison system, and program evaluation research supported its effectiveness. More recently, Kumar (2009) conducted a large random clinical trial of REBT versus a control treatment in 200 conduct disorder adolescents. The results revealed that REBT decreased the symptoms of conduct disorder and had a positive impact on comorbid symptoms.

Summary and Conclusions

Whether inmate, inpatient, or outpatient, the motivation for antisocial patients to attend and actively participate in treatment usually results from an external source (or force) pressuring the individual to "change." Therapeutic recommendations are often ultimata for losing a job, school expulsion, or going to (or returning to) prison. Treatment intervention with antisocial patients presents significant challenges, due to varied motivation, as well as the therapist's time spent managing disruptive behaviors. The therapist working with antisocial patients must possess strong therapeutic skills, clear and firm boundaries, confidence, assertiveness, and the ability to remain motivated throughout the therapeutic process. Initial treatment should focus on the treatment alliance, as this will ease the patient into becoming more comfortable and secure with exposing their vulnerabilities. The therapist should also frame the patient's problems as symptoms of a "lifestyle disorder," as it is less threatening and removes perceived judgment. Throughout the therapeutic process, continued reassertion of the collaborative nature of therapy will also assist in empowering the patient regarding issues of trust. A number of different cognitive targets have been proposed for working with this population. Clinicians would be wise to be prepared to accept that any of these targets could be operating in any particular client. Working with antisocial patients is challenging; however, the transformation of improved prosocial behaviors and consideration of others is very rewarding, for the therapist as well as the patient.

References

American Psychiatric Association (APA). (1952). *Diagnostic and statistical manual of mental disorders* (1st ed.). Washington, DC: APA.

American Psychiatric Association. (1968). *Diagnostic and statistical manual of mental disorders* (2nd ed.). Washington, DC: APA.

American Psychiatric Association. (1980). *Diagnostic and statistical manual of mental disorders* (3rd ed.). Washington, DC: APA.

American Psychiatric Association. (1987). *Diagnostic and statistical manual of mental disorders* (3rd ed., rev.). Washington, DC: APA.

American Psychiatric Association. (1994). *Diagnostic and statistical manual of mental disorders* (4th ed.). Washington, DC: APA.

American Psychiatric Association. (2000). *Diagnostic and statistical manual of mental disorders* (4th ed., text rev.). Washington, DC: APA.

American Psychiatric Association. (2013). Diagnostic and statistical manual of mental disorders (5th ed.). Washington, DC: APA.

Andrews, D. A., & Bonta. J. (2010). Rehabilitating criminal justice policy and practice. *Psychology, Public Policy, and Law, 16,* 39–55.

Beck, A. T. (1963). Thinking and depression: I. Idiosyncratic content and cognitive distortions. *Archives of General Psychiatry, 9,* 324–344.

Beck, A. T., Freeman, A., & Associates. (1990). *Cognitive therapy of personality disorders.* New York, NY: Guilford Press.

Beck, A. T., Freeman, A., Davis, D. D., & Associates. (2004). *Cognitive therapy of personality disorders* (2nd ed.). New York, NY: Guilford Press.

Beck, J. S. (2011). *Cognitive therapy: Basics and beyond* (2nd ed.). New York, NY: Guilford Press.

Burgess, P. M. (1990). Toward resolution of conceptual issues in the assessment of belief systems in rational-emotive therapy. *Journal of Cognitive Psychotherapy, 4*(2), 171–184.

Campbell, M., French, S., Gendreau, P. (2009). The prediction of violence in adult offenders: A meta-analytic comparison of instruments and methods of assessment. *Criminal Justice and Behavior, 36,* 567–590.

Cleckley, H. (1964). *The mask of sanity.* St Louis, MO: Mosby.

Cooke, D. J., & Michie, C. (2001). Refining the construct of psychopathy: Towards a hierarchical model. *Psychological Assessment, 13,* 171–188.

Cooke, D. J., Michie, C., Hart, S. D., & Clark, D. A. (2004). Reconstructing psychopathy: Clarifying the significance of antisocial and socially deviant behavior in the diagnosis of psychopathic personality disorder. *Journal of Personality Disorders, 18,* 337–357.

David, D., Freeman, A., DiGiuseppe, R. (2009). Rational and irrational beliefs: implication for clinical conceptualization and practice in psychotherapy. In D. David, S. J. Lynn, & A. Ellis (Eds.). *Rational and irrational beliefs in human functioning and disturbance; Implication for research, theory, and practice.* New York, NY: Oxford University Press.

Debidin, M., & Dryden, W. (2011). A systematic review of the literature on the use of rational emotive behaviour therapy in criminal justice work to reduce re-offending. *Journal of Rational-Emotive & Cognitive Behavior Therapy, 29*(2), 120–143; doi: 10.1007/s10942-010-0110-4

DiGiuseppe, R. (1996). The nature of irrational and rational beliefs: Progress in rational emotive behavior theory. *Journal of Rational-Emotive & Cognitive Behavior Therapy, 14*(1), 5–28.

DiGiuseppe, R., Doyle, K., Dryden, W., & Backx, W. (2013). *The practitioner's guide to rational emotive behavior therapy.* New York, NY: Oxford University Press.

DiGiuseppe, R., & McInerney, J. (1990). Patterns of addiction: A rational-emotive perspective. *Journal of Cognitive Psychotherapy, 4*(2), 121–134.

Edens, J. F. (2006). Unresolved controversies concerning psychopathy: Implications for clinical and forensic decision making. *Professional Psychology: Research and Practice, 37*, 59–65.

Edens, J. F., Poythress, N. G., Lilienfeld, S. O., & Patrick, C. (2008). A prospective comparison of two measures of psychopathy in the prediction of institutional misconduct. *Behavioral Sciences & the Law, 26*, 529–541.

Ellis, A. (1979). Discomfort anxiety: A new cognitive behavioral construct. *Rational Living, 14*, 3–8. Also in A. Ellis & W. Dryden (eds.), *The essential Albert Ellis.* New York, NY: Springer Publishing, 1990.

Ellis, A. (1994). *Reason and emotion in psychotherapy: A comprehensive method of treating human disturbance.* Revised and updated. New York, NY: Birch Lane Press.

Ellis, A., & Dryden, W. (1997). *The practice of rational emotive behavior therapy* (2nd ed.). New York, NY: Springer.

Ellis, A., & MacLaren, C. (2005). *Rational Emotive Behavior Therapy: A clinician's guide.* San Luis Obispo, CA: Impact Publishers.

Erickson, E. (1950). *Childhood and society.* New York, NY: Norton.

Freeman, A., Pretzer, J., Fleming, B., & Simon, K. M. (1990). *Clinical applications of cognitive therapy.* New York, NY: Plenum.

Gilligan, C. (1982). *In a different voice.* Cambridge, MA: Harvard University Press.

Hare, R. D. (1996). Psychopathy: A clinical construct whose time has come. *Criminal Justice and Behavior, 23*, 25–54.

Hare, R. D. (2003). *The Hare Psychopathy Checklist-Revised manual* (2nd ed.). Toronto: Multi-Health Systems.

Harpur, T. J., Hare, R. D., & Hakstian, R. (1989). Two-factor conceptualization of psychopathy: Construct validity and assessment implications. *Psychological Assessment, 1*, 6–17.

Harrington, N. (2005). Dimensions of frustration intolerance and their relationship to self-control problems. *Journal of Rational-Emotive & Cognitive-Behavior Therapy, 23*(1), 1–19.

Kagan, J. (1986). Rates of change in psychological processes. *Journal of Applied Developmental Psychology, 7*, 125–130.

Knight, K., Garner, B. R, Simpson, D. D, Morey, J. T, & Flynn, P. M. (2006). An assessment for criminal thinking. *Crime & Delinquency, 52*, 159–177.

Kohlberg, L. (1984). *The psychology of moral development.* New York, NY: Harper & Row.

Kopec, A. (1995). Rational emotive behavioral therapy in a forensic setting: Practical issues. *Journal of Rational-Emotive & Cognitive Behavior Therapy, 13*(4), 243–253.

Kuhn, T.S. (1996). *The structure of scientific revolutions.* Chicago, IL: University of Chicago Press.

Kumar, G. (2009). Impact of rational-emotive behaviour therapy (REBT) on adolescents with conduct disorder (CD). *Journal of the Indian Academy of Applied Psychology, 35* (special issue), 103–111.

Kuntz, M., Yates, K.F., Czobor, P., Rabinowitz, S., Lindenmayer, J.P., & Volavka, J. (2004). Course of patients with histories of aggression and crime after discharge from a cognitive-behavioral program. *Psychiatric Services, 55*, 654–659.

Mandracchia, J. T., Morgan, R. D., Garos, S., & Garland, J. T. (2007). Inmate thinking patterns: An empirical investigation. *Criminal Justice and Behavior, 34*, 1029–1043.

Maruna, S., & Mann, R. E. (2006). A fundamental attribution error? Rethinking cognitive distortions. *Legal and Criminological Psychology, 11*, 155–177.

Miller, W., & Rollnick, S. (2002). *Motivational interviewing: Preparing people for change* (2nd ed.). New York, NY: Guilford Press.

Millon, T., Simonson, E., Birket-Smith, M., & Davis, R.D, (1998). *Psychopathy: Antisocial, criminal, and violent behavior*. New York: Guilford Press.

Mills, J. F., Kroner, D. G., & Forth, A. E. (2002). Measures of Criminal Attitudes and Associates (MCAA): Development, factor structure, reliability, and validity. *Assessment, 9*, 240–253.

Mitchell, D., & Tafrate, R. C. (2010, June). Emerging criminal thinking patterns from factor analytic research: How well do they fit with the traditional models of irrational beliefs and cognitive distortions? In R. C. Tafrate (Chair), *CBT for criminal justice populations: Lessons learned from the United States and Canada*. Symposium conducted at the meeting of the Sixth World Congress of Behavioral and Cognitive Therapies, Boston, MA.

Mitchell, D., & Tafrate, R. C. (2012). Conceptualization and measurement of criminal thinking: Initial validation of the Criminogenic Thinking Profile. *International Journal of Offender Therapy and Rehabilitation, 56*, 1080–1102.

Nauth, L. L. (1995). Power and control in the male antisocial personality. *Journal of Rational-Emotive & Cognitive-Behavior Therapy, 13(4 Winter)*, 215–224.

Ogloff, J.R.P. (2006). Psychopathy/antisocial personality disorder conundrum. *Australian and New Zealand Journal of Psychiatry, 40*, 519–528.

Rodrigo, C., Rajapakse, S., & Jayananda, G. (2010). The 'antisocial' person: An insight in to biology, classification and current evidence on treatment. *Annals of General Psychiatry, 9*, 31.

Salekin, R.T. (2002). Psychopathy and therapeutic pessimism. Clinical lore or clinical reality? *Clinical Psychology Review, 22*, 79–112.

Simourd, D. J. (1997). The Criminal Sentiments Scale-Modified and Pride in Delinquency Scale: Psychometric properties and construct validity of two measures of criminal attitudes. *Criminal Justice and Behavior, 24*, 52–70.

Thornton, D., & Blud, L. (2007). The influence of psychopathic traits on response to treatment. In H. Herve & J.C. Yuille (Eds.), *The psychopath: Theory, research, and practice* (pp. 505–539). Mahwah, NJ: Lawrence Erlbaum Associates.

Walters, G. D. (1995). The Psychological Inventory of Criminal Thinking Styles: I. Reliability and preliminary validity. *Criminal Justice and Behavior, 22*, 307–325.

Winogron, W., Van Dieten, M., Gauzas, L., & Grisim, V. (1995). *CALM™ Controlling Anger and Learning to Manage It Program: Corrections Version*. Toronto, Ontario: Multi-Health Systems.

Wormith, J. S., Olver, M. E., Stevenson, H. E., & Girard, L. (2007). The long-term prediction of offender recidivism using diagnostic, personality, and risk/need approaches to offender assessment. *Psychological Services, 4*, 287–305.

Wright, E. M. (2009). The measurement of psychopathy: Dimensional and taxometric approaches. *International Journal of Offender Therapy and Comparative Criminology, 53*, 464–481.

Suggestions for Further Learning

Books

Beck, A.T., Freeman, A., Davis, D, & Associates. (2004*). Cognitive therapy of personality disorders* (2nd ed.). New York: Guilford Press.

Beck, J. S. (2011). *Cognitive therapy: Basics and beyond* (2nd ed.). New York, NY: Guilford Press.

DiGiuseppe, R., Doyle, K., Dryden, W., & Backx, W. (2013). *Practitioners guide to rational-emotive and cognitive behavior therapies*. New York: Oxford University Press.

DiGiuseppe, R., & Tafrate, R. (2007). *Understanding anger disorders.* New York: Oxford University Press.

Websites

Association for Behavioral and Cognitive Therapies (ABCT). A full listing of self-help books receiving the ABCT Seal of Merit can be found at: http://www.abct.org/SHBooks/
The Albert Ellis Institute: http://albertellis.org/professional-rebt-cbt/trainings/

Appendix 2.A

Intermediate Beliefs Worksheet

Pick One of The Thinking Patterns That Has Been Identified as a Problem Area: Choose from the list on the back	Identify a Real-Life Situation Where The Thinking Pattern Emerged: Specify what happened, where, and who was involved	Describe The Thinking Pattern In Detail: Create a sentence that describes how the pattern ran through your mind	Counter Response: Write a counter response to the thinking pattern. For example another way of thinking that would lead you in a different direction	Identify Choices: Now describe the choices that follow from both the original thinking pattern and the counter response	
				Original Thinking Pattern	Counter Response

Type of Belief	
Beliefs about how you may think of yourself or other people	
Criminal Associates	*My current criminal friends look out for me.* *I don't have anything in common with people who live a straight life.*
Disregard	*There's no point worrying about people you hurt.* *If people are victimized, then they deserve it.*
Emotionally Disengaged	*Don't show emotions that make you look weak.* *If I open up to someone, they will take advantage of me.*
Hostility Toward CJ Personnel	*The police are the real criminals.* *Lawyers and judges are just out for themselves.*
Overconfident	*I am a superior person.* *All women want me.*
Power and Control	*Nobody can tell me what to do.* *Other people have to listen to me.*
Beliefs about how may think about different situations	
Excitement Seeking	*I can't sit home at night, I need action.* *There is no better feeling than the rush I get when stealing.*
Exploit	*If something isn't nailed down, you should take it.* *If you can get on a government program to take care of you, you should do it.*
Hostility Toward Law and Order	*Laws are there to hurt you, not help you.* *You can't get justice from the legal system.*
Justifying	*Other people do a lot worse things than me.* *Everybody breaks the law.* *If nobody gets hurt, there's no problem.*
Beliefs about how you may solve problems and make decisions	
Cognitive Shortcut	*I attended a program in the past. They're all the same, all a waste of time. They don't do anything.* *The GED is stupid, I don't need to learn to read and do math.*
Inability to Cope	*Life has more problems than I can deal with.* *I will never be able to change.*
Poor Judgment	*No one will ever catch up to me.* *Drug use causes addiction in other people, not me.*

Appendix 2.B

Modifying Automatic Thoughts Worksheet

As you know from our discussions, certain types of thinking can lead to risky or poor decisions and bad outcomes. For that reason it is important that your thoughts about situations be as realistic as possible. In the first column on this form, please write in an automatic thought you had in a situation where you were recently tempted to make a bad decision. Make sure that you write down the part of your thinking that was leading you in a risky direction. In the second column, write in any evidence that goes against this thought. In the third column write in a new thought that fits better with the facts and would likely lead to a balanced and rational decision. First describe the situation on the line below. Then, complete the three columns.

Situation or event: _____

Automatic thought Describe the thinking in your mind which automatically occurred in this situation	*Evidence against the thought* Describe any evidence that goes against this thought or reasons why it may not be true	*Alternative belief* Write in the more realistic belief that better reflects the evidence
1. _____ _____	1. _____ _____	1. _____ _____
2. _____ _____	2. _____ _____	2. _____ _____
3. _____ _____	3. _____ _____	3. _____ _____

Appendix 2.C

Completed Modifying Automatic Thoughts Worksheet

As you know from our discussions, certain types of thinking can lead to risky or poor decisions and bad outcomes. For that reason it is important that your thoughts about situations be as realistic as possible. In the first column on this form, please write in an automatic thought you had in a situation where you were recently tempted to make a bad decision. Make sure that you write down the part of your thinking that was leading you in a risky direction. In the second column, write in any evidence that goes against this thought. In the third column write in a new thought that fits better with the facts and would likely lead to a balanced and rational decision. First describe the situation. Then, complete the three columns.

Situation or event: *Being accused of taking the magazines from the waiting room*

Automatic thought	Evidence against the thought	Alternative belief
Describe the thinking in your mind which automatically occurred in this situation	Describe any evidence that goes against this thought or reasons why it may not be true	Write in the more realistic belief that better reflects the evidence
1. You people think that just because I have gotten into trouble in the past that I am to blame for anything and everything going wrong.	1. I don't get blamed for everything. This therapist has really been good to me, seems to be on my side.	1. Sometimes people are going to accuse me of things. I don't have to overreact.
2. I was reading the magazine and must have accidently stuck it in my coat pocket.	2. I sometimes take things I want if I think it is no big deal.	2. I need to be more careful and remember it might be a big deal to somebody else.
3. But aren't the magazines there for the patients? As a patient, I was then justified in taking the magazine home to read.	3. If all the patients took the magazines there would not be any left.	3. The magazines are not mine to take. They are for everyone.

Appendix 2.D

Choice Review Worksheet

Problem	Choice	Advantages	Disadvantages
	1. E = 2. E = 3. E = 4. E =	1. 2. 3. 4.	1. 2. 3. 4.

E = Client's estimation of the effectiveness of each choice (0–100)

3

ACT for the Incarcerated

Jai Amrod and Steven C. Hayes

Overview of the Approach

The purpose of this chapter is to explain how acceptance and commitment therapy (ACT; Hayes, Strosahl, & Wilson, 2012) can be applied to incarcerated or community corrections populations. ACT is a behaviorally based approach to intervention that uses acceptance and mindfulness processes, and commitment and behavior change processes, to produce psychological flexibility. Psychological flexibility refers to a combination of openness, awareness, and active engagement (Hayes, Villatte, Levin, & Hildebrandt, 2011) in which the person is more consciously aware of the present moment, more open to the thoughts and feelings it contains, and more willing to engage in values-based actions that the situation affords.

Within an ACT approach, psychological inflexibility is argued to be the source of a significant proportion of psychopathology, due to the toxic consequences of six related processes. The first, *cognitive fusion*, refers to the tendency to allow the literal meaning of thoughts to dominate in the regulation of behavior over direct experience. This process focuses the attention of inmates on taking a stand that is "right" rather than doing what will work best over time. *Experiential avoidance* refers to the tendency to avoid difficult thoughts and feelings, even when doing so causes life harm. For example, inmates might withdraw from opportunities to grow and change rather than experience feelings of confusion or anxiety. *Loss of flexible contact with the now* refers to the inability to attend to what is present in a flexible, fluid, and voluntary way, and instead ruminate about the past or worry about the future. Inmates often have painful histories and can become stultified by difficult memories along with the associated anger, trauma, and guilt they produced. Inmates are dependent on the actions of others in the future (e.g., parole boards) and can become passive and anxious in the face of an imagined and uncertain future. *Attachment to a conceptualized self* refers to the dominance of ego-based stories. Inmates can become stuck in their view of themselves (e.g., as victims, as tough guys, and so on) even when such stories have repeated negative consequences for themselves and others. *Values problems* refer to the lack of chosen meaning in the present. This results in a lack of clear

Forensic CBT: A Handbook for Clinical Practice, First Edition.
Edited by Raymond Chip Tafrate and Damon Mitchell.
© 2014 John Wiley & Sons, Ltd. Published 2014 by John Wiley & Sons, Ltd.

sense of direction and purpose. *Inaction, impulsivity, or avoidant persistence* often dominates over committed actions, leading inmates to engage in actions that create harm or constant turmoil for themselves or others.

ACT targets these six problem areas with six methods designed to promote more open and flexible responses. *Cognitive defusion* refers to the ability to see thinking in flight and to take responsibility for it, rather than merely interacting with the world structured by thinking as if its structure were entirely external. Defusion helps inmates experience thoughts as what they are: learned, passing and doubtable events that the mind tosses to and fro quicker than we can track. *Experiential acceptance* is the process of feeling and sensing in an open and curious way. Acceptance teaches clients to see emotions and sensations for what they are and to learn from them without letting them dominate their behavior. *Present moment focus* helps develop the ability to place awareness in the now in a flexible, fluid, and voluntary way so that the internal and external environment can serve as a context for action. *A perspective taking sense of self* helps provide greater contact with conscious awareness and helps inmates contact a sense of self grounded in conscious experience and compassionate connection with others. *Identifying chosen values* helps inmates sort out authentic priorities from alien ones and to begin to set realistic and congruent goals. Finally, *committed action work* elicits preparation, both before and after release, to take steps to achieve what they want. The first four of these processes are considered mindfulness components within the model (Fletcher & Hayes, 2005), while the last four are considered to be behavioral activation methods.

Since the first book-length description of ACT (Hayes, Strosahl, & Wilson, 1999), it has been the subject of over 70 randomized trials, in nearly every major area of psychological functioning, including the range of problems commonly seen in incarcerated populations. These studies are about equally divided between those on the prevention or treatment of traditional psychiatric problems such as depression or substance abuse, and those on a range of behavioral health problems including the management of chronic diseases, and other social, educational, or practical problems such as prejudice, stress, or ability to learn (for a listing and brief descriptions of randomized controlled trials of ACT see http://contextualscience.org/ACT_Randomized_Controlled_Trials). ACT is listed as an evidence-based method by the US Substance Abuse and Mental Health Services Administration, with validation studies covering obsessive-compulsive disorder, worksite stress, and psychosis (see http://nrepp.samhsa.gov). ACT is also rated by Division 12 of the American Psychological Association in the areas of depression and chronic pain, as an intervention with modest to strong research support (see www.div12.org/PsychologicalTreatments/treatments.html). Recent meta-analyses agree that ACT is effective, with generally medium to large effect sizes as compared to wait-list or treatment-as-usual comparison groups across a wide range of problem areas (Hayes, Luoma, Bond, Masuda, & Lillis, 2006; Öst, 2008; Powers, Vörding, & Emmelkamp, 2009; see Gaudiano, 2009; Levin & Hayes, 2009, for controversies regarding this literature).

As the meta-analyses have shown, ACT has been successfully applied individually and in groups; in short-term and medium-term protocols; face to face and via books and the internet. The combination of breadth of application and flexibility of delivery makes ACT a potentially useful intervention for those who are involved in the criminal justice system. Although the behavioral elements of ACT change as various targets change, the rest of the intervention approach is very similar across problem areas. Thus, skill sets that are acquired by clinicians in learning to apply ACT to one specific type of client, are likely to be useful with other types, which considerably simplifies the problem of dissemination of evidence-based methods in the context of overtaxed systems of care in forensic settings.

Setting the Agenda: An Encouraging Stance and the Emergence of Choice

For many inmates, their current incarceration is only the latest manifestation of a lifetime of difficulties. In that context it is not surprising that many inmates feel overwhelmed and disoriented when faced with the possibility of doing notably better in handling life's challenges. Inmates may have been stuck for so long that they may not even notice that in effect they have given up on creating a fuller and more vital life in which they can make real choices that lead to workable outcomes.

In an effort to empower a sense of choice and agency, well-meaning correctional therapists sometimes tell inmates, "*you chose to come to prison.*" The problem is that this stance fails to address the common perception among incarcerated men and women that they are not good enough, and that they probably never will be. For choice to be possible, people need to deal with these toxic self-judgments. Evidence-based approaches have often done so by attempting to change self-judgments, but ACT instead attempts to reduce entanglements with them, while helping clients connect with their desire for purpose and meaning.

The basic ACT stance is less concerned with the past, and more focused on the present and future. ACT promotes a stance of compassionate awareness in the face of the inevitable pain of being human. The foundation for successfully motivating behavior change is to have clients begin to treat themselves with greater regard while also highlighting the benefit of a consciously chosen life.

Delivery of this model occurs within a therapeutic stance that we will describe in a non-technical way first (for more technical discussions of the ACT therapeutic stance see Eifert & Forsyth, 2005; Strosahl, Hayes, Wilson, & Gifford, 2004). A description of the model itself will then follow. Finally, examples will be given of specific ACT methods with incarcerated populations. These examples could also be modified for community corrections.

Being compassionate

The etymology of the word compassion means to "suffer with." The ACT therapist "suffers with" the inmate, recognizing that, although the details of suffering are unique to each person, each of us is human and pain is inevitable. We are equal, vulnerable, desiring, and mortal beings. This helps establish a more horizontal and humble relationship that fosters a sense of deep connection and avoids any sense of being "one up," which can be particularly toxic in the correctional context.

Showing how to be accepting and willing

Inmates can elicit difficult reactions in their therapists. For example, the therapist's own mind may react to inmate behavior with judgments such as "inappropriate" or "deliberately unhelpful." When this happens ACT therapists need to allow their own thoughts to come and go without taking them literally – they need to hold their own thoughts lightly. Doing so models greater psychological openness. Therapists and inmates alike have minds that insist their products are "the truth" even when buying into those products is not helpful. Similarly, it is important to develop the habit of allowing clients to experience difficult ideas and uncomfortable emotions for what they are. ACT therapists often need to resist the urge to explain away difficulties or to unnecessarily soothe difficult emotions when the going gets a little rough.

Creative and flexible responding, focused on the client's experience

The core of the ACT model is flexibility. This is true of emotions and thoughts, but it is also true of behavior. The therapist may need to develop new metaphors and exercises on the spot in response to the client's needs. A sense that interventions are canned will undermine impact. Therapeutic efforts will be futile if therapists lack the genuine humility and pragmatic flexibility to begin where each client finds himself.

Emotional, cognitive, and behavioral flexibility allows the therapist to find openings in the details presented by the client. The ACT model helps guide this process. Spontaneous jokes, critical questions, and reflection of expressed or implied feelings will be more engaging when they are responsive to the moment, but at the same time there needs to be a consistent theme that can alter the trajectory of the client's life. The ACT model can be effective in helping the inmate recognize that their old agenda just isn't going to magically work when it's failed in the past.

No arguing, sarcasm, or shaming

Lecturing and persuasion tactics by the therapist are not only likely to be resented, but will very likely foster the kind of cognitive and emotional entanglement ACT is designed to diminish. ACT attempts to create more psychological flexibility and less dominance by verbal rules and difficult emotions. It follows that therapeutic tactics that seek behavior change through the creation of more dominant verbal rules (e.g., through arguing) or through the creation of aversive emotions (e.g., through shaming and sarcasm) are ultimately counterproductive. The focus is not on having the right thought or feeling, but on how holding thoughts and feelings in particular ways brings the inmate closer to their life goals and values.

Disclosing some things about who you are

Because ACT is based on how normal psychological processes produce problems, it applies equally to therapist and inmate alike. If well timed, the therapist can disclose something of her or his own pain and suffering without becoming the focus of the session. There is a certain concern, in correctional settings, about offenders using personal information about staff against them; and, of course, therapists need to be mindful of what is judicious. At the same time, there can be immense therapeutic advantage to being seen as a real living human being rather than just another authority figure.

In addition to sharing experiences, a therapist may share what he or she is feeling in response to what a client has said. This need not be a boundaries issue or "unprofessional;" rather it can be a clear minded and appropriate way to build a therapeutic working relationship.

Psychological Inflexibility: Six Core Processes

An effective ACT therapist needs to be thoroughly familiar with the unified model of human functioning that underlies this treatment. The model itself helps the therapist identify and conceptualize relevant targets, select intervention strategies, and support new psychological patterns. Only by knowing the relevant processes that underlie psychological rigidity and flexibility is it possible for an ACT therapist to be aware of and utilize clinically meaningful interventions. The psychological flexibility model suggests that six core processes together explain much of

Table 3.1 Summary of ACT processes and interventions with the incarcerated.

Rigidity processes	Examples of common inmate statements	Flexibility processes	Examples of useful interventions
Cognitive fusion: Entangled in thoughts and feelings	"It's not right that I'm in prison, when those with bigger crimes go free" "It's not fair that I lost everything"	Cognitive defusion	Your mind is your associate, not your friend handout Passengers on the Bus metaphor
Experiential avoidance: Pushing away unwanted content	"I don't need to feel crappy if I stay high"	Experiential acceptance	Kid in the Hole metaphor Hungry Tiger metaphor
Disruption of values: Disconnected from purposeful direction	"I don't care. I'll always be (a loser, an addict, a felon)	Chosen values	Values worksheet Specifying practical goals
Lack of focused action: Doing anything and doing nothing	"I know how to make money selling drugs" "I need a disability check. I can't get a job"	Committed action	Internal Barriers worksheet To make a commitment to pre-release and post-release actions congruent with values
Attachment to the conceptualized self: Stuck in limited self-stories.	"If I wasn't a tough guy; I'd be nobody"	Perspective-taking	Identifying one's story line(s) and limits of same Chessboard metaphor (observer self)
Inflexible attention: Lacking present moment awareness	"My anger comes on in a flash out of nowhere"	Present moment focus	Attentional focus (breath or body) Locating thoughts or feelings in the body

human psychopathology and failure to thrive. Each of these six processes can be inverted to provide positive targets for the therapist attempting to increase psychological flexibility. Thus, the model of psychological problems and psychological interventions are linked in a point-by-point fashion for the ACT therapist (Table 3.1). Each of the treatment targets and corresponding interventions is described below in reference to working with offender clients.

Cognitive fusion: entangled in thoughts and feelings

In a general sense cognitive fusion refers to an overattachment to the contents of mental activity. The theory of language and cognition that underlies ACT, Relational Frame Theory (RFT: Hayes, Barnes-Holmes, & Roche, 2001), views language and higher cognition as a matter of a learned ability to relate events arbitrarily. In some contexts, as words and events are related they become bound together so tightly that their impact can be excessive – as if symbols are taken to be the whole truth. Examples of those contexts are those that support the dominance of evaluation and social approval. Cues in contexts of this kind are words such as "fair" or "right." These are extremely common terms among incarcerated populations. Inmates become overly invested in living out particular beliefs or ideas based on their notion of what's "fair" or what "should be." They are often more interested in trying to be "right" in their own mind or that of their peers than they are in doing what is effective and workable in the long term. Fusion of this kind can lead people to use ineffective strategies repeatedly.

An inmate who blackened both of his girlfriend's eyes explained his behavior in the following way: "If she hadn't cheated on me, I wouldn't be back in prison." The cognitive fusion that is going on here is entailed in the implication that her duplicitous actions could not be allowed to stand – he had no choice but to react in the way that he did. Put another way, he is fused with the thought that her "disrespectful" behavior made his assaultive behavior necessary and correct.

Fusion also shows up in the stickiness of negative self-evaluations. Many inmates have lost things that people can easily take for granted including homes, jobs, and intimate relationships. Some have diminished or destroyed relationships with family and friends. For the time being, all have lost the freedom to live in society. Under such circumstances, negative self-evaluations are rampant. When self-evaluations become properties of people, rather than indications of difficult histories or of mistakes made, their toxic impact is greatly increased. When fused, a thought such as *"I'm bad"* is no longer just a thought – it is a description of a property inherent in the person. Once there, negative self-evaluations lead easily to depression and anxiety, and foster a repeated cycle of irresponsible and self-defeating actions.

ACT does not attempt to replace negative thoughts with positive ones because RFT suggests that the attempt to do so can easily expand the networks that sustain fusion and foster the excessive impact of verbal events. Instead cognitive defusion methods are used to help see thoughts for what they are: learned, transient, and questionable verbal events produced by the "word machine." An example is *word repetition*, a technique in which difficult self-judgments are distilled down to a single word and then said aloud rapidly for 30 seconds, which research shows dramatically reduces their impact (e.g., Masuda et al., 2009). For example, when working with a court adjudicated substance abuse client, we focused on judgments that stood between him and his highest value: Being loving with his children. The thought that most disempowered him was that he was a loser and they were better off without him. We repeated the word "loser" out loud rapidly for 30 seconds. Eventually it became just a sound. The client committed to being willing to carry that word as a sound, while still reaching out to his children. When successful, defusion methods allow thoughts to simply come and go without needing to be objects of struggle.

Experiential avoidance: pushing away unwanted private content

The concept of *experiential avoidance* was introduced almost 20 years ago (Hayes & Wilson, 1994; Hayes, Wilson, Gifford, Follette, & Strosahl, 1996) to characterize the hazards of a closed and rigid approach to emotions, thoughts and bodily sensations. Experiential avoidance "occurs when a person is unwilling to remain in contact with particular private experiences… and takes steps to alter the form, frequency or situational sensitivity of these experiences even though doing so is not immediately necessary" (Hayes et al., 2012, pp. 72–73).

Distraction and thought suppression are typical avoidance strategies. In prison, one pervasive and popular pastime is to complain about the conditions of everyday institutional life. In the therapy setting, this may function in service of avoidance of cognitions related to the inmate's personal pain. A lack of focus on this pain preempts accepting it and blocks taking positive steps. In other words, an inmate's preoccupation with the difficulties of prison life serves to suppress awareness of the essential agenda of their larger life both before and following their release from prison.

Although direct control is a good way to deal with many things in our world (e.g., I can tidy up the room by vacuuming and taking out the trash), this doesn't work when it comes to private experiences, for several related reasons. Avoidance rules (e.g., "don't feel or think X, or else Y will happen") actually focus one's attention on the material they are trying to avoid, and consequently evoke what the rule was intended to avoid. Often avoidance rules point to the negative consequences of failing to avoid something (they contain an "or else" element), which tends to elicit negative emotions that are difficult to deal with. Avoidance rules are also examples of self-judgment and conditionality, which undermines self-acceptance. The ACT rule that captures the ironic effect of avoidance is "If you're not willing to have it then you have it" (Hayes et al., 1999) – in other words our own unwillingness gives psychological events control over us. Difficult thoughts and feelings tend to grow, and the preoccupation with eliminating them lead to a life that is not being fully lived.

Disruption of values: remaining disconnected from purposeful direction

Values are chosen global qualities of ongoing action that establish meaning and purpose in the present. Defined in that way values are not judgments; they are not fused or avoidant; and they are not merely matters of social compliance. They are positive choices that are inherently meaningful in the present.

When inmates lack a clear connection to their values they often instead follow the rules they have learned from the prison social milieu, in essence valuing and behaving according to arbitrary social consequences. RFT calls this type of rule following *pliance* (Hayes et al., 2001). In the prison, the inmate is subject to two local sources of pliance. The first is grounded in the need of officials to maintain the safety and security of the institution and is officially codified in the Offender Rulebook, which lists conduct violations (sometimes called "tickets" or "CDVs"). The second source of pliance can be called the inmate code of honor, the tacit rules promulgated and enforced by the inmates themselves. An example of a rule of this type is "don't snitch." This type of rebellious or resistant behavior (which is technically termed *counterpliance*) is actually pliance in a functional sense because it is based on arbitrary socially mediated consequences (Hayes et al., 1999).

Pliance is most often established under conditions of aversive control rather than positive reinforcement and as such constitutes an avoidant factor. Inmates who are caught up in pliance and counterpliance lack focus on what they want their lives to be about. To counteract these processes, the ACT therapist elicits the client's stated values, while also carefully examining the function of those statements getting at values that lie beneath the surface. In this way the inmate can identify future valued directions that come from his or her authentic priorities (Wilson & Murrell, 2004).

Lack of focused action: doing anything, doing nothing

Committed action is a values-based action deliberately linked to creating a pattern of behavior that fosters the value. Said in another way, a committed action is a specific values-based act, nested into a process of building larger and larger patterns of values-based action. When committed action is weak "the client struggles with an inability to act in effective ways or engages in impulsive acts or avoidant persistence" (Hayes et al., 2012, p. 66). The lack of an overall intention to build patterns of positive action is often easy to detect among inmate populations. When asked how they got in trouble, sometimes inmates say: "*I acted without thinking.*" When the ACT therapist explores what happened, it may turn out that what they actually mean is "*I do things without caring about what happens to myself or others.*" Often the inmate has risked harm to himself or herself, as well as others, as if it made no difference.

Committed action requires forethought and an expansion of vision across time and place. It also requires awareness of the risk inherent in committed action: the larger pattern may fail. Thus, failures in this area tend to be focused on the short term, and to lack forethought. For example, staying drugged or drunk, or both, is a common quality of action before incarceration. It is short term focused and avoids the emotional risk inherent in engaging in heartfelt committed actions linked to chosen values.

In prison, avoidant action takes other forms. For example, a prisoner may overtly proclaim that he wants no expectations placed on him. Mr M. states: "*I just want to sleep off my time.*" Ms C. explains why she prefers the locked-down unit to the freedom of movement in general population saying: "*I don't have to report to work, and they bring my food to me.*" These actions may suit them but they don't include the possibility that they could be using some of their time to lay the groundwork for their life after prison.

Assessing the inmate's values is a useful first step. But it is often the case that when the therapist questions the inmate more closely, there are glaring gaps between patterns of action and what's most important to the inmate. The therapist needs to help determine what actions the inmate is willing to commit to both before release, and within brief time frames after release, and foster chosen values.

Attachment to the conceptualized self

Self-conceptualizations are storylines that the mind has constructed about who the person is as compared to who others are. These storylines appear to be the literal truth, and as such enhance psychological rigidity. One job of the ACT therapist is to ferret out the extent to which self-conceptualizations of clients have been, in effect, self-fulfilling prophecies. Going forward, self-defeating stories need to be exposed. The case of the inmate who revealed his thought about the future: "*I'll probably just fuck it up as usual,*" provides an example of how self-defeating storylines can provide a rationale for staying stuck in a self-destructive lifestyle. Another inmate reported he lived by the dictum, "*I need to be a tough guy,*" and he said that served him well enough in his hometown when he was younger. More recently, though, by his own account, his programmed reactions had caused real harm in trying to maintain intimate relationships.

As defusion skills are acquired, the storyline as a generalization based on arbitrary linguistic processes becomes less entangling. The inmate, in turn, can view himself as having greater power to choose how he wants to behave going forward, even if it is not so easy. He can see himself as able influence future outcomes even though success is not guaranteed (Hayes & Smith, 2005). This journey is further encouraged by helping the client increase the availability and agility of perspective taking, allowing contact with a more spiritual aspect of "self" that is less bound up with narratives and is more grounded in conscious experience (Hayes et al., 2011).

Inflexible attention: lack of awareness of the present moment

Mental life largely dwells in the past or future. Inmates who can't let go of memories of the painful things that have happened to them express anger, hurt, and guilt. This is evident in their non-verbal presentation including their gait, posture, and visage, which can strike the therapist as a bold challenge. So often it's telegraphed: *"I'm dead in my tracks, and you can't make me move."* If the mind's evocation of the past or future creates malaise, so can rumination about the present. In the correctional setting, the present external conditions of incarceration can easily become miscast as problems that must be solved.

Even the possibility of release in the near future may be joyless. To begin with, "felon" can feel like an indelible brand. Also, a real or perceived lack of social competencies, the lack of resources and liberties, as well as the requirements of parole can appear to constitute a no-win "set-up."

To counter these tendencies, ACT teaches mindful awareness, which is a set of skills that trains one's attention to return to the present and to see internal states in the present. This also fosters seeing internal states for what they are: momentary and fleeting blips that are best taken lightly. To be able to observe ruminative thoughts, and to notice and accept experience as it is, rather than as the mind says it is, are characteristics shared by defusion and mindfulness skills. Flexible, fluid, and voluntary attention to the present supports and sustains these effects.

Kelly Wilson and Troy DuFrene (cited in Hayes et. al., 2012, p. 207) offer this account contrasting mindfulness with problem-solving:

> There is another mode of mind that we are interested in, which can be thought of as a *sunset mode of mind*. When you see a problem you solve it, but what do you do when you see a sunset? Or a beautiful painting? Or when you hear a beautiful piece of music? This mode of mind mostly notices and appreciates. One thing we all see in our lives is a tendency to get so caught up in problems and in the problem-solving mode that we miss a lot of sunsets.

ACT Therapy Sessions for Prison Inmates

The senior author of this chapter is a licensed psychologist who has for several years been offering ACT group therapy to inmates in the Algoa Correctional Center, a custody level two state prison located in Jefferson City, Missouri. Inmates housed in Algoa will be released within 3 years; the majority leave within a year. About one quarter of the 1500 inmates have a current Axis I disorder and have access to sessions with a licensed mental health therapist as well as ongoing psychiatric care.

The program presented below describes the basic approach, and is intended to give the correctional mental health worker who is relatively new to ACT a place to begin. For organizational purposes, the modules are grouped by the six core processes promoting psychological flexibility. The content that follows can be used in a group that meets for 10 to 12 weekly sessions. In applying this material it is best to resist the temptation to push to "cover it all" within a given session – it is more important to be true to the work than to force out a particular amount of material. Generally, these ACT groups have no more than 10 participants at any given time. It is important to allow adequate time so that group members can meaning-fully talk about issues raised, and that can vary from group to group.

Some group participants are likely to want to go further by bringing up the issues discussed in the group during their individual therapy sessions. Virtually all of the ACT material pre-sented here can easily be used in individual sessions without much modification, even with inmates who decline to be part of a group. Although it can be useful to ask group members to pay attention to certain things between group sessions, written homework generally creates resentment and resistance. With some exceptions, formal written homework is usually not worth the struggle in correctional settings.

Introduction and problem identification

Group begins with a broad introduction to ACT as an approach that addresses the practical problems that people struggle with. Our focus is not on feeling good; it is on being able to choose to live a life that works better. Group members are assured that the group will be safe in that they need not bring up personal information that they don't want others to know. They are asked to attend with the intention of trying to get involved with the exercises and meta-phors that will be presented. Also, they are asked to make the group be about what really matters in life, not about the petty and ephemeral tribulations of prison life.

The Kid in the Hole handout (see Appendix 3.A) is an adaptation of a classic ACT metaphor (Hayes et al., 1999; Zettle, 2007). Inmates are asked to jot something down about the hole they've fallen into (something other than "coming to prison"), their own impressions of that hole, and actions they've taken that were meant to help, but just made the hole deeper. Each inmate is asked to present his responses as the facilitator emphasizes that the point is not to blame oneself or others, but to stop digging so that time, attention, and hands are free to do something else.

The introductory session closes with a mindfulness exercise that lasts a few minutes long. The initial focus on attending to the breath allows group members to note the tendency of the mind to wander.

Experiential acceptance

The theme of the futility of struggle and the need to accept unwanted internal experience is concisely expressed with the metaphor of the two radio dials (Hayes & Smith, 2005): "You've been trying hard to turn down the Pain dial, but you are telling me that hasn't worked and you don't seem to be able to control it. There is another dial called the Willingness dial, how-ever, which you *can* control. It's turned up high when you are willing to accept unwanted thoughts and feelings." Two other useful methods of pointing to the futility of controlling internal experiences commonly used in this session are *The Chocolate Cake Exercise* (Hayes et al., 1999), and *The Metaphor of the Hungry Tiger* (Hayes and Smith, 2005.)

Group members are then asked to write down a thought, memory, emotion, or sensation that they have a hard time accepting, and that has cost them because they haven't faced it.

Next they are asked to fill in the following sentence: "If _____, wasn't such a problem for me, I would _____."

Let's look at Marcel's response.

MARCEL:	If guilt and anger weren't such problems for me I would lead a more productive life.
THERAPIST:	What do you mean by productive life?
MARCEL:	I would work and take care of my kids.
THERAPIST:	You stopped working and caring for kids because you felt guilty and angry?
MARCEL:	Well it's really my anger. My wife was pregnant when I came to prison. When she had the baby, it was addicted to drugs. So, all our kids were taken away from her. The kids were adopted out. I lost my parental rights because I was in prison. Every time I talk on the phone with my daughter who's been adopted, I get real angry about this situation.

A mental note has been made that Marcel first used the word "guilt" and then retracted it. In group, he prefers to lay out the problem in terms of being overwhelmed by anger toward his wife. This suggests that guilt is even more difficult for him to face (and in a later individual session this is explored, in which Marcel addresses how thoroughly he blames himself for not being there for his children). By the end of the session Marcel begins to suggest that accepting his feelings about what's happened might help him have a life more to his liking, especially after his release. The session ends with a brief summary of noting the importance of being willing to accept thoughts and feelings we don't want in service of having the life that we really do want.

Chosen values

Values work begins with a description and discussion of the difference between valued directions (works in progress across a lifetime) and goals that can be completed. Here's an illustrative example. One might have a goal of getting married to a partner. The underlying value might be to nurture a mutually loving, respectful, and intimate relationship. The goal ends on the wedding day; the underlying value requires continuing focus and care that may go on for a lifetime. Deeply held values and achievable goals provide a focus for therapy and, specifically, motivation for an inmate to undertake committed action.

The Values Worksheet (Appendix 3.B), adapted from Forsyth and Eifert (2007), can be completed by the participants in 10 or 15 minutes during a group session. By a show of hands, the facilitator can determine one value domain identified as important by most group members. Inmates then present their intentions related to that domain. This exercise serves the purpose of having each person make a statement about what she or he cares about, and of demonstrating that there are a variety of different values held within a particular domain.

The task of the therapist is to elicit deeper and more precise statements of what exactly matters to the client. An inmate may say, for example, that he wants "to be a good father." He may need encouragement to give detail and specificity to that statement, for example, "to be there for my kids by not coming back to prison; and to keep a job so I can provide for them."

At the end of the session, participants are encouraged to write down one value area that they want to begin working on. They are asked to think about two questions: (i) What can I do before I get out of prison that will move me in this direction? and (ii) What are two goals I can get started on during the first month after I get out? In the following sessions specific goals are discussed with an eye to whether they appear to be reasonably related to the underlying values as well as whether and how the inmate plans to make it happen.

The facilitator needs to be vigilant for pliance as the person may be speaking socially prescribed words without even being fully aware of what he or she really values. For example, Guy says his goal is to "spend time with my kids." But upon examination, it is evident that this is weakly held. He has no expectation of living near them, has no viable relationship with their mother, and at best envisions himself seeing them rarely. Without denigrating Guy, his therapist elicits and notes the incongruence in the situation and encourages him to focus on values he chooses, not ones he feels he must have, or ones that will look good to others. One way to assess pliance is to imagine situations with social approval removed. For example, a client may state that he values education. The therapist might ask "*if no one but you knew you had that education would it still be important?*" Pliance generally takes the form of saying what others expect or want to hear, and therapists are people too, so therapists need to take care to keep the focus on natural consequences and personal choice over pleasing the therapist.

As values choices lead to goals, the next step is to link goals to specific actions. Some of this can be carried out relatively quickly but ongoing patterns of actions may take years to unfold. Sometimes the question is phrased this way: "*You are leaving in three months. Let's say I ran into you at a Taco Bell exactly one year after your outdate. What do you expect you could actually get done during that first year? What would you want to be telling me you've done in that conversation?*"

Cognitive defusion

The purpose of the first defusion session is to begin to get some distance from the "word machine" (the mind). This is done, first, by using a "friend versus associate" analogy to create a healthy skepticism about the content the mind generates. Most inmates readily relate to the commonplace labels "friends" and "associates." The top portion of the handout found in Appendix 3.C "What Have You Learned from Your Life So Far?" spells out the importance of the message: Your mind is your associate, but it's not your friend.

The handout in Appendix 3.C also includes *The Passengers on the Bus* metaphor in an adapted and abbreviated version of those commonly presented in ACT texts (e.g., Hayes et al., 2012) By familiarizing inmates with this metaphor, the therapist creates a playful image, referring to disengaging thoughts and feelings as unruly passengers who would hijack the person's life bus if only they could. It can be useful when avoidant internal content is identified in later sessions, for example, "*There's that passenger who wants to keep your life bus from moving forward.*"

A later defusion target is "reason giving" as noted by Hayes et al. (2012): "reasons are often used by the client to offer social justification for some undesirable action or lack of action ("*I didn't go to work today because I was too depressed*"). These self-generated rules tend to combine to create a "self-story" with a predictably negative effect." (p. 259). An example of a brief exercise that can be used to defuse reason-giving is asking the person to pick a flavor of ice cream and then, in response to whatever reason is given for it, repeating the question "why?" This helps the person detect that the distance from entirely believable reasons to "I don't know" is almost always quite short, as seen by this vignette with Bert that took place in a group session.

THERAPIST:	Let's say these two paper plates had two equal-sized scoops of ice cream. The one in my left hand is vanilla, and the one in my right hand is chocolate. Which one do you choose?
BERT:	I want the chocolate.
THERAPIST:	Is it possible you could have picked the vanilla?
BERT:	Yes.
THERAPIST:	Then why did you pick the chocolate?
BERT:	Chocolate is my favorite.
THERAPIST:	Why?
BERT:	I like the way it tastes.
THERAPIST:	Why?
BERT:	Maybe it was the first I ever tasted.
THERAPIST:	Why?
BERT:	Maybe it was the first ever offered to me.
THERAPIST:	Why?
BERT:	I don't know.

Perspective taking

To encourage detachment from the conceptualized self, the notion of "story line" is introduced as a story we use to explain ourselves to others. With repetition, we come to believe our story line is what we really are. Many inmates can generate an account of one of their story lines and talk about how it has influenced their actions. By making space for a discussion of this process, they begin to see that a variety of formulations are possible and that they are more than these limited self-conceptualizations. An excellent tutorial on breaking free of story lines may be found in Chapter 11 of Strosahl and Robinson's (2008) book, *The Mindfulness and Acceptance Workbook for Depression*. As the story weakens, group members begin to see that they can create a new future even with the mind beckoning them to default to old habits. Hayes et al. (2012) suggest other useful metaphors to assist perspective taking, including the *Whole, Complete, Perfect* exercise (pp. 226–227) and the *Chessboard* metaphor (pp. 231–232). These authors also note a brief guided mindfulness exercise (p. 230) that brings attention to perspective across time, place, and person. Just asking the person to notice what is in the present moment can be a simple but powerful way to experience the observer self.

Present moment focus

There are two mindfulness practices that are used in Algoa's ACT program. The first is a basic attentional focus on the breath, noting when the mind wanders and escorting attention back to the breath. The second is bringing to mind unpleasant thoughts or memories and noting the specific location and sensations where the painful cognitions appear in the body. In addition, it can be useful to ask an inmate what his thoughts and feelings are in the present moment. If a therapist prefers other exercises for contacting the present moment, these can be used, though in the context of a time-limited ACT group inmates commonly are resistant to longer formal meditation practice.

It is useful to introduce a *very* brief mindfulness or attention-focusing exercise during the first session. If there is resistance, group members are simply asked to try the particular exercises but to give them the option to opt out. If they do so they are asked to sit quietly and not to distract group members. Inmates will sometime cooperate with short exercises when they are placed at the end of a session, so sessions are often concluded in this fashion. In this way, by the time a didactic session or two is devoted to "present moment focus" near the end of the group, clients have had some experience with exercises in a low key way that minimizes the reactivity they may have with longer formal meditation or stress reduction exercises they have been exposed to elsewhere.

Committed action

The closing sessions of the group begin with a return to a focus on values as the inmate is asked to identify an important value and to take the first steps in that direction. Group members have already identified three important values during the Chosen Values session, one of which can serve as the basis of the closing sessions. For example, after presenting a situation in which someone wants to repair a damaged relationship even though it's "scary" or very uncomfortable to do so, clients are asked: "*Why would anyone take a chance in a case like this?*" The sought-after answers generally make reference to values.

The *Internal Barriers* worksheet (Appendix 3.D) serves as a summation of key core processes that the inmate has already noted, and their therapy folder is likely to include self-reported exemplars of several of these barriers. Participants are asked to complete the worksheet with examples of as many types of barriers as they can. Responses are reviewed in session without trying to "solve" these barriers. Rather, the purpose here is to encourage the inmate to acknowledge and accept that the barriers could very well show up as they begin to take action. Of course, some clients will want to bring up external barriers such as a lack of money or reactions from others that may make progress difficult. The therapist needs to acknowledge these barriers, while resisting the temptation to offer problem-solving suggestions. Commitment to action is not a guarantee of outcomes and it does not immediately remove external barriers. What it does is empower the person to move forward in a positive direction, with the history they have.

Inmates are asked to write down one short-term goal (a goal that can be accomplished by 3 months after release) and a long-term goal, which may take many more months or even years to accomplish. To minimize pliance, the facilitator emphasizes that goals are things that "*you really want to make happen; don't write down a 'goal' just because you think it's what your family, your parole officer, or your therapist wants to hear.*"

For each goal, three actions are then listed: one that the inmate can complete prior to release; a second that can be done soon after release; and a third that can be completed within a year after release.

To close the session each participant is asked to complete this narrative and read it to the group. "*A value direction that is very important to me is _____. By (date), I am going to complete the following goal: _____. One thing I can do right away to help this happen is _____.*"

Moving from Excitement Seeking to Lasting Values: Vince's Story

During the preparation of this chapter, we noted the need to address the role of excitement-seeking in antisocial behavior. Vince, a 45-year-old man, soon to be released from prison after serving most of his 20-year sentence, agreed to be interviewed regarding his own life.

THERAPIST:	Some criminal behavior seems to be driven by excitement seeking? Tell me what led you to get involved in these types of things?
VINCE:	I think guys do these things to look good in the eyes of their friends. When I was fifteen and a half, I helped two young women move into a trailer, and I lost my virginity with them. They talked me into moving in with them and soon I was living in a trailer with five women. All my male friends started coming over and partying. Having a lot of sex with women increased my status in other people's eyes.
THERAPIST:	So you became important...?
VINCE:	Everyone looked up to me. I was the center of attention. I spent my life getting drunk and using drugs and I was an asshole.
THERAPIST:	You told me you began changing *before* you got involved in the intensive therapeutic community and acceptance and commitment therapy? Why did you decide to change in the first place?
VINCE:	I realized the women I had been with were whores and sluts and I was a slut too. I knew how to make money cutting down trees. And I had a lot of wicked cars. But due to drinking and drugs, I wrecked them all. Between the women and addictions, I went through a lot of money. And I have nothing to show for it. And I got tired of coming to prison.
THERAPIST:	So what's different now?
VINCE:	You are pressured all the time to live in other people's opinions. Now I know I don't have to live in other people's opinions to make it in life.
THERAPIST:	So what is it that *you* want in life?
VINCE:	Being prosperous..., without drugs and alcohol, and without being an asshole.

Three ACT-related insights are evident in Vince's account. The first is that excitement-seeking behavior may often be a function of pliance, that is, doing what one thinks particular others will approve of. In ACT terms, Vince's disillusionment with excitement-seeking, may be characterized as "in your pain, you find your values." Noting that trying to get the approval of his peers had led to nothing but sorrow, Vince decided to begin preparing to take action that would lead to values he truly embraced. He began by swearing off his drug of choice in prison (marijuana). He began a long-term relationship with a woman he respects and loves. He has been entrepreneurial in prison by trading his drawings and by running a "store." He lives relatively comfortably (e.g. eating more from the commissary than the chow hall). He has saved a modest sum of money for post-release and has developed several plans to sell legal products and services when he is released later this year.

The concern is often raised that some inmates will continue to choose antisocial values after release. This is undoubtedly the case. Occasionally inmates will state this point blank in individual sessions, noting that drug dealing is the most promising way for them to thrive. A mental health professional, regardless of skill or intervention, cannot expect to be effective with many of those inmates whose experience suggests change would be a mistake. However, inmates who actively seek therapy are almost always looking for change. Given limited time and resources, these are the inmates who become the focus of ACT. It is striking how often, when they are asked what they value, they speak of the need to maintain a job, to find or keep a spouse, to further their education, and to be there for their children. When these assertions are examined closely, they are infrequently a matter of pliance, most often a matter of pain and a real desire for a life that works better.

Concluding Remarks: Recognizing Relevant Processes

As an ACT therapist becomes more adept, he or she can recognize instances of psychological inflexibility as they occur and gently bring the attention of the inmate to the behavior and the function it serves. Thus an inmate who is fused with the idea that they will fail at whatever they try, may bring up a specific instance of a thought or feeling along these lines as if it is a process that must be solved before therapeutic work can be successful. The skilled ACT therapist needs to observe the event for what it is, rather than to argue with the content expressed.

The therapist competencies outlined earlier in this chapter are essential to effectively practicing ACT. Employing the metaphors and exercises found in the ACT literature without an ACT-consistent personal stance is likely to go nowhere. Inmates will detect the inconsistency. Professionals who find this approach personally incompatible with their treatment philosophy and style should not mechanically employ ACT techniques hoping they will work. At the same time, even an experienced ACT therapist can "mess up." That is part of being human, and acknowledging difficulties itself models ACT processes. Thus, it is not that the therapist needs to be a master of ACT processes to do ACT. What is important is that the therapist be committed to an open, conscious, and values-based approach to his or her own psychological events. Training in ACT, including attendance at experiential and didactic workshops, helps therapists acquire these skills. ACT sometimes requires counterintuitive actions, and a deep commitment to acceptance and mindfulness-based processes that will empower its use.

ACT provides therapists and inmates alike with a new way forward that seems to be applicable to the problems incarcerated populations face. Because of its breadth of application, and flexibility of delivery, it seems especially well suited to prison systems of care that are often overwhelmed by the level of need and limited resources. While there is research on ACT with court-adjudicated populations (e.g., Hayes et al., 2004; Luoma, Kohlenberg, Hayes, & Fletcher, 2012) it needs to be acknowledged that formal research with inmate populations is currently absent. Thus, a great deal remains to be done to learn how to fit ACT to this population and setting, and to examine its long-term effects.

References

Eifert, G. H., & Forsyth, J. P. (2005). *Acceptance and commitment therapy for anxiety disorders: A practitioner's treatment guide to using mindfulness, acceptance, and values-based behavior change strategies.* Oakland, CA: New Harbinger.

Fletcher, L. & Hayes, S. C. (2005). Relational Frame Theory, Acceptance and Commitment Therapy, and a functional analytic definition of mindfulness. *Journal of Rational Emotive and Cognitive Behavioral Therapy, 23*, 315–336.

Forsyth, J. P., & Eifert, G. H. (2007). *The mindfulness and acceptance workbook for anxiety: A guide to breaking free from anxiety, phobias and worry using acceptance and commitment therapy.* Oakland, CA: New Harbinger.

Gaudiano, B.A. (2009). Öst's (2008) methodological comparison of clinical trials of Acceptance and Commitment Therapy versus Cognitive Behavior Therapy: Matching apples with oranges? *Behaviour Research and Therapy, 47*, 1066–1070.

Hayes, S.C., Barnes-Holmes, D., & Roche, B. (2001). *Relational frame theory: A post-Skinnerian account of human language and cognition.* New York: Plenum.

Hayes, S. C., Luoma, J. B., Bond, F. W., Masuda, A., & Lillis, J. (2006). Acceptance and Commitment Therapy: Model, processes and outcomes. *Behavior Research and Therapy, 44*, 1–25.

Hayes, S. C., & Smith, S. (2005). *Get out of your mind and into your life: The new Acceptance and Commitment Therapy.* Oakland, CA: New Harbinger.

Hayes, S. C., Strosahl, K. D., & Wilson, K. G. (1999). *Acceptance and Commitment Therapy: An experiential approach to behavior change.* New York: The Guilford Press.

Hayes, S. C., Strosahl, K. D., & Wilson, K. G. (2012). *Acceptance and Commitment Therapy: The process and practice of mindful change* (2nd ed.). New York: Guilford Press.

Hayes, S.C., Villatte, M., Levin, M. & Hildebrandt, M. (2011). Open, aware, and active: Contextual approaches as an emerging trend in the behavioral and cognitive therapies. *Annual Review of Clinical Psychology, 7,* 141–168.

Hayes, S. C. & Wilson, K.G. (1994). Acceptance and Commitment Therapy: Altering the verbal support for experiential avoidance. *The Behavior Analyst, 17,* 289–303.

Hayes, S. C., Wilson, K. G., Gifford, E. V., Bissett, R., Piasecki, M., Batten, S. V., Byrd, M., & Gregg, J. (2004). A randomized controlled trial of twelve-step facilitation and acceptance and commitment therapy with polysubstance abusing methadone maintained opiate addicts. *Behavior Therapy, 35,* 667–688.

Hayes, S. C., Wilson, K. W., Gifford, E. V., Follette, V. M., & Strosahl, K. (1996). Experiential avoidance and behavioral disorders: A functional dimensional approach to diagnosis and treatment. *Journal of Consulting and Clinical Psychology, 64,* 1152–1168.

Levin, M., & Hayes, S.C. (2009). Is acceptance and commitment therapy superior to established treatment comparisons? *Psychotherapy and Psychosomatics, 78,* 380.

Luoma, J. B., Kohlenberg, B. S., Hayes, S. C. & Fletcher, L. (2012). Slow and steady wins the race: A randomized clinical trial of Acceptance and Commitment Therapy targeting shame in substance use disorders. *Journal of Consulting and Clinical Psychology, 80,* 43–53.

Masuda, A., Hayes, S. C., Twohig, M. P., Drossel, C., Lillis, J., & Washio, Y. (2009). A parametric study of cognitive defusion and the believability and discomfort of negative self-relevant thoughts. *Behavior Modification, 33,* 250–262.

Öst, L. G. (2008). Efficacy of the third wave of behavioral therapies: A systematic review and meta-analysis. *Behaviour Research and Therapy, 46,* 296–321.

Powers, M. B., Vörding, M. B. Z. S., & Emmelkamp, P. M. G. (2009). Acceptance and commitment therapy: A meta-analytic review. *Psychotherapy and Psychosomatics, 78,* 73–80.

Strosahl, K. D., Hayes, S. C., Wilson, K. G., & Gifford, E. V. (2004) An ACT primer: Core therapy processes, intervention strategies, and therapist competencies. In S. C. Hayes & K. D. Strosahl, (Eds.), *A practical guide to acceptance and commitment therapy* (pp. 31–58). New York: Springer-Verlag.

Strosahl, K. D. & Robinson, P. J. (2008). *The mindfulness and acceptance workbook for depression: Using acceptance and commitment therapy to move through depression and create a life worth living.* Oakland, CA: New Harbinger.

Wilson, K. G., & Murrell, A. R. (2004). Values work in Acceptance and Commitment Therapy. In S. C. Hayes, V. M. Follette, & M. M. Linehan (Eds.), *Mindfulness and acceptance: Expanding the cognitive-behavioral tradition* (pp. 121–151). New York: Guilford Press.

Zettle, R. D. (2007). *ACT for Depression: A clinician's guide to using Acceptance and Commitment Therapy in treating depression.* Oakland, CA: New Harbinger.

Suggestions for Further Learning

Books

Hayes, S. C., Strosahl, K., & Wilson, K. G. (2012). *Acceptance and commitment therapy: The process and practice of mindful change* (2nd ed.). New York: Guilford Press.

Luoma, J., Hayes, S. C., & Walser, R. (2007). *Learning ACT.* Oakland, CA: New Harbinger.

Hayes, S. C., & Smith, S. (2005). *Get out of your mind and into your life: The new Acceptance and Commitment Therapy.* Oakland, CA: New Harbinger.

Professional organization

Association of Contextual Behavioral Science (ACBS): a worldwide online learning and research community, and a living resource for anyone interested in basic and applied inquiries entailed by contextual behavioral science including ACT and its underlying theory of language and cognition, Relational Frame Theory (RFT) but also several other methods and approaches.

Websites

The ACBS organizational website is http://contextualscience.org/. The ACBS website lists the voluminous publications that have appeared (most in the last decade) as well as worldwide opportunities for training. The main ACBS list serve for professionals is http://tech.groups.yahoo.com/group/acceptanc eandcommitmenttherapy/, but there are several more specialized list serves as well (see ACBS website).

Journal

Although ACT studies and discourse have been published in a wide-range of professional journals, a new journal devoted specifically to contextual behavioral science is now available: the *Journal of Contextual Behavioral Science*. For more information see their website: http://www.journals.elsevier.com/ journal-of-contextual-behavioral-science/.

Appendix 3.A

Handout: The Kid in the Hole

Imagine that you're this kid who has always worn a blindfold, and has always carried around a tool bag.

Every day you go out and play in a field. It's what you've always known and you're used to playing in this field with your blindfold on and this tool bag strapped around you. Your life seems pretty good. You have a great time every day, and you start going further and further into this huge field that stretches for what seems to be forever.

What you don't know is that this field has a lot of really deep holes that are far apart from each other. So the more you run around this field, what is going to happen sooner or later...?

That's right, what happens is you fall into a big hole.

You check it out, and sure enough, you can't climb out. After a while, you open your tool bag, and it turns out the only tool in the bag is a shovel. So, in all kinds of ways, you begin shoveling.

- You dig tunnels.
- You try to mound up some dirt.
- You try cutting steps in the walls.

But the more you use the shovel, the hole you're in just keeps getting wider and deeper....
Now how does this story fit what has happened to you in your own life?

What is the hole you have fallen into?

What could you say about the hole you have fallen into in your life up 'til now?

What have you tried to do to get out of your hole that has just made the hole deeper? What have you done to try to try to solve the problem that has only made it worse?

Appendix 3.B

Values Worksheet

Pick out __three areas__ that are most important to you. For one or two of these areas, write down how you want to get moving and where you want to move toward in that area (your intention).

Work/career

Intention: Work could be a paid job, unpaid volunteer work, or taking care of a child or an elderly or dependent adult.

What's important to you about your work? What do you get out of having a job? It might be making money, being independent, or looking good in the eyes of others. It could be using your brain and/or your hands, being around other people or offering a helping hand.

How would you like to use your energy, talents, and skills productively? What would that look like? What would you do if you could be doing anything?

Intimate relationships (e.g., marriage, couples)

Intention: Intimate relationships with a partner or spouse. What kind of partner would you most like to be within an intimate relationship? What would you be doing to become close and stay close to a partner or spouse?

What type of marriage or couple relationship would you like to have? How do you want to treat your partner, or a person that you share a special commitment and bond with?

Parenting

Intention: You may have a child of your own, or take care of a child without being a bio parent. What type of parent do you want to be? How do you want to act to support your role as a parent?

How do you want to interact with your kids? How would your child see you "walk the walk" when it comes to your values here? What would others see?

What is it about being a parent that is important to you?

Education – learning and personal growth

Intention: Personal growth means getting real about yourself and developing as a human being. It can start by getting a deeper sense of who you are.

Going to school is one way to learn. Growth and learning also takes place outside of school. Would you like to sharpen skills you already have, or develop new ones? Do you enjoy learning new things? Why is learning important to you?

What skills, training, or areas of competence would you like to acquire? What would you really like to learn more about?

Health and physical self-care

Intention: How do you want to take care of yourself? Why does it matter what you eat, whether you exercise, or what you do to stay in shape?

What do you get out of staying healthy? It might be out of sheer enjoyment, in order to be successful in a physically demanding job, or to give yourself a better chance of living to a ripe old age and being around for those you love.

Being well emotionally

Intention: How and why do you want to be as fit as possible emotionally? Why is it important not to retreat from the world and all it has to offer?

The antidote to pushing the world away is to begin to practice acts of kindness and loving care –starting with yourself and expanding out to other people in your life.

What would it be like for you to learn to be kinder to yourself? How would your life be different if you were to practice acceptance and compassion toward your feelings? What is it that you like about caring for your mental well-being?

Family of origin (relationships with those besides your spouse and kids)

Intention: This domain focuses on your relationships with your sisters and brothers, parents and other relatives. What kind of relationship do you want to have with your parents or siblings? How are these roles and relationships important to you?

Is there anything missing from your life in this area that you might be able to change? How do you want to be with your brothers and sisters? If your mother or father is still alive how do you want to be with them?

Spirituality

Intention: Whether you belong to an organized religion or seek out other ways to grow in your connections with other people, the world around you or a higher power, you are connected to the spiritual part of your life.

Take a moment to reflect on your spirituality. Are there things larger than your own life that inspire you? Ask yourself: "In what, if anything, do I have faith? What is the role I would like to see spirituality play in my life and how would that show up?"

If you had this in your life, what kind of qualities would it provide for you?

Appendix 3.C

Handout: What Have You Learned From Your Life So Far?

Sometimes we think someone is our friend and we find out they are not. Sometimes we believe something is true and we find out it's not. Sometimes we think something is really important, and we find out it isn't.

Can you give an example of one of the three things above – something you used to think or believe that has changed?

Your mind is your associate, but it's not your friend. *What is the difference between an associate and a friend?" (several answers)*

Just because our mind is always hanging out with us, doesn't mean it's our friend. The mind is all the chatter that's been programmed into our head. It never stops. It comes and goes so fast that we don't even remember most of it. Sometimes our minds are good at spotting problems and figuring out how to fix them.

Sometimes the mind is not as good as it pretends to be. The mind can try to spot and fix problems that aren't even there. Sometimes when there's nothing to worry about, our minds make up things to worry about. Sometimes our minds push us to solve problems that can't be solved. Sometimes our mind calls us names if we make a mistake or forget something –names like "stupid" or "screw up." How often does your mind put you down, just because you have problems?

Your mind does the same thing that all minds do. And even though your mind is not your friend, that doesn't mean you have to fix it. The name of the game is to learn to live with your mind, but not let it keep you from making your life what you want it to be.

***** * * *

"Passengers on The Bus" metaphor (adapted from Hayes et al., 1999)

Let's say you are driving a bus which is actually your life. Along the way you've picked up a bunch of passengers, which we'll say are your thoughts, feelings, sensations in your body, memories, and things like that. So you are driving along and these passengers start telling you what you have to do, where you have to go. They yell at you: "You've got to go this way!… No, you've got to turn left!" If you don't do what they say, they are going to come up from the back of the bus.

Now, what if one day you say "I'm sick of this. I'm going to throw those guys off the bus!" You stop the bus to deal with them. Notice that the very first thing you had to do was stop. For the moment, you're not driving anywhere. Plus, these passengers are real strong and aren't going to go anywhere. You do the best you can, but it looks like you are on your way to getting beat down.

So you make a deal: If these thoughts, feelings, and memories (passengers) go sit where you can't see them, you'll do whatever you have to do to get them to leave you alone. However, when they do eventually start bothering you again, it's with the added power of the deals you've made with them.

Now the dirty little secret in this whole game is this: The power that the passengers have over you is 100% based on this: "If you don't do what we say we're coming up and making you look at us." That's it! You are the driver of your life bus. You have control. But you trade away control in these deals with the passengers.

But even though these passengers *claim* they can destroy you if you don't turn left, it has never actually occurred. These passengers can't make you do something against your will.

Appendix 3.D

Internal Barriers: Things Inside Me That Make It Hard To Live My Values

Below are some of the types of barriers that can get in the way of taking action that will be in service of your values (the direction you want to go in). If you think one of these types of barriers fits your situation see if you can write down an example or explanation.

Barrier #1:
Value Confusion: A hard time figuring out what's important to you.

Barrier #2:
Feelings, Thoughts, or Sensations that You Avoid

Barrier #3:
Feelings, Thoughts, or Sensations that You Struggle With

Barrier #4:
Reasons or Judgments You Come Up With About "Why I Can't"

Barrier #5:
The Story Line that You've Told Yourself and Others About "Who I Am "

4

Schema Therapy for Aggressive Offenders with Personality Disorders

Marije Keulen-de Vos, David P. Bernstein, and Arnoud Arntz

Interest in forensic treatment has increased considerably in recent years as evidenced by a growing literature on treatments for sex offenders and domestic violence offenders (e.g., Marshall & Serran, 2001; Murphy & Ting, 2010). However, the treatment of personality-disordered (PD) offenders is an area in need of far greater attention. Personality disorders are highly prevalent in criminal offender populations, and are associated with increased risk of violence and recidivism (Blackburn, Logan, Donnelly, & Renwick, 2003; Leistico, Salekin, DeCoster, & Rogers, 2008). This population is traditionally considered difficult to treat. In this chapter, we describe recent developments in the application of schema therapy (ST: Young, Klosko, & Weishaar, 2003) to forensic patients with PDs. ST differs from other cognitive-behavioral treatments for forensic patients in several important respects. First, unlike most other cognitive-behavioral treatments, ST was specifically developed as a treatment for PDs. It is an integrative form of therapy that combines standard cognitive-behavioral interventions with other approaches that are not traditionally used in cognitive-behavioral therapy, but are often necessary in working with patients with PDs. These include:

1. A focus on the therapy relationship to address the difficulties of these patients in forming secure attachments.
2. An emphasis on reprocessing childhood traumas, which are highly prevalent in this population.
3. The use of experiential techniques that focus on emotions to remediate the affective difficulties of these patients.

Unlike other cognitive-behavioral approaches for patients with anger and aggression problems, which are often shorter-term therapies, ST is a medium- to long-term form of psychotherapy that can last for 2 to 3 years or even longer in patients with aggressive PDs, such as Antisocial, Narcissistic, or Borderline. While ST for forensic patients can be administered in therapeutic groups (Beckley & Gordon, 2009; Farrell, Shaw & Webber, 2009;

Forensic CBT: A Handbook for Clinical Practice, First Edition.
Edited by Raymond Chip Tafrate and Damon Mitchell.
© 2014 John Wiley & Sons, Ltd. Published 2014 by John Wiley & Sons, Ltd.

Van Vreeswijk & Broersen, 2006), it is usually delivered individually, or as a combination of individual and group therapy. In keeping with the risk, need, and responsivity principles (Andrews & Bonta, 2003), longer-term therapies are justified if they can ameliorate the risk factors for violence and recidivism in otherwise difficult-to-treat patients, such as those with PDs. In fact, such longer-term treatments may prove to be cost-effective, despite their higher costs, if they can reduce rates of incarceration and recidivism. Preliminary findings in the first 30 patients to complete an ongoing randomized clinical trial of forensic inpatients with Cluster B PDs in The Netherlands support this contention: Patients who received 3 years of ST showed greater improvement in recidivism risk, and were more likely and quicker to receive permission to enter and advance through the resocialization process that can lead to release from detention, than patients receiving usual forensic treatment. Further, the full cost of delivering ST for 3 years was fully recouped by reducing patients' length of stay in the institution by just 2 months (Bernstein, Nijman, Karos, Keulen-de Vos, de Vogel, & Lucker, 2012). Although these findings were not statistically significant in this small initial sample, they suggest that the costs of delivering ST may be justified by its success in lowering recidivism risk.

In this chapter, we describe the rationale for ST, present our forensic adaptation of ST, and provide guidelines for clinical practice. The forensic ST model focuses on emotional states, known as *schema modes*, which are seen as risk factors for violence and crime. When triggered, schema modes increase the probability of aggressive, impulsive, or other antisocial behavior. By targeting these factors, schema therapists aim to reduce the patient's risk for violence and future antisocial behavior. In our experience, and based on the preliminary results of our research, therapists can indeed learn to recognize and intervene with schema modes and work more effectively with these challenging patients.

Schema Therapy Conceptual Model

Early maladaptive schemas and maladaptive coping responses

The ST theoretical model is based on the following core concepts: *early maladaptive schemas*, *maladaptive coping responses*, and *schema modes* (Rafaeli, Bernstein, & Young, 2011; Young et al., 2003). Early maladaptive schemas are self-defeating themes or patterns about oneself and one's personal relationships; they refer to maladaptive cognitive structures representing the self, others, and the environment, and relations between them. Early maladaptive schemas are trait-like, enduring entities or patterns that originate from adverse childhood experiences and early temperament; they guide people's perceptions and behavior and evolve over the course of a lifetime. Over time, they become more resistant to change and give rise to negative automatic thoughts and subjective distress. For example, early maladaptive schemas such as abandonment, social isolation, defectiveness, and mistrust/abuse can evoke emotions such as fear, sadness, and anger (Bernstein, Arntz, & de Vos, 2007; Jovev & Jackson, 2004). Young identified 18 early maladaptive schemas, which are described in Table 4.1. These schemas can be grouped into five domains, which are connected with certain basic childhood needs (also listed in Table 4.1). For example, if the need for attachment – which Young et al. (2003) posit to be one of five universal emotional needs in childhood – goes unmet to a significant degree, the result may be the development of early maladaptive schemas in the domain of "disconnection and rejection."

When early maladaptive schemas are triggered, they can give rise to strong emotions. Young et al. (2003) hypothesized that one can cope with the activation of such schemas in

Table 4.1 Schema domains and early maladaptive schemas (adapted from Young et al., 2003).

Domain: Disconnection and Rejection		

Early maladaptive schemas

1	Abandonment/Instability	The expectation that one will inevitably be abandoned
2	Mistrust/Abuse	The expectation that others will hurt, abuse, humiliate, cheat, lie, manipulate, or take advantage
3	Emotional Deprivation	The expectation that others won't meet one's need for a normal degree of emotional nurturance, empathy, and protection
4	Defectiveness/Shame	The feeling that one is defective, bad, unwanted, inferior, or invalid in important respects
5	Social Isolation/Alienation	The feeling that one is always an outsider, different and alienated from other people

Domain: Impaired Autonomy and Performance		

Early maladaptive schemas

6	Dependence/Incompetence	Expectation that one can't handle everyday responsibilities without considerable help from others
7	Vulnerability to Harm or Illness	Exaggerated fear that imminent catastrophe will strike at any time and that one cannot prevent it
8	Enmeshment/Undeveloped Self	Excessive emotional involvement and closeness with others at the expense of full individuation or normal social development
9	Failure	The belief that one has failed, or will inevitably fail, or is fundamentally inadequate in areas of achievement

Domain: Impaired Limits		

Early maladaptive schemas

10	Entitlement/Grandiosity	The belief that one is superior to others, entitled to special rights and privileges, or not bound by normal rules of social reciprocity
11	Insufficient Self-Control/ Self-Discipline	Pervasive difficulty or refusal to exercise self-control and frustration tolerance to achieve goals

Domain: Other-Directedness		

Early maladaptive schemas

12	Subjugation	Excessive surrendering of control to others because one feels coerced, to avoid anger, retaliation, or abandonment
13	Self-Sacrifice	Excessive focus on voluntarily meeting the needs of others at the expense of one's own gratification
14	Approval-Seeking/ Recognition-Seeking	Excessive emphasis on gaining approval, recognition, or attention from other people

Domain: Over-Vigilance and Inhibition		

Early maladaptive schemas

15	Negativity/Pessimism	A pervasive, lifelong focus on the negative aspects of life (e.g., pain, death, loss) while minimizing the positive or optimistic aspects
16	Emotional Inhibition	The excessive inhibition of spontaneous action, feeling, or communication
17	Unrelenting Standards/ Hypercriticalness	The belief that one must strive to meet very high internalized standards of behavior and performance
18	Punitiveness	The belief that people should be harshly punished for making mistakes

three ways: schema surrender, schema avoidance, and schema overcompensation. Schema surrender means giving in to a schema in a passive, helpless, dependent, or submissive way. For example, someone with a dependence/incompetence schema may choose partners whom they perceive to be more competent than they are, on whom they rely in a "childlike" way. Schema avoidance means avoiding people or situations that might trigger a particular schema. For example, some may avoid getting involved in intimate relationships because of a profound fear of being abandoned. Finally, schema overcompensation means doing the opposite of a schema. For example, someone with a defectiveness/shame schema might behave in a denigrating way toward others, which helps them feel superior and offsets feelings of inferiority.

Schema modes

The combination of early maladaptive schemas and maladaptive coping responses constituted the original ST conceptual model, as elaborated by Young et al. (2003). While this model proved useful for working with most PD patients, it was inadequate for patients with more aggressive PDs. These patients often have so many early maladaptive schemas that discussing them all in therapy was unmanageable. Moreover, patients with severe PDs, such as Borderline and Narcissistic, often switch or flip rapidly from one extreme emotional state to another, making it difficult for therapists to keep track of them. Young et al. (2003) introduced the concept of schema modes to help therapists monitor and work with these fluctuating states. Schema modes are defined as moment-to-moment emotional states that temporarily dominate a person's thinking, feeling, and behavior. Compared to the maladaptive schemas, which are traitlike, schema modes are statelike entities. These emotional states can either be functional or maladaptive (Young et al., 2003). We all experience a range of emotional states. However, in people with severe PDs, these states tend to be more extreme and often involve dysfunctional forms of coping. Also, in these patients, schema modes are largely dissociated from one another: When a patient is in a particular mode, he or she is quite unaware of other modes. PD patients have little control over their emotional states; therefore, they rapidly switch between emotional states.

Young and colleagues (2003) distinguish 11 schema modes that cover five mode domains; others have proposed and reported evidence for additional modes (Bamelis, Renner, Heidkamp, & Arntz, 2011; Bernstein et al., 2007; Lobbestael, van Vreeswijk, & Arntz, 2008). A complete list of modes and mode domains is given in Table 4.2. *Child* schema modes involve thinking, feeling, and acting in a childlike manner; they represent emotional reactions, such as fear, sadness, loss, anger, frustration, and loneliness, which are fundamental and universal in children. *Avoidant Coping* schema modes involve attempts to block out painful emotions, and avoid people and situations that trigger them. The *Over Compensatory Coping* schema modes involve "turning the tables" on other people, and doing the opposite of schemas, to compensate for themes such as shame, loneliness, and vulnerability. The *Surrendering Coping* schema modes reflect the tendency to submit to others in a passive, helpless, or dependent way. The *Maladaptive Parent* schema modes relate to self-directed punishment or criticism, or self-directed pressure to perform, respectively, and reflect internalized dysfunctional behavior of the parent (or other caregivers) directed toward the child. Finally, the *Healthy* schema modes express healthy, balanced, self-reflection and feelings of pleasure, spontaneous playfulness, and joy, respectively (Rafaeli et al., 2011; Young et al., 2003).

Table 4.2 Schema modes.

Child Modes	Involve feeling, thinking, and acting in a "childlike" manner
1 Abandoned/Abused Child	Feels vulnerable, overwhelmed with painful feelings, such as anxiety, depression, grief, or shame/humiliation
2 Angry Child	Feels and expresses anger in an excessive way in response to perceived or real mistreatment, abandonment, humiliation, or frustration; often feels a sense of being treated unjustly; acts like a child throwing a temper tantrum
3 Enraged Child	Feels and acts enraged for similar reasons as Angry Child, but loses control over aggression and attacks and destroys objects and humans; patients often report as if they went into a dissociative state (*"everything went black"*)
4 Impulsive Child	Acts impulsively to get needs met; can be motivated by rebelliousness against maltreatment or against internalized parental modes
5 Undisciplined Child	Acts like a spoiled child who *"wants what he wants when he wants it,"* and doesn't want to do anything he dislikes; can't tolerate the frustration of limits and discipline
6 Lonely Child	Feels lonely and empty, as if no one can understand him, sooth or comfort him, or make contact with him

Dysfunctional Coping Modes	Involve attempts to protect the self from pain through maladaptive forms of coping
7 Detached Protector	Uses emotional detachment to protect himself from painful feelings; is unaware of his feelings, feels "nothing," appears emotionally distant, flat, or robotic; avoids getting close to other people
8 Detached Self-Soother/ Self-Stimulator	Uses repetitive, 'addictive,' or compulsive behaviors, or self-stimulating behaviors to calm and sooth himself; uses pleasurable or exciting sensations to distance himself from painful feelings
9 Compliant Surrenderer	Gives in to the real or perceived demands or expectations of other people in an anxious attempt to avoid pain or to get his needs met; anxiously surrenders to the demands of others who are perceived as more powerful than himself
10 Angry Protector	Uses a 'wall of anger' to protect himself from others who are perceived as threatening; keeps others at a safe distance through displays of anger; anger is more controlled than in Angry Child Mode

Maladaptive Parent Modes	Involve internalized dysfunctional parent "voices"
11 Punitive, Critical Parent	Internalized, critical or punishing parent voice; directs harsh criticism towards the self; induces feelings of shame or guilt
12 Demanding Parent	Directs impossibly high demands toward the self; pushes the self to do more, achieve more, never be satisfied with oneself

Over-Compensatory Modes	Involve extreme attempts to compensate for feelings of shame, loneliness, or vulnerability
13 Self-Aggrandizer Mode	Feels superior, special, or powerful; looks down on others; sees the world in terms of "top dog" and "bottom dog"; shows off or acts in a self-important, self-aggrandizing manner; concerned about appearances rather than feelings or real contact with others
14 Bully and Attack Mode	Uses threats, intimidation, aggression, or coercion to get what he wants, including retaliating against others, or asserting his dominant position; feels a sense of sadistic pleasure in attacking others

Table 4.2   (*Continued*)

Over-Compensatory Modes	Involve extreme attempts to compensate for feelings of shame, loneliness, or vulnerability
15 Conning and Manipulative Mode	Cons, lies, or manipulates in a manner designed to achieve a specific goal, which either involves victimizing others or escaping punishment
16 Predator Mode	Focuses on eliminating a threat, rival, obstacle, or enemy in a cold, ruthless, and calculating manner
17 Obsessive-Compulsive Over-Controller Mode	The Obsessive type (sometimes called Perfectionistic Over-Controller) attempts to protect himself from a perceived or real threat by focusing attention, ruminating, exercising extreme control, and using order, repetition, or rituals
18 Paranoid Over-Controller Mode	Attempts to protect himself from a perceived or real threat by focusing attention, ruminating, and exercising extreme control; the Suspicious type attempts to locate and uncover a hidden (perceived) threat

Note. Modes 1, 2, 5–10, and 12–14, are adapted from Young et al. (2003).

Not all schema modes are relevant for each patient. According to ST, distinctive schema mode configurations or combinations of modes are believed to be markers of specific personality disorder pathology. For example, Borderline PD (BPD) is hypothesized to be centered around four dominant schema modes (Arntz & van Genderen, 2009; Young et al., 2003):

1. *Abused/Abandoned Child* mode, marked by feelings of abandonment or abuse.
2. *Angry/Impulsive Child* mode, characterized by uncontrolled anger or rage in response to perceived abandonment or maltreatment and rebellious impulsive need satisfaction.
3. *Punitive/Critical Parent* mode, marked by self-punitive behavior.
4. *Detached Protector* mode, which includes feelings of detachment.

Related to the focus of the present chapter, the schema modes relevant for Narcissistic PD (NPD) and Antisocial PD are described. NPD is hypothesized to be centered around the following four modes (Behary, 2008; Bamelis et al., 2011; Young & Flanagan, 1998):

1. *Self-Aggrandizer* mode, which includes the themes of grandiosity, entitlement and self-importance.
2. *Lonely/Inferior Child* mode, which includes feelings of loneliness or emptiness or inferiority.
3. *Detached Self-Soother* mode, which leads to coping by self-soothing behavior such as drug and alcohol use.
4. *Enraged Child* mode, expressing rage often towards the person who triggered these poorly tolerated feelings.

Bernstein and colleagues (2007) hypothesized that antisocial and especially psychopathic offenders make prominent use of several *forensic schema modes*, as well as modes involving overcompensation (e.g., *Self-Aggrandizer* and *Bully and Attack* modes). For example, psychopaths' crimes often include: (i) *Predator* mode, which involves cold and ruthless aggression; (ii) *Conning and Manipulative* mode, marked by deceit; and (iii) *Bully and Attack* mode, which involves aggression to assert dominance. These modes are believed to have been developed during childhood under conditions of extreme threats and humiliation (Jaffee,

Caspi, Moffitt, & Taylor, 2004; Poythress, Skeem, & Lilienfeld, 2006) and they serve as a shield to protect corresponding feelings of vulnerability, anger, and frustration (Bernstein et al., 2007). Recent research supports the contention that specific configurations of modes characterize different PDs (Bamelis et al., 2011; Lobbestael et al., 2008).

Schema therapy: forensic adaptation

There are several important adaptations to treatment that may be required when working with forensic patients. First, issues like violence and deception are far more prominent in forensic patients as compared to those in general psychiatric settings (Bernstein et al., 2007). Therapists may easily feel frightened by the potential for violence. Second, the circumstances and settings in which forensic patients are treated present special challenges that are not often seen in general psychiatry. Forensic patients are sentenced to treatment, which means that their admission is involuntary in nature. This can affect motivation and compliance with treatment, and can set up a dynamic of opposition and mistrust (Sainsbury, Krishnan, & Evans, 2004). It can also affect the therapist's motivation for providing treatment. Therapists may feel frustrated by a patient's lack of progress, or become suspicious of their motives. These issues may affect the therapeutic alliance, an aspect that has a significant influence on therapy outcome (Marshall & Serran, 2004; Ross, Polaschek, & Ward, 2008). Third, offenders have relatively limited choices regarding their treatment team; moreover, the team is also responsible for safety of the patient and his or her surroundings (McCann, Ball & Ivanoff, 2000). This may complicate patients' interactions with staff members. For example, too much attention to risk and safety issues can undermine and possibly preclude effective treatment (Norton & McGauley, 2000), while too little can also create problems.

For these reasons, we found it necessary to adapt ST to forensic settings. First, we expanded the schema mode model by adding modes that are prevalent in forensic patients, but seldom seen in general psychiatric settings. Moreover, we conceptualized these "forensic" modes as psychological risk factors for crime and violence. When these modes are triggered, they increase the probability of aggressive, impulsive, or other antisocial behavior. Thus, forensic ST focuses on ameliorating the psychological risk factors that, when triggered, can lead to criminal or violent recidivism.

As listed in Table 4.2, we added five schema modes to Young's original mode model: the Angry Protector, Conning and Manipulative, Predator, and two Over-Controller modes (*Obsessive* and *Paranoid* subtypes). As an exercise, see if you can match these forensic schema modes in Box 4.1 to case examples presented in Box 4.2. Answers are provided in Box 4.5.

Clinical Practice

ST integrates techniques from various approaches, such as cognitive, behavioral, psychodynamic and emotion-focused therapies. The initial phase of therapy is focused on assessment, education, and building a therapeutic relationship between patient and therapist. This phase concludes in an individual case conceptualization, which is used as a guideline for the treatment.

Assessment and case conceptualization

The therapist evaluates the patient's suitability for ST. Although ST was originally developed for PD patients and patients with other longstanding problems, psychiatric comorbidity with Axis I disorders and coinciding psychotropic medication is not an exclusionary criterion for ST. However,

Box 4.1   Forensic Schema Modes

(a) *Angry Protector mode* is an emotional state of controlled anger or hostility, a "wall of anger" that serves to keep people at a safe distance.

(b) *Predator mode* is a state of cold, ruthless aggression; the focus is on eliminating a threat, obstacle, or enemy, which is carried out in a callous, unfeeling and often unplanned manner.

(c) *Conning and Manipulative mode* is a state involving conning, lying, and manipulating others in order to achieve a specific goal, such as escaping punishment or victimizing others for some type of gain (e.g., material, sexual).

(d) *Over-Controller mode* involves excessive control and a focusing of attention on a real or perceived threat or danger. In the *Obsessive-Compulsive* subtype, also called the *Perfectionistic Over-Controller*, the patient attempts to exercise control through the use of order, repetition, or ritual. In the *Paranoid* subtype, the patient attempts to seek out and therefore control a source of danger or humiliation, usually by locating and uncovering a hidden (perceived) threat (Bernstein et al., 2007).

Box 4.2   Case Examples

1. Mike discovered another man in his bed with his girlfriend. The man escaped from the house, but the girlfriend stayed behind. Mike had known for a while that his girlfriend was unfaithful to him. He confronted her, but she denied it. A cold rage took over him. He decided to kill her as retaliation for her infidelity.

2. Stephen was abused by his father when he was a child. He always keeps close track of everyone, and trusts no one except his mother. He refuses to do things he cannot control. In ST, he refused to do imagery practices, stating that he didn't want to close his eyes.

3. Kevin sexually offended against a child, and was sentenced to treatment in a forensic hospital. He learned that his unsupervised leave was denied, because the "leave committee" found it unclear whether he still had sexual fantasies about children. When his psychotherapist brought up this topic, Kevin became very irritated. He said that it was obvious that no one believed him, and refused to discuss the topic further.

4. Bill was sentenced to prison for raping his girlfriend multiple times. During psychotherapy he fell in love with his female therapist. He repeatedly tried to tempt her to step out of her therapist role by asking her direct, personal questions (e.g., Are you in love with me? Do you have kids? What type of men do you like?). When the therapist told him that she is not in love with him but respected him as a person, he twisted this information and tried to use it against her by telling the nursing staff that she was in love with him and that they had a romantic relationship.

there are some comorbid conditions that may be a contraindication for ST, such as low intelligence (IQ <80), neurological impairments, autistic spectrum disorders, and certain psychotic disorders. The presence of such conditions may require modifications in standard ST techniques (e.g., avoiding using emotion-focused techniques in patients who are vulnerable to psychotic decompensation), or may suggest that other forms of therapy are indicated rather than ST.

We do not consider high levels of psychopathic traits as an exclusionary criterion for ST. Although it is commonly believed that psychopathic patients are untreatable, or that treatment actually makes them worse, there is little empirical support for this view (D'Silva, Duggan, & McCarthy, 2004). Recent studies suggest that some psychopathic patients may benefit from psychotherapy (Chakhssi, de Ruiter, & Bernstein, 2010; Skeem, Monahan, & Mulvey, 2002), a position that is consistent with our own clinical experiences, as well as the preliminary findings of our research (Bernstein,et al., 2012). Psychopathic patients do require attention to issues such as dominance, manipulation, and deception, which can arise in the therapy relationship; some adjustments in the therapist's technique are therefore necessary. Nevertheless, our experiences working with these patients lead us to be optimistic that some may be helped by treatment, a view that also needs to be tempered with realism about the challenges posed by these patients.

As with all CBT-oriented treatments, careful diagnosis and assessment are essential prerequisites for ST. The therapist begins with an initial evaluation and assesses the patient's presenting problems and goals for therapy by taking a life history and gathering information from multiple sources, including administering questionnaires, reviewing the available records, and observing the patient's behavior and emotional states. The therapist explains the ST model and schema mode language, and asks the patient to fill out certain questionnaires, such as the *Schema Mode Inventory* (SMI; Young et al., 2007) and *Young Schema Questionnaire* (YSQ; Young & Brown, 2003).

Because responses to these self-report questionnaires are often limited by a lack of patient insight (Keulen-de Vos, Bernstein, Clark, Arntz, Lucker, & de Spa, 2011; Lobbestael, Arntz, Löbbes, & Cima, 2009), the therapist also uses experiential techniques, such as imagery, to trigger schema modes. The therapist observes the patient's schemas and coping responses as they manifest themselves in the therapy sessions. Available records are then used to identify dysfunctional life patterns, using the ST conceptual model to link them to presenting problems. Relevant schema modes are identified and conceptualized in an individual case conceptualization form. These formulations are the initial focus of the treatment (Rafaeli et al., 2011; Young et al., 2003). Case conceptualizations not only guide therapeutic interventions, but also are helpful in educating patients about their problems. Furthermore, case conceptualizations are not static, but can change as the treatment progresses. For example, new information and insights may call for readjustments of the initial case conceptualization.

The case conceptualization is based primarily on schema modes, rather than early maladaptive schemas, because they reflect the combinations of certain early maladaptive schemas and maladaptive coping responses. Also, forensic patients often have so many early maladaptive schemas that discussing them all would be unmanageable. It is important to use a conceptual framework that is relatively clear, simple, and consistent. In forensic patients, schema modes serve this purpose because they describe problematic emotional states and behaviors in a manner that is straightforward, is easy for patients to understand, and gives therapists clear targets for interventions. Early maladaptive schemas and coping responses may also be examined, but are secondary to schema modes in working with forensic patients.

The case conceptualization, which is individualized for each patient, is usually represented visually, in the form of a diagram. This is illustrated in Figures 4.1 and 4.2, for a hypothetical psychopathic patient, and a narcissistic patient, respectively. The maladaptive coping modes are

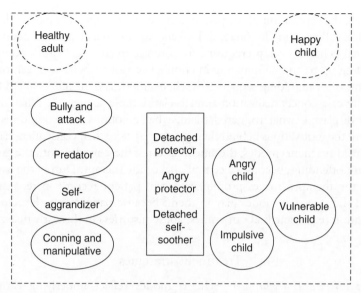

Figure 4.1 Sample case conceptualization in a psychopathic patient. Overcompensating modes on the left (in the ovals), avoidant coping modes in the middle (in the rectangle), and child and parent modes on the right (in the circles); healthy modes, if applicable, in the dashed lines.

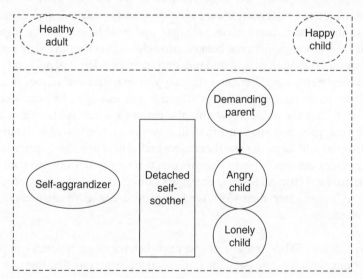

Figure 4.2 Sample case conceptualization in a narcissistic patient. Overcompensating modes on the left (in the ovals), avoidant coping modes in the middle (in the rectangle), and child and parent modes on the right (in the circles); healthy modes, if applicable, in the dashed lines.

shown in the middle and left side of the figure, while the maladaptive child and parent modes are presented on the right side. The adaptive modes are shown above the dashed line. This visual representation makes the patient's modes easier to grasp for both therapist and patient. A simplified version is often shared with patients, and can be kept on hand during sessions, so it can be referred to when needed.

In forensic ST, the explication of the patient's crimes is an important part of the case conceptualization process (Bernstein, de Jonge, & Jonkers, 2011). In fact, a clear understanding of the patient's criminal behaviors is a prerequisite for forensic treatment. "Crime scenarios," that is, the events leading up to and culminating in criminal or violent behaviors, can often be reconstructed in terms of an unfolding sequence of schema modes (Bernstein et al., 2007; Keulen-de Vos, 2013). The case conceptualization aims to clarify these sequences: What kinds of violent behavior were displayed, what triggered them, what emotions and cognitions accompanied them, what were the motivations behind them, and what were their consequences? These factors are conceptualized as schema modes; the amelioration of these modes, with the goal of reducing the risk of future offending, becomes a central goal of the therapy. During the case conceptualization phase, the therapist makes prominent use of patient records in reconstructing these sequences, and the role that modes play in them, because patients may be reluctant to share certain information (e.g., details about crimes, abuse histories) in this early phase of therapy.

Treatment strategies

Cognitive and behavioral techniques   Schema modes reflect underlying early maladaptive schemas, maladaptive coping responses, and emotional states. Therefore, ST aims to produce change at different levels: Problematic schemas need to be disputed, painful emotions to be worked through, and problematic behavior to be altered, whereas new, healthier patterns of thinking, feelings, and behaving are to be reinforced. ST uses a variety of interventions to achieve change. Cognitive interventions are used to modify patients' ways of thinking and to educate patients about their unmet needs, schemas, and maladaptive coping responses (Kellog & Young, 2006). As long as patients believe strongly in the legitimacy of certain schemas, change cannot occur. Together, patient and therapist gather evidence of pros and cons of certain schemas and coping responses. Therapists typically use cognitive techniques such as flashcards and schema diaries to increase awareness of schemas. For example, flashcards contain concise statements summarizing the evidence against the patient's schemas (Young et al., 2003). By using cognitive strategies, patients learn that, at least on an intellectual level, their underlying schemas are distorted and learn to view themselves and others in more balanced, realistic ways. Behavioral techniques are used to help patients practice new behaviors and gain confidence in consolidating behavioral change. Schema therapists can incorporate a variety of standard cognitive-behavioral techniques into their work, such as exposure, anger management, assertiveness training, and relaxation.

Experiential techniques   While traditional cognitive-behavioral techniques can play an important role in working with forensic patients, our experience suggests that they are not, in themselves, sufficient to produce deeper or more lasting change in many forensic patients with PDs. Many of these patients are highly detached from their emotions (Murphy & Vess, 2003). Cognitive therapy methods are predicated on the idea that changing thoughts leads to changes in emotions. However, detachment from emotions can render these techniques ineffective. Research suggests that "hot" cognitions – that is, cognitions that are accompanied by emotional arousal – are easier to change than "cold" ones (David & Szentagotai, 2006, Holmes & Mathews, 2005). Thus, simply talking about emotions, when this is done in a highly intellectualized or emotionally distant way, is usually insufficient to produce emotional change. ST makes prominent use of experiential techniques in order to bring emotions into active awareness and overcome emotional distance (Leahy, 2007; Mennin & Farach, 2007; Warwar, Links,

Greenberg, & Bergmans, 2008). In fact, experiential, or emotion-focused, techniques are among the hallmarks of ST, which distinguish it from more traditional cognitive-behavioral therapy approaches. Thus, while cognitive interventions lay the groundwork for awareness and insight in unhealthy schemas and modes, experiential techniques aim to consolidate this awareness on a deeper, emotional level. Moreover, forensic ST places even greater emphasis on emotion-focused techniques than is usually the case with non-forensic patients, because forensic patients are so highly detached.

Two experiential techniques in ST that are commonly used are *chair-work* and *imagery rescripting*. In chair-work, the patient switches between chairs and is invited to have dialogues between different parts of the self (Kellogg, 2004; Paivio & Greenberg, 1995). The patient sits in one chair when he or she plays a certain mode and switches chairs when a different mode is addressed or becomes active. Chair-work, which was borrowed by ST from Gestalt Therapy and Drama Therapy, makes patients' schema modes more tangible, helping them to 'feel' the mode that they are playing. The therapist can enact real scenes from the past or present, or make up scenes, "rescript" scenes to make them turn out differently, and have the patient use role playing to practice healthier attitudes and coping responses.

Imagery rescripting is a technique in which the therapist asks the patient to visualize an upsetting childhood memory or traumatic image from the past or present. The patient explores key images that are related to unmet early developmental needs, such as the need for closeness and connection, protection, the validation of feelings, and so forth. Next, the therapist intervenes in the upsetting memories by rescripting or changing the course of the original situation. A positive atmosphere is created in which the emotional needs of the patient are met in a healthy way, instead of being ignored or violated. As a result, the patient feels safer and more in control of the situation, and the underlying schemas that have been triggered via the imagery can begin to heal, as the patient's early emotional wounds are reprocessed. The patient also begins to understand the links between the past and their present situation, which he or she can feel in a vivid and immediate way (Arntz, 2011; Rafaeli et al., 2011; Smucker & Boos, 2005). Box 4.3 contains a clinical example of this technique.

Therapeutic style

The basic therapeutic style in ST is known as *limited reparenting*, because the therapist provides for some of the patients' early unmet developmental needs, within reasonable limits and boundaries. Limited reparenting means that the therapist acts like a "good enough" parent for the patient; he or she provides some of what the patient missed, in appropriate ways. For example, the therapist might provide warmth, empathy, recognition and validation of emotions, or empathic confrontation and limit setting, depending on the patient's unmet emotional needs. This therapeutic style is another feature that sets ST apart from other CBT-oriented therapies.

Limited reparenting is truly at the heart of ST. It is a defining feature of the therapy because it is incorporated into how the therapist interacts with the patient, as well as the way interventions and techniques are applied. For example, when imagery exercises involve a patient being abused as a child, the therapist uses rescripting to protect the child, to meet the need for safety that had been unfulfilled in the patient's childhood.

For limited reparenting to succeed, the therapist needs to be able to reach the patient's vulnerable side. However, forensic patients are often difficult to reach emotionally. Many of them have been exposed to violence, or have been abandoned or abused, and therefore have never experienced interpersonal relationships based on reciprocal trust and validation. These patients typically

Box 4.3   A Case Example Involving the Use of Imagery and Rescripting

Paul, a highly psychopathic patient, had refused to do imagery exercises for the first 2 years of his therapy. Finally, he agreed to do so. He closed his eyes, and brought an image to mind of having been sadistically beaten by his father, a common occurrence in his household when growing up. This time, however, when he was 14 years old, he "turned the tables" on his father, taking him by surprise and savagely beating him. This imagery exercise represented a turning point in the therapy, helping the patient to make emotional contact with the side of him that lived in terror of his father (Abused Child mode), and to recognize that he had learned to overcompensate for his fear by taking the upper hand, which usually involved aggressing against others before they could do the same to him (Bully and Attack mode).

In subsequent imagery sessions, the patient and therapist revisited these episodes, with the therapist "rescripting" the scene to protect the child and confront the abuser. In these sessions, the therapist asked the patient's permission to "enter" the image to provide for the child's needs, such as safety, comfort, and validation. In one instance, the patient and therapist arranged to have the police come to take the father away and lock him up, where he couldn't hurt the child anymore. In another session, the patient vented his anger at the father, with his therapist's support. Over a series of five of these sessions, spread over a period of several weeks, the patient gained greater freedom from the terrorizing image of his father, which he had carried with him his whole life. He reported feeling calmer, safer, and being less emotionally triggered in situations where he had previously responded with aggression.

come across in therapy sessions as hostile, mistrustful, and detached. It takes time for the patient to develop a trusting relationship with the therapist; it is not at all uncommon for it to take a year or more for these patients to form an attachment to the therapist. In addition to being patient and persistent, the therapist needs to be flexible, because basic emotional needs may differ from patient to patient, and may vary within a given patient from one session to another.

Empathic confrontation and limit setting

In order to access the patient's vulnerable side, the therapist needs to empathically confront, and at times set limits on, the patient's maladaptive coping modes, which block access to it. In *empathic confrontation*, the therapist starts by acknowledging and validating the patient's maladaptive coping modes; he or she calls the patient's attention to the modes (*I wonder which side of you this is?*) and explores the functions that they serve in an accepting and non-judgmental manner. The therapist then gently points out the maladaptive consequences of the modes, and thus stresses the necessity for change (Young et al., 2003). Sometimes, the therapist can use role-play and role-reversal as additional tools to help the patient to recognize the modes and understand their functions.

In *limit setting*, the therapist enforces limits on the patient's maladaptive modes in a clear, firm, and consequential, but non-punitive, manner. Rather than setting limits by making reference to impersonal rules (*Clinic policy states that patients can't be late for sessions*), the

Box 4.4   Case Example Involving Use of Limited Reparenting, Empathic Confrontation, and Limit Setting

Brian, an antisocial patient, was distant, hostile, and mistrustful throughout the first 6 months of the therapy. His therapist tried to remain interested, warm, and attentive, but became discouraged by the lack of progress. Eventually, she confronted him, but in an empathic way, stating that she understood the reasons for his mistrust, but that she was becoming discouraged by it. She said that she couldn't go further with him unless he was willing to take some risks to open up with her. The therapist's use of limit setting, done in a firm but caring way that also involved appropriate self-disclosure of feelings, was effective. The patient, while initially surprised, agreed to share more openly with her. Their relationship grew warmer and more comfortable, though he remained quite guarded at times. Over time, the therapist's warmth, availability, and consistency, as well as her willingness to confront the patient in a direct but non-judgmental way, helped to counteract the patient's mistrust. Eventually, he learned to rely on her for help and advice in handling difficult situations. He received permission to go on leave, and while his adaptation to life outside the institution was not easy, he continued to rely on her for periodic advice and support where needed.

therapist does so in a personal way, using self-disclosure where appropriate (*I notice that I'm getting frustrated with your coming late so often. I want to work with you, but not in this way*). Limit setting is used whenever the patient engages in behavior that is destructive to him/herself or other people, is disrespectful or transgresses boundaries, or undermines the therapy (e.g., by coming repeatedly late to sessions or missing appointments). This empathic and morally neutral approach to confronting and setting limits is especially important, because forensic patients often experience confrontation and limits as punitive, arbitrary, or unfair. In our experience, the vast majority of forensic patients respond well to these interventions, when the therapist is clear and firm, but also compassionate. Box 4.4 provides a clinical example of the use of limited reparenting, empathic confrontation, and limit setting.

Treatment motivation

In the forensic field, motivation for treatment is often considered a necessary prerequisite for starting treatment. However, forensic patients' motivation and readiness to engage in therapy is typically low (Sainsbury et al., 2004). In these cases, patients may be given short-term interventions, such as motivational interventions, to prepare them for more intensive forms of therapy. Patients who don't respond to these kinds of interventions, or who repeatedly resist efforts to engage them, are often considered "untreatable," and denied further treatment.

ST views treatment motivation as dynamic and fluctuating, rather than static and unchangeable. Furthermore, ST conceptualizes motivation and engagement in terms of schema modes that block therapeutic progress. By working with modes, ST seeks to enhance patients' motivation, a process that may be necessary over the entire course of the therapy. Various modes may interfere with patients' ability to engage in treatment. For example, the Detached Protector ("*I have no feelings*"), Self-Aggrandizer ("*I don't have any problems*"), and Paranoid

Over-Controller ("*I don't trust anyone*") modes can block patients' motivation. The goal is to work with these different schema modes so that the patient is gradually invited to switch into modes that are more productive, such as the Vulnerable Child and Healthy Adult modes, in which patients are more in touch with their underlying feelings.

Pitfalls and Recommendations

Limits and boundaries

Schema therapy requires that therapists are willing to be accessible and emotionally available to their patients, and to foster an attachment relationship with them. Furthermore, because ST is a moderate to long-term treatment, therapists must be prepared for a longer-term commitment. A common pitfall for therapists is that they are too distant or cool towards the patients, or overly critical when a patient doesn't improve quickly enough (Arntz & van Genderen, 2009; Young et al., 2003). On the other hand, some therapists have "loose" boundaries, and self-disclose or engage in other inappropriate behavior. An important modus operandi in ST should be that the therapist strikes a balance between being too close and too distant, thus having "permeable boundaries" – that is, boundaries that are firm but flexible enough to provide closeness within appropriate limits.

This pitfall is closely related to another one, namely difficulties with limit setting. Therapists need to set appropriate limits on patients' destructive and self-destructive behaviors (Arntz & van Genderen, 2009; Young et al., 2003). However, some therapists are reluctant to set limits out of fear of provoking a negative reaction; thus, they allow self-defeating, devaluing, or aggressive behavior to go on for too long. Other therapists may set too firm limits because they are too overwhelmed by the intensity of their patient's emotions or too afraid of their intimidating behavior (Young et al., 2003). Again, it is very important that therapists learn to set limits in a timely, firm, but non-punitive manner.

Forensic patients pose specific challenges for their therapists that are less often seen outside of the forensic field. For example, many narcissistic offenders have a strong Self-Aggrandizer mode, in which they behave in a devaluing and arrogant manner toward their therapists. Other offenders attempt to manipulate or deceive their therapists. For example, some forensic PD patients deliberately withhold information or respond in a socially desirable manner and present an unduly positive image of themselves; others may malinger (i.e., fake) symptoms (Keulen-de Vos et al., 2011). The schema mode model provides a means for therapists to recognize and intervene effectively when patients engage in these and other challenging behaviors.

Requirements for therapists

ST is a complex form of therapy that requires specialized training and supervision. This is especially so in the forensic field, where patients are so challenging. We recommend that therapists have 3 years of prior psychotherapy experience before they attempt to master ST (Bernstein et al., 2007). Therapists should seek training in ST through a program that is accredited by the International Society for Schema Therapy (ISST). These programs have requirements including several training days with a standardized curriculum, supervision by certified Schema Therapists, and competency ratings by independent experts. Even after receiving certification, we recommend that therapists working with forensic patients continue

Box 4.5 Answers for Matching Forensic Schema
Modes to Case Examples

a = 3
b = 1
c = 4
d = 2

to receive supervision or peer-supervision on their cases. In our experience, the ongoing support and feedback one receives in supervision is critical to achieving success in the face of the ongoing challenges that these patients present.

In the forensic field, quality assurance in the delivery of treatment is essential. Even more than in most other areas of mental health practice, a lack of adherence to the principles and practices of evidence-supported treatments can have serious consequences, when patients relapse to crime and violence. The investment in training therapists to work effectively in the forensic field is one that is likely to be repaid in the benefits it yields – not only in terms of improving the lives of patients, but in reducing the damage to lives and property, and the enormous financial costs of incarceration related to antisocial behavior.

References

Andrews, D. A., & Bonta J. (2003). *The psychology of criminal conduct* (3rd ed.). Cincinatti, OH: Anderson.

Arntz, A. (2011). Imagery rescripting for personality disorders. *Cognitive and Behavioral Practice, 18,* 466–481.

Arntz, A. & van Genderen, H. (2009). *Schema therapy for borderline personality disorder.* Oxford: Wiley-Blackwell Publishing.

Bamelis, L. L. M., Renner, F., Heidkamp, D., & Arntz, A. (2011). Extended schema mode conceptualizations for specific personality disorders: an empirical study. *Journal of Personality Disorders, 25*(1), 41–58.

Beckley, K., & Gordon, N. (2009). *Schema therapy manual.* Nottingham Healthcare NHS Trust (UK) [unpublished].

Behary, W. T. (2008). *Disarming the narcissist: surviving and thriving with the Self-Absorbed.* Oakland: New Harbinger Publications Inc.

Bernstein, D.P., Nijman, H., Karos, K., Keulen-de Vos, M.E., de Vogel, V., & Lucker, T. (2012). Schema Therapy for forensic patients with personality disorders: Design and preliminary findings of a multi-center randomized clinical trial in the Netherlands. International Journal of Forensic Mental Health, 11(4), S312–324.

Bernstein, D. P., Arntz, A., & de Vos, M. E. (2007). Schema-Focused Therapy in forensic settings: theoretical model and recommendations for best clinical practice. *International Journal of Forensic Mental Health, 6*(2), 169–183.

Bernstein, D., de Jonge, E., & Jonkers, P. (2011). Schematherapie bei forensischen Patiënten [Schema Therapy for forensic patients]. In E. Roediger & G. Jacob (Eds.), *Fortschritte der Schematherapie [Progress of schema therapy]*, pp. 198–215. Göttingen, Germany: Hogrefe.

Blackburn, R., Logan, C., Donnelly, J., & Renwick, S. (2003). Personality disorders, psychopathy and other mental disorders: co-morbidity among patients at English and Scottish high security hospitals. *Journal of Forensic Psychiatry and Psychology, 14*(1), 111–137.

Chakhssi, F., de Ruiter, C., & Bernstein, D. P. (2010). Change during forensic treatment in psychopathic versus nonpsychopathic offenders. *Journal of Forensic Psychiatry and Psychology, 21*(5), 660–682.

David, D., & Szentagotai, A. (2006). Cognitions in cognitive behavioral psychotherapies: Towards an integrative model. *Clinical Psychology Review, 26,* 284–298.

D'Silva, K., Duggan, C., & McCarthy, L. (2004). Does treatment really make psychopaths worse? A review of the evidence. *Journal of Personality Disorders, 18*(2), 163–177.

Farrell, J. M., Shaw, I. A., & Webber, M. A. (2009). A schema-focused approach to group psychotherapy for outpatients with borderline personality disorder: a randomized clinical trial. *Journal of Behavior Therapy and Experimental Psychiatry, 40,* 317–328.

Holmes, E. A., & Mathews, A. (2005). Mental imagery and emotion: a special relationship? *Emotion, 5*(4), 489–497.

Jaffee, S. R., Caspi, A., Moffitt, T. E., & Taylor, A. (2004). Physical maltreatment victim to antisocial child: evidence of an environmentally mediated process. *Journal of Abnormal Psychology, 113,* 44–55.

Jovev, M., & Jackson, H. J. (2004). Early Maladaptive Schemas and personality disordered individuals. *Journal of Personality Disorders, 18*(5), 467–478.

Kellogg, S. (2004). Dialogical encounters: contemporary perspectives on "chair-work" in psychotherapy. *Psychotherapy: Theory, Research, Practice, Training, 41*(3), 310–320.

Kellog, S. H., & Young, J. E. (2006). Schema Therapy for Borderline Personality Disorder. *Journal of Clinical Psychology, 62,* 445–458.

Keulen-de Vos, M. E., Bernstein, D. P., Clark, L. A., Arntz, A., Lucker, T., & de Spa, E. (2011). Patient versus informant reports of personality disorders in forensic patients. *Journal of Forensic Psychiatry and Psychology, 22*(1), 52–71.

Keulen-de Vos, M.E. (2013). Emotional states, crime and violence: a Schema Therapy approach to the understanding and treatment of forensic patients with personality disorders. Maastricht, NL: Datawyse / Maastricht University Press. [dissertation manuscript].

Leahy, R. L. (2007). Emotion and psychotherapy. *Clinical Psychology: Science and Practice, 14,* 353–357.

Leistico, A. R., Salekin, R. T., DeCoster, J., & Rogers, R. (2008). A large-scale meta-analysis relating the Hare measures of psychopathy to antisocial conduct. *Law and Human Behavior, 32,* 28–45.

Lobbestael, J., Arntz, A., Löbbes, A., & Cima, M. (2009). A comparative study of patients and therapists report of schema modes. *Journal of Behavior Therapy and Experimental Psychiatry, 40,* 571–579.

Lobbestael, J., van Vreeswijk, M. F., & Arntz, A. (2008). An empirical test of schema mode conceptualizations in personality disorders. *Behavior Research and Therapy, 46*(7), 854–860.

Marshall, W. L., & Serran, G. A. (2001). Improving the effectiveness of sexual offender treatment. *Trauma, Violence & Abuse, 1*(3), 203–222.

Marshall, W. L., & Serran, G. A. (2004). The role of the therapist in offender treatment. *Psychology, Crime & Law, 10*(3), 309–320.

McCann, R. A., Ball, E. M., & Ivanoff, I. (2000). DBT with an inpatient forensic population: the CMHIP forensic model. *Cognitive and Behavioral Practice, 7,* 447–456.

Mennin, D., & Farach, F. (2007). Emotion and evolving treatments for adult psychopathology. *Clinical Psychology: Science and Practice, 14,* 329–352.

Murphy, C. M., & Ting, L. (2010). The effects of treatment for substance use problems on intimate partner violence: a review of empirical data. *Aggression and Violent Behavior, 15,* 325–333.

Murphy, C., & Vess, J. (2003). Subtypes of psychopathy: proposed differences between narcissistic, borderline, sadistic and antisocial psychopaths. *Psychiatric Quarterly, 74*(1), 11–29.

Norton, K., & McGauley, G. (2000). Forensic psychotherapy in Britain: its role in assessment, treatment, and training. *Criminal Behavior and Mental Health, 10,* S82–90.

Paivio, S. C., & Greenberg, L. S. (1995). Resolving "unfinished business": efficacy of experiential therapy using empty-chair dialogue. *Journal of Consulting and Clinical Psychology, 63*(3), 419–425.

Poythress, N. G., Skeem, J. L., & Lilienfeld, S. O. (2006). Associations among early abuse, dissociation, and psychopathy in an offender sample. *Journal of Abnormal Psychology, 115,* 288–297.

Rafaeli, E., Bernstein, D. P., & Young, J. E. (2011). *Schema Therapy: Distinctive features*. New York: Routledge.

Ross, E. C., Polaschek, D. L. L., & Ward, T. (2008). The therapeutic alliance: a theoretical revision for offender rehabilitation. *Aggression and Violent Behavior, 13*, 462–480.

Sainsbury, L., Krishnan, G., & Evans, C. (2004). Motivating factors for male forensic patients with personality disorder. *Criminal Behavior and Mental Health, 14*, 29–38.

Skeem, J., Monahan, J., & Mulvey, E. (2002). Psychopathy, treatment involvement, and subsequent violence among civil psychiatric patients. *Law and Human Behavior, 26*, 577–603.

Smucker, M. R., & Boos, A. (2005). Imagery rescripting and reprocessing therapy. In: A. Freeman, M. Stone, & D. Martin (Eds.), *Comparative treatments for borderline personality disorder* (pp. 215–237). New York: Springer Publishing.

VanVreeswijk, M., & Broersen, J. (2006). *Schemagerichte Therapie in groepen [Schema Therapy in groups]*. Houten (NL): Bohn Stafleu Van Loghum.

Warwar, S. H., Links, P. S., Greenberg, L. S., & Bergmans, Y. (2008). Emotion-focused principles for working with borderline personality disorder. *Journal of Psychiatric Practice, 14*, 94–104.

Young, J.E., Arntz, A., Atkinson, T., Lobbestael, J., Weishaar, M. E., van Vreeswijk, M. F., & Klokman, J. (2007). *The Schema Mode Inventory*. New York: Schema Therapy Institute.

Young, J. E., & Brown, G. (2003). *Young Schema Questionnaire* (2nd ed.). New York: Cognitive Therapy Center of New York.

Young, J. E., & Flanagan, C. (1998). Schema-focused therapy for narcissistic patients. In E.F. Ronningstam (Ed.). *Disorders of narcissism: Diagnostic, clinical, and empirical implications* (pp. 239–262). Washington: American Psychiatric Association.

Young, J. E., Klosko, J., & Weishaar, M. (2003). *Schema Therapy: A Practitioner's Guide*. New York: Guilford.

Suggestions for Further Learning

Books

Bernstein, D. P., Arntz, A., & de Vos, M. E. (2007). Schema-Focused Therapy in forensic settings: Theoretical model and recommendations for best clinical practice. *International Journal of Forensic Mental Health, 6*(2), 169–183.

Rafaeli, E., Bernstein, D. P., & Young, J. E. (2011). *Schema Therapy: Distinctive features*. New York: Routledge.

Van der Wijngaart, R., & Bernstein, D. P. (2010). *Schema Therapy: Working with modes* [DVD series]. University of Maastricht (NL): Science Vision.

Van Vreeswijk, M., Broersen, J., & Nadort, M. (Eds.). (2012). *Handbook of Schema Therapy: Theory, research and practice*. Chichester (UK): Wiley-Blackwell Publishers.

Section 2
Criminal Thinking Models

5

An Overview of Strategies for the Assessment and Treatment of Criminal Thinking

Daryl G. Kroner and Robert D. Morgan

Overview

Criminal thinking patterns are an important consideration when working with offenders, for three reasons: (i) they have a functional role in perceptions; (ii) are predictive of antisocial and criminal behavior; and (iii) are changeable through correctional interventions. Criminal thinking is a cognitive process, which underlies a criminal lifestyle (Walters & White, 1989). The presence of criminal thinking patterns impacts the expectations that one has of a situation and the meaning that is given to a situation. When a difficult situation arises, the presence of criminal thinking patterns influences the response. It is not just difficult situations that invoke criminal thinking patterns, rather criminal thinking is ingrained and influences decisions in non-difficult times as well. For example, responses to situations of boredom or even positive rewards are influenced by criminal thinking patterns and may result in antisocial behavior. Thus, through interactions with situations, expectations, and attributed meaning, criminal thinking patterns provide a strong influence on behavior. Criminal thinking patterns are also somewhat stable. Test-retest reliability coefficients of frequently used criminal thinking scales are similar to those of other common personality scales (Knight, Garner, Simpson, Morey, & Flynn, 2006; Kroner & Reddon, 1994; Mandracchia & Morgan, 2011; Mills, Kroner, & Forth, 2002; Walters, 2002). This stability suggests that criminal thinking patterns recur regularly over time. Thus, criminal thinking patterns in the forensic arena are analogous to what, in traditional outpatient therapy settings, Beck (2011) might label "attitudes, rules, and assumptions."

With regard to prediction, the role of criminal thinking in antisocial and self-destructive behavior is empirically supported. Criminal thinking is significantly related to institutional misconduct and criminal activities (Mills, Kroner, & Hemmati, 2004; Simourd & Olver, 2002; Walters, 2002; Walters, Frederick, Schlauch, 2007; Walters & Mandell, 2007). In fact, criminal thinking is considered one of the primary four criminal risk variables (see Andrews & Bonta, 2010). Even when criminal risk levels are accounted for, criminal thinking continues to make an additional contribution to the prediction of future criminal activities (Mills et al., 2004; Walters, 2002, 2004a).

Forensic CBT: A Handbook for Clinical Practice, First Edition.
Edited by Raymond Chip Tafrate and Damon Mitchell.
© 2014 John Wiley & Sons, Ltd. Published 2014 by John Wiley & Sons, Ltd.

Criminal thinking patterns can change as a result of cognitive-behavioral therapy (CBT) intervention. Walters and colleagues have consistently demonstrated pre-to-post-test reductions in criminal thinking following a 10-week prison-based psychoeducational program (Walters, 2003; Walters, Trgovac, Rychlec, Di Fazio, & Olson, 2002). The results of cognitive-behavioral intervention among offenders with mental illness can also have a positive impact on criminal thinking patterns. Offenders who have received mental health services via cognitive-behavioral techniques have reduced criminal thinking patterns (Mandracchia & Morgan, 2012). In addition, treatment programs addressing criminal thinking lower recidivism. For example, in a community-based criminal thinking program with 331 offenders, future convictions were reduced by 20% compared with a matched comparison group (Kroner & Yessine, 2013).

Assessment

Assessment of criminal thinking is essential for determining the specific content areas that should be the treatment focus (at least initially). To adequately assess these areas we recommend using at least two of the multi-scale criminal thinking instruments described in Table 5.1. For example, using the Criminal Sentiments Scale - Modified (CSS-M; Simourd, 1997) or Measures of Antisocial Attitudes and Associates (MCAA; Mills & Kroner, 1999) combined with the Measure of Offender Thinking Styles-Revised (MOTS-R; Mandracchia & Morgan, 2011) or Psychological Inventory of Criminal Thinking Styles (PICTS; Walters, 1995) will assess a diverse combination of thinking patterns. The subscales with highest scores then become the focus of the intervention. As treatment progresses it may become apparent that another area of criminal thinking is problematic (i.e., reductions in one criminal thinking pattern may then unmask less salient criminal thinking patterns). Then a shift in treatment focus can occur, addressing other problematic areas.

It is also important to assess the change that is occurring as a result of intervention. Assessment of criminal thinking prior to the intervention can be compared to post-testing assessment results to determine effectiveness. Determining the clinical significance of the difference between pre-to-post-test scores often means going beyond simple pre-post significance testing. For thorough examination of outcome effectiveness we recommend four steps of outcome analysis. First, conduct pre-post significance testing. Second, calculate effect sizes of the pre-post differences to measure the magnitude of the effect. Third, to determine if the change is clinically meaningful, examine the pre-post changes in relation to the clinical cutoffs for the instrument being used. For example, are offenders in the clinically significant range at pre-intervention falling into the non-clinically significant range at post-testing? Finally, to ensure that interventions are producing reliable change we recommend calculating a reliable change score in order to determine (see Jacobson & Truax, 1991) the percentage of treated individuals who experienced meaningful and reliable change. Although this process may seem daunting, it is really quite simple as the results are calculated on means and standard deviations (for calculating effect sizes), a very simple statistics program (for calculating pre-post significance tests with *t*-tests or one-way analysis of variance procedures), and the use of scale reliability coefficients for calculating reliability of change estimates. Once established, this method of outcome assessment will yield solid evidence regarding the effectiveness of cognitive interventions for changing criminal thinking patterns.

Table 5.1 Empirically supported criminal thinking instruments and subscales.

Instrument	Subscales	Description
Psychological Inventory of Criminal Thinking Styles (PICTS)	Mollification	Blaming others for the negative consequences
	Cutoff	Ability to quickly eliminate or disregard the deterrents to crime
	Entitlement	Sense of ownership or special privilege
	Power Orientation	Desire to gain power or control over others
	Sentimentality	Use of good deeds to justify and excuse antisocial behavior
	Superoptimism	Unrealistic belief that the negative consequences of a criminal lifestyle will be avoided
	Cognitive Indolence	Poor critical reasoning skills
	Discontinuity	Lack of consistency in thoughts and actions
	Current	Reflects current criminal attitudes and beliefs
	Historical	Approximates past criminal attitudes and beliefs
	Proactive Criminal Thinking	Criminal Thinking that is generally independent of specific environmental cues
	Reactive Criminal Thinking	Criminal thinking that is generally in response to specific environmental cues
	Antisocial Cognition	General tendency toward criminal thinking
Measure of Criminal Attitudes and Associates (MCAA)	Number of Criminal Friends	The number of friends that the respondent reports as having engaged in criminal activity
	Criminal Friend Index	Accounts for the percentage of time spent with associates and the number of associates
	Violence	Rationalization and justification of violent behavior
	Antisocial Intent	Desire to behave in destructive or criminal ways
	Entitlement	Rationalization and justification of entitlement
	Associates	Identification with and perception of criminal associates
Criminal Sentiments Scale – Modified (CSS-M)	Law	Agreement with and adherence to established laws
	Courts	Trust in the justice system and its various components (e.g., judges, juries)
	Police	Trust and respect for law enforcement
	Tolerance for Law Violations	Acceptance of law-breaking behaviors
	Identification with Criminal Others	Perceived similarities with other people who have engaged in antisocial activities

(Continued)

Table 5.1 (*Continued*)

Instrument	Subscales	Description
TCU Criminal Thinking Scales (CTS)	Entitlement	Sense of ownership and privilege, misidentification of wants as needs
	Justification	Attributing serious antisocial acts to external circumstances
	Power Orientation	Need for power and control using aggressive means
	Cold Heartedness	Callousness, lack of emotional intimacy
	Criminal Rationalization	General negative attitude toward law and authority
Criminogenic Thinking Profile (CTP)	Disregard for Others	Lack of empathy, remorse or concern for others
	Demand for Entertainment	Impulsivity, low tolerance of boredom, need for excitement
	Poor Judgment	Underestimating negative consequences of risky behaviors
	Emotionally Disengaged	Discomfort with emotions that lead to vulnerability or intimacy
	Parasitic/Exploitative	Evading responsibility, general exploitative worldview
	Justifying	Minimization of antisocial or destructive behaviors
	Inability to Cope	Ineffective problem-solving, giving up easily
	Grandiosity	Overestimating skills, abilities, or personal qualities
Measure of Criminogenic Thinking Styles (MOTS)	Control	Power and command over the environment, others, and one's own emotions
	Cognitive Immaturity	Reliance on generalizations, rash judgments, and self-pity
	Egocentrism	Attributing others' actions to oneself

Choosing a criminal thinking instrument

With the number of criminal thinking instruments available, a decision needs to be made regarding which instrument or instruments are most appropriate. See Table 5.1 for an overview of empirically supported criminal thinking instruments and their corresponding subscales. One strategy is to incorporate a decision process summarized with the TODATE acronym: **T**ype of client, nature of **O**utcomes, **D**ecision assistance, guidance for **A**ction, **T**heory, and **E**ffort required (Kroner, Mills, Gray, & Talbert, 2011). The first question to be asked in this process is: how similar are the previously published data to the *type* of client you are working with? In answering this question, the goal is to find the instrument whose norms most closely match the type of client participating in the treatment program. Having a good match will result in a defensible choice and the testing results will be more robust over time. With instruments that have published results beyond the test manual, a more recent publication may be appropriate to be used as the normative sample.

The second stage in the process, nature of *outcomes*, deals with the purpose of the assessment. Criminal thinking programs can have multiple goals. For example, goals may include: reducing criminal thinking, changing criminal thinking to reduce institutional misconduct or recidivism, or focusing on one type of criminal thinking (i.e., entitlement) in a specialized population. The closer the previous research is to the current desired outcomes, the better. The next step to consider is how the instrument can assist in making *decisions* and communicating the results. When the pre-treatment assessment is discussed with the client to formulate content areas for intervention the more straightforward the description and interpretation of the scales, the better. As stated earlier, an instrument will have greater impact on decisions if a reliable change score has been developed because a change score will assist practitioners in determining if clinically significant before-after program change has occurred.

Guidance for *action* refers to an instrument informing the content of the intervention. The closer the content of an instrument is to the proposed interventions, the greater the utility of the instrument. With regard to *theory*, criminal thinking patterns are of a cognitive nature, but each of the published criminal thinking instruments has a unique model under which it was developed. Having consistency between the theory and treatment approach is optimal. The last criterion of *effort* refers to the ease of use of the instrument. Instruments that are easier to use, score, and interpret will likely lead to greater client compliance and fewer administrative scoring errors.

When formal assessment of criminal thinking is not an option

In most criminal justice systems, assessing the majority of offenders on criminal thinking to determine who should receive intervention is not feasible. There can be logistic issues, a lack of assessment expertise, and a lack of resources making it unrealistic to screen all offenders for criminal thinking patterns. In this type of situation, one strategy is to use basic index and demographic variables to recommend who should receive a criminal thinking intervention.

A recent study examined the relationship between index and demographic variables with criminal thinking patterns (Mandracchia & Morgan, 2012). In this study, multiple criminal thinking scales were administered (MOTS, Mandracchia, Morgan, Garos, & Garland, 2007; PICTS, Walters, 1995; CSS-M, Simourd, 1997; MCAA, Mills & Kroner, 1999). Across these measures, age, education, and the presence of a psychological disorder had the most robust relationships with criminal thinking and antisocial attitudes. Thus, being younger, less educated, and having a psychological disorder would be adequate criteria for screening offenders into criminal thinking interventions or screening for in-depth assessment of criminal thinking.

Even if index and demographic variables are used to make intervention recommendations, a measurement of criminal thinking after an initial demographic selection will be beneficial. Criminal thinking has repeatedly been shown to have incremental validity over index and demographic variables when predicting institutional outcomes (Walters & Schlauch, 2008) and ratings of risk (Simourd, 1997). Thus, a correctional system may want to have a liberal inclusion rate with the index and demographic variables and then fine tune the selection with standardized measures of criminal thinking, of which there are a number – among the scales not yet mentioned: Criminogenic Thinking Profile (CTP; Mitchell & Tafrate, 2011); Criminal Tendencies scale of the Self-Appraisal Questionnaire (SAQ; Loza, Dhaliwal, Kroner, & Loza-Fanous, 2000); Pride in Delinquency scale (PID; Shields & Whitehall, 1994); Texas Christian University Criminal Thinking Scales (TCU CTS; Knight, Garner, Simpson, Morey, & Flynn, 2006).

Conceptualizing relevant thinking targets

In keeping with the goal of simplicity, it is recommended that a maximum of three criminal thinking styles become the focus of an intervention program. Through the development of the MOTS, Mandracchia and colleagues (2007) identified three overarching criminal thinking themes from a factor analysis of thinking patterns derived from the work of Walters and Yochelson and Samenow in their work with offenders, and Beck and Ellis in their work with non-offending clients. Each criminal thinking theme is described and specific subscales that measure each theme, across different criminal thinking instruments, are identified. After describing the assessment of these themes, intervention strategies and skill-building techniques will be presented.

1. *Control.* This theme refers to the need for power and control over oneself, other people, and the environment. Offenders with this theme outwardly may seek to control others' emotions, reject established authority, and control the behavior of others through the use of sex and fear. Inwardly, offenders high in Control may neutralize their fear and anxiety by minimizing negative behaviors, dismissing anxiety-producing thoughts, and making rash decisions without considering the consequences (Mandracchia et al., 2007). Empirically supported criminal thinking patterns subsumed under this theme and scales that measure them are listed in Table 5.2.

2. *Cognitive Immaturity.* This theme is characterized by impulsivity, overgeneralization, and extreme judging. Offenders with Cognitive Immaturity may miss the forest for the trees, focusing on the details of a situation without considering the general context. They are prone to making sweeping generalizations about situations, labeling people in extreme ways, believing they know what others are thinking, minimizing their own responsibility for negative outcomes, and seeing the past as the cause of their present problems (Mandracchia et al., 2007). Table 5.2 lists the empirically supported criminal thinking patterns subsumed under this theme and scales that measure them.

3. *Egocentrism.* This theme is defined by a focus on the self across different situations and interactions. Specific patterns include attributing others' actions to oneself, expecting fair treatment from others regardless of the situation, and performing positive acts to

Table 5.2   Three overarching criminal thinking themes with corresponding scales.

Control	Cognitive Immaturity	Egocentrism
Antisocial intent (MCAA)	Demand for excitement (CTP)	Entitlement (MCAA)
Violence (MCAA)	Poor judgment (CTP)	Disregard for others (CTP)
Inability to cope (CTP)	Justify (CTP)	Grandiosity (CTP)
Power orientation (PICTS)	Mollification (PICTS)	Parasitic/exploitive (CTP)
Superoptimism (PICTS)	Cut-off (PICTS)	Entitlement (PICTS)
Attitudes toward the law,	Cognitive indolence (PICTS)	Sentimentality (PICTS)
courts, and police (CSS-M)	Discontinuity (PICTS)	Entitlement (TCU CTS)
Power orientation (TCU CTS)	Tolerance for law violations	Personal responsibility
	(CSS-M)	(TCU CTS)
Cold-heartedness (TCU CTS)	Justification (TCU CTS)	
	Criminal rationalization (TCU CTS)	

CSS-M, Criminal Sentiments Scale-Modified; CTP, Criminogenic Thinking Profile; MCAA, Measures of Criminal Attitudes and Associates; PICTS, Psychological Inventory of Criminal Thinking Styles; TCU CTS, Texas Christian University Criminal Thinking Scales.

compensate for the negative perceptions of one's criminal behaviors (Mandracchia et al., 2007). Empirically supported criminal thinking patterns subsumed under this theme and scales that measure them are also listed in Table 5.2.

Treatment content should be structured according to the three overarching criminal thinking themes outlined above. Optimally, all referred offenders should participate in some intervention focused around the Control theme because this theme appears to be most common across a wide range of offenders. Then, Cognitive Immaturity or Egocentrism, or possibly both, depending upon the offender's characteristics, would be addressed. In factor analytic research using the MOTS, Control-related patterns accounted for the majority of criminal thinking scale variance (27.1% of the total variance, whereas Cognitive Immaturity and Egocentrism accounted for 5.8% and 4.4% respectively). The MOTS Control scale also had the strongest correlations with a wide variety of other criminal thinking scales (Mandracchia & Morgan, 2011).

Within the Control theme, one or two specific criminal thinking patterns should be addressed. As noted above, once an offender has addressed the control area, efforts should focus on one or two patterns related to either Cognitive Immaturity or Egocentrism. In a minority of cases it will be optimal to address both of the latter themes. Thus, for the typical offender, there would be only three to four specific thinking patterns that are identified as targets throughout the course of treatment. Addressing different criminal thinking patterns for each offender will promote an individualized approach to the intervention, even though intervention may occur within a group setting. Although the above discussion emphasizes keeping the intervention strategies simple, the focus on the three overarching themes precludes the treatment effort from becoming too simplistic. Mitchell and Tafrate (2011) make the point that criminal thinking programs often focus on the acceptance of accountability, to the exclusion of other criminal thinking patterns. In their study using the CTP, a range of thinking patterns such as Inability to Cope, Demand for Excitement, and Disregard for Others had strong correlations with psychopathy and aggressive personality disorders, suggesting that these patterns warrant consideration in intervention programs.

Overview of Intervention Principles

Prior to addressing treatment content areas, we will cover general principles in delivering criminal thinking interventions. Within the Risk, Needs, and Responsivity framework (Andrew & Bonta, 2010, pp. 45–52), these principles fall within the Responsivity domain. Addressing criminal thinking patterns with offenders will be challenging. Unless offenders have had a previous positive experience in an intervention program to change criminogenic need areas, they will likely view the change of thinking patterns as threatening. Changing a thinking pattern is a cognitive activity and many offenders have often failed when dealing with cognitive challenges (Rutter, Gudjonsson, & Rabe-Hesketh, 2004; Sigursson, Gudjonsson, & Peersen, 2001). Typically they have not excelled in school or academic environments (Herrnstein & Murray, 1994; Muirhead & Rhodes, 1998). Thus, just addressing the area of criminal thinking will be difficult, let alone trying to change one or more thinking patterns.

1. *The need for simplicity.* The level of cognitive sophistication among offenders tends to be below average compared to other clinical populations. We draw on several sources for this conclusion. First, psychological instruments developed with non-offender samples tend to have more complex factor structures with non-offenders than with offenders (Kroner & Reddon, 1996; Kroner, Reddon, & Serin, 1992). Second, higher risk offenders typically have lower IQ levels (Block, 1995; Piquero, 2000).
2. *Stress the common.* Offenders are a heterogeneous group. Thus, the more basic the content, examples, exercises, and homework, the more offenders are going to connect with the material. This will help reduce the number of impediments to program delivery.
3. *Use fewer learning ideas.* The majority of criminal justice practitioners have post-secondary educations, and have experienced environments where learning *more* is the ideal. In contrast, the goal for offenders is to develop a *few* competencies that change their criminal thinking patterns over the long term, and will eventually impact their behavior. A focus on the simplistic, stressing the common, and using fewer learning ideas, assists with the generalizability and transporting of what is experienced and learned in the intervention to other contexts in their lives.
4. *Starting positive.* An essential component of engaging an offender to participate in an intervention program is to begin on a positive note. Given that the challenge of changing one's thinking patterns can be threatening (Walters, 2004b), an initial positive contact with an offender will likely assist in engagement and treatment retention. Beginning on a positive note can be accomplished by examining positive thinking patterns (i.e., the belief that saving for the future is beneficial) and how these positive thinking patterns are connected to positive behaviors and outcomes. In addition to beginning on a positive note, this strategy puts forward the idea of connecting a thinking pattern with a behavior or outcome. Once this is established, criminal thinking patterns can be introduced.
5. *Discuss assessment results with clients.* One way to introduce criminal thinking and the consequences of such cognitive styles is to discuss pre-test assessment measures with a client. This can be done individually or in the context of a group setting, depending on the nature of the therapeutic work. We recommend graphing the measures administered to show them, with a picture, the extent of their criminal thinking. In our experience when we use this strategy in our work with offenders with severe mental illness it invariably produces an "Ah ha" moment. The offender sees, possibly for the first time, how their

thinking is like that of other criminals, where they "spike" on their criminal thinking profiles, and thus, where the most work needs to be done. This is a rather simple strategy for getting good buy-in from at least some of the offenders in treatment.

Specific Intervention Strategies and Change Techniques

Three specific intervention strategies are proposed. Each strategy maps onto each of the three overarching criminal thinking themes previously presented (i.e., Control, Cognitive Immaturity, Egocentrism). Prior to addressing these specific intervention strategies, two helpful tools will be discussed, the *Stop Light* analogy and *case studies*.

Stop Light

As noted above, interventions are likely to be more successful if they are simple because the new skills will transfer easily to the offenders' real world. To educate offenders simply and concretely about positive functioning and negative functioning in their lives we use the Stop Light analogy. The Stop Light analogy is one that most offenders, even if they do not drive, will understand: *red light* = Stop, *yellow light* = Caution (contrary to most teenage boys interpretation that it means "go faster"), and *green light* = Go. Many aspects of offending behavior can be broken down into this simple model. Is a lifetime friend prosocial (green light) or a fellow offender (red light)? Is the offender working and pursuing career goals (green light), or not gainfully employed and with no occupational goals (red light), or unemployed (or transitioning from one job to another) with *realistic* career aspirations (yellow light)? Does the offender you are treating engage in prosocial leisure activities (green light), or have an absence of hobbies and recreational interests yet maintains a prosocial support network (yellow light), or engage in illegal activities for fun such as racing cars, using illicit substances, etc. (red light). The Stop Light analogy works for most aspects of intervening with offenders, including the work involved in cognitive change programs.

The benefit of the Stop Light analogy is that it recognizes that offenders also possess positive thinking patterns that have served them well in life. These green light thinking patterns are not to be changed but rather reinforced and used to help change the criminal thinking patterns. Therapeutically then, a focus on cognitive processes of Control, Cognitive Immaturity, and Egocentrism will be framed as red lights. Offenders can be taught the meaning and clinical presentation of these cognitive processes and shown how these patterns of thought support their criminal involvement. They should be taught that these are red light issues and provided with a mechanism for evaluating their thought patterns when interacting in the world (including dealing with problems, interpersonal interactions, and even simple goal-directed behaviors).

A note about the yellow light is warranted. The yellow light, as it pertains to criminal thinking, is, in reality, a red light for offenders in the early stages of treatment. That is, at the beginning stages of an intervention it is unlikely that an offender will be able to distinguish between what is a red versus a yellow thinking pattern. For example, you will hear offenders in the early stages of treatment state, "*I've thought this a lot* [some type of criminal thinking pattern], *but it has not had an impact on me.*" They are, in essence, trying to establish that a criminal thinking pattern is a yellow light for them and not a red light. The task of the practitioner then is to show how the thinking pattern has directly contributed to their offensive behavior (red light) or put them at risk for other criminal risk factors (e.g., substance abuse) that lead to offending behavior. Thus, the thinking pattern is a red light as it directly or indirectly contributes to offending behavior. Only when the offender recognizes their cognitive styles and is able to address them from a risk perspective does the cognitive style truly become a yellow light.

The goal then is to challenge criminal thinking (red light) and alter the criminal thinking pattern (replace with a green light thinking pattern) or alter behavior to be prosocial in spite of the criminal thinking pattern (thereby making the cognition a yellow light). This challenging of criminal thinking should be done in sessions when criminal thinking is present as well as in homework that extends into the offender's real world. As noted above, offenders need to over-learn information (Morgan, Kroner, & Mills, 2006) so that it becomes part of their natural behavior. Challenging criminal thinking as often and in as many different settings as possible will likely prove beneficial. It may also be strategic to develop a peer monitoring system within relevant interventions so offenders can be of help and be helped by one another to curb their criminal thinking and the associated antisocial behaviors.

Case studies

Cases studies are descriptions of a scenario (175 to 200 words) that highlight an issue to be discussed in the intervention. Thus, if Control thinking patterns are being addressed, then a case study involving a description of Carl and his thinking patterns of rejecting societal power, and the consequences of those patterns can be highlighted. The benefit of using a case study approach is that a criminal thinking pattern can be introduced in a relatively non-threatening manner. The example in the case study is about someone else, not the client. This allows for a discussion of the content areas before the personalizing of the criminal thinking pattern becomes the focus.

Change techniques

The proposed techniques to change criminal thinking patterns vary according to the three content areas. For those offenders with elevations with the Cognitive Immaturity theme, the change strategies are of a skills-based nature, attempting to develop prosocial thinking skills that can replace criminal thinking patterns (see Appendix 5.A for a sample Cognitive Immaturity change exercise). First, a log of the automatic Cognitive Immature thinking patterns is developed. From this log the emphasis of intervention is on development of skills to recognize and challenge these types of criminal thinking patterns. Use of these strategies is accompanied by activities geared toward developing social skills and coping strategies that are incongruent with the criminal thinking and behavior.

For those offenders with elevations with the Egocentrism theme, the interventions attempt to challenge criminal thinking patterns through changing the normative framework, goal directedness, and planfulness of the thinking patterns (see Appendix 5.B). There is a strong use of cost-benefit ratios, and the listing of pros and cons for maintaining the criminal thinking patterns. To address changing the norms of criminal thinking, a hedonistic principle of goal achievement works well. With this strategy, how criminal thinking patterns fail to attain ideal goals is central.

For those offenders with elevations with the Control theme, the intervention strategies focus on changing response decisions, responses to situations, and interpreting social cues (see Appendix 5.C). The goal is to develop alternative thinking patterns. There is an initial effort to increase the offender's willingness to consider alternative thinking patterns. Next, the use of shaping is a primary method for alternative thinking patterns to be incorporated and reinforced.

Importance of Homework

Not only is homework an ideal in CBT, but within correctional treatment, homework is one of the main predictors of treatment success (Morgan & Flora, 2002; Morgan, Flora, Kroner, Mills, Varghese, & Steffan, 2012). There are three characteristics of effective correctional homework. First, it has to be simple to complete. Essentially, the more homework that gets completed the greater the impact of the intervention. Second, the homework needs to have a real-world emphasis. Homework bridges what is learned in session with how the client is thinking and acting. If the clients are in prison, the homework should be prison-based. Third, ensuring compliance is necessary. One of the most effective techniques to ensure compliance is public commitment (i.e., asking clients to commit to completing homework in a group setting).

Length of Intervention: How Much Treatment Effort is Necessary for Changing Outcomes?

With many factors contributing to the success of correctional interventions it becomes difficult to isolate the impact of any one of these factors. With all else being equal, more than 15 sessions addressing criminal thinking patterns may be a minimal amount to have a reliable, noticeable change. In a recent analysis of a program addressing both mental health needs and criminal thinking patterns, the amount of change in criminal thinking was less (<20%) when compared to intervention strategies for changing mental health outcomes (30–40%; Morgan, Kroner, Mills, Bauer, & Serna, 2012). Another study examining the role of treatment dosage in a group intervention designed to change criminal thinking also suggested that more than 10 sessions was necessary for a change in recidivism outcomes (Kroner & Takahashi, 2012). Although approximately 10 sessions may be sufficient to allow for the expectation of a therapeutic impact, this study suggests that the more sessions completed, the greater the reduction in recidivism. Interventions with more than 15 sessions should involve a minimum two to four sessions per week.

Although a randomized clinical trial would likely assist in determining how much criminal thinking change is necessary to reduce recidivism, in most situations this is unlikely to occur. There are, though, other practical steps that could assist in improving the measurement of criminal thinking change. One step is to conduct basic test-retest assessments (no interventions) of the criminal thinking measures. Preferably this would be over the same period as the proposed criminal thinking intervention program. Similarly, using criminal thinking scales in pre- and post-testing for non-criminal thinking interventions would also be beneficial. These stability reliabilities then can be used to calculate reliable change in a criminal thinking intervention. For those involved in examining and developing appropriate criminal thinking measures, a strong reliability is of utmost importance and can be accomplished through the consideration of multiple forms of reliability. Also, when developing a change scale or index, there should be a mild inverse relationship with a risk measure. This will allow a change measure to be used in a mediation analysis, from which one can draw stronger causation conclusions about the intervention.

Retention Strategies

There are three strategies that have relevance for retaining clients in criminal thinking interventions. First, the role of criminal thinking patterns in dropping out of the intervention should be addressed. Empirically, Mitchell, Tafrate, Hogan, and Olver (2013) and Walters (2004b) have shown that criminal thinking patterns are predictive of treatment attrition. Two of the three criminal thinking patterns outlined above have relevance for preventing treatment dropout. Cognitive Immaturity, with an emphasis on impulsivity, overgeneralizations, and jumping to conclusions, may be a potential contributing factor to dropping out of an intervention program. For example, coming to a conclusion near the beginning of a program that the program is not working and impulsively dropping the program may be a criminal thinking pattern that is pertinent to dropout. This is of particular importance, as the literature on offender attrition suggests that most dropouts occur near the beginning of the program (Hiller, Knight, & Simpson, 2006). In fact, Walters (2004b) points out that in addition to the 16 dropouts from their psychoeducation program, 18 offenders dropped out prior to completing the pre-program testing. Thus, beginning the program by addressing how new thinking patterns can have positive results is of high importance in conducting criminal thinking interventions.

Similarly the theme of Control may contribute to a justification for dropping out of a program. In correctional interventions, Walters (2004b) suggests that interventions can threaten an offender's self-view, and at times become a roadblock for change. Rather than working through the threatening aspects of change, clients may provide justifications to disengage from the intervention, and possibly drop out. Thus, not only are Cognitive Immaturity and Control themes important as overall content areas for intervention, they are also relevant to practitioners' attempts to keep offenders in the program until completion.

Second, a de-emphasis on the rules within the program may be necessary as a retention strategy. A study of general intervention programs found that the ones that emphasized rules had greater involuntary attrition (Pelissier, Camp, & Motivans, 2003). Certainly, rules are necessary for delivering intervention programs, as they offer some structure to the intervention, but prioritizing and emphasizing rules can have unwanted consequences.

The third strategy, based on Walters (2004b) comment of interventions being a threat for offenders, is to begin the program by addressing prosocial and productive thinking patterns. As noted above in the overview of strategies, the focus of strength-based and desistance factors may help the offenders to more fully engage in an intervention. Tafrate et al. in Chapter 23 offer a more complete discussion of strengths-based work with offenders.

Summary

Assessing criminal thinking is relevant for the prediction of criminal outcomes and for assessing offender change in response to rehabilitative interventions. Previous research has clearly demonstrated that criminal thinking is predictive of criminal justice outcomes including recidivism (see Andrews & Bonta, 2010, for a thorough review of this literature) and institutional behavior (Mills et al., 2004; Simourd & Olver, 2002; Walters, 2002; Walters & Mandell, 2007; Walters et al., 2007). To assess criminal thinking, clinicians and researchers alike have a plethora of measures from which to choose including PICTS, MOTS-R, MCAA,

CSS-M, CTP, TCU CTS, and others. Selecting the instrument that best meets your needs is not a decision to be taken lightly and we recommend a carefully established decision-making rubric in this chapter. The criminal thinking measures discussed in this chapter have their strengths but the measures are not designed as a one-stop shop for all offenders and all clinical/research uses. Carefully selected measures (we recommend a combination of measures) will provide useful assessment information for the prediction of criminal risk, as well as rich clinical data on which to draw for purposes of intervention. In the model presented, a focus on thinking patterns that fall within the three overarching criminal thinking themes of Control, Cognitive Immaturity, and Egocentrism are recommended. Strategies for changing criminal thinking patterns include the use of Stop Light and case study techniques. Strategies for retaining offender-clients in treatment include a de-emphasis on rules, increasing awareness about the role of thinking patterns on possible treatment drop-out, and reinforcing existing prosocial thinking.

References

Andrews, D. A., & Bonta, J. (2010). *The psychology of criminal conduct* (5th ed.). New Providence, NJ: LexisNexis Group.

Beck, J. S. (2011). *Cognitive therapy: Basics and beyond* (2nd ed.). New York, NY: Guilford Press.

Block, J. (1995). On the relation between IQ, impulsivity, and delinquency: Remarks on Lyman, Moffitt, and Stouthamer-Loeber. *Journal of Abnormal Psychology, 104*, 395–398.

Herrnstein, R. J., & Murray, C. (1994). *The bell curve: Intelligence and class structure of American life.* New York: Free Press.

Hiller, M. L., Knight, K., & Simpson, D. W. (2006). Recidivism following mandated residential substance abuse treatment for felony probationers. *Prison Journal, 86*, 230–241. doi: 10.1177/0032885506287951.

Jacobson, N. S. & Truax, P. (1991). Clinical significance: A statistical approach to defining meaningful change in psychotherapy research. *Journal of Consulting and Clinical Psychology, 59*, 12–19.

Knight, K., Garner, B. R., Simpson, D. D., Morey, J. T., & Flynn, P. M. (2006). An assessment for criminal thinking. *Crime and Delinquency, 52*, 159–177. doi: 10.1177/0011128705281749.

Kroner, D. G., Mills, J. F., Gray, A., & Talbert, K. (2011). Clinical assessment in correctional settings. In T. J. Fagan and R. K. Ax (Eds.), *Correctional mental health: From theory to best practice* (pp. 79–102). Thousand Oaks, CA: Sage.

Kroner, D. G., & Reddon, J. R. (1994). Relationships among clinical and validity scales of the Basic Personality Inventory. *Journal of Clinical Psychology, 50*, 522–528.

Kroner, D. G., & Reddon, J. R. (1996). Factor structure of the Basic Personality Inventory with incarcerated offenders. *Journal of Psychopathology and Behavioral Assessment, 18*, 275–284.

Kroner, D. G., Reddon, J. R., & Serin, R. C. (1992). The Multidimensional Anger Inventory: Reliability and factor structure in an inmate sample. *Educational and Psychological Measurement, 52*, 687–693.

Kroner, D. G., & Takahashi, M. (2012). Every session counts: The differential impact of previous programmes and current programme dosage on offender recidivism. *Legal and Criminological Psychology, 17*, 136–150. doi: 10.1111/j.2044-8333.2010.02001.x.

Kroner, D. G., & Yessine, A. K. (2013, March 25). Changing risk factors that impact recidivism: In search of mechanisms of change. *Law and Human Behavior*. Advance online publication. doi: 10.1037/lhb0000022

Loza, W., Dhaliwal, G., Kroner, D. G., & Loza-Fanous, A. (2000). Reliability, construct, and concurrent validities of the Self-Appraisal Questionnaire. *Criminal Justice and Behavior, 27*, 356–374. doi: 10.1177/0093854800027003005.

Mandracchia, J. T., & Morgan, R. D. (2011). Understanding criminals' thinking: Further examination of the Measure of Offender Thinking Styles-Revised. *Assessment*, *18*, 442–452. doi: 10.1177/1073191110377595.

Mandracchia, J. T., & Morgan, R. D. (2012). Predicting offenders' criminogenic cognitions with status variables. *Criminal Justice and Behavior*, *39*, 5–25. doi: 10.117/0093854811425453.

Mandracchia, J. T., Morgan, R. D., Garos, S., & Garland, J. T. (2007). Inmate thinking patterns: An empirical investigation. *Criminal Justice and Behavior*, *34*, 1029–1043. doi: 10.1177/0093854807301788.

Mills, J. F., & Kroner, D. G. (1999). *Measures of criminal attitudes and associates: user guide*. Selby, Ontario, Canada. Available at: https://sites.google.com/a/siu.edu/corrections-and-research_lab/Downloads

Mills, J. F., Kroner, D. G., & Forth, A. E. (2002). Measures of Criminal Attitudes and Associates (MCAA): Development, factor structure, reliability, and validity. *Assessment*, *9*, 240–253.

Mills, J. F., Kroner, D. G., & Hemmati, T. (2004). The Measures of Criminal Attitudes and Associates (MCAA): The prediction of general and violent recidivism. *Criminal Justice and Behavior*, *31*, 717–733.

Mitchell, D., & Tafrate, R. C. (2011). Conceptualization and measurement of criminal thinking: Initial validation of the Criminogenic Thinking Profile. *International Journal of Offender Therapy and Comparative Criminology*. doi: 10.1177/0306624X11416197.

Mitchell, D., Tafrate, R. C., Hogan, T., & Olver, M. E. (2013). An exploration of the association between criminal thinking and community program attrition. *Journal of Criminal Justice*, *41*, 81–89.

Morgan, R. D., & Flora, D. B. (2002). Group psychotherapy with incarcerated offenders: A research synthesis. *Group Dynamics: Theory, Research, and Practice*, *6*, 203–218. doi: 10.1037/1089-2699.6.3.203.

Morgan, R. D., Flora, D. B., Kroner, D. G., Mills, J. F., Varghese, F. P., & Steffan, J. S. (2012). Treating offenders with mental illness: A research synthesis. *Law and Human Behavior*, *36*, 37–50. doi: 10.1037/h0093964.

Morgan, R. D., Kroner, D. G., & Mills, J. F (2006). Group psychotherapy in prison: Facilitating change inside the walls. *Journal of Contemporary Psychotherapy*, *36*, 137–144.

Morgan, R. D., Kroner, D. G., Mills, J. F., Bauer, R., & Serna, C. (2012). *Treating persons with mental illness that are justice involved: Preliminary fidelity data from a comprehensive treatment program*. Manuscript submitted for publication.

Muirhead, J. E., & Rhodes, R. (1998). Literacy level of Canadian federal offenders. *Journal of Correctional Education*, *49*, 59–60.

Pelissier, B., Camp, S. D., & Motivans, M. (2003). Staying in treatment: How much difference is there from prison to prison? *Psychology of Addictive Behaviors*, *17*, 134–141. doi: 10.1037/0893-164X.17.2.134.

Piquero, A. (2000). Frequency, specialization, and violence, in offending careers. *Journal of Research in Crime and Delinquency*, *37*, 392–418. doi: 10.1177/0022427800037004003.

Rutter, S., Gudjonsson, G., & Rabe-Hesketh, S. (2004). Violent incidents in a medium secure unit: The characteristics of persistent perpetrators of violence. *Journal of Forensic Psychiatry & Psychology*, *15*, 293–302. doi:10.1080/1478994032000199086.

Shields, I. W., & Whitehall, G. C. (1994). Neutralization and delinquency among teenagers. *Criminal Justice and Behavior*, *21*, 223–235.

Sigursson, J. F., Gudjonsson, G. H., & Peersen, M. (2001). Differences in the cognitive ability and personality of desisters and re-offenders: A prospective study among young offenders. *Psychology, Crime and Law*, *7*, 33–43.

Simourd, D. J. (1997). The Criminal Sentiments Scale-Modified and Pride in Delinquency Scale: Psychometric properties and construct validity of two measure of criminal attitudes. *Criminal Justice and Behavior*, *24*, 52–70. doi: 10.1177/0093854897024001004.

Simourd, D. J., & Olver, M. E. (2002). The future of criminal attitudes research and practice. *Criminal Justice and Behavior*, *29*, 427–446. doi: 10.1177/0093854802029004005.

Walters, G. D. (1995). The Psychological Inventory of Criminal Thinking Styles: I. Reliability and preliminary validity. *Criminal Justice and Behavior*, 22, 307–325. doi: 10.1177/0093854895022003008.

Walters, G. D. (2002). Current and historical content scales for the Psychological Inventory of Criminal Thinking Styles (PICTS). *Legal and Criminological Psychology*, 7, 73–86.

Walters, G. D. (2003). Changes in outcome expectancies and criminal thinking following a brief course of psychoeducation. *Personality and Individual Differences*, 35, 691–701.

Walters, G. D. (2004a). Incremental validity of the Psychological Inventory of Criminal Thinking Styles as a predictor of continuous and dichotomous measures of recidivism. *Assessment*, 12, 19–27. doi: 10.1177/1073191104270662.

Walters, G. D. (2004b). Predictors of early termination in a prison-based program of psychoeducation. *Prison Journal*, 84, 171–183. doi: 10.1177/0032885504265076.

Walters, G. D., Frederick, A. A., & Schlauch, C. (2007). Postdicting arrests for proactive and reactive aggression with the PICTS Proactive and Reactive Composite scales. *Journal of Interpersonal Violence*, 22, 1415–1430. doi: 10.1177/0886260507305556.

Walters, G. D., & Mandell, W. (2007). Incremental validity of the Psychological Inventory of Criminal Thinking Styles and Psychopathy Checklist: Screening Version in prediction of disciplinary outcome. *Law and Human Behavior*, 31, 141–157. doi: 10.1007/s109790069015-y.

Walters, G. D., & Schlauch, C. (2008). The Psychological Inventory of Criminal Thinking Styles and Level of Service Inventory - Revised: Screening Version as predictors of official and self-reported disciplinary infractions. *Law and Human Behavior*, 32, 454–462. doi: 10.1007/s10979007-9117-5.

Walters, G. D., Trgovac, M., Rychlec, M., Di Fazio, R., & Olson, J. (2002). Assessing change with the Psychological Inventory of Criminal Thinking Styles. *Criminal Justice and Behavior*, 29, 308–331. doi: 10.1177/0093854802029003004.

Walters, G. D., & White, T. W. (1989). The thinking criminal: A cognitive model of lifestyle criminality, *Criminal Justice Research Bulletin*, 4, 4–10.

Suggestions for Further Learning

Journal article

Andrews, D. A., & Bonta, J. (2010). Rehabilitating criminal justice policy and practice. *Psychology, Public Policy, and Law*, 16(1), 39–55. doi: 10.1037/a0018362.

Institution

Institute of Behavioral Research, Texas Christian University: URL: http://www.ibr.tcu.edu/pubs/recent/recent.html.

Appendix 5.A

Change Techniques for Cognitive Immaturity

1. Inform clients that effectively challenging their thinking is a skill (just like learning to monitor thinking).
2. As with any skill, it takes time to develop the skill (e.g., riding a bike took time to learn).
3. Have clients use the following Automatic Thought Log to begin monitoring their automatic thoughts:

Automatic Thought Log: To increase your understanding and insight into your thinking, document the situation that led to your automatic thoughts and subsequent feelings. You should also identify which of the eight criminal thinking styles is driving (related to) your automatic thoughts.

Date/time	Situation	Automatic thought(s)	Feeling(s)	Related criminal thought
Example: 8/7/09 (approx. 11.30 am)	Another offender cut in chow line in front of me	1. He's purposefully disrespecting me 2. He purposefully cut in line right in front of me 3. He's an asshole	Anger	Entitlement, Power Orientation

4. Facilitate a group discussion on the difficulty and effectiveness of challenging their automatic thoughts. Some questions to discuss with clients include:

   What should I do about this? What do I want to do about this?
   What would I tell a friend if he or she were in the same situation?

5. Emphasize social skills and coping strategies that lead to long-term goals.
6. Reinforce potential for change to improve probability of meeting long-term goals.

Appendix 5.B

Change Techniques for Egocentrism

1. Thinking patterns affect outcomes. Positive thinking patterns with positive outcomes, egocentric thinking patterns with long-term negative outcomes.
2. Examine the cost/benefits of potential solutions to problems through the table below:

Rating Scale: 0 = not likely, 1 = moderately likely, 2 = very likely

Solution	Will my goals be met?	Can I actually implement this solution?	Will the emotional benefits outweigh the costs?	Will the time and effort be worth the payoff?	Will my family/ friends benefit?	Will this benefit me in the short term?	Will this be in line with my morals?	Will this benefit me in the long-term?	TOTAL
1.									
2.									

3. Focus on the benefits, short-term, morals, and long-term goals.

Appendix 5.C

Change Techniques for Control

1. To develop alternative thinking patterns, teach reframing strategies. Just like a picture frame can improve the beauty of a painting, reinforcing alternative thinking patterns can lead to an opportunity for improvement. Facilitate alternative thinking patterns through discussion.
2. One central technique to reinforce clients to adopt alternative thinking patterns is to write out the beneficial alternative thinking patterns.
3. Some criteria for whether the alternative thinking pattern was beneficial:

    * Did the alternative make me feel better about the situation?

    * Will the alternative help me stay away from criminal behavior?

6

Applying CBT to the Criminal Thought Process

Glenn D. Walters

Criminal thinking encompasses both the content (what an offender thinks) and process (how an offender thinks) of criminal cognition. Whereas the previous chapter by Kroner and Morgan examined criminal thought content, the current chapter examines criminal thought process. This chapter begins with a brief overview of the role of criminal thought process in nurturing and protecting a criminal lifestyle. It then builds on this information to provide a model of CBT intervention designed to identify and challenge the criminal thought process that evolves in support of a criminal lifestyle.

Overview of Criminal Thought Process

A variety of factors contribute to crime experimentation and the initiation of a criminal lifestyle (Walters, 2012). Peer pressure, curiosity, and weak parental supervision are three particularly prominent features of criminal lifestyle development. Because criminal thought processes arise in support of a criminal lifestyle, people often start acting like a criminal long before they start thinking like one. Although I am in full agreement with the assertion that cognition and behavior are, for all intents and purposes, inseparable (Brewin, 1996), emphases shift as a criminal lifestyle unfolds. During the initiation phase of a criminal lifestyle the individual engages in crime to impress peers, relieve boredom, or because there is no parent willing or able to intervene and prevent the behavior from occurring. Over time, as a result of continued exposure to criminal role models and habitual enactment of criminal behaviors, criminal thinking styles develop as a means of supporting, rationalizing, and protecting the person's continued involvement in a criminal lifestyle. Eventually, the thinking becomes automatic and takes on a life of its own.

Walters (1990) has proposed that eight thinking styles serve as the foundation for criminal thought process in support of a criminal lifestyle. Definitions and examples of the eight criminal thinking styles can be found in Table 6.1. The Psychological Inventory of Criminal Thinking

Forensic CBT: A Handbook for Clinical Practice, First Edition.
Edited by Raymond Chip Tafrate and Damon Mitchell.
© 2014 John Wiley & Sons, Ltd. Published 2014 by John Wiley & Sons, Ltd.

Table 6.1   The PICTS thinking style scales.

Scale	TR	PV	Definition	Sample item	H-O
Mo	0.81	0.12	Justifying past criminal actions by attributing them to external factors	*"I have told myself that I would never have had to engage in crime if I had had a good job"*	P
En	0.80	0.19	Sense of privilege, ownership, and uniqueness; misidentification of wants as needs	*"The way I look at it, I've paid my dues and am therefore justified in taking what I want"*	P
Po	0.80	0.16	Desire to control social situations and attain power over others	*"When not in control of a situation I feel weak and helpless and experience a desire to exert power over others"*	P
So	0.83	0.14	Belief that one can indefinitely avoid the negative consequences of a criminal lifestyle	*"The more I got away with crime the more I thought there was no way the police or authorities would ever catch up with me"*	P
Co	0.82	0.21	Rapid elimination of common deterrents to crime with a simple phrase like "fuck it"	*"I have used alcohol or drugs to eliminate fear or apprehension before committing a crime"*	R
Ci	0.79	0.16	Lazy thinking, lack of critical reasoning, and impulsive decision-making	*"I tend to put off until tomorrow what should have been done today"*	R
Ds	0.85	0.20	Easy distractibility and failure to follow-through on good intentions	*"There have been times when I have made plans to do something with my family and then cancelled these plans so that I could hang out with my friends, use drugs, or commit crimes"*	R
Sn	0.73	0.18	Justifying criminal behavior by performing various good deeds	*"As I look back on it now, I was a pretty good guy even though I was involved in crime"*	DNH

Scale = PICTS thinking style scale; Mo = Mollification, En = Entitlement, Po = Power Orientation, So = Superoptimism, Co = Cutoff, Ci = Cognitive Indolence, Ds = Discontinuity, Sn = Sentimentality; TR = test-retest reliability after 2 weeks in 50 medium-security prison inmates; PV = mean (predictive validity) effect size (Walters, 2002) in the form of point-biserial correlations between each PICTS scale and the presence of an institutional infraction or recidivism (k = 12); Definition = description of the thinking style the scale is designed to measure; Sample Item = representative item from each scale; H-O = higher-order factor to which thinking style belongs, P = Proactive Criminal Thinking; R = Reactive Criminal Thinking; DNH = Denial of Harm.

Styles (PICTS: Walters, 1995) is an 80-item self-report measure, developed to assess these eight thinking styles. Exploratory and confirmatory factor analyses have identified two major factors (*proactive* and *reactive* criminal thinking) and two minor factors (problem minimization and problem magnification) (Walters, 1995, 2012). Item response theory (IRT) analyses have revealed that the proactive and reactive criminal thinking factors are subdimensions of criminal thinking, whereas problem minimization and magnification represent response style factors (Walters, Hagman, & Cohn, 2011). A response style is a test-taking behavior influenced by a person's attitude that can distort a test score.

The hierarchical model (see Figure 6.1) of criminal thinking postulates that four of the thinking styles (i.e., mollification, entitlement, power orientation, superoptimism) load onto a

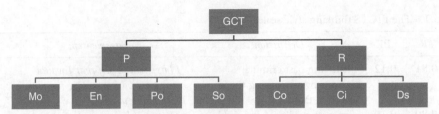

Figure 6.1   Hierarchical model of criminal thought process. GCT = General Criminal Thinking Score; P = Proactive Criminal Thinking; R = Reactive Criminal Thinking; Mo = Mollification; En = Entitlement; Po = Power Orientation; So = Superoptimism; Co = Cutoff; Ci = Cognitive Indolence; Ds = Discontinuity.

higher order proactive criminal thinking factor, and three of the thinking styles (i.e., cutoff, cognitive indolence, discontinuity) load onto a higher order reactive criminal thinking factor (Walters, 1990, 2012). These two higher order factors then load onto a superordinate factor referred to as general criminal thinking. Readers should take note of the fact that sentimentality is not included in the current version of the hierarchical model of criminal thinking proposed by Walters (2012). In a large-scale study (Walters et al., 2011) the eight PICTS sentimentality items failed to load onto either of the two thinking style second-order factors (proactive and reactive criminal thinking) or superordinate (general criminal thinking) factor. Sentimentality, it would seem, loads on a response style factor (problem minimization) rather than on a thinking style factor. Hence, problem minimization and magnification play key roles in PICTS interpretation but are not part of the criminal thought process that maintains and supports a criminal lifestyle.

Assessment: Step-by-Step Interpretation of the PICTS

Assessment of criminal thought process is best achieved by administering the PICTS to the client. When interpreting the PICTS the first step is to determine whether the results are sufficiently valid to permit interpretation. Validity with respect to a single PICTS protocol means that the results have not been unduly influenced by response style. Scales designed to assess the response styles of problem magnification (Confusion-revised: Cf-r) and problem minimization (Defensiveness-revised: Df-r) are consequently examined before interpreting the clinical or thinking style scales. Elevated scores on the Cf-r indicate levels of problem magnification and amplification sufficient to artificially elevate some of the thinking style scales (T-score ≥75 but <95) or invalidate the PICTS results (T-score ≥95).[1] Elevated scores on the Df-r indicate levels of problem minimization and defensiveness sufficient to suppress some of the thinking style scales (T-score ≥60 but <68) or invalidate the PICTS results (T-score ≥68). Table 6.2 lists the cutoffs for moderate and high elevations on the three PICTS validity scales. If scores on the Cf-r and Df-r scales are not highly elevated and fewer than 20 items are left unanswered then the practitioner can move to the next step of the interpretative process.

The second step in interpreting the PICTS is to estimate the overall level of criminal thinking by examining the General Criminal Thinking (GCT) score. T-scores of 50 or higher indicate a significant degree of general criminal thinking in that 50 represents the mean score achieved by the normative (criminal) sample. Given the apparent dimensional latent structure of the

---

[1]   T-scores are a type of standardized score with a mean of 50 and standard deviation of 10.

Table 6.2 Interpreting the PICTS validity scales.

Scale	Moderate elevation	High elevation
Don't Know (?)	10–19 items left blank	20 or more items left blank
Confusion-revised (Cf-r)	T-score of 75–94	T-score of 95 or higher
Defensiveness-revised (Df-r)	T-score of 60–67	T-score of 68 or higher

Scale = Psychological Inventory of Criminal Thinking Styles (PICTS) validity scale; Moderate elevation = interpret PICTS protocol with caution; High elevation = invalid PICTS protocol, do not interpret; T-score = standardized score with a mean of 50 and standard deviation of 10.

criminal lifestyle construct and its associated thought processes (Walters, 2007), criminal thinking is classified by trends and patterns rather than by signs and symptoms. Whereas a pattern is an idiographic comparison of a person's relative performance on several different dimensions, a trend is a normative comparison of a person's performance relative to some standard or average. The GCT score is a good indicator of general trends in criminal thinking and can range from low (T-score ≤40), to low-moderate (T-score 41–49), to high-moderate (T-score 50–59), to high (T-score ≥60). Therefore, if someone achieves a T-score of 50 or higher on the GCT we interpret this as evidence of moderate to high criminal thinking and continue to the third step of the PICTS interpretive process.

The third step in interpreting the PICTS is to conduct a pattern analysis by comparing the relative T-score elevations of the Proactive Criminal Thinking (P) and Reactive Criminal Thinking (R) scales. As was previously mentioned, pattern analysis involves an idiographic comparison of the individual's performance on several different dimensions. On the PICTS, this means comparing P and R. A difference of at least 10 points in which at least one of the scales is ≥T-score of 55 is considered significant evidence of a pattern. A difference of 6 to 9 points in which at least one of the scales is ≥T-score of 50 reveals a possible pattern. It is important to understand that proactive and reactive criminal thinking are highly correlated and that when one is high the other tends to be high and that when one is low the other tends to be low. Nevertheless, in some cases one of the scales will be significantly higher than the other. Under such circumstances, P > R means that the plotting, scheming, and calculating aspects of criminal thinking predominate; whereas R > P indicates that the emotional, spontaneous, and impulsive aspects of criminal thinking predominate.

The fourth and final step in the PICTS interpretive process is to examine the eight individual PICTS thinking style scales. This includes the four proactive scales (mollification, entitlement, power orientation, and superoptimism), the three reactive scales (cutoff, cognitive indolence, discontinuity), and the sentimentality scale (which tends to come under a third factor commonly referred to as denial of harm). Scores that are ≥T-score of 60 or ≤T-score of 40 are normally considered significant. Table 6.3 provides interpretations for high and low scores on each of the eight thinking style scales. Generally speaking, a GCT score above 50 is often accompanied by elevations of 60 or higher on one to three thinking style scales. If the T-score of the most highly elevated thinking style scale is in the upper 50s, especially if the Defensiveness scale is elevated, then it is permissible to interpret this one thinking style scale as an elevation. If more than three thinking style scales are elevated (≥T-score 60) then it is customary to focus one's interpretation on the three most highly elevated scales. As the reader can see, the PICTS is capable of providing information useful in selecting preliminary goals for intervention. Box 6.1 contains a case example.

Table 6.3 Interpretations for high and low elevations on the PICTS thinking style scales.

Scale	High (T-score ≥60)	Low (T-score ≤40)
Mollification	Looks to the environment for explanations of his/her behavior; blames own antisocial actions on external circumstances	Generally takes responsibility for his/her actions rather than blaming others; attributes actions to own choices rather than to external circumstances
Cutoff	Poor emotional control and a tendency to "fly off the handle" with minimal provocation; easily frustrated and angers quickly	Exerts good emotional control and is less likely to be viewed as impulsive compared to most offenders
Entitlement	Believes others, including society, owe him/her; often misidentifies wants as needs; views self as unique, privileged, and special	Is generally considerate of others' feelings and property; less likely to encroach on the personal space of others than most offenders
Power Orientation	Desire to be in control of situations and other people; drive for power can lead to conflict with others; argumentative and always wants things his/her way	Little interest in obtaining power and control over the external environment; gets along reasonably well with others; able and willing to compromise
Sentimentality	Superficial concern expressed for people and animals in vulnerable situations; views self as a kind of "Robin Hood" whose criminal actions are in the best interests of others	Little evidence that the individual uses concern for others to justify his/her criminal actions; in some cases, scores in this range indicate a callous disregard for the feelings of others
Superoptimism	Believes he/she can avoid the negative consequences of a criminal lifestyle indefinitely; has trouble seeing the connection between actions and consequences	Cognizant of the negative consequences of crime and is not overconfident in his or her appraisal of the chances of getting away with crime
Cognitive Indolence	Lacks critical reasoning skills; often takes shortcuts in order to achieve goals and objectives; viewed by others as impulsive and "flighty"	Less apt to be characterized by others as impulsive or lazy compared to most offenders; possesses good critical reasoning skills
Discontinuity	Has trouble following through on initially good intentions; easily distracted by events going on around him/her; may have trouble finishing what he/she has started	Focused, goal-directed, and consistent in thought and behavior; not easily sidetracked and able to follow through on initially good intentions

Intervention

Lifestyle theory (Walters, 2012) divides the change process into three phases – preparation, action, and follow-up. The term *phase* is preferred to stage because phases possess less distinct boundaries and greater cross-over than stages, and various phases of change and intervention have a high degree of overlap (see Figure 6.2). In this model, CBT can be conducted using either a group or individual format. Both formats and the three phases of lifestyle change and CBT intervention are discussed below.

Box 6.1 Fred: a Case Example

Fred is a 41-year-old single black male serving a 275-month sentence for illegal possession of a firearm. His PICTS results are presented in Table A. The first step of the interpretive process is to review the validity scales (Cf-r and Df-r). Fred's moderately elevated score on the Cf-r scale and very low Df-r score suggest that he took an open stance when responding to the PICTS, a response style that may have artificially elevated some of the clinical scales but not to the point of invalidating the protocol. A review of general criminal thinking, the second step of the interpretive sequence, reveals a strong trend toward general criminal thinking (GCT = T66). In the third step of the interpretive process we can see that the pattern of Fred's criminal thinking favors the impulsive and hot-blooded aspects of criminal thinking more than it does the calculated and cold-blooded aspects (R > P). The fourth step of the PICTS interpretive process reveals three clear thinking style scale elevations (Co, Ci, Ds > T60). Discontinuity and lack of follow-through are particularly noteworthy (Ds = T86) and along with elevations on the other two components of the reactive triad (Co, Ci), indicate poor emotional control (Co) and high impulsivity (Ci), all of which serve as preliminary goals for intervention.

Table A Fred's PICTS results.

Validity scales	
Don't Know (?)	1
Confusion-revised (Cf-r)	84
Defensiveness-revised (Df-r)	24
Higher-order factor	
General Criminal Thinking (GCT)	66
Composite scales	
Proactive Criminal Thinking (P)	58
Reactive Criminal Thinking (R)	80
Thinking style scales	
Mollification (Mo)	53
Cutoff (Co)	72
Entitlement (En)	54
Power Orientation (Po)	50
Sentimentality (Sn)	49
Superoptimism (So)	47
Cognitive Indolence (Ci)	78
Discontinuity (Ds)	86

Don't Know (?) score is in raw score format, all other PICTS scores are T-scores (mean = 50, standard deviation = 10).

Preparation phase

It is a fundamental premise of lifestyle theory that the client must be prepared for change before change can occur. One way a therapist can prepare a client for change is to adopt principles from motivational interviewing (Miller & Rollnick, 2002). Motivational interviewing

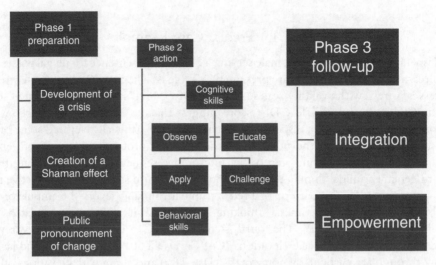

Figure 6.2   Phases and subphases of the lifestyle intervention process.

techniques, as described by Tafrate and Luther in Chapter 20, fit well into the lifestyle inter-vention format but there is a need to address other impediments to change as well. Fear of change, for instance, is a powerful disincentive. Most offenders seek treatment, not because they feel they need it, but because of external pressure from family, friends, or the criminal justice system. Fear of change is one reason why such individuals resist change. Most criminal justice clients, consequently, are in a precontemplation or contemplation stage of change when they present for treatment (Prochaska & DiClemente, 1992). In other words, they are either not considering change (precontemplation) or are extremely ambivalent about change (con-templation). Lifestyle theory proposes a three-step procedure for preparing criminal justice clients for change: amplifying crises, creating a shaman effect, and encouraging a public pro-nouncement of change.

A crisis is the perception on the part of the client that the criminal lifestyle is no longer working for them and that the not-so-good things about the lifestyle are beginning to out-weigh the good things. A crisis can be negative (loss of freedom as a result of being jailed or imprisoned) or positive (wanting to be a better role model for one's newborn child), major (facing death) or minor (series of small hassles), but in each case the individual realizes that the lifestyle is standing in the way of his/her happiness and overall life satisfaction. People who engage in a criminal lifestyle experience crises on a near-daily basis. A crisis has the power to momentarily arrest the lifestyle but because most crises are resolved relatively quickly they do not typically lead to lasting change. If the arresting process is to persist long enough to serve as the foundation for lasting change it must be developed and amplified and accompanied by the two other subphases of the preparation phase (shaman effect and public pronouncement of change). A crisis can be developed and amplified by asking the client to identify the people they have harmed, the opportunities they have missed, the relationships they have sacrificed, and the embarrassing situations they have encountered as a consequence of their involvement in crime.

Creation of a shaman effect is the second step in preparing criminal justice clients for change. Research suggests that antidepressant medication may owe at least 75% of its effi-cacy to a pharmacological placebo effect (Kirsch & Sapirstein, 1998). In that the placebo effect is mediated by the release of an endogenous opiate in the brain know as endorphin (Levine, Gordon, & Fields, 1979), some researchers believe that a similar biochemical response may be triggered by the expectation of benefit from psychotherapy (Shipley, 1988). Walters (2001) attributes the origin of the shaman effect to the expectations of efficacy mechanistic societies have for pharmacological and psychological intervention, and the reverence hunting and gathering societies have for shamanistic healers. The shaman effect prepares the client for change by promoting a sense of mastery and self-efficacy capable of converting the initial spark of a crisis into a prolongation of the lifestyle-arresting process, thereby providing the client with the opportunity to make substantial changes in behavior.

The five components of the shaman effect are delineated and defined in Table 6.4 Clients gain reassurance when they perceive that the therapist understands their inner world. Therapists can demonstrate sensitivity through accurate empathy, interpretation, and prediction. Rituals can also be used to create a shaman effect. These shamanistic rituals differ from the rituals found in a criminal lifestyle in that they foster growth rather than impede it by providing the person with a sense of personal control over their lives. One can further promote a shaman effect by enforcing the melodic requirements of speech through metaphor. A metaphor can concretize an abstract concept like criminality and provide the individual with potential avenues of change. Dialectics facilitates the development of a shaman effect by furnishing the client with a skill (thesis→antithesis→synthesis) that can be used to gain a better understanding of oneself and the surrounding environment. Finally, the attribution triad promotes a shaman effect by reminding clients that if they want to change they must acknowledge that change is necessary, that change is possible, and that they possess the skills to effect change in their lives.

The third and final step of the preparation phase of change is to encourage the client to make a public pronouncement of change in front of at least one other person, normally the therapist. Tice (1992) found that commitments made in front of an audience, even when the audience was imaginary, were stronger and more lasting than commitments made in the absence of an audience. One way clients can make a pronouncement of change in front of a therapist is to complete a change plan and share it with the therapist (Walters, 1998). A blank change plan is reproduced in Appendix 6.A of this chapter. The change plan begins as a list of

Table 6.4 Components of a shaman effect.

Component	Description
Sensitivity	Demonstration by therapist that he/she understands the client's internal frame of reference via accurate empathy, prediction, or interpretation
Ritual	External features of the therapeutic relationship (same time, same place, same people) provide client with comfort, confidence, and reassurance
Metaphor	Rhetorical and melodic requirements of speech concretize abstract concepts into tangible targets for intervention and change
Dialectics	Contrasting an idea (thesis) with its counter (antithesis) creates a synthesis capable of transcending current understanding
Attribution triad	Belief in the Necessity of Change (responsibility) Belief in the Possibility of Change (hope) Belief in One's Ability to Effect Change (confidence)

involvements, commitments, and identifications that have been problematic for the client in the past, followed by the client's plans to overcome these problematic involvements, commitments, and identifications with present substitutes and future goals. This information is then shared with the therapist, who provides the client with feedback and guidance but respects the client's position as principal architect of the change plan. With repeated administration of the change plan, future goals become present substitutes and the change plan develops and grows. The change plan, in conjunction with preliminary interpretation of the PICTS, gives rise to initial treatment goals.

Many criminal justice clients will actively resist change, associating the therapist with the legal system that has or is preparing to incarcerate them. Motivational interviewing techniques like rolling with the resistance and eliciting change talk rather than directly confronting criminal thinking are some of the best ways to deal with client resistance. In my own clinical work I have found role clarification, active collaboration, and avoidance of labels to be particularly effective in reducing the natural resistance of many criminal justice clients. Resistance often slowly dissipates once I have made it clear to clients that I am incapable of changing them, thereby clarifying my role as the facilitator of change and the client's role as the originator of change. Through development of a collaborative therapeutic relationship, the client is less likely to view the therapist as the "enemy." Of course, it is important that the therapist, when "joining" with a criminal justice client, does not lose his or her professional objectivity and "join in" or reinforce the client's criminal thinking. Finally, avoiding labels like career criminal and psychopath can help reduce resistance. In lifestyle theory, the goal is to label the lifestyle (criminal lifestyle) not the individual (lifestyle criminal).

Action phase

As was noted earlier in the section on criminal thought process, a person starts acting like a criminal before he or she start thinking like one. Variable order is reversed, however, in the case of change. This is because one must make substantial changes in thinking before a meaningful change can be anticipated in behavior. We know from research on the facilitative effect of induced compliance on cognitive dissonance (Festinger & Carlsmith, 1959) and from studies describing the salutary effects of exercise on anxiety and depression (Salmon, 2001) that behavior can change thinking. Nonetheless, when it comes to changing criminal behavior the cognitive barriers erected in support of a criminal lifestyle must come down before we can expect the individual to make a significant change in behavior. Hence, lifestyle theory concurs with contemporary cognitive-behavior theory in asserting that one of the best ways to change problematic behavior is to change problematic thinking (Beck, 1979; Ellis, 2007; Meichenbaum, 1977) because it is the problematic thinking that is supporting and protecting the problematic behavior. The action phase of CBT with the criminal thought process consists of two interrelated subphases: the cognitive skills subphase and the behavioral skills subphase.

The principal goal of the cognitive skills subphase is to identify and challenge the specific criminal thought processes that are currently maintaining the client's criminal lifestyle. A four-step procedure is recommended when conducting the cognitive skills subphase of CBT intervention. The first step is to educate the client about criminal thought process in the form of proactive and reactive criminal thinking and the eight individual criminal thinking styles (see Table 6.1). Didactic instruction, guided discussion, and reading assignments that present the client with simple descriptions of the thinking styles (see Appendix 6.B) seem to be best when implementing the first step of the cognitive skills subphase. The second step of the procedure is to provide the client with the opportunity to observe the criminal thinking styles in action. It is usually easier to see the thinking styles in others than to see it in oneself. Taped interviews with famous criminals like Charles Manson, Ted Bundy, and Jeffrey Dahmer can be found on the internet and can be used to implement the second step of the cognitive skills subphase. My preferred method is to pause the recording when a thinking style is displayed and then ask the inmate (individual) or inmates (group) with whom I am working to identify the specific thinking style, pattern, or trend being expressed. The third step of the procedure is for the client to identify the criminal thought process in him or herself. This can perhaps best be accomplished by pointing out to clients the various thinking styles that arise in their own thinking as they occur. Conducting lifestyle intervention in a group setting provides ample opportunity for feedback from both the therapist and one's peers as to the presence of the thinking styles in one's ongoing conversation. It is not until the client internalizes the process and starts identifying these thinking styles in him or herself, however, that the third step is accomplished. The fourth and final step of the cognitive skills subphase is for the client to challenge criminal thought processes and replace them with non-criminal alternatives. Two questions a client can ask him or herself to facilitate this process are: (1) *"What is the evidence in support of this belief?"* and (2) *"How will this thought benefit me in the future?"*

Whereas the cognitive skills component of the action phase of the CBT intervention seeks to identify, challenge, and change criminal thought process, the behavioral skills component is designed to alter problematic behavioral patterns. In the early stages of the action phase the emphasis is on changing criminal thinking. As one proceeds through the action phase, however, increased emphasis is placed on behavioral change: that is, getting the individual to engage in new behaviors. Two ways this can be accomplished are by employing behavioral rehearsal and homework assignments to teach and refine new skills. Behavioral rehearsal or role-playing involves teaching the client a complex social or coping skill and then practicing the skill in a controlled and safe environment, with the therapist, and perhaps other group members, providing feedback, guidance, and reinforcement. Consequently, once a complex social or coping skill is initially learned, the individual must then have the opportunity to perform and perfect the skill through practice and corrective feedback. Another way a newly acquired social or coping skill can be reinforced, modified, and sustained is by having the client complete various tasks and homework assignments. The difference between behavioral rehearsal and a task or homework assignment is that the former takes place in the therapy session under the watchful eye of the therapist and the latter takes places after the therapy appointment, while the individual is in his or her natural environment. The integration of acquired cognitive and behavioral skills begins during the final third of the action phase and becomes a point of emphasis during the follow-up phase of lifestyle intervention.

Follow-up phase

Many correctional programs fail because they lack effective follow-up or aftercare (McCollister et al., 2003). Two reasons why follow-ups are not included in an intervention are that therapists do not appreciate their importance and they do not know how to conduct a proper follow-up (Gaes, Flanagan, Motiuk, & Stewart, 1999). As the term suggests, follow-up or aftercare involves periodic interactions or booster sessions with the client after the action phase of intervention has been accomplished. For clients completing the preparation and action phases in prison, the follow-up is usually conducted by a parole/probation officer, most of whom are more familiar with corrections than counseling, or an outside consultant, most of whom are more familiar with counseling than law enforcement. Ongoing training, therefore, is vital for those carrying out the follow-up. Some therapists, regardless of their orientation, view follow-up or booster sessions as luxuries to be ignored in all but the most extreme cases. This attitude seems based, in part, on the fact that follow-up sessions are less frequent than contacts made during the preparation or action phases of intervention. Follow-up sessions may be less frequent than interventions taking place during the preparation and action phases, but they are no less intense nor are they any less important in bringing about lasting change. The two principal components or subphases of the follow-up phase are integration and empowerment.

Integration involves connecting the cognitive and behavioral components of the action phase of CBT intervention to form a seamless amalgamation of performance-enhancing skills. This integration begins near the end of the action phase but accelerates and reaches its zenith during the follow-up phase. By reminding the client about the unity and indivisibility of thought and conduct, cognition and behavior, the individual responsible for conducting the follow-up, whether a parole/probation officer or outside contractor, steers and directs the integration process. This individual might also want to share with the client the view that while cognition and behavior were given separate treatment in the first two-thirds of the action phase, such a division is arbitrary and artificial, done simply for practical reasons in that it is easier to focus on cognition and behavior separately at first and then work on their integration later. In reality, thought and conduct cannot be meaningfully disentangled in that thought affects conduct as much as conduct affects thought.

Examples (e.g.: "*Think about a time when you tried something* [behavior] *you knew you wouldn't like but to your surprise found that you liked*" [cognition]; "*Think about a time when you were angry about something* [cognition] *and how this negatively affected how you acted the rest of the day*" [behavior]) can be used to point out the "chicken and egg" nature of the cognitive-behavior relationship and encourage greater integration of the two components of the action phase: namely, cognitive and behavioral skill-building.

Empowerment is another feature of the follow-up phase of lifestyle intervention. During this subphase of CBT intervention, the focus is on building the client's confidence through success. There are several ways to promote self-efficacy, one of the more reliable routes being performance accomplishments (Bandura, 1997). Performance accomplishments are where an individual successfully performs a behavior in a real-life situation. The cognitive and behavioral skills the individual learned with the aid of instruction and modeling during the action phase of CBT intervention and then practiced by completing various homework assignments and therapist-initiated tasks can serve as the foundation for performance accomplishments. A person's daily life affords many opportunities for application of skills learned in therapy and this needs to be encouraged by whoever is conducting the follow-up. The role of the practitioner performing the follow-up intervention, then, is to provide the client with the opportunity to review and discuss his or her application efforts in a safe and secure environment; the successes the client achieves should be copiously reinforced and the less than fully successful outcomes analyzed in order to help the client identify, develop, and improve skill deficits that may be standing in the way of future performance accomplishments.

Individual Versus Group Intervention

The advantages and disadvantages of individual and group intervention often cancel each other out. In addressing criminal thought process with CBT, therefore, it is not a matter of finding the "best" approach but rather the best combination of approaches given one's current resources and circumstances. The preparation and follow-up phases are often conducted individually and the action phase collectively (in a group) because many of the preparation and follow-up subphases require a certain measure of privacy whereas the education, observation, and challenging steps of the cognitive skills substage and the behavioral rehearsal step of the behavioral skills substage are more efficiently conducted using a group format (education, challenging) or may actually profit from the presence of others (observation, behavioral rehearsal). There are always exceptions to the rule, however, and one must find the proper balance between the privacy and profundity benefits of the individual format and the social and pecuniary benefits of the group format. This is illustrated in the case of Fred (see Box 6.2), the individual whose PICTS profile was presented earlier in Box 6.1.

Box 6.2   Intervening with Fred

The author met with Fred after the latter requested an interview upon his release from the institution's lock-up unit where he spent 6 months in disciplinary segregation for attempting to assault a correctional officer. In preparing Fred for change the author helped Fred develop several preexisting crises, the most powerful being the "good time" credit Fred lost as a result of the attempted assault charge and the possibility of a new sentence should he end up assaulting a correctional officer in the future. With the lifestyle temporarily arrested, the author set out to create a shaman effect by identifying some of the criminal thinking patterns Fred displayed early in treatment (sensitivity), meeting with Fred on the same day each week (positive ritual), pointing out extremes in Fred's thinking (e.g., desire for control), and teaching him to modify these extremes via the dialectic method (thesis → antithesis → synthesis), and reinforcing Fred's belief in the necessity, possibility, and certainty of change (attribution triad). The metaphor Fred selected to represent his situation was that of being lost in the woods and needing a compass or map to get out. This metaphor, along with the increased cognitive complexity that arose through regular use of the dialectic method, helped steer Fred from the preparation phase all the way into the later stages of the action phase. The change plan that Fred used to make a public pronouncement of his intent to change listed decreases in the areas of institutional rule-breaking, commitment to aggression as a means of solving problems, and identification with his old criminal associates and peers. Fred's goals were to make a concerted effort to follow institutional rules (even those he didn't agree with), taking an anger management class, and finding a new group of associates.

The action phase of Fred's CBT intervention focused on identifying and challenging reactive criminal thinking in the form of cutoff, cognitive indolence, and discontinuity. This phase of intervention was performed primarily in a group setting where Fred and the other group members were presented with material on the criminal thinking concept, shown videos of Ted Bundy and Charles Manson in order to observe the criminal thinking styles in others, engaged in various exercises like the single pill exercise (see Appendix 6.C) designed to help clients identify the criminal thinking styles in themselves, and taught to dispute the irrational roots of their old criminal thinking styles and replace them with rational alternatives. Behavioral skills were also learned and practiced in these groups. The behavioral emphasis, though light initially, grew over the course of the action phase. Behavioral rehearsal and role playing assisted with the development of a number of social and coping skills for the purpose of teaching Fred how to more effectively manage his angry feelings and aggressive impulses. These were the tools he used to find his way out of the woods (his metaphor for the criminal lifestyle). In later points of the action phase of CBT Fred was given several homework assignments and tasks designed to start the process of cognitive-behavioral integration. For instance, he was asked to use his newly developed social skills to find a new group of associates, older inmates who did not run with gangs and who generally stayed out of trouble. Although it took several months before these individuals warmed to Fred, given his reputation for violence, he proved himself after he demonstrated that he could avoid potentially violent exchanges with both inmates and staff.

The follow-up phase of the intervention took place after Fred was released from prison and was coordinated by Fred's federal probation officer, who had received training in counseling and was familiar with lifestyle theory and the criminal thinking styles. In addition to meeting with Fred every 2 weeks, the probation officer also arranged for Fred to meet periodically with a psychologist trained in CBT who assisted Fred in the realization of the integration and empowerment goals of the follow-up intervention. This was accomplished by reviewing major events of the past month with Fred and then reinforcing him with verbal praise for the situations he handled well and pointing out alternative strategies that could have been used to more effectively handle some of the situations that did not turn out quite as well. It was during these booster sessions that the contract psychologist picked up on something that had been missed by everyone else up to that point. Fred had apparently been suffering from a central auditory processing deficit from birth that made it difficult for him to control his angry feelings and anticipate the consequences of his actions. With the help of some additional exercises and information Fred learned to control his angry emotions better and anticipate the consequences of his actions. Needless to say, this did wonders for his confidence and sense of empowerment. Fred's progress during the follow-up phase of the CBT intervention illustrates how coordinated interventions between professionals can lead to positive outcomes for clients.

Conclusion

This chapter has described how the criminal thought process can be altered with CBT. Before CBT can effectively alter the criminal thought process, however, a thorough evaluation must be conducted. Using an assessment instrument such as the PICTS to identify trends and patterns in criminal thought process helps identify preliminary goals of treatment. Upon completion of the initial evaluation, the client is prepared for change by developing and amplifying naturally occurring crises in the client's life, creating a shaman effect, and encouraging the client to make a public pronouncement for pursuing change. Preliminary goals identified from the PICTS are then modified in light of the change plan and future goals expressed by the client. During the action phase of CBT intervention the client is taught cognitive and behavioral skills and given the opportunity to practice these skills as a means of reducing his or her dependence on the criminal lifestyle in dealing with problems of everyday living. The integration of cognitive and behavioral skills, coupled with the creation of a sense of empowerment, are prominent features of the follow-up CBT phase. It should be noted, however, that these criminal thought processes have roots extending back to middle or late childhood and it will take a concerted effort on the part of both the client and therapist to first identify and then challenge these thinking styles. In the absence of a concerted effort for change on the part of both the client and therapist, the client will remain lost in the woods, to borrow a metaphor from Fred, who initially used the woods metaphor to represent his prior criminal involvements, commitments, and identifications and later to effect his escape from the criminal lifestyle.

References

Bandura, A. (1997). *Self-efficacy: The exercise of control.* New York: Freeman.

Beck, A. T. (1979). *Cognitive therapy and the emotional disorders.* New York: Meridian.

Brewin, C. R. (1996). Theoretical foundations of cognitive-behavior therapy for anxiety and depression. *Annual Review of Psychology, 47,* 33–57.

Ellis, A. (2007). *The practice of rational emotive behavior therapy* (2nd ed.). New York: Springer.

Festinger, L., & Carlsmith, J.M. (1959). Cognitive consequences of forced compliance. *Journal of Abnormal and Social Psychology, 58,* 203–210.

Gaes, G. G., Flanagan, T. J., Motiuk, L. L., & Stewart, L. (1999). Adult correctional treatment. In M. Tonry & J. Petersila (Eds.), *Crime & Justice: Prisons* (pp. 361–426). Chicago, IL: University of Chicago Press.

Kirsch, I., & Sapirstein, G. (1998). Listening to Prozac but hearing placebo: A meta-analysis of antidepressant medication. *Prevention & Treatment, 1,* art. 0002a. Retrieved June 17, 2011, from: http://academic.research.microsoft.com/Paper/5278979.aspx.

Levine, J. D., Gordon, N. C., & Fields, H. L. (1979). The role of endorphins in placebo analgesia. In J. J. Bonica, J. C. Liebeskind, & D. Albe-Fessard (Eds.), *Advances in pain research and therapy* (Vol. 3, pp. 547–551). New York: Raven.

McCollister, K. E., French, M. T., Prendergast, M., Wexler, H., Sacks, S., & Hall, E. (2003). Is in-prison treatment enough? A cost-effectiveness analysis of prison-based treatment and aftercare services for substance abusing offenders. *Law and Policy, 25,* 62–83.

Meichenbaum, D. (1977). *Cognitive-behavior modification: An integrative approach.* New York: Springer.

Miller, W. R., & Rollnick, S. (2002). *Motivational interviewing: Preparing people for change* (2nd ed.). New York: Guilford.

Prochaska, J. O., & DiClemente, C. C. (1992). Stages of change in the modification of problem behaviors. In M. Hersen, R. M. Eisler, & P. M. Miller (Eds.), *Progress in behavior modification* (pp. 184–214). Sycamore, IL: Sycamore.

Salmon, P. (2001). Effects of physical exercise on anxiety, depression, and sensitivity to stress: A unifying theory. *Clinical Psychology Review, 21,* 33–61.

Shipley, T. E. (1988). Opponent-processes, stress, and attributions: Some implications for shamanism and the initiation of the healing relationship. *Psychotherapy, 25,* 593–603.

Tice, D. M. (1992. Self-concept change and self-presentation: The looking glass self is also a magnifying glass. *Journal of Personality and Social Psychology, 63,* 435–451.

Walters, G. D. (1990). *The criminal lifestyle: Patterns of serious criminal conduct.* Newbury Park, CA: Sage.

Walters, G. D. (1995). The Psychological Inventory of Criminal Thinking Styles: Part I. Reliability and preliminary validity. *Criminal Justice and Behavior, 22,* 307–325.

Walters, G. D. (1998). Planning for change: An alternative to treatment planning with sexual offenders. *Journal of Sex and Marital Therapy, 24,* 217–229.

Walters, G. D. (2001). The shaman effect in counseling clients with alcohol problems. *Alcoholism Treatment Quarterly, 19*(3), 31–43.

Walters, G. D. (2002). Current and historical content scales for the Psychological Inventory of Criminal Thinking Styles (PICTS). *Legal & Criminological Psychology, 7,* 73–87.

Walters, G. D. (2007). The latent structure of the criminal lifestyle: A taxometric analysis of the Lifestyle Criminality Screening Form and Psychological Inventory of Criminal Thinking Styles. *Criminal Justice and Behavior, 34,* 1623–1637.

Walters, G. D. (2012). *Crime in a psychological context: From career criminals to criminal careers.* Thousand Oaks, CA: Sage.

Walters, G. D., Hagman, B. T., & Cohn, A. M. (2011). Toward a hierarchical model of criminal thinking: Evidence from item response theory and confirmatory factor analysis. *Psychological Assessment, 23,* 925–936.

Suggestions for Further Learning

Books

Walters, G. D. (1990). *The criminal lifestyle: Patterns of serious criminal conduct.* Newbury Park, CA: Sage.

Walters, G. D. (2012). *Crime in a psychological context: From career criminals to criminal careers.* Thousand Oaks, CA: Sage.

Appendix 6.A

Change Plan

Name:_____ Date:_____

Instructions: For the purposes of this plan, *involvements* are what you do and who you do it with, *commitments* are what is important to you and how you go about achieving these objectives, and *identity* is how you see yourself. List the problems you have experienced in the past with respect to crime-related involvements, commitments, and identifications in the first column. In the next column, list substitute involvements, commitments, and identifications in the present that you believe will be of assistance to you in abandoning a criminal lifestyle. In the third column, list your goals in terms of future involvements, commitments, and identifications.

	Past Problems	*Present* Substitutes	*Future* Goals
Involvements			
Commitments			
Identifications			

Appendix 6.B

Excerpt from the Lifestyle Issues Client Treatment Manual

THINKING PATTERNS

Thinking is what protects the criminal lifestyle from the reality of what you are doing to yourself and others in the name of crime. The lifestyle model identifies eight thinking patterns as critical in maintaining a criminal lifestyle. Each will be discussed briefly in this section.

Mollification: People who habitually commit crime like to avoid responsibility for their actions by "proving" to themselves and others that they had no choice but to do crime. By blaming your parents, peers, or society, however, you are failing to take responsibility for your actions. Lifestyle theory refers to this as mollification. In failing to assume responsibility for your decisions and behavior, you are eliminating potential avenues of change and intervention, which in the end only serves to protect the criminal lifestyle.

Cutoff: Commitment to a criminal lifestyle requires that you possess the ability to eliminate common deterrents to crime. The habitual criminal uses the cutoff to eliminate deterrents just as a person shuts off a light switch to darken a room. The phrase *"fuck it"* is the most common cutoff observed in inmate populations. Other cutoffs are possible, however. Some people, in fact, use drugs as a cutoff. You might use alcohol to give yourself false courage, heroin to calm you down, or cocaine to pump you up prior to committing a crime.

Entitlement: Before crime can become a reality you must grant yourself permission to commit a particular crime. Crime-involved individuals may tell themselves that they are entitled to commit crime because they've had a hard life, rough week, or bad day. Some criminals can, in fact, be rather creative in how they go about granting themselves permission to commit crime, sometimes going so far as to manipulate a conflict with a spouse or employer to justify going out and committing a crime. Entitlement often involves a sense of ownership or privilege and frequently entails the misidentification of wants as needs. Telling yourself you need something (a new car), for instance, gives you permission to get that "need" met.

Power Orientation: The thinking that governs a criminal lifestyle is not only motivated by immediate gratification, but also emphasizes interpersonal control. The criminal may attempt to counteract weak personal control by finding ways to manipulate and control others. When you are not in control of a situation you may feel powerless (zero state). By emphasizing external control (power) over internal control (self-discipline), you can put yourself in an "up" position and feel better about yourself by putting another person down.

Sentimentality: We all have a need to view ourselves in a positive, constructive light. Crime-involved individuals are no exception, and they tend to distort their thinking in order to deny self- and other-destructive behavior. Rather than making excuses because of perceived injustices, as is the pattern with mollification, sentimentality involves justifying your actions by taking note of all the positive things you have accomplished over a certain period of time. Religion, your family, and the welfare of strangers are ways one might reduce guilt through sentimentality. The major difference between sentimentality and true caring and concern is that while true caring and concern is focused on another person, sentimentality is a selfish attempt to shine a positive light on oneself by performing one or more "good deeds."

Superoptimism: Because people get away with the vast majority of their crimes they can engage in a criminal lifestyle for months, sometimes years, before experiencing the negative consequences of their lifestyle. This contributes to the formation of an attitude of invulnerability in the minds of people who are able to initially escape the physical, psychological, and legal consequences of habitual criminality, even though they may have observed many of the same consequences in others. This is because you convince yourself that you will somehow be able to escape the negative repercussions of a criminal lifestyle "for the time being." However, this only makes your eventual fall that much more dramatic.

Cognitive Indolence: People who habitually commit crime are as lazy in thought as they are in action. Like water running downhill, people involved in a criminal lifestyle take the path of least resistance, although this path is fraught with pitfalls and booby traps at every turn. If you are committed to a criminal lifestyle then you have probably taken many short-cuts, knowing full well that these short-cuts may eventually lead to disaster. However, those committed to a criminal lifestyle are much more interested in pursuing the short-term benefits of crime than worrying about the long-term effects of a criminal lifestyle. The lazy thinking that is cognitive indolence also causes many habitual criminals to take an uncritical view of their plans and ideas.

Discontinuity: People engaged in a criminal lifestyle often have trouble following through on commitments and initially good intentions. When you are engaged in discontinuity you may also have trouble remaining focused on goals because you are easily sidetracked and distracted by things going on around you. This lack of consistency in thought and behavior is called discontinuity, and is what often frustrates a person's attempts at long-term change. This lack of consistency also gives rise to a "Jekyll and Hyde" pattern in which the person wears two different masks, one when committing crime and the other when engaged in non-criminal activities.

Appendix 6.C

Single Pill Exercise

Instructions: You have to proceed cautiously with this exercise if the group you are using it with contains any individuals with serious mental health problems (particularly paranoia) or subnormal intelligence. If the members of your group or class are neither seriously mentally disturbed nor of subnormal intelligence you should be able to do the exercise without a problem, although you might want to make it clear from the beginning that this is an exercise and that you really haven't released gas into the room. Here is what you tell the group:

> "*I have good news and bad news. The bad news is that a gas has just been released into the room. This is a special kind of gas, an intelligent gas. It knows if you are currently engaged in a criminal lifestyle and it becomes poisonous for those in whom it detects the criminal lifestyle. You might be able to fool me, you might be able to fool your family, you might even be able to fool yourself, but you cannot fool the gas. If the criminal lifestyle is currently part of your life then you have anywhere from 30 minutes to an hour left to live. The good news is that I have an anecdote in my pocket, powerful enough to protect one person in the group from the gas. The question I would like answered in today's session is who should receive the pill?*"

Comment: This exercise can bring out a number of the thinking styles in group members. The most common initial thinking style is superoptimism in that some of the participants will insist that they don't need the pill because they no longer have a criminal lifestyle. Another common thinking style that arises during this exercise is sentimentality (*I should get the pill because I'm the youngest, the oldest, the one with a family*). Power orientation (*I'll just physically take the pill from you*), mollification (*you, the therapist, need the pill because you're more criminal than the rest of us in the room*), entitlement (*they owe me the pill*), and cognitive indolence (*I don't have to do anything, everything will magically work itself out*) are also frequently observed. This exercise also brings into focus the question of what exactly is a lifestyle. In other words, can you carry a criminal lifestyle with you into prison? The answer to this question is, of course, yes, because the lifestyle is a way of thinking. Some inmates can do 10 years in prison without getting a single disciplinary report but then get in trouble the first week they're on the streets. The core of a criminal lifestyle is the thinking, and it is the criminal thinking that needs to be addressed if a person is to abandon a criminal lifestyle. I normally end the session by remarking that the gas didn't work this time, so there is no need for the pill. I add, however, that the gas can serve as a metaphor for the consequences of living a criminal lifestyle and that if they do not learn how to abandon the lifestyle it could very well literally end up killing them.

7

Training Community Corrections Officers in Cognitive-Behavioral Intervention Strategies

Tanya Rugge and James Bonta

In Canada, just over 110 000 offenders were supervised in the community in the fiscal year 2010–11 (Public Safety Canada, 2011). Despite this high number, until recently, relatively little was known about the overall effectiveness of community supervision. While considerable research has been conducted over the years in terms of correctional practice with the growing "what works" literature (Andrews & Bonta, 2010a), it is only in the past few years that this knowledge is being applied in the field of probation and parole. For example, mounting evidence from the examination of correctional practice has shown that rehabilitative efforts can reduce offending, that not all rehabilitative efforts are equal, and that interventions can maximize their effectiveness through adherence to the principles of effective correctional treatment known as the Risk-Need-Responsivity (RNR) model (Andrews & Bonta, 2010a).

Based on the general personality and cognitive social learning model of criminal behavior (Andrews & Bonta, 2010a), the principles of risk, need, and responsivity have become the three foundational pillars guiding offender intervention practice today. The risk principle emphasizes the importance of directing services to higher risk offenders, the need principle underscores the criminogenic needs that should be the main targets in treatment, and the responsivity principle stresses cognitive-behavioral intervention methods to be used and optimized while ensuring that the intervention is tailored to the offender's learning style, motivation, abilities, and strengths (Andrews & Bonta, 2010a). Empirically, research has established that adherence to all three RNR principles can result in greater reductions of recidivism rates – up to 26% reductions (Andrews & Bonta, 2010b). The evidence has shown that the importance of adhering to the RNR principles is robust and applicable across various different types of treatments and services, and for all types of offenders (Andrews & Bonta, 2010a; Dowden & Andrews, 1999a; Dowden & Andrews, 1999b; Hanson, Bourgon, Helmus & Hodgson, 2009; Lowenkamp, Latessa, & Smith, 2006).

Forensic CBT: A Handbook for Clinical Practice, First Edition.
Edited by Raymond Chip Tafrate and Damon Mitchell.
© Public Safety Canada 2014. Published 2014 by John Wiley & Sons, Ltd.

Background

The examination of what happens "behind closed doors" in the area of probation and community supervision practices is relatively new (Bonta, Rugge, Scott, Bourgon, & Yessine, 2008). What is also relatively new is the question of whether adherence to the RNR principles in probation or parole is evident and if so, how these principles are applied. Research has now started to explore what constitutes "best practices" in community supervision more broadly (McNeil, Raynor, & Trottier, 2010).

Andrews and colleagues began their research on core correctional practice in Canada in the late 1970s (Andrews & Kiessling, 1980). In the mid-1990s, Trottier took elements of this core correctional practice and trained probation officers in Australia in these new techniques (Trottier, 1996). This was a starting point for investigating what takes place in the offices of probation officers when they meet with their clients. For a more thorough review of the progression of research, please see (Bonta et al., 2008).

In 2002, an examination of probation was undertaken in the province of Manitoba by Canadian researchers (Bonta, Rugge, Sedo, & Coles, 2004). While the main research question was to determine whether probation officers were adhering to the RNR principles (e.g., level of service matched to risk level, attention paid to criminogenic needs, techniques of relationship building evident, use of cognitive-behavioral techniques), a number of related factors were also examined (e.g., use of community resources). Sixty-two probation officers agreed to audiotape their supervision sessions with clients over three time periods. Audiotapes were analyzed and coded for approximately 100 variables.

Results indicated that, overall, there was minimal adherence to the RNR principles, or much less adherence than one would hope to see toward incorporating what is known about effective correctional interventions into probation services. There was only modest adherence to the risk principle, with many low-risk offenders being seen equally as often as high-risk offenders. Similarly, there was little adherence to the need principle, with only a few identified criminogenic needs being discussed during supervision sessions, and especially little attention paid to procriminal attitudes. Finally, evidence of the incorporation of the responsivity principle through the use of cognitive-behavioral techniques was negligible. While there were many unanticipated results, one of the more disappointing findings was the low proportion of probation officers focusing on procriminal attitudes and using cognitive-behavioral techniques during sessions with their clients (Bonta et al., 2008).

The results of this study prompted many more questions, particularly around the effectiveness of probation. Therefore, in 2008 a meta-analysis of community supervision outcome studies, including 15 studies from 1980 to 2006 with a total of 26 unique effect sizes, was conducted (Bonta et al., 2008). Results showed that community supervision reduced recidivism by only 2%. The findings in this study provoked a serious discussion about the discoveries, coupled with the outcomes from the Manitoba probation study. Why were probation officers not incorporating the RNR principles into their individual sessions? How would one go about assisting them in the translation of their risk-need assessment tools into case management plans? If training was to be developed, what was necessary to teach probation officers to incorporate the specific aspects of these three principles into their everyday practice? How would one ensure that cognitive-behavioral techniques were used? How could we, as researchers, aid in increasing the effectiveness of probation practices? Ultimately, how could we develop a training program that was based on the RNR principles that could improve community supervision?

The Development of the Strategic Training Initiative in Community Supervision

It took over a year for the Strategic Training Initiative in Community Supervision (STICS) to be developed. We struggled in trying to find the best solutions for the overarching questions and multiple issues that faced us in our endeavor. Table 7.1 outlines some of the program design issues and our solutions. Further information on the development of the STICS curriculum can be found in Bonta et al. (2010, 2011). After six years and over 250 probation officers successfully trained, it appears as though our solutions were successful.

Table 7.1 STICS: program design issues and solutions.

Issues	The challenge	The solution
General theory of criminal behavior	How do we bring the general theory of criminal behavior to all aspects of STICS in a coherent and cohesive manner?	Ensure STICS model and implementation permit understanding of and promote acceptance of the General Personality and Cognitive Social Learning (GPCSL) model with clear links to how it is incorporated into all practical aspects of STICS
Risk principle	How do we ensure that services focus on higher risk offenders?	Train probation officers who supervise medium- and high-risk offenders
Need principle	How do we ensure that services target criminogenic needs?	Use a validated risk-need assessment instrument to identify criminogenic needs; provide a means to transfer risk-need profiles to supervision plans; procriminal attitudes and cognitions are the primary targeted criminogenic need
Responsivity principle:	How do we ensure that services are attentive to the learning styles of the clients?	STICS model addresses: (a) relationship building, (b) cognitive-behavioral techniques, (c) relevance to the client, and (d) structure
(a) Relationship	How can POs establish a therapeutic working alliance?	Ensure STICS fosters relationship building via skills and specific processes such as collaborative goal setting and role clarification
(b) Cognitive-behavioral techniques	How do we increase the likelihood that POs use cognitive-behavioral techniques with their clients?	Provide a cognitive-behavioral model, as well as the skills, tools, and strategies necessary to utilize it in supervision with medium- to high-risk clients
(c) Relevance to client	How can we ensure that key STICS concepts and skills are used in a concrete and understandable, client-friendly fashion?	Ensure the STICS model, key concepts, skills, interventions, and materials are concrete, simple, and devoid of jargon; ensure flexibility so that STICS is useful for all types of client profiles (e.g., gender, race, mental disorder)
(d) Structuring supervision	How can we structure the supervision session and the supervision period?	Structure the individual session in four components (check-in, review, intervention, homework) and the supervision period into eight steps (from assessment to partnering with community resources)

While translating RNR into practice was difficult, one of the more challenging components pertained to the cognitive-behavioral techniques element of the responsivity principle. How could we increase the likelihood that probation officers would use cognitive-behavioral techniques with their clients? We knew that we needed to provide a cognitive-behavioral model, as well as be able to identify and teach the skills, tools, and strategies necessary for probation officers to utilize it in supervision sessions with their medium- to high-risk clients.

The original STICS project took place in three provinces of Canada: British Columbia, Saskatchewan, and Prince Edward Island, between 2007 and 2010. Eighty probation officers from these three provinces volunteered to participate in the study and after attrition, 33 probation officers formed the experimental group wherein they received a 3-day STICS training followed by both individual mentoring as well as monthly support and skill maintenance meetings for the year following participation in the initial training (19 officers were assigned to a control, routine supervision group). All probation officers also agreed to audiotape sessions with two medium-risk and four high-risk clients, over three time periods (within 1 month of starting supervision, at 3 months, and again at 6 months). Almost 300 audiotapes were received post-training. The results were very positive. Post-training recordings found significant differences between the trained probation officers and the control probation officers on the following constructs: structure, relationship, general behavioral, cognitive-behavioral, and overall effective correctional skills. Furthermore, after a mean follow-up of 2 years, the recidivism rate for the trained probation officers' clients was 25% compared to 40% for the untrained probation officers. We also compared this rate to the rate of the same probation officers prior to training. For the trained probation officers, there was a significant drop in their average recidivism rate from 47% to 25% (Bonta et al., 2010, 2011).

Since its original piloting, STICS has been taught and implemented in other contexts, with the largest being a roll-out implementation in the province of British Columbia with 400 plus probation officers (see Bonta, Bourgon, Rugge, Gress, & Gutierrez, 2013, for additional details).

Teaching Cognitive-Behavioral Interventions

As indicated earlier, there were many challenges in designing the STICS curriculum and one of the most important ones was how to teach probation officers cognitive-behavioral interventions in a form that would be successful and allow them not only to understand the techniques but also be able to teach them to their clients. We decided to break it down into various steps, each with a specific goal and assorted skills designed to achieve each goal.

Setting the stage

First and foremost was the question of "*What does cognitive-behavioral actually mean?*" to a probation officer. We now pose this question to probation officers during training sessions. The responses are varied with some of the responses touching on key components: "*if you change thinking, you can change behavior*" and "*anything learned can be changed or unlearned.*" When asked why they use cognitive-behavioral techniques, the common response is because they are told "*it works.*" A select few say they have actually seen it work with their clients. This proportion is now changing as more and more community supervision officers are exposed to trainings on how to understand and use specific cognitive-behavioral interventions with clients, and even teach these techniques and skills to others.

The STICS training explains that cognitive-behavioral interventions generally work best with offenders because they are designed to be concrete, non-verbal, practical, and structured – ultimately matching the learning style of many offenders (recall the Responsivity Principle). We teach a hands-on approach that contains four key elements or steps: (i) demonstrate the thought-behavior link; (ii) identify procriminal attitudes, thoughts, and behaviours; (iii) model and teach concrete cognitive and behavioral skills; and (iv) practice and help generalize these skills.

Demonstrate the thought-behavior link

The first and perhaps most important step is for the probation officer to show the thought-behavior link to the client – the foundation of cognitive-behavioral intervention. Thoughts direct behavior; what a person thinks influences what a person does or how a person behaves. Because of this, both the content of the thought or thinking as well as the process of thinking need to be examined by the probation officer and client if the behavior is expected to be changed. In the STICS training, we offer two detailed techniques that the officer can use with the client to accomplish teaching or establishing the thought-behavior link. Some clients, through previous programming or treatment, may already realize that their thoughts lead to their behavior. However, there will be others who feel that their behavior is caused by other people, or things outside of them that they cannot control.

If it appears that the client does not understand the thought-behavior link, we propose a technique called *Spot, the Dog*, which breaks down how one would go about teaching a dog to sit down. This visual demonstration clearly and effectively illustrates the dog's changing thought process as the sequence of events unfolds. The first time Spot is told to sit, we explain that he is likely thinking "???," but after repetition of hearing the word "*sit*" and having his bottom pushed to the floor followed by being rewarded with a cookie, the client recognizes that the reason Spot sits finally is because he thinks "*if I put my bottom on the floor, I will get a cookie*;" it is Spot's thoughts that control or direct the behavior. There are two significant messages that a client should learn during this exercise: (i) that "rewards teach" and (ii) that "punishment confuses." These two key points are intertwined throughout the training. This exercise has proven very effective with clients and this has been affirmed by hundreds of probation officers who have used this technique. Once the exercise concludes, clients are left with the understanding that what happens on the inside of their heads (i.e., their thoughts) leads directly to their behavior.

Once clients understand that what they think leads to what they do, then officers are encouraged to teach the second technique, which is called the *Behavior Sequence*. This technique reinforces the message that thoughts lead to behavior; however, it incorporates other key elements: outside context and consequences. Whereas the Spot, the Dog exercise focuses specifically on thoughts leading to behavior, the Behavior Sequence incorporates all aspects of the behavior process. If the client already has a general understanding that thoughts influence behavior, then the officer does not need to teach Spot, the Dog; they can proceed directly to teaching the Behavior Sequence.

Probation officers are taught to explain to clients that the Behavior Sequence is simply a technique that can effectively illustrate how what happens on the "outside" leads to what happens on the "inside," which leads to behavior, and then to consequences. Probation officers have found it easy to introduce the Behavior Sequence as a tool to assist clients in understanding "what's happening." In teaching the Behavior Sequence, probation officers have found it useful to examine the original offence or to examine an issue that has upset the client in some way. For the latter situation, probation officers often find it easiest to have the client tell the story and then complete the Behavior Sequence Worksheet together (see Appendix 7.A for a sample), using various parts of the story to complete the different components of the Behavior Sequence.

The visual narrative of the Behavior Sequence Worksheet breaks down the client's story of an event into four distinct parts, which we set up as columns. The first column contains the outside context of the story (or the behavior) that is being analyzed. We call these *Outside cues* and they include people, places, and things. In essence, we teach probation officers to explain to clients that outside cues are everything that is happening outside of them. The identification of outside cues helps both probation officers and clients identify thinking patterns, which in turn can help identify situations that guide future practice. The key point, which would also have been highlighted during the Spot, the Dog exercise, is that outside cues are not in the client's control – the client cannot control them, and equally important, they cannot control the client. For example, the client cannot control the behaviors of other people, just like they cannot control the weather, or make a person fall in love with them. On the other hand, outside cues cannot control the client. For example, outside cues such as other people cannot make the client do certain things – it is what the client is thinking that directs the behavior, not the outside source. Throughout the training, we teach probation officers to convey to clients that when it comes to outside cues, "*I don't control them; they don't control me.*" It is challenging for clients to differentiate between thoughts and outside cues; for example, what really was said in a circumstance versus what the client heard or thought the person meant. The discussion about outside cues starts teaching the client to separate out objective facts from cognitive interpretations or procriminal attitudes.

The next step in the sequence, *Inside cues*, consists of everything that is happening inside of the client, including their thoughts, feelings, beliefs, and values. Inside cues make up the second column of the Behavior Sequence. Examining inside cues is important because inside cues direct behavior. If the inside cues can be changed, then the behavior will change. It is absolutely key that probation officers understand this link and additionally, that they can effectively teach this connection to their clients. As a result, we spend several hours in the training working on this with the probation officers. The inside cue column is where the majority of the work will take place with the client. The key points for probation officers to understand and convey are that inside cues direct behavior and that inside cues can change. We encourage probation officers to ensure that their clients understand that "*I control my inside cues, it's my responsibility.*" Discussion about inside cues is where the identification of procriminal attitudes will occur, with more emphasis placed on how thoughts lead to behavior and where the client can start to change his or her thinking. Ultimately, it is here that the probation officer and client can begin working toward generating new prosocial thoughts to replace the procriminal thoughts, which in turn will generate alternative prosocial actions.

The third column is labelled *Behavior* and is typically the probation officer's starting point when doing a Behavior Sequence. In this column, the probation officers are encouraged to be as specific as possible when choosing the behavior that they are going to examine with the client. For example, we would argue the behavior "domestic violence" would be too vague for a probation officer to use with a client. However, the behavior "*I slapped my wife across the face*" would be detailed enough to allow for analysis of the context surrounding that event as well as the specific thoughts that were occurring in the client's mind before he raised his hand to slap her. During the practice exercises in the training, probation officers quickly realize that the more specific the behavior is when using the Behavior Sequence, the easier it will be to analyze and break down the situation. Because the target behavior is the anchor for the Behavior Sequence, we instruct probation officers to begin with this column and then work their way back to the first column, Outside cues. While this may seem peculiar, the Behavior Sequence was set up to be visually presented in chronological order: outside cues, inside cues, behavior, and consequences. However, when actually teaching or using the Behavior Sequence, it is easier to begin with the behavior and then go back to the outside cues (though in some circumstances, starting with outside cues may be all the probation officer has in terms of information). We encourage probation officers to do what works best for them given the circumstances. The key points for probation officers to understand and teach are that behavior leads to consequences and that behavior is goal-directed. The question that probation officers want to leave their client with is: "*Does what I'm doing, get me what I want?*" The goal here is to encourage the client to self-reflect and if their behavior is not resulting in the desired consequence (or does not bring them closer to their identified goal) then perhaps an alternative prosocial behavior may be a more effective choice.

The fourth and final column captures the *Consequences* of the behavior. In this discussion, we encourage probation officers to be comprehensive when eliciting consequences from their clients. For example, the apparent consequence for the client in the example above may be an assault charge and he may have lost his wife, access to his children, his friends may be upset with him, and he may lose his job as a result of a conviction. While consequences may seem straightforward, our training coaches probation officers to view consequences in various categories as they can be broken down into immediate short-term and long-term consequences. Additionally, they can also be broken down into two more groupings. The first grouping consists of *positive* and *negative*, sometimes referred to as rewards and costs. The second grouping we describe as *inside* and *outside* consequences. What was lacking in the above example were the inside consequences. What was going on inside the client's head after the behavior occurred? For example, immediately after the slap, the client may have felt powerful, thinking "*I showed her,*" but if his children saw the incident, he may have also thought "*I've been a bad father by frightening my children.*" Examining inside consequences is critical because they have a greater influence on behavior than outside consequences as they are immediate and can be self-controlled.

We instruct probation officers to work through both the inside and outside consequences with clients, as well as short-term and long-term consequences. Ultimately, did the client's behavior and the resulting consequences get the client what s/he wanted? Posing this question can be very powerful in linking a client's behavior to his or her overall goal, and therefore we suggest posing this question whenever there seems to be a disconnect between the two. This is also precisely why we encourage probation officers to spend a significant amount of time determining what the client's goals are and then working through goal setting collaboratively, preferably at the outset of probation. This allows probation officers to come back to the client-stated goal when they are analyzing whether a client's behavior got him or her closer to what they wanted. The key points for probation officers here is for them to ensure that clients understand that there are outside and inside consequences, that rewards teach and punishments confuse, and to ask "*Who controls my rewards?*" This question is posed to emphasize that they have control over many of their own rewards. We stress that probation officers should always increase the rewards they give their clients for any demonstrated prosocial thoughts or actions.

Conceptually, the Behavioral Sequence provides a visual presentation that clients can use to see the "big picture" of how things happened. The probation officer and client can then discuss how changing components within the sequence can result in more desirable consequences. In addition to examining particular behaviors, the Behavior Sequence can be used to identify and study specific attitudes, observe the consequences of individual thoughts, and enhance self-monitoring skills.

Identifying procriminal attitudes, thoughts, and behaviors

Once the thought-behavior link has been established and is understood by the client, the second step in the cognitive-behavioral intervention process is to identify attitudes, thoughts, and behaviors. In the STICS training, we define procriminal attitudes as evaluative cognitions that organize the person to act in a procriminal manner. Such cognitions bring clients closer to criminal behavior rather than closer to prosocial behavior. Not only do we want probation officers to be able to identify procriminal attitudes but also we train them to teach their clients on how to go about identifying them. In order to do this, we review various neutralization techniques (Sykes & Matza, 1957) and criminal thinking patterns within the training, and spend time working through exercises that allow probation officers to practice their skills in identifying the procriminal attitudes that they may hear from their clients. Reviewing different types of neutralizations (e.g., denial of responsibility, denial of injury, denial of victim, appeal to higher loyalty) assists probation officers in becoming more aware of the numerous rationalizations they may hear from their clients. While being able to label the specific neutralization is not critical, it can be helpful when the time comes for the probation officer to assist clients in changing the thought behind a particular neutralization. We note to probation officers that the client blaming others for their behavior, or using any other type of neutralization, are all thoughts that facilitate criminal conduct.

Once the probation officers are able to identify procriminal attitudes in a more general sense, the next step is for them to be able to recognize the procriminal attitude(s) specific to their client. In some instances, the procriminal attitudes may be obvious and abundant, particularly with high-risk clients. In such circumstances, the probation officer will have a variety of places to start. We encourage probation officers to go back to the established agreed-upon goals or work on something that seems important to the client. Client buy-in is always critical and having it can make using the various intervention techniques easier for the probation officer. In circumstances where the procriminal attitude(s) is less obvious, a Behavior Sequence Worksheet can be used to identify problematic attitudes. In fact, many probation officers have spent an entire session or more just working on the Inside cues column to discover the underlying procriminal attitude that led to the behavior being examined. The Behavior Sequence Worksheet can then also be used to show the client how changing the attitude will change the behavior.

Model and teach concrete cognitive and behavioral skills

Once steps one and two have been accomplished, the third step of this hands-on cognitive-behavioral approach is for probation officers to model and teach concrete cognitive and behavioral skills to assist the clients. Also known as cognitive restructuring, the STICS training has chosen alternative terminology that has been shown to be more comfortable to clients and is easier for them to understand. During the STICS training, we talk about the importance of terminology and emphasize that it is important to use words that the client can understand. The language used throughout the training is based on words that have been tested with hundreds of offenders and these words have been "approved" by offenders, and in some cases, even suggested by offenders.

During the cognitive restructuring component, we have chosen to use the terms *tapes* and *counters*. Tapes are basically procriminal attitudes – thoughts, attitudes, values, and beliefs that promote antisocial behavior in general and criminal behavior in particular. Counters are designed to replace the tapes (i.e., countering the tape). Countering a tape essentially means replacing the tape with a new thought to promote prosocial behavior. A counter has two parts. The first part is the expression of a new attitude, which is a prosocial alternative to the thought, opposite to the tape. We stress that this new attitude must be realistic and it must tackle the idea, value, or notion of the tape. The second part of a counter is a new behavior that should serve as a guide toward a new prosocial behavior. It should ideally be a "to-do" action, and it must be realistic to the client, believable, and doable. We often suggest that when probation officers are practicing during the training, they try to link the new thought to the new behavior with the words "*so I will…*" For example, if a client got into a fight while they were drinking and the tape is "*I was drunk*" (which is a denial of responsibility), a possible counter could be "*I am responsible for my drinking* [part one, the new attitude]…*so I will…go for an alcohol assessment and consider participating in an alcohol treatment program*" [part two, the new behavior]. This counter is realistic and doable for the client. If it is not realistic and doable for the client, we suggest continuing until a counter is developed that the client views as believable and doable.

We describe the countering process as having three steps. The first is to *catch the tape*, the second is to *counter the tape*, and the third is to *reward the counter*, ensuring that the client learns to use inside rewards (e.g., thinking "*Boy, I did a great job*") to reinforce having caught and countered the tape. Reinforcement of the positive effort put forth to counter the tape increases the chances of the client repeating the process and the behavior in the future. Throughout the training, we have always ensured that we explain the research behind every skill or technique taught. Here, we explain to probation officers that cognitive restructuring, what we call countering tapes, has shown significant reductions in recidivism (Baro, 1999; Bourgon & Armstrong, 2005; Bush & Bilodeau, 1993).

It is during the process of catching and countering tapes that it is useful for probation officers to be knowledgeable about the various types of neutralizations. For example, being able to identify if the attitude expressed is a neutralization that the client uses to excuse, minimize or avoid the costs associated with the criminal behavior (e.g., denial of responsibility, denial of injury, denial of victim, appeal to higher loyalty) will aid the probation officer in countering the tape. Other types of procriminal attitudes that probation officers may encounter include the "macho man" or "tough girl" attitude or the "system-bashing" attitude.

Exercises during the training assist probation officers in becoming skillful at countering these types of attitudes should they see them in their clients. We explain that countering can be taught and acquired but that it must be practiced and requires effort. Effective counters must be individualized to the client, as what might be effective for one client may not be effective for another. And again, we stress repeatedly the importance of rewarding the client and having the client reward themselves for countering their tapes. We even encourage probation officers to counter their own problematic thoughts in exercises during the training, which has proved to be an effective learning tool for them. We have received comments from probation officers that the process of addressing their own tapes is very helpful in mastering the skill and in teaching the clients how to do it on their own.

Practice to help generalize the skills

The last step that we teach the probation officers is how to assist clients in practicing the skills learned as well as to aid them in seeing how these skills can be generalized across different situations. As with all skills learned, the best way to master something is to practice. Therefore, we encourage probation officers to use the Behavior Sequence and practice countering pro-criminal attitudes or problematic thoughts with their clients during their individual sessions, but we also emphasize various strategies to assist in the "practicing." Specifically, we review the utility and importance of rehearsal, role-playing with clients, and assigning homework. We suggest that each client leave the session with a "to-do" action (e.g., write down five tapes and generate counters, follow up with a community resource, explain and practice a time-out with a spouse), which the probation officer will follow up on at the next session.

As with other skills, we speak to the research that supports the importance of practice and rehearsal, both for probation officers and their clients. We stress that learning through repetition is particularly important for clients trying to learn new thinking and new ways of behaving and equip probation officers with a few different ways to accomplish this last step of practicing and generalizing. For example, we encourage practicing within the individual sessions; this could be spending a session or more just countering various tapes. Another strategy encouraged is role-playing with the client. Probation officers certainly learn the effectiveness of role-plays during the training as they do them repeatedly to practice the skills.

We explain that role-playing is a cognitive-behavioral technique used to practice new skills and is helpful for clients in assessing themselves and/or the situation. They can assess their inside cues or the outside cues using this technique. The instructions we provide about how to effectively use role-plays include: (i) identify the goal of the role-play (e.g., is it to practice a skill or is it to assess something?); (ii) discuss the context of the situation to be role-played so that outside cues can be established; (iii) during the role-play, encourage the client by rewarding small, positive steps; (iv) the probation officer can model the desired behavior and then the client can work toward it through graduated practice; and (v) feedback after the role-play is vital for helping to shape future behavior, reinforcing skill-building, and identifying new areas for improvement. We outline multiple situations where role-plays can be an effective practice technique with clients (e.g., speaking to an angry spouse, job interview, saying no to friends).

A third method of practicing is that of assigning homework after every session. This allows the client to practice the technique outside of the probation office but still allows for preparation and debriefing with the probation officer. As with role-playing, we emphasize the importance of identifying the goal of the homework (e.g., self-monitoring, skill practicing, or resource building) and rewarding positive steps. We stress collaboration with the clients on the goal and the task to ensure buy-in. Attention should be paid to any responsivity issues (e.g., learning disorder, literacy) and probation officers are encouraged to personalize the assignment to the client. Creativity can be fun, and homework does not need to be what one would envision receiving in school. Even if the client goes home and thinks about something for the next session, that can be useful. Lastly, homework review and feedback at the next session is critical. Nothing can damage a relationship like the client working hard at the homework and then the probation officer not asking about it or failing to remember to review the homework at the next session.

The importance of the relationship

While teaching cognitive-behavioral intervention skills and practicing proficiency are vitally important, neither will be possible without the foundation of a positive relationship between the probation officer and his/her client. The responsivity principle posits that cognitive-behavioral interventions are the most effective with offenders and that strategies should be tailored to the personal factors of the client. Throughout the STICS training, we emphasize that this principle is all about creating the most effective learning or change environment for the client. A probation officer can be responsive to the client's way of communicating, learning, and understanding the world in a number of ways. We explain that building rapport with the client in order to have some influence on what will be learned is critical. If the client does not like the probation officer, then the client will likely not listen to him or her; this makes it difficult to teach the client a skill.

We also promote direct learning through evidence-based interactions and exercises. For example, the client can be encouraged to change by the content of the probation officer's messages and the use of rewards and costs. The underlying foundation is the development of an effective relationship, evidencing elements such as firm-but-fair, genuineness, honesty, warmth, and empathy. We stress to probation officers that as change agents, they really only have one thing at their disposal every day: their words. What they say and how they say it are critically important. The training outlines the difference between supervision goals (i.e., completing supervision without incident, complying with the conditions of probation, etc.) and therapeutic goals (i.e., addressing criminogenic needs, and in some situations non-criminogenic needs), and highlights creating an environment where the probation officer's interpersonal influence on clients can be enhanced. Probation officers can then use their influence to gradually sway the client toward prosocial conventions. While the majority of probation officers generally have quite good relationship skills, time is still spent on practicing the skills of active listening, respectful responding, and giving feedback as well as how to model prosocial behavior, and give effective reinforcement and disapproval, all toward developing and maintaining a good collaborative and therapeutic relationship.

Within the relationship factor, role clarification on the part of probation officers, where they can explain their dual role as officer of the court and as helper, is highlighted. Various components of role clarification are outlined for the probation officers to practice, and then the significance of collaborative goal setting is reviewed. This component, along with a good relationship, provides a firm foundation from which probation officers can move toward using the cognitive-behavioral techniques. Having an agreed-upon goal will always allow a place for probation officers to return to or to build upon as they teach the various cognitive-behavioral skills to the client.

One of the questions we often hear from probation officers during training is "*How do I sell or get the client to agree to listen to new information or learn a new skill?*" Finding the right time to ask is important. For example, a good time may be when the client is expressing frustration or regret about not getting something s/he wants; a desire to change him/herself, what s/he does, or how s/he feels; confusion about why s/he behaves the way s/he does; difficulty achieving a goal; or pride in behaving prosocially. Even if no ideal time presents itself, probation officers should always begin by asking the client if s/he is interested in listening to some new information. We impart that probation officers emphasize they want to teach the client something that can be of benefit to him or her.

As the training comes to a close, probation officers are reminded that changing attitudes and thoughts is like building a house. First, they need to build a foundation, then erect the walls, then add the roof. Each component or part of the house depends upon what precedes it. This analogy explains the STICS model. The first step is to build the relationship. Once the relationship is developing, the four steps of cognitive-behavioral intervention can begin. Probation officers can move forward demonstrating the thought-behavior link; work with clients to identify procriminal attitudes, thoughts, and behaviors while minding the relationship; model and teach concrete cognitive and behavioral skills; and finally practice and help the client generalize these skills beyond the probation office.

The Challenge of Integrating Cognitive-Behavioral Techniques into Offender Supervision

Generally speaking, the main concerns we hear from probation officers relate to workload and their ability to master the skills enough so that they can teach them to their clients. Regarding workload, we do recognize that practicing the skills learned in STICS will take some time, but we encourage probation officers to implement one skill at a time rather than everything all at once. For example, after the training, many probation officers return to their offices and start by changing their introductions, incorporating role clarification and collaborative goal setting into the sessions with new clients. For others, they may return and ask a long-standing client if they can try something new with them that they just learned in training. Because we anticipated workload being an issue, all managers have been required to participate in the training so that they would be aware of the time required for probation officers to practice these skills. What we have heard from probation officers is that once the skills are learned, less time will need to be spent with the clients, especially those at lower risk.

We have also proposed a session breakdown based on 30 minutes (as the Manitoba study indicated that the average session was just under that; Bonta et al., 2008). We suggest that at least half of that time go toward teaching a skill or intervention to the client. We also ask probation officers to enter each session with a plan of what they would like to achieve. Even if an acute need presents itself and the intervention cannot be taught, a plan of where the probation officer would like to go or what s/he would like to teach allows the probation officer to prepare in advance and seek out opportunities during the session to incorporate new skill building. Our feedback has been that this is doable and effective from a probation officer's perspective.

In terms of having the probation officers be able to practice and master the skills, we made sure that probation officers would be given the opportunity for further skill development after the initial STICS training. We were clear from the beginning that STICS consisted of two parts: the initial training and then at least a year of monthly half-day support meetings and various opportunities to practice skills. Trained officers could receive individual feedback on their skill development by submitting audio recordings of them using the skills, and everyone receives a one-day refresher course approximately 8 months following the training. In our current provincial-roll in British Columbia, the refresher courses now take place at 6 months following the original training and every 8 months thereafter. There are also specially trained coaches within each probation office whom newly trained probation officers can consult when trying techniques for the first time.

While only a portion of the STICS techniques were discussed here, it is hoped that a flavor of the training was communicated to readers. Given the context of this book, we chose to focus on the cognitive-behavioral techniques we teach in STICS. We explain to probation officers that the cognitive-behavioral techniques reviewed above are effective and basically add more tools to their existing toolbox of skills. While we cannot expand here, it is important to note that the teaching of cognitive-behavioral techniques is coupled with other important strategies during the training. For example, we discuss the risk principle, and how probation officers can go about ensuring they spend the most time with their higher risk clients. We discuss the need principle with them, ensuring they are skillful at identifying criminogenic needs as well as being able to distinguish stable needs from acute needs. We propose methods to prioritize needs and offer a tool to assist in the translation of information provided by their risk-need assessment into a workable action plan for the period of supervision. While each skill builds on another throughout training, and we do suggest a certain order, once all skills are learned, we explain that the techniques can be used in different circumstances depending on how the probation officer, or client, would like to proceed. There is no one right answer for what skill to use when. And as with the clients, we encourage probation officers to reward themselves for the steps that they themselves make in mastering the skill of teaching cognitive-behavioral techniques to their clients.

Conclusion

It was over 10 years ago that our team began investigating the effectiveness of community supervision. It has been quite a journey since then; however, we feel that progress has certainly been made. We have moved from probation services lowering recidivism by about two percentage points to 14.5 percentage points for STICS-trained probation officers. A training program has been developed that is clearly based on the RNR principles with specific emphasis on teaching probation officers to incorporate cognitive-behavioral techniques into their supervision sessions with clients. Probation officers who come from various backgrounds have all been able to practice the skills taught in the STICS training, and clients with various verbal and intellectual abilities are able to understand the concreteness of the skills taught to them. While only about 500 probation officers have been trained to date, the results are very promising and we continue to hear from probation officers that the STICS model is effective in facilitating change in their clients, and we have the evidence to support this (Bonta et al., 2010). Furthermore, we have heard from probation officers that this model also brings additional job satisfaction to them personally. Implementation of the STICS model through these probation officers is a baby step toward changing and improving community supervision practices in Canada.

Authors' Note and Acknowledgements

The opinions expressed herein do not necessarily represent the views of Public Safety Canada. Correspondence can be addressed to Tanya Rugge, Public Safety Canada, 340 Laurier Avenue West, Ottawa, Ontario, Canada, K1A 0P8 or by email to Tanya.Rugge@ps.gc.ca. We would like to acknowledge the significant contributions of Guy Bourgon and Leticia Gutierrez as integral members of the Strategic Training Initiative in Community Supervision team.

References

Andrews, D. A. & Bonta, J. (2010a). *The psychology of criminal conduct* (5th ed.). New Providence, NJ: LexisNexis Matthew Bender.

Andrews, D. A. & Bonta, J. (2010b). Rehabilitating criminal justice policy and practice. *Psychology, Public Policy and Law, 16,* 39–55.

Andrews, D. A. & Kiessling, J. J. (1980). Program structure and effective correctional practices: A summary of the CaVic research. In R.R. Ross & P. Gendreau (Eds.), *Effective correctional treatment* (pp. 439–463). Toronto: Butterworth.

Baro, A. L. (1999). Effects of a cognitive restructuring program on inmate institutional behaviour. *Criminal Justice and Behaviour, 26,* 466–484.

Bonta, J., Bourgon, G., Rugge, T., Gress, C., & Gutierrez, L. (2013). Taking the leap: From demonstration project to real world implementation. *Justice Research and Policy, 15,* 1–19.

Bonta, J., Bourgon, G., Rugge, T., Scott, T-L., Yessine, A., Gutierrez, L., & Li, J. (2010). *The Strategic Training Initiative in Community Supervision: Risk-Need-Responsivity in the real world.* User Report 2010–01. Ottawa: Public Safety Canada.

Bonta, J., Bourgon, G., Rugge, T., Scott, T-L., Yessine, A., Gutierrez, L., & Li, J. (2011). An experimental demonstration of training probation officers in evidence-based community supervision. *Criminal Justice and Behavior, 38,* 1127–1148. doi: 10.1177/0093854811420678

Bonta, J., Rugge, T., Scott, T., Bourgon, G., & Yessine, A. (2008). Exploring the black box of community supervision. *Journal of Offender Rehabilitation, 47,* 248–270. doi: 10.1080/10509670802134085.

Bonta, J., Rugge, T., Sedo, B., & Coles, R. (2004). *Case management in Manitoba probation.* User Report 2004–01. Ottawa: Public Safety Canada.

Bourgon, G. & Armstrong, B. (2005). Transferring the principles of effective treatment into a "Real World" prison setting. *Criminal Justice and Behavior, 32,* 3–25.

Bush, J. & Bilodeau, B. (1993). *Options: A cognitive change program.* Longmont, CO. National Institute of Corrections.

Dowden, C., & Andrews, D. A. (1999a). What works for female offenders: A meta-analytic review. *Crime and Delinquency, 45,* 438–452.

Dowden, C., & Andrews, D. A. (1999b). What works in young offender treatment: A meta-analysis. *Forum on Corrections Research, 11,* 21–24.

Hanson, R. K., Bourgon, G., Helmus, L., & Hodgson, S. (2009). *A meta-analysis of the effectiveness of treatment for sexual offenders Risk, need and responsivity.*: User Report 2009-01. Ottawa, Public Safety Canada.

Lowenkamp, C. T., Latessa, E. J., & Smith, P. (2006). Does correctional program quality really matter? The impact of adhering to the principles of effective intervention. *Criminology & Public Policy, 5,* 575–594.

McNeill, F., Raynor, P., & Trotter, C. (2010). *Offender supervision: New directions in theory, research and practice.* Willan Publishing.

Public Safety Canada (2011). *Corrections and conditional release statistical overview 2009.* Ottawa: Public Safety Canada.

Sykes, G.M., & Matza, D. (1957). Techniques of neutralization: A theory of delinquency. *American Sociological Review, 22,* 664–670.

Trottier, C. (1996). The impact of different supervision practices in community corrections. *Australian and New Zealand Journal of Criminology, 29,* 1–18.

Appendix 7.A

Behavior Sequence Worksheet

Outside Cues	Inside Cues	Behavior	Consequences	
Situation, people, places & things:		Be specific	Outside Rewards	Inside Rewards
			Outside Punishments	Inside Punishments

Part II

CBT Interventions for Common Criminal Justice Problem Areas

Section 1

Two Perspectives on the Treatment of Anger

8

Anger Management for Offenders
A Flexible CBT Approach

Howard Kassinove and Michael J. Toohey

On December 11, 2007, after a heated argument with his wife, Jose Toxtle took a knife and thrust it eight times into her body, killing her. The immediate cause was his discovery that she was having an affair with a man she met on the internet. He begged her, on his knees, to stay with him. However, she responded by saying that he had a small penis and therefore he could not satisfy her sexually. Toxtle was convicted of murder in the second degree.

Nassau County, District Attoney's Office (http://www.nassaucountyny.gov
/agencies/DA/NewsReleases/2008/062408toxtle.html)

Although anger can be a useful emotion, it becomes a problem when it is frequent, intense, enduring, or is expressed with aggression. Further, the definitions and interrelationships of anger, aggression, and hostility are confusing. Scientists and practitioners alike often use the terms interchangeably, which stands in the way of treatment progress. In this chapter, we define these terms and review some fundamental characteristics of anger. We then describe the relationship of anger to aggression, make the case that anger management is effective, and describe an anger episode model that is used to help offenders understand their own anger experiences. Finally, we describe an anger treatment program and suggest two unexplored but possibly helpful interventions.

Anger is a "negative phenomenological feeling state that motivates desires for action, usually against others, which aim[s] to warn, intimidate, control, attack or gain retribution" (Kassinove & Tafrate, 2006a, p. 4). It is a self-perceived state that is associated with misappraisals and dichotomous (black or white) thinking about the triggering agent, the importance of the event, the capacity to cope with the event, and justice-oriented demands. There are verbal labels about the intensity of the felt anger (*I am really pissed*), attributions of blame as to who caused the anger (*He made me feel so bad*), overgeneralizations about the importance or meaning of the event (*Man, my whole life fell apart*), and occasional fantasies of revenge (*When she's not expecting it, I'll get even for what she did*). Finally, anger is typically associated with physiological changes such as an increased heart rate, sweating, and so forth. Perhaps the most

Forensic CBT: A Handbook for Clinical Practice, First Edition.
Edited by Raymond Chip Tafrate and Damon Mitchell.
© 2014 John Wiley & Sons, Ltd. Published 2014 by John Wiley & Sons, Ltd.

important problem associated with dysfunctional anger is its tendency to limit the capacity for problem-solving, as the angry person sees only one solution and acts impulsively on that solution.

Aggression refers to *gross motor behavior* that is intentionally aimed against another person. Although violent behavior is often impulsive, the motor actions are purposeful and may range from pushing marital partners, to road rage, to beating up others as part of gang violence. As noted in the definition given above, anger can motivate aggressive actions that intimidate or control others or are for the purpose of retribution. With respect to criminal justice offenders there are some additional considerations. Some offenders are psychotic, or suffer from post-traumatic stress disorder (PTSD), or are otherwise overwhelmed and unaware of their actions at the moment. Later, they may admit to their actions, albeit with excuses for their behavior. Others forever deny their aggressive actions, as the justice system creates a strong reinforcement system to deny responsibility – even after conviction.

We use the term "hostility" to refer to those underlying attitudes and beliefs that set the stage for anger and aggression. These include both role expectations for spouses and children and others (expressed in attitudes such as *Women should do what they are told* and *An eye for an eye and a tooth for a tooth*), and specific anger-producing criminogenic thinking patterns that are seen in forensic populations (see Kroner and Morgan, Chapter 5; Walters, Chapter 6; Rugge and Bonta, Chapter 7). Expectations play a major role in anger and aggression, and we use the term hostility to refer to those cognitive predispositions (attitudes, thoughts, beliefs, and ideas) that lead to the interpretation of life events as unacceptable and that may be followed by anger and aggression.

Returning to the case of Mr. Toxtle, described above, it is likely that he was aware of his anger, thought that his wife's evaluation of his penis was *terrible*, thought she *should not* have said what she did, believed that she caused his anger, decided that he could not cope with her words and behavior, and believed that she either loved him or she did not. He likely had attitudes about the proper role of a wife and he was, no doubt, physiologically aroused and he responded impulsively – giving little thought to alternative ways of resolving the problem. Although there were other stressors in his life, including occupational problems, his angry solution to the problem led to a highly undesirable outcome for all involved.

Characteristics of Anger

Although anger does not regularly lead to aggression, aggression is regularly *preceded* by anger. This represents a major reason that anger itself, in addition to aggression, requires treatment in aggressive forensic populations. Anger problems have been linked to adjustment in prison, disciplinary problems, assaults, and violence, and it is an important predictor of aggression in incarcerated adolescents (Cornell, Peterson, & Richards, 1999). Anger is associated with physical assaults on care staff (Gentry & Ostapuik, 1989), and institutional staff members rate anger as the primary problem in secure psychiatric facilities (Rice, Harris, Quinsey, & Cyr, 1990). Kroner and Reddon (1995) found that interpersonal problems in prisoners were strongly related to anger expression and arousal, and holding anger in was significantly related to other dimensions of psychopathology. Anger may be part of a general heightened emotional responsivity in some offender populations (Howells, Day, & Wright, 2004), and anger appears to be a particularly important emotion in residential settings with offenders.

There are differences between the occurrence of healthy, regulated anger and maladaptive, dysregulated anger. In community samples, anger occurs about once a week and lasts for about an hour. It is verbally reported to feel less strong than rage, but stronger than annoyance. Anger seems to emerge as a moral judgment about actions thought to be wrong (Averill, 1983). Mostly, regulated anger is expressed verbally through assertive statements such as "*I was really annoyed when you said that to me.*" There may be also occasional yelling, arguing, or sulking. In contrast, anger becomes problematic when it disrupts daily functioning due to increases in intensity, frequency of occurrence, duration, rumination, and/or problematic expressive patterns.

Anger can be evaluated in multiple ways including through self-reports, changes in physiology (e.g., heart rate, blood pressure), and/or behavioral observations. Clinically, however, anger management therapists typically rely on self-reports. Such reports may occur during unstructured clinical interviews or while completing psychometric tests such as the Novaco Anger Expression Inventory (Novaco, 2003), the State Trait Anger Expression Inventory (Spielberger, 1999), or the Anger Disorders Scale (DiGiuseppe & Tafrate, 2004).

This approach, however, is not without problems. Findings from an unpublished study by Toohey, Tirnady, and McCabe (2011), show that probationers who are mandated to anger management psychotherapy significantly under-report their anger. Although it is possible that probationers are less aware of their anger, it seems more likely that they try to show their therapists that they do not have an anger problem. Probationers (and others at the pre-sentencing stage) know that anger management therapists may be required to send reports back to the court. Thus, we agree with the recommendation of Novaco (2003) that concurrent measures are important when paper-and-pencil measures are used in forensic settings. A social desirability measure, staff ratings, and clinical interviews will help to round out judgments about anger. Forensic CBT practitioners would be wise to understand the long history of disappointment with self-report data. Much evidence suggests that people simply do not know much about their inner lives (Schwarz, 1999; Wilson & Nisbett, 1978). They give different responses based on how questions are worded and with regard to the perceived consequences of their verbalizations. Clinicians are left with the usual conundrum that self-reports, while not very reliable or predictive, represent the primary method of social discourse and psychotherapeutic interchange.

With regard to characteristics of anger, it is also useful to note that feelings and expressions vary demographically. As noted by Day (see Chapter 18), it is wise to recognize cultural differences when planning anger management interventions. Overall, the demographic composition, and educational attainment and literacy levels of the prison population, are quite different from that of the general community. The prison population is more likely to be male, minority, young, less educated, and less literate. In addition, the Haigler, Harlow, O'Connor, and Campbell (1994) report found that significantly more inmates reported a learning disability or a comorbid mental or emotional condition. Certainly, it would be wise to take these findings into account as interventions are developed. Successful anger management practitioners will consider such factors as underlying attitudes and role expectations, culturally relevant examples presented for discussion, the content of role-plays, and the reading level of assigned written materials.

Does Anger Management Work?

Six meta-analyses with adults have concluded that anger management is effective (Beck & Fernandez, 1998; Bowman-Edmondson & Cohen-Conger, 1996; Del Vecchio & O'Leary, 2004; DiGiuseppe & Tafrate, 2003; Saini, 2009; Tafrate, 1995). Practitioners who are seeking institutional and financial support for their programs would be wise to use the results of these analyses to reinforce the conclusion that anger management works. Generally, positive results have been reported for interventions that are based on self-statement change, reduction of physiological arousal, and behavioral skill building. Also of importance, DiGiuseppe and Tafrate (2003) suggested that treatment gains were maintained at follow-up, and Saini (2009) concluded that anger reduction can occur in as little as eight sessions. Of course, not everyone agrees with these conclusions and some authors have questioned the efficacy of treatment in offender populations. Olatunji and Lohr (2004–5), for example, consider that many of the positive effects can actually be attributed to non-specific factors such as attention, warmth, positive regard, and so forth. As advice for practitioners who operate daily in the trenches, we recommend paying close attention to these non-specific factors as well as to those techniques that seem to be effective. Howells et al. (2005) and Heseltine, Howells, and Day (2010) have also questioned the efficacy of anger management in offender populations. They concluded that such programs increase knowledge about anger but they do not decrease anger expression. We think the pessimism expressed by some of these authors is legitimate. As noted by Novaco (1997) and others, forensic CBT often has to be delivered to persons with low motivation, resistance, avoidance, histories of failure, institutionalization, and social rejection. We noted above that such persons are also likely to present with less educational attainment and more limited literacy skills. It is hard to legitimately use the positive results found in the six meta-analyses when generalizing to such persons. Yet, it is the job of CBT practitioners to deliver the best available services based on current evidence. The anger episode model and the treatment program that we describe below hopefully meet this standard.

Some General Remarks

We want to note that most of our professional experiences have been with criminal justice system probationers, others referred by the judicial system, community residents, mental health outpatients, and college students. Clearly, the individual settings in which readers work will have contingencies that require modifications of our recommendations. Because forensic CBT for anger may be delivered in settings with various levels of behavioral restriction for service recipients, flexibility and practicality are the norm. For example, when anger management services are delivered by prison mail for violent offenders, rather than face-to-face, the program rules will be quite different than when delivered to adults on probation or parole in community settings.

As noted above, some authors disagree with the idea of anger treatment. In addition to questions about efficacy, their argument is that anger is a natural and useful response to threat. As with the useful parts of anxiety, to treat it as a disorder to be fixed is to deny its role in helping us survive. We agree that both anger and anxiety can serve us well in times of threat. Perhaps it is not appropriate to think of them as disorders. Yet, when they become dysregulated, as is often the case in forensic populations, the call for remedial action to protect the public is reasonable.

Finally, a related issue has been presented by Brodsky (2011). He believes, and we agree, that psychology has been more successful in developing new behaviors than in extinguishing old ones. Thus, treatments are more likely to be successful if they aim to develop better responses to aversive or threatening stimuli than to eliminate dysfunctional ones. Many of our recommendations are consonant with this idea.

The Anger Episode Model

Anger is partly inherited and partly learned by interactions with the environment. On one hand, we are all still subject to that automatic and useful "fight or flight" reaction. However, maladaptive and excessive anger are also learned through modeling and conditioning. The modeling effect has been well known since the classic experiment of Bandura, Ross, and Ross (1961) in which children who watched videos of an adult being aggressive toward a Bobo doll were later more aggressive with the doll themselves. Many forensic clients live in environments where there are significant displays of anger and aggression (gangs, dysfunctional families, and so forth). Thus, there are lots of opportunities to model antisocial and non-helpful behavior. With regard to direct conditioning we can consider the case of Juan, a grocery store owner. During a disagreement with his employee, Juan may become angry and show it with a raised voice, verbal putdowns, threats, gesturing, and so forth. The employee does not want to be fired and, feeling intimidated, he may then apologize. Juan is reinforced for expressing anger, and the verbal expression becomes part of his repertoire of behavior that is then elicited in similar situations.

Fortunately, individuals with anger difficulties are not *always* angry. Anger occurs in *episodes* that come and go, in response to various provocations, and the episodes differ in terms of intensity, frequency, duration, and expression. Even Mr. Toxtle, who murdered his wife, was surely kind and considerate on occasion. And the ruthless dictators of history, such as Stalin and Hitler, certainly had some moments of calm and kindness. Inmates, even those with significant behavioral problems, have been known to treat prison cats with great tenderness and affection. Therefore, it is not helpful to think of anyone as an *angry person* since that suggests the person is always angry. And it is unrealistic for a practitioner to have the goal of making a person *not angry*. Giving a blanket diagnosis of "angry," or suggesting that the person *has* an "intermittent explosive disorder," does not identify the specific behaviors to be understood and remediated. Consequently, we use an applied behavioral analysis approach to identify the cognitive, verbal, and motor behaviors that occur *when* a person is angry and then use that analysis to generate change techniques from a menu of options.

In 1995, Kassinove proposed a model for the typical anger episode. It was then expanded and revised with Tafrate in 2002 (Kassinove & Tafrate, 2002) and 2009 (Tafrate & Kassinove, 2009). The model considers individual episodes of anger and comprises the following five stages: trigger, appraisal, experience, expression, and outcome (Figure 8.1).

Triggers

The trigger is the stimulus that begins the anger episode. *Anything* can serve as an anger trigger, even something that might be objectively pleasing. Of course, there are the common anger triggers to which most of us respond such as traffic jams, being ignored, verbal put-downs, and various kinds of disrespect. As noted, there are also anger triggers that are intended to be positive. For example, a boss may compliment an employee by telling her that she looks appealing in her new dress. She might become angry with the "compliment," viewing it as demeaning and inappropriate. Kassinove served as chairperson of his university department for many years. He once gave what he considered to be a compliment to a faculty member by indicating that she did a wonderful service by working with students from a local high school. She, however, became quite offended indicating her belief that he was trying to pigeonhole her as being capable of working *only* with teenage students. So, it is useful to know that what

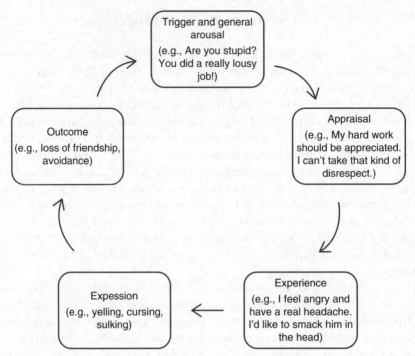

Figure 8.1 Anger Episode Model. From Kassinove & Tafrate (2009), reproduced with permission of Impact Publishers.

is one person's treasure is another person's trigger. Internal stimuli (i.e., Skinner's private events) can also serve as anger triggers. As an example, we have had cases where adults were angered in response to an *imagined* amorous transgression or an *imagined* misdeed by a friend. Finally, we note that regardless of the objective circumstances, people are often more sensitive to potential anger triggers when they are mentally or physically uncomfortable, or threatened (Anderson, 1989; Engin, Keskin, Dulgerler, & Bilge, 2010; Rotton, Frey, Barry, Milligan, & Fitzpatrick, 1979). In some ways, the easiest prevention for the emergence of anger is to assure a high-quality environment (clear air, appropriate temperature, no negative smells) and appropriate levels of sleep, food, and recreational opportunities. A reduction of noise, clearly a problem in many secure facilities, would also help.

Appraisals

Next in the anger sequence are the appraisals. These are beliefs the person has about the trigger. Since people view situations differently, they become angrier or less angry in the same objective situation. Based on the work of Ellis (1994), and other CBT pioneers, Kassinove and Tafrate posit that it is often not the *trigger* that directly leads to anger, but the *evaluation* or *appraisal* of the trigger. Ellis stated that four specific beliefs lead to dysfunctional anger. They are related to the placement of demands on the trigger (e.g., *She should listen to me because I am her husband!*), magnifying events out of proportion, or awfulizing (e.g., *It is terrible that he disrespected me!*), an intolerance for frustration or a belief in having no capacity to deal with unpleasant events (e.g., *I can't stand how mean she was!* or *I can't take that rejection*), and globalizing (e.g., *He is completely rotten for standing me up!*). Of these, it is having demands about how others should or must act that seem to be most important in the generation of anger. During the intervention phase forensic clients are asked to consider that others are free to act as they want, although *hoping* they act in wanted ways is reasonable. They are also taught that to view *unpleasant* events as *awful* does not help and that they *can* tolerate lots of unpleasantness. Thus, they are shown that they have many *more coping resources* than they know. Finally, they learn to evaluate *behaviors* (e.g., *The way she acted when she saw Mary in the mall was bad*) rather than to generalize about total personhood (e.g., *She is such a bitch!*).

Experiences

Directly influenced by the appraisal, the personal experience refers to the subjective awareness of anger (e.g., *I am feeling really pissed off!*), the physiological reactions (tense stomach, heightened alertness, rapid heartbeat, sweating, and so forth), and some new thoughts about the trigger (e.g., *Okay, I am going to kill that bitch!*). The anger experience is often associated with hurtful images and fantasies of revenge.

Expressions

The public expression of anger is typically the reason that offenders come to our attention. These expressions are typically verbal (e.g., *If you keep this up you will be very sorry!*) or physical (e.g., pointing, shoving, pushing, glaring, breaking an object, throwing an object against a wall, etc.). Alternatively, anger can be held in, not expressed, and even resolved over time. But for criminal offenders such as gang members or violent batterers, there is significant reinforcement from peers, family members, and others that keep the outward expression strong and constant, making intervention difficult. Although some adults appear for treatment because they made verbal threats that led to orders of protection against them, the majority come because of physical actions. Ultimately, the main focus for forensic CBT therapists will be to work on the *expression* of anger.

Outcomes

Outcomes can be short-term or long-term, and positive or negative. Some outcomes of anger expression, especially those in the short term, are positive. They include behavioral compliance by the target of the anger and the positive effects that come from the release of adrenaline and other hormones that give a sense of power. In cases of domestic violence, angry verbalizations may lead to behavioral compliance. There may be a similar result when an angry parent threatens a child. These short-term outcomes are intermittently reinforcing and lead to the continued use of anger to intimidate and control others. The longer-term outcomes are often quite negative and may include criminal justice system involvement, relationship and occupational difficulties, and medical problems such as an increased risk of heart disease and stroke (Williams, Paton, Siegler, Eigenbrodt, Nieto, & Tyroler, 2000). It is important that forensic anger management recipients learn to differentiate the sometimes positive and immediate outcomes of their anger displays from longer-term and often negative outcomes. Finally, the outcomes of anger may serve as triggers for additional anger episodes. For example, angry folks often blame others for causing their anger and that may lead others to be even more disrespectful to the angry person. For that reason, the anger model is presented in a circular fashion.

Before we show how to use the anger model as an aid to intervention, we again note that it is best to address anger in a behavioral, applied behavior analysis framework and to place focus on the expressive portion of the anger episode model. In recent years, there has been a return to a focus on insight in anger management therapy and, as we noted above, some scholars (Howells et al., 2005; Heseltine et al, 2010) believe that it is only knowledge that is learned. Knowledge about anger, and helping forensic patients learn the model, is important. In that sense, anger management *classes* are useful. The authors of this chapter, however, strongly recommend putting the B back into CBT, and emphasize an orientation toward *behavior*. Anger management *therapy*, by trained practitioners, is more likely to be helpful.

Using the Model to Guide Interventions

We now address the standard interventions for anger, in terms of their corresponding stages in the anger episode. Then, we review some potentially useful and unexplored anger management adjuncts.

Preparation

Success is almost impossible if offenders (i) are not *aware* of their dysfunctional anger, and (ii) are not *motivated* to reduce it. In offender populations, anger and aggression have been normalized. Offenders come from subgroups where yelling, screaming, verbal putdowns, threats, and aggression have been modeled by family members and peers, and/or they have received direct reinforcement for their own negative actions from gang members and others. When this is added to the anger and violence they see on television, read about in the news, or hear in music, they come to believe this is the norm in human interactions.

The first goal, then, is to have them discover how much anger they feel when compared to others. This can be done by direct discussion and by keeping a log that describes daily anger. However, this is often fruitless because offenders perceive such discussions as being part of a top-down relationship in which they are being told how dysfunctional they are by a representative of the criminal justice system. A better approach is to use standardized psychological anger measures, since the results can be framed as objective and not coming from the clinician. If the client scores in the higher ranges on total or subtest scores, it can serve as a wake-up call to show that by comparison with others an anger problem does exist. Clinicians may find the Anger Disorders Scale (DiGiuseppe & Tafrate, 2004), the State-Trait Anger Expression Inventory (Spielberger, 1999), or the Novaco Anger Inventory and Provocation Scale (Novaco, 2003) to be useful in this regard. A video demonstration showing how this approach was highly successful in a 31-year-old angry man can be found in Kassinove and Tafrate (2006b).

Once there is awareness of a personal anger problem, the issue of "wanting" to work on the problem arises. Although lack of motivation (or outright resistance) is a dilemma for all anger patients, it is an issue of particular relevance for court-mandated cases since they are not participating in anger management voluntarily. Motivation enhancement can be tackled with a standard motivational interviewing approach(Miller & Rollnick, 2002, 2013). The goal at the early stage of intervention is to encourage offenders to talk in favor of changing; that is, to increase specific verbalizations about reducing anger and to decrease verbalizations about staying the same (e.g., *That's just the way I am. Everyone in my family is a hothead*). In our experience, some useful prompts for an unmotivated forensic patient are:

"Tell me a bit more about your anger."
"What is life like when you are not angry?"

"People handle their anger differently. What are some of the good and bad things about your reactions?"

"How might your anger affect your life in two or three years from now?"

"What would your life be like if you reacted with less anger?"

"In what way would you like your anger to have improved after completing this program?"

Again, the purpose of these statements is to promote change-talk. Examples of questions that discourage change-talk would be, *"Why don't you work on your anger?"* or *"Why can't you be less angry?"* We discourage these questions because they are phrased in ways such that the answers would address reasons in favor of *remaining* angry. Better phrased questions would be: *"How would it help you to work on your anger?"* or *"If you decided to do it, what steps might you take to work on your anger?"* Both of these questions promote answers in favor of working on anger (i.e., change-talk).

Psychoeducation

Following increases in awareness and motivation, people are more willing to learn some of the basic facts about anger and to begin intervention strategies. The order in which the interventions are best taught is debatable and it may change depending upon the individual's circumstances. The program actually presents a menu of interventions. The CBT practitioner is expected to select those best suited for each offender. For the purposes of this chapter, we will present the interventions in the order that they apply to the anger episode model.

Before true intervention, however, comes education and fact acquisition. We use visual aids to be sure that both parties are conceptualizing what is happening in the same way. Three aids are important. First, there is a large visual on our office wall that depicts the Anger Episode Model, as shown in Figure 8.1. This allows for the development of a non-threatening educational perspective. The model is explained in an impersonal manner, with little initial reference to the offender's personal behavior.

Second, we also have a large visual of an Anger Thermometer on the wall (Kassinove & Tafrate 2002; Figure 8.2). Most people have a poor emotional vocabulary and find it hard to distinguish among annoyance, anger, and rage. Indeed, they sometimes cannot differentiate anger from anxiety or from more general upset. The Anger Thermometer is used to indicate that emotions on the anger spectrum can range from inappropriately low, to appropriately moderate, to inappropriately strong. By showing a set of different words that may be used to communicate different levels of arousal, they begin to differentiate their own arousal levels in the presence of aversive triggers. The thermometer can be jazzed up with pictures and it may be translated into different languages for non-English speakers. Also, if age, educational, and/or literacy levels are low, the words can be modified. The goal, however, is always the same. Teach an emotional vocabulary so that, in times of conflict, assertive rather than aggressive verbalizations are possible.

Third, once the psychoeducation phase is complete, we use a two-page Anger Episode Record (Figure 8.3). Initially, this is used to review anger episodes within the treatment or case management session. Later, clients can be asked to fill it out on their own, close to the time when an anger episode occurred. The record is then discussed in session.

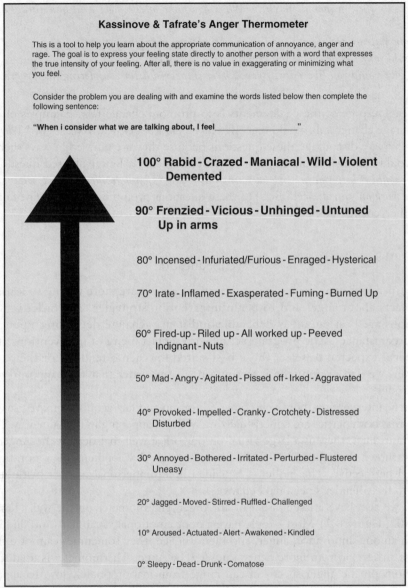

Kassinove & Tafrate's Anger Thermometer

This is a tool to help you learn about the appropriate communication of annoyance, anger and rage. The goal is to express your feeling state directly to another person with a word that expresses the true intensity of your feeling. After all, there is no value in exaggerating or minimizing what you feel.

Consider the problem you are dealing with and examine the words listed below then complete the following sentence:

"When i consider what we are talking about, I feel_____"

100° Rabid - Crazed - Maniacal - Wild - Violent Demented

90° Frenzied - Vicious - Unhinged - Untuned Up in arms

80° Incensed - Infuriated/Furious - Enraged - Hysterical

70° Irate - Inflamed - Exasperated - Fuming - Burned Up

60° Fired-up - Riled up - All worked up - Peeved Indignant - Nuts

50° Mad - Angry - Agitated - Pissed off - Irked - Aggravated

40° Provoked - Impelled - Cranky - Crotchety - Distressed Disturbed

30° Annoyed - Bothered - Irritated - Perturbed - Flustered Uneasy

20° Jagged - Moved - Stirred - Ruffled - Challenged

10° Aroused - Actuated - Alert - Awakened - Kindled

0° Sleepy - Dead - Drunk - Comatose

[Howard Kassinove Ph.D. and Raymond Chip Tafrate, Ph.D Anger Management The Complete Treatment Guidebook for Practicioners © 2002]

Figure 8.2   Anger Thermometer. From Kassinove & Tafrate (2002), reproduced with permission of Impact Publishers.

Intervention proper

The first stage of the anger episode model is the anger trigger. In community environments, some triggers can simply be changed to reduce anger. Since high heat, noise, crowding, and smelly substances have been shown to increase anger responses, turning on an air conditioner (or going to an air-conditioned mall), reducing crowding at work, or cleaning the environment can provide some relief. Arguments between co-workers can be minimized by assigning

Name _____ Date _____

Anger Episode Record: Triggers+ Appraisals→ Experiences→ Expressive Patterns→ Outcomes

Directions. Fill out one record, completely, for each episode of anger that you experienced.

Triggers Describe the event(s)

This anger episode occurred on:
Monday Tuesday Wednesday
Thursday Friday Saturday Sunday

This anger episode occurred in the:
Morning Afternoon
Evening Late at night

This anger episode occurred:
At home At work
Other

The target of my anger was: _____

The situation surrounding my anger was: _____
_____

+

Appraisals Place a check next to each thought that you have/ had about the trigger.

___ *Awfulizing* (e.g. I thought this was one of the worst things that could be happening)

___ *Low frustration tolerance* (e.g. I thought I could not handle or deal with this situation)

___ *Demandingness* (e.g. I thought the other person should have acted differently)

___ *Oher rating* (e.g. I thought the other person was "bad," "worthless," or, an "asshole, "# @ "%&," etc.)

___ *Self-rating* (e.g. Deep down I thought I was less important or worthwhile)

___ *Distortion* (e.g. My thinking became distorted I didn't see things clearly)

___ *Unfairness* (e.g. I thought the other person acted unfairly)

___ *Revenge* (e.g. I thought the other deserves to suffer or be punished)

___ *Other* _____

___ *Other* _____

Experiences

How *intense* was your anger in this situation?

0   mild   moderate   strong   100
none   extreme

How long did your anger last?

___ minutes   ___ hours   ___ days

What physical sensations did you experience *(place a check next to each physical sensation you experienced):*

___ Muscle tension
___ Rapid heart rate
___ Headache
___ Upset stomach
___ Flushing
___ Trembling

___ Fluttering in stomach
___ Nausea
___ Rapid breathing
___ Tingling sensations
___ Feelings of unreality
___ Dizziness

___ Sweating
___ Indigestion
___ Diarrhea
___ Positive energy
___ Fatigue

Figure 8.3 Anger Episode Record. From Kassinove & Tafrate (2002), reproduced with permission of Impact Publishers.

Expressive Patterns

[Place a check next to each behavior you engaged in during this anger episode]

___ **Aversive verbalizations** (e.g. yelling, screaming, arguing, threatening, making sarcastic, nasty or abusive remarks)

___ **Bodily expressions** (e.g. rolling eyes, crossing arms, glaring, frowning, giving a stem look)

___ **Physical aggression** (e.g. fight, hit, kick, push, or shove, someone; break, throw, slam, or destroy an object)

___ **Passive retaliation** (e.g. say something bad or do something secretly harmful the person; deliberately not follow rules)

___ **Hold anger in** (e.g. keep things in and boil inside; harbor grudges and not tell anyone)

___ **Avoidance** (e.g. Escape or withdraw from the situations; distract myself by reading, watching TV, or listening to music etc.)

___ **Try to resolve the situation** (e.g. compromise, discuss, or come to some agreement with the person)

___ **Substance use** (e.g. drink beer or alcohol; take medications; aspirin, valium, etc; take other drugs-marijuana, cocaine, etc.)

___ **Other** _____

Outcomes

How do you feel after the anger passed? (Check all that apply)

___ Irritated/Annoyed	___ Relieved	___ Depressed
___ Satisfied	___ Disgusted	___ Happy
___ Sad	___ Triumphant	___ Concerned
___ Joyous	___ Guilty/Ashamed	
___ Foolish	___ Anxious/Fearful	

What other feelings did you have after the anger passed? _____

List the positive short-term outcomes of this anger episode:

List the positive long-term outcomes of this anger episode:

How did this anger episode affect relationship(s) with others?

This episode had a *(check one)* ___ negative ___ positive

impact on a: ___ Work/professional relationship
___ Social/friendship
___ Romantic relationship
___ Family relationship
___ Other

List the negative short-term outcomes of this anger episode:

List the negative long-term outcomes of this anger episode:

Figure 8.3   (*Continued*)

them to different parts of a factory or to different shifts. Environmental manipulations, such as changing the classrooms of adolescents, moving to a different city or school, or assigning a different job can lead to less anger. Certainly, for financial or custodial reasons, some of these *trigger changes* cannot be achieved in incarceration facilities. Often, however, they can be accomplished with probationers, parolees, and forensic outpatients. When possible, they do provide problem relief. As one famous example, we note the case of Steve Jobs, the genius who developed the Apple computer. Possessing a distasteful personality and poor personal hygiene that led to many disagreements, he was assigned to work in the night shift at the Hewlett Packard company early in his career. The goal was to let him do his work while keeping him away from others (Isaacson, 2011).

Unfortunately, many triggers are not easily changeable. In cases where change is not possible and continued problem behaviors may have additional legal consequences (e.g., in a fit of anger, punching a child who won't stop arguing), two solutions are to *escape* from or to *avoid* the trigger. These temporary solutions do not solve the actual problem (i.e., leaving the room when a friend is demeaning solves the immediate problem, but it doesn't stop his aversive talking in the future). Instead, they provide some degree of breathing room until more effective anger management interventions can be taught.

Sometimes, a repetitive problematic trigger is clearly identified and anger emerges quickly as a sort of *automatic pilot response*. In one case, in a public and crowded mall, an offender noticed that her boyfriend often looked glaringly at other women. She immediately started making demeaning and sarcastic remarks to her boyfriend, such as, "*What makes you think she'd be interested in a pig like you?*" They began to argue and it became heated. She threw a cell phone at him. The police were called and eventually a restraining order prevented her from seeing the (former) boyfriend. In such cases, social problem-solving (D'Zurilla & Goldfried, 1971; Huband, McMurran, Evans, & Duggan, 2007) can be useful to help offenders determine the most practical reaction to perceived aversive situations. In social problem-solving, a series of possible reactions are created for dealing with aversive triggers. In the case given above, the offender could have shouted at the boyfriend, hit him, asked him to stop, used assertive verbal communications to express her feeling, written a letter later to express herself, and so on. Then, the potential positive and negative outcomes of each of those alternatives are discussed. With the clinician, a "best" solution is agreed upon and implemented. By guiding them through social problem-solving, clients learn how to attempt to change or respond to a trigger in a thoughtful, premeditated, and non-impulsive manner. The goal is to stop the automatic pilot reaction and become more thoughtful about solutions.

A note is in order here about conflict management goals. Most offenders, indeed most people, think of conflict in terms of power and control. Thus, they seek a *win–lose* outcome in which they get their way and the other person caves in, agrees, complies, and changes. In traditional conflict management theory and training, it is recognized that the best goal in conflict is a *win–win* strategy in which both parties benefit by the agreed problem solution. This is the typical case when a contractor wants to do a job for a homeowner, who wants a lower price. They both win when the price is lowered and the contractor is hired. Understandably, offenders have often grown up in environments where win–lose solutions have been reinforced and it will be difficult to change their thinking in short intervention programs. Nonetheless, it is helpful to bring this topic up for discussion. It may also be useful for therapists to model personal stories of conflicts where both parties achieved their goals (e.g., *My spouse wanted a new TV and I wanted to go on a vacation. We decided to buy the TV first, but planned a specific trip for three months in the future, after we saved some money, so that we would both have something to look forward to*). It may also be helpful to ask non-incarcerated offenders to watch specific movies that can be discussed in session (such as the 2011 film *Win Win*, which models the theme that success and virtuous behavior can go hand-in-hand.

Unfortunately, there will be times when a trigger cannot be changed or avoided, as when a boss in a failing business requires an employee to work overtime or on a Saturday, without extra compensation. When such situations occur, it may be helpful to invoke an intervention involving the next step of the anger episode model, the evaluation, or *appraisal*, of the trigger. Interventions, such as rational emotive behavior therapy (REBT; Ellis, 1994) and cognitive therapy (CT; Beck, 1976), focus on changing distorted thoughts and replacing them with more realistic ones. They are important in anger management as they convey the message that it is not only the trigger (e.g., the boss, the spouse, or the adolescent child) that leads to feeling angry, it is also the thoughts about the trigger. The implication is that it is not the world that determines anger, but people/offenders themselves. And, if unrealistic thoughts are changed (e.g., *Damn, she never listens to me. I can't take it anymore. She should listen to what I say!*) then anger can be reduced. Kroner and Morgan (see Chapter 5) and Walters (see Chapter 6) address the hypothesis that offenders may have different patterns of thinking and traditional cognitive interventions may address incorrect targets. This possibility, if empirically supported, would lead to further studies that can examine whether changing such specific thoughts will actually reduce offender misbehaviors. In our experience, offenders often have demands about how others *should* behave and these are worthy targets for change.

Of note, although standard *forgiveness interventions* address multiple stages of the anger episode model, they include cognitive components such as understanding forgiveness, deciding to forgive, and challenging distorted thoughts about the aversive trigger through REBT, CT, or perspective-taking techniques. In the latter, people are asked to tell about the event from the trigger's or offending person's perspective. Perspective-taking typically leads to a better understanding of the aversive behavior of others by considering their points of view.

There will be situations when offenders have trouble adapting to a trigger and/or challenging their thoughts so that anger does not emerge when the trigger reappears. At those times, therapeutic techniques that address the third stage of the model, the anger experience, are required. These techniques help offenders reduce their already developed anger experiences. Two interventions, *progressive muscle relaxation* (PMR; Jacobson, 1925/1987) and *diaphragmatic breathing* (Fried, 1993), aim to reduce physiological arousal and are based on the notion that it is impossible to feel relaxed and angry simultaneously. In PMR, patients are instructed to systematically tense and relax each of their major muscle groups in order to practice how to relax in the presence of aversive stimuli. Ideally, once they become proficient at being able to relax, they will be able to do it when feeling tense in the moment due to anger. Diaphragmatic breathing is similar but focuses on taking long, slow breaths from the diaphragm (as opposed to the quick, sharp breaths from the chest associated with anger arousal) to create a relaxed response.

A related technique that reduces the anger experience is *barbing* (Kassinove & Tafrate, 2002; Tafrate & Kassinove, 1998). Barbing is a type of exposure in which people habituate to verbal anger triggers, or *barbs*, by repeatedly facing them. In other words, if a person typically becomes angry when called an "asshole," the practitioner (with the consent of the client) might barb the person by repeatedly calling him an "asshole" until the word essentially loses its meaning. Learning to dissociate feeling angry when hearing the barb in session can reduce the anger experience when the barb is heard in the real world. More detailed discussions on the use of exposure strategies are provided in Kassinove and Tafrate (2011) and Tafrate and Kassinove (2009).

Finally, there are interventions that focus on the expression of anger. These are based on the idea that anger is a survival emotion that will always be with us. Therefore, the goal is to learn to express it in a civilized way so that it will be helpful in relationships, rather than harmful. The classic intervention focuses on increasing assertive expressions of anger and reducing aggressive behavior. *Assertiveness* (Wolpe, 1990) refers to the direct, honest, and appropriate expression of anger. Typically, patients are first taught to differentiate being assertive from being verbally aggressive and being passive. The educational piece is important as it first shows that there are variations in possible reactions to aversive stimuli. It is noted that aggressive responses typically escalate reactions and, while they may lead to short-term compliance, the long-term outcome is poor interpersonal relationships. Then, it is noted that passivity is also not good as there is value in standing up for personal rights. The person thus sees that the therapist agrees with the importance of a solid response to being rejected, avoided, threatened, put down, called names, and so forth. Being on the same side with regard to the importance of a response can build the therapeutic alliance. Following this short education piece, assertiveness training proper can begin.

There are two components in an assertive expression of anger: (i) a "*when . . ., then I feel*" statement describing the feeling that occurred during the specific situation, and (ii) a request for help. Consider this poor marital interaction between Mary and Francisco, in which Mary is verbally aggressive:

MARY: Francisco, you are late again. Why the hell does this keep happening? You just keep doing what you want and paying no attention to me!

FRANCISCO: Just go to hell! I don't need your crap when I walk in the door.

Mary's prompt was based on her legitimate annoyance, but it pushed Francisco away. Now, consider this passive reaction by Mary:

MARY: Oh, Hi Francisco, do you want your dinner now?

FRANCISCO: Yes I do. I am going to wash up first.

MARY: (Thinking to herself: That bastard. He doesn't even apologize for coming home late. I may be better off with another guy who will care more about my feelings.)

In this case, Mary's passivity leads her to fume inside and to think about leaving Francisco. Finally, let's take a look at this example in which Mary is assertive:

MARY: Francisco, I'm happy to see you. But, to be honest, I feel annoyed when you come home late without calling first. It's probably not good to talk about this now. I think it would be better if we talked about it after dinner. Is that okay by you?

Now, Mary has expressed her feeling in a *when . . ., then I feel* manner. She has also requested that they talk about the problem later that night. Mary has not stuffed up her feelings and she has not exploded at him. Her statement is meant to clearly express her feeling, why she feels that way, and how she can be helped. Moreover, the statement is best said as calmly as possible, at normal volume. If the statement is screamed or coated in sarcasm then the delivery will overpower the message itself, invalidating its content.

In many situations, assertive expressions have the best chance of yielding positive results for conflict resolution. We think it is one of the most powerful interventions available and it is part of many anger intervention programs. Much has been written about how to understand and do assertiveness training since it was proposed by Wolpe and others. We recommend Alberti and Emmons' *Your Perfect Right* (2008) as an excellent self-help book for use in anger management therapy. Nevertheless, a caveat about assertiveness is in order. This text is geared toward forensic CBT, which is a broad area ranging from outpatient offenders to adults in maximum security facilities. There have been no studies, to our knowledge, confirming the utility of assertiveness in moderate to maximum security facilities. In fact, it could be dangerous in such facilities to use assertive statements such as, *"When you took my towel I felt unhappy and I'd like to talk with you about that"* or *"When you called my wife a doozy, I felt angry."* These statements could easily be perceived as an indication of weakness. As usual, in the end it will be up to the practitioner to decide if assertiveness training is useful for any particular offender in a specific environment.

Unexplored Interventions

We now turn to two unevaluated, but possibly helpful, anger interventions. Music as a potential intervention has been ignored in the professional anger management literature. Yet, studies have shown that listening to music is already a "lay" therapeutic practice that is used to attenuate negative mood states by both adults and adolescents (North, Hargreaves, & Hargreaves, 2004; Sloboda, 1992). Slow, relaxing music may lead to less impulsivity and more thoughtfulness about actions. Patel (2012), of the California Neurosciences Institute, believes that music is related to social bonding, and that synchronizing to a musical beat promotes positive and more cooperative social interactions toward people outside of the musical context. In incarceration settings, inmates and correctional officers congregate in public spaces. Music may have the ability to slow behavior, affect likability, and reduce negative affect. In such settings, it might be worthwhile to consider playing slower, relaxing pieces in the background. Some suggestions would be slower versions of Bizet's *Intermezzo (*Sandstrom & Russo, 2010), Barber's 1936 *Adagio for Strings*, and Vivaldi's *1742 Concerto for Two Mandolins & Strings in G Major* (Siemer, 2005). In contrast, it would be a bad decision to play faster angry songs such as Apocalyptica's *Refuse/Resist* (Tamir & Ford, 2009) or popular songs that are played in gyms to assist with faster and harder workouts. Even putting on soothing Enya music in the background when a couple is arguing may change their mood and conflict resolution behaviors. Music has the potential to become a useful tool in anger management therapy because of its ease of access, low cost, and demonstrated efficacy in other populations. We ask the following questions: Would it be useful to have softer and slower music piped into custodial facilities? Would it be useful to have softer and slower music playing during outpatient anger management sessions? Would it be useful to have softer and slower music introduced into work or school environments where there is the potential for conflict? These are empirical questions to be answered in controlled studies. At this point, we simply ask the reader to be aware of the potential of music in anger management programs.

According to a report from the Pew Research Center (Lenhart, Kahne, Middaugh, Macgill, Evans, & Vitak, 2008), survey data indicate that 97% of teenagers play video games. Although many games involve racing or puzzles, it is well known that others are quite violent in their content. Anderson and colleagues (2010) go so far as to conclude that exposure to violent video games is a causal risk factor for aggressive behavior, aggressive cognition, and aggressive affect. If violent video games promote anger and aggression, it may be possible that prosocial games can reduce negative feelings and behaviors. Such games are characterized by the lack of the death of characters, lack of sudden and loud noises, and absence of conflict. Indeed, evidence for this hypothesis has already been provided by Greitmeyer, Osswald, and Brauer (2010), who found that playing prosocial video games was positively related to prosocial affect and that playing such games increases empathy and helping others. Thus, we ask readers to consider the value of promoting the availability and use of prosocial video games for the treatment of anger and aggression in offender populations.

Group Work

There are potential advantages of employing a group treatment program for anger management. The opportunity to practice less angry responses to verbal provocations no doubt makes assertiveness training more helpful and can be of benefit during perspective-taking exercises. Also, when discussing personal anger problems, group members may accept both critical and constructive feedback from peers more readily than from the group leader. This may be especially true when the leader is perceived to be an authority figure and the angry person has a history of rebellion against authority. Also, some intervention components, such as relaxation training and psychoeducation, can be easily applied to multiple recipients. And, obviously, group treatment is more cost-effective than individual treatment.

At the same time, there are downsides to group treatment that may not appear in study results. When using PMR and diaphragmatic breathing, responses can easily be performed by all members of the group. However, if relaxation is paired with imagery, the imagined scenes have to be appropriate for all group members. Similar concerns will emerge when trying to help group members become less reactive to verbal barbs. Those barbs have to be appropriate to all group members or boredom will emerge. Keeping up the energy in groups is dependent upon the materials being consistently of interest to all group members. As another consideration, group treatment may simply be unappealing to some participants because of social anxiety or suspiciousness. Finally, in forensic settings, group treatment may be unacceptable as high-risk prisoners may not be allowed to congregate with each other. A colleague of ours, who works in a maximum security facility, and is in this situation, currently delivers anger management services by prison mail. Group treatment with his inmates is impossible.

Conclusion

For people who have difficulty controlling their anger or aggressive behavior, effective interventions exist. We take the position that anger occurs episodically. It begins, heightens, is experienced and expressed, and ends. With the reinforced guidance of a CBT practitioner, offenders can identify triggers and inappropriate appraisals, review the personal experience and expression of anger, and evaluate the outcomes of feeling and expressing anger. Interventions can aim to challenge distorted thinking, reduce the anger experience, replace aggressive verbal expressions with ones that are more assertive, and reduce dysfunctional behavior. Based upon clinical experience and meta-analytic results, techniques we recommend include learning when to avoid problematic situations, learning how to escape from aversive situations, viewing aversive situations as unpleasant without magnifying them out of proportion, reducing demands about how others act, reducing physical arousal, expressing anger in an assertive manner, and developing a willingness to forgive and move forward in relationships. Although not yet fully investigated, listening to slower and more relaxing forms of music and playing prosocial video games may also be helpful.

The more offenders become aware of and understand their anger, the more likely they will be able to reduce it in the future. However, awareness and understanding are not enough. Practitioners will be much more effective if they work, work, work – and then work some more – with offenders until their automatic anger reactions to aversive stimuli are replaced by reactions that are more likely to lead to conflict resolution. As we have learned from applications of CBT in other clinical areas, practice makes better!

In the end, forensic practitioners will have to be creative as they deliver anger management services. Research results often use paper and pencil measures of anger, small sample sizes, and participants who are more literate, less disturbed, and in better environmental circumstances than offenders seen by forensic CBT practitioners. Yet, based on current empirical data and personal experiences, we are optimistic that much can be accomplished in the unique cases seen daily by practitioners across a range of forensic settings.

References

Anderson, C. (1989). Temperature and aggression: Ubiquitous effects of heat on occurrence of human violence. *Psychological Bulletin, 106*, 74–96.

Anderson, C. A., Shibuya, A., Ihori, N., Swing, E. L., Bushman, B. J., Sakamoto, A., Rothstein, H. R., & Saleem, M. (2010). Violent video game effects on aggression, empathy, and prosocial behavior in Eastern and Western countries: A meta-analytic review. *Psychological Bulletin, 136* (2), 151–173.

Averill, J. R. (1983). Studies on anger and aggression: Implications for theories of emotion. *American Psychologist, 38* (11), 1145–1160.

Bandura, A., Ross, D., & Ross, S. A. (1961). Transmission of aggression through imitation of aggressive models. *Journal of Abnormal and Social Psychology, 63*, 575–582.

Beck, A. T. (1976). *Cognitive therapy and the emotional disorders.* New York: International University Press.

Beck, R., & Fernandez, E. (1998). Cognitive behavioral therapy in the treatment of anger: A meta-analysis. *Cognitive Therapy and Research, 22*, 63–74.

Bowman-Edmondson, C., & Cohen-Conger, J. (1996). A review of treatment efficacy for individuals with anger problems: Conceptual, assessment, and methodological issues. *Clinical Psychology Review, 16*, 251–275.

Brodsky, S. L. (2011). *Therapy with coerced and reluctant clients.* Washington, DC: American Psychological Association.

Cornell, D. G., Peterson, C. S., & Richards, H. (1999). Anger as a predictor of aggression among incarcerated adolescents. *Journal of Consulting and Clinical Psychology, 67* (1), 108–115.

Del Vecchio, T., & O'Leary, K. D. (2004). The effectiveness of anger treatments for specific anger problems: A meta-analytic review. *Clinical Psychology Review, 24*, 15–34.

DiGiuseppe, R., & Tafrate, R. (2003). Anger treatment for adults: A meta-analytic review. *Clinical Psychology: Science and Practice, 10*, 70–84.

DiGiuseppe, R., & Tafrate, R. (2004). *Anger Disorders Scale.* North Tonawanda, NY: Multi-Health Systems (MHS).

D'Zurilla, T. J., & Goldfried, M. R. (1971). Problem solving and behavior modification. *Journal of Abnormal Psychology, 78*, 107–126.

Ellis, A. (1994). *Reason and emotion in psychotherapy: Revised and updated.* New York: Carol Publishing.

Engin, E., Keskin, G, Dulgerler, S., & Bilge A. (2010). Anger and alexithymic characteristics of the patients diagnosed with insomnia: A control group study. *Journal of Psychiatric and Mental Health Nursing, 17* (8), 692–699.

Fried, R. (1993). The role of respiration in stress and stress control: Toward a theory of stress as a hypoxic phenomenon. In P.M. Lehrer & R.L. Woolfolk (Eds.), *Principles and practices of stress management* (pp. 301–331). New York: Guilford Press.

Gentry, M. R., & Ostapuik, E. B. (1989). Violence in institutions for young offenders. In K. Howells & C. R. Hollin (Eds.), *Clinical approaches to violence* (pp. 250–266). Chichester, UK: John Wiley & Sons, Ltd.

Greitmeyer, T., Osswald, S., & Brauer, M. (2010). Playing prosocial video games increases empathy and decreases schadenfreude. *Emotion, 10* (6), 796–802.

Haigler, K., Harlow, C., O'Connor, P. E., & Campbell, A. (1994). *Literacy behind prison walls.* Washington, DC: National Center for Education Statistics/U.S. Department of Education.

Heseltine, K., Howells, K., & Day, A. (2010). Brief anger interventions with offenders may be ineffective: A replication and extension. *Behavior Research and Therapy, 48* (3), 246–250.

Howells, K., Day, A., Williamson, P., Dubner, S., Jauncey, S., Parker, A., & Heseltine, K. (2005). Brief anger management programs with offenders: Outcomes and predictors of change. *Journal of Forensic Psychiatry and Psychology, 16* (2), 296–311.

Howells, K., Day, A., & Wright, S. (2004). Affect, emotions and sex offenders. *Psychology, Crime and Law, 10*, 179–195.

Huband, N., McMurran, M., Evans, C., & Duggan C. (2007). Social problem-solving plus psychoeducation for adults with personality disorder: Pragmatic randomised controlled trial. *British Journal of Psychiatry, 190*, 307–313.

Isaacson, W. (2011). *Steve Jobs.* New York, NY: Simon & Schuster.

Jacobson, E. (1925/1987). Progressive relaxation. *American Journal of Psychology, 100* (3/4), 522–537.

Kassinove, H., & Tafrate, R. (2002). *Anger management: The complete treatment guidebook for practitioners.* Atascadero, CA: Impact Publishers.

Kassinove, H., & Tafrate, R. (2006a). Anger related disorders: Basic issues, models, and diagnostic considerations. In E. Feindler (Ed.), *Anger-related disorders: A practitioner's guide to comparative treatments* (pp. 1–27). New York, NY: Springer.

Kassinove, H., & Tafrate, R. (2006b). *Anger management video program: An instructional guide for practitioners.* Atascadero, CA: Impact Publishers.

Kassinove, K., & Tafrate, R. (2011). Application of a flexible, clinically driven approach for anger reduction in the case of Mr. P. *Cognitive and Behavioral Practice, 18*, 222–234.

Kroner, D. G., & Reddon, J. R. (1995). Anger and psychopathology in prison inmates. *Personality and Individual Differences, 18*, 783–788.

Lenhart, A., Kahne, J., Middaugh, E., Macgill, A., Evans, C., & Vitak, J. (2008). *Teens, video games, and civics.* Pew Internet. Available at: http://pewresearch.org/pubs/953/.

Miller, W. R., & Rollnick, S. (2002). *Motivational interviewing: Preparing people for change.* New York: Guilford.

Miller, W. R., & Rollnick, S. (2013). *Motivational interviewing: Helping people change* (3rd ed.). New York, NY: Guilford Press.

North, A. C., Hargreaves, D. J., & Hargreaves, J. J. (2004). Uses of music in everyday life. *Music Perception, 22*, 41–77.

Novaco, R. W. (1997). Remediating anger and aggression with violent offenders. *Legal and Criminological Psychology, 2*, 77–88.

Novaco, R. W. (2003). *The Novaco Anger scale and Provocation Inventory (NAS-PI).* Los Angeles, CA: Western Psychological Services.

Olatunji, B., & Lohr, J. (2004–5). Nonspecific factors and the efficacy of psychosocial treatments for anger. *Scientific Review of Mental Health Practice, 3*, 3–18.

Patel, A. D. (2012). Solving music's mysteries. *APS Observer, 25* (6), 28–29.

Rice, M. E., Harris, G. T., Quinsey, V. L., & Cyr, M. L. (1990). Planning treatment programs in secure psychiatric facilities. In D.N. Weisstub (Ed.), *Law and mental health: International perspectives, Vol. 5*, (pp. 162–230). New York, NY: Pergamon Press.

Rotton, J., Frey, J., Barry, T., Milligan, M., & Fitzpatrick, M. (1979). The air pollution experience and physical aggression. *Journal of Applied Social Psychology, 9*, 397–412.

Saini, M. (2009). A meta-analysis of psychological treatment of anger: Developing guidelines for evidence based practice. *Journal of the American Academy of Psychiatry and the Law, 37*(4), 438–441.

Sandstrom, G. M. & Russo, F. A. (2010). Music hath charms: The effects of valence and arousal on recovery following an acute stressor. *Music and Medicine, 2*(3), 137–143.

Schwarz, N. (1999). Self-reports. *American Psychologist, 54*, 93–105.

Siemer, M. (2005). Mood-congruent cognitions constitute mood experience. *Emotion, 5*(3), 296–308.

Sloboda, J. A. (1992). Empirical studies of emotional response to music. In M.R. Jones & S. Holleran (eds.), *Cognitive bases of musical communication* (pp. 33–46). Washington, DC: American Psychological Association.

Spielberger, C. D. (1999). *The State-Trait Anger Expression Inventory-2 (STAXI-2): Professional manual.* Odessa, FL: Psychological Assessment Resources (PAR).

Tafrate, R. (1995). Evaluation of treatment strategies for adult anger disorders. In H. Kassinove (Ed.), *Anger disorders: Definition, diagnosis, and treatment* (pp. 109–113). Washington, DC: Taylor & Francis.

Tafrate, R., & Kassinove, H. (1998). Anger control in men: Barb exposure with rational, irrational, and irrelevant self-statements. *Journal of Cognitive Psychotherapy, 12*, 187–211.

Tafrate, R., & Kassinove, H. (2009). *Anger management for everyone: Seven proven ways to control anger and live a happier life.* Atascadero, CA: Impact Publishers.

Tamir, M., & Ford, B. Q. (2009). Choosing to be afraid: Preferences for fear as a function of goal pursuit. *Emotion, 9*(4), 488–497.

Toohey, M., Tirnady, R., & McCabe, J. (2011). The use of self-report in the assessment of anger in probationers. Unpublished manuscript.

Williams, J. E., Paton, C. C., Siegler, I. C., Eigenbrodt, M. I., Nieto, F. J., & Tyroler, H. A. (2000). Anger proneness predicts coronary heart disease risk: Prospective analysis from the Atherosclerosis Risk in Communities (ARIC) study. *Circulation, 101*, 2034–2039.

Wilson, T., & Nisbett, R. (1978). The accuracy of verbal reports about the effect of stimuli on evaluations and behavior. *Social Psychology, 41*, 118–131.

Wolpe, J. (1990). *The practice of behavior therapy* (4th ed.). New York, NY: Pergamon.

Suggestions for Further Learning

Books

Alberti, R. E., & Emmons, M. (2008). *Your perfect right: Assertiveness and equality in your life and relationships.* Atascadero, CA: Impact Publishers.

Kassinove, H., & Tafrate, R. (2002). *Anger management: The complete treatment guidebook for practitioners.* Atascadero, CA: Impact Publishers, Inc.

Kassinove, H., & Tafrate, R. (2009). Anger. In D. McKay, J. Abramowitz, & S. Taylor (Eds.), *Cognitive-behavioral therapy for refractory cases* (pp. 297–323). Washington, DC: American Psychological Association.

Tafrate, R. C., & Kassinove, H. (2009). *Anger management for everyone: Seven proven ways to control anger and live a happier life.* Impact Publishers: Atascadero, CA.

Walen, S. R., DiGiuseppe, R., & Dryden, W. (1992). *A practitioner's guide to rational-emotive therapy* (2nd ed.). New York: Oxford University Press.

Journal article

Kassinove, H., & Tafrate, R. (2010). Application of a flexible, clinically driven approach for anger reduction in the case of Mr. P. *Cognitive and Behavioral Practice, 18*, 222–234.

9

Contextual Anger Regulation Therapy (CART)

An Acceptance-Based Treatment for Domestic and Non-Domestic Violent Offenders

Frank L. Gardner and Zella E. Moore

Clinically problematic anger and its frequent behavioral manifestation of aggressive/violent behavior is a serious yet understudied problem. While there is a great deal of evidence to implicate anger as a serious *personal health* problem leading to conditions such as cardiovascular disease (Sirois & Burg, 2003), its behavioral manifestations also pose a serious *public health* problem resulting in significant personal and societal costs in terms of judicial and other public health outcomes (Corso, Mercy, Simon, Finklestein, & Mercy, 2007). Despite a myriad of personal and public health consequences, few interventions directly target and address the psychopathological processes and outcomes of a clinically angry clientele. Therefore, this chapter presents an empirically informed acceptance-based behavioral approach for the treatment of problematic anger; and in particular, the treatment of the aggressive and violent behaviors frequently associated with anger, which is most often the primary reason for referral to treatment. We begin with the theoretical and empirical foundations underlying our treatment protocol, which is known as contextual anger regulation therapy (CART); provide an introduction to the treatment; follow with a descriptive presentation of the modular intervention, including goals and strategies of each module; and conclude with additional considerations for working with this unique and challenging clinical population.

Theoretical and Empirical Foundations

Contextual anger regulation therapy (CART; Gardner & Moore, 2008, 2014) has been developed over the last nine years in response to the absence of clearly efficacious psychological treatments for anger and violence (Santanello, Moore, & Gardner, 2004). Despite many years of research, a careful perusal of professional reviews reveals mixed support for the efficacy of treatments for anger/violence. A recent review of treatments for perpetrators of intimate partner violence (IPV) found recidivism rates approximating 30–40% within 6 months of treatment, regardless of the type

Forensic CBT: A Handbook for Clinical Practice, First Edition.
Edited by Raymond Chip Tafrate and Damon Mitchell.
© 2014 John Wiley & Sons, Ltd. Published 2014 by John Wiley & Sons, Ltd.

of intervention strategy (Stover, Meadows, & Kaufman, 2009). Reviews that include anger interventions for non-IPV perpetrators have found only slightly more encouraging results. For example, a series of meta-analyses (Del Vecchio & O'Leary, 2004; DiGiuseppe & Tafrate, 2003; Saini, 2009) suggest moderate effect sizes across a variety of anger interventions. However, at least one review suggested that traditional cognitive-behavioral therapy (CBT) treatments for anger/ violence demonstrate a level of efficacy that could be attributed to non-specific factors such as the therapeutic alliance rather than specific treatment techniques (Olatunji & Lohr, 2005).

Considering the significant negative consequences of clinical anger and its behavioral manifestations, and the limitations of existing anger interventions, we developed the treatment approach known as contextual anger regulation therapy (CART; Gardner & Moore, 2008, 2014). CART is built upon our theoretical model for understanding the relationship between anger and aggression/violence. This model, referred to as the anger avoidance model (AAM; Gardner & Moore, 2008), is grounded in empirical advances regarding the role of deficits in emotion regulation in problematic human behavior (Aldao, Nolen-Hoeksema, & Schweizer, 2010), as well as the ascendance of acceptance-based behavioral approaches in understanding and treating a wide range of psychopathological conditions (Kashdan, Barrios, Forsyth, & Steger, 2006).

The AAM suggests that clients manifesting significant problems with anger-related pathology, including aggressive and/or violent behavior, often have broad deficits in emotion regulation and thus manifest a highly developed intolerance for the experience of anger (Gardner, Moore, & Dettore, 2012; Patel, Cuccurullo, Foy, Gardner, & Moore, 2009). This, in turn, results in substantial efforts to avoid and/or escape that intolerable experience. As such, aggressive/violent behavior can be seen as an extreme behavioral form of antecedent- or response-based emotion regulation efforts. That is, aggressive/violent behavior is used as an effort to modify situations in order to reduce the experience of negative affect that these situations evoke. This could be seen prior to the experience of emotion, as an antecedent-based emotion regulation strategy, or following the onset of an emotional experience, as a response-focused emotion regulation strategy. As an example of aggressive/violent behavior that reflects an antecedent-based emotion regulation strategy, a client may raise her voice and make verbal threats at the onset of an interaction with a partner in order to prevent the occurrence of a conversation about an emotionally evocative topic. An example of a response-focused strategy might be a situation in which, when becoming angry, a client pushes a partner out of the way and leaves the room. In the first instance, the aggressive behavior was utilized to avoid the onset of an emotional experience, while in the second example, relatively similar behavior was utilized following the occurrence of an emotion as a means of escaping from the experience of that emotion. Aggression/violence is therefore utilized as a means of either preventing intolerable anger from occurring (avoidance) or making the intolerable anger stop (escape) by altering the immediate environmental "cause" of the anger. Based on the AAM, and given the rapidly evolving evidence for the potential of specific psychological factors inherent in acceptance-based behavior therapies to impact aggressive/violent behavior, CART (Gardner & Moore, 2008) was carefully developed to treat this challenging clinical phenomenon.

CART for "Anger Management" and Interpersonal Violence

CART was conceived in 2004 as an alternative treatment for clients being referred for "anger management" and/or interpersonal/domestic violence (Gardner & Moore, 2010). While court systems typically make a distinction between treatments for anger management and IPV, in our experience, both non-intimate violence and IPV clients often share deficits in emotion regulation and possess an inability to regulate what they perceive as intolerable affect.

Anger management: Practically and theoretically untenable

We have found that most "anger management" referrals follow non-intimate/non-domestic violence offenses, such as altercations with individuals in social interactions, situations such as "road-rage," or extreme aggressive behaviors at the workplace. While most of these referrals are court-mandated, some come from Employee Assistance Programs (EAPs) or are initiated by family/friends. An extremely small number of our clients have sought treatment via self-referral with no outside pressure or requirement. The term "anger management" has been historically used as a catchphrase for any intervention whose primary purpose is the development of strategies to limit, reduce, eliminate, or in some way control the experience of anger, with the associated assumption that this would culminate in reduced aggressive or violent behaviors. It seems to be based on a basic belief/assumption that anger is essentially a problematic emotion, which must be controlled in order for violent behavior to be eliminated. In essence, from the anger management perspective, anger results in violence.

We view the concept of anger management as practically and theoretically untenable, and destructive as a term for professional use. First, we believe that it is fundamentally incorrect to view anger as an emotion that needs to be "managed," as no one has ever gotten into trouble with legal authorities for *experiencing* the emotion of anger. Rather, individuals encounter such legal consequences based on their subsequent *behavior*, or rather, the *expression* of anger. In addition, from a theoretical position, the idea that in order to behave differently one must manage how one feels is inherently problematic, as anger is a normal and naturally occurring emotion that will and should be present in human beings.

The message espoused in most anger management programs, that anger is the problem, has led many clients to believe that anger is inherently bad and therefore must be avoided or denied at all costs. Based upon our own data (Gardner, Dettore, Moore, & Foy, 2010; Smyth, Dettore, Gardner, & Moore, 2010), consistent with recent trends in psychopathology in general (Barlow, Allen, & Choate, 2004; Kashdan et al., 2006), and with previous studies with anger-related client populations (Davey, Day, & Howells, 2005), it is clear that the inhibition/non-acceptance/non-experience of emotion, particularly anger, is more related to psychopathology and problematic behavior than the full and tolerated experience and appropriate expression of emotion. As such, CART can best be understood not as an anger management intervention, despite the fact that many referrals come via this generic description. Rather, CART is a behavioral intervention designed to enhance the full and appropriate experience *and* appropriate behavioral expression of anger.

With regard to the treatment of IPV, two fundamentally distinct traditions have emerged. As a basic presentation, the first tradition is equivalent to the anger management model, in which anger reduction (with the assumption of violence reduction) has been provided in the context of psychological treatment in which strategies to better manage anger and enhance appropriate interpersonal communication are provided to offending clients. The second tradition, based on feminist psychology, (i) holds an underlying assumption that domestic violence is not a reflection of a psychological disorder/issue, but rather, is a reflection of paternalistic and control-based learned attitudes and behaviors in a male dominated society (Pence & Paymar, 1993), and (ii) posits that IPV should be seen and responded to based upon this foundational understanding.

Fundamental similarities between IPV and non-IPV anger clients

The question of intervention choice for IPV (also referred to as domestic violence) is complex, with both scientific and sociopolitical realities (Dutton & Corvo, 2007). While a full discussion of this topic is well beyond the scope of this chapter, and in fact is covered in detail by Ronan, Maurelli, and Holman (see Chapter 11) and Eckhardt, Crane, and Sprunger (see Chapter 10) in the present text, two important points are relevant to CART. First, empirical data indicate that traditional treatments of IPV, whether based on the feminist-oriented Duluth model (Pence & Paymar, 1993) or cognitive-behavioral therapy, are generally ineffective. In fact, a recent review of interventions for IPV concluded that current interventions for perpetrators of IPV have a limited impact on repeat violence, with most interventions reporting minimal benefits above the effect of arrest alone (Stover et al., 2009). In addition, as previously noted, Stover and colleagues found that recidivism rates for these interventions approximated 30–40% within 6 months, regardless of the intervention strategy used. Second, a recent study from our own clinic with both domestic and non-domestic violent offenders (Gardner et al., 2012) suggested that while there are very minor differences between individuals mandated for anger management as a result of IPV versus non-IPV, there are significantly greater fundamental similarities between the two groups. For example, both populations largely appear to have experienced significant amounts of child maltreatment (of somewhat different types), and most importantly, possess broad difficulties in emotion regulation. Consistent with the AAM, it is these particular difficulties that mediate the relationship between childhood maltreatment and anger-related problems, thereby suggesting that targeting deficits in emotion regulation would be appropriate for both populations.

The Duluth-based models of IPV intervention have eschewed consideration of psychological variables such as anger as allowing for "excuse making" and avoidance of responsibility for problematic patriarchal attitudes and behaviors (Pence & Paymar, 1993). The underwhelming empirical data on current IPV intervention approaches (Babcock, Green, & Robie, 2004; Stover et al., 2009), along with evidence suggesting that patriarchal attitudes are not predictive of IPV (Dutton & Corvo, 2007), certainly suggest that alternative models need to be considered. This issue does not, however, have to be an all-or-nothing proposition. Recently, we suggested that our AAM, along with the data with regard to emotion regulation difficulties among violent offenders (IPV in particular), could be interpreted in a manner consistent with a rapprochement between the Duluth model-based interventions and psychological interventions (Gardner et al., 2012). We propose that IPV may be seen as an effort to avoid or escape from angry emotions, and thus, while the aggressive/violent behavior may at times take the overt *form* of control/dominance, it may instead be the result of significant deficits in emotion regulation and thus serve the *function* of a dysfunctional effort to regulate intolerable affect.

Based upon these considerations with regard to both traditional anger management and intimate partner/domestic violence populations, the CART protocol was constructed, and is described in detail throughout the remainder of this chapter.

CART: Program Goals and Treatment Modules

CART is at its foundation an acceptance-based behavioral therapy in the tradition of acceptance and commitment therapy (ACT; Hayes, Strosahl, & Wilson, 2012) and mindfulness-based cognitive therapy (MBCT; Segal, Williams, & Teasdale, 2002). In addition, it incorporates a number of strategies and techniques found in emotion-focused therapy (Elliot, Watson, Goldman, & Greenberg, 2004), functional analytic psychotherapy (FAP; Kohlenberg & Tsai, 1993), and more recent unified/transdiagnostic protocols (Barlow et al., 2004). It operates within an emotion regulation framework in which emotion regulation is defined as the capacity to be aware of, tolerate, utilize, modulate when necessary, and appropriately express emotion (verbally and behaviorally), with an emphasis on the emotion of anger. It is from this emotion regulation perspective that the title "contextual anger regulation therapy" evolved. Importantly, the goal is *not* anger regulation from the traditional view, where "regulation" would be seen as an equivalent term to anger "control," "management," or "reduction." Rather, the use of the term stems from this more contemporary view of emotion/anger regulation. This emotion regulation framework is the underlying foundation of CART and directly informs the fundamental CART treatment goals, which are the:

1. Enhanced capacity to be aware of, accept/tolerate, and understand anger as a normal and necessary emotional experience.
2. Enhanced capacity to reflect upon and utilize the information provided by emotions (anger in particular), as well as modulate anger when necessary or when experienced as extreme, to solve problems and manage interpersonal conflict.
3. Enhanced flexibility of available behavioral actions (including enhanced skills) in response to anger-eliciting situations (which are also consistent with personal values), culminating in enhanced interpersonal effectiveness and quality of life.

CART is most often delivered in individual sessions, although a discussion of modifications necessary for use in a group-session format and across ages will be provided later in this chapter. The CART protocol consists of nine modules, which are grouped in a specific sequence and are conceptualized as distinct components requiring full completion before moving on to each subsequent module. Each module contains specific treatment objectives (in direct support of the treatment goals stated above), and each treatment objective is built upon the treatment objectives achieved in earlier modules. In addition to the advantages of any structured manualized treatment, which include sequential understanding of material, systematic client development, skill building, etc., where one skill-set builds upon the next, the purpose and advantage of a modular approach to psychological treatment is that the therapist is provided with a strategic and tactical structure for therapy, while still allowing for the flexibility required when working with the wide array of client types that present for treatment. As such, the nine modules can be expected to take anywhere from 9 to 20 sessions to complete, although a shortened version required in contexts necessitating brief structured treatment is provided elsewhere (Gardner & Moore, 2014). What follows is a presentation of the nine modules, including strategic goals, strategies, and tactics employed in each. To illustrate the CART approach, a sanitized case will be presented across all nine modules, and the full course of treatment will be described.

Module 1: Psychoeducation, values identification, and motivation enhancement

The primary objectives of this introductory module are to foster an understanding of: (i) the AAM model; (ii) how the issues and behaviors that have led clients into treatment can be explained by the AAM; (iii) the historical roots of the presenting problems; (iv) the benefits (short-term) and costs (long-term) of clients' current behavioral patterns; (v) what is truly desired and what really matters in the clients' lives (i.e., values identification); (vi) what the CART protocol is and how it differs from traditional anger management or other related interventions that clients may have previously experienced or of which clients have heard; and (vii) how, if relevant, treatment fits into clients' personal (court/family) mandates.

When all of these specific objectives are fully addressed, clients should be left with an enhanced sense of hope, a means of thinking differently about their current problems and future possibilities, and the foundation of a sound and effective working alliance with their therapist. These three important characteristics have previously been identified as being related to positive therapeutic outcomes (Castonguay & Beutler, 2006). As the reader can see, there are aspects of early treatment within CART Module 1 that are typically found in motivational interviewing (Miller & Rollnick, 2002), dialectical behavior therapy (DBT; Linehan, 1993), ACT (Hayes et al., 2012), and more traditional forms of CBT. The crucial difference is the use of the AAM as the focal point of these discussions in order to provide a context for clients in terms of their current problem, its genesis, and the treatment to come.

The three basic therapeutic strategies utilized in Module 1 are:

1. Explanation of the AAM in plain language, with an emphasis on integrating the client's history and presenting problem into the description. In order to appropriately present the AAM, we encourage readers to become fully familiar with the AAM and utilize it as a template for their initial discussion and presentation to their client.

2. Identification of personal values (i.e., be a good father/husband, be a good friend and colleague) as anchor points for guiding future behavioral choices (Wilson & Murrell, 2004). While there are a number of questionnaire-based strategies for determining client values that can serve to guide behavioral choices (Gardner & Moore, 2014; Wilson & Murrell, 2004), it is also quite common for these values to be determined in an open and direct discussion. Yet regardless of format utilized, we do suggest one particular caution: we encourage clinicians to carefully distinguish between *goals*, which typically are either achieved or not achieved (e.g., getting a promotion at work), and *values*, which are never fully achieved, but rather are constantly worked toward (e.g., being a good parent). See Amrod and Hayes in Chapter 3 for a detailed discussion on applying ACT principles such as values clarification to offender clients.

3. Compare and contrast the benefits of values-based behavior versus emotion-driven behavior. When employing this therapeutic strategy, the therapist typically reviews the costs and benefits of actions taken in the clients' lives to date, and in particular, those actions that resulted in judicial or personal difficulties and/or referral for treatment. In general, the benefit of emotion-driven behavior is some immediate reduction of negative affect (such as anger), while the costs are most often longer-lasting significant life difficulties. In contrast, the benefit of values-based behavioral choices is likely to be a greater likelihood of creating the life that is desired (i.e., better relationships, work outcomes, family life), while the cost is likely to be an immediate short-term discomfort during the experience of negative affect (such as anger). While the reader might notice some similarity to the goals and strategies of motivational interviewing (Miller & Rollnick, 2002) in this description, it should be pointed out that unlike motivational interviewing, this discussion tends to be more directive and incorporates the concept of personal values as a behavioral anchor for use throughout the CART program.

Module 1: Client example   Tom, a 26-year-old African-American male, was referred by the court for "domestic violence counseling." The referral followed an incident during which he pushed his wife in the midst of an argument in which she "would not stop harassing [him]." This was the second time he was referred for psychological intervention following a domestic violence charge; on the first occasion, 3 years earlier, he was referred to a traditional anger management program, which consisted of a 3-hour class. Following intake after the present offense, Tom was diagnosed with Personality Disorder NOS, and he demonstrated marked difficulties with emotion regulation in various aspects of his life.

Tom's Module 1 experience consisted of two sessions. In the first session of Module 1, Tom was presented with how the assessment data and his personal history fit into the anger avoidance model. He had described substantial emotional abuse and neglect by both his mother and father when growing up, had learned to scan his environment for evidence that someone might be trying to harm him, and learned that experiencing and/or expressing anger, and emotion in general, was dangerous (e.g., he would be treated much worse by his parents if he expressed or demonstrated any outward signs of emotion). He learned to deal with interpersonal conflict by avoiding it, or walking away from it, and would feel as though he would "lose his mind" if unable to "get away" when experiencing conflict and associated emotions. Tom was readily able to see that his aggressive behavior was an effort to escape from these situations, and was able to provide numerous similar examples. Tom understood but was skeptical about the idea that treatment would focus on allowing him to become more tolerant of anger and other emotions, and clearly saw the difference between this approach and previous anger management. Session 2 of Module 1 was devoted to the discussion and identification of personal values, including making the distinction between acting in the service of such values versus acting in the service of avoiding or escaping emotions such as anger. The importance of values was presented as essentially being the reason for Tom to engage in treatment. In essence, it was explained that our goal was not simply to have him not reoffend, but rather, to enhance the quality of his life in some tangible and important ways. As the clinician and Tom moved through this process, Tom identified the primary values of being a good husband and father, and being a friend and co-worker that people could count on and see as consistently professional (note: Tom was an electrician). At this point, the goals of Module 1 had been achieved, and the module was therefore deemed complete.

Module 2: Using the therapeutic relationship to recognize and modify clinically relevant behavior

The primary objectives of Module 2 are: (i) the identification of in-session behaviors that are directly relevant to identified out-of-session client problem behaviors; and (ii) consistent and appropriate therapeutic responses to these clinically relevant behaviors such that the client has the opportunity to learn new and more appropriate interpersonal behaviors.

As previously noted, CART incorporates a strong and ever-present interpersonal component in its treatment package. The interpersonal focus in CART is modeled after Kohlenberg and Tsai's functional analytic psychotherapy (1993). At the core of this approach is an understanding that the client's interpersonal difficulties will manifest themselves within treatment sessions, and in particular, with respect to the therapist as a discriminative stimulus for negative affect, anticipatory cognitions, and problematic interpersonal behavior.

Module 2 is a natural continuation of Module 1, and the interpersonal strategies of this module continue as a foundation of CART throughout the course of treatment. A focus on the interpersonal aspect of treatment is particularly important at the beginning of the treatment process, as in-session client reactions/behaviors in response to session time/scheduling, cancellation of sessions, payment, therapist questions, style, gender, race, etc., typically arise early in treatment. This offers a wonderful opportunity to note clinically relevant behavior, which can be defined as within-session behavior that corresponds either directly or in more subtle ways to problematic behaviors described/known to occur outside of therapy. Early inclusion of this core interpersonal aspect allows the therapist to address clinically relevant behavior in a structured, systematic, and ongoing manner.

So, for example, a hostile behavioral style (and associated heightened anger) upon being confronted by the therapist for being late to a session is particularly noteworthy when seen in a client who has been referred for intimate partner violence. In addition, the therapist must be willing to confront the client with the behavior in a firm yet non-hostile manner, while making the connection between this behavior and the behavior that brought him or her into treatment.

Module 2: Client example   Tom arrived 30 minutes late to the third treatment session, and was told that he only had 20 minutes remaining for his session. He became agitated and began raising his voice to the clinician. Following a reiteration of the clinic policies (which had already been presented as part of the first session), his behavior in response to being frustrated was pointed out, including the similarity of this behavioral style to the behavior that got him into trouble to begin with. This exchange would become a pattern within treatment; whenever his behavior toward the (female) therapist was similar in class and function to the behavioral difficulties that he manifested outside of treatment, such similarities would be immediately pointed out and discussed. It should be noted that when Tom manifested more appropriate in-session interpersonal behavior when frustrated, it too would be pointed out and reinforced. While in this case Module 2 only consisted of one session, the clinician should remember that this module could be the singular focus of multiple sessions or even no distinct sessions, but will always emerge at various times during the entire treatment process whenever clinically relevant behavior is manifested during a session. There is no clear time for the goals of this module to be fully attained, as identifying clinically relevant behaviors (both negative and positive variants) should occur throughout treatment.

Module 3: Developing mindful emotion awareness

The primary objectives of Module 3 are to: (i) increase non-judging present-moment awareness of emotional experiences, including the cognitive, subjective, physiological, and related behavioral action tendencies associated with those experiences; and (ii) increase understanding of internal experiences such as thoughts, feelings, and bodily sensations as transient events that are both informative and passing.

The core therapeutic focus of this module is a process by which the client becomes more comfortable with having, observing, and remaining in increasingly longer contact (without avoidance or escape) with the various components of the emotional experience. This process begins with education about emotion, including its adaptive value and occasional maladaptive outcomes. This is followed by education about emotion awareness/mindfulness, and then progressively moves through a series of mindfulness-enhancing exercises. These exercises are intended to help the client disengage from automatic behavior; learn to non-judgmentally observe and enhance awareness of external and internal experiences; remain in contact with uncomfortable internal experiences; and focus attention to relevant cues and redirect attention when distracted.

As a central component of CART, the development of enhanced mindfulness requires extensive in- and out-of-session practice opportunities. Examples of both an initial mindfulness exercise (Introduction to Mindfulness Exercise; see Appendix 9.A) and a more advanced exercise (Mindfulness of the Breath Exercise; see Appendix 9.B), used both in- and out-of-session, are provided at the conclusion of this chapter. Mindfulness exercises are intended to promote the full experience of anger and related cognitive, affective, and physiological processes. Most importantly, enhanced mindful awareness disrupts the avoidance/escape process, and thus directly targets the core pathological process of clinical anger.

Module 3: Client example Module 3 (session 4) began with a discussion intended to provide basic education about emotion in general, including its adaptive value and occasional maladaptive outcomes. Efforts were made to integrate Tom's own experiences into this discussion, such as his thoughts of being mistreated, his physiological response of flushed face and/or tightened muscles, and the aggressive actions of raising his voice when feeling angry at work. This was contrasted with the more adaptive message that anger can provide, which might simply be that an important issue needs to be addressed. This discussion lasted an entire session.

In the next session of Module 3 (session 5), the therapist focused on the importance of non-judging awareness/mindfulness of Tom's thoughts and emotions, not as internal experiences to be immediately and automatically reacted to, but rather as experiences to notice and reflect upon. This was discussed as a necessary first step toward the goal of responding to the needs and demands of a situation, and in turn what Tom might want out of that situation (based upon his personal values). This was contrasted with automatically responding in order to avoid or escape from his thoughts and feelings. The session ended with a presentation of a mindfulness exercise, and a request for home practice of the exercise. Continuing with Module 3, the sixth session discussed Tom's experience of, and frustration with, trying mindfulness exercises between sessions (which were attempted, although not at the daily frequency that was requested). The entire session was committed to this discussion and further in-session mindfulness exercise practice. Finally, a seventh session was devoted to this topic, as Tom's between-session practice was discussed and the experiences that he had with noticing and not reacting to various thoughts and feelings were reinforced and explored. It was at this point, with mindfulness being practiced and relatively understood, that the clinician deemed Tom ready to move on to the next module.

Module 4: Cognitive defusion and the reduction of problematic rule-governed behavior

The therapeutic objectives of Module 4 include: (i) understanding the concept of cognitive fusion and its relationship to aggressive/violent behavioral patterns; (ii) developing an awareness of relevant internal rules (schemas) and their associated automatic (fused) behaviors; and (iii) decentering from anger-related cognitions/rules.

In this module, the therapeutic strategy of cognitive defusion (Hayes et al., 2012) is front and center in the CART program. Cognitive *fusion* is the process by which individuals respond to their thoughts as though they are absolute truths/realities that most often involve immediate (and usually a rigid and narrow range of) behavioral responses. Individuals experiencing clinical anger typically come to treatment with very specific internal rule systems/schemas. When triggered, these internal rule systems result in rapid and automatic behavioral responses, most often functioning as a means of avoiding or escaping from emotional experiences deemed as intolerable. Many of these behaviors are highly self-destructive. In turn, cognitive *defusion* is the process by which individuals develop the capacity to decenter, or distance themselves from their own cognitive processes. That is, individuals come to view their thought processes as simply what their mind is telling them at that particular moment, and not as an absolute truth/reality to which they must respond. The decentering process is what some theorists believe is the mechanism by which traditional cognitive restructuring/reappraisal techniques may actually work (Segal et al., 2002). Cognitive defusion begins with, and is enhanced by, the development of mindfulness (see Module 3), and increasingly allows clients to slow down, recognize their internal dialogue, make informed personal behavioral choices, and not be automatically rule-driven in their behavioral pursuits. It should be noted that these thoughts/ rules are not confronted by logical analysis or Socratic dialogue with the goal of changing, reducing, or eliminating them, as is commonly seen in traditional cognitive-behavioral interventions. Rather, the goal is to develop a capacity to view cognitions as simply something that our mind tells us (i.e., what we think, not what *is* or what we *are*), something that will always come and go in our mind, something that can be observed, and something that does not necessarily require any action.

Module 4: Client example   In the first session of Module 4 (session 8), the clinician began by reinforcing the importance of: (i) noticing the rules that often direct immediate behavior, and (ii) beginning the process of seeing them as a reflection of "what the mind is telling" Tom, rather than as a reflection of something absolute to which he must instantly respond. Based upon previous discussions and Tom's own experience with mindfulness exercises, he started to develop an awareness that rules such as *"No one is going to talk to me or treat me this way!"* (and its many variants), consistently appeared with his anger. The clinician reminded Tom that anger has cognitive, physiological, and subjective elements (as discussed during the emotion education phase of treatment), and an important goal in their work together was for him to notice these different aspects of emotion. The clinician pointed out how Tom's history resulted in the tendency for his mind to engage in these rules, and that while these rules may have had some adaptive value as a child, they now often lead to overreactions that are inconsistent with his stated values in life. During this and the next session (session 9), Tom and the clinician worked toward decentering from these thoughts, viewing them simply as learned responses his mind would frequently tell him.

In essence, Tom began to develop the capacity to view his thoughts as something that will always come and go, that can be noticed, and that do not require an immediate response. As part of this process, the therapist utilized a version of an exercise described by Hayes and associates (1999) in which Tom repeated the phrase *"No one will talk to me this way!"* over and over again (30 repetitions) until the words began to lose their meaning. Tom was asked to repeat this exercise at least once daily. He understood the purpose, and while he found the exercise somewhat silly at first, he in fact engaged in the exercise on a daily basis. At this point, the therapist believed that Tom was fully engaged in the defusion process and understood its importance, and thus decided to progress to the next treatment module. Importantly, readers should note that no effort was made to directly *challenge* or *change* the content of Tom's thought processes. Rather, the goal was for Tom to become aware of, and ultimately decenter from, these thoughts, and by doing so, slow the automatic behavioral responses that these thoughts had previously triggered.

Module 5: Understanding anger and anger avoidance

The primary therapeutic objectives of Module 5 are to: (i) develop an understanding of anger as a normal and unavoidable emotion, and the inherent problem with viewing anger as something to be feared and avoided; (ii) develop an understanding of the common misconceptions about anger, such as that it inevitably leads to aggression if not controlled, that venting is both healthy and necessary, and that overt behavioral displays of anger are necessary; (iii) develop an understanding of the costs of efforts to avoid the experience of anger; and (iv) develop the capacity to tolerate the experience of anger without engaging in avoidance or escape strategies.

In this module, the primary therapeutic strategy focuses on enhanced acceptance of anger as an inevitable and naturally occurring emotion, and differentiates the cost of experiencing anger from the cost of efforts to avoid or escape the experience of anger. In addition, common misconceptions about anger, such as its lack of utility, its natural association with aggression, and its need to be vented, are discussed and corrected in order to allow a new non-adversarial relationship with anger to develop. The goal is understanding that what is needed is a new way of *relating* to anger, instead of feeling less anger. As the experience of anger is normalized, the client also begins to recognize that the primary clinical problem is the effort to not experience anger, and not the anger itself. This begins the process by which anger avoidance/escape behaviors are naturally replaced with the opposite-action (Linehan, 1993) of experience and non-response.

Module 5: Client example   Module 5 (session 10) began with a focus on anger as an emotion, including a careful delineation of the thoughts and physiological reactions that would signal the occurrence of anger. While Tom initially saw anger as an enemy to be defeated, the clinician noted the adaptive value of anger as a signal that something of importance needs to be addressed. Importantly, this session discussed the misconception that anger causes violence, and highlighted the reality that violence is a result of the desire to avoid or escape the feeling of anger. This discussion set the stage for the 11th session, during which the therapist led Tom through a consideration of the costs associated with attempting to avoid feeling angry, including reduced time with family and distant relationships with co-workers. Tom was asked to make a concerted effort to spend more time with family and co-workers, continue to notice the thoughts and emotions that come and go during these experiences, and arrive at the next session ready to discuss the challenges and successes associated with the inevitable increase in anger and frustration that would result from being fully engaged in life. This assignment set the stage for the beginning of the next CART module.

Module 6: Acceptance and anger regulation

The therapeutic objectives of Module 6 are to: (i) enhance the capacity to tolerate/accept the presence of anger, even when intensely experienced; (ii) develop the capacity to distinguish between those behaviors aimed at avoiding the experience of anger, and those behaviors in the service of personal values (i.e., engaging in behavior that is intended to live a life consistent with what one values and desires); and (iii) develop the capacity to modulate (i.e., downregulate) anger when necessary, *not* for the purpose of feeling better, but rather, for the purpose of actively pursuing personal values.

In this module, the intent is to further hone the ability, which began in Module 5, to experience anger without the need for previously automatic avoidance or escape behaviors.

The primary therapeutic strategy includes continuing encouragement related to the acceptance and tolerance of anger (Egbert et al., 2009). The resultant willingness to remain in contact with these experiences also increases the likelihood that appropriate decision-making and values-based behavior will begin to emerge and will be naturally reinforced in the environment. In essence, during this module, the client engages in what can be thought of as systematic in- and out-of-session exposure-type exercises, in which increasingly difficult (i.e., anger-evoking) situations are experienced and tolerated. Herein, a greater understanding of the various cognitions, emotions, and physical sensations associated with anger tend to evolve, and thus the process of modifying the prior stimulus functions of anger begins.

Of course, there are circumstances in which overly intense episodes of anger may interfere with optimal behavioral responding, and thus, there is often a need to develop appropriate *values-based* self-soothing skills. The distinction between values-based self-soothing and non-values-based self-soothing relates primarily to the function of each. For example, a client using a brief deep breath relaxation exercise to lower his level of affect, with the intent of continuing with a difficult but necessary conversation with a relationship partner, is markedly different in function from the same client using a relaxation exercise to both reduce the negative affect and cut short (and thus escape from) that same conversation. In these cases, values-based behavioral approaches aimed at downregulating the excessively intense experience of anger are presented, such as the use of brief breathing exercises. As noted in the example above, it is important that self-soothing techniques be carefully utilized, as care must be taken not to inadvertently promote an alternative means of avoidance. It is imperative that these brief emotion modulation skills be presented in a manner consistent with values-based behavior in the face of the intense experience of anger, rather than in the service of avoiding or escaping from the anger. As such, it is also important that these efforts be introduced *after* anger distress tolerance has already been enhanced.

Module 6: Client example   In the first session of Module 6 (session 12), Tom discussed his preliminary efforts at engaging in activities that would predictably result in some degree of anger and frustration, both at home and at work. Predictably, Tom did not "push the envelope" too hard, and only presented one example in which he had a drink after work with co-workers and listened to them complain about work and the company's management. While this would typically lead to some anger for him, as he would often be chided for following the rules and being the bosses "pet," Tom stayed for several hours, tolerated the comments, noticed his thoughts and emotions, and even said that at one point he laughed out loud when he realized that what he was doing in his head sounded like a therapy session with the clinician. He was proud that he was able to tolerate the anger, although he admitted it was not very intense. After reinforcing these efforts, the clinician worked with Tom to establish a more challenging series of exposure-based activities, mostly involving family activities (e.g., a full family day out; a difficult discussion with his wife about family finances). These events were discussed, and a goal was set to both notice the internal events and remain focused on family-enhancing behaviors that Tom indicated he would like to achieve.

During the next session (session 13), Tom discussed his family outing, which went fairly well. He did become angry several times, and except for one moment when he scolded his 8-year-old son a bit too loudly, he indicated that the day went well, and his wife was shocked at how well he acted all day. Tom suggested that he allowed himself to feel angry and was surprised that it came in spurts and did not last all day. However, Tom did not have the conversation with his wife about the family's finances. He suggested that although he intended to, he became so angry at the thought of the conversation that he put it off. The financial discussion was subsequently role-played during the session, and the clinician suggested to Tom that he could consider utilizing a brief mindfulness exercise prior to the conversation as a way of decentering from the natural array of thoughts and emotions that would occur.

Between sessions 13 and 14, Tom was successful at having the conversation with his wife, and during session 14, he stated that the conversation went very well. Tom was again surprised that he was able to carry out the entire conversation despite becoming angry, and verified that he maintained his composure throughout and finished the discussion on a positive note. At this point, the clinician judged that it was time to progress to the next treatment module.

Module 7: Commitment to values-based behavior

The therapeutic objectives of Module 7 are to: (i) develop a connection between personal values and specific behaviors; (ii) develop an understanding that the experience of intense anger can occur *at the same time* as effective values-based behaviors; (iii) develop a behavioral activation plan for values-based behaviors; and (iv) identify specific skill deficits in need of correction.

As the tolerance of anger has been enhanced, the therapeutic focus moves to the ongoing commitment to the pursuit of meaningful personal values through the activation of values-based behaviors. In this module, the distinction between goals and values is once again reiterated and reinforced. Specifically, goals have a clear end point, yet values have no end point and require ongoing action and attention. As such, what is desired is a consistent approach to engaging in those behaviors that optimize quality of life. The therapist encourages the client to increase his or her willingness to act in accordance with his or her stated values *while* being angry, and thus the client is encouraged to confront important yet previously avoided situations. When confronted rather than avoided through the use of a systematic behavioral activation plan, new emotional meanings are developed in response to these important life situations, and increasingly, a sense of personal effectiveness is established. Finally, as the client is now attempting to navigate through (rather than avoid) important life situations, skill deficits in communication, conflict management, and problem-solving that are likely to interfere with desired positive interpersonal outcomes will inevitably be identified.

Module 7: Client example During the next three sessions (sessions 15, 16, and 17), Tom and the clinician worked at establishing a series of activities that would promote his stated values even further, and discussed the likelihood and ultimately the reality of experiencing anger during these activities. Tom systematically increased his family and work activities consistent with his values, and began to understand, from actual experience, that he could feel angry and still engage in these activities. While he reported that he would occasionally catch himself acting on his emotion, he gradually developed the capacity to notice his anger and make values-based choices rather than reacting with the intent to escape from the emotional state. Once these activities were well underway, the therapist moved to the next module, as it had become clear that Tom lacked some basic skills in conflict management/problem-solving.

Module 8: Interpersonal skills training

The therapeutic objectives of Module 8 are to: (i) enhance interpersonal problem-solving skills; (ii) enhance communication and assertiveness skills; and (iii) enhance conflict management skills, as appropriate.

In this module, the primary therapeutic strategy is the presentation and learning of the basic interpersonal skills necessary for the ongoing and lifelong pursuit of an optimized values-based quality of life. In this regard, the development of specific skills related to problem-solving, communication, and/or conflict management will be directly addressed and trained. These skills are taught and practiced within sessions and utilized between sessions, with follow-up feedback and then additional practice. At this point in the CART program, these skills are the focus of treatment because they can most effectively be addressed following the appropriate development of mindful emotional awareness and greater anger tolerance/acceptance. The development of more effective "positive" interpersonal behaviors increases the likelihood that the client will receive naturally occurring positive reinforcement within his or her environment and will therefore be more likely to remain values-based in his or her behavioral choices moving forward.

Module 8: Client example   In Module 8 (sessions 18 and 19), the clinician worked with Tom to develop a greater capacity to: (i) listen; (ii) reflect, so as to convey to someone else (e.g., his wife) that he was listening and understood; and (iii) express his thoughts and feelings in a constructive and positive way. This was modeled by the clinician, role-played within session, and then practiced between sessions. Tom was eager to try this new approach with his wife, and felt more comfortable having important discussions with the addition of this new skill-set. During these two sessions, the idea that the completion of treatment was "just around the corner" was discussed. While Tom indicated some trepidation, he was also eager to complete the course of treatment, and his court mandate. Following these two sessions, the clinician embarked upon the final CART module.

Module 9: Integration, relapse prevention, and treatment termination

The therapeutic objectives of Module 9 are: (i) the identification and in vivo practice of responding to future anger-inducing triggers, and the discussion of appropriate responses to possible challenges and lapses; (ii) the development of an action plan for continued use of CART principles and strategies once treatment is complete; and (iii) proactive treatment termination.

The therapeutic strategy utilized in Module 9 is the development of a plan to deal with the myriad of stressors that one will face, respond to inevitable challenges and lapses, and systematically approach the termination of treatment as a beginning and not an ending. Central is the development of an action plan for the continued use of CART principles. This action plan should include ongoing self-monitoring, self-reflection, and self-correction. In this regard, the therapist works with the patient to: (i) identify and practice appropriate responses to potential anger-inducing situations that have not been previously attended to during treatment; (ii) discuss the likelihood of occasional lapses; and (iii) develop specific plans to ensure that these inevitable lapses do not become more extreme relapses of old behavioral patterns. Finally, it is important for the therapist to provide an open dialogue about ending the formal therapy process, note the availability of future sessions if needed, encourage clients' readiness to work at CART principles on their own, and reinforce the idea that the difficulties that brought them into treatment can be effectively managed with ongoing attention and care. Most clients presenting with clinical anger have come from early environments that were emotionally abusive and/or neglectful, and thus, treatment termination must be addressed openly and honestly so as to promote a new and healthy interpersonal experience.

Module 9: Client example   In the final session (session 20) of treatment, the clinician reviewed Tom's course in treatment, discussed potential future triggers for Tom to consider and of which to be aware, and reminded Tom of the specific skills and ongoing exercises that were likely to continue his personal development. A specific list of exercises and activities were written down, and Tom was asked to reflect on the list on a weekly basis to ensure continued commitment to his personal development. Continued self-care was compared to a diabetic individual who must accept that personal health required constant care and attention to basic daily actions. Tom was also reminded that the clinician would be available in the future if he required any booster sessions.

For the comprehensive and detailed step-by-step manualized CART protocol, including client forms, additional case studies, and outcome research, readers are referred to Gardner and Moore (2014).

Frequent Questions about Using Acceptance-Based Approaches with Offenders

Now that we have described the nine CART modules and provided a brief case example to illustrate the sequenced approach to treatment, it may be helpful to address a few questions that are frequently asked regarding the use of an acceptance-based approach with offender populations.

The first question that often arises is: What do you do when offender clients do not take defusion exercises or other exercises seriously? The reality is that mandated offenders often come to therapy with questionable motivation for change, and are similarly suspicious and/or skeptical of psychological treatments of any kind. As such, in CART Modules 1 and 2, it is important to provide a context for intervention; work to develop a reason for clients to come to weekly sessions (and do between-session activities) aside from the mandate by the court; and allow clients to see that the model of treatment provided to them makes sense, fits with their history and experience, and can be utilized for an enhanced quality of life. Usually, clients come to treatment after several efforts at traditional anger management interventions, which were largely ineffective. Thus, the presentation of a model that does not view anger as an enemy to be the target of treatment, but rather, focuses on developing a greater capacity to behave in a manner consistent with what the clients want their life to be (with or without the presence of anger), appears, in our experience, to be more likely to result in a buy-in from clients.

Lack of client progress is a common concern for clinicians. As such, students and professionals often ask: How do I deal with a lack of client progress during treatment, and specifically, what do I do if a client becomes stuck in a particular module? It has been our experience that the most common reason for a client to become stuck in a given module is that the clinician is choosing an overt lecturing style with an associated lack of experiential engagement. The clinician should look to develop client skills by using a non-lecturing tone, by incorporating the client's own experience, by creatively presenting material, and by directly addressing between-session exercise non-compliance, which is an important clinically relevant behavior.

Therapy is certainly not always a comfortable endeavor. Module 2 in particular can bring about client reactivity and natural confrontation because its primary focus is on the identification of in-session behaviors that are directly relevant to identified out-of-session problematic behaviors. In many cases, this means that the client's interpersonal difficulties will come to the forefront within treatment sessions, which commonly occurs when the therapist is a discriminative stimulus for negative affect, anticipatory cognitions, and problematic inter-personal actions. What can be done to address this issue? The therapist is encouraged to consistently and appropriately respond to these clinically relevant behaviors so the client has the opportunity to learn new and more appropriate interpersonal behaviors. If the clinician inconsistently addresses these behaviors, it may appear to the client as if the therapist is simply "being difficult" when he or she does attempt to enforce such client awareness and change. It has been our experience that when clinicians engage appropriately in the process (i.e., directly and without excessive personal affect or ego involvement), it results in better client outcomes and is not in any way associated with attrition. In fact, our experience has taught us that clients who are not appropriately challenged by both session content and real personal engagement when their in-session behavior warrants it, are likely to view therapy as unhelpful.

Another common question surrounds the idea that some offender problem behavior appears to be more oriented around "approach behavior" than "avoidant behavior," and thus might be the result of excitement related to fighting or engaging in violence, or pleasure in hurting or controlling others. We believe this is a reality with which any psychological treatment for offender populations must deal. As presented in our initial publication on the anger avoidance model (Gardner & Moore, 2008), we suggest that problems related to aggressive/violent behavior can be seen as consisting of two distinct subtypes. The first subtype, which we refer to as *reactive* aggression, reflects aggressive/violent behavior that is a reaction (i.e., that is an emo-tion regulatory response) to anger, in which the primary goal is avoidance of, or escape from, "intolerable" emotional experiences. By contrast, we refer to the second type as *instrumental* (predatory) aggression, in which the primary goal is the attainment of some form of personal gain (material items, pleasure, excitement, etc.). We suggest that while some of the techniques (especially those seen in Module 2) may be appropriate for this latter subtype of aggressive clients, CART has been developed primarily for the former type, which in our experience constitutes by far the most common type of referral in an outpatient setting.

One final point that is often raised by professionals is that some offender clients' values are antisocial in nature (e.g., to be seen as tough and streetwise; to "keep it real"; to be feared by rival gang members). So, how is this dealt with in terms of chosen values in the CART model? CART seeks to promote an overall enhanced life for clients. As such, it is important to promote values that can reasonably be expected to optimize clients' overall life circumstances. Similarly, the clinician cannot be expected to fully comprehend the life circumstances and needs of clients who come from low socioeconomic environments with a lack of opportunity and a community culture that includes violence, and yes, even gang membership.

In such circumstances, the issue is whether the client can come to recognize the distinction of life circumstances, that is, those that require the attitudes and behaviors consistent with "street survival," and those for which street survival attitudes and behaviors would be coun-terproductive. For example, such clients would be assisted in the development of, and would work toward, values and associated behaviors at home and with family that would produce improved functioning in this domain, without necessarily seeking to change street attitudes and behaviors (which the client might factually view as necessary for personal survival). This requires a level of stimulus discrimination that the client often does not naturally manifest, and in some cases, these non-street values and associated behaviors may generalize further. However, our experience has been that there are very few things that a clinician can do that will reduce credibility and make successful treatment less likely than to pontificate to clients with a significantly different life circumstance than most of us could ever imagine, about how their day-to-day street behavior and attitudes should be modified.

Suggested Modifications for Group Therapy

While CART has been designed primarily for adult clients seen in individual therapy, recent research (Dettore, Lee, & Gardner, 2012) adapted the program for a nine-session school-based group program with middle-school children. In addition to adaptations necessary to make the modules developmentally appropriate for a child population, two macro-level adaptations were made to make the program more "group friendly." These group-oriented adaptations were such that Module 2 (using the therapeutic relationship to recognize and modify clinically relevant behavior) and Module 9 (integration, relapse prevention, and treatment termination) were excluded from the program, although the concepts were integrated where appropriate in other modules. In addition, all other modules other than 3 and 7 were arranged to be single-session modules. Modules 3 (mindful emotion awareness) and 7 (commitment to values-based behavior) were each expanded to two sessions each. These changes were made because Modules 2 and 9 were deemed least likely to be effectively managed in a group format; it was determined that a nine-session protocol would be most appropriate for the site in question; and our experience has been that Modules 3 and 7 typically take more than a single session to adequately address, and are essential steps in the CART process. Therefore, the nine-session group-based adaptation in use thus far has been:

- Session 1: Module 1
- Sessions 2 and 3: Module 3
- Session 4: Module 4
- Session 5: Module 5
- Session 6: Module 6
- Sessions 7 and 8: Module 7
- Session 9: Module 8

While this group-based iteration of CART was developed specifically for a middle-school population, it is the overall strategy that we suggest when seeking to use the CART protocol in a group format, especially when the treatment length is time-limited/restricted. As can be seen, CART has been developed as a *modular* treatment approach intended to allow for maximum flexibility across clinical populations and contexts. The one caution we offer is that the *sequence* of modules should always remain fixed, as the modules have been designed to build upon each other. Thus, rather than nine truly unique, totally independent units, they all have some degree of necessary and appropriate overlap. As such, changing the sequencing is very likely to create a confusing and ineffective connection of related topics. While we view nine sessions as the likely minimum for a group intervention, it may be somewhat shorter if the group session is conducted in a 2-hour rather than a 1½-hour period of time. CART has been devised for maximum therapist flexibility, and we therefore encourage creative modifications within modules to fit the needs of specific situational contexts as long as the essential sequencing of topics remains constant.

Outcome Research

CART was developed in standard clinical practice at two urban university-based anger/violence treatment programs over a 9-year period (to date) that has included over 200 clinic patients, most of whom were court mandated for a variety of violent offenses. There have been two structured open trials of CART. The first trial, which is ongoing, involved 45 adult clients (to date) mandated for domestic/intimate partner violence intervention. At intake, clients completed a variety of measures related to anger, violent behavior, symptom distress, quality of life, difficulties in emotion regulation, and psychological flexibility. Thirty-two of the 45 clients (71%) completed at least eight sessions of the program. Results showed that at the completion of the CART program, participants showed significantly enhanced experiential acceptance, emotion regulation skills, and quality of life; and reduced the scope of situations that were triggers of aggressive responding (Gardner, Moore, & Pess, 2012). Further, CART processes that are targeted as primary mechanisms of aggressive/violent behavior, such as experiential avoidance and difficulties in emotion regulation, demonstrated change by mid-treatment, while the measures of outcome (i.e., quality of life, scope of aggressive-inducing situations) demonstrated more change toward the end of treatment. This is consistent with the AAM and the basic principles of CART. Importantly, in contrast to the previously noted studies using traditional CBT interventions, which found a 30–40% recidivism rate within 6 months of arrest for interpersonal violence (Stover et al., 2009), only one (3%) of the 45 CART participants who have to date completed the open trial have reoffended across this same period of time (up to 6 months post-completion). Additional data collection and follow-up continue. With protocol development representing Phase 1 of CART development, research, and utilization, open trial studies represent Phase 2 of an outcome research program that will soon culminate in a randomized controlled trial (Phase 3) comparing CART with traditional CBT interventions.

The second open trial of CART consisted of a developmentally modified group intervention provided in an urban school system (Dettore et al., 2012). In this study, 12 African-American fifth grade males (ages 10–12) in a self-contained class and previously classified by the school as emotionally disturbed (demonstrating chronic levels of physical and verbal aggression with frequent school suspensions), took part in a nine-session group-based CART program. Following the intervention, these students demonstrated significant increases in concentration, academic functioning, and higher-order cognitive skills, and reduced levels of aggressive and impulsive behaviors, as measured by teacher reports. Possibly the greatest indicator of treatment success, however, is the fact that the school district has requested that this program be extended throughout their school system and across multiple age groups.

The coming years will see a larger number of trials of CART, as we continue to educate and train clinicians to utilize this comprehensive and evidence-informed treatment approach.

Summary and Concluding Remarks

The primary goals of contextual anger regulation therapy are the development of basic emotion regulation skills of emotional acceptance/tolerance and awareness, and importantly, the promotion of positive values-driven behaviors culminating in enhanced quality of life. The techniques utilized in CART, such as mindfulness, cognitive defusion, values-based behavioral activation and commitment, emotional acceptance, and interpersonal problem-solving, are all incorporated with the ultimate goal of helping clients function better through enhanced emotion regulation, while still inevitably experiencing anger and other affective states. We do not help them become less angry (although often, paradoxically, they do), we help them *function better* despite negative affective states such as anger. CART ultimately seeks to help clients reach for something better in life, and not simply feel better in some immediate, transient way. We have previously described this process as *life* management rather than *anger* management (Gardner & Moore, 2014). This fundamental notion is at the heart of contextual anger regulation therapy.

Authors' Note

Correspondence concerning this article should be addressed to Frank L. Gardner, PhD, professor and Director, Department of Advanced Studies in Psychology, Nathan Weiss Graduate College, Kean University, 1000 Morris Avenue, Union, New Jersey, United States, 07083. Phone: (908) 737-5862. Fax: (908) 737-5895. E-mail: fgardner@kean.edu

Zella E. Moore, PsyD, is an associate professor in the Department of Psychology at Manhattan College in New York City, New York.

References

Aldao, A., Nolen-Hoeksema, S., & Schweizer, S. (2010). Emotion regulation strategies across psychopathology: A meta-analytic review. *Clinical Psychology Review, 30,* 217–237.

Babock, J. C., Green, C. E., & Robie, C. (2004). Does batterers' treatment work? A meta-analytic review of domestic violence treatment. *Clinical Psychology Review, 23,* 1023–1053.

Barlow, D. H., Allen, L. B., & Choate, M. L. (2004). Toward a unified treatment for emotional disorders. *Behavior Therapy, 35,* 205–230.

Castonguay, L. G., & Beutler, L. E. (2006). Principles of therapeutic change: A task force on participants, relationships, and techniques factors. *Journal of Clinical Psychology, 62,* 631–638.

Corso, P. S., Mercy, J. A., Simon, T. R., Finklestein, E. A., & Mercy, T. R. (2007). Medical costs and productivity losses due to interpersonal and self-directed violence in the United States. *American Journal of Preventive Medicine, 32*(6), 474–482.

Davey, L., Day, A., & Howells, K. (2005). Anger, over-control, and serious violent offending. *Aggression and Violent Behavior, 10,* 624–635.

Del Vecchio, T., & O'Leary, D. (2004). Effectiveness of anger treatments for specific problems: A meta-analytic review. *Clinical Psychology Review, 24,* 15–34.

Dettore, M. M., Lee, E. F., & Gardner, F. L. (2012, February). *Acceptance-based group treatment for externalizing behaviors in an urban elementary school.* Paper presented at the annual convention of the National Association of School Psychologists, Philadelphia, PA.

DiGiuseppe, R., & Tafrate, R. (2003). Anger treatment for adults: A meta-analytic review. *Clinical Psychology: Science and Practice, 10,* 70–84.

Dutton, D. G., & Corvo, K. (2007). The Duluth model: A data-impervious paradigm and a failed strategy. *Aggression and Violent Behavior, 12,* 859–867.

Egbert, L., Ruvo, J., Dettore, M., McCarthy, J., Gardner, F. L., & Moore, Z. E. (2009, November). *Experiential acceptance as a mechanism of change in the treatment of court mandated violent offenders.* Paper presented at the annual conference of the Association for Behavioral and Cognitive Therapies, New York, NY.

Elliot, R., Watson, J. C., Goldman, R. N., & Greenberg, L. S. (2004). *Learning emotion focused therapy: The process experiential approach to change.* Washington, DC: American Psychological Association.

Gardner, F. L., Dettore, M. M., Moore, Z. E., & Foy, T. (2010, June). *Contributions of experiential avoidance and emotion regulation to anger symptom severity.* Paper presented at the triennial conference of the World Congress of Behavioral & Cognitive Therapies, Boston, MA.

Gardner, F. L., & Moore, Z. E. (2007). *The psychology of enhancing human performance: The Mindfulness-Acceptance-Commitment (MAC) approach.* New York: Springer Publishing Company LLC.

Gardner, F. L., & Moore, Z. E. (2008). Understanding clinical anger and violence: The anger avoidance model. *Behavior Modification, 32*(6), 897–912.

Gardner, F. L., & Moore, Z. E. (2010, November). Collaborating with an office of probation and parole on the treatment of court-mandated violent offenders. In Z. E. Moore (Chair), *Cognitive-behavioral assessment and treatment of criminal justice populations: Implications for cross-discipline dissemination and collaboration*. Symposium presented at the annual convention of the Association for Behavioral and Cognitive Therapies, San Francisco, CA.

Gardner, F. L., & Moore, Z. E. (2014). *Contextual Anger Regulation Therapy: A Mindfulness and Acceptance-based Approach*. New York, NY: Routledge/Taylor & Francis.

Gardner, F. L., Moore, Z. E., & Dettore, M. (2012a). *The relationship between anger, early aversive history, and emotion regulation difficulties in domestic and non-domestic violent offenders*. Manuscript submitted for publication.

Gardner, F. L., Moore, Z. E., & Pess, R. (2012b, November). *A pilot study examining the effectiveness of anger regulation therapy (ART) for the treatment of interpersonal partner violence*. Paper presented at the annual convention of the Association for Behavioral and Cognitive Therapies, National Harbor, MD.

Hayes, S. C., Strosahl, K. D., & Wilson, K. G. (1999). *Acceptance and Commitment Therapy: An experiential approach to behavior change*. New York: Guilford Press.

Hayes, S. C., Strosahl, K. D., & Wilson, K. G. (2012). *Acceptance and commitment therapy: The process and practice of mindful change*. New York: Guilford Press.

Kashdan, T. B., Barrios, V., Forsyth, J. P., & Steger, M. F. (2006). Experiential avoidance as a generalized psychological vulnerability: Comparisons with coping and emotion regulation strategies. *Behaviour Research and Therapy, 44*, 1301–1320.

Kohlenberg, R. J., & Tsai, M. (1993). Functional analytic psychotherapy: A radical behavioral approach to treatment and integration. *Journal of Psychotherapy Integration, 4*, 175–201.

Linehan, M. M. (1993). *Skills training manual for treating borderline personality disorder*. New York: Guilford Press.

Miller, W. R., & Rollnick, S. (2002). *Motivational interviewing: Preparing people for change* (2nd ed.). New York: Guilford Press.

Olatunji, B. O., & Lohr, J. M. (2005). Nonspecific factors and the efficacy of psychosocial treatments for anger. *The Scientific Review of Mental Health Practice*. Available at: http://www.srmhp.org/0302/anger.html

Patel, H. J., Cuccurullo, L. J., Foy, T. R., Gardner, F. L., & Moore, Z. E. (2009, November). *The role of experiential avoidance in the manifestation of internalized and externalized anger*. Paper presented at the annual conference of the Association for Behavioral and Cognitive Therapies, New York, NY.

Pence, E., & Paymar, M. (1993). *Education groups for men who batter: The Duluth model*. New York: Springer.

Saini, M. (2009). A meta-analysis of the psychological treatment of anger: Developing guidelines for evidence-based practice. *Journal of the American Academy of Psychiatry and the Law, 37*, 473–488.

Santanello, A., Moore, Z. E., & Gardner, F. L. (2004, November). *Are there empirically supported treatments for anger?: Toward the development of a university based center for the treatment and study of anger*. Paper presented at the annual conference of the Association for Advancement of Behavior Therapy, New Orleans, LA.

Segal, Z. V., Williams, M. C., & Teasdale, J. D. (2002). *Mindfulness based cognitive therapy for depression: A new approach to preventing relapse*. New York: Guilford Press.

Sirois, B. C., & Burg, M. M. (2003). Negative emotion and coronary disease: A review. *Behavior Modification, 27*, 83–102.

Smyth, E. J., Dettore, M., Gardner, F. L., & Moore, Z. E. (2010, November). *Emotion dysregulation as a mediator between early maladaptive schemas and anger*. Paper presented at the annual convention of the Association for Behavioral and Cognitive Therapies, San Francisco, CA.

Stover, C. S., Meadows, A. L., & Kaufman, J. (2009). Interventions for intimate partner violence: Review and implications for evidence-based practice. *Professional Psychology: Research and Practice*, *40*, 223–233.

Wilson, K. G., & Murrell, A. R. (2004). Values work in acceptance and commitment therapy: Setting a course for behavioral treatment. In S. C Hayes, V. M. Follette, & M. M. Linehan (Eds.), *Mindfulness and acceptance* (pp. 120–151). New York: Guilford.

Suggestions for Further Learning

Books

Gardner, F. L., & Moore, Z. E. (2014). *Contextual Anger Regulation Therapy: A Mindfulness and Acceptance-based Approach*. New York, NY: Routledge/Taylor & Francis.

Hayes, S. C., Strosahl, K. D., & Wilson, K. G. (2012). *Acceptance and Commitment Therapy: The process and practice of mindful change* (2nd ed.). New York, NY: Guilford Press.

Appendix 9.A

Introduction to Mindfulness Exercise

This short exercise will help clients focus on where they are right now and why they are here. This exercise should take about five minutes to complete. Just like with any other exercise or activity, ask clients whether they are willing to do it before you start. We suggest that therapists read the instructions to clients in a slow and soft fashion.

1. Go ahead and get in a comfortable position in your chair. Sit upright with your feet flat on the floor, your arms and legs uncrossed, and your hands resting in your lap. Allow your eyes to close gently [pause 10 seconds]. Take a couple of gentle breaths: in ... and out—in ... and out. Notice the sound and feel of your own breath as you breathe in [pause] and out [pause 10 seconds].
2. Now turn your attention to being inside this room. Notice any sounds that may occur inside the room [pause] and outside [pause 10 seconds]. Notice how you are sitting in your chair [pause 10 seconds]. Focus on the place where your body touches the chair. What are the sensations there? How does it feel to sit where you sit? [pause 10 seconds] Next, notice the places where your body touches itself [pause 10 seconds]. Notice the spot where your hands touch your legs. How do your feet feel in the position that they are in? [pause 10 seconds] What sensations can you notice in the rest of your body? If you feel any sensations in your body, just notice them and acknowledge their presence [pause 10 seconds]. Also notice how they may, by themselves, change or shift from moment to moment. Do not try to change them [pause 10 seconds].
3. Now let yourself be in this room. See if you can feel the investment of you and I in this room—what we are here for [pause 10 seconds]. If you are thinking this sounds weird, just notice that and come back to the sense of integrity in this room. Be aware of the value that you and I are serving by being here [pause 10 seconds]. See if you can allow yourself to be present with what you are afraid of. Notice any doubts, reservations, fears, and worries [pause 10 seconds]. See if you can just notice them, acknowledge their presence, and make some space for them [pause 10 seconds]. You don't need to make them go away or work on them [pause 10 seconds]. Now see if for just a moment you can be present with your values and commitments. Why are you here? Where do you want to go? What do you want to do? [pause 10 seconds]
4. When, you are ready, let go of those thoughts and gradually widen your attention to take in the sounds around you [pause 10 seconds] and slowly open your eyes with the intention to bring this awareness to the present moment and the rest of the day.

Appendix 9.B

Mindfulness of the Breath Exercise

This brief exercise will help you expand upon your mindfulness skills, and will allow for further development of mindful awareness and attention. This exercise should take no more than 20-minutes to complete. It is suggested that this exercise be completed at a slow pace.

Please find a comfortable position to sit. Notice the position of your body, particularly your legs, hands, and feet. Allow your eyes to close gently [pause 10 seconds].

Take several deep breaths and notice the air going in and out of your body. Notice the sound and feel of your own breathing as you breathe in [pause] and out [pause]. Allow your focus of attention to be on your abdomen rising and falling with each breath [pause 10 seconds].

As you continue to breathe in and out, imagine that there is a pencil in your hand and that you are drawing a line upward with each inhale, and then a line downward with each exhale [pause 10 seconds]. Imagine the picture that these lines would create [pause 10 seconds].

As you slowly continue to breathe in and out, notice that you may become aware of a variety of thoughts and emotions that enter and leave your mind. Simply notice them as though they are part of a parade, gently allow them to pass and once again focus on your own breathing and all the sensations that come [pause 10 seconds]. Having a variety of thoughts and emotions is not incorrect or in any way a problem, but simply reflects the reality of the human mind. There is no need to change, fix, or in any way attempt to control these experiences. Simply note the parade of thoughts in your mind and refocus on your own breathing [pause 10 seconds].

Allow yourself to continue to breathe gently in and out, focusing your thoughts on the physical sensations of each breath that you take. Whenever you are ready, slowly open your eyes, become fully aware of your physical surroundings, and continue your day.

Section 2

Two Perspectives on the Treatment of Intimate Partner Violence

10

CBT for Perpetrators of Intimate Partner Violence

The "I³" Approach

Christopher I. Eckhardt, Cory A. Crane,
and Joel G. Sprunger

Surveys of adults conducted in the United States and elsewhere indicate that intimate partner violence (IPV) occurs at an alarmingly high frequency across a multitude of age groups, across both sexes, and at high rates among individuals of all ethnic, racial, and cultural backgrounds (for a review, see Jose & O'Leary, 2009). According to the most recent survey of US adults (Black et al., 2011), almost 7 million women and 5.5 million men experience physical violence, stalking, or rape from an intimate partner each year. Rates of psychological aggression are somewhat normative in most community and clinical samples, with 75% of males and 80% of females reporting psychological aggression perpetration (e.g., Jose & O'Leary, 2009). Large-scale surveys, longitudinal studies, and meta-analytic reviews indicate that rates of physical and psychological IPV perpetration are roughly similar between males and females, with a trend toward showing higher perpetration rates among females (especially young adults) (e.g., Archer, 2000; Ehrensaft, Moffitt, & Caspi, 2004). This finding has been quite controversial in branches of the IPV field that have traditionally assumed IPV to be solely defined as male-to-female abuse (Dutton & Nicholls, 2005; Felson, 2002). In general, rates of IPV are higher in clinical samples, with perpetration prevalence rates ranging from 35 to 50% for male-to-female IPV and 37 to 57% for female-to-male IPV (e.g., Cascardi, Langhinrichsen, & Vivian, 1992).

Given the widespread prevalence of IPV and the serious physical, psychological, and inter-personal consequences experienced by victims of such abuse (Golding, 1999), it is critical to examine the effectiveness of attempts by the criminal justice system to rehabilitate IPV offenders. Over the last 30 years, states have passed laws criminalizing IPV and mandating some form of immediate incarceration of the offender as well as some type of longer-term intervention for both offenders and victims. At least 1000 such programs are currently in operation in the United States (Adams & Cayouette, 2002), most of which serve predominantly court-mandated populations and are primarily focused on men who have assaulted women. Although a range of program philosophies and practices exist, programs for perpetrators of IPV, often labeled "Batterer Intervention Programs" (BIPs), tend to advocate an open

Forensic CBT: A Handbook for Clinical Practice, First Edition.
Edited by Raymond Chip Tafrate and Damon Mitchell.
© 2014 John Wiley & Sons, Ltd. Published 2014 by John Wiley & Sons, Ltd.

admissions group modality for a widely varying length of time (8 to 52 weeks). Traditionally, programs have been structured around the assumption of a gender-themed root cause of IPV, such that the patriarchal nature of societal and institutional structures rewards male domination, and justifies any means (including physical aggression) that reinforce male power, control, and privilege (e.g., Dobash & Dobash, 1979). This heuristic represents a starting point for many intervention programs for IPV perpetrators and embodies the current dominant approach (i.e., the Duluth model; see Pence & Paymar, 1993). Thus, it follows that intervention programs will be largely focused on psychoeducational reprogramming of (male) offenders rather than psychotherapeutic change, with violence reduction best achieved by exposing patriarchal/ misogynistic attitudes, encouraging accountability and personal responsibility for coercive tactics in relationships, and promoting more gender-egalitarian behaviors. While many of the core assumptions of this approach have been heavily criticized (e.g., Dutton & Nicholls, 2005; Straus, 2010), most existing intervention programs and state coalitions against domestic violence espouse some variation of this conceptual framework (Maiuro & Eberle, 2008).

A second "traditional" model of BIP emerged from an integration of Duluth model and couples' therapy techniques in the early 1980s and is more consistent with the therapeutically oriented cognitive-behavioral therapy (CBT) model. The therapeutic CBT model expands the range of attitudinal variables beyond those surrounding patriarchal socialization and includes additional factors empirically associated with IPV, such as emotion dysregulation and faulty relationship skills (e.g., Dutton, 1986; Feazell, Mayers, & Deschner, 1984; Saunders, 1984; Sonkin, Martin, & Walker, 1985). In contrast to the feminist-informed model (which also labels itself a CBT approach), BIPs based on the therapeutic CBT model include core assumptions and components borrowed from basic cognitive therapies for psychopathology (e.g., Beck, 1976) that achieve the goal of behavior change through a collaborative therapeutic relationship, exposure and disputation of distorted cognitions, and various problem-solving and mood regulation techniques. CBT programs for IPV perpetrators have continued to develop over the last 20 years and have been widely applied (e.g., Hamberger, 1997; Murphy & Eckhardt, 2005; Stosny, 1995; Wexler, 2006).

Given the widespread adoption of BIPs across the country, one would assume that there is solid evidence for their effectiveness at preventing new episodes of IPV. However, literature reviews conclude that BIP interventions are associated with only small average reductions in IPV (e.g., Babcock, Green, & Robie, 2004; Davis & Taylor, 1999). In a review of 22 studies that used quasi- or true experimental designs and police or partner reports of violence recidivism, effect sizes for IPV intervention on violence cessation ranged from 0.09 to 0.34 (Babcock et al., 2004). In randomized experiments, men assigned to BIPs had average violence recidivism rates about 5% lower than men assigned to control conditions. From a meta-analysis with more restrictive criteria for study inclusion, Feder and Wilson (2005) drew equally pessimistic conclusions. In randomized experiments, IPV intervention had no overall effect on subsequent physical assault according to victim reports (Cohen's $d = 0.01$) and a small effect according to official criminal reports ($d = 0.26$), leading the authors to conclude that "the existing evidence cannot ensure that these programs are, in fact, helpful and not harmful" (p. 257). In a recent review of all controlled studies of BIP, Eckhardt et al. (2013) similarly concluded that there is as much evidence in favor of the effectiveness of BIPs as there is against, with most studies of BIP effectiveness suffering from substantial methodological limitations.

Thus, the empirical status of BIPs is decidedly uncertain, despite the enormous public health and safety concerns about IPV and the promise that such interventions have in rehabilitating offenders. At best, the effectiveness literature suggests that men who complete traditional group programs are only slightly more likely to refrain from IPV than men assigned to minimal interventions. At worst, a near majority of men mandated to attend such groups do not complete them, and in some studies treatment completers fare no better or slightly worse than men assigned to non-BIP interventions. These conclusions have led many in the field to question whether intervention programs for partner violence waste valuable resources and create a false sense of security among victims who expect the abusive partner to change as result of attending a BIP (Jackson et al., 2003).

Therefore, the time is ripe to develop, evaluate, and disseminate alternative intervention programs for partner abusive individuals in order to enhance victim safety. Indeed, reviews suggest that alternative approaches to traditional models of BIP have thus far yielded promising effects on violence reduction (Eckhardt et al., 2013). In the present chapter, we present an alternative to traditional BIP programming that is centered on a novel model of IPV etiology – the Instigating-Impelling-Inhibiting, or I³, model (Finkel & Eckhardt, 2013) – that also utilizes components of therapeutic CBT and motivational interviewing. We present this I³-informed CBT model as follows. First, we will review the I³ model of IPV risk and illustrate why it holds promise as a guiding framework for understanding IPV etiology and intervention. Second, we will discuss the conceptual application of this framework to intervention. Third, we will identify practical intervention techniques aligned with each dimension in the I³ model. We conclude by discussing the implications of this model for program development and BIP effectiveness research.

The Instigating-Impelling-(Dis)Inhibiting Model of IPV (I³ Theory)

IPV scholars have identified a wealth of risk factors for IPV perpetration, as evidenced by numerous meta-analyses and qualitative reviews of this literature (e.g., Schumacher, Feldbau-Kohn, Slep, & Heyman, 2001; Stith, Rosen, McCollum, & Thomsen, 2004). While the list of risk factors seems to get longer with each new literature review, little progress has been made in integrating these risk factor lists and in demonstrating possible functional interconnections among them. As noted many years ago by Straus and Gelles (1988, p. 159):

> No single factor such as male dominance or growing up in a violent family has been shown to account for more than a small percentage of the incidence of…spousal abuse. However, a study of the potential effect of 25 such 'risk factors' (Straus, Gelles, & Steinmetz, 1980) indicated that in families where only one or two of the factors existed there were no incidents of wife beating during the year studied. On the other hand, wife beating occurred in 70% of the families with 12 or more of the factors….Thus, the key to unraveling the paradox of wife beating appears to lie in understanding the interplay of the numerous causal factors.

Understanding this interplay of risk factors is precisely the purpose of I³ theory.

I³ theory is a recently developed meta-theory for systematically investigating factors related to IPV etiology (Finkel, 2007; Finkel, DeWall, Slotter, Oaten, & Foshee, 2009; Finkel & Eckhardt, 2013). I³ theory is an integrative model that is centered on a simple yet clinically important core assumption – the probability of IPV perpetration increases when environmental triggers and aggressive urges overcome an individual's ability to counteract these urges. The model gets its name from the first letters of the three process categories in which IPV risk factors are classified: Instigation, Impellance, and Inhibition. These three categories make up the *process level* of the model; the factors contained within each of the three categories are considered at the *construct level*; the indices for the specific constructs in each process category reflect the *operation level*. Analyses at these three conceptual strata provide a wealth of information for clinicians and researchers that has traditionally been lacking in a literature that has commonly favored static lists of risk factors as opposed to dynamic models of IPV risk.

Instigation

Instigation is defined in the I^3 model as the exposure to discrete social dynamics that normatively trigger an urge to become aggressive (Finkel & Eckhardt, 2013). IPV does not occur in a vacuum and typically occurs in commonly occurring social contexts involving provocation. A critical assumption is that IPV requires an instigating context, with such instigating factors representing the starting point for a process analysis of IPV perpetration risk. These provocations may be direct or indirect in nature (Slotter & Finkel, 2011). Whereas *direct* instigation involves the target in the provoking event (e.g., an intimate partner is attacked after an insulting statement), *indirect* instigation occurs when actions from another source evoke an aggressive urge toward not only the third-party provocateur, but the intimate partner as well (e.g., work conflicts that spill over into partner interactions). Given that over 80% of IPV incidents are preceded by a verbal argument (Greenfield et al., 1998), both direct and indirect sources of instigation, as well as other impellance risks reviewed below (e.g., trait anger), may be sufficient to trigger an urge to aggress.

Impellance

The process category of impellance contains the lion's share of risk factors associated with IPV perpetration. Impellance is defined as dispositional or situational factors that psychologically prepare an individual to experience a strong urge to aggress when encountering instigation in a particular context (Finkel & Eckhardt, 2013). There are four types of impelling risk: distal, dispositional, relational, and situational. *Distal* factors are those that represent aspects of an individual's evolutionary or cultural heritage that make the individual more likely to experience a powerful urge to be aggressive when encountering instigation, such as the "culture of honor" observed in Southern US males (Nisbett & Cohen, 1996).

Dispositional impelling factors are relatively stable individual differences that prepare a person to experience a powerful urge to aggress when confronted with a particular instigator in a particular context. Dispositional hostility (Norlander & Eckhardt, 2005), trait anger (Anderson & Bushman, 2002; Eckhardt, Barbour, & Stuart, 1997), and elevated testosterone levels (Dabbs, Frady, Carr, & Besch, 1987) are examples of fairly static individual differences that interact with instigation to produce aggressive behavior.

Factors classified as *relational* impellances are the dyadic characteristics of the relationship between two intimate partners that increase the likelihood of experiencing a powerful urge to behave aggressively. Some relational elements known to be conducive to IPV are target-specific jealousy (Dutton, van Ginkel & Landolt, 1996) and insecurity in the relationship (Carney & Buttell, 2005). Dissatisfaction with extant power dynamics in the potentially abusive relationship dyad is a strong predictor of partner violence (Ronfeldt, Kimerling, & Arias, 1998).

Situational factors, the final type of impellance risk, are momentarily activated cognitive, affective, or physiological factors that make people likely to experience a powerful urge to aggress when confronting a particular instigator in a particular situation. An example of an internal situational influence for committing aggression is the experience of physical pain (Berkowitz, 1998). External situational contributions include exposure to violent media (Anderson & Bushman, 2001; Anderson, Carnagey, & Eubanks, 2003) and hot temperatures (Anderson, Anderson, Dorr, DeNeve, & Flanagan, 2000). These factors are the most transient of the impellances, but their consideration is vital to an accurate index of a person's likelihood to commit acute acts of violence against their partner.

Instigation × impellance

Impellances act as a catalyst for instigating influences. An impellance can be likened to a pool of gasoline; alone, it cannot cause a fire, but introduce a lit match and the combination produces an inferno exponentially quicker and more severe than the match would have been able to achieve in the same amount of time. A person may have a substantial propensity toward behaving in an aggressive manner, but in the absence of instigation toward aggression, that person will show no behavioral indication of such dispositions. The combined aggressive influence of instigation and impellance comprises the *urge readiness* of an individual, or the collective urge that one has toward behaving aggressively. A person's urge readiness is context-specific, so the particular interactional dynamic existing between instigation and impellance may be highly idiographic. An individualized treatment approach that identifies and acknowledges the magnitude of influence contributed by these interacting components is key, and would otherwise be missed in a one-size-fits-all intervention approach.

The significance of an impelling factor is dependent on the specific instigation. As mentioned above, an impelling factor is not "ambulatory" and requires an instigating factor to provide the initial velocity toward a display of aggression. An instigating factor must be compatible with an impelling factor for that impellance to provide a contribution to that person's urge to aggress. Another way of looking at it is in terms of relevance: a person with very little sense of commitment to their relationship (relational impellance) may not respond to target-specific jealousy (instigation) any more than the average person. However, that same individual would be more likely to respond with greater aggression when provoked (instigation) by the target because they do not have an interest in preserving the relationship and will not temper their aggressive solution to a perceived personal insult. These examples illustrate that impellances toward IPV perpetration rely on relevant sources of instigation. Therefore, having a greater number of impellances increases the risk of encountering compatible instigating factors and, therefore, experiencing a greater magnitude of urge readiness.

Inhibition

The focus among IPV researchers and clinicians has typically been confined to analyzing IPV risk in terms of either the quantity of impellers present in a given offender, or in an analysis of an instigation × impellance interaction (e.g., trait anger and sexual jealousy situations). However, such analyses omit a critical factor in understanding IPV – most people report successful inhibition of violent urges (Finkel et al., 2009). Thus, anger-prone individuals do not *always* attack a partner even when provoked; on most occasions, even those at high risk for violence inhibit such impulses. Since the I³ meta-theory conceptualizes IPV as most likely when aggressive urges override one's inhibitory capabilities, I³ theory places an emphasis on examining the presence of factors that promote self-regulation (i.e., inhibition) or that interfere with self-control (disinhibition) (Finkel & Eckhardt, 2013).

Disinhibiting factors also fall into four subtypes: distal, dispositional, relational, and situational. *Distal* disinhibitors are aspects of one's evolutionary or cultural heritage that weaken a person's likelihood of overriding aggressive urges. Cultural or societal norms that condone or do not directly disapprove of IPV perpetration would fall into this subtype of disinhibitor. *Dispositional* disinhibitors are those that are relatively stable individual differences that diminish a person's ability to override an aggressive urge. Examples of factors classified as dispositional disinhibitors include those related to poor executive functioning (Giancola, 2000), such as the inability to perceive accurate outcomes of violence (Slaby & Guerra, 1988), high impulsiveness (Denson, DeWall, & Finkel, 2012), and low dispositional self-control (Finkel & Campbell, 2001). *Relational* disinhibiting factors are characteristics of the relationship that decrease the likelihood of overriding an urge to be aggressive, such as having low empathy for a specific partner (Richardson, Green, & Lago, 1998) and little commitment to the relationship (Slotter & Finkel, 2011). *Situational* disinhibiting factors are momentarily activated cognitive, affective, or physiological experiences that hinder a person's ability to override an aggressive urge. These influences, by nature, are dynamic and highly dependent on the immediate context of the individual. Situational disinhibitors include specific environmental influences and immediate internal states.

Alcohol intoxication is a prime example of a situational disinhibitor for IPV (Eckhardt, 2007; Leonard, 2005). Alcohol intoxication produces key neuropsychological changes that alter executive functioning and impede self-regulatory capacities. In addition, alcohol tends to produce a cognitive myopic effect (Giancola, Josephs, Parrott, & Duke, 2010), whereby an intoxicated individual restricts the processing of social information to the most salient cue present in that situation; in relationship conflicts, these salient cues tend to center on hostile communication, interpersonal threat, and aggressive methods of problem-solving, thus creating the framework for an aggressive response.

Inhibiting factors are viewed in the I^3 model as protective factors, or factors that increase the likelihood that a person will be able to resist their urge readiness to aggress. Just as an individual's urge readiness is the sum of influence from the instigating and impelling factors, the difference between inhibiting and disinhibiting influences can be defined as a person's *urge impedance*, or their total capacity to diminish aggressive urges. Self-regulatory capabilities are not static, but fluid in nature, relying on cognitive resources to function optimally (Baumeister, Vohs, & Tice, 2007). Acts of self-regulation consume available resources, so each consecutive thwarting of aggressive urges decreases the "fuel" available to inhibit the next impulse. In this sense, each repetition of self-control is a greater situational disinhibiting factor than the previous instance.

Process interaction

The I^3 model allows for simultaneous analysis of the total immediate risk for IPV perpetration by accounting for factors of the various types within each process category (i.e., the three "I"s). The total idiosyncratic contribution of impellance for a person may include both distal and proximal factors. For instance, the total impellance for a particular individual may have the distal influence of the "culture of honor," the dispositional influence of trait anger, the relational influence of earning wages lower than those of his partner, and the situational influence of a hot environmental temperature. Acknowledgment of the influence contributed by factors of differing temporal stability informs treatment efforts regarding long-term versus critical incident targets of intervention. Thus, the advantage to using I^3 theory in clinical decision-making rests in its interactional framework. The model suggests that clinicians could predict, with greater accuracy, whether a given interaction between intimate partners will be violent versus non-violent if they can discern the strength of instigation, impellance, and inhibition; in other words, knowledge of these three processes, and of the interplay among them, may be both *necessary and sufficient* for predicting IPV perpetration.

Pre-Treatment Assessment According to I³ Theory

The clinical utility of the I³ meta-theoretical framework is apparent in its amenability toward a process-level, individualized assessment of risk for a given client. In order to take full advantage of the model, the clinician must conduct a thorough and detailed pre-treatment assessment of the factors that pertain to the client. Information from a detailed interview will help the clinician to categorize the reported factors into the three process categories. A collection of corroborating evidence – self-report, partner-report, criminal records – will help the clinician to construct an accurate model of the magnitude of influence toward or against IPV that is associated with each construct in each of the three processes. With these estimates of magnitude, the clinician can begin to construct an individual treatment plan based on the client's idiosyncratic risk and protective factors.

With this in mind, we present an IPV case recently seen by one of us (C.C.) that demonstrates how therapists may use the I³ model to conceptualize a case of male-to-female IPV.

Overview of case

GM was a 42-year-old Caucasian American male who was mandated to treatment following a domestic violence offense and reported a history of frequent bidirectional partner violence with his current partner. He had lived with his 58-year-old girlfriend for 12 years and was supported by her income as well as monthly Social Security Disability Insurance (SSDI) that he received for chronic neck and back pain. Assessment of GM included a detailed conceptualization of the influences that increased his risk for IPV perpetration, organized around each of the I³ processes.

Instigation. In terms of instigation factors, at the outset of treatment, the client reported that he experienced direct instigation, in the form of verbal and physical aggression on a weekly basis. His partner's aggression was often motivated by the client's own impulsive and immature behavior, which included staying out for days gambling with their joint funds and drinking to excess before returning home broke (but sober). GM also reported being easily frustrated by indirect instigators that included loud, intrusive neighbors, hostile calls from debt collectors, and inconsiderate drivers.

Impellers. GM completed intake measures and provided daily tracking assessments, which provided valuable information on various types of impelling factors that may have contributed to his perpetration of IPV. Distally, the client's genogram revealed that he had been raised the only child in an intact home by relationally abusive parents, both of whom abused alcohol. Dispositionally, GM had also earned success and accolades as a particularly aggressive, semi-professional hockey player who retired following a back injury in his early twenties. He reported a long history of anger control problems and aggressive impulsivity, as evidenced by two or three bar fights per year since age 17, four physical encounters with neighbors over a 3-year period, and a fight with his best friend that resulted in several broken bones. This suggests an overall propensity to experience and react with anger to interpersonal challenges. Relationally, GM further reported low self-esteem as a result of his perceived financial dependence upon his partner and the sexual side effects of his psychotropic medications. He reported that arguments with his partner about money or sexual performance were common situational impellers. Situationally, the client's daily logs indicated that his anger and irritability increased on days when he experienced marijuana withdrawal resulting from limited funds. Finally, GM suffered from chronic pain but could not be prescribed opiates due to his history of drug dependence. The client reported heightened pain with cold temperatures and was also uncomfortable in warm temperatures due to obesity. The client stated that he was in a state of constant discomfort and irritation that could be temporarily alleviated by self-medication with marijuana.

Dis(inhibition). GM reported that he had not experienced negative consequences for his violent behavior prior to his IPV arrest. The client reported that his experience of excitement during bar fights would override the pain experienced during each altercation, and that his relationship aggression would result in either "*getting my way*" or enhancing attachment. The client was not concerned about his partner leaving, nor was he aware that he could be arrested for partner violence without the cooperation of his partner. Further, the client described his commitment to the relationship in practical terms, stating that she financially supported him and that his relationship alternatives were limited. GM had incurred multiple concussions while practicing and playing hockey, possibly accounting for a degree of his poor executive functioning and impulsivity. Further impairing the client's ability to inhibit aggression was chronic alcohol and cocaine abuse. GM reported that he was drunk before every bar fight and that at least 25% of his partner aggression occurred within the context of alcohol consumption.

The I^3 model allows the therapist to impose a coherent risk-process model to assist in the conceptualization of treatment strategies for this case. The case of GM suggests that he experiences frequent urges to aggress given a range of direct and indirect provocations with his partner and in situations likely to lead to interpersonal violence (e.g., bars). He is generally irritable and quick to anger, and has a long history of using aggression as a problem-solving strategy. His chronic pain and bouts of cannabis withdrawal both increase risk of aggression, as well as limit the extent to which he can inhibit aggressive urges. GM has additional self-control deficiencies related to his low level of commitment to his relationship, his lack of respect for his partner, and likely cognitive disturbances resulting from head trauma and years of substance abuse. In the sections below, we outline how to conceptualize cases of IPV similar to GM's according to the I^3 approach.

I^3 Theory-Informed CBT Treatment for IPV Offenders

Treatment logistics

We will now turn our attention toward an I^3 theory-informed approach to the treatment of intimate partner violence. IPV interventions often range from 8 to 52 weekly sessions of 45–60 minutes depending on the specific agency, existing state guidelines, and other criminal justice factors. However, as no significant benefits have been associated with programs that

Table 10.1 The case of GM: risk factors for intimate partner violence according to I³ theory.

Instigation	Impellance	(Dis)inhibition
Financial disputes	Family of origin violence	Expectations of violence
Verbal victimization	Alcoholic parents	Poor self-control
Physical victimization	Dispositional aggressivity	Low partner empathy
Chronic pain	Dispositional anger	No risk of retaliation
Loud noises	Low self-esteem	Relationship stability
Intrusive neighbors	Cannabis withdrawal	Limited alternatives
Debt collectors	Impulsivity	Head trauma
Road rage	Aggressive sports culture	Alcohol abuse
Extreme gambling losses	Low frustration tolerance	Cocaine abuse

enforce lengthier durations, we recommend a 12-session course of treatment. Case conceptualization according to the I³ model is undertaken in order to provide a more detailed and idiographic understanding of how to promote readiness to change in the presence of specific risk and protective factors. For example, case conceptualization would look similar to Table 10.1 for the case of GM. A full review of measures designed to assess these constructs with IPV perpetrators is beyond the scope of the current chapter (for a review, see Murphy & Eckhardt, 2005).

This section of the chapter is structured around individual rather than group treatment because of the empirically supported benefits of individual over group IPV interventions (for a review, see Murphy & Meis, 2008). Regarding the logistics of individual sessions, we present a consistent format across treatment. The first 5 minutes of each session is devoted to introducing the learning topic, briefly describing the rationale as it relates to the client's personal goals, and providing the client with one to three relevant goals that they should be able to achieve by the end of the session. Following the introduction, 15 minutes are allotted to review the previous session and assigned homework. The skills training and acquisition component of the session occupies 20 minutes. Each session concludes with 15 minutes of skills rehearsal as well as a 5-minute discussion of how and when homework will be completed.

While the I³ theory-informed treatment model for IPV is designed to be individualized, this does not preclude the possibility of administering group treatment. As previously discussed, most IPV treatment is currently administered in a group setting, despite the limitations of group work (Austin & Dankwort, 1999). Suggested modifications for group therapy include conducting an individual motivational enhancement session, prior to the first group session, in which the client undergoes a complete psychosocial assessment, receives initial feedback, and is encouraged to provide personalized treatment goals. Clients should be approached individually throughout treatment to check in on the progress they perceive having made in pursuit of their personalized goals. Groups should remain relatively small (four to eight clients) to encourage participation and individual focus. The 5-15-20-15-5 minute divisions may still be applied to group interventions with greater focus upon generalized goals during the discussion of skills and paired problem-solving and role-play activities during the practice component. The group counselor must take care to recognize variability in readiness to change within the group. When possible, clients should be assigned to groups based upon reported readiness to change. Counselors should also include group building exercises to foster group cohesion. The counselor should not reveal client information disclosed during individual sessions with the group as such breaches of confidentiality may well harm rapport and adversely affect individual participation.

Additionally, couples-based IPV interventions, such as integrative behavioral couples therapy, have demonstrated unique benefits in modifying maladaptive behaviors that emerge from interactive processes within dyads (e.g., O'Farrell, Murphy, Stephan, Fals-Stewart, & Murphy, 2004). The I³ model may be particularly well suited to address treatment needs within couples reporting bidirectional IPV. Ronan, Maurelli, and Holman (see Chapter 11) discuss a couples-based IPV approach in further detail.

General motivational enhancement structure

As with any approach, I³ would suggest that before any specific behavior change techniques are applied, it is first beneficial to assess and enhance motivation to engage in behavior change efforts. This may be particularly true for the court-ordered offender whose primary motivation to comply with treatment is external, such as the threat of adverse financial and legal consequences for non-compliance (Murphy & Baxter, 1997). Beyond increasing session attendance, high levels of motivation should be encouraged to: (i) increase attention during sessions in an effort to facilitate the acquisition of basic skills; (ii) convey the importance of homework and in vivo practice exercises in effecting positive cognitive and behavioral change; (iii) reduce resistance to treatment; and (iv) promote movement through stages of change (Murphy & Eckhardt, 2005).

Techniques borrowed from Miller and Rollnick's (2002, 2013) motivational interviewing (MI) approach have received empirical support for increasing IPV perpetrators' readiness to change problem behaviors prior to or during the first treatment session (for a review, see Eckhardt et al., 2013). These benefits are further enhanced when integrated with motivational enhancement techniques throughout the course of the broader CBT intervention. Incorporating MI techniques boosts treatment compliance both in and outside of sessions, as evidenced by improved session attendance and outside help seeking (Musser, Semiatin, Taft, & Murphy, 2008). Examples of MI adaptations to the IPV population can be found in the appendices to this chapter, and are based upon a recent treatment manual for IPV offenders (Murphy & Eckhardt, 2005).

Briefly, our approach adopts the core motivational interviewing tenet that clients who engage in self-destructive behaviors experience ambivalence about efforts to change. Clients typically understand that IPV has resulted in negative consequences across multiple domains (loss of relationship, legal consequences) but also perceive their behavior as adaptive in some way (a necessary and unavoidable way to manage a difficult situation). Using MI, counselors attempt to help the client resolve ambivalence and come to the conclusion that selecting alternative, prosocial, pro-relationship behaviors will produce results consistent with personally established goals.

First, counselors avoid shaming clients through the attribution of blame or the use of judgmental and critical responses as this may make ambivalent clients defensive of their past behavior and more resistant to treatment. Alternatively, the counselor acknowledges the client's autonomy and responds empathically toward concerns through active listening techniques (i.e., open-ended questions, affirmations of change talk, reflections, summarizations), while avoiding confrontation. A problem-solving framework can be applied and reinforced to help the client generate lists of positive and negative consequences for various behavioral responses to conflict in pursuit of prosocial decision-making. The counselor then works with the client to generate explicit goals for treatment and gradually reduce perceived obstacles to resolve ambivalence and further promote sustained motivation following treatment. The motivational enhancement session may conclude with a general change plan worksheet (see Appendix 10.A). Clients capable of reporting their own goals to reduce violence and improve a current or future relationship will be more invested in achieving those goals than clients instructed to change certain behaviors by the courts or a counselor. Additional efforts may be taken to bolster a client's motivation to change (see Appendix 10.B for an additional motivational enhancement exercise). We recommend that the 30–60-minute motivational interview occur either during a pretreatment intake or the first individual treatment session.

I³ model components

Instigation   Following the motivational enhancement session, the counselor and client work together to identify typical stimuli that normatively instigate or trigger the urge to aggress. To a large extent, acute incidents of IPV involve problematic interactions, often with difficult individuals who may be entrenched in interaction dynamics that are highly provoking. This provocation-focused session helps the client to recognize situations, individuals, and specific events that will likely elicit anger and increase the risk of aggression based upon previous experiences. Later sessions introduce specific cognitive and behavioral skills to help clients reduce the risk of aggressing in high-risk situations.

There are a number of psychoeducational techniques to identify and modify the distal contexts that increase the likelihood of IPV. We suggest that this session begins with the construction of a genogram, or family tree, in which the counselor and client interact to develop a clear understanding of the patterns of substance use, psychopathology, marital conflict, and divorce across the client's known family members. Social learning perspectives suggest that this exercise may help the client identify familial relationship patterns that influence their own interactions. The exercise may also contribute to establishing rapport with the client, and encourages the client to consider his or her own involvement in violent events in a manner that is non-threatening and indirect. The client is then asked to identify personal patterns of aggression as related to general instigators (see Appendix 10.C for a worksheet to facilitate this process). Consistent with the I³ model, patterns of aggression following arguments, self-esteem threats, and victimization are brought to the client's awareness. Similarly, the client's motivation to aggress, such as control, jealousy, or the desire to avoid an aversive argument, is explored.

Self-monitoring forms can be assigned as homework and reviewed in-session, to address substance use, anger, and aggression as well as more broadly to help clients recognize high-risk situations. This exercise is particularly beneficial for clients who initially have difficulty understanding the relationships between thoughts, emotions, and behaviors. Self-monitoring should be assigned as homework for two to four sessions (see Appendix 10.D for a sample self-monitoring worksheet).

Once contexts that increase the likelihood of IPV have been identified, the focus of subsequent sessions can turn to stimulus control and efforts to modify such contexts, at least to the extent that situations can indeed be changed. Typically, efforts to terminate conflictual relationships and change disruptive patterns of daily life, especially if these patterns are highly associated with IPV, should be encouraged. Changes may include restructuring job demands, avoiding social hour after work, better regulation of one's sleep, and sometimes relationship separation.

Impellance   In cases where it is not feasible to end a problematic relationship, the focus diverts to cognitive and behavioral modifications of interactional *impellers*, factors that increase the urge to aggress upon exposure to instigators. Additionally, clients work to develop inhibitory strategies that will eventually lessen the probability of IPV during relevant interpersonal situations.

Reducing the influence of individual, situational, and relational impelling risk factors is of critical importance for IPV perpetrators, as most individuals will either remain in the abusive relationship or at least engage in future relationships with another partner. The literature on risk factors for partner violence suggests that IPV perpetrators bring a number of aggresso-genic affective and cognitive traits to their close relationships (Stith et al., 2004). Anger is the affective state that has been most robustly associated with general aggression and IPV (for a review, see Norlander & Eckhardt, 2005). It is recommended that counselors begin the discussion of the influence of anger on IPV with a didactic component describing the physiological response of the sympathetic nervous system following provocation. Essentially, anger provocation activates the physiological cues that are consistent with fight-or-flight preparation, such as increased heart rate, rapid breathing, and the excretion of sweat. The ease with which this system may be activated influences the likelihood of aggression following provocation. The client may be able to associate anger with their own aggression and provide examples of personal coping strategies that have helped them de-escalate dangerous situations in the past. Relaxation techniques should then be introduced as a method to activate the parasympathetic nervous system and reduce the physiological urge to aggress. The client may learn to implement diaphragmatic breathing, progressive muscle relaxation, relaxational imagery, self-talk, and mindfulness-based meditation techniques. The common thread across relaxation techniques involves clients removing themselves from the current argument or anger-provoking situation.

Once the client understands the relationship between affect and aggression, the counselor may choose to introduce cognition and cognitive styles as a strong correlate of angry affect, thus completing the thoughts-feelings-behaviors triad. The significance of attitudes and cognitive distortions as strong correlates of IPV is evident both in terms of empirical evidence (for a review, see Stith et al., 2004) and in the fact that *all* treatment approaches attempt to achieve non-violence through modification of faulty attitudes and beliefs. Efforts to restruc-ture IPV-supportive cognitions may begin with an introduction to the cognitive biases and irrational beliefs commonly associated with IPV (for a review, see Murphy & Eckhardt, 2005). These include arbitrary inference, overgeneralization, dichotomous thinking, hostile attri-bution biases, and demandingness (e.g., "*my partner needs to be nice to or respect me*" or "*my partner must not care about me since I got this horrible birthday gift*"). Examples of thinking errors may be collected from or provided to the client after each is described in general terms. In addition, self-monitoring forms (see Appendix 10.D) may be adapted for clients to complete between sessions in order to provide a more proximal assessment of these cognitive processes relative to the eliciting situation.

Following the discussion of thinking errors and their bidirectional effects on both affect and behavior, the counselor can introduce methods to challenge problematic thinking patterns. For a complete list of these techniques, see more detailed descriptions in Eckhardt and Schram (2009) and Murphy and Eckhardt (2005). Briefly, the focus follows a traditional CBT frame-work of disputing faulty beliefs, examining alternative "rational" beliefs, and practicing the substitution of thinking errors with these more rational thoughts through exercises both in and out of session. Disputing questions include those that reduce certainty (e.g., "*Am I 100% sure that this is true?*"), elicit alternative information (e.g., "*Is there evidence for or against this conclusion?*"), and reduce negative affect related to the consequences of a perceived problem (e.g., "*Would I be able to cope with this if it is true?*"). Again, the client should be encouraged to provide examples of thinking errors that provoke anger or an urge to aggress against a partner. The counselor can then help the client dispute each thinking error and generate rational counter-thoughts to mitigate the possibility of cognitive impellers resulting in aggression following future instigation. Homework should be assigned and reviewed for comprehension over subsequent sessions (see Appendix 10.E for a worksheet used in cognitive restructuring).

However, cognitive restructuring only partially addresses many of the more common relational impellers that have been observed in violent couples, such as jealousy, resentment, and a perceived imbalance of power. Restructuring exercises only reach the client, not the partner, and fail to address all aspects of ongoing problematic interactions and pervasive relationship dissatisfaction. The further reduction of IPV risk through relational impellers may be achieved through fostering greater appreciation for one's partner using couples training exercises and improving communication through standard CBT social skills training. Specifically, relationship satisfaction enhancement techniques should be reviewed, encouraging the client to recognize and appreciate pleasant behaviors performed by a current or future partner (see Appendix 10.F for a sample exercise). Additionally, clients should be encouraged to plan enjoyable activities with their partners (see Appendix 10.G). Such skills produce the dual benefits of increasing both relationship satisfaction and egalitarianism.

Further, social skills training should address proper communication of negative affect, standard assertiveness training, and appropriate techniques to request and reject assistance as methods of reducing belligerent communication styles within the relationship. Communication skills training may result in greater openness to partner influence, emotional availability, and receptiveness to criticism. Clients should be given the opportunity to simulate these skills through role-playing exercises with the counselor (for specific techniques, see Murphy & Eckhardt, 2005).

Inhibition   As noted above, it is perhaps unreasonable to presume that IPV offenders must never have an aggressive cognition or revenge-filled thought following treatment. Research suggests that such processes are common in intimate relationships but that it is normative to inhibit such thoughts (Finkel et al., 2009). Thus, a central responsibility for the counselor working with IPV offenders is, in part, to build the client's problem-solving and inhibitory skills so that they are able to reduce such urges when they arise. Treatment goals in the inhibition process therefore involve two different but complementary approaches to risk reduction. First, I³-informed treatment aims to limit behaviors and interactions that lead to disinhibition. Second, treatment aims to develop and train skills that promote self-regulatory capabilities (i.e., inhibition).

As noted in a previous section, frequent efforts of IPV offenders to exert some degree of control in their often chaotic and unstable lives lead to frequent depletion of the finite personal resources available to maintain effective self-regulation. Thus, efforts to manage high anger and aggressive imagery will drain regulatory strength; during a subsequent negative interaction with an intimate partner, the individual will have impaired self-control and existing impellers may exert a more direct influence on behavior. The intensity of stressors as well as the amount of available self-control resources required to cope with them differ from one person to the next. The relaxation techniques and couples satisfaction training previously described combined with brief self-management training should be discussed with the client as methods of countering disinhibition resulting from the depletion of self-regulatory resources.

In addition, IPV offenders have high rates of alcohol and substance use relative to the general population (Leonard, 2005). Given the negative impact of alcohol intoxication on self-control, it is essential for treatment programs to deal effectively with co-occurring substance use problems among IPV offenders. Indeed, alcohol treatment alone has proven effective at reducing the occurrence of IPV (for a review, see Murphy & Ting, 2010). So great is the co-occurrence of IPV and substance use disorders that effective integrated treatments have been designed to address both behaviors concurrently (e.g., Easton et al., 2007). Although a full integration of substance use treatment is beyond the scope of the present chapter, counselors should be aware that many IPV clients could benefit from discussing issues related to substance use recovery, emergency planning, and relapse prevention.

Treatment targeted toward the promotion of inhibition to reduce the risk of future violence makes use of multiple CBT-informed strategies. In addition to relaxation skills, problem-solving skills should be discussed at length with all clients. Clients are provided with a standardized process through which they may identify a problem, generate a list of possible behavioral responses, decide upon a course of action based upon the logical consequences of each option, and evaluate the consequences of the selected behavior to inform future decision-making in comparable situations (see Appendix 10.H for a sample problem-solving worksheet). The promotion of such self-awareness is designed to reduce the perception of positive outcomes following violent behavioral decisions. Counselors should issue problem-solving homework assignments to solidify comprehension (see Appendix 10.I for a sample homework assignment).

Other methods of increasing inhibition and subsequently reducing disinhibition should be utilized in treatment when deemed necessary by the counselor. The use of empathy training, perspective taking, and constructive discussions of relationship expectancies may increase relational inhibition, while normalizing prosocial relationship behaviors, such as self-control training and problem-solving therapies, can increase distal inhibition. Finally, emergency planning can be used to prepare for particularly challenging discussions or substance use relapse in an effort to increase situation-specific inhibition.

Clearly, I^3 processes are not mutually exclusive. Many of the risk factors and interventions overlap across processes. Beyond the main effects of the I^3 processes in the above treatment description, the theory advances hypotheses about interactions on all levels that should be considered during individual case formulation and treatment planning. Under the current model, an individual who has successfully limited instigation and impellance while optimizing inhibition will be the least likely to reoffend. Additionally, individuals with high dispositional aggression, alcohol intoxication, and depleted self-regulation are more likely to aggress following provocation than without provocation, and clients with anger disorders are more likely to aggress following tasks that deplete self-regulation. For a comprehensive review of two- and three-way interaction effects as well as the empirical evidence supporting them, see Finkel and Eckhardt (2013).

Summary

Substantial progress has been made in the development of interventions for individuals who assault their relationship partners. Over time, there has been a notable shift away from narrowly focused, unidimensional ideologies, towards etiology and intervention models that offer broader viewpoints concerning risk factors for IPV and how this understanding of risk relationships may translate into more focused interventions for perpetrators (Dutton & Corvo, 2006). In the present chapter, we attempt to add to this emerging literature by outlining how a promising process dynamic risk model of IPV etiology – I^3 (Finkel & Eckhardt, 2013) – may be integrated with a motivational enhancement-based CBT approach for IPV offenders (Murphy & Eckhardt, 2005). In this approach, we advocate organizing behavior change efforts around the three central processes of I³: Instigation, Impellance, and Inhibition. CBT-based techniques to modify instigators include various forms of stimulus control, whereas more traditional cognitive restructuring and emotion control elements form the basis of techniques designed to modify factors that impel IPV. Problem-solving and self-control replenishing techniques can assist in building the client's self-regulatory skills, and elimination of the disinhibiting effects of substance misuse can further generate more efforts to regulate behaviors in close relationships. Further investigation is needed to evaluate the active components of this approach, and to examine factors that predict its effective implementation.

References

Adams, D., & Cayouette, S. (2002). Emerge – A group education model for abusers. In E. Aldarondo & F. Mederos (Eds.), *Programs for men who batter: Intervention and prevention strategies in a diverse society* (pp. 4.1–4.32). Kingston, NJ: Civic Research Institute.

Anderson, C., Anderson, K., Dorr, N., DeNeve, K., & Flanagan, M. (2000). Temperature and aggression. *Advances in Experimental Social Psychology, 32*, 63–133.

Anderson, C., & Bushman, B. (2001). Effects of violent video games on aggressive behavior, aggressive cognition, aggressive affect, physiological arousal, and prosocial behavior: A meta-analytic review of the literature. *Psychological Science, 12*, 353–359.

Anderson, C., & Bushman, B. (2002). Human aggression. *Annual Review of Psychology, 53*, 27–51.

Anderson, C., Carnagey, N., & Eubanks, J. (2003). Exposure to violent media: The effects of songs with violent lyrics on aggressive thoughts and feelings. *Journal of Personality and Social Psychology, 84*, 960–971.

Archer, J. (2000). Sex differences in aggression between heterosexual partners: A meta-analytic review. *Psychological Bulletin, 126*(5), 651–680.

Austin, J. B., & Dankwort, J. (1999). Standards for batterer programs: A review and analysis. *Journal of Interpersonal Violence, 14*, 152–168.

Babcock, J. C., Green, C. E., & Robie, C. (2004). Does batterer's treatment work? A meta-analytic review of domestic violence treatment. *Clinical Psychology Review, 23*, 1023–1053.

Baumeister, R. F., Vohs, K. D., & Tice, D. M. (2007). The strength model of self-control. *Current Directions in Psychological Science, 16*(6), 351–355.

Beck, A. (1976). *Cognitive therapy and the emotional disorders.* Oxford, UK: International Universities Press.

Berkowitz, L. (1998). Affective aggression: The role of stress, pain, and negative affect. In R. Geen, & E. Donnerstein (Eds.), *Human aggression: Theories, research, and implications for social policy* (pp. 49–72). San Diego, CA: Academic Press.

Black, M.C., Basile, K.C., Breiding, M.J., Smith, S.G., Walters, M.L., Merrick, M.T., Chen, J., & Stevens, M.R. (2011). *The National Intimate Partner and Sexual Violence Survey (NISVS): 2010 Summary Report.* Atlanta, GA: National Center for Injury Prevention and Control, Centers for Disease Control and Prevention.

Carney, M., & Buttell, F. (2005). Exploring the relevance of attachment theory as a dependent variable in the treatment of women mandated into treatment for domestic violence offenses. *Journal of Offender Rehabilitation, 41*, 33–61.

Cascardi, M., Langhinrichsen, J., & Vivian, D. (1992). Marital aggression: Impact, injury, and health correlates for husbands and wives. *Archives of Internal Medicine, 152*, 1178–1184.

Dabbs Jr., J., Frady, R., Carr, T., & Besch, N. (1987). Saliva testosterone and criminal violence in young adult prison inmates. *Psychosomatic Medicine, 49*, 174–182.

Davis, R. C., & Taylor, B. G. (1999). Does batterer treatment reduce violence. *Women & Criminal Justice, 10* (2), 63–93.

Denson, T., DeWall, C., & Finkel, E. (2012). Self-control and aggression. *Current Directions in Psychological Science, 21* (1), 20–25.

Dobash, R. E., & Dobash, R. (1979). *Violence against wives: A case against the patriarchy.* New York: Free Press.

Dutton, D. (1986). Wife assaulter's explanations for assault: The neutralization of self-punishment. *Canadian Journal of Behavioural Science, 18*(4), 391–390.

Dutton, D. G. & Corvo, K. (2006). Transforming a flawed policy: A call to revive psychology and science in domestic violence research and practice. *Aggression and Violent Behavior, 11,* 457–483.

Dutton, D., van Ginkel, C., & Landolt, M. (1996). Jealousy, intrusiveness and intimate abusiveness. *Journal of Family Violence, 11,* 411–423.

Dutton, D. G., & Nicholls, T. L. (2005). The gender paradigm in domestic violence research and theory: Part 1 – The conflict of theory and data. *Aggression and Violent Behavior, 10,* 680–714.

Easton, C. J., Mandel, D. L., Hunkele, K. A., Nich, C., Rounsaville, B. J., & Carroll, K. M. (2007). A cognitive behavioral therapy for alcohol-dependent domestic violence offenders: An integrated substance abuse–domestic violence treatment approach (SADV). *American Journal on Addictions, 16,* 24–31.

Eckhardt, C. I. (2007). Effects of alcohol intoxication on anger experience and expression among partner assaultive men. *Journal of Consulting and Clinical Psychology, 75* (1), 61–71.

Eckhardt, C., Barbour, K., & Stuart, G. (1997). Anger and hostility in maritally violent men: Conceptual distinctions, measurement issues, and literature review. *Clinical Psychology Review, 17* (4), 333–358.

Eckhardt, C., Murphy, C., Whitaker, D., Sprunger, J., Dykstra, R., & Woodard, K. (2013). The effectiveness of intervention programs for perpetrators and victims of intimate partner violence. *Partner Abuse, 4,* 196–231.

Eckhardt, C., & Schram, J. (2009). Cognitive behavioral interventions for partner abusive men. In P. Lehmann (Ed.), *Interventions for intimate partner violence: A strengths approach.* NY: Springer.

Ehrensaft, M. K., Moffitt, T. E., & Caspi, A. (2004). Clinically abusive relationships in an unselected birth cohort: Men's and women's participation and developmental antecedents. *Journal of Abnormal Psychology, 113* (2), 258–270.

Feazell, C. S., Mayers, R. S., & Deschner, J. P. (1984). Services for men who batter: Implications for programs and policies. *Family Relations, 33,* 217–223.

Feder, L., & Wilson, D. B. (2005). A meta-analytic review of court-mandated batterer intervention programs: Can courts affect abusers' behavior? *Journal of Experimental Criminology, 1,* 239–262.

Felson, R. B. (2002). *Violence and gender reexamined.* Washington, DC: American Psychological Association.

Finkel, E. (2007). Impelling and inhibiting forces in the perpetration of intimate partner violence. *Review of General Psychology, 11* (2), 193–207.

Finkel, E., & Campbell, W. (2001). Self-control and accommodation in close relationships: An interdependence analysis. *Journal of Personality and Social Psychology, 81,* 263–277.

Finkel, E. J., DeWall, C. N., Slotter, E. B., Oaten, M., & Foshee, V. A. (2009). Self-regulatory failure and intimate partner violence perpetration. *Journal of Personality and Social Psychology, 97* (3), 483–499.

Finkel, E. J., & Eckhardt, C. I. (2013). Intimate partner violence. In J. Simpson, & L. Campbell (Eds.), *The Oxford handbook of close relationships* (pp. 452–474). New York: Oxford University Press.

Giancola, P. (2000). Executive functioning: A conceptual framework for alcohol-related aggression. *Experimental and Clinical Psychopharmacology, 8,* 576–597.

Giancola, P., Josephs, R., Parrott, D., & Duke, A. (2010). Alcohol myopia revisited: Clarifying aggression and other acts of disinhibition through a distorted lens. *Perspectives on Psychological Science, 5,* 265–278.

Golding, J. M. (1999). Intimate partner violence as a risk factor for mental disorders: A meta-analysis. *Journal of Family Violence, 14* (2), 99–132.

Greenfield, L. A., Rand, M. R., Craven, D., Klaus, P. A., Perkins, C. A., Ringel, C., Warchol, G., Maston, C., & Fox, J. A. (1998). *Violence by intimates.* Washington, DC: U.S. Department of Justice, Bureau of Justice Statistics.

Hamberger, L. K. (1997). Cognitive behavioral treatment of men who batter their partners. *Cognitive and Behavioral Practice, 4* (1), 147–169.

Jackson, S., Feder, L., Forde, D. R., Davis, R. C., Maxwell, C. D., & Taylor, B. G. (2003, June). *Batterer intervention programs: Where do we go from here?* (Special NIJ Report). Washington, DC: National Institute of Justice, U.S. Department of Justice.

Jose, A., & O'Leary, K. (2009). Prevalence of partner aggression in representative and clinic samples. In K. O'Leary, & E. M. Woodin (Eds.), *Psychological and physical aggression in couples: Causes and interventions* (pp. 15–35). Washington, DC: American Psychological Association.

Leonard, K. (2005). Editorial: Alcohol and intimate partner violence: When can we say that heavy drinking is a contributing cause of violence? *Addiction, 100,* 422–425.

Maiuro, R. D., & Eberle, J. A. (2008). State standards for domestic violence perpetrator treatment: Current status, trends, and recommendations. *Violence and Victims, 23* (2), 133–155.

Miller, W. R., & Rollnick, S. (2002). *Motivational interviewing: Preparing people for change* (2nd ed.). New York: Guilford.

Miller, W. R. & Rollnick, S. (2013). *Motivational interviewing: Helping people change* (3rd ed.). New York: The Guilford Press.

Murphy, C. M. & Baxter, V. A. (1997). Motivating batterers to change in the treatment context. *Journal of Interpersonal Violence, 12,* 607–619.

Murphy, C. M., & Eckhardt, C. I. (2005). *Treating the abusive partner: An individualized cognitive-behavioral approach.* New York: Guilford Press.

Murphy, C. M., & Meis, L. A. (2008). Individual treatment of intimate partner violence perpetrators. *Violence and Victims, 23,* 173–186.

Murphy, C. M., & Ting, L. A. (2010). Interventions for perpetrators of intimate partner violence: A review of efficacy research and recent trends. *Partner Abuse, 1* (1), 26–44.

Musser, P.H., Semiatin, J.N., Taft, C.T., & Murphy, C.M. (2008). Motivational interviewing as a pre-group intervention for partner violent men. *Violence and Victims, 23,* 539–557.

Nisbett, R., & Cohen, D. (1996). *Culture of honor: The psychology of violence in the South.* Boulder, CO: Westview.

Norlander, B., & Eckhardt, C. (2005). Anger, hostility, and male perpetrators of intimate partner violence: A meta-analytic review. *Clinical Psychology Review, 25,* 119–152.

O'Farrell, T. J., Murphy, C. M., Stephan, S. H., Fals-Stewart, W., & Murphy, M. (2004). Partner violence before and after couples-based alcoholism treatment for male alcoholic patients: The role of treatment involvement and abstinence. *Journal of Consulting and Clinical Psychology, 72,* 202–217.

Pence, E., & Paymar, M. (1993). *Education groups for men who batter: The Duluth model.* New York: Springer.

Richardson, D., Green, L., & Lago, T. (1998). The relationship between perspective-taking and non-aggressive responding in the face of an attack. *Journal of Personality, 66,* 235–256.

Ronfeldt, H., Kimerling, R., & Arias, I. (1998). Satisfaction with relationship power and the perpetration of dating violence. *Journal of Marriage and the Family, 60,* 70–78.

Saunders, D. G. (1984). Helping husbands who batter. *Social Casework,* 65 (6), 347–353.

Schumacher, J. A., Feldbau-Kohn, S., Slep, A. M. S., & Heyman, R. E. (2001). Risk factors for male-to-female partner physical abuse. *Aggression and Violent Behavior, 6,* 281–352.

Slaby, R., & Guerra, N. (1988). Cognitive mediators of aggression in adolescent offenders: I. Assessment. *Developmental Psychology, 24,* 580–588.

Slotter, E., & Finkel, E. (2011). I³ theory: Instigating, impelling, and inhibiting factors in aggression. In P. Shaver & M. Mikulincer (Eds.), *Human aggression and violence: Causes, manifestations, and consequences* (pp. 35–52). Washington, D.C.: American Psychological Association.

Sonkin, D. J., Martin, D., & Walker, L. E. (1985). *The male batterer: A treatment approach*. New York: Springer.

Stith, S. M., Rosen, K. H., McCollum, E. E., & Thomsen, C. J. (2004). Treating intimate partner violence within intact couple relationships: Outcomes of multi-couple versus individual couple therapy. *Journal of Marital and Family Therapy, 30* (3), 305–318.

Stosny, S. (1995). *Treating attachment abuse: A compassionate approach*. New York: Springer.

Straus, M. A. (2010). Thirty years of denying the evidence on gender symmetry in partner violence: Implications for prevention and treatment. *Partner Abuse, 1* (3), 332–362.

Straus, M. A., & Gelles, R. J. (1988). *Intimate violence*. New York: Simon & Schuster.

Straus, M. A., Gelles, R. J., & Steinmetz, S. K. (1980). *Behind closed doors: Violence in the American family*. New York: Doubleday/Anchor.

Wexler, D. B. (2006). *Stop domestic violence: Innovative skills, techniques, options, and plans for better relationships (group leader's manual)*. New York: W. W. Norton & Co.

Suggestions for Further Learning

Books

Finkel, E. J., & Eckhardt, C. I. (in press). Intimate partner violence. In J. Simpson, & L. Campbell (Eds.), *The Oxford handbook of close relationships*. New York: Oxford University Press.

Murphy, C. M., & Eckhardt, C. I. (2005). *Treating the abusive partner: An individualized cognitive-behavioral approach*. New York: Guilford Press.

Research project

Eckhardt, C., Murphy, C., Whitaker, D., Sprunger, J., Dykstra, R., & Woodard, K. (in press). The effectiveness of intervention programs for perpetrators and victims of intimate partner violence: Findings from the Partner Abuse State of Knowledge Project. *Partner Abuse*.

Appendix 10.A

Motivating Change

Worksheet 1: The Change Plan

Things that I would like to improve about my relationship or myself in relationships:
1.
2.
3.

I want to change these things so that:
1.
2.
3.

I may need help making this change and can rely on:
1.
2.
3.

To accomplish these goals, I will:
1.
2.
3.

Appendix 10.B

Motivating Change

Worksheet 2: Future Self Letter

Future Self Assignment[1]   During the next week, I want you to imagine that a year has passed and that you're now in a non-violent relationship. It could be with your current or a future partner. As this new you, write a two paragraph letter to the old you, the one who is in treatment now. Write about what your life is like. Include reasons that you stopped the violence a year earlier, what your lifestyle has become, and the benefits you enjoy from non-violence. Mention in your letter any problems that you faced during the past year while becoming non-violent and describe how you dealt with them. Describe yourself in this new relationship as clearly as you can. It may help you to think about the following categories as you visualize yourself in the future: friendships, health, employment, recreational activities, general lifestyle satisfaction, children, parents, and how you were at the beginning of your relationship.

---

[1]   Adapted from Easton's Substance Abuse-Domestic Violence (SADV) Treatment Manual (Easton et al., 2007).

If you would prefer, draw a picture, sketch, or create a painting of this image of yourself in the future, rather than depicting it in writing. Choose whatever medium will allow you to see another possibility for yourself.

We think you will find this an extremely useful exercise. The purpose is to get you to start visualizing your journey and ultimate goal. Having a clearer picture of where you're going and why, as well as how to get there, will be useful in the months ahead. At our next session, we will talk about the future you foresee for yourself.

Appendix 10.C

Understanding Patterns of Conflict

Worksheet 1: Aggression Self-Awareness Record

As a method of increasing your awareness about your own patterns of aggression during conflict, please use the following chart to identify conflict-related situations, thoughts, feelings, and consequences. It will be difficult to start but once you've developed the routine of paying more attention, it will become easier to record and understand the ways in which you personally tend to aggress.

Trigger: What types of events or interactions tend to make you angry or feel aggressive (e.g., arguing about money, loss, frustration at work, remembering bad conversations, alcohol, etc.)?

1. _____

2. _____

Thoughts and Feelings: What do you notice about how you are thinking and/or feeling in relation to the trigger(s) you have identified (e.g., thoughts of being worthless, disrespected, threatened, and feelings of sadness, anger, and fear)?

1. _____
2. _____

Behavior: What did you do when you were thinking and feeling these ways (e.g., smoked, drank, walked away, blocked the exit, ignored others)?

1. _____
2. _____

Positive Consequences: What good came from your behavior (e.g., I felt better for a while)?

1. _____
2. _____

Negative Consequences: What negative things happen as a result of your responses? (e.g., I felt badly, I was arrested, I am more alone now)?

1. _____
2. _____

Appendix 10.D

Understanding Patterns of Conflict

Worksheet 2: Self-Monitoring Record – Relationship Conflict

Trigger	Thoughts and Feelings	Behavior	Positive Consequences	Negative Consequences

Appendix 10.E

Cognitive Restructuring

Thinking Error	Disputing Questions	Rational Thought	Consequence
The guy that texted my wife wants to sleep with her.	What evidence is there against this? Could I cope with this if it were true?	She's never cheated on me. I've been nervous over nothing in the past. Sure, it doesn't mean he has a chance with her.	I felt relieved and a bit closer to my wife. We did not have a fight that lasted all night and I got to watch the Red Wings play.

Appendix 10.F

Relationship Building

Worksheet 1: Recognizing Good Behavior[1]

We sometimes focus on the negatives in life and in our own relationships. We often forget that our significant others are our partners. People who, despite their flaws, help us in many ways every day. They might give us a concerned look when we get bad news, thank us for something that we do, finish a little housework, or take care of our children when we are unable to. Over the next week, look hard for your own partner's helpful or considerate behaviors and write down one thing that you appreciate each day. Once you've written the behavior down, be sure to take a moment to thank your partner for their help.

Day	Good Behavior
Sunday	
Monday	
Tuesday	
Wednesday	
Thursday	
Friday	
Saturday	

---

[1] Adapted from Easton's Substance Abuse-Domestic Violence (SADV) Treatment Manual (Easton et al., 2007).

Appendix 10.G

Relationship Building

Worksheet 2: Pleasant Activities[1]

In developing a non-violent relationship, it is important to identify activities that bring you pleasure in your relationship. All too often, we focus on the negatives while ignoring the things that make us truly happy. For this assignment, identify something enjoyable to do with your partner every day. Choose something that won't take a lot of time, effort, or money but that both you and your partner might enjoy. This could involve taking a walk together, making a meal, playing cards or a board game, trading compliments, etc. Ask your partner to help you generate the list of activities.

Day	Planned Activity	Follow-Up: What Happened?
1.		
2.		
3.		
4.		
5.		
6.		
7.		

[1] Adapted from Easton's Substance Abuse-Domestic Violence (SADV) Treatment Manual (Easton et al., 2007).

Appendix 10.H

Problem-Solving

Worksheet 1: The Steps of Problem Solving[1]

1. Is there a problem? Recognize that a problem exists. We get clues from our bodies, thoughts, feelings, behavior, reactions to others, and the way that others react to us.
2. What is the problem? Identify the problem. Describe the problem as accurately as you can. Break it down into manageable parts.
3. What can I do? Consider various approaches to solving the problem. Brainstorm to think of as many solutions as you can. Consider acting to change the situation and/or changing the way you think about the situation.

[1] Adapted from Easton's Substance Abuse-Domestic Violence (SADV) Treatment Manual (Easton et al., 2007).

4. What will happen if…? Select the most promising approach. Consider all the positive and negative aspects of each possible approach, and select the one likely to solve the problem.
5. How did it work? Assess the effectiveness of the selected approach. After you have given the approach a fair trial, does it seem to be working out? If not, consider what you can do to improve the plan or switch to an alternate response.

Practice exercise   Select a problem that does not have an obvious solution. Describe it accurately. Brainstorm a list of possible solutions. Evaluate the possibilities, and number them in order of your preference.

Identify the problem: _____

List brainstorming solutions: _____
_____
_____

Appendix 10.I

Problem-Solving

Worksheet 2: Problem Solving Homework

Problem:	
Calm	1. Give yourself some time alone. 2.
Options	1. 2. 3. 4.
Consequences	How will you feel? How will others feel? Think both short and long-term See sub-table below
Decide/Execute	Which option is best?
Evaluate/Plan	How did it go? What would you do if you could try again?

Consequences sub-table:

Option	(+) Consequences	(−) Consequences
1.		
2.		
3.		
4.		

11

A Couples-Based Violence Reduction Approach to Curbing Intimate Partner Assault

George F. Ronan, Kimberly Maurelli,
and Krista M. Holman

Brief Review of Traditional Approaches

The treatment of intimate partner violence (IPV) has generally focused on the separate treatment of victims and perpetrators, and some have cautioned against the use of conjoint treatment (Heru, 2007; La Taillade, Epstein, & Werlinich, 2006). Arguments against couples-based treatment for IPV stem from concerns about the safety of the victim. Having a a victim disclose information about the perpetrator's misbehavior during a conjoint session could result in untoward repercussions from his/her partner such as further violence within the home or the victim accepting responsibility for the actions of the perpetrator (Heru, 2007; Stith & McCollum, 2009). Thus, many have espoused the use of gender-specific group or individual protocols for the treatment of IPV.

Traditional gender-specific group or individual treatments for perpetrators focus on altering two factors that correlate with IPV: negative attitudes toward women and communication skills deficits (Eckhardt & Schram, 2009; Robertson & Murachver, 2007). As an example, the Duluth model conceptualizes IPV as arising from learned behaviors including intimidation, power and control, and the socially supported degradation of women (Lehmann & Simmons, 2009). Consistent with this formulation, treatment focuses on increasing batterers' responsibility for male-to-female IPV, providing psycho-education, and challenging dysfunctional attitudes and beliefs (Gondolf, 2007). However, support for interventions based on the Duluth model is limited (Babcock, Green, & Robie, 2004; Stover, Meadows, & Kaufman, 2009) and the empirical basis behind some of the underlying assumptions has been questioned. Date and Ronan (2000), for instance, found no differences between attitudes toward women when comparing incarcerated males with a history of domestic violence to incarcerated males with a history of only male-to-male violence, and incarcerated males with no history of violence. Interestingly, the two violent samples did demonstrate significantly poorer interpersonal problem-solving

Forensic CBT: A Handbook for Clinical Practice, First Edition.
Edited by Raymond Chip Tafrate and Damon Mitchell.
© 2014 John Wiley & Sons, Ltd. Published 2014 by John Wiley & Sons, Ltd.

skills than the sample with no history of violence. These findings suggest that attitudes toward women and IPV covary based on their relationship to a third factor (interpersonal problem-solving skills), as opposed to having a general causal relationship.

Cognitive-behavioral approaches conceptualize IPV as resulting from problematic thoughts, attitudes, and actions (Eckhardt & Schram, 2009). Consistent with this conceptualization, treatment focuses on teaching adaptive skills such as anger reduction, conflict management, and positive behavioral exchanges (Lehmann & Simmons, 2009). The focus on teaching interpersonal skills derives from an underlying assumption that batterers have communication skills deficits (Eckhardt & Schram, 2009). However, some research suggests that perpetrators' problematic communication is a function of difficulty in managing high-conflict situations, as opposed to a general communication skills deficit. As an example, Ronan, Dreer, Dollard, and Ronan (2004) found that violent couples' use of effective communication strategies varied as a function of the topic discussed. Couples used significantly fewer effective positive communication strategies when discussing high-conflict scenarios in comparison to when they were discussing pleasant or low-conflict scenarios (Ronan et al., 2004). This suggests that difficult interactions in these couples might not be caused by communication skill deficits per se, but rather are a function of particularly poor skills for managing high-conflict situations.

Rationale for a Couples Approach

Male-only IPV treatment programs have not been found to significantly reduce IPV (Babcock et al., 2004). The reason for their limited success might relate to the high dropout rate, with some programs yielding dropout rates as high as 60% (Rondeau, Brodeur, Brochu, & Lemire, 2001). Male-only treatment groups might also have limited effectiveness because they are not addressing issues relevant to IPV, such as negative interaction patterns that are occurring within intimate relationships (La Taillade et al., 2006). Furthermore, these groups can have iatrogenic effects as group members may bond together and become more supportive of IPV-related attitudes and behaviors (Stith & McCollum, 2009). Similarly, perpetrators court-ordered to treatment can be resentful towards their partners, and this can cause violence to escalate especially if the victim is living within the home (Stith & McCollum, 2009). Because of these drawbacks, research has begun to focus on couples-based treatment programs (Fals-Stewart, Klostermann, & Clinton-Sherrod, 2009; La Taillade et al., 2006; Stith & McCollum, 2009).

Brief Review of Couples-Based Treatments

Couples-based IPV treatments allow problematic relationship dynamics to be addressed while remediating skill deficits and providing safety planning to promote healthy relationship functioning (Stith & McCollum, 2009). Numerous forms of couples-based IPV treatment have been developed. For instance, the Domestic Violence Focused Couples Treatment (DVFCT), developed by Stith, McCollum, and Rosen, is a solution-focused treatment approach to address IPV that can be carried out in a group-based or individual couples format (Stith & McCollum, 2009). This program represents a hybrid of a gender-specific group and couples-based treatment for IPV, as it begins with a 6-week gender-specific group treatment. The sessions are co-facilitated by male and female treatment providers who meet with male and female clients separately during the first 6 weeks to provide psychoeducation to partners regarding IPV and to increase the comfort level of partners. These initial sessions are used to screen for safety concerns to ensure that couples-based treatment is appropriate. These initial sessions also strive to increase the ability of each partner to accept responsibility for his/her own actions, provide a context for rapport building between partners and treatment providers, and develop treatment goals (Stith & McCollum, 2009).

The 6-week gender-specific group treatment phase is followed by 12 weeks of couples-based treatment. These sessions are solution-focused and discussions revolve around successes in order to identify appropriate behaviors and improvements, and emphasize movement toward the couples' relationship goals (Stith & McCollum, 2009). Couples participating in a group format of DVFCT were found to have lower 6-month recidivism rates (25%) than couples participating in a single-couple format of DVFCT (43%) or a comparison group (66%), lending some support to the effectiveness of DVFCT in reducing IPV (Stith, Rosen, McCollum, & Thomsen, 2004).

The Couples Abuse Prevention Program (CAPP), developed by Epstein and colleagues (2005), is a 10-week CBT-based treatment program that focuses on providing psychoeducation, skill-building (e.g., anger management skills, communication skills, problem-solving skills, stress reduction skills), thought challenging (e.g., cognitive restructuring of negative attributions and dysfunctional beliefs), and increasing positive behavioral exchanges (La Taillade et al., 2006). As part of an ongoing research study, couples who seek services at the University of Maryland, College Park, report IPV, and who consent to participation, are randomly assigned to receive either CAPP or treatment as usual (TAU). Pilot data indicate that both CAPP and TAU resulted in significant increases in relationship satisfaction and significant decreases in some forms of psychological abuse (e.g., partner hostile withdrawal; Epstein et al., 2005). Couples participating in CAPP evidenced significant decreases in their use of negative communication, whereas those participating in treatment as usual did not (Epstein et al., 2005). Neither treatment protocol resulted in significant decreases in the use of physical aggression; however, Epstein and colleagues (2005) described this null finding as related to a low base rate of physical aggression in their sample.

Treatments to address co-occurring IPV and substance use concerns in a couples context are also available. Behavioral couples therapy (BCT) involves working with couples to improve relationship dynamics that are conducive to abstinence-based living (O'Farrell, 1999). Although not designed to specifically address IPV, BCT teaches useful skills that are amenable to reducing IPV such as coping strategies for relationship problems, strategies to increase positive interactions, and precautions for the non-abuser to take to remain safe if his/her partner relapses (Fals-Stewart et al., 2009). Rates of IPV have been shown to significantly decrease following BCT, and couples completing BCT have been shown to evidence significantly less IPV after treatment completion relative to couples completing individual treatment (Chase, O'Farrell, Murphy, Fals-Stewart, & Murphy, 2003; Fals-Stewart, Kashdan, O'Farrell, & Birchler, 2002; O'Farrell, Murphy, Stephan, Fals-Stewart, & Murphy, 2004).

Rationale for the Violence Reduction Program

In comparison to conditions like generalized anxiety and major depression wherein the symptoms occur on a frequent or even daily basis, IPV is a low-frequency, high-amplitude phenomenon. That is, interpersonal violence occurs at a low base rate, but when interpersonal violence occurs the impact is significant. In fact, it is rare to find people who engage in interpersonal violence on even a weekly basis, and those who do often spend considerable amounts of time in prison and are unlikely to be treated in an outpatient setting. The intermittent nature of violence suggests that the factors interacting to produce interpersonal violence are not likely to be constantly in play. This suggests IPV is unlikely to be a sole function of person or environmental variables that are consistently operating on or within the person.

The overall approach used in the Violence Reduction Program is consistent with a General Aggression Model (GAM; Anderson & Bushman, 2002; Anderson & Carnagey, 2004). The GAM is a social-cognitive developmental model designed to integrate theories of human aggression into a coherent framework (Dewall & Anderson, 2011). The basic GAM also examines how aggression unfolds in the context of a single social interaction (Anderson & Bushman, 2002). The three main components of the model are: (i) personal and situation variables; (ii) internal states; and (iii) appraisal and decision-making processes. The GAM has explained incidents of aggression in numerous contexts including intimate partner violence, violence between groups, violence resulting from global climate change, and suicide (DeWall & Anderson, 2011; DeWall, Anderson, & Bushman, 2011). Interestingly, the model also explains high rates of non-violence in certain cultures (DeWall et al., 2011). The GAM provides a useful framework for understanding human aggression as it subsumes many theories of aggression into a coherent whole.

The GAM suggests that as individuals learn to engage in the reappraisal process and identify alternative solutions to conflicts, their likelihood for aggression decreases. A core unique feature of our Violence Reduction Program is the explicit focus on training in social problem-solving skills to increase couples' ability to deal with high-conflict situations. Similar to other approaches that have received support in the research literature, our program is a couples-based intervention that incorporates well-tested cognitive and behavioral principles to promote healthy relationship functioning and decrease aggressive behavior. Specific procedures include conducting a detailed case conceptualization, maintaining positive motivation to change, enhancing couples-based problem-solving skills, training in arousal reduction and emotion regulation, and other training to foster successful coping in high-conflict situations.

Components of The Violence Reduction Program

Screening couples

The court commonly requires personal protection or no-contact orders for adjudicated cases of domestic violence. Therefore, it is important to carefully screen cases to identify those for which a treatment-based exception to a no-contact order would be appropriate. The court is unlikely to grant exceptions based on a poor case analysis. Data from our clinic indicate that the majority of people court-ordered into treatment for interpersonal violence do not intend to continue a relationship with the victim of the violence. While the reasons for this are varied, the most frequently reported reason has to do with the victim or the perpetrator no longer wanting to maintain any interaction with their partner. These cases are not appropriate for couples-based interventions. There are, however, cases where the couples plan to continue their relationship; oftentimes these dyads have ignored the no-contact order and are already engaged in frequent contact or have resumed living together. Simply asking perpetrators about their current relationship with the victim is often enough to identify their current relationship status. This latter group represents the cases that we have considered for couples-based treatment. Couples who voluntarily participate in treatment designed to decrease their levels of interpersonal violence might also reflect a group appropriate for a couples-based approach. Finally, occasionally people who have completed gender-specific training are developing new intimate relationships and request couples-based treatment to help reduce the probability of domestic violence occurring within this new relationship. Regardless of the reason for referral, participants considering the use of a couples-format to reduce interpersonal violence undergo additional screening to determine their eligibility for couples-based treatment.

Research on IPV typologies has generally found evidence for different forms and functions of interpersonal violence. Two commonly discussed forms of interpersonal violence are dispositional and situational (Babcock, Canady, Graham, & Schart, 2007). Dispositional IPV is indicated when there is a clearly identifiable perpetrator and victim, the abuse is asymmetrical and carried out almost exclusively by the perpetrator against the victim, and the abuse occurs in a context of power and control (Stith & McCollum, 2009). Gender-specific group or individual treatment may be the best choice when dispositional IPV is prevalent. Gender-specific group or individual treatment provides more safeguards to keep the victim safe, and allows the perpetrator to address issues related to power and control. In contrast, situational IPV is characterized by symmetrical and reciprocal abuse occurring within the relationship. Both partners engage in abusive behaviors and these behaviors are often part of a more pervasive negative interaction cycle that includes psychological abuse, negative reciprocity, and arguments that quickly escalate. Some have posited that a general lack of skills for managing high-conflict situations might be operative (Babcock et al., 2007; Stith & McCollum, 2009). If the couples want to stay together, acknowledge that IPV is a problem within their relationship, are willing to work toward having healthy relationships, and are experiencing situational IPV, couples-based IPV treatment might be appropriate (La Taillade et al., 2006; Stith & McCollum, 2009).

Prior to engaging in treatment, couples are interviewed individually and conjointly to identify areas of contention, safety concerns, and to assess the level of violence in the relationship. Each partner receives safety planning and information on community resources. Couples are instructed to contact law enforcement personnel if they feel at risk. Both partners must agree that they will call the police if intimate partner violence develops. Couples are informed that any violation of the no-violence contract results in a discontinuation of the couples-based intervention, with the perpetrator being placed in a non-couples-based treatment protocol, and any community corrections personnel assigned with monitoring the perpetrator receiving written notification of the change in treatment focus. There is zero tolerance for physical violence or threats of physical violence between partners during the treatment program, which promotes victim's safety and clarifies the direct consequences for any acts of relationship violence. Consistent with numerous other couples-based approaches, couples in this program use time-out contracts for dealing with intense emotions and sign a no-violence contract that is enforced throughout treatment (La Taillade et al., 2006). Couples are discouraged from engaging in name calling, belittling, or other forms of verbal aggression; however, this behavior is not regulated by the no-violence contract because of differences in opinion regarding what constitutes verbal aggression, and concern regarding couples refusing to comply with this requirement. Couples are taught more effective forms of communication and throughout the treatment program their use of verbal aggression is expected to decrease.

One of the measures used by our clinic to screen all perpetrators of violence is the HCR-20: Assessing Risk for Violence (Webster, Douglas, Eaves, & Hart, 1997). The HCR-20 is a structured clinical interview used to screen violent offenders. The interview items reflect three broad categories that assess 10 historical risk factors, five clinical factors, and five current risk factors for future violence. Other screening measures include the Structured Clinical Interview for DSM-IV Axis II Personality Disorders (First, Gibbon, Spitzer, Williams, & Benjamin, 1997) and various standardized measures of aggression and relationship distress and violence (e.g., Conflict Tactics Scale – Revised: Straus, Hamby, Boney-McCoy, & Sugarman, 1996; Dyadic Adjustment Scale: Spanier, 1976). These self-report measures are administered again at post-treatment to help determine the degree of change.

Setting treatment goals

Each partner's participation in defining treatment goals is essential, and goal setting at the beginning of treatment occurs in several contexts. We have found it useful to have couples discuss their goals for treatment during individual and conjoint sessions. Discussion of goals during individual sessions allows each partner to raise concerns that they might not be currently comfortable voicing in front of their partner (Stith, McCollum, & Rosen, 2011). The treatment provider's goal is to coach the partner on how to address the issue during conjoint sessions in a manner that is more likely to lead to joint problem-solving versus high levels of arousal and affect escalation. One strategy that seems to help is organizing goals along a time continuum from short-term to long-term (see Nezu & Nezu, 1989). Oftentimes, short-term goals focus on making basic changes in the participants' interaction patterns and daily behaviors, whereas long-term goals target larger changes in the structure of their relationship. After meeting with each partner individually, the treatment provider helps each partner discuss their concerns as a dyad and conjointly develop treatment goals. The treatment provider is responsible for helping the couple to manage goal setting in high-conflict areas. Throughout treatment we actively discourage couples from engaging in any vituperative exchanges. Stopping such exchanges and modeling appropriate communication skills helps to set the tone for learning how to effectively manage conflicts.

During goal setting the treatment provider acts as a coach to help the couple develop realistic, specific, and measurable goals (La Taillade et al., 2006). Many different strategies can be used to help identify goals. For instance, we sometimes ask partners to think about times when their relationship was better and to describe what was different. General responses such as "*We used to talk about everything*" are common, and the treatment provider's goal is to operationalize vague responses into more concrete targets for treatment. Another strategy can be to have partners discuss their values to help them define what they want to accomplish in treatment. For instance, if the couple identified family involvement as a value and acknowledged that their actions were not consistent with this value, then the treatment provider would help the couple develop a goal that moves them in this direction such as spending time engaged in fun family activities three times per week.

Other strategies involve the use of hypothetical scenarios to generate ideas about how a relationship could change. Commonly used strategies involve use of hypothetical vignettes such as the miracle question (De Jong & Berg, 1998) or asking, "*What in your relationship would change if a magic wand made everything better?*" These techniques require each partner to imagine their life without their current problems and to describe how their day-to-day interactions would be different. Because it is common for each member of the dyad to have different opinions about what needs to change, it is best to have each partner answer these questions. This process can also result in vague statements such as "*We'd get along better*" or

"*We'd be happier together.*" Once again, it is the treatment provider's responsibility to coach the couple to define these changes in more concrete, unambiguous terms. Most often this entails describing reasonable expectations for change, as well as the duration, intensity, frequency, and context of the to-be-changed behaviors. The treatment provider also provides guidance as the couple synthesizes their differing views and identifies common goals. Without clearly articulated goals, it is difficult or impossible to determine progress.

The treatment provider's case conceptualization establishes an initial order for addressing treatment goals. The initial case conceptualization is presented to the couple and provides a rationale for why it might be more helpful to address certain goals first. For instance, if the case conceptualization suggests that a couple is entrenched in negative interaction patterns that have persisted for many months or years, then training in joint problem-solving skills might be unsuccessful because partners are unwilling to listen to each other or consider the other's opinion. A focus on decreasing their negative interactions, increasing their positive interactions, and creating a safe environment might be required prior to training in conflict management or joint problem-solving skills (Baucom, Epstein, La Taillade, & Kirby, 2008). Just as goal setting is considered to be a dynamic process, goal implementation is also a dynamic process and goals are revisited throughout treatment.

Although we emphasize allowing the couple to develop their own goals with the treatment provider taking on the role of coach and guide, ending violence remains an overarching goal. During the first goal-setting session most couples generate the goal of ending violence. However, if a couple does not generate this goal on their own it is the treatment provider's job to discuss the issue with them and ensure that they are willing to work towards this goal. As noted above, zero tolerance for violence is required and couples are required to sign a contract indicating that they will not engage in any acts of physical violence (La Taillade et al., 2006). If couples are unwilling to adopt this approach, we recommend against their being seen together for treatment and a referral for individual treatment is made. Clearly adopting a stance of zero tolerance for violence at the start of treatment communicates that violence in the relationship is unacceptable and that treatment will not enable either partner to continue engaging in violent behavior.

Treatment goals evolve throughout the course of treatment. We have found it useful to review established goals regularly, rather than conceptualizing goal setting as a one-time occurrence that takes place at the beginning of treatment. This approach allows for the frequent assessment of each partner's satisfaction with treatment goals and treatment progress, and to identify areas of concern or need for goal modification in order to meet each partner's needs.

Maintaining motivation for treatment

Conducting an analysis of each partner's readiness to change can facilitate treatment motivation. Readiness to change often varies between and within dyads. Various readiness-to-change questionnaires can be helpful in assessing each partner's level of motivation (e.g., McConnaughy, Prochaska, & Velicer, 1983; Meis, Murphy, & Winter, 2010). We use the Stages of Change Questionnaire (McConnaughy, Prochaska, & Velicer, 1983, 1989) to provide an estimate of each individual's stage of change at the beginning of treatment. We have found it important to present this material in as concrete a manner as possible so we have developed a video that we use to explain how readiness to change can influence openness to treatment. The video contains eight vignettes that depict individuals interacting with a "therapist" and discussing the reasons for coming into treatment. Each vignette depicts an individual in a specific stage of change. For example, in the precontemplative vignettes, individuals present in a blaming and hostile manner and do not take responsibility for their role in the incident that resulted in them being court-ordered to attend treatment. They deny having an anger problem and justify their use of aggression during the incident. Each vignette is presented and the couple is asked: (i) What stage of change the person is in? (ii) How motivated is the person for treatment? (iii) How likely is it that the person will be able to change? and (iv) Why are they likely to change or not?

While enhancing readiness to change can have a positive impact on treatment completion and skill acquisition for people who initially score low on such measures, the research has generally not supported conceptualizing readiness to change from a stage model when dealing with adjudicated violent offenders. Ronan, Gerhart, Bannister, and Udell (2010) found readiness to change did not progress in a linear manner and varied at different points in treatment. Shifts in readiness to change at pre-treatment and post-treatment failed to predict skill acquisition. There appear to be a variety of factors that impact on readiness to change in people convicted of domestic violence, such as time since conviction, type of problem targeted for change, and ongoing relationship satisfaction. Ideally, as couples implement new strategies and successfully resolve conflicts, the improvement in relationship functioning becomes self-reinforcing and motivates their continued behavior change.

Our experience has been that most couples entering treatment are uncertain about the change required, and this lack of knowledge has considerable impact on their readiness to change. If one person of the dyad displays uncertainty about a commitment to change it is important to uncover, normalize, and address the reasons for this skepticism. Providing a clear rationale for the treatment process and goals of treatment can help to enhance motivation to change and foster the development of a therapeutic alliance (Gurman, 2008; Lehmann & Simmons, 2009). We have found values clarification to be a useful strategy to help couples become more aware of problems and increase motivation to change. The goal is to help members of the dyad identify their personal values and their relationship values, and to assess the degree to which their behaviors map onto their values. Values clarification can often provide a sense of purpose and a rationale for making difficult changes (Hayes, Strosahl, Bunting, Twohig, & Wilson, 2004). We ask each partner to complete a values clarification exercise similar to that described by Wilson, Sandoz, Kitchens, and Roberts (2010). A copy of the exercise we use is presented in Appendix 11.A.

During this exercise, each partner is asked to identify things that are important to him/her (e.g., being a good mother, being a good husband) and indicate how much his/her actions reflect this value (Strosahl, Hayes, Wilson, & Gifford, 2004). Oftentimes, clients will state that they value being a good partner and will acknowledge that their behavior does not always reflect this value. It is helpful to ask partners to clarify what behaviors reflect this value and what behaviors might go against this value. Through this process, couples are able to identify goals for change that will help them live more aligned with their values (Strosahl et al., 2004). Referring to these values periodically throughout treatment can help maintain the couple's motivation to change.

Strategies for change

After the initial screening the focus shifts to training in change strategies. The majority of couples seen in our clinic are ready for action-oriented change strategies, as opposed to those designed to move them out of the contemplation stage. A social problem-solving framework

(Nezu, 2004) is used to organize change strategies. The basic goal is to help couples to work together to effectively resolve daily hassles and larger, more long-term problems to decrease the likelihood of relying on aggressive or violent problem-solving strategies. Couples develop a productive orientation toward dealing with relationship problems and develop the realistic skills necessary to resolve current and future problems. Below we provide an outline of skills that are typically taught during the course of treatment.

Problem orientation phase   Positive self-efficacy and outcome expectancies facilitate adaptive coping with problems and reduce affective distress, whereas negative self-efficacy and expectancies about problem-solving outcomes facilitate poor strategies for solving problems and increase affective distress (Bandura, 1997). Targets for treatment during this phase involve changing emotional reactions and outcome expectancies that arise when dealing with relationship problems, and the shaping of a rational problem-solving style.

Changing thoughts and emotions related to relationship problems involves a shift from the belief that relationship problems indicate personal failures to an acceptance that relationship problems are normative. Exploring each partner's learning history, with a particular focus on how their parents resolved marital problems and how problems were managed in past relationships, can create an understanding of how their current relationship expectancies and problem-solving skills were learned. Understanding the genesis of relationship expectancies and problem-solving skills tends to decrease dysfunctional personal attributions for current relationship concerns. During this exploration it is important to avoid "gunny sacking" or having partners simply provide lists of times when they felt wronged in the past. The goal is to foster a movement away from ascribing relationship problems to stable personal or external factors, and toward more changeable processes such as learning.

Exercises that leverage cognitive dissonance can facilitate attitude change by having couples discuss real problems they are experiencing while the treatment provider plays "devil's advocate" by arguing why the problems can never be resolved. The couple's job is to argue why the problems are solvable. Regardless of the strategies employed, the goal is to move the couple toward an understanding that relationship problems are a normal part of life, that skills for resolving relationship problems in a non-violent manner can be learned, and that spending time resolving relationship problems will enhance their relationship.

Couples with a negative orientation toward problem-solving often believe that the same problems will keep recurring, problems in the relationship are abnormal and a sign of failure, and that they lack the skills necessary to resolve relationship problems in a healthy manner. A negative orientation toward problem-solving leads to entrenched and non-productive patterns of interaction. Couples commonly interpret strong emotional reactions, failure to immediately have one's needs met, and a partner's dissatisfaction as a global sign that the relationship is dysfunctional. The role of the treatment provider is to reconceptualize these reactions as commonly occurring experiences that serve as a cue that problems exist. Reframing these reactions can help to decrease the intensity of the emotions experienced when problems arise. Encouraging couples to generate examples of when they successfully solved problems together can help to modify negative attributions about their joint problem-solving abilities.

If couples repeat the same pattern of behaviors when attempting to resolve relationship problems, we highlight for them that this reflects a specific problem-solving style. Nezu (2004) identified two problematic problem-solving styles: *avoidant* and *impulsive/careless*. Couples who adopt an avoidant style delay solving problems until the problems intensify or worsen. This avoidant style is often reflected by a statement like "*We'll just have to see what happens.*"

We find it important to help couples rethink this style and we might comment "*nothing begets nothing*," or "*I wonder if adopting a more active strategy could be more helpful?*" It is important to have couples approach, as opposed to avoid, relationship problems.

When confronted by distressing or high-conflict situations, couples who employ an impulsive/careless style often act on the first solution that comes to their mind. In couples with a history of aggressive responding, it is common for the initial solution to a high-conflict situation to be an emotionally derived response best characterized as malicious, aggressive, or violent. Couples that demonstrate an impulsive/careless approach often benefit from training in emotion regulation strategies such as arousal reduction or mindfulness-based interventions. We routinely train such couples in controlled breathing and relaxation exercises as a means of controlling their arousal levels and inhibiting their impulsivity. As noted previously, we often reframe negative affect as a cue that a problem exists, thereby reconceptualizing emotional reactions as part of the problem-solving process rather than a problem in and of itself. Action-oriented strategies designed to decrease impulsive responding include training in conflict management and the use of positive reinforcement. One conflict management strategy we have found useful is to train partners to repeat or reflect back requests. This provides the partner time to think about the request and also acknowledges that the request was heard. Partners are also taught behavioral principles of reinforcement and employ these principles to shape desired behaviors. For instance, if one partner likes when her spouse helps with the dishes, she would reward him by saying or doing something he would like, such as saying thank you or engaging in another positive exchange. Behavioral exchanges such as these provide short-term gains and promote bonding, which is essential for partners to work together to effectively resolve relationship concerns (Hamel, 2005).

The overall goal during this phase of treatment is to have couples adopt a rational problem-solving style whereby they engage in systematic application of effective problem-solving strategies. Modification of negative attitudes about relationship problems is also accomplished through instruction in effective problem-solving skills. The next phase of treatment involves training couples in these skills for resolving problems.

Problem-solving skills phase During this phase of treatment couples receive training in defining and formulating relationship problems, generating solutions to relationship problems, and in deciding which solutions to implement. Effective strategies suggested for resolving problems have been reasonably well articulated (e.g., American Psychological Association, 2008; D'Zurilla & Nezu, 2010). Training in assertiveness, conflict management, and other coping skills is interwoven into this training. Learning new skills instills confidence in a discouraged couple.

A typical strategy involves having each partner develop a list of problems that resulted in past arguments and ranking the problems using a four-point scale to indicate the degree to which discussing the problem results in an argument. Our experience is that violent couples can typically identify these "hot button" problems. If couples have difficulty generating a list of problems that resulted in past arguments, then problems identified during agenda setting can be used, or the treatment provider can provide a list of problems commonly reported by violent couples (we use the Couple Arguments Scale, presented in Appendix 11.B). The treatment provider guides the couple in discussing differences in the problems identified by each partner and encourages a comparison of the ratings. Comparison of the ratings facilitates a discussion of problems that each partner considers significant and fosters an understanding of each partner's point of view. Difficulties arise when one partner is unwilling to accept a problem identified by their mate or discounts their partner's rating. Communication training and empathic listening skills are often taught during this exercise.

A hierarchy of the aggregated problem ratings is developed to train couples in several key strategies used to define problems. It is common to begin training with the problem rated least likely to result in an argument and to work up the hierarchy. Couples are trained to "stop and think" when they identify a problem and to separate facts from assumptions. Additional strategies include having the couple ask the following questions when confronted by a problem: "*What is the problem? Who has the problem? When is it a problem? Where is it a problem?*" The aim is to have each problem stated in concrete terms. Instead of vaguely defining a problem as "*We have a terrible relationship*," the couples are encouraged to describe the specific nature of the problem such as "*We fight whenever we are paying the bills and talk about money.*" Another important component is to identify the problem-solving goal. One way to figure out the goal is to ask, "*What will be different when the problem is solved?*" For instance, "*How do we keep from fighting when we talk about finances?*"

The same issues used to train couples in defining and formulating problems are used to train couples in how to generate solutions to problems and how to decide on which solutions to use for resolving them. It is common for couples who have experienced violence to go with the first solutions that come to mind. For couples with recent histories of negative interactions, the most readily available solutions are often emotion-based and less effective than solutions that arise from deliberate thought and mutual decision-making. Couples are taught that the more ideas they generate the greater the likelihood of effectively resolving the problem. This is based on the role played by availability heuristics and because several ideas with low individual ratings can often be combined to result in a strategy with high efficacy for problem resolution. For example, a couple experiencing financial difficulties may find that monitoring their spending is not enough to correct the problem but can be part of an effective strategy when combined with other solutions, such as paying off high-interest credit cards and using cash rather than debit or credit cards.

Another important component involves training couples in separating idea production from decision-making. Oftentimes couples try to generate ideas and evaluate the ideas simultaneously and this results in their dismissing ideas that could prove useful. This process is operative when one partner generates potential solutions to problems while the other partner argues why the ideas are inadequate. A better approach is to encourage each partner to generate as many ideas as possible and save comments on the utility of each idea until the decision-making phase. When discussing solutions to problems it is important for the treatment provider to keep the above-mentioned principles in mind and to reinforce the generation of many possible solutions to each problem.

Training in a utility model of decision-making takes place after couples have generated solutions for resolving a problem. Couples are taught to rate each solution for the degree to which it meets several criteria including: short-term benefit; long-term benefit; consistency with each partner's values; emotional cost; time/effort required; financial cost; effects on family; and effects on friends. The highest rated solutions combine to develop a strategy that enhances the probability of both short-term and long-term gains. Couples often develop strategies that require training in assertiveness, communication, or conflict management skills prior to implementation with a high fidelity. Role-playing is used to train these interpersonal skills, and we have developed a video to highlight the importance of mastering these skills.

The video contains 10 vignettes that depict individuals involved in interpersonal conflicts. Each vignette focuses on a different aspect of the problem-solving model or interpersonal skills and highlights problems that can arise when these skills are not used. For example, one vignette depicts a couple involved in an argument, talking over one another, and visibly not listening to each other as the argument escalates. This video is used to highlight the importance of effective communication skills and reflective listening. Group members are asked to discuss: (i) What happened in the video? (ii) What was the problem? (iii) What made the problem worse? and (iv) What might have helped the problem?

In addition to training in interpersonal skills and problem-solving, sometimes the solution requires more long-term inputs that might involve consultation with other treatment providers. For example, a couple with a blended family and discrepant parenting styles might report that discussions about discipline strategies frequently escalate to aggressive exchanges. The couple might identify the following short-term strategies for discussing discipline strategies: (i) remain seated at opposite ends of the kitchen table when discussing discipline strategies; (ii) agree that child discipline strategies must be discussed prior to their being used; (iii) listen to each other's opinions about parenting strategies for two minutes without interruption and then allow the other person two minutes to share their opinion; and (iv) maintain a focus on the desired behavioral outcome. An associated long-term strategy might involve participating in a parent-training program. For helpful criteria for developing problem-solving worksheets see the Marital Problem Solving Worksheets Guidelines in Appendix 11.C.

Throughout treatment the focus is on teaching couples how to implement effective problem-solving skills. Attitudes, beliefs, and emotions that interfere with effectively resolving relationship problems are also changed. Couples are reinforced for their attempts and successes at resolving relationship problems in a rational manner. The learning of effective problem-solving skills is directly assessed in session and in the real environment through the use of homework assignments. Treatment is complete when couples and the treatment provider agree that the couple has learned the skills necessary to engage in joint problem-solving without violence, and both partners feel comfortable implementing the skills in their everyday interactions and during high-conflict situations.

References

American Psychological Association (2008). *Systems of Psychotherapy Video Series: Problem Solving Therapy*. Washington, DC: APA Press.

Anderson, C. A., & Bushman, B. J. (2002). Human aggression. *Annual Review of Psychology, 53*, 27–51. doi: 10.1146/annurev.psych.53.100901.135231

Anderson, C. A., & Carnagey, N. L. (2004). Violent evil and the general aggression model. In A. Miller (Ed.), *The social psychology of good and evil* (pp. 168–192). New York, NY: Guilford Publications.

Babcock, J. C., Canady, B., Graham, K. H., & Schart, L. (2007). The evolution of battering interventions: From the dark ages into the scientific age. In J. Hamel & T. Nicholls (Eds.), *Family therapy for domestic violence: A practitioner's guide to gender-inclusive research and treatment* (pp. 215–244). New York, NY: Springer.

Babcock, J. C., Green, C. E., & Robie, C. (2004). Does batterers' treatment work? A meta-analytic review of domestic violence treatment. *Clinical Psychology Review, 23*, 1023–1053. doi: 10.1016/j.cpr.2002.07.001

Bandura, A. (1997). *Self-efficacy: The exercise of control*. New York: W. H. Freeman.

Baucom, D. H., Epstein, N. B., La Taillade, J. J., & Kirby, J. S. (2008). Cognitive-behavioral couple therapy. In A. S. Gurman (Ed.), *Clinical handbook of couple therapy* (4th ed., pp. 31–72). New York, NY: Guilford Press.

Chase, K. A., O'Farrell, T. J., Murphy, C. M., Fals-Stewart, W., & Murphy, M. (2003). Factors associated with partner violence among female alcoholic patients and their male partners. *Journal of Studies on Alcohol, 64,* 137–149.

Date, A., & Ronan, G. F. (2000). An examination of attitudes and behaviors presumed to mediate partner abuse: A rural incarcerated sample. *Journal of Interpersonal Violence, 15,* 1140–1155. doi: 10.1177/088626000015011002

De Jong, P., & Berg, I. K. (1998). *Interviewing for solutions.* Pacific Grove, CA: Brooks/Cole.

DeWall, C. N., & Anderson, C. A. (2011). The General Aggression Model. In P. R. Shaver & M. Mikulincer (Eds.), *Human aggression and violence: Causes, manifestations, and consequences* (pp. 15–33). Washington, D.C.: American Psychological Association.

DeWall, C. N., Anderson, C. A., & Bushman, B. J. (2011). The General Aggression Model: Theoretical extensions to violence. *Psychology of Violence, 1,* 245–258. doi: 10.1037/a0023842

D'Zurilla, T. J., & Nezu, A. M. (2010). Problems solving therapy. In K. S. Dobson (Ed.), *Handbook of cognitive-behavioral therapies* (3rd ed., pp. 197–225). New York, NY: Guilford Press.

Eckhardt, C. I., & Schram, J. (2009). Cognitive behavioral interventions for partner-abusive men. In P. Lehmann & C. A. Simmons (Eds.), *Strengths-based batterer intervention: A new paradigm in ending family violence* (pp. 137–188). New York, NY: Springer.

Epstein, N. B., Werlinich, C. A., La Taillade, J. J., Hoskins, L. H., Dezfulian, T., Kursch, M. K., et al. (2005, October). *Couple therapy for domestic abuse: A cognitive-behavioral approach. Paper presented at the annual convention of the American Association for Marriage and Family Therapy,* Kansas City, MO.

Fals-Stewart, W., Kashdan, T. B., O'Farrell, T. J., & Birchler, G. R. (2002). Behavioral couples therapy for drug-abusing patients: Effects on partner violence. *Journal of Substance Abuse Treatment, 22,* 87–96. doi: 10.1016/S0740-5472(01)00218-5

Fals-Stewart, W., Klostermann, K., & Clinton-Sherrod, M. (2009). Substance abuse and intimate partner violence: In K. D. O'Leary & E. M. Woodin (Eds.), *Psychological and physical aggression in couples: Causes and interventions* (pp. 251–270). Washington DC: American Psychological Association.

First, M. B, Gibbon, M., Spitzer, R. L., Williams, J. B., & Benjamin, L. S. (1997). *User's Guide for The Structured Clinical Interview for DSM-IV Axis II Personality Disorders.* Arlington, VA: American Psychiatric Publishing.

Hamel, J. (2005). *Gender-inclusive treatment of intimate partner abuse: A comprehensive approach.* New York, NY: Springer.

Hayes, S. C., Strosahl, K. D., Bunting, K., Twohig, M., & Wilson, K. (2004). What is acceptance and commitment therapy? In S. C. Hayes & K. D. Strosahl (Eds.), *A practical guide to acceptance and commitment therapy* (pp. 1–30). New York, NY: Springer.

Heru, A. M. (2007). Intimate partner violence: Treating abuser and abused. *Advances in Psychiatric Treatment: Journal of Continuing Professional Development, 13,* 376–383. doi: 10.1192/apt.bp.107.003749

Gondolf, E. W. (2007). Theoretical and research support for the Duluth model: A reply to Dutton and Corvo. *Aggression and Violent Behavior, 12,* 644–657. doi: 10.1016/j.avb.2007.03.001

Gurman, A. S. (2008). Integrative couple therapy: A depth-behavioral approach. In A. S. Gurman (Ed.), *Clinical handbook of couple therapy* (4th ed., pp. 383–423). New York, NY: Guilford Press.

La Taillade, J. J., Epstein, N. B., & Werlinich, C. A. (2006). Conjoint treatment of intimate partner violence: A cognitive behavioral approach. *Journal of Cognitive Psychotherapy: An International Quarterly, 20,* 393–410. doi: 10.1891/jcpiq-v20i4a005

Lehmann, P., & Simmons, C. A. (2009). The state of batterer intervention programs: An analytical discussion. In P. Lehmann & C. A. Simmons (Eds.), *Strengths-based batterer intervention: A new paradigm in ending family violence* (pp. 3–38). New York, NY: Springer.

McConnaughy, E. A., Prochaska, J. O., & Velicer, W. F. (1983). Stages of change in psychotherapy: measurement and sample profiles. *Psychotherapy: Theory, Research and Practice, 20*, 368–375. doi: 10.1037/h0090198

McConnaughy, E. A., Prochaska, J. O., & Velicer, W. F. (1989). Stages of change in psychotherapy: A follow-up report. *Psychotherapy, 26*, 494–503. doi: 10.1037/h0085468

Meis, L. A., Murphy, C., & Winter, J. J. (2010). Outcome expectancies of partner abuse: Assessing perpetrators' expectancies and their associations with readiness to change, abuse, and relevant problems. *Assessment, 17*, 30–43. doi: 10.1177/1073191109343514

Nezu, A. M. (2004). Problem-solving and behavior therapy revisited. *Behavior Therapy, 35*, 1–33.

Nezu, A. M., & Nezu, C. M. (1989). *Clinical decision making in behavior therapy: A problem-solving perspective.* Champaign, IL: Research Press.

O'Farrell, T. J. (1999). Behavioral couples therapy for alcoholism and drug abuse. *Psychiatric Times, 16*. Retrieved from http://www.psychosocial.com/addiction/bct.html

O'Farrell, T. J., Murphy, C. M., Stephan, S. H., Fals-Stewart, W., & Murphy, M. (2004). Partner violence before and after couples-based alcoholism treatment for male alcoholic patients: The role of treatment involvement and abstinence. *Journal of Consulting and Clinical Psychology, 72*, 202–217. doi: 10.1037/0022-006X.72.2.202

Robertson, K., & Murachver, T. (2007). Correlates of partner violence for incarcerated women and men. *Journal of Interpersonal Violence, 22*, 639–655. doi: 10.1177/0886260506298835

Ronan, G. F., Dreer, L. E., Dollard, K. M., & Ronan, D. W. (2004). Violent couples: Coping and communication skills. *Journal of Family Violence, 19*, 131–137. doi: 10.1023/B:JOFV.0000019843.26331.cf

Ronan, G., Gerhart, J., Bannister, D., & Udell, C. (2010). Relevance of stage of change analysis for violence reduction. *Journal of Forensic Psychiatry and Psychology, 21*, 761–722. doi: 10.1080/14789949.2010.483285

Rondeau, G., Brodeur, N., Brochu, S., & Lemire, G. (2001). Dropout and completion of treatment among spouse abusers. *Violence and Victims, 16*, 127–143.

Spanier, G. B. (1976). Measuring dyadic adjustment: New scales for assessing the quality of marriage and similar dyads. *Journal of Marriage & the Family, 38*, 15–28. doi: 10.2307/350547

Stith, S. M., & McCollum, E. E. (2009). Couples treatment for psychological and physical aggression. In K. D. O'Leary & E. M. Woodin (Eds.), *Psychological and physical aggression in couples: Causes and interventions* (pp. 233–250). Washington D.C.: American Psychological Association.

Stith, S. M., McCollum, E. E., & Rosen, K. H. (2011). *Couples therapy for domestic violence: Finding safe solutions.* Washington, DC: American Psychological Association.

Stith, S. M., Rosen, K. H., McCollum, E. E., & Thomsen, C. J. (2004). Treating intimate partner violence within intact couple relationships: Outcomes of multi-couple versus individual couple therapy. *Journal of Marital and Family Therapy. Special Issue: Implications of Research with Diverse Families, 30*, 305–318. doi: 10.1111/j.1752-0606.2004.tb01242.x

Stover, C., Meadows, A. L., & Kaufman, J. (2009). Interventions for intimate partner violence: Review and implications for evidence-based practice. *Professional Psychology: Research and Practice, 40*, 223–233. doi: 10.1037/a0012718

Straus, M. A., Hamby, S. L., Boney-McCoy, S., & Sugarman, D. B. (1996). The revised Conflict Tactics Scales (CTS2): Development and preliminary psychometric data. *Journal of Family Issues, 17*, 283–316. doi: 10.1177/019251396017003001

Strosahl, K. D., Hayes, S. C., Wilson, K. G., & Gifford, E. V. (2004). An ACT primer: Core therapy processes, intervention strategies, and therapist competencies. In S. C. Hayes & K. D. Strosahl (Eds.), *A practical guide to acceptance and commitment therapy* (pp. 31–58). New York, NY: Springer.

Webster, C. D., Douglas, K. S., Eaves, D., & Hart, S. D. (1997). *HCR-20: Assessing risk for violence. Version 2.* Burnaby, BC, Canada: Simon Fraser University and Forensic Psychiatric Services Commission of British Columbia.

Wilson, K. G., Sandoz, E. K., Kitchens, J., & Roberts, M. (2010). The valued living questionnaire: Defining and measuring valued action within a behavioral framework. *The Psychological Record, 60*, 249–272.

Suggestions for Further Learning

Books

Ronan, G.F., Dreer, L., Maurelli, K., Ronan, D. W., & Gerhart, J. (2013). Practitioner's Guide to Empirically Supported Measures of Anger, Aggression, and Violence. New York, NY: Springer.

Stith, S. M., McCollum, E. E., & Rosen, K. H. (2011). *Couples therapy for domestic violence: Finding safe solutions.* Washington, DC: American Psychological Association.

Journal articles

Gerhart, J. I., Ronan, G.F., Russ, E.U., & Seymour, B. (2013). The moderating effects of Cluster B personality traits on violence reduction training: A mixed model analysis. *Journal of Interpersonal Violence, 28,* 45–61.

Ronan, G. F., Gerhart, J., Banister, D., & Udell, C. (2010). Relevance of a stage of change analysis for violence reduction training. *Journal of Forensic Psychiatry and Psychology, 21,* 761–772.

Appendix 11.A

Values Assessment Exercise

Please complete the following using three different steps:

Complete the first column using a scale of 1 to 10, with 1 indicating "not important at all" and 10 indicating "extremely important" and rate how important the value is to you.

Complete the second column, using a scale of 1 to 10, with 1 indicating "never do anything related to that value" to 10 "always act in accordance with that value" and rate how often you act consistent with the value.

Complete the third column by subtracting column 1 from column 2. This score will indicate how closely aligned your behaviors are with your values.

Value	Importance score	Action score	Discrepancy score (+ or −)
I value having good health			
I value being a good parent			
I value being a good partner (marriage/intimate relationship)			
I value being a good friend			
I value being a good son/daughter			
I value being a good grandson/daughter, uncle, aunt, nephew, niece, cousin			
I value being a good employee			
I value the environment and nature			
I value animals			
I value art and music			
I value knowledge/learning			
I value financial security (retirement, money for kid's college)			
I value having pleasure and fun			
I value material things (cars, clothes)			
I value fame			
I value justice/fairness			
I value charity/community service			
I value diversity/multiculturalism			
I value inner peace			
I value physical beauty			
Other values:			
Other values:			

Appendix 11.B

Couple Arguments Scale

The following is a list of problems that many couples face. We would like you to rate how often a discussion of the problem listed below results in an argument. If problems other than those listed below result in arguments, please list them in the space provided.

4. Always Results in an Argument
3. Sometimes Results in an Argument
2. Rarely Results in an Argument
1. Never Results in an Argument

____ My mate is unfaithful to me.
____ My mate is critical of me.
____ My mate wants too much contact with me.
____ My mate wants too little contact with me.
____ My mate is sexually distant.
____ My mate is not affectionate.
____ I am ashamed of my mate's occupation.
____ My mate doesn't make enough money.
____ My mate doesn't care well for the children.
____ My mate is attracted to others.
____ My mate doesn't support my ambitions.
____ I have different beliefs from my mate.
____ My mate and I have problems with money.
____ My mate and I disagree about whether to have children.
____ I dislike my mate's friends.
____ My mate doesn't like my friends.
____ My mate nags me frequently.
____ My mate does not help with household chores.
____ My mate has different religious beliefs.
____ I dislike dealing with my mate's parents or in-laws.
____ My mate has different goals, values, and things believed to be important.
____ My mate makes major decisions without discussing the matter with me beforehand.
____ My mate doesn't spend much of his/her free time or leisure time with me.
____ My mate and I have differing philosophies in life.
____ Other problems _____

Appendix 11.C

Marital Problem-Solving Worksheets Guidelines

Problem orientation

Briefly describe the situation:

How do you know you have a problem?

1. What are your thoughts?
2. What are your behaviors/physical actions?
3. What are your emotions/feelings?

Defining and formulating problems

Briefly describe the problem (remember to be concrete and specific):

1. What are the facts?
2. What are the assumptions?
3. Answer these questions:
   a. Who has the problem?
   b. What is the problem?
   c. Where is it the problem?
   d. When is it a problem?
4. What is your goal?

Generation of alternatives

Remember: Don't judge, be creative. Be concrete and always ask yourself, "*Does this alternative help me meet my goal?*"

The goal for resolving this problem is:

List ideas for solving the problem:

Decision-making

Rate all solutions with a plus or minus according to the criteria below:

List of solutions	Short term	Long term	Time/ effort	Feelings	Morals	Physical well-being	Money	Family	Friends	Society	Total	Will it work?

Solution implementation and verification

Briefly describe the problem:

Briefly describe the strategy for resolving the problem:

Briefly describe what you expect to happen:

Briefly describe what actually happened:

What's next?

Section 3

Two Perspectives on the Treatment of Addictions

12

An Integrated REBT-Based Approach to the Treatment of Addicted Offenders

F. Michler Bishop

Therapy and counseling until very recently were mostly psychodynamic and still are in many institutions. Specific, research-based ways to help people change and/or accept the way they think, feel, and behave were not at all prevalent 30 years ago and are still not the norm.

Cognitive-behavioral therapy (CBT) and its most prominent variations, cognitive therapy (CT), rational emotive behavior therapy (REBT), mindfulness-based CBT, dialectical behavior therapy (DBT), and acceptance and commitment therapy (ACT), all offer an advantage to clients who have multiple psychological and behavioral issues (Landenberger & Lipsey, 2005; Lipsey, Landenberger, & Wilson, 2007). What clients learn about better regulating their emotions can be directly applied to regulating their urges to drink or engage in other types of self-destructive and addictive behaviors.

REBT, in particular, is very user friendly. People understand what it is to think and act irrationally. They also understand the need to practice if they want to get better at something, whether it be basketball, anger management, or sobriety. Finally, REBT works extremely well in groups, and a tremendous amount of helpful material (e.g., worksheets, articles, podcasts, self-help books) can be easily accessed and used by correctional counselors, therapists, and psychologists.

The present chapter outlines an integrated, REBT-based, motivation-enhancing approach to treating addiction problems in offenders in community corrections and prison-based settings. The approach is integrated in two ways. First, all good therapy integrates four basic components: (i) an empathetic style leading to an effective therapeutic relationship; (ii) a discussion of past events helping to motivate clients in the present; (iii) effective evidence-based techniques; and (iv) a focus on future goals and values. There is ample research demonstrating that an empathetic style is critical to building an effective, therapeutic working relationship. In addition, addictions often have their roots in the past. Exploring the past with clients helps motivate them to free themselves from present-day, destructive responses. However, too much focus on the past is often inefficient and ineffective. Consequently, the bulk of the chapter focuses on a second kind of integration; the integration of techniques clustered under six headings: behavioral, emotive, cognitive, interpersonal, spiritual/existential,

Forensic CBT: A Handbook for Clinical Practice, First Edition.
Edited by Raymond Chip Tafrate and Damon Mitchell.
© 2014 John Wiley & Sons, Ltd. Published 2014 by John Wiley & Sons, Ltd.

and chemical/nutritional. In sum, effective techniques, taught in an empathetic manner, with respect for past events and with a focus on future goals and values, enhance a person's motivation to change, and make therapy faster and more effective.

Conceptualizing Motivation for Addicted Offenders

With clients who are involved in the criminal justice system, the goal of the first session is to get a second session. Practitioners who work in the field of addictions have to work to motivate their clients to return. Clients will not do things that are discomforting and perhaps frightening – such as trying to get through a day without prescription medications like Xanax and Oxycontin or alcohol (or all three) – without having some very good reasons for doing so. What might motivate an offender to learn a better way to manage his or her addictive problems and negative emotions? There must be a sense that all the work – because it does take a lot of work, week in and week out, to learn various REBT techniques – will pay off in the future. Many REBT and CBT practitioners who treat addictive disorders have wisely embraced motivational interviewing (MI) and integrated it into their practices. Although MI is not synonymous with the Rogerian approach to therapy, it is client-centered and shares some of its underlying principles. For example, a principle underlying all Rogerian therapy is that humans are basically good. Give them a setting (your office) where they can experience "unconditional regard" and they will gradually figure out how to improve their lives. Miller and his associates (Miller & Rollnick, 2002) clearly embrace this view. They have worked primarily with problem drinkers, and the approach appears to work especially well with such clients. On the other hand, there are clients who can benefit from a more direct, coaching-like approach. A baseball player could, theoretically, figure out how to hit the ball better, but direct coaching will definitely speed up the learning process. The therapeutic alliance often develops more quickly and more sturdily when therapists offer concrete techniques, and REBT has many such techniques to offer.

REBT was not initially designed with motivation as a central focus. Ellis (1962, 1994) started working with people with sexual problems who presumably wanted (i.e., they were motivated) to get over their problems. Similarly, anyone who volunteered at Ellis' famous and long-running Friday night workshops was already motivated to change; he or she wanted a push, and Ellis was more than willing to oblige, with a combination of explicit REBT/CBT techniques and with many empathetic and encouraging jokes and smiles. He was well aware that clients had to commit to practicing the techniques he taught them and that motivation was definitely necessary. He would often say, "*You can do whatever you want, but if you want to be HAPPIER* [BIG smile toward the client], *practice this exercise 10 times a day – or 10,000 times a day!*" But motivation was not central to his approach, and he spoke little about it.

It is helpful to think of clients with addictive problems as coming in three varieties, based loosely on the Stages of Change model (Prochaska, DiClemente & Norcross, 1992). Some clients do not see themselves as having a substance abuse problem; from their perspective, it is the police or their spouse who has a problem. However, most clients are ambivalent. They know they have a problem but are conflicted. They want to go on drinking/using as long as they can get away with it *and* they want better relationships and, in general, a less miserable life. Finally, some clients have an addictive problem, and they acknowledge that fact *and* they want to change. But they have not been able to do so.

Most clients with an addiction have multiple problems. They use crack, abuse alcohol, gamble, get in fights, have difficulties with their relationships, and break the law in a variety of ways. However, they may not be in the same stage of change on each problem. That is, they may acknowledge that they have a problem with heroin, but they do not think that they have a problem with alcohol, anger management, or gambling. They have even more difficulty acknowledging that they may have been grappling with other forms of mental illness for a long time, for example, dysthymia, attention-deficit hyperactivity disorder, post-traumatic stress disorder, and bipolar disorders. With respect to some problems, they are not motivated at all to change; with respect to others, they are under-motivated; and with respect to still others, they are motivated, although not on all days and in all settings.

The past can be used to motivate the present. One of the distinguishing features of REBT is the view of how past experiences and struggles affect present emotions and behaviors. Ellis focused on the current problem and what clients were *saying to themselves* about past events. But in considering past experiences, some people have a lot more to "tell" about than others, and what they have to overcome may challenge and overwhelm them. Criminal justice involvement may be one result. No one likes to be a prisoner either literally or figuratively. Once clients start to grapple with their past and acknowledge that their reactions to past events may be undercutting their efforts to change, they frequently become more motivated to learn *how* to free themselves from these reactions.

Personality disorders may make treatment more challenging, and practitioners will certainly encounter offenders who will meet the DSM-IV-R criteria for antisocial, narcissistic, borderline, and/or histrionic personality disorder (Wulach, 1988). Many years ago Yochelson and Samenow (1976, 1977) coined the term "criminal personality" for such people. Others use the term "psychopath." The potential for rehabilitating such people is probably slim, but, at the same time, the proportion of such people in a correctional facility may be small. There is a much larger group of people who are open to if not overtly motivated to better manage their emotions and lives in order to move forward. Specifically, many of the people who were incarcerated in the past 20 years for drug possession and other drug-related offenses do not have a "criminal personality" and/or meet the DSM-IV-R criteria mentioned above. However, as has been pointed out by a number of researchers (e.g. Dadds et al., 2009), some clients who exhibit psychopathic characteristics, especially males, learn as they grow older how to "talk the talk" and act *as if* they empathize and feel as other humans do. In working with forensic populations, this is something that therapists and counselors need to keep in mind.

An Integrated, Six-Pronged Approach

The most significant change in psychotherapy over the past 50 years has been the movement away from a reliance on insight as the mechanism of change. Historically, it was believed that if people understood why they did what they did, they would change. The predominant focus now is on *how*, and the focus of most cognitive and behavioral research has been on developing evidence-based, effective techniques.

Techniques should be used with two goals in mind: (i) increasing and maintaining motivation to change, and (ii) teaching clients how to manage aspects of their lives better:

- the way they think, feel, and behave;
- their interpersonal relationships;
- their use of chemicals, both legal and illegal, and their nutritional habits;
- their relationship to a higher power or higher principles, including long-term goals and values.

The remainder of this chapter is devoted to outlining a variety of techniques in each area. Of course, doing anything in one domain, for example, learning to do an ABC exercise, affects the other domains. Just because I have placed an exercise in the cognitive domain does not mean it will not affect the way a client feels or acts; it will.

Prong 1: behavioral techniques

The goal of the treatment for addictions is *behavior* change. Without necessarily realizing it, many therapists want to help their clients *feel* better. However, that goal may get in the way of helping their clients *behave* better. In fact, learning to moderate or overcome an addictive behavior almost always involves increased *discomfort*, rather than feeling better, especially in the first few days, weeks, and months. Consequently, in all sessions including the first one, the focus should be on the behavioral goal and on techniques designed to achieve it. The following five tools may help.

(a) Set goals   What does your client want? What is the goal of therapy? Psychoanalytic therapy was predicated on the theory that client problems were fueled by repressed material. Clients were not asked what they wanted to work on because they *could not* know what they needed to work on. The theory made that clear. The problem had been repressed many years and thus could not be known. A patient couldn't just consciously state it. Rogers and Ellis (and Adler before them) did not accept this theory. They believed in asking clients what they wanted to work on and proceeding from there.

Good treatment inevitably inquires about a person's goals and values. Therapists used "value clarification" exercises in the 1960s and 1970s, and Ellis in almost every demonstration and lecture spoke about the importance of having an "all-consuming vital interest" in one's life, but there was no effort to build empirical support for this position. ACT is currently perhaps the most explicit and overt about the importance of values, and Hayes and his colleagues (Hayes, Strosahl, & Wilson, 1999) have done the important work of building an empirical base of support for such an approach. Amrod and Hayes (see Chapter 3) discuss the use of ACT with offenders in further detail.

Goal setting is particularly important in the treatment of addictions. Does the client want to stop or moderate? Clients who are incarcerated may still find a way to access a variety of drugs, so the question is not absurd even in prison. And once out of prison, what are the goals?

The extent to which a practitioner can develop an effective therapeutic relationship in a correctional setting may depend more on his or her own qualities, characteristics that Rogers referred to as genuineness, authenticity, and the capacity to give unconditional regard. Certainly, Rogers' *unconditional regard* and Ellis's *unconditional self-acceptance* and *unconditional other acceptance* when demonstrated by a therapist will encourage clients, even correctional clients, to be more forthcoming and work more seriously. Of course, some clients may try to take advantage of this type of therapeutic stance, and many will also test it.

(b) Develop a plan   Once goals are established, it may be helpful to develop a plan. The seven questions in Box 12.1 have been found very useful not only for assessing a client's commitment to change but also for increasing the likelihood that a client will get the behavior change that he or she wants. If that happens, all the discomforts inherent in going for treatment will have paid off.

> ### Box 12.1   Seven Questions to Help Develop a Plan for Change
>
> 1. *"What do you want?"* Ask the client to specify in detail what he/she wants to do... to moderate or stop completely? And if moderation is the goal, what would that look like? Clients are notoriously vague regarding specific behavior change.
> 2. *"When and where do you want the change to occur? In what settings? At what time of day?"*
> 3. *"How committed are you to this change, between 0 and 100?"* This will give you an idea of how serious a client is about this change plan.
> 4. *"How likely is it that you will stick to your plan, between 0 and 100?"* This provides another way of assessing intent.
> 5. *"How might you derail the plan?"* or *"What might you tell yourself to derail it?"*
> 6. *"What might you do (or we do) to increase the likelihood that you will stick to your plan?"*
> 7. *"What have we agreed on?"* This provides a final opportunity to assess whether or not the client is just going along with you or is really interested in changing a behavior.

(c) Teach relaxation techniques   When clients learn how to do deep diaphragmatic breathing or some other form of relaxation technique, they can manage their emotions better. There is now evidence that any repetitive practice, including meditation, prayers, even jogging, has a calming effect on the mind. The impact often lasts from 4 to 8 hours. During that period, people can think straighter and feel better, thereby decreasing the likelihood that they will turn to addictive behaviors to change their feelings.

(d) Encourage exercise   Author and Association for Behavioral and Cognitive Therapies award winner Anne Fletcher (2002) interviewed approximately 250 recovering addicts to find out how they had become sober, hence the title of her book, *Sober for Good*. She was once asked, "What did you discover that you had not expected?" She answered immediately, "Exercise. Almost everyone said that exercise was critical to his or her own recovery."

(e) Routinely assign homework   Homework has always been an integral part of REBT because it is assumed that clients have to practice in order to change an overlearned, harmful behavior. What they gain from a session of therapy will not be sufficient. Practicing *how* to think and feel and behave differently between sessions is vital.

One homework assignment that can be introduced early in treatment is to have the client maintain a log, such as a Drinking Log. A log is simply a record or tool to self-monitor behavior. Outside of a correctional setting, drinking logs are often very helpful at the beginning of therapy, not only as an assessment tool but also to help clients become more mindful of their behavior. The same technique can be very helpful with other types of behaviors, for example, with anger episodes. Although clients are routinely told not to change their behavior but only to record it, including the time and place, the behavior often changes dramatically just by bringing more mindfulness to the situation.

How information from the log is processed at the next therapy session can be very important. Clearly, clients may feel shame about what the log reveals and be hesitant to talk about it. The key is to be clear that you suggested the exercise to help both of you understand how serious the problem is, where and when it occurs, etc. As MI therapists know, how a therapist asks questions has a dramatic impact on the way a client feels and the kind of answers he or she gives. Closed-ended questions (questions that lead to yes/no answers) like: "*Did you complete the log?*" will probably a cause a client to feel as if he or she is being interrogated. Open-ended question such as "*What did you find?*" said in a non-judgmental tone work better.

Keeping a log often quickly moves people from wondering if they have a problem to actively wanting to do something about it. From a Stages of Change perspective, they move one or two stages. Such exercises also bring back attention and energy (mindfulness) to an activity that has become automatic.

Another homework assignment is called Sobriety Sampling. What is it like to go without a behavior even for a short while? What is it like to give up something for a day or every other day or for a week or a month? Many religions ask followers to give up something for a period of time. For example, Catholics at one time did not eat meat for the 40 days before Easter. Fasting, theoretically, brings communities together and helps individuals remember what they value and what is important to them.

Many clients with an addiction strongly believe that they cannot stand the discomfort of going a time period without taking a Vicodin or watching porn or having a drink. Sobriety sampling provides them with an opportunity to experiment. *How* can they best deal with the inevitable discomfort? They can practice observing their discomfort and responding in a different way. They can work on what REBT calls "low frustration tolerance" and DBT calls "distress tolerance." Sobriety sampling gives them a chance to learn *how* to respond to the discomfort with new, non-addictive behaviors, often planning ahead to do so. In doing so, they become more aware (and more mindful) of their own agency or self-efficacy, that is, the feeling that they *can*, in fact, do something difficult and uncomfortable, even perhaps intensely uncomfortable.

Prong 2: emotive techniques

Ellis (1962, 1994) initially called his type of treatment rational therapy, but quickly changed it to rational *emotive* therapy, recognizing the key role emotions play in human lives (changing it again in 1993 to rational emotive *behavioral* therapy after people pointed out for years the number of behavioral exercises and homework assignments he advocated). To this day, the most popular cognitive-behavioral therapies continue to implicitly discount the importance of emotions and to focus more on the cognitive and behavioral lives of their clients.

People engage in addictive behaviors to change the way they feel. They either want to feel better because they are experiencing some kind of negative emotion and they want to make it go away, or they want to feel better because they think – even though they feel good – that they should feel even better. People like the effect of addictive substances in the short run but not in the long run. For this reason, addictive behaviors are extremely difficult to change, even in the face of repeated, serious negative consequences, such as losing a job, the end of a relationship, and/or jail.

Although therapists need to focus on behavioral change, addictive behaviors are fueled by emotions. It is critically important to focus on the fuel as well as on the behavior. What will help cripple the fuel line? Three elements: (i) help the client become more aware of what he or she is feeling; (ii) help the client become more aware of the connection between his or her feelings and behaviors (and thinking/evaluating); and (iii) teach the client new ways to manage or accept common, everyday emotions. The following three exercises may help this process.

(a) Explore and decide on reasonable emotional goals   Emotional goals are common but not always recognized. A cognitive goal in therapy may be to think straighter, with fewer cognitive distortions or irrational beliefs. A behavioral goal may be to stop using crack. What are the emotional goals? In my office and in workshops, I ask people what they would like to feel in a normal day. Relaxed, calm, happy, appreciated, satisfied, and engaged are some of the common responses. Then I ask them how they felt the day before at the same time period. Anxious, irritated, tense, depressed, angry, and unsatisfied are common answers. There is a significant disconnect between what people report wanting to feel and what they actually feel.

Some of my clients try to fix that problem with pot or alcohol or some kind of off-label use of prescription medications. They think other people like you and me are relaxed and happy, so they want to be relaxed and happy. When I inform them that I am not feeling either of those emotions at that moment in the session, they are often surprised. At that point, we begin to work collaboratively on what might be reasonable emotional goals for them to shoot for... without using addictive behaviors to avoid or fix the problem. Then we discuss various ways they might accept or manage emotions that are negative and unpleasant but are, in fact, appropriate for what is going on. The ABC technique (see below) when practiced and learned provides them with a powerful tool to not get so upset in the first place and, if they do, provides a way to calm down.

(b) Rational Emotive Imagery (REI)   Can a client change the way he or she responds emotionally? Many psychodynamically trained therapists scoff at such an idea. But Ellis (1962, 1994) strongly believed that emotional responses, like behaviors, are learned and overlearned. To respond differently, a client has to practice learning a new response. But emotions often well up so quickly and are difficult to work on in the moment. REI provides a technique to help *feel different*, in response to a trigger situation that people can practice in their own time and space.

Ellis included REI in every demonstration of REBT. If the problem was anger management, he encouraged the client to imagine the typical trigger situations and to make herself feel intensely angry. When she had done so, she was told to raise her finger. Then he would instruct her to change her emotion to just intense concern and irritation (or what some REBT-ers call "functional anger"). Once she had indicated that she had done so, she was to raise her finger again. Then he asked her to explain *how* she had done it. He would then tell the person to do REI 10 times a day, and sometimes include a "reward" if she did it and a "penalty" if she did not. Prisoners have plenty of opportunities to get enraged or feel disrespected and/or to feel shame. They can do this exercise in their imagination many times a day and de-condition (unlearn) their typical emotional response and learn a new one. (Note: A discussion regarding what constitutes reasonable emotional goals should precede teaching the client REI.)

(c) Shame attacks   Shame underlies much addictive behavior but may not be discussed by counselors. Ellis advocated doing "shame attacks" to work on – again at one's own time and place – de-awfulizing shame. Partly to make his presentations lively, funny, and memorable, Ellis advocated what often sounded like fraternity hazing stunts, for example, *"Go into a pharmacy and, in an extra loud voice, ask for a gross of condoms...extra small!"* But shame attacks do not have to be of that nature. They can involve behaviors like having a client tell someone or a group that he or she has relapsed or talking about a traumatic event in the past.

Counselors in correctional facilities, especially working with younger prisoners, have often noted that their clients would do better if they experienced a little more shame and guilt. This is undoubtedly correct for some people, including people in prison. Consequently, deciding when and how much to work on shame requires careful ongoing assessment.

Prong 3: cognitive techniques

No doubt language constitutes humans' most powerful tool for change, including change in interpersonal relationships and self-change. Learning how to better manage behaviors, emotions, and even thoughts involves the use of language. The same is true for becoming better at interacting with other human beings. Everybody talks to himself or herself, and not in a psychotic manner. Consequently, Ellis (1962, 1994) and later Beck (1976) and others (Hayes et al., 1999; Linehan, 1993) based the focus of therapy on helping people change the way they talk to themselves.

Ellis maintained that the thoughts that caused the most problems were better thought of as *beliefs* – not simply *automatic thoughts* – because people were emotionally invested in them. Like religious beliefs, they believed them deeply and were often very resistant to changing them. Of course, all cognitive techniques also affect the way people feel and behave. I have categorized various techniques as "cognitive" or "emotive," simply because they seemed to more directly affect that aspect of human functioning. The following cognitive techniques may be helpful.

(a) ABC(DE) technique Many years ago, Ellis (1962, 1994) created the ABC technique. He created a self-help tool, something that psychoanalysts at the time thought simply ridiculous. It was, and is, extremely user friendly and works with individuals and especially well in groups. The first part, the ABC part, helps people learn to "diagnose" how their thinking is contributing to a current problem. The second part, the DE part, helps them develop ways to cope better going forward. The technique gives people not only a sense of control over the mayhem in their lives but also some modicum of real control. The ABC technique also helps therapists refocus an individual or group session that is wandering off track. A sample *ABCDE* worksheet is provided in Appendix 12.A.

Generally, it is best to start with the C. The C stands for **C**onsequence, an unfortunate word choice. Many of our clients immediately think of the consequences of drinking or drugging, like receiving a "driving under the influence" (DUI) citation and getting incarcerated. Time should be spent helping clients learn that the "C" usually stands for an unwanted behavior (like drinking) or emotion (like feeling angry or anxious). In some people, it may be obsessive thinking. Then work back in time and try to uncover the *B*s, the **B**eliefs, both rational and irrational or helpful and unhelpful, that contribute to, for example, drinking or feeling angry.

Finally, you will probably wind up talking about the *A*, the **A**ctivating event. But the whole session will not be devoted to "what happened" (the activating event), which is one of the strengths of the ABC technique. It helps people focus on what they *can* change, not on the past, which they cannot change. Some of the most typical irrational beliefs exhibited by people who get in trouble with addictive behaviors are presented in Box 12.2.

Rational beliefs (e.g., "*A drink would help me feel better*") are often mingled in with irrational beliefs. Working collaboratively with the client, a therapist's job is to help the client discover what is often hiding underneath what appear to be rational beliefs. For example, the unstated but implicit second half of the above belief is the irrational component "*and I can get away with it.*"

Box 12.2   Common Irrational Beliefs Associated with Addiction

1. *"I can get away with it."* This is not only the most common belief among prisoners but also among clients who have never been incarcerated. This belief almost always goes hand in hand with the next very common belief.
2. *"It won't matter."*

Other very common beliefs include…

3. *"I deserve it."*
4. *"I'm going to drink or use anyway, so I might as well not torture myself."*
5. *"I'll just have one (and feel the way I want to feel)."* Then when that doesn't work: *"I'll just have one more (and feel the way I want to feel)."* And when that doesn't work: *"I'll just have one more."* Eventually the internal chemistry changes so much that the game is over.
6. *"I can't stand the discomfort anymore,"* or *"I won't be able to stand the discomfort."*
7. *"I can stop any time."*
8. *"I'll stop tomorrow."*
9. *"I have not had something to drink for 15 days. Clearly, I have got it beat. I don't have a problem anymore."*
10. *"Everybody does it."*
11. *"If I don't use, I'll lose all of my friends."*
12. *"Screw it!"*

REBT therapists urge people to identify and question their irrational or automatic, distorted beliefs. However, it is important to acknowledge that the beliefs held by many prisoners about the fairness and reasonableness of the policies that imprisoned them are also held by many reasonable, presumably rational people outside of correctional facilities around the globe. In the United States, policies are definitely extreme compared to the rest of the world. For the past 20 years, partly as a result of the War on Drugs, the United States has imprisoned more citizens than any other country; at year end 2011, 492 sentenced prisoners per 100 000 US residents were incarcerated (Carson & Sabol, 2012). No other country approaches our numbers. England's rate of incarceration per 100 000 people is 154 and Germany's is 83 (International Centre for Prison Studies, 2013). In 2009, 18% of people incarcerated in US state prisons were serving time for drug-related crimes (Guerino, Harrison, & Sabol, 2011). In 2010, 48% of all inmates in federal prisons were serving time for drug-related crimes (Carson & Sabol, 2012). Therapists sometimes mistake clients' disagreement regarding policy issues as indicators of irrational or criminal thinking.

Clients (and therapists) love to focus on uncovering their irrational beliefs. In fact, doing the ABC part may feed into narcissistic tendencies of some clients. But doing the *DE* part of the ABC tool determines whether the exercise is helpful or not. The *D* stands for **D**isputing or debating the irrational/dysfunctional beliefs to help fortify the healthier, more rational/reasonable part of someone's thinking. The process of disputing questions the validity or helpfulness of a specific belief.

Ellis, who developed the ABC technique and wanted people to be able to learn it and remember it, was looking for a word that began with a D. "Disputing" fit the bill. And Ellis's style was often very direct and confrontational, reflecting both his belief that a good therapist, at times, could be most helpful using such a style, but also reflecting the culture of his south Bronx upbringing. But in his hands, the style was compassionate and empathetic, and clients felt supported and helped, partly because Ellis smiled and joked at the same time.

A style such as Ellis's will not work in the hands of most therapists. It will sound too aggressive and combative, but the idea of being direct and not wasting time has merit. Moreover, it is critical for clients to learn to examine and question – if not dispute – the rationality and helpfulness of their beliefs. A therapist can adopt a style and tone that fits their client. With someone racked by guilt and shame, gently asking, "*How has that helped in the past?*" in response to the belief "*I can get away with it,*" may work best. It is an open-ended question, and it may help a client to begin to take some responsibility for questioning the beliefs that support an addictive behavior. However, with another client, a much more forceful "*How the beep has that worked in the past?*" may get better results. It is, for some, a very appealing, no-nonsense approach. It can be especially effective with clients who have grown up in tough neighborhoods and are not particularly fond of "shrinks." That may explain why some therapists find REBT so effective in correctional settings.

The disputing or debating or questioning of beliefs can be done in many ways. Beck's CT tends to use a more empirical approach: "*Where is the evidence that he* [e.g. a fellow inmate] *hates you?*" Ellis thought what he called a more "philosophical" and "elegant" approach was better: "*So let's assume that he hates you? Then what?*" He would then often ask something like: "*Why is that so awful?*" and/or "*Why can't you stand that?*" and/or "*How does that make your life a beeping failure?*" Both approaches can be combined with a humorous style.

Regardless of how the therapist frames it, the D part should be a question: "*How is that belief helpful? How has that worked out in the past? Is there any evidence that everyone should appreciate what you have done? What do you mean by 'beep it'*"?

Some clients skip over the D and go directly to the E: more Effective thoughts/beliefs, emotions, and behaviors. What could they think *instead* that would be more helpful, given their long-term goals and values? This may lead to helpful ways of thinking about a fellow inmate: "*He has always acted that way and will probably always act that way in the future. I cannot change it.*" Similarly, the therapist and client (or the group) can work together to figure out what someone could *feel* instead. And, ultimately, what someone could *do* instead.

The ABC technique motivates clients to try to change. It offers a way to feel, think, and behave differently. It provides hope that therapy may actually pay off. And it is not solely dependent on a therapist or counselor.

(b) The choice clock   As many readers know, Ellis (1962, 1994) asserted that human emotional and behavioral problems spring primarily from irrational thinking. People may have a knee-jerk, conditioned response to someone else's behavior, but they have a choice: they can crank it up, get more emotionally upset and behave accordingly; they can crank it down, calming themselves down; or they can stay where they are. Using a clock metaphor and a metaphorical crank, may help. In Figure 12.1, at the 12 o'clock position, engaging in some form of demandingness will definitely cause someone to "crank it up": "*He shouldn't have dissed me.*" At the 3 o'clock position, he can make things worse (hotter) by exaggerating the negative: "*It's awful.*" At the 6 o'clock position, your client can add the idea, "*I can't stand it anymore,*" and, finally, at the 9 o'clock position, he can throw in some self-criticism and self-pity: "*This crap only happens to me. I'm such a jerk.*" Then, cranking it up more: "*I'm such a jerk. It's the end. I can't take it anymore. Oh my god, everything happens to me. Life sucks (as it shouldn't)….*"

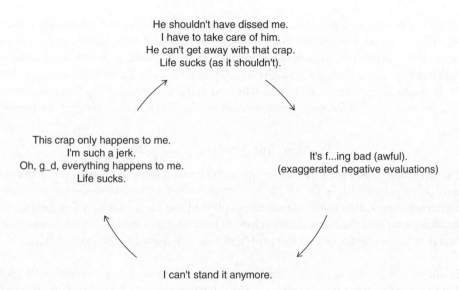

He shouldn't have dissed me.
I have to take care of him.
He can't get away with that crap.
Life sucks (as it shouldn't).

This crap only happens to me.
I'm such a jerk.
Oh, g_d, everything happens to me.
Life sucks.

It's f...ing bad (awful).
(exaggerated negative evaluations)

I can't stand it anymore.

Figure 12.1   Choice clock.

(c) Unconditional self-acceptance (USA) and unconditional other acceptance (UOA)   Unconditional self-acceptance and unconditional other acceptance represent a radical, revolutionary philosophy, but one found in Christianity and some other religions. In a nutshell, if someone behaves badly, he or she may damn the behavior but not his or her entirety. "*Judge the sin, not the sinner*," Christians say. Some Buddhists advocate letting go of evaluating (Ellis used the term "rating") and blaming altogether, no matter what.

Clearly, most humans have an immense capacity for self-blame and guilt. So teaching them to stop rating themselves or others every time they rate a behavior may be very therapeutic and reduce the negative impact of guilt and shame. However, I have sat next to someone who I know committed a serious crime and heard his interpretation of this philosophy which was: "*I may have done a bad thing, but I am not a bad person. In fact, I have done a lot of good things, so I know I am a good person.*" I pointed out that rating oneself positively just because you behaved well was not part of USA; however, this did not alter the client's perspective. In sum, in the wrong hands, this philosophy can be used to excuse anything.

What Bradshaw (2005) called "toxic shame" often fuels lapses and relapses. When people are learning a new way to behave, they make mistakes. If they feel overwhelmed with shame, the likelihood is that they will go on behaving badly in a desperate attempt to avoid feeling so awful. Helping them learn to rate behaviors and not their entire selves will help them accept themselves as they change. Helping them learn to rate the behaviors and not the entire selves of others, will help them be less angry.

(d) Mindfulness exercises   While it can be argued that meditation and other mindfulness exercises should be placed in the behavioral category rather than the cognitive, a case can also be made for their conceptualization as cognitive activities. The Buddha and his followers recognized the "chattering" quality of the human mind: "*This fickle, unsteady mind, difficult to guard, difficult to control, the wise man makes straight, as the fletcher straightens the arrow…Difficult to grasp, exceedingly subtle is this mind. It is ever in quest of delight. Let the wise man keep watch over it… A guarded mind brings happiness.*"

In response to this awareness, Buddhists developed techniques to help people calm down their thinking. Several research studies have demonstrated the effectiveness of meditation for substance abuse problems, including its application with prison populations (Bowen et al., 2006; Witkiewitz & Marlatt, 2004; Zgierska, Rabago, Chawla, Kushner, Koehler, & Marlatt, 2009). It is also interesting to note that when Niebuhr first penned the Serenity Prayer, the first line was originally: "*God grant me the serenity of 'mind' to accept the things I cannot change.*"

Prong 4: interpersonal techniques

For the vast majority of people, relationships are key to a sense of well-being. But because we are so interdependent with other people, our relationships are often the source of many negative activating events. It is our ideas about people and the ideas that we think people have of us that create much of the havoc in ourselves and in our relationships. The following are suggestions that help people work on the problems that they have in their relationships.

(a) Facilitate attendance in self-help and other groups   Although many people with addictive problems do not like attending 12-step and Self-Management and Recovery Training (SMART Recovery®) meetings, it is clear that they are extremely helpful for those who like them. Although developed from a different perspective, many aspects of 12-step philosophy are consistent with CBT principles. The connection between 12-step philosophy and CBT is colorfully illustrated in some of the popular 12-step slogans (e.g., "*90 meetings in 90 days;*" "*Easy does it, but do it;*" "*Live and let live;*" "*Get your feet to a meeting and your mind will follow*").

One alternative to 12-step self-help is SMART, an REBT-based community-based support group. Unlike 12-step groups, spirituality is not central to SMART's program. In addition, the terms "addict" and "alcoholic" are not used, participants do not have to embrace the disease model of addictions, there are no sponsors, and participants are not encouraged to attend for life, even though some members attend for years. SMART Recovery is an abstinence-based program (those who want to moderate their drinking are encouraged to go to Moderation Management meetings) and is organized around four modules called: (i) Building and Maintaining Motivation; (ii) Coping with Urges; (iii) Managing Thoughts, Feelings and Behaviors; and (iv) Living a Balanced Life. Many extremely useful tools and worksheets are available online for downloading at www.smartrecovery.org. For correctional populations, an audio-video program has been developed called Inside Out. Unfortunately, to date, it has not been widely marketed to, or adopted by, correctional facilities.

Attending self-help meetings helps people learn better ways to deal with many life problems in addition to addiction. SMART Recovery meetings, because they encourage cross-talk, like good group therapy, provide a different kind of practice as compared with 12-step meetings, which are more overtly supportive. Many people can benefit from both 12-step and SMART.

(b) Role-playing   Role-playing helps individuals practice thinking and behaving differently. There are many ways role-playing can be set up. For example, place two chairs (one behind the other) either in the middle of a group or in your private office. In the beginning, the client sits in the front seat. Then the therapist or group leader sits in the other seat, right behind the client's right shoulder. From that position, it is easy to play the "addictive voice," whispering in his or her ear while the client tries to counter with a "healthy" voice in response. After some moments of role-playing, the therapist and client can switch seats (and roles). Subsequently, other group members can be encouraged to exchange places with one of the people in an attempt to do a

better job of either defeating the client's "healthy" voice or defeating the "addictive" voice. The psychodramatic quality of this exercise always captures a group's attention.

(c) Spousal involvement   Many studies suggest that involving significant others in treatment leads to better results. This may be difficult or impossible to arrange in some correctional environments but may be very important when preparing to live outside prison walls. For example, O'Farrell and his associates (O'Farrell & Clements, 2012; O'Farrell & Murphy, 1995) have shown that a simple contract between a man and his significant other results in a significant drop in domestic violence. Meyers and Wolfe's (2004) book based on community reinforcement and family therapy (CRAFT), *Get Your Loved One Sober: Alternatives to Nagging, Pleading, and Threatening*, is an excellent resource currently available for family members and friends.

(d) Social skills training   Many people in prison have never learned how to interact with others effectively, especially when they are feeling angry, anxious, or awkward. Explicitly training them and giving them extensive practice – often through role-playing – in how to respond to various situations has been shown to help people do better in terms of drinking and drugging less (Chaney, 2003). What could they say if someone says to them: "*You're a beeping a**hole.*" What could they say when they are back in their neighborhood and someone asks: "*Do you want something to drink?*" How could they respond if they get a job but arrive late one day and their supervisor asks: "*Why were you late?*" Group members can take turns role-playing such common situations. They can also suggest other situations that the therapist may not know are problematic for a given client.

Prong 5: spiritual/existential "techniques"

The key to significant, difficult behavior change is motivation. As noted in the beginning of this chapter, people will not change or maintain a change without very good reasons to do so, usually in the form of new goals for their lives. Part of therapy's popularity is that good therapists, no matter which school they feel closest to – Rogerian, Adlerian, REBT, ACT, DBT, existential, gestalt, reality, to name some of the most popular – almost always get into conversations about existential and spiritual issues. What does a client still hope to do with his life? What did he hope for 10 or 20 years ago? How has he figured out how to accept the gap, assuming there is a gap, between what he wants or wanted and what he has? The following four approaches may help; many others are available online (see www.smartrecovery.org and www.hazelden.org).

(a) Help clients practice what can be helpful in their religions (if they are religious)   A high percentage of Americans and perhaps even a higher percentage of the inmate population are religious. Some inmates have deeply hurt other people. Therapists may help clients learn to accept themselves in spite of their past behaviors, but, for some clients, only religious organizations and religious leaders can provide relief from the shame and guilt that they harbor for their past misdeeds.

(b) Wisdom stories   All religions have "wisdom stories" or "teaching stories" designed to help people accept the realities of life and to give them hope that a better future is possible. Hope helps motivate people to try again, to make a stronger effort. Bertrand Russell asserts that people gave up Stoicism and adopted Christianity because living conditions became so difficult in the crumbling Roman Empire that they could not live without the belief that something better was in store. Christians, Muslims, Buddhists, Hindus, and many other religious believers

are motivated to try to do better in life because they believe that what they do in this life will affect, either positively or negatively, what happens in the next life. Counselors and therapists who do not hold beliefs common to their client can still work effectively by respecting the fact that no one has scientific evidence to prove or disprove some religious beliefs.

Many religious stories are very cognitive behavioral in nature and can be applicable to people from a variety of faiths. For example, in the New Testament, Christ convinces a bunch of men not to stone Mary Magdalene (*"He who has not sinned, cast the first stone"*). The story goes on to tell us that although the old men left first, even the young men finally were moved to drop their stones and leave...to accept that all people behave badly at some points in their lives. Then Christ goes over to Mary and extends his hand. He does not judge her. Nor does he tell her to judge herself (for being an adulteress or a prostitute; it is unclear what she is accused of). He also does not tell her to sleep on a brick and to eat bread and water for 6 months to punish herself. He simply tells her to change her behavior: *"Go and sin no more."* As many inmates are religious, understanding the nature of acceptance and forgiveness in the major religions may be helpful to being a more effective therapist.

(c) Values clarification exercises Values clarification exercises were developed in the late 1960s to help individuals and members of a group become clearer about what they would like to strive to do with their lives (Simon, Howe, & Kirschenbaum, 1972). One simple exercise that can be done in individual or group treatment is to ask clients to write their own obituary: it may help them focus more on the future and less on taking care of their present needs. A second exercise is to ask clients what they would do if they won $43 million dollars when they got out of prison: the answer can clarify what clients value when financial considerations are taken out of the equation.

A third useful values clarification exercise was develop by the creator of reality therapy, William Glasser (1989). He liked to ask his clients three questions: *"What do you want? What are you doing? How do you like it?"* The first question is the tricky one because most people have conflicting wants. For example, they want to both express their anger *and* stay out of trouble at the same time. They want to drink a lot and womanize *and* maintain a good relationship with their girlfriend. The three questions are useful because they are easy to remember and they force people to look at what they are doing, and think about whether the results are in line with their long-term goals and values.

Prong 6: chemical "techniques"

(a) Medication Medications for addictions can be helpful for some clients (e.g., Anton et al., 2006). Some medications are specifically designed to help clients cope with the urge to drink or use, such as Antabuse (disulfiram), naltrexone (Vivitrol, an injected version), and Campral (acamprosate) for alcohol abuse and dependence; methadone and buprenorphine, for opioid addiction; and Zyban and Chantix for nicotine dependence. Selective serotonin reuptake inhibitors (SSRIs) have also been shown to reduce the number of days drinking and the intensity of drinking episodes. Medical researchers and some doctors are also exploring the effectiveness of off-label uses for medications originally designed for other purposes, such as topiramate (an antiseizure medication), baclofen (an antispasm medication), and ondansetron (an antinausea medication used to treat the side effects of chemotherapy).

(b) Nutrition and sleep Many clients with an addiction eat poorly, not fully understanding the effect bad nutrition has on moods, energy levels, and, more importantly, the ability to

manage their behaviors better, and more effectively to exhibit self-control or self-regulation. For example, low glucose levels in the blood have been shown to negatively affect the ability to self-regulate a number of different behaviors, including drinking (Gaillot et al., 2007). In addition, most people do not yet understand the impact of sleep loss on performance and self-regulation and do not take seriously the importance of getting the sleep that they need to function well. Research into how addictive behaviors disrupt sleep is still sparse, but alcohol negatively affects sleep quality, leading to mood disorders in some people, which may, in turn, lead to an increase in alcohol and drug consumption.

Individual Versus Group Work

Both individual and group therapy have a place in the treatment of addictions. Since shame often fuels addictive behaviors, some individuals will never talk in group about something dreadful that has happened in the past, such as being sexually abused. In such cases, individual sessions may be critical to success. But group sessions provide the best setting to learn new interpersonal skills and to get feedback from other human beings. SMART Recovery meetings, in general, tend to discourage people from talking at length about the past. In contrast, 12-step programs have created settings and traditions in which people may talk openly about their past wrenching experiences. Some combination of the two approaches works best. Individual stories help a group pull together and empathize with each other, and ABC(DE) exercises help group members focus on how to understand a member's contributions to the current problem and work out better responses in the future. In sum, a supportive workshop-like setting may be the most effective group format.

Professional Burnout, the Internist Model, and Zen Caring

Clients with addictive problems often lapse and relapse. These periods sap hope and motivation from clients, and can have a similar effect on practitioners. How can practitioners prevent professional burnout? Exploring the beliefs that lead to burnout will help. Many therapists, consciously or unconsciously, have beliefs about certain clients that may seem reasonable but are probably irrational. Ultimately, they will lead to feelings of hopelessness, helplessness, resentment, and despair regarding one's work. Over the years, I have watched my own feelings and thoughts as I waited for a client to come to a session. Some of the thoughts include: (i) *"He'll never change,"* (ii) *"I can't help this person. I don't know what to do,"* (iii) *"She relapsed again. I can't do this. I am not a good counselor,"* (iv) *"This is pointless and stupid. We are doing revolving door therapy,"* (v) *"I hate working with him,"* and (vi) *"She is so negative and passive aggressive, I dread having to see her."*

The above is only a very partial list, but it includes some common practitioner beliefs. Lapses and relapses are seen as evidence of failure, even though lapses and relapses are extremely common with *all* serious health issues. O'Brien and McClellan (1996) have shown that many chronic illnesses, including addictions, have similar relapse rates. Yet practitioners are often extremely hard on themselves. As an antidote, consider the "internist model." Internists also work with chronically ill patients; however, they rarely get exasperated or feel like quitting. Unlike some therapists and psychiatrists, they do not yell at or shame their patients for relapsing. Why? Because they accept that people often do not change their lifestyles and that their conditions sometimes worsen. They continue to work with patients because they hope something they say or do may help.

Another recommendation is to practice "Zen caring": that is, be helpful but not invested in your clients' successes or failures. They will not find that you are elated when they are doing well nor irritated or disappointed when they lapse or relapse. Simply be there. The analogy of a ski instructor may be helpful. If a client really wants to get better at skiing, it is very helpful to find a good instructor. Usually, like a good CBT therapist, the instructor will ask the client what he or she wants to accomplish, that is, his or her goal for the lessons. Then the instructor sets about trying to figure out what might help most. If the client falls or fails to practice between lessons, good instructors will not show disappointment or irritation. They will just continue to work with their client.

Conclusion

The emphasis in this chapter has been on goal-focused techniques and on an integrated, REBT-based, motivation-enhancing approach. The techniques are designed to solve a problem, to help clients build a bridge between where clients are and where they want to be. To help clients become and remain motivated and to make therapy faster and more efficient requires integrating the four building blocks of good psychotherapy: empathy, respect for the impact of past events on the present, a focus on future goals and values, and effective, preferably, evidence-based techniques.

References

Anton, R. F., O'Malley, S. S., Ciraulo, D. A., Cister, R. A., Couper, D., Donovan, D. M., et al. (2006). Combined pharmacotherapies and behavioral interventions for alcohol dependence: The COMBINE study: A randomized controlled trial. *Journal of the American Medical Association, 295*, 2003–2017.

Beck, A. T. (1976). *Cognitive therapy and the emotional disorders*. New York: International Universities Press.

Bowen, S., Witkiewitz, K., Dillworth, T. M., Chawla, N., Simpson, T. L., Ostafin, B. D., et al. (2006). Mindfulness meditation and substance use in an incarcerated population. *Psychology of Addictions, 20*, 343–347.

Bradshaw, J. (2005). *Healing the shame that binds you*. Deerfield Beach, FL: Health Communications, Inc.

Carson, E. A., & Sabol, W. J. (2012). *Prisoners in 2011*. Washington, DC: Bureau of Justice Statistics.

Chaney, E. F. (2003). Social skills training. In R. K. Hester & W. R. Miller (Eds.), *Handbook of alcoholism treatment approaches: Effective alternatives* (3rd ed., pp. 13–64). Boston: Allyn & Bacon.

Dadds, M. R., Hawes, D. J., Frost, A. D., Vassallo, S., Bunn, P., Hunter, K., & Merz, S. (2009). Learning to 'talk the talk': the relationship of psychopathic traits to deficits in empathy across childhood. *Journal of Child Psychology and Psychiatry, 50*, 599–606.

Ellis, A. (1962). *Reason and emotion in psychotherapy*. New York: Lyle Stuart.

Ellis, A. (1994). *Reason and emotion in psychotherapy* (Rev. and updated ed.). New York: Birch Lane Press.

Fletcher, A. M. (2002). *Sober for good: New solutions for drinking problems – advice from those who have succeeded*. New York: Houghton Mifflin Harcourt.

Gaillot, M. T., Baumeister, R. F., DeWall, C. N., Maner, J. K., Plant, E. A., Tice, D. M., Brewer, L. E., & Schmeichel, B. J. (2007). Self-control relies on glucose as a limited energy source: Willpower is more than a metaphor. *Journal of Personality and Social Psychology, 92*, 325–336.

Glasser, W. (1989). Control theory. In W. Glasser (Ed.), *Control theory in the practice of reality therapy*. New York: Harper & Row.

Guerino, P., Harrison, P. M., & Sabol, W. J. (2011) *Prisoners in 2010*. Washington, DC: Bureau of Justice Statistics.

Hayes, S. C., Strosahl, K. D., Wilson, K. G. (1999). *Acceptance and commitment therapy: An experiential approach to behavior change.* The Guilford Press.

International Centre for Prison Studies. (2013). World prison brief. Retrieved from http://www. prisonstudies.org/info/worldbrief/

Landenberger, N. A., & Lipsey, M. W. (2005). The positive effects of cognitive-behavioral programs for offenders: A meta-analysis of factors associated with effective treatment. *Journal of Experimental Criminology, 1,* 451–476.

Linehan, M. M. (1993). *Cognitive-behavioral treatment of borderline personality disorder.* New York: Guilford.

Lipsey, M. W., Landenberger, N. A., & Wilson, S. J. (2007). Effects of cognitive-behavioral programs for criminal offenders. *Campbell Systematic Reviews, 6.*

Meyers, R. J. & Wolfe, B.L. (2004). *Alternatives to nagging, pleading and threatening: Help for you and your problem drinker.* Center City, MN: Hazelden Publications.

Miller, W. R., & Rollnick, S. (2002). *Motivational interviewing: Preparing people to change addictive behavior* (2nd ed.). New York: Guilford.

O'Brien, C. P., & McLellan, A. T. (1996). Myths about the treatment of addiction. *Lancet, 347,* 237–240.

O'Farrell, T. J., & Clements, K. (2012). Review of outcome research on marital and family therapy in treatment for alcoholism. *Journal of Marital and Family Therapy, 38,* 122–144.

O'Farrell, T. J., & Murphy, C. M. (1995). Marital violence before and after alcoholism treatment. *Journal of Consulting and Clinical Psychology, 63,* 256–262.

Prochaska, J. O., DiClemente, C.C., & Norcross, J. C. (1992). In search of how people change: Applications to addictive behaviors. *American Psychologist, 47,* 1102–1114.

Simon, S. B., Howe, L. W., & Kirschenbaum, H. (1972). *Values clarification: A handbook of practical strategies for teachers and students.* New York: Hart Publishing Co.

Witkiewitz, K., & Marlatt, G. A. (2004). Relapse prevention for alcohol and drug problems: That was Zen, this is Tao. *American Psychologist, 59,* 224–235.

Wulach, J. (1988). The criminal personality as a DSM-III-R antisocial, narcissistic, borderline, and histrionic personality disorder. *International Journal of Offender Therapy and Comparative Criminology, 32,* 185–199.

Yochelson, S., & Samenow, S. (1976). *The criminal personality: Vol. 1. A profile for change.* New York: Jason Aronson.

Yochelson, S., & Samenow, S. (1977). *The criminal personality: Vol. 2. The change process.* New York: Jason Aronson.

Zgierska, A., Rabago, D., Chawla, N., Kushner, K., Koehler, R., & Marlatt, A. (2009). Mindfulness meditation for substance use disorders: A systematic review. *Substance Abuse, 30,* 266–294.

Suggestions for Further Learning

Book

Bishop, F. M. (2001). *Managing addictions: Cognitive, emotive, and behavioral techniques.* Northvale, NJ: Jason Aronson, Inc.

Websites

Albert Ellis Institute, www.albertellis.org

SMART Recovery® website for numerous self-help forms and therapist aides (www.smartrecovery.org).

YouTube playlist of Acceptance and Commitment Therapy exercises: http://www.youtube.com/playlist?list=PL69FA6D311F0C0C7B

Institution

The Albert Ellis Institute (www.albertellis.org) for training and CBT/REBT materials.

Appendix 12.A

Doing an ABC for an Addictive or Avoidant Behavior

(1) Start at C. (2) Move back in time. Fill in B and then A. (3) Improve the future. Do D and E.

A. Activating Event(s)/Contributing Factors/"Triggers"

*(These can be **internal**, e.g.., physical or emotional feelings – or **external**, <u>real or imagined or anticipated</u>)*

B. Beliefs

(What did you tell yourself so that you could have a drink, use, gamble, engage in unsafe sex, procrastinate, etc.? Look for some of the typical unhelpful/irrational/dysfunctional beliefs: "I can get away with it." "I'll just have two." "It won't matter." "I'm just going to do it anyway, eventually." "Beep it.")

C. The Problem Behavior(s) - drinking, drugging, sexting, etc. (or emotions, e.g., anger, depression, anxiety; or thinking, e.g., OCD-ish thinking)

D. Disputes

(Write questions here that help you dispute or question the helpfulness, rationality, or validity of some of the beliefs you wrote in B, above. For example: What do you mean by "I can get away with it"? "How has that worked in the past?" "Where is the evidence that 'it doesn't matter'?")

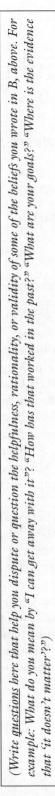

E. More <u>Effective</u> thoughts (e.g., counter statements to the Bs, above), behaviors (things you could do instead), and feelings – which will increase the likelihood that you will stick to your plans and goals.

("I may be able to get away with it tonight, but I won't always, and the tradeoff is not worth it.")
(Things you could do: Exercise. Fill out a worksheet. Do a CBA. Call a friend. Go to a meeting.)

13

Social and Community Responsibility Therapy (SCRT)

A Cognitive-Behavioral Model for the Treatment of Substance-Abusing Judicial Clients

Kenneth W. Wanberg and Harvey B. Milkman

No man is an island entire of itself; any man's death diminishes me, because I am involved in mankind, and therefore never send to know for whom the bell tolls; it tolls for thee.

John Donne, 1572–1631

There is a robust relationship and striking similarities between substance abuse and criminal conduct (Wanberg & Milkman, 2008). Drug-involved offenders comprise the majority of incarcerates. From 70 to 90% of offenders report use of illicit drugs during their lifetime, 50–70% have a lifetime diagnosis of substance abuse or dependence, and 50–80% were under alcohol and other drug (AOD) influence when arrested for their offense. The high-risk situations and thought sequences that portend reoffending and relapse are parallel and potentiating. Substance use and abuse contribute significantly to the risk of recidivism. All offender risk assessment instruments include measures of past and recent substance abuse. In response to this combination of substance abuse and criminal conduct, cognitive-behavioral therapy (CBT) has become an effective approach in preventing relapse and recidivism.

The essence of what happens in CBT is cognitive-behavioral restructuring. There are two traditional CBT foci for the process of this restructuring: (i) changing or replacing internal cognitive structures, also known as cognitive restructuring; and (ii) the restructuring of relationships with others, best known in the literature as social skills training. The utilization of these two approaches in traditional CBT is egocentric: primarily concerned with alleviating the problems and psychological pain of individuals and helping them have better psychosocial outcomes. In correctional treatment, the egocentric focus is important. Judicial clients have intrapersonal problems that need to be resolved in order to reduce stress, tension, depression, and other psychological maladies that prevent normal and healthy functioning. As well, judicial clients are in need of improved interpersonal relationships for more meaningful and satisfactory living.

Forensic CBT: A Handbook for Clinical Practice, First Edition.
Edited by Raymond Chip Tafrate and Damon Mitchell.
© 2014 John Wiley & Sons, Ltd. Published 2014 by John Wiley & Sons, Ltd.

However, given that these two traditional CBT approaches are egocentric-oriented, a paradigm shift is suggested in their utilization with judicial clients. To effectively address antisocial patterns and substance abuse, the egocentric goal of helping clients resolve their psychological problems and pain must be integrated with a well-defined and consistent *sociocentric* approach that includes a psychology of caring and a focus on developing thinking and behaviors that result in moral and social responsibility toward others, the community, and society as a whole.

We recommend the CBT model be adjusted and expanded to address antisocial and criminal thinking within a sociocentric therapeutic framework. Cognitive restructuring must focus not just on establishing self-control for positive personal outcomes, but also on changing criminal and antisocial thinking to gain prosocial outcomes. Social skills training must focus on not just improving social relationships for egocentric gain, but also help achieve positive outcomes for others within the context of interpersonal relationships. Finally, this paradigm shift involves a third dimension of correctional CBT: focusing on developing cognitive-behavioral skills that help judicial clients restructure their relationship with their community and society at large.

This chapter provides a systematic treatment of the use of sociocentric approaches with substance-abusing judicial clients. It outlines specific CBT-based strategies that facilitate change from antisocial to prosocial thinking and behavior and that focus on the development of moral and social responsibility toward others, the community, and society at large. Although neuro-biological (Leshner, 2006) characteristics of the "addicted brain" indicate caution over labeling substance abuse as a "moral problem," the reality is that substance abuse has clear moral ramifications in that it causes pain and suffering annually to millions of individuals and an annual cost to American society of around $511 billion dollars (Crime News, 2010). In comparison, the estimated cost of a catastrophic hurricane is $50 billion (Eltman & Hays, 2012).

We start with a case example that is not associated with any specific person but represents a composite of events, thoughts, emotions, and actions commonly found in judicial clients (Box 13.1). This narrative will be referenced throughout the chapter to illustrate the general principles of our model, *social and community responsibility therapy* (SCRT). Then we will outline several conceptualizations that are typical for judicial clients such as Larry and offer some tools practitioners can use to change beliefs and behaviors. Finally we will emphasize the three components of our treatment model: promoting prosocial cognitions, fostering responsible relationships, and building a sense of connection and caring with the larger community.

The Cognitive-Behavioral Map

Figure 13.1 provides a Cognitive-Behavior Map (CB Map) for learning and change that gives judicial clients a clear and distinct tool for understanding and managing mental, emotional, and behavioral responses to external and internal events and for changing cognitive structures that can lead to positive and prosocial outcomes (Milkman & Wanberg, 2012; Wanberg & Milkman, 1998, 2006, 2008; Wanberg, Milkman, & Timken, 2005). Although we look at this map from the perspective of offender treatment, it can be used as a practical guide for all persons who seek to have positive outcomes and make cognitive-behavioral changes to prevent negative outcomes in daily living. The application of the CB Map is based on six assumptions.

1. External or internal (inside memories and feelings) stimuli can trigger cognitive structures – thought habits, rules, values and attitudes, and core beliefs – that lead to criminal conduct and substance abuse.

Box 13.1   The Case of Larry

Larry is a 31-year-old skilled fabricator of counter tops who grew up in a modest suburban community. His father is a heavy equipment operator who worked out of state much of the time, spending little time with his sons. His mother worked as a teacher's aid. Larry always felt the pressure to be like his older brother, who did well in school and athletics, and is a successful high school teacher. He felt his brother had all the breaks. "I never had any. I always felt dumb."

Larry started using marijuana at age 13, drinking at 16, was convicted of Driving While Intoxicated at 17, was caught breaking into a convenience store with friends at 18, and placed on probation for a year. For the next 10 years, Larry was into cocaine (when he could afford it) and methamphetamine; but alcohol was his mainstay. He drank daily, and went on monthly binges. "Only way I could forget. I deserved some fun." He was always high or drinking when committing a crime. He received two more DWIs before age 22. He eluded treatment but had to take a 6-week DWI education class. He engaged in periodic stealing, went from job to job, could not manage his money, had two accidents when speeding, could not plan ahead, and most of his friends and role models had problems with the law. He did feel bad about a girl hurt in one of the car accidents. He never felt bad about stealing and thought "they had more than they deserved. Anyway, I didn't know who they [his victims] were."

He had a job with a fabrication contractor who was good to Larry and liked his work. The owner had expensive equipment in his shop. Larry thought "this stuff would be easy to sell. Some big bucks." He had second thoughts because he knew the owner was having a hard time making ends meet in the business. But Larry needed cash. He cased the place, saw no surveillance cameras, quit his job, and a week later he and a friend burglarized the building stealing $100,000 of equipment. In the process of selling it he was caught and convicted of grand theft and burglary. Because of his record he was sentenced to a year in prison, during which time he went through a CBT program for substance abusing offenders.

Larry was completing his first year of parole, was clean and sober, and was law-abiding. As part of his aftercare program, he was seeing a counselor twice a month and attending Alcoholics Anonymous (AA). On his way for an appointment with his parole officer (PO), his car stalled. He thought "I'll never make it on time." "Just bad luck – that's why I've had problems." "I've never had a fair shake" (a core belief), "I've never been treated fairly." "The world sucks." "No one gives a crap." He felt a lot of anger, hopelessness. His first thought was of Tim – an old crime buddy. "I'll call him, he'll help." Tim was there in 20 minutes, but too late for Larry to make the appointment and it meant he would be late for work.

Larry had missed two appointments but had "good reasons." The PO didn't like it: "Told me I'm on the line, third strike and I'm back in. But, I've done nothing wrong." Tim put on the heat: "Screw 'em. He'll put you in the slammer. Time you stopped f***in' around. I'm heading to LA tomorrow. Couple jobs we can do there. Take a ride." Larry was feeling the pressure. He thought about getting high. He thought: "My PO will revoke. If he does, I'll go back to prison. Just as well split."

Other thoughts rushed in. "But what about Susan [Larry's wife]. She's pregnant. First time I've been happy. I've always treated my women bad. My drinking hurt them. Different with Susan. I owe her. Don't want to hurt her. She's a good woman. She doesn't deserve this. My kid's going to need a good dad. I don't want to go back to prison." Then he thought some more. "My PO, He's been good to me. I like the way he handles himself. Maybe he won't revoke." He thought about his treatment and Nancy his counselor in his program in prison. "She treated me fair. She took time with me. That cog stuff really helped. But she had it tough, being a woman working with all those hoods. I'd let her down." Then his sponsor flashed through his mind. "Why didn't I call him?" He looked at Tim, felt bad for him. "He's lonely. He's a loser, can't get it together." But some counter thoughts. "But what the hell. Where'll all that get me now? My PO will never understand. It's too late. Going with Tim will solve that."

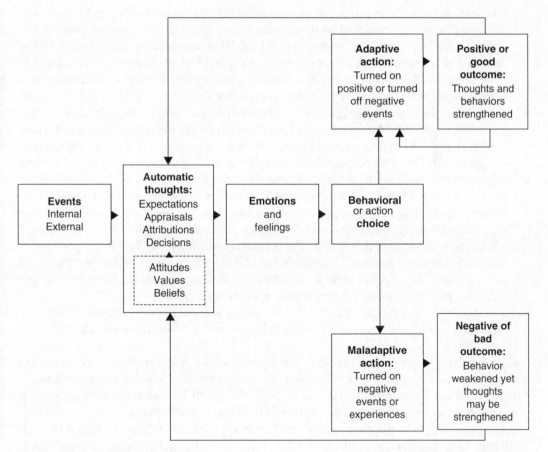

Figure 13.1 The Cognitive-Behavioral Map for learning and change. Copyright K. W. Wanberg & H. B. Milkman (1998, 2006, 2008); K. W. Wanberg, H. B. Milkman, & D. Timken (2005) (used with permission of the authors).

2. Patterns of AOD misuse and criminal conduct are determined by the cognitive structures activated by cognitive processes. A first step of correctional treatment is for clients to identify thought habits, attitudes, and the core beliefs that lead to substance abuse and criminal conduct. Since there is often a "millisecond" between the thought and emotional-behavioral outcome, it is often necessary first to identify the emotional response and then work back to the underlying thought or thoughts leading to the emotion. The goal is to move from "automatic shifting" to conscious and "manual" shifting in thought processing.
3. Thought habits, underlying attitudes, values, rules, and core beliefs, can be changed through a variety of cognitive restructuring skills and techniques. The guiding principle is that we can change, better manage, and choose our thoughts and our beliefs. We consciously choose our behavioral responses.
4. The restructuring of antisocial, criminal, and substance abuse thinking and underlying beliefs will result in positive emotional and behavioral (prosocial) outcomes. Cognitive structures can lead to both positive and negative emotional outcomes (e.g., anger, resentment, guilt, depression, joy, happiness, contentment) and positive and negative behavioral outcomes (e.g., being prosocial, drug free, substance abuse, criminal conduct).
5. The outcomes of those actions reinforce internal thoughts, underlying beliefs, and the mediating structures that lead to those behaviors. When the outcomes are positive, the behaviors leading to the outcomes are reinforced. When the outcomes are negative (being arrested), this should decrease the probability of the behavior repeating itself. This does not always happen. Behaviors that result in bad outcomes are often repeated because negative (maladaptive) outcomes can strengthen the cognitive structures that lead to those behaviors. Unless the thought habits and underlying beliefs are changed, there is a high probability that negative behaviors resulting from these structures will continue to occur. There is a return arrow from positive outcome back to adaptive positive action (upper right corner of Figure 13.1) but no comparable return arrow in the lower right of Figure 13.1, from negative outcomes back to negative maladaptive behavior or action. But, there are return arrows leading back to automatic thoughts from both positive outcomes and negative outcomes. Thus, there are two reinforcement pathways: (i) behaviors are reinforced because they lead to desirable outcomes; (ii) behaviors are reinforced regardless of the outcomes, if the cognitive structures that lead to the behaviors are reinforced. This is the principle of self-reinforcement. Of course, a common paradoxical effect is that, in the thinking of the judicial client, the negative behaviors (antisocial) often result in short-term gain and are viewed as positive outcomes (benefits from committing a crime).
6. A response to a specific situation or event can lead to four outcomes: activation of cognitive structures; emotional reactivity; resulting behavior; and the consequence of that behavior.

Let's use Larry's story as an example. The external event of not making it to see his PO activates cognitions (e.g., the core belief "*bad things happen to me, I've never had a fair chance*") that sets off angry feelings that could lead to Larry going with Tim, which in the long run will result in negative outcomes. However, in Larry's thinking, it could lead to the short-term outcome of not going back to prison. Larry could choose to restructure his thinking and not go with Tim. Unless automatic thinking and core beliefs and thought structures change, Larry will go with Tim and merely repeat the cycle. The short-term positive outcome – not going back to prison – will merely reinforce the thoughts and core beliefs that lead to going with Tim. If going with Tim results in being put back in prison, the thoughts "*they've put me back in prison without giving me a chance*" and the core belief "*I've never had a fair shake. I've never been treated fairly*" get reinforced. Whether the outcome is positive or negative, the cognitive structures leading to the outcome get reinforced.

Addressing Recidivism and Relapse (R&R) in Correctional Treatment

Recidivism prevention is often addressed within the framework of relapse prevention, assuming, with substance-abusing judicial clients, that if relapse is prevented, recidivism is also prevented. However, many offenders reoffend but do not relapse and vice versa.

Recognizing that the process of recidivism differs from the process of relapse with respect to the specific triggers, we provide a model for relapse and recidivism prevention based on the concepts in the CB-Map (Wanberg & Milkman, 1998, 2008) and on Marlatt's (1985) relapse prevention coping skills model. This approach differentiates between the triggers or high-risk exposures for relapse and those for recidivism.

Our SCRT model shows that judicial clients will tend to experience an increased sense of self-efficacy when they effectively use coping skills to manage high-risk exposures that challenge their effort to live a drug-free and crime-free life. We refer to high-risk exposures as high-risk thinking, feelings, and beliefs that can lead to relapse and recidivism. Examples of high-risk exposures are provided in Figure 13.2, which shows that effective management of these exposures decreases the probability of reoffending, strengthens the cognitive-behavioral changes that prevent recidivism, and enhances prosocial attitudes and behavior. Those with ineffective coping skills, when confronted with high-risk exposures, may lack the ability to change thoughts and behaviors to prevent recidivism. This can result in what Marlatt calls the rule violation effect: violating the rule of living crime free leads to thinking: "*might as well go all the way.*" If the client derives positive gain from criminal thinking (expectancy outcomes) or actual reoffending (e.g., money, power, status with peers), the criminal thinking and behavior are reinforced.

Both relapse and recidivism are based on not handling the high-risk exposures outlined in Figure 13.2. Relapse and recidivism prevention is based on effective management of these exposures using cognitive-behavioral restructuring skills as outlined in Figure 13.3. These two figures can be utilized in helping judicial clients develop a plan for relapse and a plan for recidivism prevention based on their own high-risk exposures and the cognitive-behavioral restructuring skills needed to address these exposures.

Judicial clients who effectively manage high-risk exposures will experience an increase in self-efficacy, an important concept in the Marlatt relapse model and most CBT models. Self-efficacy (referred to as self-mastery in our model), or the perception or judgment that one can manage high-risk exposures and prevent relapse and recidivism, is an important part of CBT (Abrams & Niaura, 1987; Bandura, 1977a, 1995, 1997; Beck, Freeman, Davis, et al., 2004; Freeman, Pretzer, Fleming, & Simon, 1990; Goldfried, 1995; Marlatt, 1985; Wanberg & Milkman, 2006, 2008; Wilson & O'Leary, 1980). Bandura sees self-efficacy as the unifying construct of the social-cognitive framework of therapy that strengthens self-control (Bandura, 1977a, 1978).

Now, what about Larry? What are his high-risk exposures? His high-risk situations, thoughts, feelings, and core beliefs? Use Figure 13.2 to chart Larry's high-risk exposures and Figure 13.3 as a guide to formulating specific skills he might use to prevent recidivism and relapse and experience an increase in self-efficacy. The rest of this chapter will provide some of these answers.

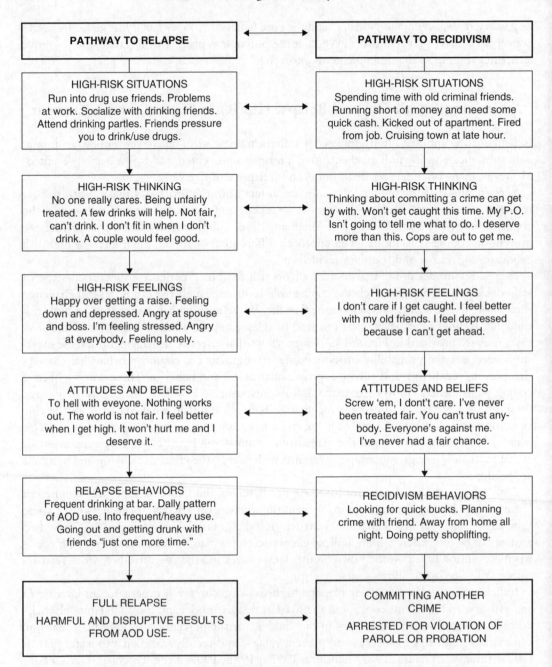

Figure 13.2 Cognitive-behavioral pathways for relapse and recidivism. AOD, alcohol and other drug; P.O., probation officer. Copyright K. W. Wanberg & H. B. Milkman (2006, 2008) (used with permission of the authors).

Practitioner Tools for Helping Judicial Clients Change

There are a number of general but essential tools that facilitate prosocial change in correctional clients. A few of these are identified in Box 13.2 (Milkman & Wanberg, 2005, 2012; Wanberg & Milkman, 1998, 2006; 2008; Wanberg, Milkman & Timken, 2005).

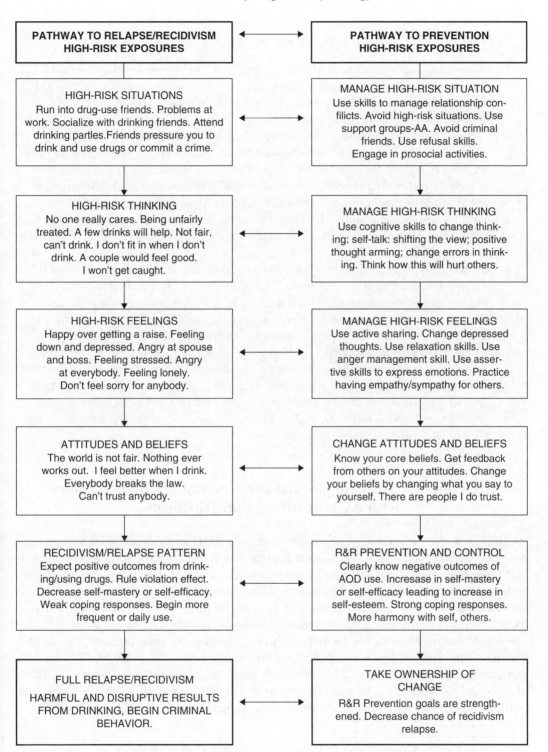

Figure 13.3 Cognitive-behavioral pathways for relapse and recidivism (R&R) prevention. AOD, alcohol and other drug. Copyright K. W. Wanberg & H. B. Milkman (2006, 2008) (used with permission of the authors).

Box 13.2   SCRT Practitioner Tools

1. **A cognitive-behavioral map for change** similar to the one provided in Figure 13.1 identifies the targets for change. The CB Map can become a tool for daily use by clients helping to create awareness of ways to prevent relapse and recidivism (R&R) and to generate positive outcomes.

2. **A plan for change** provides clients with a structure to define: (i) specific problem areas to be addressed (e.g., being influenced by antisocial peers); (ii) change goals; (iii) methods to address the problem areas (e.g., interactive refusal skills); and (iv) identify desired outcomes. The plan for change addresses R&R prevention and other problem areas such as mental health issues and relationship problems that impact R&R.

3. **Weekly risk management charting** by clients that record high-risk exposures encountered during the week such as criminal associates, skills used to manage those exposures, and outcomes.

4. **Thinking reports and re-thinking reports** (Wanberg & Milkman, 2006, 2008) address specific situations, experiences, or problems encountered during the week that lead to positive or negative outcomes. The CB Map provides the elements of the thinking report: event, thoughts, attitudes and beliefs, feelings, and outcomes. The re-thinking report restructures an experience to generate positive outcomes.

5. **Interactive self-assessments** (Wanberg & Milkman, 2006, 2008) are used throughout treatment and involve having clients identify how the session concepts and topics apply to their lives. Clients rate themselves on a scale of 1 to 10 as to their level of understanding of, and ability to use, the concepts and skills being learned. The process involves receiving feedback from counselors and group members as to their involvement around session material.

Strategies for Increasing Social and Community Responsibility with AOD-Involved Judicial Clients

We now look at some specific strategies for addressing AOD and criminal thinking and conduct that emphasize the sociocentric treatment approach. We shift the paradigm of the two traditional CBT approaches of cognitive restructuring and social skills training to specifically address criminal thinking and conduct in terms of two components of SCRT: *prosocial cognitive restructuring*, and *relationship responsibility therapy*. We also add a third component that focuses on restructuring the client's relationship with the community: *community responsibility therapy*. As illustrated in Figure 13.4, these three approaches have the primary goals of preventing relapse and recidivism and facilitating a meaningful and responsible life. The model's platform is cognitive self-control and self-management that can result in the positive outcome of successful community re-entry and reintegration. We now summarize some of the strategies of these three systematic components which provide the structure of SCRT.

Component 1: Prosocial cognitive restructuring

There are five primary goals for using prosocial cognitive restructuring in the treatment of criminal conduct and co-occurring substance abuse. The first is to have clients move from

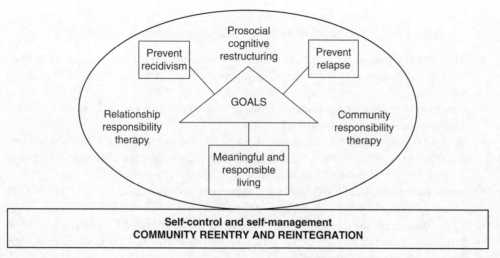

Figure 13.4   Social and community responsibility therapy goals and skills. Copyright K. W. Wanberg & H. B. Milkman (2006, 2008); K. W. Wanberg, H.B. Milkman, & D. Timken (2005) (used with permission of the authors).

"automatic shifting" to "manual shifting" in order to get prosocial outcomes. It involves consciously "putting one's hands on" the process of shifting thoughts and beliefs to learn mental self-control and guide the change process. The second goal is to change the proximal structures (thoughts), intermediary (attitudes, values, rules), and distal or deeper structures (core beliefs) that lead directly to substance abuse and criminal conduct relapse and recidivism.

The third goal of prosocial cognitive restructuring is to help clients manage emotional states that can lead to relapse and recidivism. Both negative emotional states (depression) and positive emotional states (elation and joy) can increase the risk of relapse (Hodgins, el Guebaly, & Armstrong, 1995; Marlatt & Witkiewitz, 2005). Negative emotional states such as depression and anxiety have been found to increase the probability that clients will drop out of treatment and reoffend (Hiller, Knight, & Simpson, 1999; Moos, Finney, & Moos, 2000).

The fourth goal is the provision of an atmosphere charged with prosocial modeling (Andrews & Bonta, 2003; Bandura, 1965, 1977b, 1997). Agents of prosocial growth and change who interact with judicial clients (e.g., counselors, case managers, probation and parole officers, mental health workers) are the key models for high standards of moral principles, empathic understanding, respect for their community, and compassion for others. There is strong research support for the efficacy of modeling within the therapeutic relationship and its positive effect on treatment retention and outcome (for a summary of this literature see DeMuro, Wanberg & Anderson, 2011; Wanberg & Milkman, 2008).

The fifth goal addresses the judicial client's deficits in moral responsibility and prosocial reasoning and thinking that lead to consistent criminal belief patterns and habits causing harm to others and the community. We define moral responsibility as: respecting the rights of others, being account-able to the laws of society, having positive regard for and caring about the welfare and safety of others, and contributing to the good of society. For the substance-abusing judicial client, these deficits are infused with thought habits that lead to substance abuse. Prosocial cognitive restructur-ing involves a number of specific sociocentric-oriented strategies to change antisocial, criminal, and AOD-oriented thinking and beliefs. Some of these are summarized below.

Box 13.3 Cognitive Restructuring Skills for Use in SCRT

- Thought stopping and thought braking. When having thoughts that can lead to negative or bad outcomes, shout "stop" or imagine a big STOP sign (e.g., *"I've got to go with Tim."*).
- Countering or arguing against the thought: *"Can't trust anybody."* Counter: *"I think I'm starting to trust my counselor."*
- Shifting the view: Looking at situations in more than one way. View: *"Tim is my way out of going to prison."* Shift: *"If I go see my PO, maybe the worst that can happen is to get another year of parole."*
- Empathic reflection: Thinking from another person's position: *"I know my PO has got his job to do."* *"What will this do to Susan?"*
- Sympathic reflection: He looked at Tim and felt bad for him. *"He's lonely."*
- Planting a positive thought: *"My PO said 'third strike I'm out. But he's been fair. I think he's a fourth strike guy."*
- Taking responsibility and seeing your part in both good and bad outcomes. For bad outcomes: *"I've treated women badly. I hurt them."* For good outcomes: *"Different with Susan. I owe her."*
- Logical (sensible) study or going to court with your thoughts. This involves arguing against thinking and behavior that can lead to a bad outcome and arguing for thinking that leads to a good outcome (e.g., *"Going with Tim, he's a loser." "My PO, he's been fair. Maybe he won't revoke."*).
- Making thoughts weaker or stronger. Involves punishing negative thoughts and rewarding positive thoughts. Punish: *"I'm going with Tim. But then I'll end up back in prison for sure. That's dumb."* Reward: *"My kid's going to need a good dad. I don't want to go back to prison. That's better for everybody."*

Cognitive restructuring skills   There are a number of sources that identify specific cognitive restructuring skills used in CBT (J. S. Beck, 1995, 2011; Burns, 1999; Bush & Bilodeau, 1993; Bush, Glick & Taymans, 2002; Kaplan & Laygo, 2003; Leahy, 1996, 2003; McMullin, 2000; Monti, Rohsenow, Colby, & Abrams, 1995; Wanberg & Milkman, 1998, 2008). These skills are utilized in prosocial cognitive restructuring in order to change criminal and antisocial thinking in order to get prosocial outcomes. These can also be referred to as restructuring self-talk. Several are described in Box 13.3.

Cognitive Assessment Guide   A first step in prosocial cognitive restructuring is to have clients identify their specific criminal, antisocial, and AOD use thought habits and core beliefs. The worksheet in Table 13.1 is helpful in this step. For example, the criminal act that led to the client's last arrest can be listed as the target behavior. The key cognitive assessment questions are: What were the client's thoughts, attitude, and core beliefs at the time of the act?

Once criminal and substance abuse thought habits are identified, it is helpful for clients to determine into which category of thought structures they fall (e.g., expectancies, appraisals, decisions, or attributions). A thought habit *"I can get by with it"* would be an expectation. Those recurring patterns of thought habits and beliefs that are high-risk exposures for relapse and recidivism can then be worked on. Treatment is then directed at enhancing conscious

Table 13.1 Cognitive Assessment Guide using Larry's case as an example.

Target behavior: Resolve the issue with Larry's PO that he will miss his appointment because of car breaking down			External/internal events: Car breaking down on way to PO appointment	
Thought (automatic) habit	*Attitudes and core beliefs*	*Emotional outcomes*	*CB restructuring skills*	*Expected outcome(s)*
I'll never make it on time; my third strike, I'm going back to prison, I'm going to run with Tim (appraisal structures)	The world sucks: Bad things always happen to me, I've never had a fair chance in life	Anger, frustration, and hopelessness	STOP the negative thinking RELAX: a few deep breaths COUNTER: I've had some good things happen recently LOGIC: If I run now, it's a matter of time before I get caught and it will be worse	Telling Tim I'm not going with him Resolving the car problem and going to the PO's office, even though late Explaining to the PO what happened and accepting the consequence

PO, probation officer.

awareness of the activation of these thought structures and then utilizing restructuring to replace these structures with those that lead to prosocial outcomes.

Table 13.1 presents a *Cognitive Assessment Guide* that examines a specific external event that Larry faced. Now, pick another event from Larry's case and identify the target outcome behavior for that event. Complete the thought (automatic) habits, attitudes, and core beliefs that might be going on in Larry during that event. Then, identify the emotional outcomes and the CB restructuring skills that can lead to an expected positive outcome. A blank copy of the *Cognitive Assessment Guide* is provided in Appendix 13.A.

By having clients do this exercise repeatedly, they will begin to identify and recognize their specific thought habits and patterns and core beliefs that lead to criminal conduct and substance abuse, and in the course of treatment, practice cognitive-restructuring skills to change those cognitions. Then, when confronted with high-risk exposures that trigger these cognitions, they can go to a "manual shifting" process, work at managing and changing these cognitions, and reduce the probability of relapse and recidivism.

Thought mapping and belief searching   Figure 13.5 provides a tool and an illustration for identifying core beliefs related to thought habits; or if certain core beliefs are identified, searching for criminal or substance use thoughts that can emerge from the core beliefs. This helps identify criminal thinking and belief patterns. Unless core beliefs are changed, it is difficult for clients to move from criminal thinking and conduct toward a pattern of prosocial thinking and conduct.

Recognizing and changing errors in thinking   Identifying and changing thinking errors is an important component of CBT (A. T. Beck, 1976; Burns, 1999; Leahy, 2003; Marlatt, 1985; Yochelson & Samenow, 1976, 1977; Wanberg & Milkman, 1998, 2008). This involves learning to recognize thinking errors by being critical of one's cognitive and behavioral responses and then using self-talk cognitive restructuring skills, such as those identified in Box 13.3, to challenge the error: Larry thinks: "*My PO never supports me.*" Challenge: "*He has*

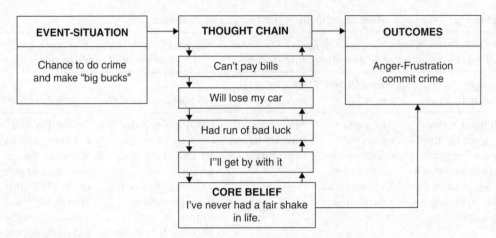

Figure 13.5 Thought mapping and belief searching. Copyright K. W. Wanberg & H. B. Milkman (2006, 2008) (used with permission of the authors).

cut me some slack." Larry thinks: *"Won't hurt to call Tim."* Challenge: *"Getting together with Tim means trouble."* It is essential that clients understand specific antisocial and criminal thoughts that result from specific thinking errors.

Once criminal or AOD abuse thoughts related to a specific thinking error are identified, the next step is to replace those thoughts with prosocial thinking: Thinking error: *"I deserve more than this"* (fair deserts). Prosocial correction: *"There are a lot of people worse off than me."* Some other examples of thinking errors are: power thrust (*"I'm better than others"*); victim stance (*"I've never had a fair chance"*); demand (*"I want it now"*); just deserts (*"They deserve it"*); cheated (*"I had more coming"*); magnify (*"Nobody understands me"*); catastrophize (making mountains out of molehills).

Values and morals clarification and character building   A thread that runs through correctional treatment is enhancing moral values and strengthening moral character (Little & Robinson, 1986; Ross, Fabiano & Ross, 1986; Ross & Hilborn, 2005; Wanberg & Milkman, 1998, 2006; Wanberg, Milkman, & Timken, 2005; Yokley, 2008). This is a gradual process that cannot be accomplished by preaching morality. As noted earlier, change is also accomplished through the provider modeling prosocial and moral thinking, talking, and acting. It is also accomplished through challenging clients to look at their values and moral stances. The importance of moral and character development in establishing a prosocial and positive relationship with others and the community is supported by a long history of investigation and research (e.g., Arbuthnot & Gordon, 1986; Bandura, 1977b; Colby & Kohlberg, 1987; Erickson, 1959, 1968; Hare, 1970; Hoffman, 1984, 1987; Kohlberg, 1964, 1981; Peterson & Seligman, 2004; Piaget, 1932).

A start is for clients to understand the meaning of antisocial and prosocial attitudes, and moral character, and then to identify their personal values, morals, and the standards of conduct they expect of others. For example, since freedom is an important value of judicial clients, a session should be devoted to identifying what freedom means to each of them. This is followed by identifying what thoughts and behaviors support the maintenance of freedom.

The value or moral dilemma exercise helps clients confront the conflict between their own values and morals and those of others. It is useful to highlight the discrepancy between a value they hold and their internal moral stance. The key elements of this exercise are: (i) present the moral dilemma; (ii) describe the moral conflict and dilemma of the central character; (iii) have group members take a position and then argue their position; (iv) look at the consequence of each position; and then (v) use problem-solving skills to resolve the dilemma.

For example, Larry's boss tells him late Friday afternoon that he wants him to go to a neighboring state to work for a month. His pay will be doubled. But if he wants the opportunity, he has to leave that evening to start the job on Sunday morning. Larry has been short of cash and he needs the extra money to pay a month of back rent and other bills. His parole order forbids him from going out of state without the permission of his PO, who is out of town and can't be reached until Monday. His PO has already given him three strikes. Does he go and take the chance his PO will understand when he calls him on Monday? What does he do?

Component 2: Relationship responsibility therapy

Emerging out of social learning theory (Bandura, 1977b), social skills training has solid empirical evidence supporting its efficacy in improving and increasing the effectiveness of relationships, reducing psychological symptoms, and increasing adherence to treatment involvement (e.g., Monti, Abrams, Kadden, & Cooney 1989; Monti et al., 1995; Segrin, 2003). Social skills training is widely applied to a variety of psychosocial problems (Segrin, 2003). Its substantive approach began with assertiveness training (Alberti & Emmons, 1995; Lange & Jakubowski, 1976). In traditional cognitive-behavioral therapy, social skills training is essentially egocentric. It has the goal of increasing the client's ability to engage in appropriate and effective interactions and communication with others and "more satisfying, effective, and enjoyable interactions with other people" (Segrin, 2003, p. 385).

Within the framework of SCRT, we see social skills training as relationship responsibility therapy, focusing on helping judicial clients develop prosocial and responsible thinking and behavior in their relationship with others (family members, intimate partners, co-workers, etc.). This involves respecting the rights of those they relate to, being concerned about their safety and welfare, and focusing on positive outcomes for others. As Beck et al. (2004) note, treatment of antisocial personality disorder will focus on improving moral and social behavior through enhancement of cognitive functioning and fostering interpersonal consideration. This is a main component of our criminal conduct and substance abuse curriculum for judicial clients (Wanberg & Milkman, 1998, 2006, 2008) and in our education and treatment curriculum for impaired driving offenders (Wanberg, Milkman, & Timken, 2005) and our *Criminal Conduct and Substance Abuse Treatment Program for Adolescents* (Milkman & Wanberg, 2012). Yokley (2008) also addresses this area in his *Social Responsibility Therapy for Adolescents and Young Adults* (2008). Several methods of building and maintaining responsible relationships are summarized.

Self-evaluation Self-assessment of the impact of substance abuse and criminal conduct on relationships involves: (i) identifying persons affected by the client's substance abuse and criminal conduct; (ii) recognizing the degree of emotional and physical harm or pain each person suffered; and (iii) identifying the response of others to the client's substance abuse and criminal conduct. The direct victims of criminal conduct are sorted out from those indirectly affected. This self-assessment can engender significant affective responding in some clients. Thus, it is recommended that this exercise be conducted by experienced counselors within a strong supportive therapeutic environment.

Empathy building and training   This is a crucial component in offender and antisocial treatment and change. Empathy has a strong relationship with prosocial and moral conduct (Eisenberg & Miller, 1987; Hoffman, 1984, 1987), motivates altruistic and moral behavior (Bohart & Greenberg, 1997; Hoffman, 1984, 1987), has a strong inverse relationship with aggression (Feshbach, 1984, 1997), is relational, and involves contextual awareness (O'Hara, 1997). Whereas egocentric empathy helps individuals know another person so as to have a more enriching and meaningful relationship with that person, sociocentric empathy provides relational awareness, knowing the relationships we participate in, with the prosocial goal of mutual benefit. O'Hara calls this mutual empathy (1997).

A single construct that accounts for a significant amount of antisocial conduct and criminal behavior is low self-control. An important component of low self-control is *lack of empathy*, self-centeredness, indifference and insensitivity to the suffering and plight of others, and not identifying with or putting oneself in the place of others (Gottfredson & Hirschi, 1990). It is of note that since empathy is contextual and circumstantial, empathy and prosocial conduct could have an inverse relationship. For example, a gang member may have a strong empathic response to another gang member, but still engage in antisocial and criminal acts that harm others. Strategies for empathy training are discussed later in this section.

Sympathy training   A companion of empathy building, sympathy training is an important component in developing prosocial attitudes and self-control. John Shlien (1997), as a student in the 1950s, had an ongoing dialogue with Carl Rogers around the concept of empathy. He argued that "empathy alone without sympathy may be harmful" (p. 67) and sympathy takes us to a higher state of moral development.

Often, the boundaries between sympathy and empathy are vague. However, there are some guidelines that distinguish between the two. Empathy can occur before the fact. One can have empathy before seeing a person hurt; or for someone or a community and have no emotional attachment to that entity. It is understanding, it is cognitive: "Your pain, my head." It is also about someone who is hurt or understanding the needs of another person. It helps prevent behaviors that cause pain and promotes behaviors that result in the positive benefit of others. Larry thinks: "*But what about Susan.*" "*My PO would be let down.*" "*My child needs a good dad.*"

Sympathy involves emotions and occurs after the fact: it is having compassion and feeling sorry for someone who has been injured. Sympathy is "your pain, my emotions." Sympathy brings an emotional commitment to being prosocial and caring, and responsible living. It provides the compassion component to moral responsibility. Larry thinks: "*I feel bad for Tim. He can't get it together.*"

There are a number of relationship responsibility therapy methods that facilitate and enhance prosocial empathic and sympathic responding within the sociocentric treatment context. These are summarized in Box 13.4. Although all of these techniques are used in empathy training, some can be used for enhancing sympathy responding as well.

Reflect on Larry's case and the application of prosocial cognitive restructuring and relationship responsibility training. What kind of understanding does Larry have around how his AOD use relates to his criminal conduct and impacts others? Evaluate his capacity for empathy and sympathy for others. What were some of the empathy and sympathy responses that he had? What specific relationship responsibility skills does he need to use to deal with Tim's pressure? Now, imagine you are Larry's therapist and he decides to go see you after resolving the pressure from Tim. Try and imagine the process of having him describe the prosocial cognitive restructuring he had to do in order to deal with Tim and then get to your office. Consider the skills Larry

Box 13.4 Empathy and Sympathy Training Strategies

1. **Communication skills training** has two dimensions: active sharing that promotes self-awareness and active listening that promotes other-awareness. Active listening provides a platform for empathy training and being sociocentric. Communication skills are at the core of learned empathy, which "is a basic form of social communication" (Feshbach, 1997, p. 33). Practicing active listening should be an integral part of treatment sessions.

2. **Cognitive analysis training** (Feshbach, 1984) involves analyzing non-verbal behavior (e.g., the meaning of facial expressions). This can be done through identifying the thoughts and emotions being expressed in pictures or by characters in an audio-suppressed video. Clients also judge the perceptual accuracy of their analysis. Other cognitive analysis exercises include non-verbal communication training and vicarious problem-solving (solving someone else's problems).

3. **Interpersonal and relationship problem-solving and negotiation** go beyond egocentric problem-solving and require a mutual agreement as to what is the problem, possible solutions, and a win-win or mutually satisfying outcome. The important prosocial ingredient is that the client wants the other person(s) to be part of the problem-solving and to have a positive outcome.

4. **Perspective taking** should start with non-threatening interactions such as taking the perspective of another group member explaining his or her problem. This can move to taking the perspective of individuals in the client's personal life, such as looking at an interpersonal conflict from the perspective of the other person. Assessing perceptual accuracy is a part of this process.

5. **Giving and receiving reinforcement and praise** are based on the communication skills of active sharing and active listening and enhance empathy and prosocial responding in interpersonal interactions (Monti et al., 1989, 1995; Ross et al., 1986; Wanberg & Milkman, 1998, 2008). Giving praise brings a client to focus on the other person; receiving compliments requires actively listening to the other person's perceptions.

6. **Managing anger in relationships** involves the use of both prosocial cognitive restructuring and the above described relationship responsibility therapy strategies. It includes basic anger management skills: knowing the anger triggers and being mindful of one's angry thoughts and feelings, using relaxation skills and self-talk to maintain self-control, communicating angry thoughts and feelings, knowing when a dead-end has been reached and when to use time-out, identifying relationship problems that underlie the anger, listening to and understanding the other person's response to the anger, taking the other person's perspective, and mutually rewarding resolution of the problem.

7. **Role-playing and role-reversal**. Role-playing sets up the condition whereby the client can demonstrate a problem or conflict and then demonstrate specific thoughts and behaviors that can lead to a positive outcome. Role-reversal is one of the most effective techniques in empathy and sympathy training and involves the client taking the role of the other person in the role play process (e.g., the client assumes the role of the intimate partner when role-playing a conflict episode with that partner. It is an operational way of having clients "walk in the shoes of someone else").

8. **Doubling** involves a client reflecting what another client is saying. For example, during a role-play while one client is talking with someone playing the role of his/ her intimate partner, another group member will stand by the client and reflect out loud what the client may be thinking or feeling. If the client says: "*you really don't listen to me*," the double might say, "*and you really don't understand me.*" It is best that the counselor demonstrate this technique before having clients use it. It is effective in empathy training in that the double takes the perspective of another individual with whom there is no emotional involvement. It is also helpful in sympathy training in that the double can feel the hurt and pain of another person.

9. **Feeling-thought sharing** involves having group members share their thoughts and emotions about someone expressing sadness and hurt in a group. Sympathy training would ask: "*How do you feel about Donna's sadness over her loss?*" Empathy training would ask: "*What are your thoughts about Donna's sadness?*" In this approach, it is best to have group members first share their feelings; then their thoughts.

10. **Responding to vignettes** that portray individuals who are having positive (just found a job) or negative experiences (an injury or mishap). The goal is for clients to identify the prosocial element of their responses and then whether they are sympathic, empathic, or both.

11. **Modeling** of sympathy and empathic responding by the counselor (Bandura, 1965).

would need to use to deal with his PO, and set up a role-play situation where Larry practices both problem-solving and communication skills to gain a positive outcome with his PO.

Component 3: Community responsibility therapy

Criminal conduct and substance abuse alienate clients from the community. Placement in the judicial system removes the offender from the community, either through incarceration or structured judicial supervision. Therefore, the ultimate goal in correctional treatment is to facilitate prosocial re-entry into the community.

Prosocial cognitive restructuring focuses on replacing antisocial and criminal thinking and behavior with prosocial thinking and behavior. Relationship responsibility therapy focuses on being responsible in relationships. Community responsibility therapy focuses on restructuring the client's relationship with the community with the goal of living according to the values and laws of society and being a responsible member of the community. This is a main component of our criminal conduct and substance abuse treatment curriculum (Milkman & Wanberg, 2012; Wanberg & Milkman, 1998, 2006, 2008). A few methods and approaches for building community responsibility are summarized.

Integrating the correctional with the therapeutic   Effective correctional treatment brings together the judicial and therapeutic processes (Andrews & Bonta, 2003; Taxman, 2004). Sanctioning becomes effective when it is integrated with correctional treatment. Treatment becomes more effective when it is integrated with the sanctioning process. Correctional treatment is both client centered and society centered. The provider has two clients, the offender and the community, and wears two hats, the correctional and the therapeutic. The treatment provider works closely with judicial supervisors in achieving the goal of having clients successfully meet the terms and conditions of the court and re-enter the community. When a treatment agency or counselor accepts a judicial client, that agency agrees to help administer the judicial sentence – to engage in the sanctioning process.

This is a paradigm shift for traditional treatment approaches in that correctional treatment must involve punishment or sanctioning. The shift requires a close working relationship between the provider and the judicial system. From the start, clients are informed that the treatment provider represents both the community and the client. The client agrees to this condition by signing a consent for release of information to the judicial system allowing the provider to inform the court (community) of the client's progress.

Through integrated structured supervision, the treatment provider is involved in the client's judicial supervision through periodic meetings between client, treatment provider, and judicial supervisor. This creates a working partnership among the three stakeholders. The goal is to facilitate client rapport with the judicial and therapeutic systems.

Self-assessment of antisocial behavior   The literature reflects differences among experts as to how many offenders fit the DSM-IV (American Psychiatric Association, 1994, 2000) diagnosis of Antisocial Personality Disorder (APD), varying from 40% to 80% (see Richards, 2004). On close scrutiny, most if not all offenders would meet at least one, if not two, and most would meet three of the DSM-IV and DSM-5 criteria (American Psychiatric Association, 2013). Our position is that all offenders fit an antisocial personality pattern, which we define as irresponsible behavior that goes against the norms and rules (or laws) of society and disregards and/or violates the rights of others. There are also different patterns of antisocial personality within the offender population just as there are different levels and categories of criminal behavior as defined by state and Federal statutes. Box 13.5 provides a list of antisocial characteristics taken from the DSM-IV and DSM-5 criteria, and sociopathy, and antisocial characteristics as described in several textbooks on abnormal psychology (e.g., Butcher, Mineka, & Hooley, 2010; Sarason & Sarason, 2005; Seligman, Walker, & Rosenhan, 2001).

An important goal of correctional treatment is to help clients understand their own unique antisocial pattern of going against society. This can be done in a group session that focuses specifically on antisocial behavior and uses the specific antisocial markers provided in Box 13.5. Within the framework of interactive self-assessment, clients share which and how many characteristics they fit, and receive feedback from the group around their findings. Clients can give an item a score of 1 if they fit it and zero if they do not.

Assessment of prosocial strengths   This can be done by clients identifying the characteristics in Box 13.5 that they think they do not fit, indicated by the number of zero scores, which provides a measure of prosocial strengths. It can also be useful for the group to redefine each of the items in prosocial terms (e.g., item 12 is rephrased: Prosocial and law-abiding friends; see Chapter 14 (Marshall & O'Brien) and Chapter 21 (Fortune & Ward) for coverage of other strength-based approaches).

Assessment of client's criminal conduct and impact on the community   This is accomplished by having clients construct a criminal conduct history log. Clients list *only* the crimes for which they were arrested or charged and include: type of crime, arrest year, months on probation, months served in jail or prison, months on parole, was AOD use involved in the offense, specific victim(s), and estimated cost of the crime to the community. Clients often have

Box 13.5   Characteristics of the Antisocial Personality Pattern

1. Repeated acts of non-conformity to social norms and laws.
2. Impulsivity and failure to plan ahead.
3. Patterns of deceit, lying, conning for personal gain.
4. Maladaptive anger.
5. Low frustration tolerance.
6. Poor problem-solving in relationships.
7. Irresponsibility in finances, relationships, society obligations.
8. Inability or unwillingness to delay gratification.
9. Irritability, aggressiveness, repeated physical fights and assaults.
10. Reckless disregard for the safety of others.
11. Denial of personal responsibility and blaming.
12. Antisocial and criminal associates.
13. Manipulative and exploitive relationships and using others for selfish reasons.
14. Lack of empathy for others.
15. Lack of remorse and guilt around hurting or mistreating others.
16. Self-centered and aggrandizement of self and inflated self-view.
17. Failure to sustain consistent work behavior.
18. Taking risks that puts oneself in danger without seeing possible outcomes
19. Hard time or unable to form an intimate relationship where both receive equal benefits.

problems identifying victims in that some offenses do not involve an individual victim per se. However, every crime has a victim or victims, and the community is a victim of every crime.

Community-oriented empathy and sympathy   Community-oriented empathy is an awareness that one is part of the community and society and understands the problems and difficulties of a community. Community-oriented sympathy involves feeling the pain and hurt of a community or society (e.g., a country suffering from war, a community suffering from riots or being the victim of a hurricane). Both processes build an understanding that when the community is hurt, "I am also hurt."

Having judicial clients develop empathy and sympathy beyond non-personal relationships is a difficult task. It is more abstract and less concrete than interpersonal empathy training. However, there are some specific strategies that help clients learn community-oriented empathy and sympathy. The construction of the criminal history log, described above, can also facilitate understanding of how the community was a victim of the client's criminal conduct. This can be expanded to having clients evaluate the impact of their substance abuse on the community. *Media-reflection exercises* involve showing the group a video or movie of a country or city ravaged by war or a natural disaster and having group members identify their empathic and sympathetic responses.

Prosocial treatment groups and the therapeutic community   These provide an effective microcosm for learning to be productive members of the group, which can generalize to the community at large (Deitch, Carleton, Koutsenok, & Marsolais, 2002; DeLeon, 2000; Inciardi, Martin, & Butzin, 2004; Wexler, Melnick, Lowe, & Peters, 1999). They also provide an environment within which clients learn community-oriented empathy and prosocial responsibility.

Preventing violence and aggression   Although many judicial clients do not commit a crime of violence, an area of concern is providing sessions for all clients that focus on the prevention of violence and aggression. In addition to the direct victim of a violent crime, the community is also a victim. All criminal conduct, whether involving violence or not, is an attack on the integrity and moral fiber of the community. Thus, all judicial clients can benefit from the core therapeutic principles that focus on the prevention of aggression and violence.

Re-entry and reintegration programs and aftercare   As noted, entrance into the judicial system alienates offenders from the community, including those placed on probation, and the ultimate goal is for clients to re-enter and reintegrate into the community. Treatment providers and judicial workers can facilitate the client's involvement in both formal aftercare programs and informal community reinforcement programs such as Alcoholics Anonymous (AA). The research is clear: judicial clients engaging in re-entry and aftercare programs following treatment have a much higher probability of living crime- and drug-free (Inciardi, Surratt, Martin, & Hooper, 2002; Wexler, 2004).

Contributing to the good of the community   Required or volunteer community service programs provide opportunity for clients to return good to the community. Such programs should be therapeutically structured and involve group processing to gain the full impact of community service involvement.

Giving and receiving support and continuing care   This represents a lifestyle alternative for clients and facilitates community reintegration. It is time and research tested that openness to and receiving support from others enhances positive treatment outcomes. This support goes beyond formal treatment. Community reinforcement approaches are effective in helping clients sustain ownership of change (Sisson & Azrin, 1989; Smith & Meyers, 1995). This is achieved through involvement in self-help groups and aftercare services. Individuals who have made and sustained change also strengthen their own change by giving support to others who are attempting to live crime- and drug-free. Role modeling, mentoring, and 12-step work are powerful ways to reinforce ownership of change and strengthen prosocial behavior and community responsibility.

Larry's Story Revisited

The three SCRT components of prosocial cognitive restructuring, relationship responsibility therapy, and community responsibility therapy have been presented and a number of strategies for the application of these components described. So let us return to Larry's story. He used his cognitive-behavior skills that he had learned in therapy and told Tim he wasn't running, called his PO, and scheduled a session with his therapist that evening. We now briefly outline the appropriate application of SCRT components to the session.

- Using basic counseling skills, Larry is given time to share his thoughts and emotions about the experience and is provided with positive reinforcement for his achievement.
- Use the CB Map (Figure 13.1) to review the episode and identify the event, his automatic thoughts (*"just as well split," "I'll go back to prison"*), his emotions, and behavioral choices that could have led to a negative outcome. Use the thought-mapping and belief-searching

to facilitate this process (see Figure 13.5). Use Figure 13.2 to identify the high-risk exposures that Larry faced. As part of this process, help him to identify some of his thinking errors (e.g., "*My PO will never understand.*").

- Using the CB Map, repeat the process and have Larry identify some of the prosocial thoughts that led to the positive outcome (*"What about Susan? She's a good woman", "My PO, he's good to me"*) and the core belief that he has been treated fairly by others in his life (his wife, counselor, etc.). Identify some of the skills he used, such as Countering – "*My PO, told me I'm on the line, he'll revoke,*" but "*he's been good to me, he understands, maybe he won't revoke;*" or Thinking Their Position such as "*But what about Susan?*"
- Focus on relationship responsibility strategies, which would include empathy and sympathy training around his thoughts about and relationship with his wife, therapist, PO, AA sponsor, and communication skills training that would involve role-playing Larry going home and actively sharing his experience with Susan and actively listening to her thoughts and emotions.
- Finally, the SCRT objective of bringing together the correctional and therapeutic processes is implemented by having Larry identify how he can repair the relationship with his PO (and the correctional system) and then, during the therapy session, have Larry call his PO to set up a meeting for him and his therapist to meet with the PO. To prepare for that, set up a role-play episode for Larry to rehearse his interaction with his PO. The session ends with the therapist again providing positive reinforcement for the way Larry handled this critical event in his life.

Concluding Remarks

The main thesis of this chapter is that to effectively address antisocial and criminal attitudes and conduct, the egocentric therapy goal of helping clients resolve their psychological problems and pain must be integrated with a well-defined and consistent sociocentric approach that includes a psychology of caring and a focus on developing thinking and behaviors that result in moral and social responsibility toward others, the community, and society as a whole. Thus, correctional treatment is both client and society centered. The primary goals that guide correctional treatment are: preventing relapse and recidivism, and facilitating meaningful and responsible living, which take into account the safety and welfare of others and society. The ultimate goal is successful reintegration into the community.

Within the framework of a sociocentric approach, SCRT comprises three components. First, traditional CBT restructuring is reframed as prosocial cognitive restructuring, which focuses on identifying and replacing antisocial and criminal thinking and beliefs with prosocial cognitive structures that lead to responsible behavior toward others and the community. Second, traditional CBT social skills training is redefined as relationship responsibility therapy, which focuses on developing prosocial and responsible thinking and behavior in relationship with others (family members, intimate partners, co-workers, etc.) with the goal of enhancing positive outcomes resulting in benefit for all parties involved.

The third component of our SCRT model is fostering community responsibility and helping judicial clients to restructure their relationship with the community. This involves having clients define their past involvement in criminal conduct and substance abuse, identify the impact of this involvement on others and the community, and developing skills to enhance empathic and sympathic responding within relationships and the larger community. Clients gain a good grasp of their antisocial attitudes and conduct, their prosocial strengths, and then learn approaches and skills to enhance prosocial and morally responsible behavior. SCRT focuses on helping clients identify and learn to manage high-risk exposures that lead to relapse and recidivism. An overarching theme is the integration of the therapeutic and correctional systems through developing a working partnership among the three stakeholders: the client, the treatment provider, and the judicial system, which represents the community.

The facilitation of SCRT is enhanced when clients are involved in programs that give back to the community. Successfully integrated interventions that promote prosocial cognitions, enhance responsibility in personal relationships, and promote community responsibility, form the foundation of a model for helping judicial clients live crime- and drug-free and meaningful lives.

References

Abrams, D. B., & Niaura, R. S. (1987). Social learning theory. In H. T. Blane & K. W. Leonard (Eds.), *Psychological theories of drinking and alcoholism* (pp. 131–178). New York: Guilford.

Alberti, R. E., & Emmons, M. L. (1995). *Your perfect right: A guide to assertive living* (7th ed.). San Luis Obispo, CA: Impact Publishers.

American Psychiatric Association. (1994). *Diagnostic and statistical manual of mental disorders* (4th ed.). Washington, DC: Author.

American Psychiatric Association. (2000). *Diagnostic and statistical manual of mental disorders* (4th ed., text revision). Washington, DC: Author.

American Psychiatric Association (1994). *Diagnostic and statistical manual of mental disorders* (5th ed.). Washington, DC: Author.

Andrews, D. A., & Bonta, J. (2003). *The psychology of criminal conduct* (3rd ed.). Cincinnati, OH: Anderson.

Arbuthnot, J., & Gordon, D. A. (1986). Behavioral and cognitive effects of a moral reasoning development intervention for high-risk, behavioral-disordered adolescents. *Journal of Consulting and Clinical Psychology, 54*, 208–216.

Bandura, A. (1965). Influence of models' reinforcement contingencies on the acquisition of imitated responses. *Journal of Personality and Social Psychology, 1*, 589–595.

Bandura, A. (1977a). Self-efficacy: Towards a unifying theory of behavioral change. *Psychological Review, 84*, 191–215.

Bandura, A. (1977b). *Social learning theory.* Englewood Cliffs, NJ: Prentice-Hall.

Bandura, A. (1978). The self-system in reciprocal determination. *American Psychologist, 33*, 344–358.

Bandura, A. (Ed.) (1995). *Self-efficacy in changing societies.* New York: Cambridge University Press.

Bandura, A. (1997). *Self-efficacy: The exercise of control.* New York: Freeman.

Beck, A. T. (1976). *Cognitive therapy and the emotional disorders.* New York: International Universities Press.

Beck, A. T., Freeman, A., Davis, D. D., & Associates. (2004). *Cognitive therapy of personality disorders* (2nd ed.). New York: The Guilford Press.

Beck, J. S. (1995). *Cognitive therapy: Basics and beyond.* New York: Guilford.

Beck, J. S. (2011). *Cognitive therapy: Basics and beyond* (2nd ed.). New York: Guilford.

Bohart, A. C., & Greenberg, L. S. (1997). Empathy and psychotherapy: An introductory overview. In A. C. Bohart, & L. S. Greenberg (Eds.), *Empathy reconsidered: New directions in psychotherapy* (pp. 3–31). Washington, DC: American Psychological Association.

Burns, D. D. (1999). *Feeling good: The new mood therapy* (revised and updated). New York: Avon Books.

Bush, J. M., & Bilodeau, B. C. (1993). *Options: A cognitive change program.* Washington, DC: National Institute of Corrections.

Bush, J. M., Glick, B., Taymans, J. (2002). *Thinking for a change: Integrative Cognitive Behavioral Program.* Washington, DC: National Institute of Corrections.

Butcher, J. N., Mineka, S., & Hooley, J. M. (2010). *Abnormal psychology.* Boston: Allyn & Bacon.

Colby, A., & Kohlberg, L. (1987). *The measurement of moral judgement. Vol. 1: Theoretical foundations and research validation.* Cambridge: Cambridge University Press.

Crime News. (2010). *Substance abuse costs $511 Billion: A cost-benefit analysis.* Retrieved from: http://www.crimeinamerica.net/2010/03/22/substance-abuse-costs-511-billion-a-cost-benefit-analysis-crime-news

Deitch, D. A., Carleton, S., Koutsenok, I. B., & Marsolais, K. (2002). Therapeutic community treatment in prisons. In C. G. Leukefeld, F. Tims, & D. Farabee (Eds.), *Treatment of drug offenders: Policies and issues* (pp. 127–137). New York: Springer Publishing Company, Inc.

DeLeon, G. (2000). *The therapeutic community: Theory, model and method.* New York: Springer Publishing Co.

DeMuro, S. A., Wanberg, K. W., & Anderson, R. (2011). Driving while impaired (DWI) intervention service provider orientations: the scales of the DWI Therapeutic Educator Inventory (DTEI). *Substance Abuse, 32,* 225–237.

Eisenberg, N., & Miller, P. (1987). Empathy, sympathy, and altruism: Empirical and conceptual links. In N. Eisenberg & J. Strayer (Eds.), *Empathy and development* (pp. 292–316). New York: Cambridge University Press.

Eltman, F., & Hays, T. (2012, November 8). New York hurricane damage could cost $33 billion says Governor Cuomo. *The Huffington Post.* Retrieved from: http://www.huffingtonpost.com/2012/11/08/new-york-hurricane-damage-costs-cuomo_n_2094008.html

Erikson, E. H. (1959). *Childhood and society* (2nd ed.). New York: Norton.

Erikson, E. H. (1968). *Youth and crisis.* New York: Norton.

Feshbach, N. D. (1984). Empathy, empathy training and the regulation of aggression in elementary school children. In R. M. Kaplan, V. J. Konecni, & R. W. Novaco (Eds.), *Aggression in children and youth.* The Hague: Martinus Nijhoff.

Feshbach, N. D. (1997). Empathy: The formative years – implications for clinical practice. In A. C. Bohart & L. S. Greenberg (Eds.), *Empathy reconsidered: New directions in psychotherapy* (pp. 33–62). Washington, DC: American Psychological Association.

Freeman, A., Pretzer, J., Fleming, B., & Simon, K. M. (1990). *Clinical applications of cognitive therapy.* New York: Plenum.

Goldfried, M. R. (1995). *From cognitive-behavioral therapy to psychotherapy integration: An evolving view.* New York: Springer.

Gottfredson, M., & Hirschi, T. (1990). *A general theory of crime.* Palo Alto, CA: Stanford University Press.

Hare, R. D. (1970). *Psychopathy: Theory and research.* New York: Wiley.

Hiller, M. L., Knight, K., & Simpson, D. D. (1999). Prison-based substance abuse treatment, residential aftercare, and recidivism. *Addiction, 94,* 833–842.

Hodgins, D. C., el Guebaly, N., & Armstrong, S. (1995). Prospective and retrospective reports of mood states before relapse to substance use. *Journal of Consulting and Clinical Psychology, 63,* 400–407.

Hoffman, M. L. (1984). Moral development. In M. H. Bornstein & M. E. Lamb (Eds.), *Developmental psychology: An advanced textbook* (p. 279). Hillsdale, NJ: Lawrence Erlbaum.

Hoffman, M. L. (1987). The contribution of empathy to justice and moral judgment. In N. Eisenberg & J. Strayer (Eds.), *Empathy and its development* (p. 47). New York: Cambridge University Press.

Inciardi, J. A., Martin, S. S., & Butzin, C. A. (2004). Five-year outcomes of therapeutic community treatment of drug-involved offenders after release from prison. *Crime & Delinquency, 50,* 88–107.

Inciardi, J. A., Surratt, H. L., Martin, S. S., & Hooper, R. M. (2002). The importance of aftercare in a corrections-based treatment continuum. In C. G. Leukefeld, F. Tims, & D. Farabee (Eds.), *Treatment of drug offenders: Policies and issues* (pp. 204–216). New York: Springer Publishing Company, Inc.

Kaplan, A., & Laygo, R. (2003). Stress management. In W. O'Donohue, J. E. Fisher, & S. C. Hayes (Eds.), *Cognitive behavior therapy: Applying empirically supported techniques in your practice* (pp. 411–416). Hoboken, NJ: John Wiley & Sons, Inc.

Kohlberg, L. (1964). Development of moral character and moral ideology. In M. L. Hoffman & L. W. Hoffman (Eds.), *Review of child development research, Vol. I* (pp. 383–431). New York: Russell Sage Foundation.

Kohlberg, L. (1981). *The philosophy of moral development.* San Francisco, CA: Harper & Row.

Lange, A. J., & Jakubowski, P. (1976). *Responsible assertive behavior.* Champaign, IL: Research Press.

Leahy, R. L. (1996). *Cognitive therapy: Basic principles and applications.* Northvale, NJ: Jason Aronson, Inc.

Leahy, R. L. (2003). *Cognitive therapy techniques: A practitioner's guide.* New York: The Guilford Press.

Leshner, A. (2006). *Addiction is a brain disease. Issues in Science and Technology.* University of Texas at Dallas.

Little, G., & Robinson, K. (1986). *How to escape your prison: A moral reconation therapy workbook.* Memphis, TN: Eagle Wing Books.

Marlatt, G. A. (1985). Relapse prevention: Theoretical rationale and overview of the model. In G. A. Marlatt & J. R. Gordon (Eds.), *Relapse prevention: Maintenance strategies in the treatment of addictive behaviors* (pp. 3–70). New York: Guilford.

Marlatt, G. A., & Witkiewitz, K. (2005). Relapse prevention for alcohol and drug problems. In G. A. Marlatt & D. M. Donovan (Eds.), *Relapse prevention* (2nd ed., pp. 1–44). New York: Guilford Press.

McMullin, R. E. (2000). *The new handbook of cognitive therapy techniques.* New York: W. W. Norton.

Milkman, H. B., & Wanberg, K. W. (2005). *Criminal conduct and substance abuse treatment for adolescents: Pathways to self-discovery and change – The provider's guide.* Thousand Oaks, CA: Sage Publications.

Milkman, H. B., & Wanberg, K. W. (2012). *Criminal conduct and substance abuse treatment for adolescents: Pathways to self-discovery and change – The provider's guide* (2nd ed.). Thousand Oaks, CA: Sage Publications.

Monti, P. M., Abrams, D. B., Kadden, R. M., & Cooney, N. L. (1989). *Treating alcohol dependence: A coping skills training guide.* New York: Guilford.

Monti, P. M., Rohsenow, D. J., Colby, S. M., & Abrams, D. B. (1995). Coping and social skills training. In R. K. Hester & W. R. Miller (Eds.), *Handbook of alcoholism treatment approaches: Effective alternatives* (2nd ed., pp. 221–241). Boston: Allyn & Bacon.

Moos, R. H., Finney, J. W., & Moos, B. S. (2000). Inpatient substance abuse care and the outcome of subsequent community residential and outpatient care. *Addiction, 95,* 833–846.

O'Hara, M. (1997). Relational empathy: Beyond modernist egocentrism to postmodern holistic contextualism. In A. C. Bohart & L. S. Greenberg (Eds.), *Empathy reconsidered: New directions in psychotherapy* (pp. 295–320). Washington, DC: American Psychological Association.

Peterson, C., & Seligman, M. E. P. (2004). *Character strengths and virtues: A handbook and classification.* New York: Oxford University Press.

Piaget, J. (1932). *The moral judgement of the child.* London: Routledge & Kegan Paul.

Richards, H. J. (2004). How psychopathic? A critical consideration for offender treatment. In K. Knight & D. Farabee (Eds.), *Treating addicted offenders: A continuum of effective practices.* Kingston, NJ: Civic Research Institute.

Ross, R. R., Fabiano, E. A., & Ross, R. D. (1986). *Reasoning and rehabilitation: A handbook for teaching cognitive skills.* Ottawa, Ontario: University of Ottawa.

Ross, R. R., & Hilborn, J. (2005). *Reasoning and rehabilitation 2: Short Version for Adults – A handbook for teaching prosocial competence.* Ottawa, Ontario: Cognitive Centre of Canada.

Sarason, I. G., & Sarason, B. R. (2005). *Abnormal psychology: The problem of maladaptive behavior* (11th ed.). Englewood Cliffs, NJ: Prentice-Hall.

Segrin, C. (2003). Social skills training. In W. O'Donohue, J. E. Fisher, & S. C. Hayes (Eds.), *Cognitive behavior therapy: Applying empirically supported techniques in your practice* (pp. 384–390). Hoboken, NJ: John Wiley & Sons, Inc.

Seligman, M. E. P., Walker, E. F., & Rosenhan, D. L. (2001). *Abnormal psychology* (4th ed.). New York: W. W. Norton.

Shlien, J. (1997). Empathy in psychotherapy: A vital mechanism? Yes. Therapist's conceit? All too often. By itself enough? No. In A. C. Bohart & L. S. Greenberg (Eds.), *Empathy reconsidered: New directions in psychotherapy* (pp. 63–80). Washington, DC: American Psychological Association.

Sisson, R., & Azrin, N. (1989). The community reinforcement approach. In R. K. Hester & W. R. Miller (Eds.), *Handbook of alcoholism treatment approaches* (pp. 242–258). New York: Pergamon.

Smith, J. E., & Meyers, R. J. (1995). The community reinforcement approach. In R. K. Hester & W. R. Miller (Eds.), *Handbook of alcoholism treatment approaches: Effective alternatives* (2nd ed., pp. 251–266). Boston: Allyn & Bacon.

Sovereign, R. G., & Miller, W. R. (1987). *Effects of therapist style on resilience and outcome among problem drinkers.* Paper presented at the Fourth International Conference on Treatment of Addictive Behaviors, Bergen, Norway.

Taxman, F. S. (2004). Reducing recidivism through a seamless system of care: Components of effective treatment, supervision, and transition services in the community. In K. Knight & D. Farabee (Eds.), *Treating addicted offenders: A continuum of effective practices* (pp. 32-1–32-12). Kingston, NJ: Civic Research Institute.

Wanberg, K.W. & Milkman, H. B. (1998). *Criminal conduct and substance abuse treatment: Strategies for self-improvement and change.* Thousand Oaks, CA: Sage Publications.

Wanberg, K. W. & Milkman, H. B. (2006). *Criminal conduct and substance abuse treatment: Strategies for Self-Improvement and Change – Pathways to responsible living, Participant's workbook.* Thousand Oaks, CA: Sage Publications.

Wanberg, K. W. & Milkman, H. B. (2008). *Criminal conduct and substance abuse treatment: Strategies for Self-Improvement and Change – Pathways to responsible living, Provider guide.* Thousand Oaks, CA: Sage Publications.

Wanberg, K. W., & Milkman, H. B. (in press). Effective approaches for criminal conduct and substance abuse treatment: Contributions of the science of what works. *Journal of Community Corrections.*

Wanberg, K. W., Milkman, H. B., & Timken, D. (2005). *Driving with care: Education and treatment of the impaired driving offender – Strategies for responsible living and change.* Thousand Oaks, CA: Sage Publications.

Wexler, H. K. (2004). An integrated approach to aftercare and employment for criminal justice clients. In K. Knight & D. Farabee (Eds.), *Treating addicted offenders: A continuum of effective practices* (pp. 34-1–44-6). Kingston, NJ: Civic Research Institute.

Wexler, H. K., Melnick, G., Lowe, L., & Peters, J. (1999). Three-year reincarceration outcomes for Amity in-prison therapeutic community and aftercare in California. *Prison Journal, 79*(3), 321–336.

Wilson, G. T., & O'Leary, K. D. (1980). *Principles of behavioral therapy.* Englewood Cliffs, NJ: Prentice-Hall, Inc.

Yochelson, S., & Samenow, S. E. (1976). *The criminal personality, Vol. I: A profile for change.* New York: Jason Aronson.

Yochelson, S., & Samenow, S. E. (1977). *The criminal personality, Vol. II: The change process.* New York: Jason Aronson.

Yokley, J. M. (2008). *Social and responsibility therapy for adolescents and young adults: A multicultural treatment manual for harmful behavior.* New York: Routledge.

Suggestions for Further Learning

Books

Milkman, H. B., & Wanberg, K. W. (2012). *Criminal conduct and substance abuse treatment for adolescents: Pathways to self-discovery and change – The provider's guide* (2nd ed.). Thousand Oaks, CA: Sage Publications.

Wanberg, K. W., & Milkman, H.B. (2008). *Criminal conduct and substance abuse treatment: Strategies for self-improvement and change – Pathways to responsible living, Provider guide.* Thousand Oaks, CA: Sage Publications.

Appendix 13.A

Cognitive Assessment Guide

Name:	I.D.	Provider:	Date:

Target behavior:			External/internal events:	
Thought habit (automatic)	Attitudes and core beliefs	Emotional outcomes	CB restructuring skills	Expected outcome(s)

Target behavior:			External/internal events:	
Thought habit (automatic)	Attitudes and core beliefs	Emotional outcomes	CB restructuring skills	Expected outcome(s)

Target behavior:			External/internal events:	
Thought habit (automatic)	Attitudes and core beliefs	Emotional outcomes	CB restructuring skills	Expected outcome(s)

Section 4

Two Perspectives on the Treatment of Sexual Aggression

14

Balancing Clients' Strengths and Deficits in Sexual Offender Treatment

The Rockwood Treatment Approach

William L. Marshall and Matt D. O'Brien

Introduction

Sexual offending is a serious and relatively frequently occurring social problem. According to Bagley (1991) up to 33% of males and 50% of females reported being sexually abused as children, with most of these assaults occurring before 12 years of age. In the United States in 2004, more than 84 000 children were victims of sexual abuse (U.S. Department of Health and Human Services, 2006). A comprehensive telephone survey indicated that 32% of women and 14% of men suffered sexual victimization during childhood (Briere & Elliot, 2003) with Finkelhor (1984) reporting similar data.

Similarly the rape of adult women appears to be disturbingly high across all nations (van Dijk & Mayhew, 1992). W. L. Marshall and Barrett (1990) extracted data from official records in Canada during 1988, and multiplying this rate by four (the lower estimate of under-reporting derived from surveys), produced an estimated 75 000 adult female victims of rape for that year. This is consistent with other studies in which as many as 30% of women reported being sexually assaulted at some point in their adult lives (Russell, 1984).

As we will see, when treatment is appropriately implemented, it markedly reduces recidivism among these offenders (Hanson et al., 2002; Lösel & Schmucker, 2005) and thus reduces the number of future victims. Effective intervention also saves considerable money that otherwise would be spent on investigations and judicial processes as well as on incarceration and victim costs (W. L. Marshall, 1992; Prentky & Burgess, 1990).

Overview of the Rockwood Psychological Services (RPS) Approach

Program development and procedural features

Rockwood Psychological Services (RPS) treatment programs for sexual offenders were first developed in the early 1970s (W. L. Marshall, 1971) as an application of the emerging behavior therapy movement. While other programs at that time focused on either simply eliminating

Forensic CBT: A Handbook for Clinical Practice, First Edition.
Edited by Raymond Chip Tafrate and Damon Mitchell.
© 2014 John Wiley & Sons, Ltd. Published 2014 by John Wiley & Sons, Ltd.

deviant sexual interests (Bond & Evans, 1967) or on also enhancing appropriate interests (Marquis, 1970), the early RPS program incorporated both these aims as well as employing procedures to increase the client's self-confidence and relationship skills. Over the years the targets addressed in RPS programs expanded as a result of clinically derived hunches that were subsequently subjected to empirical examination and as a result were either discarded or incorporated as fixed features of the program. These developments were periodically reported (W. L. Marshall, Earls, Segal, & Darke, 1983; W. L. Marshall & Williams, 1975) culminating in a series of three books: the first described the procedures used to change the treatment targets and the evidence supporting these procedures (W. L. Marshall, Anderson, & Fernandez, 1999); the second described the need to integrate cognitions, behaviors, and emotions (W. L. Marshall, Marshall, Serran, & Fernandez, 2006); and the most recent one provided the overall integration of the program within a strength-based approach (W. L. Marshall, Marshall, Serran, & O'Brien, 2011). Each of these books provides the evidence base for all aspects of our programs.

Our programs operate in community outpatient settings, in psychiatric inpatient facilities, and in prisons. In each of these settings the program is essentially the same, except that in our community program we typically see clients just once per week, while in institutional settings the frequency of sessions varies from twice per week (for moderate-risk offenders) to three times per week (for high-risk and high-moderate-risk offenders). Evidence from basic psychological research on what has been called "massed versus spaced practice" (see W. L. Marshall, Marshall, Serran, & O'Brien, 2011, for a summary of this research) indicates the need to space learning sessions in order to allow participants to consolidate what they have learned. This evidence indicates that having more than three sessions per week does not produce any additional gains in outcome. Additionally, on the basis of the evidence indicating the negative impact of overtreating offenders, we typically involve moderate-risk clients in treatment for 4–6 months, and higher-risk clients for 6–10 months. It is important to note that sexual offenders who have significant anger or substance abuse problems will also be expected to enter other programs for these additional difficulties as well as the sexual offender-specific program. RPS programs employ one or two therapists (depending upon available resources) addressing eight to ten clients at time, and they function as open-ended (or rolling) groups. In open-ended programs, a new client replaces each graduate once the graduate has successfully addressed each criminogenic issue to the satisfaction of the therapist. To determine whether or not the client has effectively addressed each issue, we employ our empirically validated Therapist Rating Scale, which is available free-of-charge from our website: www.rockwoodpsyc.com.

We operate three different kinds of programs, each of which follows the same model. Our full treatment program, which we refer to as the Regular Program, covers all aspects of the components necessary to achieve effective treatment. An almost identical program is run for convicted sexual offenders who, nevertheless, categorically deny having ever committed an offense: we refer to this as our Deniers' Program. It covers exactly the same issues in exactly the same way as the Regular Program except that we present the goal to the offenders as equipping them with the skills necessary to meet their needs prosocially so that they will never again be at risk to be falsely accused of offending. Finally, we have a special program aimed at preparing incarcerated sexual offenders for their subsequent full treatment programs, which may or may not be at an institution where RPS programs operate. We call this our Preparatory Program, which is rather brief and is simply intended to engage and motivate clients. Each of these programs will be described in the present chapter.

Motivation and engagement

Like most offenders, men who commit sexual crimes are characteristically poorly motivated for treatment. As a result, many refuse the offer of treatment, while those who accept an offer typically do so for externally motivated reasons such as to secure early release from confinement, or to be allowed to reunite with their families. We use motivational interviewing skills (Miller & Rollnick, 2002; Miller & Rose, 2009) when we offer clients a place in treatment. This appears to be effective since in our prison programs, 96.2% of all available sexual offenders accept the offer. This motivational style continues throughout all aspects of the programs but is particularly emphasized in the initial phase. Again, this appears to be effective as the drop-out rate from the RPS prison programs is slightly under 3%. Tafrate and Luther (see Chapter 20) discuss integrating motivational interviewing in offender CBT treatment in more detail.

In addition to the use of motivational interviewing skills, we also engage clients by describing treatment as aimed at providing skills and self-confidence to achieve a better quality of life than they had prior to their conviction. We do this when we offer treatment and we repeat it at the first treatment session. Mann and Webster (2002) showed that a significant number of sexual offenders who admitted to having a problem but refused an offer of treatment, said they did so because they believed treatment would simply involve addressing their offending behavior; what they said they wanted was treatment that would give them a better life.

Our overall approach to treatment is strength-based and derives from the emerging literature in positive psychology (Linley & Joseph, 2004; Snyder & Lopez, 2005) and the basic tenets of effective treatment delivery (see W. L. Marshall, Fernandez, et al., 2003, for a review of the general therapeutic process literature). Our view is that sexual offenders engage in inappropriate behaviors because their problematic backgrounds (see Starzyk & Marshall, 2003, for a review) have not equipped them with the capacities to meet their needs in prosocial ways. None of this means we excuse sexual offenders. We insist they take responsibility for their futures and we require them to take the necessary steps to ensure they do not again harm innocent people, but we do so in an empathic, warm, and rewarding way. Our latest book (W. L. Marshall, Marshall, Serran, & O'Brien, 2011) provides detailed descriptions of our approach and includes both its theoretical underpinnings and our outcome evaluations.

The decision to develop the Preparatory Program was related to research demonstrating that programs designed to introduce and prepare participants increase the effectiveness of group treatment for various psychological problems (Mayerson, 1984). Other studies demonstrated that preparatory programs increase self-disclosure and self-exploratory verbalizations (Garrison, 1978), as well as increase participation (Conyne & Silver, 1980) and motivation (Curran, 1978). In essence, this early intervention aims to reduce resistance, demonstrate that treatment can be a positive experience, orient participants to working in a group setting, help clients become more comfortable discussing difficult issues, and increase hope and motivation for change. Offenders participating in this program have been judged by subsequent therapists to be better participants in full sexual offender treatment programs.

Phases of the RPS programs

We conceptualize our Regular and Deniers' Programs as having three phases: Phase 1 is aimed at the engagement of the client; Phase 2 addresses factors that are known to predict reoffending in untreated sexual offenders (so-called "criminogenic factors"); and Phase 3 integrates what they have learned into a set of self-management plans.

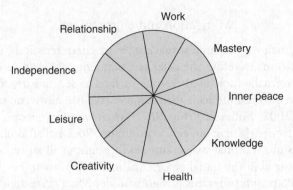

Figure 14.1 The Good Lives Wheel.

As noted above, we start by identifying the goal of our treatment program as the development of the skills, self-confidence, and emotional capacities necessary to have a better life. We use a Good Lives Wheel (see Figure 14.1) to illustrate the goals of their personal Good Lives Model (GLM; Ward, 2002). In conjunction with this we ask clients to provide an autobiography. We do so in order to help them identify both areas of strength and areas where they need further development. We focus treatment on these latter areas and utilize their strengths to implement treatment strategies. See Fortune and Ward (Chapter 21) for a full discussion of the Good Lives Model .

Phase 1 In this phase we address issues that are not necessarily criminogenic (i.e., have not been shown to predict reoffending) but are both self-enhancing and non-threatening. For example, sexual offenders typically display low self-esteem and experience high levels of shame (L. E. Marshall, Marshall, Bailey, Mailett, & Sparks, 2012). Both these features have been shown in the general psychological literature to be significant obstacles to engagement in learning any new skill (Baumeister, 1993; Tangney & Dearing, 2002). As a result, we deploy strategies to overcome these problems in this first phase of treatment. We also begin the processes involved in teaching effective coping strategies since inadequate responses to stressors are common among sexual offenders, and again this target is seen by offenders to be non-threatening and self-enhancing.

In this first phase, we avoid speaking about, or having them identify, any aspect of their offending behavior. To reiterate, our goal in this first phase is winning their confidence, developing their trust in the therapist and the program, and convincing them that they have the capacity to change. The approach we adopt in all aspects of the program is both strength-based and motivational. We emphasize known features of effective therapists such as being warm, empathic, rewarding, and somewhat directive (see W. L. Marshall & Burton, 2010; Marshall, Burton, & Marshall, 2013, for detailed summaries of the general clinical literature and specific studies of sexual and non-sexual offenders).

Phase 2 In this phase we target known criminogenic features. Andrews and Bonta (2006) have shown that effective treatment programs for any type of offender must address these features; that is, those behavioral, cognitive, and emotional deficits that predict reoffending in untreated offenders. Hanson, Bourgon, Helmus, and Hodgson (2009) have confirmed this observation with sexual offender treatment programs. Accordingly, we focus on

Box 14.1 Criminogenic Factors Related to Sexual Offending

Cognitive factors:

- emotional congruence with children
- hostility toward women
- lack of concern for others
- offense supportive attitudes

Relationship problems:

- lack of intimacy
- insecure attachments
- emotional loneliness

Self-regulation issues:

- emotional dysregulation

Sexual factors:

- sexual preoccupation
- sexual preference for children
- sexualized violence

Low self-esteem/shame

providing the skills necessary to overcome these deficits. Fortunately, there is now available convincing evidence on what constitutes criminogenic factors in sexual offenders (see Hanson, 2006; Mann, Hanson, & Thornton, 2010, for a summary of these findings). Established treatment targets are described in Box 14.1. As we will see in more detail later in this chapter, we have developed strategies for effectively addressing these crucial treatment targets.

Phase 3 In this phase the aim is to assist each offender in the generation of plans for the continued development of his life goals. Taking his Good Lives Wheel from Phase 1, where he described the deficits in the areas of the GLM, each offender identifies the skills and confidence he has developed throughout the treatment program. Next he is assisted in selecting two, or at most three, areas of his GLM that he intends to work on shortly after his release. The client is asked to generate the steps that will lead to attaining these immediate goals and to identify how he will continue to develop in these and other areas over the rest of his life. Since idle time represents a risk for sexual offending, we typically encourage each offender to select use of leisure time as one of the targets for immediate attention. He is encouraged to select at least two leisure activities that he enjoys, or believes he will enjoy, and then to identify how he will pursue these activities. Quite often, sexual offenders have job histories, or educational histories, that appear to represent functioning well below their actual capacities, so they are also assisted in identifying job skills training or educational upgrading as other paths on which to immediately concentrate.

We also encourage clients to turn their attention, over time, to the other areas identified in the GLM that are in need of development. This helps them to recognize that treatment represents just the beginning of a lifetime effort to develop a better, more fulfilling life. All too often offenders view discharge as indicating that their efforts at change are over whereas our view is that so long as they keep earnestly developing their GLM, they are more likely to achieve life satisfaction and, thereby, become less likely to reoffend.

In terms of the development of warning signs indicating that the client is moving toward a risk of reoffending after discharge, and the corresponding generation of relapse prevention plans, we encourage clients to limit their range of warning signs and relapse prevention plans to a sensible and manageable number. In our view most programs for sexual offenders require clients to generate far too many warning signs and a correspondingly extensive set of relapse prevention plans. We want our clients to generate manageable and easy to remember plans to avoid reoffending.

Associated with these plans, we ask each client to name a limited group of people who will be able to offer support upon his discharge. For each of these supports, we ask the client to indicate what area of functioning each identified person will assist him with. Again we do not want clients to overdo these plans, since having too many supports is likely to reduce the effectiveness of each support and may overwhelm the client by having him attempt to utilize, or report to, each of these people. And, of course, too many supports may reduce his own efforts by becoming too reliant on others.

As a last step in preparing for discharge, we ask the client to identify where he will live, who he will live with, and what he will do to generate an income. In considering each of these aspects of his discharge plans, we ask the client to ensure that none of these plans will place him in a context where he may have access to potential victims. We point out that even if he is not tempted to offend, certain circumstances may place him at risk to be accused of offending, which, given his past record, might be readily believed.

In addition to the RPS programs noted above, we have found that our program is easily adapted to fit the needs of offenders with cognitive problems (i.e., those with low IQs, with brain injury, with dementia, and with learning disabilities) as well as those with serious mental disorders (i.e., severe Axis 1 or Axis 2 disorders). We will not describe these specific adaptations for the cognitively disordered or mentally disordered clients in this chapter as we have not yet evaluated them.

Treatment targets

Andrews and Bonta (2006) have described the "Principles of Effective Offender Treatment" derived from a series of meta-analyses, and Hanson et al. (2009) have shown that these same principles apply to sexual offender treatment. The series of meta-analyses conducted by Andrews and his colleagues (see Andrews & Bonta, 2006, for a summary), revealed that three concepts define effective treatment: what they call the Risk-Need-Responsivity (RNR) principles. The risk principle indicates that treatment is most effectively applied to high-risk offenders, although this appears to be more of an administrative guide than a factor that produces significant change. The needs principle, however, when appropriately applied, explains a significant amount of the treatment-induced changes. This principle requires that treatment be directed at factors that are known to predict reoffending; that is, criminogenic factors (as already noted in Box 14.1). The responsivity principle is discussed below.

As we noted earlier, we also target self-esteem and shame, neither of which have yet been shown convincingly to be criminogenic. We target these features because they have been demonstrated to impede treatment engagement. As it turns out, low self-esteem and shame are highly correlated (L. E. Marshall et al., 2012), so that by increasing self-esteem, shame is reduced.

Baumeister and his colleagues (Baumeister, Heatherton, & Tice, 1993; Baumeister, Smart, & Boden, 1996) have shown that high levels of self-esteem are associated with aggression, and Bushman (Bushman, Baumeister, Thomaes, Begeer, West, & Ryu, 2009) repeated this observation. While some may interpret these findings to indicate that efforts to raise the self-esteem of sexual offenders is unwise, that would only be true if these efforts were directed at increasing self-esteem to above normative limits. The latter is not our goal, and our previous research has shown that our procedures improve the self-esteem of sexual offenders to a level of a standard deviation of about 0.5 below the normative average and that none scored above this level.

Procedures for changing treatment targets

In the general clinical literature, Norcross (2002) has shown that the deployment of effective procedures to change problematic behaviors accounts for some 15% of the treatment benefit for Axis 1 and Axis 2 disorders. As far as we could determine there is no evidence that explicitly evaluates the contributions to treatment effectiveness derived from procedures with offenders of any kind, including sexual offenders. There is, however, evidence on the value of some procedures for producing the desired changes on specific treatment targets. We will describe these procedures and their effectiveness in changing the targets.

Self-esteem   Our approach to enhancing self-esteem derives from studies we conducted much earlier with very low self-esteem community-based non-offenders (W. L. Marshall & Christie, 1982; W. L. Marshall, Christie, Lanthier, & Cruchley, 1982). In these studies, and in our subsequent treatment of sexual offenders, we employed three procedures: (i) helping clients identify and then increase the range and frequency of modestly enjoyable activities; (ii) helping them identify and increase their range and frequency of social activities; and (iii) having each client increase the daily frequency of positive self-statements. To achieve this latter goal we ask each client, with the group's assistance, to identify five or six positive qualities about himself. Once these are identified, we ask him to rehearse statements describing these qualities several times each day. We (W. L. Marshall, Anderson, & Champagne, 1997) have shown that these three procedures increase the self-esteem of sexual offenders up to the normative mean on an established measure.

Self-regulation issues   Evidence from the general experimental literature (Gross, 2007) suggests that an important key to behavioral self-regulation is emotional regulation. Emotional dysregulation typically arises from maladaptive responses to life's problems. Thus deficiency in coping skills (which is identified as criminogenic) appears to be a significant factor in producing emotional and, therefore, behavioral dysregulation. Training in adaptive coping skills (i.e., problem-solving strategies) is therefore an important component in instilling appropriate

View of others

		Able to give love	Unable to give love
View of Self	Lovable	SECURE	DISMISSIVE
	Unlovable	PREOCCUPIED (Anxious/ambivalent)	FEARFUL

Figure 14.2   Model of attachment styles. Adapted from Bartholomew and Horowitz (1991).

behavioral management skills. We implement the problem-solving strategies described by D'Zurilla (1986) employing a variety of role-playing and reverse role-playing practices. We have shown this to effectively increase the coping skills of sexual offenders (Serran, Firestone, Marshall, & Moulden, 2007). Pfäfflin, Böhmer, Cornehl, and Mergenthaler (2005) have shown that encouraging offenders to express emotions during treatment is significantly related to producing beneficial changes, presumably as a result of providing opportunities to practice, obtain feedback, and thereby modify their emotional responses. As a result, we actively encourage emotional expression throughout treatment and provide feedback and discussion about the appropriateness of each display of emotion. In addition, when impulsivity is chronic or particularly problematic, we employ aspects of Ross and Fabiano's (1985) Reasoning and Rehabilitation training, which essentially involves appropriate feedback about problematic responding and reinforcement for more restrained behavior.

Relationship problems   We (W. L. Marshall, 1989, 1993; W. L. Marshall & Marshall, 2000, 2010) have proposed that the relationship problems evident in sexual offenders derive from insecure attachment styles and poor intimacy skills resulting in emotional loneliness. Included in sexual offenders' lack of capacity to form intimate relationships are poor and disrespectful communication skills, deficits in empathy, low self-worth, distrust of others, fear of self-disclosure, jealousy, and a failure to develop mutually enjoyable leisure interests with their partners.

The first step in our approach to enhancing intimacy skills is to describe Bartholomew and Horowitz's (1991) two-dimensional model of attachment. Figure 14.2 shows our adaptation of this model. We then ask each client to indicate which category he believes describes his characteristic past relationships and to provide illustrations of his past intimate behaviors. The therapist assists the client in recognizing that he can change his attachment style by learning appropriate skills. The group is then encouraged to examine the potential benefits of being in an effective intimate relationship. We assist this process by outlining the known psychological and health benefits resulting from high levels of intimacy (see W. L. Marshall, Bryce, Hudson, Ward, & Moth, 1996, for these details).

Throughout the whole process of treatment, we encourage the development of communication skills and we insist on, and model, respectful interactions between all group members. Role-plays may be developed so that an individual client can rehearse respectful and empathic communications and appropriate self-disclosures. This can be done with another group member playing the role of his actual, or potential partner. To this point, the group has already begun the processes necessary to enhancing a sense of self-worth, which typically reciprocally inhibits distrust and facilitates confident expressions of feelings. Of course, these are further enhanced during the focus on intimacy. In addition, we encourage each client to identify leisure activities that he and his partner might enjoy together. Evidence from the intimacy literature and the relationship counseling literature (Christensen et al., 2004; Epstein & Baucom, 2002) indicates that the more enjoyable activities couples engage in, the stronger their intimate bond.

While jealousy is a common and destructive problem among men who have poor relationships, it appears to primarily result from either their own unfaithfulness or from their lack of self-worth. Our program, as we have shown, addresses self-worth. Unfaithfulness seems to be driven by both a sense of unworthiness as an intimate partner, and a lack of relationship satisfaction. As a result of the processes described above aimed at increasing relationship skills and personal confidence, we rarely have to address jealousy in any great detail. When we do have to, we help the client distinguish between feelings of distress generated by the actual unfaithfulness of his partner, and what is referred to as "suspiciousness" or "unfounded" jealousy. Discussion centers around what course of action is appropriate when actual unfaithfulness occurs, and how to overcome a disposition to be suspicious. In the latter case it requires further building of self-worth, particularly within the specific context of relationships. We (W. L. Marshall et al., 1996) have shown that this intimacy training package effectively enhances the skills and confidence that are essential for effective relationships and reduces feelings of emotional loneliness.

Sexual factors The first step in addressing sexual issues in our program begins with discussions and education on what constitutes healthy sexuality. Clients are provided with summaries of what is known about the behaviors and attitudes that maximize sexual satisfaction and these are discussed by the group. Part of the goal of this activity is to overcome prudishness and inhibitions about the range of activities that facilitate effective sexual relations. We do this because we have shown (L. E. Marshall, O'Brien, Woods, & Nunes, 2011) that sexual offenders have markedly strict ideas about what sexual practices are commonly practiced and deemed acceptable and enjoyable by most couples. Of course this section of our program is also meant to allay their fears about how their partners might respond to their request for commonly practiced sexual activities such as oral sex, and the exploration of various positions for vaginal intercourse. It is also meant to educate them about the practices that are likely to maximize their partner's sexual satisfaction. Finally, this section of our program serves to make them more comfortable with discussing sex in the group, which facilitates their more open discussion of their deviant sexual interests.

One of the most common concerns about sexual offenders is their supposedly deviant sexual interests. However, in terms of assessing these deviant proclivities, such interests have been identified in only a limited percentage of sex offenders. Phallometric evaluations (i.e., measures of changes in erectile responses, sometimes called penile plethysmography, or simply PPG) have been the standard measure of sexual interests. These evaluations have identified deviance in a limited number of rapists, in even fewer incest offenders, and in approximately 50% of men who molest other people's children (W. L. Marshall & Fernandez, 2003). It appears that deviant interests are most likely to be manifest at phallometric assessments among those non-familial child molesters who have multiple victims. This suggests that deviant interests are learned (see W. L. Marshall & Eccles, 1993, for a discussion) and so can be unlearned. This, however, is not a universally held opinion (see Seto, 2008). In addition, some, albeit few, sexual offenders display limited sexual interest in adult partners. Both these problems (i.e., arousal to deviant acts and lack of arousal to appropriate partners), if present, need to be addressed in treatment.

Behavioral procedures have been developed to address both deviant interests and a lack of appropriate interests (see W. L. Marshall, O'Brien, & Marshall, 2009). While there are a range of procedures, our preferred strategy is to use a combination of two that serve to change both these targets. Masturbation, being a natural and an almost universal practice among males (Leitenberg, Detzer, & Srebnik, 1993), serves as the vehicle for altering these problematic patterns of sexual interests. Sexual offenders with deviant interests are encouraged to follow a particular set of procedures whenever they masturbate; during the excitatory and plateau stage of sexual arousal (see Masters & Johnson, 1966), the client is asked to use whatever fantasy he wishes to become aroused. Once aroused he is advised to switch to a previously identified set of appropriate fantasies. If he begins to lose arousal, he is told to shift back to a deviant image and, once re-aroused, to then switch to the appropriate thoughts. After a man has achieved orgasm, he enters what Masters and Johnson call the "refractory period" – a time when sexual interests are markedly diminished. During the refractory period, which typically lasts for at least 20 minutes, the client is instructed to rehearse, out loud or subvocally, every variation he can generate on his deviant fantasies. Rehearsing appropriate fantasies prior to orgasm is meant to enhance the sexual valence of these images, while associating deviant fantasies with refractory unresponsiveness is intended to produce extinction. This latter process has been called "satiation therapy" (W. L. Marshall, 1979). We (Marshall, O'Brien, & Marshall, 2009) have described a body of evidence supporting the efficacy of this combined procedure.

While changing deviant interests has been seen as the critical intervention with sexual offenders, such interests are not all indicative of reoffending; that is, they are not all criminogenic. It is primarily deviant interests in male children that are criminogenic and, even then, they are not strong predictors. On the other hand, evidence of sexual preoccupation, manifested by a variety of repetitive sexual activities over which the man claims little control, is a strong predictor of sexual recidivism (Hanson, 2006) and must, therefore, be a target of treatment. We (L. E. Marshall & Marshall, 2006; L. E. Marshall, Marshall, Moulden, & Serran, 2008) have shown that as many as 35–40% of sexual offenders meet criteria for sexual preoccupation. It is, therefore, a significant treatment issue.

Although there are no empirically established procedures for dealing with sexual preoccupation, we have assumed this feature would be equally responsive to our program for sexual offenders. Since a significant number of the clients in our outcome studies met criteria for sexual addiction, and our program effectively reduced reoffending, it seems safe to assume that various features of our program attenuate sexually addictive propensities. Other authors (Delmonico & Griffin, 2008) have similarly suggested that the elements in programs for sexual offenders meet the treatment needs of sexual addicts. However, when these problems seem so pronounced that a client cannot properly focus on treatment, we refer him to the institution's psychiatrist to administer one of the current selective serotonin reuptake inhibitors. Once the behavior is attenuated by these medications, and the client is effectively attending to treatment, the drugs are gradually withdrawn.

Cognitive factors We have left this topic to the last section of Phase 2 for two reasons. First, there are many empirically unsound assumptions common in the literature regarding the need to address a broad range of so-called "cognitive distortions." Second, it seems to us to be quite artificial, if not inappropriate, to address these issues independent of the context in which they might arise. Many, indeed most, sexual offender programs err in addressing a variety of non-criminogenic cognitions and attitudes, and they do so in a separate module that removes these issues from their natural context. This latter strategy makes it easy for the offenders to express appropriate thoughts and feelings because the issues that characteristically elicit dysfunctional ideas are not present. For example, negative attitudes toward women are most likely to be manifest when the discussions focus on sex or on relationship issues.

An additional problem we have with most sexual offender programs is that they are not really "cognitive-behavioral" despite the descriptor they apply to their approach. Fernandez, Shingler, and Marshall (2006) showed by detailed analyses that almost all such programs employed few, if any, behavioral strategies. The majority of programs are, in fact, almost entirely cognitive and many carefully avoid the expression of emotions, which is so essential to behavioral changes becoming entrenched dispositions. In any event, the primary problem with most programs is that they address far too many non-criminogenic cognitions and attitudes and that they deal with all treatment targets in a strictly cognitive, if not objective, manner.

As was noted in Box 14.1, very few cognitions and attitudes are, in fact, criminogenic. We will point to those that are *not* but that are nevertheless common targets in sexual offender programs. For example, we (W. L. Marshall, Marshall, & Kingston, 2011; W. L. Marshall, Marshall, & Ware, 2009) have described a body of empirical literature indicating that making excuses for, or justifying, wrongful behavior is both healthy and surprisingly likely to reduce future wrongdoing. Even among offenders of all types, those who attempt to excuse their crimes, or dismiss their responsibility for their offenses, are less likely to reoffend than those who immediately take full responsibility (Maruna, 2001). While it might fit with common sense, and our natural desire, to have wrongdoers take responsibility for their past crimes, it apparently is not an effective strategy.

As a result of these considerations we do not require sexual offenders to acknowledge responsibility for their past. We do insist on them taking responsibility for their future by initiating actions and formulating plans that will give them a more satisfying life free of crime. Consistent with this, and unlike most sexual offender programs, we do not ask offenders to provide an account of their sexually abusive acts that match the details provided by victims and police (see W. L. Marshall, Marshall, & Ware, 2009, for the specific reasons behind this). Thus, we challenge only those views that the evidence tells us predict reoffending or interfere with effective relationships. As noted, we do this within the context of the treatment program where these distorted thoughts and attitudes arise. Our challenges to client thinking are somewhat akin to cognitive restructuring strategies, but these challenges are always done in a supportive, empathic, and respectful style. Unfortunately, it is common in sexual offender programs to employ a strongly confrontational approach to address dysfunctional cognitions despite the fact that such a style *reduces* treatment effectiveness (W. L. Marshall, 2005).

Critical Aspects of Treatment Delivery

In Andrews and Bonta's (2006) description of the effective principles of offender treatment, they distinguish within the responsivity principle between a *specific* and a *general* component. The specific component of the responsivity principle requires therapists to adjust their approach to the unique features of each client. This requirement matches what in the clinical literature is referred to as "flexibility" and is concerned with the way in which treatment is delivered.

The most important feature of the general component of responsivity is embodied in what Andrews and Bonta call the Core Correctional Practices (CCPs). These practices require therapists to be warm, empathic, respectful, and supportive, and to model and reinforce prosocial attitudes and behaviors. These features are matched by what are known to be effective ways of delivering treatment for all types of Axis 1 and Axis 2 disorders (Luborsky, 1994; Martin, Garske, & Davis, 2000; Norcross, 2002). Not only does the presence of these therapist qualities and style markedly enhance the effectiveness of treatment, it also reduces the number of clients who drop out of treatment (Beckham, 1992; Piper et al., 1999). This is an important observation since sexual offenders who drop out of treatment have higher reoffense rates than do those who refuse to enter treatment (Browne, Foreman, & Middleton, 1998; Lösel & Schmucker, 2005; McGrath, Cumming, Livingston, & Hoke, 2003).

Consistent with Andrews and Bonta's notion of the CCPs, we (W. L. Marshall, Serran, Fernandez, et al., 2003; W. L. Marshall, Serran, Moulden, et al., 2002) have shown that when therapists working with sexual offenders are warm, empathic, rewarding, and directive, the benefits derived from treatment are maximized. When therapists are confrontational, rather than being supportively challenging, treatment benefits are markedly diminished. In his examination of the views of sexual offenders concerning their effective experience of treatment, Drapeau (2005) found that the most important component was said to be the therapist's delivery. The clients declared that effective therapists were those who were warm, empathic, non-judgmental, and honest. They indicated they wanted to be challenged but they wanted this to be done in a caring and respectful way. They emphatically declared that a confrontational style led them to either react angrily or to withdraw and discount the value of treatment. Finally, the clients said they wanted to be part of all the major decisions in treatment and they indicated that the collaborative identification of the targets and treatment goals generated a greater commitment to the program on their part.

On a similar issue, Beech and his colleagues (Beech & Fordham, 1997; Beech & Hamilton-Giachritsis, 2005), using Moos's (1986) Group Environmental Scale, examined the relationship between the group climate and beneficial changes in prison programs and in treatment groups in the community. They found that when groups were "Cohesive" and "Expressive," positive treatment changes were maximized. Cohesiveness refers to the way group members work together, are mutually supportive, challenge one another respectfully, and form bonds with each other. Expressiveness describes groups that are verbally and emotionally expressive. Note here again the importance of emotional expression. Pfäfflin et al. (2005) showed that it was only when clients indicated an understanding of issues *concurrent with emotional expression*, that beneficial changes occurred.

Clearly the way in which treatment is delivered is critical to its effectiveness with sexual offenders. Indeed, our own studies demonstrated that the presence of positive therapist qualities accounted for between 30% and 60% of the benefits derived from treatment. Our guess is that these qualities facilitate the establishment of the appropriate group climate and motivate clients to commit to treatment. Under these circumstances the fusion of emotion and understanding, so critical to treatment benefits, is all but certain to occur.

Group Versus Individual Treatment

Relatively little research attention has been paid to whether group therapy is more beneficial than individual therapy (Serran, Marshall, Marshall, & O'Brien, 2013). In the only article we could find, Abracen and Looman (2004) examined the relative efficacy of programs for high-risk incarcerated sexual offenders that either included a combination of group and individual work, or involved individual therapy alone. They found no significant differences between these two approaches. This is similar to findings in the general clinical literature. For example, McRoberts, Burlingame, and Hoag (1988) conducted a meta-analysis of studies that reported evaluating the differential outcome between individual and group therapy. They found both to be equally effective across most mental health issues such as post-traumatic stress disorder (PTSD), social phobia, psychotic disorders, anxiety disorders, obsessive-compulsive disorder (OCD), and aggression. Individual therapy appeared to be somewhat more effective for treating depression, whereas group therapy appeared more effective in treating clients with substance use problems, and with various stress-related disorders.

As indicated earlier in this chapter, the Rockwood sexual offender programs designed to address criminogenic needs are typically delivered in group settings, usually with 8–10 men in each at any one time. Group therapy appears to be the most common form of sexual offender treatment (McGrath, Cumming, Burchard, Zeoli, & Ellerby, 2010). For example, two large-scale meta-analyses examining treatment outcome with sexual offenders (Hanson et al., 2002; Lösel & Schmucker, 2005) found that out of 112 studies examined, only eight were solely focused on individual work while another eight primarily, though not exclusively, addressed the relevant issues in individual sessions. In an extensive survey of programs for sexual offenders in North America, 89.9% were found to be group-based (McGrath, Cumming, & Burchard, 2003). In addition to Sawyer's (2002) point that this is clearly the most economical way in which to deliver treatment, there are a number of other important justifications for group programs.

Glaser and Frosh (1993) noted that compared with treatment delivered on an individual basis, group treatment provides clients with the opportunity to offer support for each other – helping others in an active way, rather than being a passive recipient of treatment. Indeed, as we have seen, the cohesive nature of effective group treatment is a key to its success. The social cohesiveness inherent in good-quality group therapy also provides the opportunity to develop key life skills relating directly and indirectly to a number of dynamic risk factors (e.g., relationship stability, general social competence, and empathy). This available social support typically also helps clients to cope with issues addressed in the group. Fuhriman and Burlingame (1994) have also suggested that there are certain aspects of therapy that are enhanced through its delivery in a group, including: vicarious learning, role flexibility, altruism, and situation re-enactment (both through role-plays and general group dynamics). Anecdotal evidence from our group members typically supports Yalom's (1995) observation that clients most commonly identify peer feedback as the most important source of therapeutic help. This is not to negate the role and value of the therapist in the group. As we saw earlier, sexual offenders have judged the role of the therapist to be crucial to any benefits they derived from treatment. Success is clearly not simply bound up in whether treatment is delivered in a group or an individual setting, but has as much to do with the skills of the therapist delivering the treatment.

For many clients it is clear that group treatment can help them develop skills that the individual treatment delivery format cannot provide practice in, including: receiving support from others; providing support to others; developing some degree of intimacy in relationships; self-disclosing to others; increasing confidence in relating to other adults; practicing coping strategies; being challenged to adopt more functional thinking styles; and adopting more pro-social attitudes. Other benefits include: the ability to share more personal issues due to feeling more comfortable with peers who have similar problems; reinforcing learning by having to explain it to others; deriving greater benefits due to repeated exposure to important ideas and concepts; and reassurance that clients are not the only ones to have thought and behaved in such ways. Of course, an important method of obtaining information about the relative merits of group and individual treatment is to ask the clients. Garrett, Oliver, Wilcox, and Middleton (2003) found that 46% of sexual offenders who had received group treatment said that they preferred this option, while another 34% said they would accept either group or individual treatment. These clients said they appreciated hearing the experiences and perspectives of others in the group.

It is worth considering the effects on the therapist of running group treatment as opposed to individual treatment. In effective group therapy the necessary challenges, to existing thinking and behavior, are most effectively provided by the other group members. With no others to aid this process in one-to-one therapy, the therapist has the sole responsibility for challenging clients and he/she may not be perceived by the client to be as credible as fellow offenders. These circumstances of individual therapy are more likely than a group setting to produce therapist frustration with recalcitrant clients and thereby result in the emergence of a confrontational style, which has been shown to reduce effectiveness.

As a number of authors have pointed out, the research indicates that conducting some form of treatment, be it individual or group based, is significantly more effective than conducting no treatment at all (Bednar & Kaul, 1994; Fuhriman & Burlingame, 1994; Lambert & Bergin, 1994). As Schwartz (1995) suggests, it is not so much the choice between group or individual therapy that may present problems but rather the combination of the two approaches that might be most troubling. She notes that adding individual treatment to group work may allow the client to form a bond with the therapist that may undermine effective participation in group.

Some authors have expressed concerns about delivering sexual offender treatment in a group setting. For example, Brown (2005) suggested that group therapy could encourage the worsening of deviant arousal through the discussion of offense details and fantasies, as well as the chance that group members might facilitate subsequent offending through deviant peer networks established in the group. There is no evidence that either of these outcomes occur. Our programs positively mitigate against the emergence of these features because we do not require group members to provide a detailed offense disclosure or an in-depth overview of their fantasies. Instead we focus more on addressing dynamic risk factors. As Mann and Webster (2002) note, many of those who have committed sexual offenses present as being fearful of joining a group program for a number of reasons, including: fear of being identified in a prison setting as a sexual offender; fear of confidentiality breaches; fear of being criticized by their peers; lack of trust in key professionals; and prior negative experiences in group treatment. As those authors point out, however, it is commonly found that anxiety levels dissipate after spending time in a group. It is also our contention that social anxiety should actually be seen as a strong reason for joining a group. Dealing with these potential obstacles prior to entering group treatment is one of the benefits of a preparatory program.

While we prefer group treatment for many reasons (e.g., efficiency and demonstrated efficacy), there do not seem to be any obvious impediments to effective individual treatment. So long as sexual offender treatment addresses the known criminogenic features, employs empirically sound procedures, and delivers treatment in an effective way, there is no reason to suppose that individual treatment will not result in reduced recidivism.

Are Sex Offender Treatment Programs Effective?

While the above descriptions may seem to some readers to be sensible and likely to succeed, others may quite reasonably be skeptical. Therefore it is necessary to conduct evaluations of long-term outcome to determine whether or not the RPS programs are effective.

Sufficient numbers of evaluations of sexual offender treatment programs have appeared in the literature to justify subjecting them to meta-analyses. While some early meta-analyses offered encouraging findings, there were problems in the selection processes used to identify programs included in these quantitative reviews. Fortunately three more recent meta-analyses employed sound selection criteria (i.e., each study had to provide a matched untreated comparison group, and had to employ official recidivism data). These studies have been generally accepted as providing reasonable bases upon which to estimate overall treatment effectiveness. The first of these studies was described by Hanson et al. (2002) involving 43 programs containing 5078 treated offenders and 4376 untreated offenders. Overall the results revealed that 12.3% of the treated clients reoffended over a 5-year follow-up while 16.8% of the untreated men were recidivists. Examining only CBT programs ($k = 13$), the results were more impressive: 9.9% treated clients and 17.3% untreated clients reoffended. Lösel and Schmucker (2005) found remarkably similar results among 80 studies involving over 22 000 sexual offenders, approximately half of whom were treated (11.1% reoffended) and half untreated (17.5% reoffended). Finally Hanson et al. (2009) found similar results in a somewhat smaller analysis.

In terms of RPS programs specifically, we have conducted appraisals of each of the programs described in this chapter. Unfortunately, because we are so effective in recruiting offenders into the program, there are insufficient numbers available to serve as an untreated comparison group for the Regular Program. We have, accordingly, employed actuarial risk assessment instruments to estimate the expected rates of recidivism against which to compare the actual reoffense rates of our treated group. Elsewhere we (W. L. Marshall & Marshall, 2007) have described our justification of this strategy but we realize that some readers will find this a less than optimal solution. At present, we are in the process of identifying a matched untreated group from an almost identical companion institution.

Over a 5.4-year follow-up of 535 clients who completed the RPS Regular Program between 1991 and 2001, 3.2% reoffended sexually compared with an expected reoffense rate (based on their STATIC-99 scores, Hanson & Thornton, 1999) of 16.8%. At this first evaluation, these treated sexual offenders also committed further non-sexual, non-violent offenses; 13.6% of the treated group reoffended non-sexually compared with an expected rate (based on the LSI-R, Andrews & Bonta, 1995) of 40.0%. At a subsequent 8.4-year follow-up of these same 535 sexual offenders, we found that 5.6% were identified as sexual reoffenders against an expected rate of 23.8%. At this 8.4-year follow-up, 8.4% of the 535 sexual offenders were identified as having committed non-sexual violent offenses while their expected rate for these offenses (based on their SORAG scores – see Quinsey, Harris, Rice, & Cormier, 2006) was 34.8%. Using similar strategies to evaluate our Deniers' Program, we have determined that the treated group showed a sexual reoffense rate of 2.5% over 3.5 years follow-up against an expected rate of 13%.

Thus, if readers accept the basis upon which we have estimated untreated reoffense rates for our clients, then clearly our programs are effective. Of course some authors (e.g., Seto et al., 2008) have suggested that convincing evidence of treatment effectiveness can only be derived from a randomized controlled trial (RCT). While we agree that such a study might be more convincing we (W. L. Marshall & Marshall, 2007) have pointed to problems in implementing a RCT evaluation, not the least of which is that, as in our settings, those who provide funds for treatment are unlikely to permit the implementation of a study that deliberately withholds treatment from a significant number of offenders who are a danger to the public.

Conclusions

Our experience and currently available evidence suggests that adopting a strength-based approach to the treatment of sexual offenders is likely to maximize effectiveness. A strength-based approach derived from positive psychology (Linley & Joseph, 2004; Snyder & Lopez, 2005) coupled with motivational interviewing (Miller & Rollnick, 2002; Miller & Rose, 2009) offers a paradigmatic shift in the way sexual offenders are dealt with in treatment. This new approach embodies all that is currently known about the most effective way to deliver treatment and this requires therapists to be warm and empathic, to be supportive and respectful when challenging the offenders, and to model and reward prosocial attitudes and behaviors. Our program, which embodies these features, is the only one of this kind to have been evaluated. So far, the results seem to us to offer strong support for our approach. We believe that the widespread adoption of similar strength-based approaches would be effective with all types of offenders, particularly given the generalized effects of our program beyond just reductions in sexual offense recidivism to reductions in general and violent reoffending as well.

References

Abracen, J., & Looman, J. (2004). Issues in the treatment of sexual offenders: Recent developments and directions for future research. *Aggression and Violent Behavior: A Review Journal, 9*, 229–246.

Andrews, D. A., & Bonta, J. (1995). *LSR-I: The Level of Supervision Inventory.* Toronto: Multi-Health Systems.

Andrews, D. A., & Bonta, J. (2006). *The psychology of criminal conduct* (4th ed.). Cincinnati, OH: Anderson Publishing.

Bagley, C. (1991). The long-term psychological effects of child sexual abuse: A review of some British and Canadian studies of victims and their families. *Annals of Sex Research, 4*, 23–48.

Bartholomew, K., & Horowitz, L. M. (1991). Attachment styles among young adults: A test of a four-category model. *Journal of Personality and Social Psychology, 61*, 226–244.

Baumeister, R. F. (Ed.). (1993). *Self-esteem: The puzzle of low self-regard.* New York: Plenum Press.

Baumeister, R. F., Heatherton, T. F., & Tice, D. M. (1993). When ego threats lead to self-regulation failure: Negative consequences of high self-esteem. *Journal of Personality and Social Psychology, 64*, 141–156.

Baumeister, R. F., Smart, L., & Boden, J. M. (1996). Relation of threatened egotism to violence and aggression: The dark side of high self-esteem. *Psychological Review, 103*, 5–33.

Beckham, E. E. (1992). Predicting drop-out in psychotherapy. *Psychotherapy, 29*, 177–182.

Bednar, R., & Kaul, T. (1994). Experiential group research: Can the canon fire? In A.E. Bergen & S.L. Garfield (Eds.), *Handbook of psychotherapy and behaviour change* (pp. 631–663). New York: John Wiley & Sons, Inc.

Beech, A. R., & Fordham, A. S. (1997). Therapeutic climate of sexual offender treatment programs. *Sexual Abuse: A Journal of Research and Treatment, 9*, 219–237.

Beech, A. R., & Hamilton-Giachritsis, C. E. (2005). Relationship between therapeutic climate and treatment outcome in group-based sexual offender treatment programs. *Sexual Abuse: A Journal of Research and Treatment, 17*, 127–140.

Bond, I. K., & Evans, D. R. (1967). Avoidance therapy: Its use in two cases of underwear fetishism. *Canadian Medical Association Journal, 96*, 1160–1162.

Briere, J., & Elliott, D. M. (2003). Prevalence and psychological sequelae of self-reported childhood physical and sexual abuse in a general population sample of men and women. *Child Abuse & Neglect: The International Journal, 27*, 1205–1222.

Brown, S. (2005). *Treating sex offenders: An introduction to sex offender treatment programmes.* Devon, UK: Willan.

Browne, K. D., Foreman, L., & Middleton, D. (1998). Predicting treatment dropout in sex offenders. *Child Abuse Review, 7*, 402–419.

Bushman, B. J., Baumeister, R., Thomaes, S., Begeer, S., West, S., & Ryu, E. (2009). Looking again, and harder, for a link between low self-esteem and aggression. *Journal of Personality, 77*, 427–446.

Christensen, A., Atkins, D. C., Berns, S., Wheeler, J., Baucom, D. H., & Simpson, L. E. (2004). Traditional versus integrative behavioral couple therapy for significantly and chronically distressed married couples. *Journal of Consulting and Clinical Psychology, 72*, 176–191.

Conyne, R. K., & Silver, R. J. (1980). Direct, vicarious, and vicarious-process experiences: Effects on increasing therapeutic attraction. *Small Group Behavior, 11*, 419–429.

Curran, T. (1978). Increasing motivation to change in group treatment. *Small Group Behavior, 9*, 337–348.

Delmonico, D. L., & Griffin, E. J. (2008). Online sexual offending: Assessment and treatment. In D. R. Laws & W. T. O'Donohue (Eds.), *Sexual deviance: Theory, assessment & treatment* (2nd ed., pp. 459–485). New York: Guilford Press.

Drapeau, M. (2005). Research on the processes involved in treating sexual offenders. *Sexual Abuse: A Journal of Research and Treatment, 17*, 117–125.

D'Zurilla, T. J. (1986). *Problem-solving therapy: A social competence approach to clinical intervention.* New York: Springer Publishing.

Epstein, M. B., & Baucom, D. H. (2002). *Enhanced cognitive-behavioral therapy for couples: A contextual approach.* Washington, DC: American Psychological Association.

Fernandez, Y. M., Shingler, J., & Marshall, W. L. (2006). Putting "behavior" back into the cognitive-behavioral treatment of sexual offenders. In W. L. Marshall, Y. M. Fernandez, L. E. Marshall, & G. A. Serran (Eds.), *Sexual offender treatment: Controversial issues* (pp. 211–224). Chichester, UK: John Wiley & Sons, Ltd.

Finkelhor, D. (1984). *Child sexual abuse: New theory and research.* New York: Free Press.

Fuhriman, A., & Burlingame, G.M. (1994). Group psychotherapy: Research and practice. In A. Fuhriman & G.M. Burlingame (Eds.), *Handbook of Group Psychotherapy* (pp. 3–40). New York: John Wiley & Sons, Inc.

Garrett, T., Oliver, C., Wilcox, D.T., & Middleton, D. (2003). Who cares? The views of sexual offenders about the group treatment they receive. *Sexual Abuse, 15*, 323–338.

Garrison, J. E. (1978). Written vs verbal preparation of patients for group psychotherapy. *Psychotherapy: Theory, Research & Practice, 15*, 130–134.

Glaser, D., & Frosh, S. (1993). *Child sexual abuse* (2nd ed.). Basingstoke, England: Macmillan.

Gross, J. J. (Ed.). (2007). *Handbook of emotion regulation.* New York: Guilford Press.

Hanson, R. K. (2006). Stability and change: Dynamic risk factors for sexual offending. In W. L. Marshall, Y. M. Fernandez, L. E. Marshall, & G. A. Serran (Eds.), *Sexual offender treatment: Controversial issues* (pp. 17–31). Chichester, UK: John Wiley & Sons, Ltd.

Hanson, R. K., Bourgon, G., Helmus, L., & Hodgson, S. (2009). The principles of effective correctional treatment also apply to sexual offenders: A meta-analysis. *Criminal Justice and Behavior, 36*, 865–891.

Hanson, R. K., Gordon, A., Harris, A. J. R., Marques, J. K., Murphy, W. D., Quinsey, V. L., & Seto, M. C. (2002). First report of the Collaborative Outcome Data Project on the Effectiveness of Psychological Treatment of Sex Offenders. *Sexual Abuse: A Journal of Research and Treatment, 14*, 169–194.

Hanson, R. K., & Thornton, D. (1999). *Static 99: Improving actuarial risk assessments for sex offenders.* User Report 99-02. Ottawa: Department of the Solicitor General of Canada. Available at: http://www.publicsafety.gc.ca/serv/srch/index-eng.aspx?q=static+99

Lambert, M. J., & Bergin, A. E. (1994). The effectiveness of psychotherapy. In A.E. Bergin & S.L. Garfield (Eds.), *Handbook of psychotherapy and behaviour change* (4th ed., pp. 72–113). New York: John Wiley & Sons, Inc.

Leitenberg, H., Detzer, M. J., & Srebnik, D. (1993). Gender differences in masturbation and the relation of masturbation experience in preadolescence and/or early adolescence to sexual behavior and sexual adjustment in young adulthood. *Archives of Sexual Behavior, 22,* 87–98.

Linley, P. A., & Joseph, S. (Eds.). (2004). *Positive psychology in practice.* Hoboken, NJ: John Wiley & Sons, Inc.

Lösel, F., & Schmucker, M. (2005). The effectiveness of treatment for sexual offenders: A comprehensive meta-analysis. *Journal of Experimental Criminology, 1,* 117–146.

Luborsky, L. (1994). The benefits to the clinician of psychotherapy research: A clinician-researchers view. In P. F. Talley, H. H. Strupp, & S. F. Butler (Eds.), *Psychotherapy research and practice: Bridging the gap* (pp. 167–180). New York: Basic Books.

Mann, R. E., Hanson, R. K., & Thornton, D. (2010). Assessing risk for sexual recidivism: Some proposals on the nature of psychologically meaningful risk factors. *Sexual Abuse: A Journal of Research and Treatment, 12,* 191–217.

Mann, R. E., & Webster, S. (2002, October). *Understanding resistance and denial.* Paper presented at the 21st Annual Research and Treatment Conference of the Association for the Treatment of Sexual Abusers, Montreal.

Marquis, J. N. (1970). Orgasmic reconditioning: Changing sexual object choice through controlling masturbation fantasies. *Journal of Behavior Therapy and Experimental Psychiatry, 1,* 263–271.

Marshall, L. E., & Marshall, W. L. (2006). Sexual addiction in incarcerated sexual offenders. *Sexual Addiction & Compulsivity: The Journal of Treatment and Prevention, 13,* 377–390.

Marshall, L. E., Marshall, W. L., Bailey, W., Mailett, G., & Sparks, J. (2012). *Self-esteem and shame in sexual offenders: Pre and post-treatment data.* Manuscript in preparation.

Marshall, L. E., Marshall, W. L., Moulden, H. M., & Serran, G. A. (2008). The prevalence of sexual addiction in incarcerated sexual offenders and matched community nonoffenders. *Sexual Addiction and Compulsivity: The Journal of Treatment and Prevention, 15,* 271–283.

Marshall, L. E., O'Brien, M. D., Woods, M., & Nunes, K. (2011a, November). *Sexual attitudes in sexual offenders and two comparison groups.* Paper presented at the 30th annual conference of the Association for the Treatment of Sexual Abusers, Toronto, Canada.

Marshall, W. L. (1971). A combined treatment method for certain sexual deviations. *Behaviour Research and Therapy, 9,* 293–294.

Marshall, W. L. (1979). Satiation therapy: A procedure for reducing deviant sexual arousal. *Journal of Applied Behavioral Analysis, 12,* 377–389.

Marshall, W. L. (1989). Invited essay: Intimacy, loneliness and sexual offenders. *Behaviour Research and Therapy, 27,* 491–503.

Marshall, W. L. (1992). The social value of treatment for sexual offenders. *Canadian Journal of Human Sexuality, 1,* 109–114.

Marshall, W. L. (1993). The role of attachment, intimacy, and loneliness in the etiology and maintenance of sexual offending. *Sexual and Marital Therapy, 8,* 109–121.

Marshall, W. L. (2005). Therapist style in sexual offender treatment: Influence on indices of change. *Sexual Abuse: A Journal of Research and Treatment, 17,* 109–116.

Marshall, W. L., Anderson, D., & Champagne, F. (1997). Self-esteem and its relationship to sexual offending. *Psychology, Crime & Law, 3,* 161–186.

Marshall, W. L., Anderson, D., & Fernandez, Y. M. (1999). *Cognitive behavioural treatment of sexual offenders.* Chichester, UK: John Wiley & Sons, Ltd.

Marshall, W. L., & Barrett, S. (1990). *Criminal neglect: Why sex offenders go free.* Toronto: Doubleday.

Marshall, W. L., Bryce, P., Hudson, S. M., Ward, T., & Moth, B. (1996). The enhancement of intimacy and reduction of loneliness among child molesters. *Legal and Criminological Psychology, 1,* 95–102.

Marshall, W. L., & Burton, D. (2010). The importance of therapeutic processes in offender treatment. *Aggression and Violent Behavior, 15,* 141–149.

Marshall, W. L., Burton, D. L., & Marshall, L. E. (2013). Features of treatment delivery and group processes that maximize the effects of offender programs. In J. L.Wood & T. A.Gannon (eds.), *Crime and crime reduction: The importance of group processes* (pp. 159–176). London: Routledge.

Marshall, W. L., & Christie, M. M. (1982). The enhancement of social self-esteem. *Canadian Counsellor, 16,* 82–89.

Marshall, W. L., Christie, M. M., Lanthier, R. D., & Cruchley, J. (1982). The nature of the reinforcer in the enhancement of social self-esteem. *Canadian Counsellor, 16,* 90–96.

Marshall, W. L., Earls, C. M., Segal, Z. V., & Darke, J. (1983). A behavioral program for the assessment and treatment of sexual aggressors. In K. Craig & R. McMahon (Eds.), *Advances in clinical behavior therapy* (pp. 148–174). New York: Brunner/Mazel.

Marshall, W. L., & Eccles, A. (1993). Pavlovian conditioning processes in adolescent sex offenders. In H. E. Barbaree, W. L. Marshall, & S. M. Hudson (Eds.), *The juvenile sex offender* (pp. 118–142). New York: Guilford Press.

Marshall, W. L., & Fernandez, Y. M. (2003). *Phallometric testing with sexual offenders: Theory, research, and practice.* Brandon, VT: Safer Society Press.

Marshall, W.L., Fernandez, Y.M., Serran, G.A., Mulloy, R., Thornton, D., Mann, R.E., & Anderson, D. (2003a). Process variables in the treatment of sexual offenders. *Aggression and Violent Behavior: A Review Journal, 8,* 205–234.

Marshall, W. L., & Marshall, L. E. (2000). The origins of sexual offending. *Trauma, Violence, & Abuse, 1,* 250–263.

Marshall, W. L., & Marshall, L. E. (2007). The utility of the Random Controlled Trial for evaluating sexual offender treatment: The gold standard or an inappropriate strategy? *Sexual Abuse: A Journal of Research and Treatment, 19,* 175–191.

Marshall, W. L., & Marshall, L. E. (2010). Attachment and intimacy in sexual offenders: An update. *Sexual and Marital Therapy, 25,* 86–90.

Marshall, W. L., Marshall, L. E., & Kingston, D. A. (2011b). Are the cognitive distortions of child molesters in need of treatment? *Sexual Aggression, 17,* 118–129.

Marshall, W. L., Marshall, L. E., Serran, G. A., & Fernandez, Y. M. (2006). *Treating sexual offenders: An integrated approach.* New York: Routledge.

Marshall, W. L., Marshall, L. E., Serran, G. A., & O'Brien, M. D. (2011c). *Rehabilitating sexual offenders: A strength-based approach.* Washington, DC: American Psychological Association.

Marshall, W. L., Marshall, L. E., & Ware, J. (2009a). Cognitive distortions in sexual offenders: Should they all be treatment targets? *Sexual Abuse in Australia and New Zealand, 2,* 70–78.

Marshall, W. L., O'Brien, M. D., & Marshall, L. E. (2009b). Modifying sexual preferences. In A. R. Beech, L. A. Craig, & K. D. Browne (Eds.), *Assessment and treatment of sex offenders: A handbook* (pp. 311–327). Chichester, UK: John Wiley & Sons, Ltd.

Marshall, W. L., Serran, G. A., Fernandez, Y. M., Mulloy, R., Mann, R. E., & Thornton, D. (2003b). Therapist characteristics in the treatment of sexual offenders: Tentative data on their relationship with indices of behaviour change. *Journal of Sexual Aggression, 9,* 25–30.

Marshall, W. L., Serran, G. A., Moulden, H., Mulloy, R., Fernandez, Y. M., Mann, R. E., & Thornton, D. (2002). Therapist features in sexual offender treatment: Their reliable identification and influence on behaviour change. *Clinical Psychology and Psychotherapy, 9,* 395–405.

Marshall, W. L., & Williams, S. (1975). A behavioral approach to the modification of rape. *Quarterly Bulletin of the British Association for Behavioural Psychotherapy, 4,* 78.

Martin, D. J., Garske, J. P., & Davis, M. K. (2000). Relation of the therapeutic alliance with outcome and other variables: A meta-analytic review. *Journal of Consulting and Clinical Psychology, 68,* 438–450.

Maruna, S. (2001). *Making good: How ex-convicts reform and rebuild their lives.* Washington, DC: American Psychological Association.

Masters, W., & Johnson, B. (1966). *Human sexual response.* Boston: Little, Brown.

Mayerson, N. G. (1984). Preparing clients for group therapy: A critical review and theoretical formulation. *Clinical Psychology, Review, 4,* 191–213.

McGrath, R.J., Cumming, G.F., & Burchard, B.L. (2003a). *Current practices and trends in sexual abuser management: Safer Society 2002 Nationwide Survey.* Brandon, VT: Safer Society Press.

McGrath, R. J., Cumming, G. R., Burchard, B. L., Zeoli, S., & Ellerby, L. (2010). *Current practices and emerging trends in sexual abuse management.* Brandon, VT: Safer Society Press.

McGrath, R. J., Cumming, G., Livingston, J. A., & Hoke, S. E. (2003b). Outcome of a treatment program for adult sex offenders: From prison to community. *Journal of Interpersonal Violence, 18,* 3–17.

McRoberts, C., Burlingame, G.M., & Hoag, M.J. (1988). Comparative efficacy of individual and group psychotherapy: A meta-analytic perspective. *Group Dynamics: Theory, Research, and Practice, 2,* 101–178.

Miller, W. R., & Rollnick, S. (Eds.). (2002). *Motivational interviewing: Preparing people for change* (2nd ed.). New York: Guilford Press.

Miller W.R., & Rose, G.S. (2009). Toward a theory of motivational interviewing. *American Psychologist, 64,* 527–537.

Moos, R. H. (1986). *Group Environment Scale manual* (2nd ed.), Palo Alto, CA: Consulting Psychologists' Press.

Norcross, J. C. (2002). Empirically supported therapy relationships. In J. C. Norcross (Ed.), *Psychotherapy relationships that work: Therapist contributions and responsiveness to patient needs* (pp. 3–10). New York: Oxford University Press.

Pfäfflin, F., Böhmer, M., Cornehl, S., & Mergenthaler, F. (2005). What happens in therapy with sexual offenders? A model of process research. *Sexual Abuse: A Journal of Research and Treatment, 17,* 141–151.

Piper, W. E., Ogrodniczuk, J. S., Joyce, A. S., McCallum, M., Rosie, J. S., O'Kelly, J. G., & Steinberg, P. I. (1999). Prediction of dropping out in time-limited interpretive individual psychotherapy. *Psychotherapy: Theory, Research and Practice, 36,* 114–122.

Prentky, R. A., & Burgess, A. W. (1990). Rehabilitation of child molesters: A cost-benefit analysis. *American Journal of Orthopsychiatry, 60,* 80–117.

Quinsey, V. L., Harris, G. T., Rice, M. E., & Cormier, C. A. (2006). *Violent offenders: Appraising and managing risk* (2nd ed.). Washington, DC: American Psychological Association.

Ross, R. R., & Fabiano, E. (1985). *Time to think: A cognitive model of delinquency prevention and offender rehabilitation.* Johnson City, TN: Institute of Social Sciences and Arts.

Russell, D. E. H. (1984). *Sexual exploitation: Rape, child sexual abuse and workplace harassment.* Thousand Oaks, CA: Sage Publications.

Sawyer, S. (2002). Group therapy with adult sex offenders. In B. K., Schwartz & H. Cellini (Eds.), *The sex offender: Current treatment modalities and systems issues* (Vol. 4, pp. 14.1–14.15). Kingston, NJ: Civic Research Institute.

Schwartz, B. K. (1995). Group therapy. In B.K. Schwartz & H. Cellini (Eds.), *The sex offender: Corrections, treatment and legal practice* (Vol. *1*, pp. 14.1–14.15). Kingston, NJ: Civic Research Institute.

Serran, G. A., Firestone, P., Marshall, W. L., & Moulden, H. (2007). Changes in coping following treatment for child molesters. *Journal of Interpersonal Violence, 22,* 1199–1210.

Serran, G. A., Marshall, W. L., Marshall, L. E., & O'Brien, M. D. (2013). Group or individual therapy in the treatment of sexual offenders. In L. A. Craig, L. Dixon, & T. A. Gannon (Eds.), *What works in offender rehabilitation: An evidence based approach to assessment and treatment* (pp. 452–467). Chichester, UK: Wiley-Blackwell.

Seto, M. C. (2008). *Pedophilia and sexual offending against children: Theory, assessment, and intervention.* Washington, DC: American Psychological Association.

Seto, M. C., Marques, J. K., Harris, G. T., Chaffin, M., Lalumière, M. L., Miner, M. H., Berliner, L., Rice, M. E., Lieb, R., & Quinsey, V. L. (2008). Good science and progress in sex offender treatment are intertwined: A response to Marshall & Marshall (2007). *Sexual Abuse: A Journal of Research and Treatment, 20*, 247–255.

Snyder, C. R., & Lopez, S. J. (Eds.) (2005). *Handbook of positive psychology.* New York: Oxford University Press.

Starzyk, K. B., & Marshall, W. L. (2003). Childhood and family personological risk factors for sexual offending. *Aggression and Violent Behavior, 8*, 93–105.

Tangney, J. P., & Dearing, R. L. (2002). *Shame and guilt.* New York: Guilford Press.

U.S. Department of Health and Human Services – Administration on Children, Youth and Families (2006). *Child maltreatment 2004.* Washington, DC: National Institute of Justice.

van Dijk, J. J. M., & Mayhew, P. (1992). *Criminal victimization in the industrialized world: Key findings of the 1989 and 1992 International Crime Surveys.* The Hague: Netherlands Ministry of Justice, Department of Crime Prevention.

Ward, T. (2002). Good lives and the rehabilitation of offenders: Promises and problems. *Aggression and Violent Behavior, 7*, 513–528.

Yalom, I .D. (1995). *Theory and practice of group therapy* (4th ed.). New York: Basic Books.

Suggestions for Further Learning

Books

Marshall, W. L., Marshall, L. E., Serran, G. A., & O'Brien, M. D. (2011). *Rehabilitating sexual offenders: A strength-based approach.* Washington, DC: American Psychological Association.

Beech, A. R., Craig, L. A., & Browne, K. D. (2009). *Assessment and treatment of sex offenders: A handbook.* Chichester, UK: Wiley-Blackwell.

Laws, D. R., & O'Donohue, W. T. (2008). *Sexual deviance: Theory, assessment and treatment.* New York: Guilford Press.

15

Recidivism Risk Reduction Therapy (3RT)

Cognitive-Behavioral Approaches to Treating Sexual Offense Behavior

Jennifer Wheeler and Christmas Covell

Introduction

Development and goals of the 3RT model

Some individuals participate in therapy after they have been caught engaging in illegal sexual behavior. The underlying goal of therapy for sexual offense behavior is to reduce a person's likelihood of engaging in such behavior again. Currently, there is no "gold standard" for treating sexual offense behavior, although cognitive-behavioral approaches, especially Relapse Prevention (RP), have dominated the field in recent decades. In this chapter, we describe one such cognitive-behaviorally based approach to treating sexual offense behavior, called *recidivism risk reduction therapy* (3RT; Wheeler & Covell, 2005; Wheeler, George, & Stephens, 2005a; Wheeler, George, & Stoner, 2005b). 3RT was developed in an effort to respond to the limitations of relapse prevention approaches, and to incorporate "best practices" that have been identified by more recent clinical research. Specifically, 3RT was developed to accomplish the following goals:

1. To address identified limitations of the popular – but insufficient – RP model for sexual offense treatment.
2. To explicitly incorporate the "doing what works" approach to sexual offense treatment (specifically the Risk-Need-Responsivity model).
3. To employ dynamic risk assessment as the dominant conceptual framework for treatment planning and implementation.
4. To utilize other existing empirically based practices, and apply these to the behavioral, emotional, and cognitive deficits that are associated with sexual offense behavior.

Forensic CBT: A Handbook for Clinical Practice, First Edition.
Edited by Raymond Chip Tafrate and Damon Mitchell.
© 2014 John Wiley & Sons, Ltd. Published 2014 by John Wiley & Sons, Ltd.

Addressing limitations of the RP model for sex offense treatment   When cognitive-behavioral (CBT) approaches gained popularity in the twentieth century, these approaches were soon applied to the treatment of sexual offense behavior. Most significantly, after RP emerged in the 1980s as an adjunct approach for addictive behaviors, it was conceptualized and adapted as a potential treatment for sexual offense behavior (Pithers, Marques, Gibat, & Marlatt, 1983). Subsequently, RP became the treatment for sexual offenders most widely used in the late twentieth century (Laws, Hudson, & Ward, 2000a). Currently, RP continues to be a prominent, if not dominant, approach to sexual offense treatment (see Newring, Loverich, Harris, & Wheeler, 2009).

However, since its application nearly 30 years ago, important limitations in RP for sexual offense behavior have been identified (e.g., Hanson, 2000; Hudson, Ward, & Marshall, 1992; Laws, 1995, 2003; Thornton, 1997, as cited in Laws (2003); Ward & Hudson, 1996a, 1996b, 1998, 2000; Ward, Louden, Hudson, & Marshall, 1995; Wheeler, 2003; Wheeler, George, & Marlatt, 2006). Furthermore, research has strongly suggested that RP may not be a universally successful, or necessary, approach for reducing recidivism rates among all participants (Marques, Wiederanders, Day, Nelson, & Van Ommeren, 2005).

Among the criticisms of RP for the treatment of sexual offense behavior are the following:

- RP was never intended to be a *primary* treatment approach in the field of addictions (i.e., to facilitate therapeutic change), but rather, as an *adjunct* approach, intended to follow and support a primary treatment (Wheeler, 2003; Wheeler, George, & Marlatt, 2006); therefore, RP is misapplied if used as a primary treatment approach for sexual offense behavior.
- RP for sexual offense behavior has historically placed undue emphasis on the presumption that sex is used as an "avoidance-based" coping strategy (i.e., to avoid negative emotional states), and thus may have erroneously ignored the unique reinforcing properties of sexual behavior (Hudson et al., 1992; Ward & Hudson, 1996a, 1996b, 1998, 2000; Ward et al., 1995; Wheeler, 2003; Wheeler et al., 2006); therefore, treatment for sexual offense behavior requires due consideration of sexual offending as an "approach-based" behavior.
- For some clients, RP may feel more like a "one size fits all" or "cookie-cutter" approach to treatment that does not always respond to their individual needs. For example, not all clients have a pattern of offense behavior that would accurately be described as a "cycle," and not all clients are motivated by underlying "deviant" sexual interests; therefore, treatment for sexual offense behavior requires more ideographic clinical conceptualization and treatment delivery.

Given these and other limitations of the RP approach to sex offense treatment (see Laws, 2003, for a review of these limitations), 3RT was developed to improve upon the RP treatment model in the following ways:

- 3RT was developed as a primary treatment approach, designed to target the underlying (and often long-standing) problematic attitudes, lifestyles, and behaviors associated with sexual offense behavior.
- 3RT has an "approach-based" treatment emphasis that incentivizes prosocial lifestyles and behavioral goals (in contrast to "avoidance-based" approaches, such as RP).
- 3RT is a flexible and ideographic treatment program that can respond to the individual needs of each client, and can readily incorporate new research as this becomes available.

In addition to addressing some of the limitations of RP, 3RT retains some important features of the RP model that earned RP such widespread support, specifically:

- 3RT is based on cognitive-behavioral treatment theory and techniques, and includes clear tasks, goals, and assignments, making it "user-friendly" for clinicians and clients who are already familiar with CBT/RP.
- 3RT has "face validity," in that the stated goal of 3RT is to *reduce recidivism risk* (just as the stated goal of RP was to prevent relapse). Such face validity should increase the value of such a treatment approach in the eyes of stakeholders and policy-makers.
- 3RT focuses on those aspects of a client's life that are relevant to reoffense risk, with the exception of those aspects determined to be responsivity needs that interfere with effective treatment delivery (see Covell & Wheeler, 2011, for a summary of responsivity considerations in the delivery of sexual offense treatment).

Incorporating the "doing what works" approach to sexual offense treatment   Despite some early pessimism about the effectiveness of offender rehabilitation (e.g., Lipton, Martinson, & Wilks, 1975; Martinson, 1974), subsequent and more methodologically rigorous empirical research has determined which treatment approaches and techniques have demonstrated effectiveness in facilitating offender change and associated reductions in recidivism. In other words, research has debunked the myth that "nothing works," and has additionally identified "what works" to reduce general criminal recidivism.

A model of effective correctional programming was originally proposed by Andrews, Bonta, and Hoge (1990), incorporating the conclusions of the research literature on "what works" to reduce criminal recidivism. This model comprised three basic principles for effective offense-specific treatment, known as the *risk principle, need principle*, and *responsivity principle*.

The risk principle describes the importance of providing a level of treatment services commensurate with an individual's risk for reoffense. Simply put, higher risk offenders require more resources and intensive services than lower risk offenders. The emphasis of the risk principle is not only on allocating sufficient treatment and risk-management resources to higher-risk offenders, but also ensuring that lower-risk offenders are not unduly "overtreated," resulting in the misappropriation of limited resources that should be allocated to higher-risk offenders.

The need principle proposes that effective treatment should target an individual's criminogenic needs (i.e., those factors about their lifestyle and personality that are statistically associated with increased risk to reoffend, also known as dynamic risk factors). The emphasis of the need principle is not only on the importance of targeting dynamic risk-needs to reduce recidivism risk, but also on the importance of *avoiding* focus on *non*-criminogenic needs, as this would not be anticipated to impact recidivism, and would therefore be an inefficient use of scarce clinical resources.

The responsivity principle generally proposes that clinicians use empirically based treatment techniques, and discourages the use of poorly theorized or invalid approaches (e.g., masturbatory satiation), as well as administering treatment programs in a "one size fits all" approach. On an individual level, the responsivity principle also proposes that clinicians tailor treatment delivery to accommodate the individual needs, abilities, and learning style of each client (e.g., creating performance-based homework assignments for clients who cannot read).

Together, these three principles of "doing what works" to reduce criminal recidivism helps clinicians identify *who* to treat, *what* specific problems to treat, and *how* to treat individuals with criminal offense histories. Treatment programs that employ this model have demonstrated greater reductions in recidivism compared to programs using only sanctions, or inappropriate or vague treatment approaches, and have demonstrated success with a variety of offender populations (Andrews, Dowden, & Gendreau, 1999; Dowden & Andrews, 1999a; 1999b; 2000; 2003).

Although it was originally developed for the general criminal population, the Risk-Need-Responsivity (RNR) model has since been reconstructed for its specific application to sexual offense behavior (Ward, Melser, & Yates, 2007). In the sex-offense-specific RNR model, treatment targets may include relevant non-criminogenic needs, if this would be expected to increase the client's treatment motivation and engagement, and/or to improve therapeutic alliance. In a recent meta-analysis, Hanson, Bourgon, Helmus, and Hodgson (2009) identified reductions in recidivism for sexual offense treatment programs employing the RNR model, demonstrating the applicability of the model to this population.

In addition to an increased emphasis on the therapeutic alliance, Ward and colleagues also emphasize the use of "approach" versus "avoidance" treatment goals (e.g., Good Lives Model; Ward & Marshall, 2004). For example, clients are more likely to pursue a behavioral goal focused on developing long-term, healthy relationships with adults, rather than a goal of simply avoiding relationships with children. Such an emphasis on approach-oriented goals supports efforts to reduce a client's risk, as achievement of these goals inherently interferes with antisocial and/or otherwise maladaptive lifestyle patterns often associated with offending (e.g., in order to develop prosocial peer relationships, it is necessary to avoid negative peer relationships).

3RT and the RNR model Given the importance of "doing what works" to reduce rates of criminal recidivism, 3RT was specifically developed to incorporate the RNR model into the treatment of sexual offense behavior. Consistent with the risk principle, 3RT allows clinicians to tailor the level of services to the level of risk of a given client, such that clients who are identified as higher risk receive more services than lower risk clients. Consistent with the need principle, 3RT allows clinicians to address only those risk-need areas that are relevant to a given client, and modify treatment targets as clients' needs change, and/or as the empirical research dictates (i.e., dynamic risk factors; see below). Consistent with a *general responsivity principle*, 3RT allows clinicians freedom to utilize existing cognitive-behavioral treatment strategies that have empirically demonstrated success at facilitating therapeutic change, and apply new techniques as these are developed and validated. Consistent with an *individual responsivity principle*, a client's individual needs and abilities are explicitly identified and addressed. This is consistent with growing research on the importance of meeting the needs of each individual to maximize therapeutic outcomes in sexual offense treatment (Hanson et al., 2009; Harkins & Beech, 2007; Kennedy, 2000; Looman, Dickie, & Abracen, 2005; Marshall et al., 2005).

3RT explicitly incorporates dynamic risk factors (DRFs) as the dominant framework for sexual offense treatment. For over a decade, research on sexual offense behavior has increasingly identified factors that are statistically associated with an individual's risk for sexual reoffense. Specifically, research has revealed two types of risk factors: *static risk factors* and *dynamic risk factors*. Static risk factors refer to those aspects of a client's history that are statistically associated with increased risk to reoffend, which *cannot be changed*. Examples include the number of prior convictions, a history of any stranger victims, or a history of any male victims. Although static risk factors are important for sex offender risk management (so that treatment services can be appropriately allocated according to risk), static factors are not *directly* targeted in treatment, because these factors cannot be changed. Dynamic risk factors refer to those aspects of a client's environment, lifestyle, or personality that are statistically associated with increased risk to reoffend and are *amenable to change*. Examples include sexual arousal to "deviant" stimuli (e.g., prepubescent children), negative emotionality (e.g., hostility, paranoia), or substance dependence.

DRFs include two types (Hanson & Harris, 2000): *Stable* DRFs exist for months, or even years, prior to sexual offense behavior (e.g., a lack of stable, long-term romantic relationships). Accordingly, if a stable dynamic factor can be reduced or eliminated in therapy (e.g., by increasing skills for maintaining long-term relationships), this may result in long-term change in an individual's reoffense risk. *Acute* DRFs occur in the days, hours, or even minutes prior to sexual offense behavior (e.g., conflict with an intimate partner). Acute risk factors may be an indicator that a reoffense is imminent, and thus are of great importance to community supervisors; by comparison, stable DRFs may be more important to therapists, who are attempting to facilitate long-term behavioral changes in their clients.

Although research on DRFs is an ongoing process, preliminary findings provide a basic framework for integrating DRFs into approaches to sex offense treatment. Given their statistical relationship to recidivism, and their amenability to change, DRFs are increasingly being regarded as high-priority targets for treatment interventions in sex offense treatment (e.g., Good Lives Model: Ward & Marshall, 2004; VRS-SO, Wong & Olver, 2010).

With regard to sexual offense behavior, DRFs appear to be associated with one of two broad categories: *deviant sexual interests* and an *antisocial orientation* (Hanson & Morton-Bourgon, 2004; Hanson & Bussière, 1998; Hanson & Harris, 2001; Hudson, Wales, Bakker, & Ward, 2002; Quinsey, Lalumiere, Rice, & Harris, 1995; Roberts, Doren, & Thornton, 2002). Examples of stable DRFs for sexual offense recidivism are presented in Box 15.1.

Given the statistical relationship between DRFs and sexual offense recidivism, 3RT was specifically developed with DRFs as the central, organizing framework for treatment planning and delivery. First, in 3RT, the "pre-treatment" phase involves a period of assessment, during which a client's DRFs are identified and conceptualized as a "cluster" of problematic thoughts, feelings, and/or behavior(s), that can be addressed in therapy. Clinicians identify the various thoughts, feelings, and behaviors that comprise clients' DRFS, and these problem behaviors become the focus of therapeutic change. Conceptualizing DRFs as "clusters" of maladaptive thoughts, feelings, and behaviors is particularly useful, because there are many existing, empirically based or validated cognitive-behavioral techniques for addressing similar symptoms that appear in the context of other disorders.

Second, after a client's DRFs have been identified and conceptualized as problem behavior(s), the goal of the treatment phase of 3RT is to teach clients how to replace their maladaptive thoughts and behaviors with more adaptive thoughts and behaviors. For example, a client's arousal to children might be reduced during treatment, but this treatment gain is unlikely to be maintained if arousal to an appropriate alternative is not also pursued (such as consensual sex with an adult). This "approach-based" therapeutic strategy follows the basic behavioral

Box 15.1   Dynamic Risk Factors for Sexual Offending

- Sexually deviant interests, sexual preoccupation
- Lack of stable long-term romantic relationships
- Attitudes supporting of sexual offending
- Negative emotionality, aggression, impulsivity, substance use, problem-solving deficits
- Lack of prosocial peer relationships and activities
- Rule violation/lack of cooperation with supervision

principle that it is ineffective to help a client discontinue a problematic behavior without also helping them to learn an alternative response to that behavior. This process, of identifying a problem behavior, discontinuing it, and replacing it with a more effective response, can also be described as "skills training"; that is, an approach to teaching clients how to be more prosocial and generally more effective in their day-to-day lives. As such, the 3RT model conceptualizes many of an offender's dynamic risk-needs as "skills deficits," which can be targeted using existing skills training approaches (the application of specific skills training techniques to target DRFs is described later in this chapter). By integrating dynamic risk assessment with strategically applied treatment techniques, 3RT offers a new approach to sex offense treatment that is grounded in cognitive-behavioral theory and empirically based practice, and entirely consistent with the RNR principles of effective offender change programs.

Overview of the 3RT Model

The 3RT model comprises three phases: (i) *Pre-Treatment*, (ii) *Treatment*, and (iii) *Post-Treatment*. The primary mechanism for change occurs during the Treatment phase, whereas the Pre- and Post-Treatment phases are designed to prepare for effective treatment delivery, and to develop RP strategies, respectively. The duration of each phase may vary from program to program, and from client to client. Timeframes are provided in this chapter simply as reference points, as there are no hard-and-fast rules about how long each phase should/will take. For example, a client may spend relatively less time in treatment if he is generally functioning well, has few dynamic risk-needs, is low risk to reoffend, and is motivated to participate in treatment; whereas a client may spend relatively more time in treatment if he has a major mental health or personality disorder, numerous dynamic risk-needs, a more complicated offense history, and presents as unmotivated to participate in treatment.

Each phase comprises specific components, which may occur concurrently or consecutively, and may be delivered in group or individual formats, depending on the resources available in a given treatment program. Box 15.2 outlines the key components of each phase.

Box 15.2   Phases of 3RT

1. **Pre-Treatment phase**
   (a)   Informed consent
   (b)   Intake assessment
   (c)   Case conceptualization and treatment planning
   (d)   Concurrent orientation sessions
2. **Treatment phase**
   (e)   General cognitive-behavioral skills training sessions
   (f)   Sex-offense-specific cognitive-behavioral skills training sessions
   (g)   Concurrent individual therapy sessions
3. **Post-Treatment phase**
   (h)   Relapse prevention sessions
   (i)   Community transition sessions
   (j)   Concurrent individual sessions

Pre-Treatment Phase

Prior to beginning treatment, all clients participate in the approximately 4–8-week Pre-Treatment phase. The goals of the Pre-Treatment phase are to: (i) obtain clients' informed consent to participate in treatment; (ii) determine the level of resources that should be allocated to each client based on their assessed risk to sexually reoffend; (iii) assess clients' dynamic risk and responsivity needs; (iv) conceptualize clients' offense histories in the broader context of their overall life functioning; (v) formulate idiographic treatment plans designed to target each clients' specific strengths and limitations; and (vi) orient clients to the content, process, and rationale for treatment. In addition, clients in this phase may receive motivation-enhancing interventions, particularly when there is evidence that they are reluctant to collaboratively engage in their own treatment.

Intake assessment

Assessment of dynamic risk-needs   The focus of the pre-treatment intake assessment is identifying clients' stable DRFs. DRFs are used as a guiding conceptual framework for describing clients' problem behavior and formulating goals for treatment. There are numerous existing resources for assessing DRFs associated with general criminal recidivism (e.g., Level of Service Inventory – Revised: Andrews & Bonta, 1995; Psychopathy Checklist – Revised, 2nd edition: Hare, 2003; *Diagnostic and Statistical Manual* (4th edition, text revision): American Psychiatric Association, 2000; the Violence Risk Scale (VRS): Wong & Gordon, 2001; IORNS: Miller, 2006), and sexual-offense-specific recidivism (e.g., SONAR: Hanson & Harris, 2000b; Stable-2007 and Acute-2007: Hanson, Harris, Scott, & Helmus, 2007; Multiphasic Sex Inventory: Nichols & Molinder, 1984, 2000; VRS-SO: Wong & Olver, 2010). In 3RT, items from these measures (particularly the Stable-2007, given the measure's strong empirical support) have been adapted, combined, and expanded from their original form into meaningful treatment constructs, to form the foundation for relevant goals and interventions for targeting DRFs.

As previously described, DRFs for sexual offense recidivism generally fall into one of two domains that are broadly associated with "sexual deviance" and/or general "antisociality." In 3RT, these two broad domains are referred to as *erotopathic risk-needs* and *antisocial risk-needs*. Each of these domains contains subcategories that describe the kinds of problematic thoughts, emotions, and behaviors that characterize that area. Each subcategory includes numerous factors, each of which can be conceptualized as a DRF that can be targeted in treatment.

Erotopathic risk-needs   In 3RT, the term *erotopathic*[1] *risk-needs* is used as a collective term, to refer to any thoughts, feelings, behaviors, and relationships that are associated with a client's problematic, inadequate, or otherwise maladaptive sexual/romantic relationships. Some clients may outright reject or avoid romantic intimacy with consenting same-aged peers, whereas other clients may simply lack effective skills for developing and maintaining

---

[1] "Erotopathic" is a neologism coined by the authors specifically for 3RT. It is adapted from the roots "Eros," connoting romantic love/romantic intimacy, and "-pathic," connoting disease; in other words, "erotopathic" refers to the notion that clients may be exhibiting evidence of "diseased" displays of love and romantic intimacy.

Box 15.3 Erotopathic Category Characteristics

1. **Sexual self-regulation deficits**:
   - Sexual preoccupation/sex drive
   - Sex as coping
   - Deviant sexual interests
   - Disinhibited sexual behavior/sexual "acting-out"
   - Instrumental use of sex
   - Sexual secrecy/deceit
   - Hypo- and/or over-controlled sexual behavior
   - Sexual dysfunction/inadequacy/knowledge deficit
2. **Romantic intimacy deficits**:
   - Lack of lovers/intimate partners
   - Emotional identification with children
   - Developmental identification with teenagers
   - Use of violence or other behavioral extremes with partner
   - Hostile masculinity
   - Sexual objectification of intimate partners
   - Oppression/rejection of female sexuality
   - Sexual orientation and/or gender identity issues
3. **Attitudes supportive of sexual offending**:
   - Sexual entitlement
   - Misinterpretation/misattribution of social/sexual cues
   - Externalized/uncontrollable causal attributions for offense
   - Global, fixed attitudes regarding sociosexual behavior
   - Justifications/rationalizations/minimization/distraction

such relationships. Whatever the nature of the "erotopathic" deficit, the critical question for treatment planning is: What precludes this client from developing and maintaining an adaptive, loving relationship with a consenting, peer-aged partner? Note that all clients who have been diagnosed with a paraphilia will have dynamic risk-needs in the erotopathic domain.

The erotopathic domain is divided into three categories. The first, *sexual self-regulation deficits*, comprises risk-needs related to poorly controlled expression of sexual impulses. The second, *romantic intimacy deficits*[2], is concerned with the ability to form and maintain close, intimate relationships with consenting, peer-aged sexual partners. The third, *attitudes supportive of sexual offending*, are those that excuse, permit, or condone such behavior, including justifications, rationalization, and minimization of offense behaviors. Specific characteristics related to each category are presented in Box 15.3.

Antisocial risk-needs In 3RT, the term "antisocial" is used collectively to refer to any of the thoughts, feelings, behaviors, and relationships that are associated with a client's generally

---

[2] In 3RT, romantic intimacy is conceptualized as distinct from other forms of intimacy, requiring specific social and emotional skills beyond those required for other forms of social/emotional intimacy (e.g., with friends, family).

Box 15.4 Antisocial Category Characteristics

1. **General self-regulation deficits**:
   - Impulsive acts
   - Poor cognitive problem-solving skills
   - Negative emotionality/hostility
   - Substance abuse/dependence</bbl>
2. **General social functioning deficits**:
   - Significant non-prosocial influences
   - General social rejection/loneliness
   - Lack of concern for others
   - Antisocial/asocial attitudes/orientation
   - Antisocial/asocial occupation/activities
   - Lifestyle instability/chaos/irresponsibility
3. **Rule violation/lack of cooperation:**
   - Non-cooperation with supervision
   - Passive or non-participation in prior treatment
   - Lack of insight about/knowledge of own risk factors
   - Unrealistic long-term goals/release plans

"non-prosocial" lifestyle. Some clients may outright reject/avoid a prosocial lifestyle, whereas other clients may lack effective skills to develop and maintain stable, prosocial peers and activities. Whatever the nature of the psychological deficit, the basic question for treatment planning is: What precludes this client from developing and maintaining a stable, responsible, prosocial lifestyle?

In our model, the antisocial domain is divided into the following three categories. The first, *general self-regulation deficits*, refers to a client's ability to self-monitor and inhibit antisocial/asocial thoughts and behaviors. The second, *general social functioning deficits*, is concerned with evidence of impairments in a client's ability to/attitude toward developing and maintaining a prosocial lifestyle. The final category, *rule-violation/non-compliance*, refers to impairment in a client's ability to conform to/comply with demands and/or expectations of others, particularly those who are in a position of authority. Box 15.4 presents specific characteristics of the three antisocial categories.

Assessment of responsivity needs Responsivity refers to the delivery of treatment programs in a manner that is consistent with the abilities and learning style of a client. A client's individual features may influence how they will respond to efforts to modify their problematic thoughts and behaviors. Addressing responsivity issues enhances the effective treatment of dynamic risk-needs, and accordingly, reduces recidivism; therefore, effective treatment programs must respond to individual characteristics of the client and be guided by their preferred learning styles, abilities, and cultural needs. Kennedy (2000) has summarized the importance of addressing responsivity needs as follows: "If the responsivity principle is not adhered to, treatment programs can fail, not because they do not have therapeutic integrity or competent therapists, but rather because [clients'] responsivity related barriers, such as cognitive/intellectual deficits, were not addressed."

Orientation sessions

3RT orientation sessions are psychoeducational in nature, and cover a broad range of topics to help clients understand what they can expect from treatment, and why treatment will be beneficial to them. The purpose of these groups is to help clients understand that treatment is not something that happens *to* them, rather, it is a process in which they are active and collaborative participants. Furthermore, helping clients understand the rationale for their treatment should be associated with increased buy-in from the clients, increased credibility for therapists and the therapy process, and should enhance the therapeutic alliance. Topics in orientation include: the history of sex offense treatment as well as an overview of DRFs, CBT, and dialectical-behavioral therapy (DBT).

Orientation sessions can be conducted in individual or group formats, depending on the resources available in a given treatment program and the responsivity needs of a particular client. Because these groups are psychoeducational in nature and do not require clients to disclose information about themselves, orientation groups can be "mixed"; that is, two or more clients could be placed in an orientation group together, regardless of otherwise clinically significant differences in their offense histories, demographic characteristics, dynamic risk-needs, etc. However, it is recommended that the orientation groups be "closed" groups; that is, more like a "class" with closed enrollment, so that all group members need to start and finish orientation together, because each session builds upon what was covered in the previous session.

Treatment Phase

The Treatment phase utilizes CBT interventions focused on skills acquisition and generalization, in an effort to target DRFs. As previously described, DRFs are used as a guiding conceptual framework; therefore, the primary goal of the Treatment phase is to target each client's dynamic risk factors. In other words, by the end of the Treatment phase, clients should have developed new ways of thinking and behaving that would be expected to mitigate their risk to reoffend in the future. The Treatment phase includes two therapeutic modalities: skills training sessions, and individual therapy sessions.

Skills training in 3RT: Conceptualizing DRFs as skill deficits

In some traditional approaches to treatment for sexual offenses, much emphasis has been (quite understandably) placed on getting the clients to *stop* exhibiting problematic thoughts, feelings, and behavior (e.g., stop having deviant fantasies, stop having rape-supportive attitudes, stop sexually offending). In 3RT, there is, of course emphasis on stopping the problem behavior; however, emphasis is also placed on what the client is going to do *instead* of the problematic thoughts, feelings, and behaviors. In 3RT, the goal of all of the treatment interventions is to decrease/eliminate the problem behavior(s) *and* replace the problem behavior(s) with more adaptive behavior(s).

This emphasis on increasing clients' use of alternative (and more adaptive) behaviors is based on the basic behavioral principle that it is ineffective to expect a client to cease an over-learned behavior without teaching them a behavior to replace their old behavior. If a client does not learn and practice a new, alternative response, it is expected that their old, over-learned behavior will eventually re-emerge, particularly when the client is under duress or a

Box 15.5   Steps in Addressing DRFs

Step 1: Identify the problem behavior
Step 2: Identify the "function" of the problem behavior
Step 3: Identify a more adaptive/less harmful behavior
Step 4: Identify skills required to use alternative response
Step 5: Implement treatment to help client develop these skills

heightened state of arousal (e.g., anger, sexual arousal). This means that clients must have opportunities to practice new, alternative behaviors.

Box 15.5 provides a brief overview/summary of how a client's behavior might be conceptualized in terms of dynamic risk, and in turn, how this dynamic risk-need might be addressed in treatment through skills training.

During the Treatment phase, clients participate in two rounds of cognitive-behavioral skills training. Each round of skills training is approximately 6 months long, and is organized into the four skills training modules that target problematic: (i) thoughts, (ii) emotions, (iii) behaviors, and (iv) relationships.

Similar to the orientation sessions delivered during the Pre-Treatment phase, skills training sessions are largely didactic in nature, and clients are not expected to divulge personal information about their offense histories in the context of skills training. In this sense, these sessions are more like a hands-on educational class than a therapy process group; however, they are still considered therapy, because these sessions are a vital aspect of facilitating positive, prosocial change in our clients.

Skills training sessions are not the time for clients to share or discuss intimate personal problems or crises they might be having (individual sessions serve this function; see below). To help facilitate this boundary between individual therapy and skills training sessions, it is very important that skills training sessions are as distinctly separate from individual sessions as possible. This separation can be accomplished in a number of ways, such as by using a skills trainer who is not also the individual therapist, holding the skills sessions on a different day/time than individual sessions, or holding the skills training sessions in a room other than the therapy office.

Skills training sessions can be conducted in individual or group formats, depending on the resources available in a given treatment program. They should be "closed" groups, so that all group members start and finish each module together (because each session builds upon what was covered in the previous session). New group members could join an existing group at the beginning of each of the four modules. The training sessions can be conducted by the individual therapist, but if there are adequate resources available, then it is recommended that these sessions are conducted by a separate skills trainer (or ideally, two skills trainers per group). Skills trainers should plan to spend about 5 or 6 weeks per module, which means that all four modules would be completed in about 6 months, presuming weekly sessions.

Adapting DBT skills training for 3RT

One useful set of skills training techniques are those provided in the *Skills Training Manual for Dialectical Behavioral Therapy* (DBT; Linehan, 1993). DBT has demonstrated empirical success in reducing the maladaptive behaviors of individuals with borderline personality disorder (Linehan et al., 1991), as well as with other clinical populations, including forensic populations (see Dimeff & Koerner, 2007). More recently, increased consideration has been given to the applicability of DBT skills to the treatment of sexual offense behavior (e.g., Hover, 1999; Hover & Packard, 1998, 1999; Wheeler et al., 2005b). In addition, Quigley (2000) and Shingler (2004) provide detailed reviews of the theoretical and practical compatibilities between DBT and sexual offense treatment.

DBT modules target treatment needs that are directly relevant to DRFs associated with sexual offense behavior, including problematic thoughts (e.g., "deviant" sexual fantasies; antisocial attitudes; attitudes supportive of sexual offending; sexual entitlement), problematic emotions (e.g., "deviant" sexual interests/arousal; loneliness, anger/hostility; suspiciousness/mistrust), problematic behavior (e.g., sexual dysregulation/hypersexuality; use of sex as a coping strategy; aggression/violence; impulsivity; antisocial behavior; substance abuse; unstable/parasitic lifestyle; rule violation), and problematic relationships (e.g., emotional identification with children; unstable/chaotic/lack of romantic relationships; intimacy deficits; social isolation; antisocial peer relationships; lack of concern for others).

Specifically, we generally recommend that the first round (approximately 6 months) of skills training in 3RT involve "standard" DBT skills training, without specific reference to sex-offense-specific treatment needs. Clients who have difficulty openly discussing or admitting to their sexual offense behavior, or clients who may be resistant to participating in sex-offense-specific therapy, may especially benefit from participation in treatment that "meets them where they are at"; that is, they may be willing to make changes in their lives, but not yet ready to address their offense-specific needs. Further, making these changes may facilitate shifts in attitude or tolerance for vulnerability that allow for a willingness to more directly explore and/or address sex-offense-specific issues and risk-needs.

Sex-offense-specific skills training

Despite its theoretical and practical compatibility with the needs of this population, DBT does not address some of the specific treatment needs of clients who have engaged in sexual offense behavior. For example, DBT does not specifically include interventions for managing problematic sexual thoughts, feelings, and behaviors, or for managing specific antisocial thoughts, feelings, and behaviors. Therefore, 3RT includes a skills training program that is based on DBT skills training, but specifically modified to address clients' dynamic risk-needs.

As previously described, erotopathic risk-needs (i.e., maladaptive sexual/romantic behaviors) and antisocial risk-needs (i.e., maladaptive social behaviors and lifestyle) form the foundation of skills training sessions. Clients participate in skills training sessions specifically tailored to target erotopathic and/or antisocial risk-needs. Thus, skills training sessions are taught using the *Skills Training Manual for Dialectical Behavior Therapy* (Linehan, 1993), aided by additional teaching notes, discussion points, and activities specifically designed to target these types of DRFs. Clients may be assigned to one or both types of skills training sessions, as their stable-dynamic risk-needs warrant.

3RT-E skills training sessions In 3RT erotopathic (3RT-E) skills training sessions, clients learn skills to monitor their arousal, reduce problematic thought patterns, and replace these maladaptive thoughts and behaviors with more effective methods of sexual self-monitoring and regulation. Overall, clients develop skills to establish and maintain adaptive, satisfying intimate relationships with consenting, peer-age partners. Framed largely in terms of Stable-2007 DRFs

(Hanson et al., 2007), the following erotopathic dynamic factors have been associated with an increased risk for sexual reoffending:

- Deviant sexual interests (e.g., sexual interest in children, any paraphilic interest, sexual preoccupation).
- Deviant sexual preferences (e.g., any deviant sexual preference, sexual preference for children).
- Lack of romantic partner (e.g., no relationships, or a history of unstable relationships).
- Intimacy deficits (e.g., loneliness/social isolation, emotional identification with children, conflicts with intimate partners).
- Attitudes supportive of sexual crimes (e.g., rape-supportive attitudes, attitudes supportive of child molestation, sexual entitlement).

When conceptualized as skill deficits, one approach to targeting these deficits is to help the client develop skills for maintaining satisfying and prosocial intimate/sexual relationships. The goal of 3RT-E skills training groups is to help clients develop at least some of the skills described below.

To improve *sexual self-monitoring skills*, participants learn skills for monitoring their own arousal processes (e.g., sexual thoughts, subjective arousal, sensory perceptions, and physical sensations) and to objectively perceive stimuli in their environment (e.g., describing sexual stimuli without interpreting or judging them). These skills are designed to specifically target maladaptive patterns of sexualized thoughts and behaviors that contribute to offenders' maladaptive sexual self-regulation (e.g., an expectation that sexual activity will eliminate subjective feelings of distress), and replace these with more effective methods for sexual self-monitoring and regulation.

To improve their *sexual/emotion regulation skills*, participants learn skills to identify, label, monitor, and control their sexual feelings, as well as potentially destructive emotions inherent to being involved in romantic relationships (e.g., jealousy, insecurity, mistrust, anger). Participants learn to monitor their sexual arousal and other physiological reactions, and label the physiological responses accordingly. They also learn to reduce their vulnerability to certain emotional states, including sexual arousal. Finally, they learn to develop skills to de-escalate their arousal and/or emotions as indicated.

To reduce their *maladaptive use of sexual thoughts and behaviors as a coping strategy*, participants learn skills to identify their maladaptive sexual coping strategies and replace these with more effective coping techniques. In addition to developing skills for acute coping responses, 3RT-E skills include a broader emphasis on how to reduce the overall distress in the client's life by increasing (non-harmful and non-sexual) behaviors that the client finds pleasurable or otherwise rewarding.

To decrease their *maladaptive romantic/sexual relationships and interactions*, participants learn and practice skills to engage in prosocial intimate interactions and relationships. Ideally, these skills directly target those skills necessary for forming and maintaining healthy romantic relationships (e.g., dating, terminating relationships, intimacy building, acquiring mutual consent). These skills are modeled and rehearsed in group (in role-plays), and in vivo (through homework assignments or group outings).

3RT-A skills training sessions In 3RT antisocial (3RT-A) skills training sessions, clients learn to observe and describe their own internal processes, reduce problematic thought patterns, and replace these maladaptive thoughts and behaviors with more effective means of regulating their general thoughts, emotions, and behavior. Overall, clients develop skills to establish and maintain prosocial behaviors, attitudes, and relationships, and to generally function more effectively in society. Again, framed largely in terms of Stable-2007 DRFs, the following "antisocial" dynamic factors have been associated with an increased risk for sexual reoffending:

- Lack of prosocial influences (e.g., antisocial peer influences, absence of prosocial peer influences).
- Negative emotionality (e.g., hostility/irritability, suspiciousness/mistrust).
- Substance abuse/dependence (including any substance abuse and being intoxicated at the time of the offense).
- Problem-solving deficits.
- Rule violation (including non-compliance with supervision, treatment rules/expectations; release violations).

Conceptualized as skill deficits, one approach to reduce the risks associated with these factors is to help the client develop skills for maintaining a stable, prosocial lifestyle; that is, a lifestyle that supports individual responsibility and accountability, prosocial attitudes and relationships, and compliance with rules and structure, by developing at least some of the skills described below.

To improve *general self-monitoring skills*, participants learn skills for observing and describing their own internal processes (e.g., thoughts and beliefs, sensory perceptions, physical sensations) and objectively perceive stimuli in their external environment (e.g., observing and describing, without interpretation or judgment). Ideally, these cognitive skills target antisocial thought patterns (e.g., attitudes, beliefs, distortions) that contribute to offenders' self-regulation deficits, and replace these maladaptive cognitions with more effective methods for self-monitoring and regulation.

To decrease *antisocial emotional difficulties* (e.g., misplaced or excessive irritability, hostility, suspiciousness, mistrust) and improve their overall emotion regulation skills, participants learn skills to identify, label, monitor, and control their feelings and emotional responses. They learn to differentiate emotional responses, including physiological responses, and label them accurately. They develop skills to de-escalate their emotions as needed, as well as techniques for reducing their overall vulnerability to negative emotionality.

To decrease *maladaptive coping strategies* (e.g., substance abuse; violence), participants learn skills to replace impulsive and harmful behaviors with more effective coping responses. They learn skills to improve their tolerance for life's inevitable distress, as well as skills to take care of themselves in an effort to reduce their vulnerability to distress.

To decrease *antisocial relationships and activities*, participants learn and practice skills to help them function more effectively in a prosocial environment. For example, they learn techniques for effective communication, problem-solving, assertiveness, and conflict resolution, with an emphasis on learning to interact with others in a mutually respectful way. Importantly, these skills are designed to help individuals identify their goal(s) in a given interaction and to effectively address these needs while attending to the wants/needs of the other person in the interaction, without violating the rights/needs of others. These skills are modeled and rehearsed in groups (in role-plays), and in vivo (through homework assignments or group outings). Participants should also have increased involvement in prosocial activities (e.g., employment, joining an athletic team, developing a hobby) to increase contact with prosocial peers.

3RT: Individual therapy sessions

The purposes of individual therapy sessions are to provide clients with the opportunity to address their specific dynamic risk-needs, and apply the skills they are learning to their own functioning (e.g., using weekly diary cards, activity logs, and/or other home-practice activity). In addition, individual sessions provide a format for clients to address significant life events and crises as these arise (and conduct functional analyses of problem behavior) and opportunities for behavioral rehearsal and feedback (i.e., role-plays).

One therapeutic activity/intervention that is effectively conducted during individual sessions is a *functional analysis* (also known as a behavior chain analysis, or BCA) of a client's problematic behavior. Specifically, the client can learn in-depth about the thoughts and feelings associated with their behavior, and how each interacts with the other. This information is critical to help clients understand their own vulnerabilities and identify points for intervention.

Another therapeutic activity best suited for individual sessions is the creation, assignment, and subsequent review of *home-practice activities*, including diary cards, activity logs, or other home-practice activities. Each week, the therapist considers what important skills the client is working on, and develops activities to increase the client's opportunities to practice these skills between sessions. The activity is clearly explained to the client, and explicitly related to their treatment needs. Prior to ending the session, therapist and client engage in some pre-emptive troubleshooting to identify potential barriers to completing the assignments, and how these might be minimized or eliminated altogether. Most importantly, therapists then review the client's progress toward completing this activity in the next therapy session, while continuing to address any barriers to completing assignments and implementing/practicing skills outside formal treatment sessions.

One example of a home-practice activity that therapists can assign each week is a *diary card*, or activity log. These are sheets that identify each day of the week, and specific tasks that are to be charted, logged, or documented, day-by-day. For example, therapists might ask clients to keep track of the skills they are using each day, how they are spending their time on an hour-by-hour basis, or to log the frequency of their sexual thoughts and behaviors (e.g., an "arousal log"). The purpose of these logs should be explained clearly to the client, and the logs should be reviewed with the client in the following session. For some clients, the purpose of keeping such records may be to help them develop a more accurate appraisal of the frequency with which they engage in certain activities, whereas for other clients it may be to increase their accountability for how they are spending their time. What is most important is that the therapeutic rationale for keeping the log is clear to the therapist and the client, and that the log is reviewed after it has been completed.

Post-Treatment Phase

In 3RT, the Post-Treatment phase can be conducted in the form of weekly individual sessions, or in the form of facilitator-led groups. This phase may involve less face-to-face time with therapists, and increased face-to-face time with the correctional staff or social workers coordinating the clients' transition. Community transition planning does apply to clients who are participating in treatment in community settings (reviewed in more detail later in this section). This phase can integrate other adjunct groups, services, and interventions, such as chaperone/

supervisor training, family reunification therapy, and role-plays for job interviewing and making disclosures.

The two primary goals of clients in the Post-Treatment phase are to: (i) complete a *RP Plan* that includes their acute DRFs, and (ii) identify their basic logistical needs in the community (and/or away from professional supports and supervision) and their *community transition plan* for addressing these needs (e.g., residential, employment, financial, social/emotional). Clients should be provided with outlines and guidelines for completing both a RP plan and a community transition plan, and the differences between each plan should be clearly explained to them.

Relapse prevention planning

As noted earlier, RP (Marlatt & Gordon, 1985) was initially applied to sexual offense treatment as a primary treatment modality; however, this was not the purpose or intent of the original RP model as it was developed in the field of addictions. Because of this long-standing misapplication of RP, as well as other critiques of how RP has been applied to sexual offense treatment over the last few decades (e.g., Laws, 2003; Stoner & George, 2000; Ward et al., 1995; Wheeler, 2003), we advocate for the return of RP to the role for which it was originally developed: that is, as an adjunct approach to help clients maintain the successful progress they have made in treatment.

RP and its application to sexual offense behavior has been described elsewhere (e.g., Laws, Hudson, & Ward, 2000b; Wheeler et al., 2005a, 2005b), and will not be reviewed in detail here. Instead, we will briefly review some of the key concepts and RP terminology, and offer approaches to effectively integrating RP as a maintenance strategy following treatment for sexual offense behavior.

Key RP concepts and terminology Historically, sexual offense behavior has been conceptualized as a harmful behavior that supersedes healthier ways of responding to sexual urges and/or coping with unwanted emotions. For any given client, their offense behavior was presumed to follow a prototypic progression, commonly referred to as his relapse "cycle." Accordingly, an early objective of RP has been to identify the client's "cycle"; that is, the unique chain of cognitive, behavioral, and environmental events that have been associated with his past offense behavior, and are presumed to be associated with future offenses. After the client's "cycle" was identified, interventions were developed to interrupt this pattern and prevent the client from progressing from a "lapse" to a "relapse." In RP, the relapse "cycle" involves interacting constructs that, left unchecked, will facilitate a relapse (i.e., the commission of a new sexual offense). Some of the most important of these constructs are described in Box 15.6.

Updating RP planning with DRFs Historically, programs employing RP to treat sexual offense behavior have required that clients create a RP plan as part of their treatment. Most RP plans are likely to include the identification of the problematic factors in Box 15.6, along with their appropriate interventions. We advocate for the use of RP plans that also devote substantial attention to the DRFs for sexual offense recidivism. Specifically, we propose a two-part approach to RP planning, with the first part targeting stable DRFs and the second part targeting acute DRFs. A sample RP plan outline following our model is presented in Appendix 15.A.

Box 15.6   Relapse Prevention for Sexual Recidivism

1. **Chronic lifestyle imbalances and/or acute triggering events**: These activate the "chain" of maladaptive thoughts and behaviors that precede a sexual offense (e.g. conflict with an intimate partner; job loss).
2. **Seemingly unimportant decisions**: Decisions that support the commission of a sexual offense (e.g., ruminating about a conflict with a romantic partner; putting himself in a place where he has access to a potential victim).
3. **Lapse**: With regard to sexual offense behavior, a lapse has been defined as "offense precursor activities" (e.g. Laws, 2003), such as using pornography, indulging in deviant masturbatory fantasies, or cruising for potential victims.
4. **The abstinence violation effect (AVE)**: A cognitive and affective event that is hypothesized to occur following a lapse. The AVE refers to an individual's recognition that he/she has broken a self-imposed rule; that is, by having engaged in one act of the prohibited behavior, his/her commitment to abstinence has been violated. According to the RP model, an individual's response to this violation can determine whether the lapse turns into a full-blown relapse (Marlatt & George, 1984; Marlatt & Gordon, 1985), and therefore plays a critical role in the relapse cycle.
5. **The problem of immediate gratification (PIG)**: The process of attending to positive aspects of the prohibited behavior, and ignoring the negative consequences. The PIG can occur before or after a lapse; therefore it can increase the risk of a high-risk situation leading to a lapse, in addition to increasing the risk of a lapse becoming a full-blown relapse (see Marlatt, 1989).
6. **High-risk situations (HRS)**: Factors are present that have been historically associated with the decision to commit a sexual offense (e.g., feeling sexually aroused; being alone with a potential victim).

Community transition planning

The nature of a client's "transition" back into the community varies tremendously, depending on the client's sentence structure, developmental stage, socioeconomic status, social support, and risk level. For example, an adult client who is transitioning back into the community for the first time following a 10-year prison sentence will have different needs from an adult client who has served his entire sentence in the community and is transitioning from supervision and treatment services. Similarly, an adult client who is transitioning from a group home into independent housing will have vastly different treatment needs from a juvenile client who is transitioning from a group home back into their family home. In community transition groups, clients focus on refining and progressively generalizing their skills to a broad variety of "real life" situations and settings in the community independent of treatment and treatment professionals, through practice, troubleshooting, and observations of other group members. Some clients, such as those with greater risk- and/or responsivity-needs, may benefit from ongoing individual sessions during the Post-Treatment phase.

Residential considerations and DRFs   Some fortunate clients may have stable homes in which to reside, while other clients may be homeless. Managing the residential needs of

Box 15.7   Community Transition Plan Domains

- Living/residential
- Employment
- Financial
- Educational
- Leisure/recreational activities
- Social support/family/peer relationships
- Romantic/sexual relationships
- Psychological/mental health needs
- Physical/medical needs
- Spiritual needs
- Family reunification planning

clients who have engaged in sexual offense behavior has become a controversial topic in recent decades, as new laws continue to emerge that restrict where such persons can reside. Many communities are – quite understandably – unhappy about the prospect of "sex offenders" residing there, and may go to great lengths to prevent them from moving in. Similarly, communities may become outraged to learn that a homeless "sex offender" is living in a local motel, being paid for with their tax dollars. The cumulative effect of these concerns can lead to the creation of *iatrogenic dynamic risk-needs*: that is, we as a community can actually create situations that result in an increase in a client's risk. When a client lacks stable housing, this will likely be associated with an increase in their overall lifestyle instability. Furthermore, when clients do not have a stable residential address, this makes it extremely difficult, if not impossible, for law enforcement personnel to monitor these offenders in the community, further increasing the potential risk to the community. Thus, communities who "banish" offenders from residing there may be para-doxically increasing the risk that these offenders will sexually recidivate.

Conversely, increasing a client's lifestyle stability in the community should be associated with a reduction in that client's risk to the community. The more opportunities a client has to participate in prosocial activities, and form relationships with prosocial peers, the less likely the client is to engage in an irresponsible or even antisocial lifestyle. Accordingly, clients who are participating in community transition sessions should be identifying how they can maximize their opportunities for prosocial influences, while simultaneously avoiding situations that may increase their stable and acute dynamic risk-needs. Examples of areas to consider in community transition planning are included in Box 15.7.

At treatment termination, clients are expected to be skilled at identifying potential risk-needs that may be associated with each of these aspects of their lives in the community. For example, a client who has a history of grooming children with whom he has no prior rela-tionship will need to identify leisure and recreational activities that are prosocial, but that do not involve children. Some clients may not be able to return to their previous careers (e.g., healthcare providers, clergy, teachers/coaches), and thus may have to make a signifi-cant change in their vocational status. Some clients may have victims in the family home, or victim-aged children in the family home, and thus may require intensive reunification therapy prior to returning to these residences. Even clients who have no history of committing offenses against children may need to participate in reunification before moving back to the family home after a prolonged absence, to help family members effectively cope with this adjustment.

One promising model for facilitating clients' effective and prosocial transition into the community is a restorative justice program called Circles of Support and Accountability (COSA; Wilson & Prinzo, 2001). Briefly, COSA programs comprise groups of community volunteers (the inner circle) who are provided with support and training from professionals (the outer circle), to assist an individual with a history of sexual offending in reintegrating into the community following a period of detention or incarceration. Volunteers assist an individual in meeting their practical needs (employment, housing, medical care, etc.), provide support for the individual's efforts to meet their needs and solve problems in a prosocial manner, and intervene on their stable and acute dynamic risks associated with their historical offense patterns (for more information on COSA programs, see Hanvey, Philpot, & Wilson, 2011; Wilson, McWhinnie, Picheca, Prinzo, & Cortoni, 2007; Wilson & Prinzo, 2001).

Treatment Completion

In sexual offense therapy, the notion of treatment completion is complex, primarily because clients who are court-ordered into treatment may have artificially imposed treatment termination dates (e.g., based on the date they are released from prison or from community supervision). There are many terms that a particular program might use to refer to the point at which a client stops receiving treatment services, including treatment "completion," "discharge," "termination," and "graduation." Therapists should be aware that these terms are not synonymous, and that there are clinically meaningful differences between them. In fact, terms such as graduation and completion may be misleading, contributing to the false impression that therapy is like a "class," with a clear beginning and end, and/or that there is a fixed and terminal nature to a client's risk and capacity/need for change, such that they are no longer at risk for engaging in sexual behavior problems.

In truth, clients' progress, change, and the nature and degree of their individual risk-needs vary and are influenced by their current circumstances. Accordingly, we are well aware that change will continue to occur with clients, and that they will encounter or create situations and circumstances that are destabilizing or risky for them, which may necessitate a return to treatment or increased support.

In 3RT, a client's "termination" is described in behaviorally specific terms (rather than a categorical label), and depends on the circumstances of the program. For instance, if a client completes all of his or her treatment goals, and no further therapeutic services are indicated at that time, they may be described as having "completed the goals identified at the outset of treatment." If a client has made some progress in treatment, but is being released and still has some ongoing treatment needs, then they might be described in 3RT as having "completed some treatment targets, but still in need of treatment for the following needs...." Therefore, rather than using a vague blanket term such as "treatment completion," 3RT therapists are encouraged to be specific about *what* a client has "completed" – whether that is a specific intervention (e.g., six sessions of skills training) or a particular treatment target (e.g., reduce deviant arousal by 10%).

Summary

This chapter describes 3RT, a cognitive-behavioral approach to treating sexual offense behavior. 3RT uses DRFs as the organizing framework for treatment planning and delivery, and draws upon existing CBT techniques, such as DBT skills, to target these risk factors. 3RT is a highly flexible and adaptive approach that can be easily tailored to meet the needs of individual clients, including adults and juveniles, males and females, in inpatient and outpatient settings. In this way, 3RT offers therapists a straightforward and empirically derived approach to reduce recidivism risk in clients who have exhibited sexual offense behavior.

References

American Psychiatric Association. (2000). *Diagnostic and statistical manual of mental disorders* (4th ed., text revision). Washington, DC: American Psychiatric Association.

Andrews, D. A., & Bonta, J. (1995). *The Level of Service Inventory – Revised*. Toronto, Canada: Multi-Health Systems.

Andrews, D. A., Bonta, J., & Hoge, R. D. (1990). Classification for effective rehabilitation: Rediscovering psychology. *Criminal Justice & Behavior, 17,* 19–52.

Andrews, D. A., Dowden, C., & Gendreau, P. (1999). Clinically relevant and psychologically informed approaches to reduced reoffending: A meta-analytic study of human service, risk, need, responsivity, and other concerns in justice contexts. Unpublished manuscript. Ottawa, ON: Carleton University.

Covell, C., & Wheeler, J. (2011). Application of the responsivity principle to treatment of sexual offense behavior. *Journal of Forensic Psychology Practice, 11*(1), 61–72.

Dimeff, L. A., & Koerner, K. (2007). *Dialectical behavior therapy in clinical practice: Applications across disorders and settings.* New York: Guildford.

Dowden, C., & Andrews, D. A. (1999a). What works for female offenders: A meta-analytic review. *Crime and Delinquency, 45,* 438–452.

Dowden, C., & Andrews, D. A. (1999b). What works in young offender treatment: A meta-analysis. *Forum on Corrections Research, 11*(2), 21–24.

Dowden, C., & Andrews, D. A. (2000). Effective correctional treatment and violent reoffending: A meta-analysis. *Canadian Journal of Criminology, 42,* 449–476.

Dowden, C., & Andrews, D. A. (2003). Does family intervention work for delinquents? Results of a meta-analysis. *Canadian Journal of Criminology and Criminal Justice, 45,* 327–342.

Hanson, R. K. (2000). What is so special about relapse prevention? In D. R. Laws, S. M. Hudson, & T. Ward (Eds.), *Remaking relapse prevention with sex offenders: A sourcebook* (pp. 27–38). Thousand Oaks, CA: Sage.

Hanson, R. K., Bourgon, G., Helmus, L., & Hodgson, S. (2009). The principles of effective correctional treatment also apply to sexual offenders: A meta-analysis. *Criminal Justice & Behavior, 36,* 865–890.

Hanson, R. K., & Bussière, M. T. (1998). Predicting relapse: A meta-analysis of sexual offender recidivism studies. *Journal of Consulting and Clinical Psychology, 66,* 348–362.

Hanson, R. K., & Harris, A. J. R. (2000). Where should we intervene? Dynamic predictors of sexual offense recidivism. *Criminal Justice & Behavior, 27*(1), 6–35.

Hanson, R. K., & Harris, A. J. R. (2000b). *The Sex Offender Need Assessment Rating (SONAR): A method for measuring change in risk levels* (User Report 2000–01). Ottawa: Public Safety and Emergency Preparedness Canada.

Hanson, R. K., & Harris, A. J. R. (2001). A structured approach to evaluating change in risk levels. *Sexual Abuse: A Journal of Research and Treatment, 13* (3), 105–122.

Hanson, R. K., Harris, A. J. R, Scott, T-L., & Helmus, L. (2007). *Assessing the risk of sexual offenders on community supervision: The Dynamic Supervision Project.* Retrieved from http://www.publicsafety.gc.ca/res/cor/rep/_fl/crp2007-05-en.pdf

Hanson, R. K., & Morton-Bourgon, K. (2004). *Predictors of sexual recidivism: An updated meta-analysis* (User Report 2004-02). Ottawa: Public Safety and Emergency Preparedness Canada. Retrieved from http://www.publicsafety.gc.ca/res/cor/rep/_fl/2004-02-pred-se-eng.pdf

Hanvey, S., Philpot, T., & Wilson, C. (2011). *A community-based approach to the reduction of sexual re-offending: circles of support and accountability.* London and Philadelphia: Jessica Kingsley Publishers.

Hare, R. D. (2003). *The Hare Psychopathy Checklist-Revised: Second Edition.* Toronto: Multi-Health Systems.

Harkins, L., & Beech, A.R. (2007). A review of the factors that can influence the effectiveness of sexual offender treatment: Risk, need, responsivity, and process issues. Aggression and Violent Behavior,12 (6), 615–627

Hover, G. R. (1999). Using DBT skills with incarcerated sex offenders. *ATSA Forum, 11* (3).

Hover, G. R., & Packard, R. L. (1998, October). *The effects of skills training on incarcerated sex offenders and their ability to get along with their therapist.* Poster presented at the 17th Annual Research and Treatment Conference of the Association for the Treatment of Sexual Abusers, Vancouver, British Columbia.

Hover, G. R., & Packard, R. L. (1999, September). *The treatment effects of dialectical behavior therapy with sex offenders.* Paper presented at the 18th Annual Research and Treatment Conference of the Association for the Treatment of Sexual Abusers, Lake Buena Vista, FL.

Hudson, S. M., Ward, T., & Marshall, W. L. (1992). The abstinence violation effect in sex offenders: A reformulation. *Behavior Research and Therapy, 30* (5), 435–441.

Hudson, S.M., Wales, D.S., Bakker, L., & Ward, T. (2002). Dynamic risk factors: The Kia Marama evaluation. *Sexual Abuse: A Journal of Research and Treatment, 14* (2), 103–119.

Kennedy, S. M. (2000). Treatment responsivity: Reducing recidivism by enhancing treatment effectiveness. *Forum on Corrections Research, 12,* 19–23.

Laws, D. R. (1995). Central elements in relapse prevention procedures with sex offenders. *Psychology, Crime, & Law, 2,* 41–53.

Laws, D. R. (2003). The rise and fall of relapse prevention. *Australian Psychologist, 38* (1), 22–30.

Laws, D. R., Hudson, S. M., & Ward, T. (2000a). The original model of relapse prevention with sex offenders. In D. R. Laws, S.M. Hudson, & T. Ward (Eds.), *Remaking relapse prevention with sex offenders: A sourcebook* (pp. 2–24). New York: Guilford Press.

Laws, D. R., Hudson, S. M., & Ward, T. (2000b) *Remaking relapse prevention with sex offenders: A sourcebook.* Thousand Oaks, CA: Sage.

Linehan, M. M. (1993). *Skills training manual for treating borderline personality disorder.* New York: Guilford.

Linehan, M. M., Armstrong, H. E., Suarez, A., Allmon, D., & Heard, H. L. (1991). Cognitive-behavioral treatment of chronically parasuicidal borderline patients. *Archives of General Psychiatry, 48,* 1060–1064.

Lipton, D.S., Martinson, R., & Wilks, J. (1975). *The effectiveness of correctional treatment: A survey of treatment evaluation studies.* New York: Praeger.

Looman, J., Dickie, I., & Abracen. J. (2005). Responsivity issues in the treatment of sexual offenders. *Trauma, Violence, and Abuse, 6* (4), 330–353.

Marlatt, G. A. (1989). Feeding the PIG: The Problem of Immediate Gratification. In D.R. Laws (Ed.), *Relapse prevention with sex offenders* (pp. 56–21). New York: Guilford.

Marlatt, G. A., & George, W. H. (1984). Relapse prevention: Introduction and overview of the model. *British Journal of Addictions, 79,* 261–273.

Marlatt, G. A., & Gordon, J. R. (1985). *Relapse prevention: Maintenance strategies in the treatment of addictive behavior.* New York: Guilford Press.

Marques, J. K., Wiederanders, M., Day, D. M., Nelson, C., & Van Ommeren, A. (2005). Effects of a relapse prevention program on sexual recidivism: final results from California's Sex Offender

Treatment and Evaluation Project (SOTEP). *Sexual Abuse: A Journal of Research and Treatment,* *17*(1), 79–107.

Marshall, W. L., Ward, T., Mann, R. E., Moulden, H., Fernandez, Y. M., Serran, G., & Marshall, L. E. (2005). Working positively with sexual offenders: Maximizing the effectiveness of treatment. *Journal of Interpersonal Violence, 20,* 1096–1114.

Martinson, R. (1974). What works? Questions and answers about prison reform. *The Public Interest,* pp. *22–54.*

Miller, H. (2006). A dynamic assessment of offender risk, needs, and strengths in a sample of pre-release general offenders. *Behavioral Sciences and the Law, 24,* 767–782.

Newring, K. A. B., Loverich, T. M., Harris, C. D., & Wheeler, J. G. (2009). Relapse prevention. In W. T. O' Donohue & J. E. Fisher (Eds.), *General principles and empirically supported techniques of cognitive behavior therapy: Applying empirically supported techniques in your practice* (2nd ed.), (pp. 520–531). Hoboken, NJ: John Wiley & Sons, Inc.

Nichols, H. R., & Molinder, I. (1984). *The Multiphasic Sex Inventory manual.* Available from: Nichols and Molinder, 437 Bowes Drive, Tacoma, WA 98466, USA.

Nichols, H. R., & Molinder, I. (2000). *The Multiphasic Sex Inventory-II manual.* Available from: Nichols and Molinder, 437 Bowes Drive, Tacoma, WA 98466, USA.

Pithers, W. D., Marques, J. K., Gibat, C. C., & Marlatt, G. A. (1983). Relapse prevention with sexual aggressives: A self-control model of treatment and maintenance of change. In J. G. Greer & I. R. Stuart (Eds.), *The sexual aggressor* (pp. 124–239). New York: Van Nostrand Reinhold.

Quigley, S. M. (2000). Dialectical behavioral therapy and sex offender treatment: An integrative model. *Dissertation Abstracts International, 60* (9), 4904B.

Quinsey, V. L., Lalumiere, M. L., Rice, M. E., & Harris, G. T. (1995). Predicting sexual offenses. In J. C. Campbell (Ed.), *Assessing dangerousness: Violence by sexual offenders, batterers, and child abusers* (pp. 114–137). Thousand Oaks, CA: Sage.

Roberts, C. F., Doren, D. M., & Thornton, D. (2002). Dimensions associated with assessments of sex offender recidivism risk. *Criminal Justice and Behavior, 29,* 569–589.

Shingler, J. (2004). A process of cross-fertilization: What sex offender treatment can learn from dialectical behavior therapy. *Journal of Sexual Aggression, 10* (2), 171–180.

Stoner, S. A., & George, W. H. (2000). Relapse prevention and harm reduction: Areas of overlap. In D. R. Laws, S.M. Hudson, & T. Ward (Eds.), *Remaking relapse prevention with sex offenders: A sourcebook* (pp. 56–75). Thousand Oaks, CA: Sage.

Ward, T., Louden, K., Hudson, S. M., & Marshall, W. L. (1995). A descriptive model of the offense chain for child molesters. *Journal of Interpersonal Violence, 10,* 452–472.

Ward, T., & Hudson, S. M. (1996a). Relapse prevention: A critical analysis. *Sexual Abuse: A Journal of Research and Treatment, 8,* 177–200.

Ward, T., & Hudson, S. M. (1996b). Relapse prevention: Future directions. *Sexual Abuse: A Journal of Research and Treatment, 8,* 249–256.

Ward, T., & Hudson, S. M. (1998). A model of the relapse process in sexual offenders. *Journal of Interpersonal Violence, 13,* 700–725.

Ward, T. & Hudson, S.M. (2000). A self-regulation model of relapse prevention. In D. R. Laws, S. M. Hudson, & T. Ward (Eds.), *Remaking relapse prevention with sex offenders: A sourcebook* (pp. 79–101). New York: Guilford Press.

Ward, T., & Marshall, W. L. (2004). Good lives, aetiology and the rehabilitation of sex offenders: A bridging theory. *Journal of Sexual Aggression, 10,* 153–169.

Ward, T., Melser, J., & Yates, P. (2007). Reconstructing the Risk-Need-Responsivity model: A theoretical elaboration and evaluation. *Aggression and Violent Behavior, 12,* 208–228.

Wheeler, J. G. (2003). The abstinence violation effect in a sample of incarcerated sexual offenders: A reconsideration of the terms lapse and relapse. *Dissertation Abstracts International, 63* (8), 3946B.

Wheeler, J. G., & Covell, C. (2005). *Stable dynamic risk-need rating manual: For treatment planning, delivery, and progress evaluation.* Unpublished manual.

Wheeler, J. G., George, W. H., & Marlatt, G. A. (2006). Relapse prevention for sexual offenders: Considerations for the Abstinence Violation Effect. *Sexual Abuse: Journal of Research and Treatment*, *18* (3), 233–248.

Wheeler, J. G., George, W. H., & Stephens, K. (2005a). Assessment of sexual offenders: A model for integrating dynamic risk assessment and relapse prevention approaches. In D. M. Donavan & G. A. Marlatt (Eds.), *Assessment of addictive behaviors* (2nd ed., pp. 392–424). New York: Guilford Publications.

Wheeler, J. G., George, W. H., & Stoner, S. A. (2005b). Enhancing the relapse prevention model for sex offenders: Adding recidivism risk reduction therapy (3RT) to target offenders' dynamic risk needs. In G. A. Marlatt & D. M. Donavan (Eds.), *Relapse prevention* (2nd ed., pp. 333–362). New York: Guilford Publications.

Wilson, R. J., McWhinnie, A., Picheca, J. E., Prinzo, M., & Cortoni, F. (2007). Circles of support and accountability: Engaging community volunteers in the management of high-risk sexual offenders. *The Howard Journal of Criminal Justice*, *46*, 1–15.

Wilson, R. J., & Prinzo, M. (2001). 'Circles of support: A restorative justice initiative.' *Journal of Psychology and Human Sexuality*, *13*, 59–77.

Wong, S. C. P., & Gordon, A. (2001). The Violence Risk Scale. *Bulletin of the International Society for Research on Aggression*, *23* (2), 16–20.

Wong, S. C. P., & Olver, M. E. (2010). The Violence Risk Scale and the Violence Risk Scale-Sex Offender Version. In R. Otto & K. Douglas (Eds.), *Handbook of violence risk assessment*. New York: Routledge.

Suggestions for Further Learning

Journal articles

Covell, C., & Wheeler, J. (2011). Application of the responsivity principle to treatment of sexual offense behavior. *Journal of Forensic Psychology Practice*, *11* (1), 61–72.

Hanson, R. K., Bourgon, G., Helmus, L., & Hodgson, S. (2009). The principles of effective correctional treatment also apply to sexual offenders: A meta-analysis. *Criminal Justice & Behavior*, *36*, 865–890.

Shingler, J. (2004). A process of cross-fertilization: What sex offender treatment can learn from dialectical behavior therapy. *Journal of Sexual Aggression*, *10* (2), 171–180.

Research report

Hanson, R. K., & Morton-Bourgon, K. (2004). *Predictors of sexual recidivism: An updated meta-analysis* (User Report 2004-02). Ottawa: Public Safety and Emergency Preparedness Canada. Retrieved from http://www.publicsafety.gc.ca/res/cor/rep/_fl/2004-02-pred-se-eng.pdf

Website

See Behavioral Tech LLC website (http://behavioraltech.org/) for resources for live and web-based training, therapeutic tools, and research on applications of dialectical behavioral therapy (DBT).

Appendix 15.A

Sample Relapse Prevention Outline

Part I: stable dynamic risk-needs[3]

1. Have the client re-read their Intake Assessment and Treatment Plan. Ask the client to identify each of the stable dynamic risk factors (DRFs) that were identified at intake, and explain the relationship of each stable DRF to their sexual offense behavior:[4]
   - What factors were observable? (how would someone else have been able to identify that they were present?).
   - What factors were unobservable? (i.e., no one else but the client could know that they were present).
2. Have the client identify specific goals, targets, and shaping techniques that were used in treatment, and explain which were effective at reducing their dynamic risk-needs, and why:
   - How can they tell that [a particular technique] was effective?
   - How can they tell that [a particular target or goal] had been reached?
3. For each stable DRF, ask the client to describe themselves at intake and then compare themselves to their current status. Instruct them to be behaviorally specific, without evaluation or judgment:
   - In what areas do they continue to have stable dynamic risk-needs?
   - Which stable dynamic risk-need is most vulnerable to relapse?
   - How can they continue to target these needs after they have transitioned to the community?
   - Are there any needs that they have now that they didn't have at the beginning of treatment? (e.g., by virtue of having lost a job, or not having a home in the community).
4. Have the client identify how they would know if they were exhibiting a "relapse" in each of the stable dynamic risk-need areas that were identified at intake. Have the client make a list of each stable dynamic risk-need, and specific observable indicators that they might be relapsing in each area.
5. For each potential relapse, have the client identify a step toward intervention (e.g., identify a skill learned in treatment that was effective at reducing that dynamic risk-need over time).
6. Have the client rank their stable DRFs in order, from most vulnerable to relapse to least vulnerable to relapse.
7. Have clients identify friends, family, co-workers, and supervisors who should be provided with a copy of this list.
8. Have the client role-play how they will explain this list to each person to whom they give it.

Part II: Acute dynamic risk-needs factors

1. Have the client define the following terms for themselves and their offense behavior:
   - Acute triggering events
   - Seemingly unimportant decision (SUD)

[3] In RP terminology, stable DRFs would be consistent with "Chronic Lifestyle Imbalances."
[4] Not all risk factors will be relevant to every offense; in 3RT, there is no presumption that every offense represents the same "cycle" as other offenses, but rather, that offenses reflect underlying problematic patterns in lifestyle and personality – that is, DRFs.

- Lapse
- Abstinence violation effect (AVE)
- The problem of immediate gratification (PIG)
- High-risk situations (HRS)
- Relapse

2. Have the client make a list of each potential acute DRF that is relevant to his or her needs, and specific observable indicators of their escalation.

3. For each potential acute risk area, have the client identify a step toward immediate intervention (e.g., call their therapist).

4. Have the client rank their acute DRFs in order, from most vulnerable to escalation to least vulnerable to escalation.

5. Have clients identify friends, family, co-workers, and supervisors who should be provided with a copy of this list.

6. Have the client role-play how they will explain this list to each person to whom they give it.

Part III
Tailoring CBT to Special Forensic Populations

16
Advancing the Use of CBT with Justice-Involved Women

Marilyn Van Dieten and Erica King

This chapter will briefly describe the major concerns raised by feminist scholars and practitioners regarding the development and delivery of cognitive-behavioral therapy (CBT) interventions for justice-involved women. A brief overview of the empirical evidence in support of a gendered approach will be provided and a series of guiding practices for the use of CBT with this population will be proposed. Finally, we will look at how gender-informed strategies can be integrated within CBT programs and interventions to enhance outcomes with justice-involved women.

CBT as an Evidence-Based Practice

CBT interventions are among the most frequently used approaches with criminal justice-involved clients. The popularity of programs based on the fundamental principles of CBT such as modeling, reinforcement, and behavioral and cognitive change can be largely attributed to the fact that they are amenable to outcome evaluation and consistently demonstrate favorable results with this population across settings and researchers (Andrews & Bonta, 2010; Landenberger & Lipsey, 2005). Correctional programs such as Reasoning and Rehabilitation (Ross & Fabiano, 1985; Tong & Farrington, 2006), Thinking for a Change (Bush, Glick, & Taymans, 1996), Aggression Replacement Training (Goldstein, Glick, Reiner, Zimmerman, & Coultry, 1987), Controlling Anger and Learning to Manage It (Winogron, Van Dieten & Gauzas, 2004), and Moving On (Van Dieten, 2010; Van Dieten & MacKenna, 2001) are manualized with clearly defined outcomes that permit ongoing monitoring of program success by staff and researchers. CBT programs also target some of the major criminogenic needs or challenges faced by correctional clients including critical reasoning, problem-solving, emotional regulation, and social competence. Finally, CBT programs can be delivered by staff that do not possess counseling backgrounds. In fact, individuals can be trained to deliver these programs

Forensic CBT: A Handbook for Clinical Practice, First Edition.
Edited by Raymond Chip Tafrate and Damon Mitchell.
© 2014 John Wiley & Sons, Ltd. Published 2014 by John Wiley & Sons, Ltd.

with relative ease, and accreditation standards as well as protocols for continuous quality improvement have been well-established by many agencies (Barnoski, 2004; Hanson, 2010).

The widespread use and evaluation of CBT programs has resulted in a rich literature that is currently used to guide implementation efforts. Landenberger and Lispsey (2005) conducted a meta-analysis of 58 studies of the effects of CBT on the recidivism of adult and juvenile offenders. They found that the most powerful program components contributing to variations in treatment effects included emotional regulation, with specific attention to anger control and interpersonal problem-solving. They also confirmed that CBT programs have the greatest impact when delivered to clients who are considered at greatest risk for future criminal behavior and who face a number of personal and life challenges. Finally, they discovered that quality implementation (including training and ongoing supervision to monitor program fidelity) was critical to ensure reductions in recidivism.

Despite the growing popularity of CBT programs in corrections, concern has been expressed regarding the wholesale acceptance of this approach across criminal justice populations – particularly with women. Feminist scholars argue that a reliance on CBT fails to address broader systemic issues (poverty, victimization, etc.), which are seen as central to criminal behavior (Bloom, Owen, & Covington, 2003; Pollack, 2005; Turnbull & Hannah-Moffat, 2009). Other writers have raised concerns that the adoption of CBT programs that were initially designed for males is not appropriate for criminal justice-involved females (Bloom et al., 2003).

Using CBT with Justice-Involved Women

There are two broad areas of concern expressed by feminist scholars with respect to using CBT in the rehabilitation of justice-involved women: (i) the lack of attention given to context in the development and maintenance of criminal behavior, and (ii) the tendency by professionals and program developers to overlook scientific findings related to gender and their importance in forensic treatment.

Context matters

The mandate of correctional practice is often depicted as a pendulum that swings between two opposing philosophies: punishment and rehabilitation. Since the 1990s, as rehabilitation gained momentum, the principles associated with the Risk-Need-Responsivity (RNR) model have dominated correctional reform efforts. This model was developed by researchers who systematically reviewed the available research and discovered that programs with specific components, now commonly referred to as the *principles of effective intervention*, were more likely to garner favorable results (Andrews & Bonta, 2010). The first component is known as the *risk principle* and refers to targeting offenders who are in greatest need of intervention and who are most likely to recidivate. The *need principle* is the second component and underscores the importance of targeting dynamic risk factors (or criminogenic needs) in correctional settings. Criminogenic needs, such as antisocial attitudes and poor problem-solving, are factors that have been statistically linked to criminal conduct. When these need areas are targeted appropriately in treatment (e.g., through techniques such as modeling), the likelihood of committing further crime is diminished. The final component of the RNR model is the *responsivity principle*, which can be further conceptualized as having *general* and *specific* subcomponents.

The underlying premise of the general responsivity principle is that certain evidence-based approaches like CBT are most likely to reduce recidivism with justice-involved populations. The specific responsivity principle asserts that client factors such as motivation, cognitive ability, gender, ethnicity, and cultural background may require a differential response from professionals to enhance opportunities for learning and engagement. The three core principles of effective intervention have been integrated into correctional policy and practice throughout North America and have undoubtedly contributed to the shift from "punishment to rehabilitation" (Cullen, 2002).

At the level of professional practice, the seminal work of Andrews and Bonta (2010) has accelerated the use of an array of tools, techniques, and strategies that are now routinely used by correctional staff. There is no question that the RNR model was instrumental in the popularization of CBT in correctional settings. In fact, by the mid-1990s, CBT programs were the intervention of choice in corrections and it was not uncommon for therapists to use the theoretical models underlying CBT as an explanation for criminal behavior (Samenow, 1984, 1991). Samenow (1991) argued that biological, psychological, and sociological explanations failed to account for the fact that many individuals make "willful decisions to choose a life of crime, regardless of their personal and/or socio-economic background" (p. 18). In his book, *Changing Criminal Thinking*, Sharp (2000) contends that offenders are afflicted with "stinking thinking" that includes rationalizing, justifying, blaming, accusing, and seeing oneself as a victim. The elimination of "criminal thinking" is often the central goal of treatment, particularly with sex offenders and violent offenders, and the primary method to achieve this outcome is to identify "criminal thinking" and to confront it immediately and directly (Maruna & Mann, 2006).

The primary emphasis on antisocial attitudes, thinking errors, and other criminogenic needs as an explanation for criminal behavior is also at the heart of the feminist critique (Bloom et al., 2003). In mainstream correctional theories such as RNR, contextual issues such as poverty, racism, victimization, and unemployment are either disregarded or minimized as explanatory factors. Hannah-Moffat (2004, 2006) argues that by focusing on criminogenic needs such as "criminal thinking" and decontextualizing criminal conduct, we are unjustifiably assigning most blame and responsibility to the individual. As a result, individuals rather than structural factors become the focus of intervention, suggesting that the remedy is simply a matter of altering a person's choices, thoughts, and feelings. Implicit in this paradigm is the belief that it is up to the individual to demonstrate a capacity for self-change regardless of the fact that many clients are returning to the very circumstances (i.e., poverty, unemployment, unsafe housing, domestic violence, etc.) they faced when convicted. Therefore, feminist scholars advocate a more holistic approach designed to address change at multiple levels including the development of adaptive strategies, opportunities for educational and vocational development, and the expansion of natural supports and professional connections (Bloom et al., 2003; Goodkind, 2005).

Feminist scholars have also demonstrated the importance of context in understanding criminal behavior perpetrated by women and girls. Recent advances in research suggest there are gender differences in the circumstances and nature of criminal conduct, and additionally highlight the presence of female-specific risk factors (Wright, Salisbury, & Van Voorhis, 2007). For example, women are less likely than men to have extensive criminal histories and are more likely to be arrested for non-violent crimes (West, Sabol, & Greenman, 2010). The vast majority of incarcerated women have also experienced chronic and pervasive childhood abuse, which places them at elevated risk for further victimization and the perpetration of violence (Henning,

Jones, & Holdford, 2003; Widom, Czaja, & Dutton, 2007). These findings have added fuel to the feminist argument that by denying the impact of past victimization in treatment contexts we are essentially communicating to women that they are responsible for any current failings. In fact, it is not unusual for program facilitators to ignore disclosures of past victimization at the risk of feeding into offender denial or rationalizations for criminal conduct.

Despite concerns levied by some feminist scholars around the use of CBT and other psychological interventions with justice-involved women, we maintain that these approaches are an important and critical component to offender programming, particularly when attentive to contextual factors and integrated within a more holistic framework. In other words, we recognize that there is room to advance the capacity for individuals to change while acknowledging the circumstances and situations that bring women into contact with the justice system. In the next segment, we will expand this discussion by focusing more closely on the pathways and specific needs that have been identified for women offenders.

Gender matters

The second major concern voiced by feminist scholars is the relative lack of attention focused on gender and other responsivity factors such as race, ethnicity, and social class (see Day, Chapter 18, for a discussion on culturally responsive CBT). Though the available evidence is preliminary, there are two bodies of research that demonstrate the importance of gender. First, there is some research to suggest a gendered pathway into crime (Daly, 1992; Reisig, Holtfreter, & Morash, 2006). Daly derived five typologies to demonstrate how women enter the justice system. Women categorized as "Street Women" have been abused and neglected in childhood, have run ran away from home as juveniles, and have a history of substance abuse/prostitution, and an extensive history of involvement in petty crime. A second group, "Harmed and Harming Women," have also experienced pervasive childhood abuse, have a history of acting out violently, may abuse substances as a coping strategy, and experience mental health issues. The third typology includes women who become "Drug Connected" in the context of their relationships with intimate partners. A fourth typology focuses on "Battered Women" who are arrested when retaliating or engaged in acts of self-defence. Finally, there appears to be a group of women who are "Economically Motivated" in their criminal behavior.

A second body of research identifies differences in risk factors, criminogenic needs, and strengths between justice-involved men and women. The seminal work of Salisbury and Van Voorhis (2009), Jones (2012), and other scholars suggests that there are some risk factors that are more salient for females. Factors that have consistently emerged in the research suggest that pervasive childhood abuse and neglect, current victimization, relationship dysfunction, parental stress, housing safety, mental health history and the presence of symptoms related to depression/anxiety and psychosis/suicidal ideation are predictive of negative criminal justice outcomes for women in institutional and community settings. These authors have also explored the impact of strengths on outcomes and have found that women with higher levels of self-efficacy, family support, parental involvement, and educational assets are at lower risk for recidivism.

Despite a growing body of literature and a rising population of justice-involved females, correctional policy in general continues to devalue the significant role that gender plays both in directing one's pathway to crime and in determining the focus of intervention. In fact, relatively little effort has been made to develop programs that accommodate potential differences in the needs of females or to modify programs that were initially designed for males. Correctional agencies tend to adopt not only the same delivery style but also the content of CBT programs without regard to gender, age, ethnicity, and culture (Nagayama Hall, 2001). For example, Thinking for a Change is one of the most popular cognitive-behavioral interventions with adult offenders. Developed by Bush et al. (1996), this program uses a combination of approaches that include cognitive restructuring, social skills training, and problem-solving to address the criminogenic needs of offenders (Milkman & Wanberg, 2007). While the skills taught in this program hold relevance for women, women offenders and staff have often reported that the rationale for behavior rehearsal within sessions is often based on a male narrative.

The promise of this and other CBT programs for enhancing the lives of offenders is not debated here. However, consistent with the responsivity principle discussed earlier, we argue that the incorporation of a gender-informed approach can enhance outcomes with women. The precedent for this consideration is well-established in both cognitive theory and practice. For example, a number of writers have demonstrated how early applications of CBT were customized to help women challenge and transcend limiting beliefs based on marginalized viewpoints of the "fairer sex" as less competent, intelligent, and entrepreneurial (Davis & Padesky, 1984; Kopala & Keitel, 2003). Kopala and Keitel (2003) described this as "helping women use their differential personal or 'underground' power more effectively" (p. 8). We also suggest that by incorporating content that relates to women and the various situations, circumstances, behaviors, and motivations that lead them into the justice system, we are more likely to engage women and facilitate the use of personal change strategies.

Over the years, we have spoken with a number of state-wide facilitators and program managers who have successfully implemented CBT programs. Recently, we conducted a series of semi-structured interviews with six facilitators who were formally trained to deliver Thinking for a Change (a gender-neutral program) and Moving On (a gender-responsive cognitive curriculum). We identified a number of recurring themes in facilitators' responses. First, each of the facilitators felt strongly that the skills and strategies introduced during CBT groups were important for both males and females. Second, when using the gender-neutral program, facilitators reported that they often found themselves translating and adapting the material to make it more relevant for women. As reported by one facilitator, "*women can't see themselves*" when they participate in this program. Most found themselves changing the examples, role-plays and activities, to more fully engage the women. Third, facilitators felt that verbatim adherence to content in the gender-neutral program was over-emphasized and the manner of delivery was underemphasized. Facilitators were routinely told to stick closely to the materials, read from the manuals, and not modify any of the examples. They found that the women often complained about how the content was structured and requested more time to process activities and translate what they had learned to real-life experiences. In contrast, training in the gender-responsive curriculum focused in equal measure on program content and approach. In fact, facilitators are trained to adopt a collaborative, relational mode of delivery. The response from the women to this more "relational" facilitation style was highly favorable. Not only did participation increase, but when women were encouraged to explore and personalize the program content, they became more mindful of the connection between thoughts, feelings, and behaviors. They were more likely to describe ways that they could transfer knowledge and skills to their lives outside of the group.

The Promise of a Gendered Approach to CBT

There is a small but emerging body of research that demonstrates the impact of gendered treatment with justice-involved women (Blanchette & Brown, 2006). Gehring and Bell (2008) and Gehring, Van Voorhis, and Bell (2009) have summarized the existing research and have found several CBT programs designed exclusively for women offenders. A brief description of each program and a summary of the outcome research are presented below.

Moving On (Van Dieten, 2010; Van Dieten & MacKenna, 2001) is one of the first CBT programs designed exclusively for justice-involved women. This program has been used in community and institutional settings across North America. It was developed to address crimi-nogenic needs, to mobilize natural and professional supports, and to strengthen and build a number of cognitive skills including emotional regulation, interpersonal competence, and self-efficacy. The program was evaluated by Gehring et al. (2009) using a matched control sample to compare outcomes of 300 women who received traditional probation and 300 women who received the program. Women in the treatment group demonstrated significant reductions in recidivism at 6, 12, and 30 months follow-up.

Helping Women Recover: A Program for Treating Substance Abuse (Covington, 2008) and Beyond Trauma (Covington, 2003) are manualized programs that were adapted for justice-involved women. Both can be delivered conjointly or as stand-alone treatments. The goals of the first program are to reduce substance use, encourage participation in aftercare program-ming, and to reduce the likelihood of further justice involvement. The second program helps clients develop effective coping skills, build healthy relationships, and encourage the development of interpersonal support networks. Both programs incorporate cognitive-behavioral skills training, mindfulness techniques, meditation, education, and other relational strategies. In a randomized experimental study, Messina, Grella, Cartier, and Torres (2010) found that women who participated in the Helping Women Recover and Beyond Trauma group were significantly less likely than the comparison group receiving standard treatment to be reincarcerated during a 12-month follow-up period.

Seeking Safety (Najavits, 2002) is a manualized program using an integrative cognitive-behavioral therapy approach to address substance abuse and post-traumatic stress disorder (PTSD). This program is appropriate for use on an individual or group basis and covers 25 topics (asking for help, coping with triggers, etc.) that are designed to provide clients with stabilization skills and coping strategies that facilitate personal safety and abstinence from sub-stance use. Several outcome studies have been conducted to evaluate Seeking Safety with incarcerated women (Zlotnick, Johnson, & Najavits, 2009; Zlotnick, Najavits, Rosenow, & Johnson, 2003). Although the first evaluation of Seeking Safety did not include a control group, researchers found improvements in PTSD and trauma-related symptoms, as well as additional positive outcomes including social adjustment, a decrease in alcohol and drug abuse, and improvements in problem-solving skills. A second study by Zlotnick et al. (2009) consisted of a randomized controlled pilot study comparing a Seeking Safety group to a con-trol group receiving 30 hours of residential substance abuse treatment. Women in both condi-tions showed significant improvements, at 12 weeks after intake and 3 and 6 months after release from prison. Women in the Seeking Safety group demonstrated improvement on PTSD symptoms over time, whereas decreases in alcohol use were greater for the control group. However, women who attended a greater number of Seeking Safety sessions demonstrated better results on both substance use and PTSD symptoms.

Despite a dearth of controlled clinical trials, CBT programs designed for women are emerging, and some empirical support does exist for the application of gender-informed CBT programs. Clinical practices and methods used by developers of gender-informed programs will be explored more fully in the next section.

Advancing the Use of CBT with Justice-Involved Women

There is surprising richness and consistency in the literature with respect to what comprises a gender-responsive approach. For example, almost without exception, authors of programs like Seeking Safety, Helping Women Recover, and Moving On (Covington, 2008; Najavits, 2002; Van Dieten, 2010) incorporate the use of relational-cultural and strengths-based theories (Miller, 1986; Miller & Stiver, 1997; Smith, 2006). Drawing from our review of this literature and experience in writing and delivering programs for women and girls, it is our position that there are a number of guiding practices that can be implemented to complement and advance the use of CBT with this population. We have organized these into two broad categories: (i) approach and (ii) methods of intervention.

The approach: what should the intervention feel like?

Build a working relationship. "Basic capacities of human relating – warmth, affirmation and a minimum of attack and blame may be at the center of effective psychotherapeutic intervention" (Najavits and Strupp , 1994, p. 21). Almost without exception, gender-informed programs place an emphasis on the application of relational-cultural theory (RCT). The core tenets of RCT were first articulated by a group of feminist theorists at the Stone Centre, Wellesley College in Massachusetts (Jordan, 2000; Jordan, Kaplan, Miller, Stiver, & Surrey, 1991; Miller, 1986). RCT assumes that to be emotionally healthy, the client must maintain mutually satisfying and respectful relationships with those around them. This is important for males but is argued to be particularly important for women, who are socialized to desire and value connection throughout their lifespan. Miller and Stiver (1997) suggest that many women experience what is termed *disconnection* by the time they reach adolescence or early adulthood. Disconnections are not uncommon in relationships but can create stress and impact one's self-concept and behavior. For many justice-involved women, relational disruptions begin with exposure to violence and may persist into adulthood in the context of unhealthy romantic attachments, subjugation to criminal romantic partners, criminal behavior, substance abuse, and poor decision-making (e.g., Cernkovich, Lanctôt, & Giordano, 2008; Chesney-Lind, 2006; Salisbury & Van Voorhis, 2009).

RCT practitioners work intentionally to model empathy, genuineness, and positive regard, and to encourage the reciprocation of these behaviors. These qualities have long been regarded as critical to forming a "therapeutic alliance." Further, there is evidence to suggest that the quality of this relationship (i.e., client perceptions of empathy, acceptance, and warmth) accounts for a large proportion of treatment variance across a wide range of interventions and disorders (Lambert, 1992). In fact, research suggests that the therapeutic relationship makes substantial and consistent contributions to psychotherapy outcome independent of specific type of treatment (Miller, Taylor, & West, 1980).

Most cognitive theorists acknowledge the importance of the therapeutic relationship as a precursor to the effective implementation of CBT (see, e.g., Cloitre, Cohen & Koenen, 2006;

Cloitre, Stovall-McClough, Miranda, & Chemtob, 2004; Kuyken, Padesky & Dudley, 2009). Given the central role that relationships play in female socialization and development, as well as a pathway to crime, we hold that working toward a therapeutic alliance should be an overarching goal rather than a precursor to intervention. This may be particularly important when working with women who have suffered a history of abuse and trauma. Mickelson, Kessler, and Shaver (1997) have presented data that show women who have experienced interpersonal trauma during childhood are more likely to demonstrate an avoidant attachment style in relationships. Accordingly, it is not uncommon for women to express the desire for connection while simultaneously conveying strong fears of rejection or distrust.

> *Sometimes the counselors are good and sometimes they don't care...but even if I like them – I won't let anyone get close to me for a very, very, long time.... Whenever they get too close I push back...I just can't – won't let anyone know stuff they can hold over me again...*
>
> Nadine

Nadine and many justice-involved women are mandated to participate in correctional programs. This coercive element and a variety of practical, psychological, and cultural barriers can have a detrimental impact on the working relationship between practitioner and client. We strongly encourage staff to be mindful of changes in client behavior. Evidence of resistance, or what is often labeled as "manipulation" or "drama" among women offenders, can be used as a signal to the practitioner to place emphasis on reconnecting. We also believe that our work entails providing the client with the skills necessary to recognize and create productive and healthy relationships. Essentially, the practitioner and client should work together to develop a strong and secure relationship that serves as a model for future relationships. This connection then provides a reference for the client that can be used by her to compare other relationships and to determine if they are healthy or destructive (Cloitre, Cohen, & Koenen, 2006; Van Dieten, 2010).

Adopt a strengths-based approach All women – regardless of their level of risk or crime committed – have strengths that can be mobilized to enhance positive outcomes. CBT has long been considered a deficit-based model of intervention with the goal of providing clients with a variety of adaptive skills. The positive psychology movement along with the influential work of Werner and Smith (1992) have shifted many CBT practitioners and theorists to focus either exclusively on strengths or to recognize the value in using an integrative approach. There is also a growing body of research that supports the use of strengths-based approaches like motivational interviewing (MI) in combination with cognitive behavioral treatments (Moyers & Houck, 2011). MI was developed to enhance intrinsic motivation to change. The emphasis on starting where the client is and eliciting "change talk" or her reasons for change have been demonstrated to promote engagement and decrease resistance. MI is now frequently used to prepare participants for treatment and has been demonstrated to contribute to higher completion and retention rates in programs for substance abusers (Miller, Yahne, & Tonigan, 2003; Moyers & Houck, 2011). Tafrate and Luther (see Chapter 20) discuss how to integrate MI into forensic practice.

A recent monograph written by Smith (2006) provides a comprehensive exploration of the history and theory underlying a strengths-based approach. She defines a strength as "that which helps a person to cope with life or that which makes life more fulfilling for oneself or others." MI and other strengths-based approaches and resiliency models have become increasingly popular in corrections not only as a "readiness component for treatment"; strengths and protective factors now appear in a number of standardized risk-need assessments (Barnoski, 1998; Robinson 2002) and case work models for both youths and adults (Van Dieten & Robinson, 2009). Werner and Smith (1992) have demonstrated that protective factors can serve as buffers to mediate the impact of adversity and may have a more profound influence on criminal justice outcomes than specific risk factors. Salisbury and Van Voorhis (2009) and our own research (Robinson, Millson, & Van Dieten, 2010) confirm the importance of protective factors in reducing the impact of risk and in creating a more optimistic outlook among practitioners who work with justice-involved women.

Finally, a number of strengths-based treatment approaches have emerged such as the Good Lives Model (GLM: Ward, 2010). Fortune and Ward (see Chapter 21) describe GLM in greater detail. GLM is premised on the belief that by working with the offender to build capabilities and strengths, we are more likely to reduce the offender's risk of reoffending. Sorbello, Eccleston, Ward, and Jones (2002) argue that an emphasis on criminogenic needs may fail to capture many of the real-life issues faced by justice-involved women. They suggest that by focusing on the enhancement of strengths we can better assist women to lead a more fulfilling and balanced life. For example, as a woman's ability to engage in meaningful interactions with others increases, she is more likely to thrive in the community, which in turn reduces recidivism. The use of a strengths-based approach is also well-grounded in the treatment of trauma (Cloitre et al., 2006; Covington, 2003). The CBT model developed by Cloitre et al. (2006) requires the professional to acknowledge that trauma, abuse, and negative environmental factors such as poverty can have an adverse impact on the lives of women. It also encourages the professional to view behavioral and emotional reactions typically labeled as non-adaptive through a strengths-based lens. For example, by shifting the conversation away from asking a woman how she has been damaged by trauma, we can uncover her coping strategies. If one of these is self-harm, we can explore the reasons she values this strategy, explore the benefits of changing, and eventually introduce alternative options.

The practitioner who uses a strengths-based approach recognizes the client's struggles and at the same time sends a clear message of optimism and hope. This requires the practitioner to build a relationship with each client in the early stages of intervention that "conveys a respect for her struggles" (Smith, 2006, p. 16). It also necessitates that the practitioner listen attentively for the exceptions or times when the client felt in control. By working intentionally to identify and then reinforce the use of these existing strategies, we build promise and support self-efficacy. Box 16.1 contains a brief transcript of a facilitator working in a community setting and using a strengths-based approach while delivering Moving On, a gender-responsive program described earlier in this chapter.

At the beginning of this interaction, the facilitator intentionally acknowledged Nadine's feelings and reflected her concerns. The facilitator then deliberately elicited strategies that were used that night to defuse a high level of stress and conflict. This technique, which is seminal in solution-focused therapy, is called "looking for solution patterns or the search for exceptions" (de Shazer, 1985, 1988). The use of this strategy helped Nadine to feel a sense of hope and some optimism about her ability to manage stress. This will not necessarily translate into enhanced parenting or relapse prevention skills, but it gives Nadine a sense of control over her behavior and may prompt her to consider additional intervention and/or options for support.

Box 16.1   Sample Dialogue Using a Strengths-Based Approach

FACILITATOR: Would someone be willing to share an event over the last week that you found to be extremely pleasant or extremely challenging?

NADINE: Yeah! My kids are completely out of control...

FACILITATOR: You're struggling right now with managing the kids...

NADINE: Yeah! Mostly it's my son.... He just won't listen to me – I tell him to stop hitting his brother and he keeps on hitting him...until I get good and angry and go in and grab him out of the room.

FACILITATOR: He pushes you to your last limit.

NADINE: I don't know – sometimes I really feel like I need a "hit" just to get through the night with these kids.

FACILITATOR: You get so frustrated that it triggers an urge to use...and yet, you didn't use...

NADINE: Yeah! I'm really trying not to give in...I just don't know what to do.

FACILITATOR: I guess I'm curious – tell me what you did that night to keep the stress in check.

NADINE: I put the youngest under my arm and we went into the bedroom. I knew I had to keep him safe and I also knew that if he was with me – I would be safer. We read a story together.... Ten minutes later my oldest – who is completely out of control – came into the room and laid on the floor. We all fell asleep. I guess the fight went out of him.

FACILITATOR: You were able to not only manage your stress and urge to use but you also helped your son to calm down.

NADINE: Yeah – I guess I never thought about it like that.

Focusing on "coping" gives both the woman and the practitioner a different lens through which to view difficult past events. This approach is particularly relevant when working with justice-involved women, who do not have control over many of the adversities they have experienced, but can begin to identify and value the ways they have already managed (and even solved) the problem(s) that led to their correctional involvement. Readily integrated into CBT, the use of a strengths-based approach enhances engagement and contributes to immediate and promising outcomes for clients and staff (Benedict, 2005; Van Dieten, 2010). As such, we believe that the incorporation of this approach into assessment and treatment is critical to advance our work with justice-involved women.

Foster collaboration   To work successfully with clients, we need to understand and value how they experience the world and their right to determine the best course of action. Collaboration is considered a key factor and core practice in the effective delivery of CBT (Beck, 1995) and a number of other therapeutic approaches including relational-cultural therapy (Miller, 1986), motivational interviewing (Miller & Rollnick, 2002), narrative therapy (White & Epston, 1990), and solution-focused therapy (Berg & deShazer, 1993). Though the definition of this concept varies to some extent, most authors describe collaboration as a "partnership" that honors the strengths of both parties.

In CBT, the professional brings knowledge, skills, theory, and an understanding of techniques and strategies that have contributed to favorable outcomes with clients. Equally important are the experiences and resources that the client brings as an "expert in her own life" (Gilbert, 1980). Consistent with the principle of autonomy/support in motivational interviewing, we encourage facilitators to avoid giving unsolicited advice and solutions, and not to take control of the session without seeking permission from the client to ensure that the client has the opportunity to make decisions regarding the use of various techniques and the direction of treatment.

We believe that the use of a collaborative approach is essential when working with justice-involved women to model and build a mutually respectful and empathic relationship. Collaboration also supports self-sufficiency. According to Seligman (1972), exposure to adverse life events can result in a pervasive sense of powerlessness or "learned helplessness." Correctional environments tend to place a strong emphasis on control and this can further intensify these negative feelings and beliefs. Providing women with decision-making power can serve to promote a sense of personal accomplishment and self-efficacy. An excellent example within corrections is mandated attendance and reporting. Treatment providers are typically required to provide documentation to referral agents that the client is attending and participating in treatment. In many programs, "mandated participation" is defined by the client's willingness to participate in all group exercises and activities. Facilitators who deliver a gender-responsive program provide information about attendance; however, how participation is assessed and the expectations around participation are conveyed quite differently. One of the primary goals of a gender-responsive approach is to help women develop a sense of personal power and boundaries around what, how much, and with whom they share information. Therefore, women are invited to participate in all activities and their decision to do so or not is always respected and honored.

Probation staff, parole officers, and other criminal justice practitioners often work with clients who are mandated to complete a variety of court-ordered conditions, which may be overwhelming for the client or incongruent with her goals and priorities. In this situation, the professional is faced with honoring the client's decision and at the same time, preparing her to address simultaneous demands. Box 16.2 contains a transcript of a probation officer working with a client named Tina and using several strategies to remain relational, strengths-based, and collaborative.

There are a number of strategies that can be readily implemented by correctional professionals that are consistent with a relational, strengths-based, and collaborative approach and that do not circumvent correctional policy and practice. These might include: giving justice-involved women the power to determine which elements of the court order to focus on first; working to set the goals for intervention; exploring the benefits of making a change or attending a program; exploring and resolving practical and emotional barriers for group participation; and asking the client for feedback about the helpfulness of the intervention. These are just a few strategies that convey respect and enhance motivation.

The methods of intervention: what should the intervention look like?

Gender, socialization, social roles, poverty, and minority status play a central role in feminist theory, and the awareness of how each dimension impacts personal growth and well-being is often the primary focus of intervention. These dimensions are not typically viewed as foundational to CBT interventions (Beck, 1995). However, the advantages of integrating them into practice have been explored by a number of CBT theorists (Cloitre et al., 2006; Hurst & Genest, 1995). Davis and Padesky (1984) described several benefits that can be derived by actively exploring and validating the impact of these variables. Importantly, these dimensions provide a framework to identify and alter discordant and dysfunctional thoughts or beliefs. We

Box 16.2 Tina and Her PO

Tina is a 34-year-old woman who has been charged with shoplifting and theft. This is her fourth criminal conviction. She has met with her current probation officer (PO) on two previous occasions. During the first two sessions the PO oriented her to the supervision process and completed a standardized risk/needs assessment. In this session the PO provides the client with feedback and then works collaboratively to identify the target of intervention.

PO: Tina – the last time we met – I asked you a lot of questions about your family, friends, your experiences growing up and we talked about what brought you here. I had a chance to go through your file and I wanted to spend some time just summarizing what I have heard and read. As I listened to you last week I was struck by the fact that you have a number of strengths and resources. Let's start with family...You talked a lot about how important your children are to you, how they help to ground you, keep you focused and remind you about how blessed you are...

TINA: Yeah...my kids are amazing...[becomes tearful]

PO: There is nothing more important...You also have a very close relationship with your sister – as I recall you described her as your best friend...you also mentioned that she is a really strong support in helping you with the kids. Sound right?

TINA: She is always there for me. She is taking care of my kids right now and she told me she will stand by me no matter what.

PO: A person you can count on...

TINA: I'm not sure I will ever be able to pay her back – she has rescued me so many times.

The PO continues to review strengths and to seek clarification and encourage Tina to add new information while proceeding across each of the domains of the assessment instrument: (i) Family, (ii) Friends and Community Resources (spiritual, medical, mental health, etc.), (iii) Vocational (e.g., employment and education), and (iv) Personal (internal strengths including coping strategies, social and cognitive skills, interests, hobbies, talents, etc.). After completing the review, the case manager provides a summary of strengths and then moves on to focus on challenges.

PO: Tina...It's clear that you have a lot of strengths – your kids, your sister, your neighbors, your desire to work,...You really want things to be different...During our interview last week you also mentioned some challenges...things that seem to get into your way and that brought you here.

TINA: Yeah...

PO: A few things stuck out for me – the fact that you are really struggling to make ends meet financially. You mentioned that you have not been employed for some time, that you get little to no support from the kids' fathers, and that when you feel the bills piling up you get overwhelmed.

TINA: It's been so rough lately...I get social assistance but it's not enough and Cindy's dad stopped paying child support when he lost his job.

PO: Money is even tighter than usual...

TINA: Yeah...I know that doesn't give me the right to steal from other people...I just get so depressed...

PO: The second challenge is related to the first one – because when you are really overwhelmed you just can't move...you feel that everything is hopeless and it's hard to come up with solutions – legal solutions to manage your problems.

TINA: Yeah…I know I should be on medication for depression because it helps but since I moved here last year I haven't been able to find a doctor.

PO: So…there are a few things that are keeping you stuck…there is the financial stress which leaves you feeling overwhelmed and then you get so down you don't feel you have any options. Where do you think we should start – what do you feel we should focus on first in the case plan?

TINA: I need to learn to manage my depression…I hate the way I feel right now…I cry all the time and I know my kids are scared…

The PO acknowledges the challenges that Tina is facing and that led to her current arrest. She also recognizes that to successfully complete her supervision order Tina has a number of court-ordered conditions with time restrictions – such as repayment of a fine and finding employment. The PO remains aware of these issues and at the same time encourages her client to set the agenda – focus on a target that she feels is most important and critical to her success. Tina and the PO work together to frame the goal and to identify action steps that can be completed for the next meeting.

have found this framework extremely useful in correctional settings because as staff listen and explore how the client experiences these dimensions, they are able to develop a deeper understanding of this population. They also become more aware of the cultural stereotypes and personal biases that impact how they interact and respond to women. This may be particularly important for practitioners working with women in correctional settings in building awareness of how women in corrections are marginalized through poverty, racial inequality, lack of jobs and resources, and the stigma associated with criminal justice involvement. Unlike a diagnosis of depression, which can be presented to a client to explain a particular set of symptoms, use of labels such as "offender," "criminal," or "prisoner" connote a person who is "bad" by virtue of her behavior. There is also considerable pressure placed on all correctional staff to hold women accountable for their "bad" behavior and to be on guard for women who use the past to excuse or justify their "badness" and manipulate others. As a result, many staff disregard or override the impact of adverse life circumstances, thereby losing the opportunity not only to connect with women but also to provide them with cognitive reappraisal and other adaptive skills.

In many correctional settings, staff are trained to work with the client to identify and change attitudes that support or condone criminal behavior. Antisocial attitudes or pro-criminal sentiments have been identified by researchers as important predictors of criminal behavior and consequently a critical target for intervention (Andrews & Bonta, 2010). A popular strategy used to address this target is cognitive restructuring. Essentially staff and clients are cued to listen for negative statements about the law, conventional pursuits and values, the victim, and the individual's ability or willingness to change behavior. Some programs work with the client to label the antisocial belief as a thinking error and then provide them with the tools to challenge and change faulty beliefs. An example of this methodology is illustrated in Box 16.3. A comprehensive list of common thinking errors related to criminal justice clients is available from Barnhart (2010) at http://www.corrections.com/tracy_barnhart.

The method of intervention outlined in Box 16.3 is congruent with prevailing correctional culture. However, we would like to propose an alternative approach whereby the focus of intervention is less on labeling Danielle's thinking errors and more about the circumstances that

Box 16.3 The Case of Danielle – A Traditional and Non-Gendered Conceptualization of Criminal Thinking

Danielle has been convicted on four occasions since the age of 16. Her current charges include drug possession and assault. According to her pre-sentence report, Danielle was placed into foster care at the age of 10. She was removed from the home after verified reports of sexual abuse by her stepfather and maternal neglect. Danielle ran from foster care at the age of 15 and lived on the streets for two years until she met Angel. During the course of her relationship with Angel, the police were called to their apartment on three different occasions in response to emergency calls from neighbors. Danielle verified that she and Angel loved each other but that he was often upset with her behavior. On the night she was charged, they were drinking heavily when Angel confronted her about a bill that she had not paid. Danielle reported that she was unable to stop him from hitting her and that while being strangled she grabbed a knife from the kitchen table and lashed out in self-defence. Angel sustained a life-threatening injury and was rushed to the hospital in a taxi while Danielle pressed a cloth to his wound. She was apprehended at the hospital later that night and subsequently convicted of a felony assault.

In conceptualizing thinking errors and focusing exclusively on Danielle's crime – "assault causing bodily harm" – and her self-reported claim of self-defense, we can identify two thinking errors that characterize her criminal thinking: "justifying" (blaming others or making excuses for our behavior) and "victim stance" (wanting others to feel sorry for us or convincing ourselves that it was the other person's fault). Once the thinking error has been identified we can work with Danielle so that eventually she may openly admit responsibility for her behavior and then develop the strategies necessary to avoid similar situations in the future.

have brought Danielle to the system and that are likely to bring her back. This method holds Danielle accountable while recognizing the importance of gender and context. If we accept that gender matters, we begin with an understanding that the context in which violence is committed by women is more likely to be relational or directed toward family members and intimate partners, and committed reactively rather than instrumentally (Rossegger et al., 2009). It is also important to be mindful that women who have a history of childhood abuse are at elevated risk for revictimization, including date rape and intimate partner violence (Widom et al., 2007). According to Cloitre et al. (2006), the desire to pursue relationships is based on a "healthy impulse to engage" (p. 15). However, Danielle and many women who have experienced trauma in childhood are exposed to abusive models and negative ways of relating to others and this becomes normative.

Understanding context provides us with the opportunity to explore more fully not only the circumstances that led to Danielle's arrest but the beliefs that guide her behavior in relationships with others. To work effectively with Danielle, we will need to build and model a professional relationship based on trust, respect, and mutual empathy. Once we have engaged Danielle, we can work intentionally to change how she relates to others.

Cognitive intervention can help women to become more mindful about how past events impact their lives and guide future expectations and behaviors. When intervening with

Danielle, we start from a strengths-based position. For example, Danielle's desire to have a relationship with Angel can be perceived as normal in that it is based on a need for connection and intimacy. She valued her relationship with Angel because he protected her from life on the streets and provided her with the first home she had ever had. Danielle accepted his need to dominate and she responded to repeated physical assaults because she learned that compliance was in her best interest and convinced herself that being hit was acceptable. She was perplexed by the incident resulting in her criminal charge because when she stabbed Angel, he was strangling her and she felt her life was at risk.

The patterns of coping used by Danielle are not unusual for a survivor of abuse. How we engage with other people and stay in relationships is learned over time. Danielle has experienced abusive relationships most of her life so it is not surprising that her personal expectations and behaviors are primarily negative. The goal of intervention should be less about labeling Danielle's survival instincts as "excuses" and more about the way she perceives herself within a relationship, who she relates to, and the way that she relates to others. The professional is encouraged to give her the opportunity to discuss the situation without prematurely labeling her actions and beliefs or testing the validity of her feelings. The intervention can then unfold in four stages: Safety, information, strategies, and supports. Once Danielle feels safe and indicates the desire to focus on her relationship with Angel, the practitioner can move to provide psychoeducational information on the causes, consequences, and effects of abuse. The third stage of intervention would be to introduce cognitive reappraisal, emotional regulation, and other cognitive skills that will enhance interpersonal competence. One of the most powerful strategies that we can give to women is the ability to reframe or replace cognitions that are harmful and self-sabotaging. Finally, it is critical to expand Danielle's support system and to connect her with people or to activities that will provide modeling that is safe, empathic, and respectful.

Increase personal agency and expand resources   A gender-informed approach to CBT requires that every skill taught, every scenario and narrative that is introduced, and every strategy that is practiced reflects the experiences faced by justice-involved women. While the skills may be similar to those encouraged in a gender-neutral program, the context in which a woman would apply them is largely gendered.

One of the most exciting aspects of using a gender-informed approach to CBT is that it provides women with an array of adaptive strategies that build personal agency; subjective awareness that one is initiating, executing, and controlling one's actions in the world (Bandura, 1992). When using CBT, the professional has the opportunity to demystify the treatment process. We do this by introducing strategies that address all levels of functioning – physiological, cognitive, and emotional – and give women the opportunity to practice using them. Clients are also asked to evaluate the usefulness of each strategy across a variety of contexts and settings, and to choose the ones they are willing to continue to use and practice. In Box 16.4, we have listed some of the major cognitive skills that are introduced and practiced during Moving On (Van Dieten, 2010).

Earlier we discussed the importance of relationships in the psychological and emotional growth of women: a critical outcome of a gender-informed approach is to assist women to build and form connections in the community that are healthy, prosocial, and supportive. Assisting women to develop meaningful relationships with family and friends, and to access mainstream services and community resources is an aspect of a gender-responsive approach to CBT. Women are also encouraged to participate in the community by helping to define group

Box 16.4   CBT Skills in the "Moving On" Program

Skills to build social competence

- Empathy
- Active listening
- Assertiveness skill steps
- Saying "No"
- Defusing anger
- Receiving criticism
- Giving feedback

Skills for emotional regulation

- Identify and label feelings
- Reflection diary
- Four steps to identify and change harmful self-talk
- Emotional SOS
- Grounding techniques
- Abdominal breathing
- Peaceful scene visualization
- Passive muscle relaxation
- Self-soothing activities
- Stress reduction activities

Skills to enhance self-sufficiency and personal agency

- Decision-making
- Problem-solving
- Goal-setting
- Change Plan

norms and to propose solutions that expand trust and cohesion and to give back to the community in a reparative way by helping other women identify resources and strategies that might lead to healthier outcomes.

Bridging: Where Context and Content Meet

Bringing context into treatment means that professionals have awareness of the impact of gender and culture. Davis and Padesky (1984) initiated a discussion of content areas that can be explored in an effort to increase awareness of how women view themselves, others, and the world and when their beliefs are discordant with prevailing culture. We have expanded the original dimensions proposed by these authors to reflect the experiences of justice-involved women. In Appendix 16.A we list the context, common reactions, and prevailing beliefs held by women, and provide a list of interventions that can be used to supplement and reinforce the use of CBT reappraisal, interpersonal, self-regulation, and problem-solving skills.

Changing the Culture of Criminal Justice Organizations to be More Responsive to Women

We maintain that an integrated CBT approach can play a vital role in promoting organizational change by helping line staff in the use of more effective gender-informed strategies and skills. For example, we now believe that for many women, incarceration resonates closely with experiences of childhood abuse and that practices routinely used to manage offender behavior (e.g., isolation, increased supervision, loss of contact with children and family, diminished access to resources) can actually trigger women to use maladaptive survival mechanisms such as anger, rage, and self-harm. These behaviors often lead to more severe punishment, increased isolation, and the escalation or renewed use of harmful strategies. Programming also presents a risk for women in that most gender-neutral curricula tend to ignore past victimization. In the worst-case scenario, women are blamed and retraumatized by correctional staff who fail to consider the gendered elements that led to their offending behavior in the first place. In the best-case scenario, women comply with program expectations but often don't internalize the content because they do not fully see their narratives as women represented in the content.

Over the last decade, we have seen an increase in the number of facilities that offer formal treatment to help women reduce trauma-related symptoms and to regulate emotional and behavioral reactions (Gehring et al., 2009). Unfortunately, the sense of safety and stabilization experienced by women who participate in individual counseling or treatment groups can be almost immediately negated when they return to their units and encounter line staff and/or other women who lack the skills or understanding to respond in a helpful way. Green, Miranda, Daroowalla, and Siddique (2005) suggest there is a growing awareness and appreciation that the violence experienced by justice-involved women needs to be addressed both directly in treatment and when managing offender behavior. The response from a variety of government agencies across the United States and Canada – see, e.g., Substance Abuse and Mental Health Services Administration (SAMHSA), the National Institute of Corrections (NIC), the Correctional Services of Canada (CSC) – has been the development of departmental resources and specialized training for staff working with justice-involved women.

The first step in this process requires that agencies and professionals identify cognitive-behavioral programs and other interventions that are gender-informed and that target essential need areas. For example, women who have a history of victimization, PTSD, anxiety, or depression appear to benefit from cognitive interventions that focus on safety and stabilization. In a series of studies conducted by Cloitre et al. (2006) with childhood abuse survivors, results supported an emphasis on building a therapeutic alliance and providing women with emotional regulation skills before participating in treatment for trauma. Dialectical behavior therapy as described by Linehan (1993) can be particularly helpful at this stage in that professionals are explicitly trained to remain focused on these objectives (e.g., the establishment of day and night rhythms, appropriate self-care including adequate food and rest, structuring of daily activities, identifying people or agencies that can serve as sources of support). The second step is to cross-train all professionals who work with justice-involved women (Goodkind, 2005; Green et al., 2005; Schram, Koons-Witt, & Morash, 2004). This helps staff to become more mindful of the circumstances and specific challenges that place females at risk for an adverse reaction. Training line staff in the various tools and strategies introduced to women during treatment can also be helpful to promote a common language and to encourage skill transfer.

Final Remarks

Cognitive-behavioral therapy continues to be the most studied and frequently used treatment modality with males and females across correctional settings. Unfortunately, many correctional agencies persist in placing women into intervention programs that are gender neutral and that fail to address their differential needs. In this chapter, we explored two areas that can be developed to advance the use of CBT with justice-involved women. First, we encouraged a relational, strengths-based, and collaborative approach when implementing CBT. Second, we demonstrated that by exploring the impact of gender and context, we can more fully address the realities of women's lives, help them to mobilize existing strengths, and provide them with an array of personal and social options that can mitigate risk and enhance outcomes.

There is, however, a final cautionary remark. Relatively speaking, we still lack significant research on interventions with this population. The traditional and ultimate benchmark of success when evaluating the efficacy of a CBT program in corrections is a measure of impact on recidivism. Given that the base rates for women's reoffending tend to be quite low, researchers are starting to adopt additional outcome measures to demonstrate impact. For example, we routinely encourage facilitators of Moving On to complete a series of tools to assess participant progress with respect to the objectives of the session. Namely, change is monitored during each client contact along three dimensions: success or progress in goal achievement; demonstration of adaptive skills or application of information; and the identification of natural and/or formal supports. Based on the innovative work of Duncan, Miller, and Sparks (2004) we have also developed a series of client-centered performance measures for Moving On. At the end of every session, women are given the opportunity to reflect on their successes and to provide feedback related to group facilitation, the relevance of the content, and to rate the value or helpfulness of specific cognitive techniques and strategies. By acknowledging the importance of gender and allowing it to inform program design and delivery, women are not only likely to show reductions of recidivism, they are also more likely to become thriving, contributing members of society.

References

Andrews, D. A., & Bonta, J. (2010). *The psychology of criminal conduct* (5th ed.). New Providence, NJ: Matthew Bender & Company, Inc.

Bandura, A. (1992). Exercise of personal agency through the self-efficacy mechanism. In R. Schwarzer (Ed.), *Self-efficacy: Thought control of action* (pp. 3–38). Washington, DC: Hemisphere Publishing Corp.

Barnhart, T. (2010). *Thinking errors defined*. National Institute of Corrections. Retrieved from: http://nicic.gov/Library/024287

Barnoski, R. (1998). *Validation of the Washington State juvenile court assessment: Interim report*. Document ID: 98-11-1201. Washington State Institute of Public Policy.

Barnoski, R. (2004). *Outcome evaluation of Washington State's research-based programs for juvenile offenders*. Document ID: 04-01-1201. Olympia, WA: Washington State Institute for Public Policy.

Beck, J. S. (1995). *Cognitive therapy: Basics and beyond*. New York: The Guilford Press.

Benedict, A. (2005). Five CORE practice areas. *CORE gender-responsive assessment*. Core Associates. Available at: http://cjinvolvedwomen.org/sites/all/documents/Five%20Core%20Practice%20Areas1-08.pdf

Berg, I. K., & deShazer, S. (1993). Making numbers talk: Language in therapy. In S. Friedman (Ed.), *The new language of change: Constructive collaboration in psychotherapy*. New York: The Guilford Press.

Blanchette, K., & Brown, S. L. (2006). *The assessment and treatment of women offenders: An integrative perspective*. Chichester, UK: John Wiley & Sons, Ltd.

Bloom, B., Owen, B., & Covington, S. (2003). *Gender-responsive strategies: Research, practice, and guiding principles for women offenders*. Washington, DC: U.S. Department of Justice, National Institute of Corrections. Retrieved from: http://www.nicic.org/pubs/2003/018017.pdf.

Bush, J., Glick, B., & Taymans, J. (1996). *Thinking for a change: An integrated cognitive behavior change program*. Longmont, CO: National Institute of Corrections.

Cernkovich, S. A., Lanctôt, N., & Giordano, P. C. (2008). Predicting adolescent and adult antisocial behavior among adjudicated delinquent females. *Crime & Delinquency, 54*, 3–33. doi: 10.1177/0011128706294395.

Chesney-Lind, M. (2006). Patriarchy, crime, and justice: Feminist criminology in an era of backlash. *Feminist Criminology, 1*, 6–26. doi: 10.1177/1557085105282893.

Cloitre, M., Cohen, L. R., & Koenen, K. (2006). *Treating survivors of childhood abuse: Psychotherapy for the interrupted life*. New York: The Guilford Press.

Cloitre, M., Stovall-McClough, C., Miranda, R., & Chemtob, C. M., (2004). Therapeutic alliance, negative mood regulation, and treatment outcome in child abuse-related posttraumatic stress disorder. *Journal of Consulting and Clinical Psychology, 72*, 411–516.

Covington, S. S. (2003). *Beyond trauma: A healing journey for women* (facilitator's guide). Center City, MN: Hazelden.

Covington, S. S. (2008). *Helping women recover: A program for treating substance abuse. Special edition for the criminal justice system*. San Francisco: Jossey-Bass.

Cullen, F. T. (2002). *Rehabilitation and corrections programs. Crime and public policy* (2nd ed.). San Francisco, CA: ICS Press.

Daly, K. (1992). Women's pathways to felony court: Feminist theories of lawbreaking and problems of representation. *Review of Law and Women's Studies, 2* (11), 11–52.

Davis, D., & Padesky, C. (1984). Enhancing cognitive therapy with women. In A. Freeman, K. Simon, L. Beutler, & H. Arkowitz (Eds.), *Comprehensive handbook of cognitive therapy*. New York: Plenum Press.

de Shazer, S. (1985). *Keys to solution in brief therapy*. New York: Norton.

de Shazer, S. (1988). *Clues: Investigating solutions in brief therapy*. New York: Norton.

Duncan, B. I., Miller, S. D., & Sparks, J. (2004). *The heroic client: A revolutionary way to improve effectiveness through client-directed, outcome-informed therapy*. San Francisco, CA: Josey Bass.

Garcia, M. (2012). Improving access to services for female offenders returning to the community. National Institute of Justice, Office of Justice Programs. Retrieved from: http://www.nij.gov/nij/journals/269/female-offenders.htm.

Gehring, K., & Bell, V. (2008). *Gender-responsive assessments and approaches*. Cincinnati, OH: University of Cincinnati Press.

Gehring, K., Van Voorhis, P., & Bell, V. (2009). *"What works" for female probationers? An evaluation of the Moving On program*. Cincinnati, OH: University of Cincinnati Press.

Gilbert, L. (1980). Feminist therapy. In A. Brodsky & R. Hare-Mustin (Eds.), *Women and psychotherapy* (pp. 245–265). New York: Guilford.

Gilligan, C. (1982). *In a different voice*. Harvard University Press.

Goldstein, A., Glick, B., Reiner, S., Zimmerman, D., & Coultry, T. (1987). *Aggression replacement training*. Champaign, IL: Research Press.

Goodkind, S. (2005). Gender-specific services in the juvenile justice system: A critical examination. *Affilia, 20*, 52–70.

Green, B., Miranda, J., Daroowalla, A., & Siddique, J. (2005). Trauma exposure, mental health functioning, and program needs of women in jail. *Crime and Delinquency, 51*, 133–151.

Hannah-Moffat, K. (2004). Criminogenic need and the transformative risk subject: Hybridizaton of risk/need in penalty. *Punishment and Society, 7*, 29–51.

Hannah-Moffat, K. (2006). Pandora's box: Risk/need and gender-responsive corrections. *Reactions Essay, 5* (1), 183–192.

Hanson, K. (2010). Accreditation standards for correctional programs. *Research Summary, 10* (1), Ottawa: Public Safety Canada.

Henning, K., Jones, A., & Holdford, R. (2003). Treatment needs of women arrested for domestic violence: A comparison with male offenders. *Journal of Interpersonal Violence, 18*, 839–856.

Hurst, S., & Genest, M. (1995). Cognitive-behavioural therapy with a feminist orientation: A perspective for therapy with depressed women. *Canadian Psychology/Psychologie Canadienne, 36* (3), 236–257. doi: 10.1037/0708-5591.36.3.236.

Jones, N. (2012). Merging theoretical frameworks to inform risk assessment for the young female offender. *Dissertation Abstracts International Section A: Humanities and Social Sciences, 73* (4-A), 1567.

Jordan, J. V. (2000). The role of mutual empathy in relational/cultural therapy. *Journal of Clinical Psychology, 56*, 1005–1016.

Jordan, J. V., Kaplan, A. G., Miller, J. B., Stiver, I. P., & Surrey, J. L. (1991). *Women's growth in connection: Writings from the Stone Center*. New York: Guilford Press.

Kopala, M., & Keitel, M. (2003). *Handbook of counseling women*. Thousand Oaks, CA: Sage Publications, Inc.

Kuyken, W., Padesky, C., & Dudley, R. (2009). *Collaborative case conceptualization: Working effectively with clients in cognitive-behavioral therapy*. New York: Guilford Press.

Lambert, M. J. (1992). Implications of outcome research for psychotherapy integration. In J. C. Norcross & M. R. Goldstein (Eds.), *Handbook of psychotherapy integration* (pp. 94–129). New York: Basic Books.

Landenberger, N. A., & Lipsey, M. W. (2005). The positive effects of cognitive-behavioral programs for offenders: A meta-analysis of factors associated with effective treatment. *Journal of Experimental Criminology, 1*, 451–476.

Linehan, M. M. (1993). *Cognitive-behavioral treatment of borderline personality disorder*. New York: Guilford Press.

Maruna, S., & Mann, R. (2006). A fundamental attribution error? Rethinking cognitive distortions. *Legal and Criminological Psychology, 11*, 155–177.

Messina, N., Grella, C., Cartier, J., & Torres, S. (2010). A randomized experimental study of gender-responsive substance abuse treatment for women in prison. *Journal of Substance Abuse Treatment, 38* (2), 97–107.

Mickelson, K. D., Kessler, R. C., & Shaver, P. R. (1997). Adult attachment in a nationally representative sample. *Journal of Personality and Social Psychology, 73* (5), 1092–1106.

Milkman, H., & Wanberg, T. (2007). *Cognitive behavioral treatment. A review and discussion for correctional professionals*. Washington, DC: National Institute of Corrections. NIC Accession Number: 021657.

Miller, J. B. (1986). *What do we mean by relationships? Working Paper Series, No. 33*. Wellesley, MA: Stone Center.

Miller, W. R. & Rollnick, S. (2002). *Motivational interviewing: Preparing people to change* (2nd ed.). New York: Guilford.

Miller, J. B., & Stiver, I. P. (1997). *The healing connection: How women form relationships in therapy and in life*. Boston, MA: Beacon Press.

Miller, W. R., Taylor, C. A., & West, J. C. (1980). Focused versus broad-spectrum behavior therapy for problem-drinkers. *Journal of Consulting and Clinical Psychology, 48*, 590–601.

Miller, W. R., Yahne, C. E., & Tonigan, J. S. (2003). Motivational interviewing in drug abuse services: A randomized trial. *Journal of Consulting and Clinical Psychology, 71*, 754–763.

Miller-Karas, E., & Everett, G. (2005). *Trauma first aide manual*. Santa Fe, NM: Trauma Resource Institute

Moyers, T. B., & Houck, J. (2011). Combining motivational interviewing with cognitive behavioral treatments for substance abuse: Lessons from the COMBINE research project. *Cognitive and Behavioral Practice, 18* (1), 38–45.

Nagayama Hall, G. (2001). Psychotherapy research with ethnic minorities: Empirical, ethical, and conceptual issues. *Journal of Consulting & Clinical Psychology, 69* (3), 502–510.

Najavits, L. (2002). *Seeking Safety: A treatment manual for PTSD and substance abuse.* New York: Guilford Press.

Najavits, L., & Strupp, H. H. (1994). Differences in the effectiveness of psychodynamic therapists: A process-outcome study. *Psychotherapy, 31,* 114–123.

Pollack, S. (2005). Taming the shrew: Regulating prisoners through women-centered mental health programming. *Critical Criminology, 13,* 71–87.

Reisig, M. D., Holtfreter, K., & Morash, M. (2006). Assessing recidivism risk across female pathways to crime. *Justice Quarterly, 23,* 384–405. doi: 10.1177/0093854809349438.

Robinson, D. (2002). *Scoring manual for the Youth Assessment and Screening Instrument: YASI.* Ottawa, Ontario: Orbis Partners, Inc.

Robinson, D., Millson, B., & Van Dieten, M. (2010). *An outcome evaluation of the Women Offender Case Management Model implemented by the Connecticut Court Support Services Division.* Washington, DC: National Institute of Corrections.

Ross, R. R., & Fabiano, E. A. (1985). *Time to Think: A cognitive model of delinquency prevention and offender rehabilitation.* Johnson City, TN: Institute of Social Sciences and Arts.

Rossegger, A., Wetli, N., Urbaniok, F., Elbert T., Cortoni, F., & Endrass, J. (2009). Women convicted for violent offenses: Adverse childhood experiences, low level of education and poor mental health. *BMC Psychiatry, 81* (9). doi: 10.1186/1471-244X-9-81.

Salisbury, E. J., & Van Voorhis, P. (2009). Gendered pathways: A quantitative investigation of women probationers' paths to incarceration. *Criminal Justice and Behavior, 36,* 541–566. doi: 10.1177/0093854809334076.

Samenow, S. (1984). *Inside the criminal mind.* New York: Crown Publishers.

Samenow, S. (1991). Correcting errors of thinking in the socialization of offenders. *Journal of Correctional Education, 42* (2), 56–58.

Schram, P. J., Koons-Witt, B. A., & Morash, M. (2004). Management strategies when working with female prisoners. *Women & Criminal Justice, 15* (2), 25–50.

Seligman, M. E. P. (1972). Learned helplessness. *Annual Review of Medicine, 23,* 407–412.

Sharp, B. D. (2000). *Changing criminal thinking: A treatment program.* Landham, MD: American Correctional Association.

Smith, E. J. (2006). The strength-based counseling model. *The Counseling Psychologist, 34,* 13–79.

Sorbello, L., Eccleston, L., Ward, T., & Jones, R. (2002). Treatment needs of female offenders: A review. *Australian Psychologist, 37* (3), 196–205.

Spohn, R. E., (2000). Gender differences in the effect of child maltreatment on criminal activity over the life course. In G. L. Fox & M. L. Benson (Eds.), *Families, crime and criminal justice* (pp. 207–231). Amsterdam: JAI.

Tong, L. S. & Farrington, D. (2006). How effective is the "Reasoning and Rehabilitation" programme in reducing reoffending? A meta-analysis of evaluations in four countries. *Psychology, Crime & Law, 12* (1), 3–24.

Turnbull, S., & Hannah-Moffat, K. (2009). Under these conditions: Gender, parole and the governance of reintegration. *British Journal of Criminology, 49,* 532–551. doi: 10.1093/bjc/azp015.

Van Dieten, M. (2010). *Moving On: A program for women at risk.* City Center, MN: Hazelden Publishing.

Van Dieten, M., & MacKenna, P. (2001). *Moving On facilitator's guide.* Toronto, Ontario: Orbis Partners, Inc.

Van Dieten, M., & Robinson, D. (2009). Effective correctional treatment: What is the state of the art? In Rhine, E. & Evans, D. (Eds.), *Research into practice: Bridging the gap in community corrections.* Annapolis, MD: ACA.

Ward, T. (2010). The Good Lives model of offender rehabilitation: Basic assumptions, etiological commitments, and practice implications. In F. McNeill, P. Raynor, & C. Trotter (Eds.), *Offender supervision: New directions in theory, research and practice* (pp. 41–64). Devon, UK: Willan Publishing.

Werner, E. E. & Smith, R. S. (1992). *Overcoming the odds: High-risk children from birth to adulthood.*
Ithaca: Cornell University Press.

West, H. C., Sabol, W. J., & Greenman, S. J. (2010). *Prisoners in 2009.* Retrieved from: http://bjs.ojp.
usdoj.gov/content/pub/pdf/p09.pdf.

White, M., & Epston, D. (1990). *Narrative means to therapeutic ends.* New York: WW Norton.

Widom, C. S., Czaja, S. J., & Dutton, M. (2007). Childhood victimization and lifetime revictimization.
Child Abuse & Neglect, 32, 785–796.

Winogron, B., Van Dieten, M., & Gauzas, L. (2004). *Controlling anger and learning to manage it.*
Toronto: Multi-Health Systems.

Wright, E. M., Salisbury, E. J., & Van Voorhis, P. (2007). Predicting the prison misconducts of women
offenders: The importance of gender-responsive needs. *Journal of Contemporary Criminal Justice,
23* (4), 310–340.

Zlotnick, C., Johnson, D., & Najavits, L. (2009). Randomized controlled pilot study of cognitive-
behavioral therapy in a sample of incarcerated women with substance abuse disorder and PTSD.
Behavior Therapy, 40, 325–336.

Zlotnick, C., Najavits, L., Rosenow, D., & Johnson, D. (2003). A cognitive-behavioral treatment for
incarcerated women with substance abuse disorder and post-traumatic stress disorder: Findings
from a pilot study. *Journal of Substance Abuse Treatment, 25,* 99–105.

Suggestions for Further Learning

Websites

National Institute of Corrections (NIC) – part of the United States Department of Justice, Federal
Bureau of Prisons. The NIC provides support programs to assist federal, state, and local corrections
agencies. Additionally the NIC provides funds to support programs that are in line with its key ini-
tiatives. For a complete list of online resources go to http://nicic.gov/

Orbis Partners Inc., of Ottawa, Ontario, provides consulting to criminal justice and social service organizations and agencies. This agency provides opportunities for individuals and organizations to receive
training in gender-informed intervention programs and practices. www.orbispartners.com

National Resource Center on Justice Involved Women – a resource for professionals, policymakers, and
practitioners who work with adult women involved in the criminal justice system. The center offers
an array of readings, training resources, and opportunities for technical assistance. www.cjinvolved-
women.org

Association of Programs for Female Offenders – http://www.apfonews.org/

Appendix 16.A

Reactions by Justice-Involved Women to Frequently Experienced Situations and Circumstances: Treatment Implications and Suggested Interventions

CONTEXT	COMMON REACTIONS FROM JUSTICE-INVOLVED WOMEN	INTERVENTIONS TO SUPPLEMENT AND REINFORCE THE USE OF CBT
Parenting		

North American culture has endorsed the belief that parenting and child care are primarily a woman's responsibility. Although this belief is shifting, women still assume the bulk of second-shift work.
 	
When incarcerated, many women do not see their children, may lose custody of their children, and/or have severely jeopardized the connection with their children (Wright et al., 2007).
	▪ High levels of anxiety regarding the safety and custody of children
	▪ High levels of shame regarding impact of her behavior on children
	▪ Perceptions of failure and worthlessness because of what has happened to children
	▪ Lack of confidence in ability to manage the behavior of her children or to meet their emotional needs
		Build skills to promote healthy parent-child relationships and to support the caregivers/mentors of children.
		▪ Parenting skills programs
		▪ Skills programs for caregivers of children while mother is incarcerated
		▪ Skills programs that support caregiver and mother in co-parenting until reunification
		▪ Prison-based nursery programs
		▪ Legal aid to address custody and family reunification issues
		▪ Reunification programs:
		   o visits
		   o creative contacts
		▪ Literacy and family strengthening programs (e.g., Words Travel)
		▪ Mentoring programs for children of prisoners

Other Relationships		
Interpersonal attachments are fundamental to a woman's self-concept (Gilligan, 1982). Kohlberg's theory of moral development may be less applicable to women who frequently violate personal values to protect loved ones and preserve relationships even when unhealthy (Wright et al., 2007). Females are socialized to be attuned to other's emotions, notice relationship problems and try to solve them (Benedict, 2005).	▪ Disconnections with family and friends due to criminal behavior ▪ Belief that her needs are less important than other people's (children, husband, partner, friends, etc.) ▪ Belief in the "importance" of preserving a relationship regardless of the consequences	Assess existing relationships and provide the opportunity for women to define the qualities and characteristics of a healthy relationship. ▪ Build skills to enhance social competence (assertiveness, negotiation, conflict resolution, etc.) ▪ Access to models of healthy relationships ▪ Information on establishing and maintaining boundaries ▪ Safety planning

(Continued)

Appendix 16.A *(Continued)*

CONTEXT	COMMON REACTIONS FROM JUSTICE-INVOLVED WOMEN	INTERVENTIONS TO SUPPLEMENT AND REINFORCE THE USE OF CBT
Victimization		
Women are more likely to be abused by someone they know. A very large number of women offenders report past and present victimization experiences (e.g., physical, sexual, and emotional violence) (Widom et al., 2007).	▪ PTSD ▪ Strong feelings of guilt, depression, self-blame ▪ Belief that intimate partner violence is deserved ▪ Belief that being alone or single means that she is unlovable and undeserving ▪ Inability to trust ▪ Inability to set boundaries ▪ Inability to claim a healthy relationship ▪ Increased risk for rape, domestic violence ▪ Increase risk to perpetrate violence or self-harm	Provide resources and information about trauma impact, effects and consequences. Introduce stabilization skills including self-regulation and problem-solving. ▪ Information on intimate partner violence ▪ Safety planning ▪ Information to evaluate early warning signs of healthy vs unhealthy relationships ▪ Information about power and control and its manifestations of abuse across sexual orientation, culture, race, religion ▪ See mental health treatment below
Physical Functioning		
Physical attractiveness plays a significant role in shaping a woman's sense of personal worth. Women are also concerned about physical functioning and discomfort associated with menstruation, pregnancy, child birth (Davis & Padesky, 1984). Women in prison are stripped of beauty products and served food with high caloric content. Changes to skin, hair and body are not unusual (Bloom et al., 2003; Schram et al., 2004). Women express concerns about both the lack of quality and availability of medical and dental services. Many women face chronic medical issues such as TB, HIV, hepatitis, and diabetes (Bloom et al., 2003; Schram et al., 2004).	▪ Strong concerns about body and attractiveness, somatic complaints including dysmorphia not uncommon ▪ Distrustful of medical providers ▪ Wary of expertise and competence ▪ Concerns about long-term health and chronic medical care	General information on physical health, nutrition, sexuality and self-care. ▪ Physical exercise ▪ Yoga ▪ Meditation and relaxation ▪ Mindfulness techniques ▪ Media literacy and social action projects designed to counteract objectification and sexualization of women in media ▪ Adjustments to prison "allowable property lists"

Appendix 16.A *(Continued)*

CONTEXT	COMMON REACTIONS FROM JUSTICE-INVOLVED WOMEN	INTERVENTIONS TO SUPPLEMENT AND REINFORCE THE USE OF CBT
Mental Health and Substance Use		

A very large number of women offenders have mental health issues including depression, anxiety, PTSD and co-occurring disorders (Wright et al., 2007).
 	
A very large number of women offenders have a history of substance abuse issues emerging as a result of victimization and trauma (Covington, 2003, 2008; Spohn, 2000).
	▪ Hyperarousal (hyperactive, hypervigilance, anxiety and panic, rage)
	▪ Depression, disconnection, exhaustion, fatigue, numbness
	▪ Strong feelings of despair, fear, and hopelessness
	▪ Inability to trust
	▪ Stigma associated with participation in treatment
	▪ Strong cultural messages to remain silent
		Provide access to information and a variety of professional services.
		▪ Stabilize woman with emotional regulation and interpersonal skills
		▪ Provide information on anxiety, depression, substance use
		▪ Intensive therapy (individual and or group counseling) to address mental health needs:
		  ○ Narrative techniques and exposure therapy for women who wish to address trauma
		  ○ Inpatient and outpatient substance abuse treatment
		▪ Access to medical and psychiatric services as needed

Community Living and Work		
Women have a much shorter tradition of work outside of the home and despite the fact that more and more women are joining the labor force there is still considerable inequity in pay and in status. Many women offenders lack marketable work skills and are not able to earn a living wage. Many have financial responsibilities for their children and other family members (Bloom et al., 2003; Green et al., 2005). Women transitioning from prison often prioritize employment and safe housing as the most critical need areas to ensure successful re-entry (Garcia, 2012).	▪ Fear, shame and uncertainty about the future ▪ Feelings of guilt and powerlessness to provide for self and family ▪ Anxiety with respect to entering the workforce ▪ Stigma associated with lack of ability and achievement	Facilitate connections to vocational services and safe, drug-free, and affordable housing. ▪ Assess and build marketable skills ▪ Explore job training programs ▪ Introduce career interest inventories ▪ Explore specific employment programs ▪ Provide case management services to assist with housing ▪ Assist with identification (social security cards, license, birth certificate)

17

CBT with Juvenile Offenders

A Review and Recommendations for Practice

Eva Feindler and Alison M. Byers

Overview: Treatment Versus Punishment

According to the 2009 Uniform Crime Report issued by the FBI, teenage violent offenses have become considerably less serious and less frequent. In fact the volume and impact of serious crime has dropped dramatically from nearly one-third of total offenses in the 1960s to one-sixth today (Federal Bureau of Investigation, 2009). Violent offenses and property offenses for youth have diminished about 40% from the high rates reported in the late 1960s. Influenced certainly by greater policing of domestic disturbances and policy shifts away from vague status offenses toward charging specific crimes, these reductions may also be influenced by the responsiveness of the mental health and education communities in the development and implementation of prevention and intervention programs.

While there are multiple theories that attempt to explain delinquency, a preponderance of theorists agree that delinquent behavior is a result of a complex interaction between individual predispositions, external situations, close interpersonal and/or familial influences in a young person's life (e.g. religion/education), as well as the neighborhood, economy, culture, and the society in which the youths are immersed. There are some factors, which function as risks, pushing juveniles toward crime and some that function as protective mechanisms steering them away from delinquency. Given that there are so many varied explanations for the creation of delinquency, it is not surprising that there are also a multitude of proposed solutions, or responses, to delinquent behavior. For the discussion in this chapter we will be focusing on the use of various forms of cognitive-behavioral therapy (CBT) as a means of treating juveniles who have at least one arrest and are adjudicated delinquent by the courts, and therefore have some ongoing contact with the juvenile correctional system. Practitioners of varied backgrounds, working in community or in residential settings, will hopefully find these resources beneficial.

Estimates vary widely but there is strong agreement that 50–75% of the one million juveniles being processed through the juvenile justice system have at least one diagnosable mental disorder. Among those with at least one diagnosis, 25% are found to have a "severe" disorder

Forensic CBT: A Handbook for Clinical Practice, First Edition.
Edited by Raymond Chip Tafrate and Damon Mitchell.
© 2014 John Wiley & Sons, Ltd. Published 2014 by John Wiley & Sons, Ltd.

(Cocozza & Skowyra, 2000). This is significant because having high proportions of offenders with serious mental health needs challenges the ability of the juvenile justice system to provide proper assessment, treatment, and safety, both for diagnosable youths as well as non-diagnosable offenders. Currently in the juvenile correctional system a preponderance of facilities are oriented toward a "punishment" or control and containment model, as compared to a treatment model, and philosophically these concepts are often in conflict and do not peacefully coexist. Despite mounting evidence, less than 5% of eligible and psychologically needy children in the juvenile justice system are currently receiving evidence-based treatments (Greenwood, 2008).

Part of the problem is the complexity in defining whom the juvenile justice system *primarily* serves. Some would argue that the needs of the public are paramount and that youthful offenders, like their adult counterparts, need to be held responsible for their actions and face consequences, and that the juvenile correctional system's primary function is to protect society from further harm by offenders. These theories focus on the concept that offenders have free will and are actively choosing to engage in delinquent behavior, and therefore policy responses should be limited largely to punishment, incapacitation of the offender, and deterrence.

A competing argument is that human behavior is affected by multiple factors and that society is better served by having the juvenile justice system recognize the emotional, psychological, educational, and/or developmental needs of young clients. Theoretically, addressing the previously unmet needs of juveniles at a young age is, in the long run, the ultimate benefit to society by cutting short a life of crime. These opposing philosophies can be oversimplified by calling them punishment versus rehabilitation, although some would argue that many of these young offenders have never been "habilitated" in the first place and are therefore in desperate need of treatment by the time they are first arrested. Given the many pressures faced by state governments across the country, everyone would agree that the juvenile justice system across the board is taxed almost to the breaking point. Given that fact, there is reasonable debate as to whether the juvenile justice system is the best place for youths with severe mental health needs, particularly given the conflicting demands of containment and treatment. However, there are currently few options other than programs under the purview of the courts or the social services system. There are a wide variety of programs in existence and they vary by:

1. Level of security ranging from maximum security to probation.
2. Duration of the program.
3. Residential placement versus community outpatient.
4. Availability and intensity of mental health treatment.
5. Voluntary versus court ordered.

Challenges in Implementing Juvenile Forensic Programs

The idea of integrating more mental health treatment into the provision of services to youths involved in delinquent or criminal activity works well in theory; however, there are numerous issues, both practical and theoretical, that get in the way of implementation. As noted above, the mental health model and the juvenile justice model have competing priorities. The most basic distinction is the need for safety as opposed to treatment. In its most basic form, the juvenile justice system adopts a "safety-first" model, which largely endorses control and/or punishment. In this model, when a youth is in custody, acting out behavior is likely to result in access to services being reduced. Ironically, often these are the very services the youth may need in order to improve behavior in the long run, such as recreation, sports, educational support, counseling or rehabilitation services, or positive peer socialization. On the other hand, mental health practitioners recognize that these additional services provide the scaffolding that supports the growth and healing in children struggling with mental health issues and therefore see these not as extra privileges to be lost but rather essential tools to heal.

From a public safety perspective, the mental health and treatment needs of juveniles must be balanced with the public safety needs and the demands of accountability and consequences for their actions. In the mental health system, it is clear who the client is. In the correctional system, multiple, sometimes competing needs must be considered simultaneously. Toward this end, it should be noted that some mental health models are better at taking these competing demands into account than others. For example, in dialectical behavior therapy (DBT: Linehan, 1993a), a key focus is on addressing life-threatening behaviors. DBT allows negative behaviors to be reframed in the context of a mental health symptom model, keeps the focus on the reduction of negative behavior, and keeps both client and community safe, while supporting the needs of the client and not endorsing "punishment." Another example is that in a therapeutic model, "resistance" is considered normal behavior from a teenage client. The therapist is expected to work through a client's reluctance, anger, and opposition, not penalize the client for non-compliance. Trained clinicians are capable of recognizing that some acting-out behavior is acceptable and even helpful. In the juvenile justice system this behavior is penalized given that it is interpreted in a way that categorizes a youth as problematic and oppositional.

The ability of a practitioner to engage a youthful offender in a productive and caring way depends in part on their training. CBT is intended to be implemented by trained mental health practitioners, often individuals who have at least a college degree if not a master's degree or doctorate in counseling, social work, or psychology. The fundamentals of CBT include case conceptualization, treatment planning, goal setting, session structure, identifying and responding to automatic thoughts, using homework, and using behavioral interventions. While there is no minimum amount of training required to implement CBT, the authors assume that practitioners have at least one full semester of didactic training by a licensed professional, with accompanying supervision for casework in order to be prepared to cope with the complexities of implementation with difficult clients. Proper training increases the likelihood that clinicians will understand the subtle nuances of, and adherence to, protocols and manuals. For clinicians who are just starting to work with CBT or just starting to work with youthful offenders, it is strongly advised that there be appropriate supervision in place to support staff and ensure the best possible treatment for the youths.

Group therapy can be cost-effective. Adolescents respond very well to the group setting wherein peer support and the group process allows for productive exploration of social roles and rules, which can lead to greater growth than would be possible in individual counseling. However, group therapy also presents several obstacles. Practitioners should understand that the group should be structured and guided by the therapist and that there is an expectation that the therapist will use modeling and operant strategies. A good facilitator will know how to use the group setting to maximize peer support, encourage leadership, facilitate new relationships and prosocial roles, and modulate feedback (Rose & Church, 1998).

In addition to helping the group get oriented, setting goals and expectations, building cohesion, and enhancing motivation, the leaders will also need to look out for the potentially negative iatrogenic effects of group treatment. To this end, it is vital that facilitators be aware that there is the possibility of a "deviant peer contagion" effect, which can result from a group of delinquents negatively influencing each other and succumbing to competing reinforcement contingencies as they bond, show off, or otherwise try to use the group setting for purposes other than therapeutic treatment (Dishion, McCord, & Poulin, 1999). However, a well-trained, properly supervised therapist can intervene early at the first sign that members are sabotaging the group process.

Assessing Treatment Needs

One of the factors found to be key to successful treatment of juvenile offenders is the goodness-of-fit between the youth and the program to which he/she has been adjudicated. Youths need to be evaluated for a wide array of factors and then should, ideally, be matched to a program that will address their needs. In addition to identifying symptoms of conduct disorder or oppositional defiant disorder, a good intake should cover the areas listed below:

- Potential mental health diagnoses, particularly depression (and suicidality), and anxiety.
- The presence of substance use and/or abuse.
- Trauma history (especially intrafamilial and community violence).
- Familial support and supervision, and patterns of family interaction/punishment.
- Academic issues, including language and learning obstacles.
- Patterns of peer interaction, both prosocial and antisocial.

For professionals who have been assigned to work with adjudicated youths, and who may not have access to, or familiarity with, psychodiagnostic screening assessments, there are some tools available freely on the web, which can be useful in identifying problem areas (See Boxes 17.1 and 17.2). Several others have been included in the appendix and can be reproduced.

In general, a cognitive-behavioral approach assesses an adolescent's skill deficits and factors that provoke antisocial and immature behaviors and that reinforce and maintain poor adjustment across time and contexts. Most intervention programs include a behavioral assessment phase to help understand an adolescent's discrete patterns and deficit areas, and then a skills-based learning program focused on cognitive and behavioral changes as well as on emotion regulation. Many treatment programs are multi-component and teach new skills using modeling, role-play, guided homework, and positive reinforcement for approximations to the desired prosocial behaviors. A list of core cognitive-behavioral skills typically covered in programs is provided below:

- Training on general thinking and decision-making: Stopping and thinking before acting, generating alternative solutions, evaluating consequences, and making decisions about appropriate behavior.
- Cognitive restructuring: Activities and exercises aimed at recognizing and modifying the distortions and errors that characterize criminogenic thinking.
- Interpersonal problem-solving: Training in problem-solving skills for dealing with interpersonal conflict and peer pressure.
- Social skills: Training in prosocial behaviors, interpreting social cues, and taking other persons' feelings into account.
- Anger control: Training in techniques for identifying triggers and cues that arouse anger and maintain affective arousal.
- Moral reasoning: Activities designed to improve the ability to reason about right and wrong behavior and raise the level of moral development.

Box 17.1   General Assessment Resources

Bright Futures produces a number of helpful tools for professionals that can be accessed for free on the web; see: http://www.brightfutures.org/mentalhealth/pdf/tools.html#professionals

In addition, The California Evidence-Based Clearinghouse for Child Welfare has a number of free assessment devices that you can use if you simply contact the individual who created the screening tool directly; see: http://www.cebc4cw.org/assessment-tools/

The Pediatric Symptom Checklist is a psychosocial screen designed to facilitate the recognition of cognitive, emotional, and behavioral problems so that appropriate interventions can be initiated as early as possible; see: http://www.brightfutures.org/mental health/pdf/professionals/ped_sympton_chklst.pdf

A good tool to use to get a fairly complete overview of the child is the Child and Adolescent Needs and Strengths (CANS-MH). The CANS-MH is a comprehensive assessment of psychological and social factors for use in treatment planning. Domains assessed include general symptomology, risk behaviors, developmental functioning, personal/interpersonal functioning, and family functioning. The CANS-MH is intended to support case planning and evaluation of service systems. See: http://www.praed foundation.org/CANS-MH%20Manual.pdf

Box 17.2   Specialized Assessment Resources for Juveniles

Substance Use/Abuse
A really good comprehensive site regarding youth and drinking can be found at The National Institute on Alcohol Abuse and Alcoholism, where you can download a screening tool and a brief intervention. Go to: http://pubs.niaaa.nih.gov/publications/Practitioner/YouthGuide/YouthGuide.pdf

Depression
The Center for Epidemiological Studies Depression Scale for Children can be found at: http://www.brightfutures.org/mentalhealth/pdf/professionals/bridges/ces_dc.pdf

Foster Care
For children in foster care the American Academy of Pediatrics has developed a website with some useful resources: http://www.aap.org/en-us/advocacy-and-policy/aap-health-initiatives/healthy-foster-care-america/Pages/Mental-and-Behavioral-Health.aspx

Trauma
For a download of one trauma survey from the Veterans Administration, please see: http://www.ptsd.va.gov/PTSD/professional/pages/assessments/assessment-pdf/TESI-C.pdf

A trauma-focused CBT manual and discussion (includes the adolescent version of the UCLA PTSD Index for Adolescents and the scoring protocol) can be found at: http://www.nctsn.org/nctsn_assets/pdfs/TF-CBT_Implementation_Manual.pdf

Also, the Child Exposure to Domestic Violence Scale can be obtained from: http://www.mincava.umn.edu/cedv/cedv.pdf

The Department of Veterans Affairs has a comprehensive list of many scales that can be used to assess childhood trauma such as the Child Trauma Interview. For a direct link to their page go to: http://www.ptsd.va.gov/professional/pages/assessments/child-trauma-ptsd.asp

In addition, the Trauma History Checklist and Interview (Habib & Labruna, 2006), is included in the appendix of this chapter.

Anxiety

The SCARED (Screen for Child Anxiety Disorders) from the University of Pittsburgh Department of Psychiatry can be found at: http://www.wpic.pitt.edu/research/AssessmentTools. There are child and parent forms along with scoring information on the website.

Family/Marital Assessment

The Family Advocacy Support Tool (FAST) is the family version of the Child and Adolescent Needs and Strengths (CANS) family of planning and outcome management tools. A large number of individuals have contributed to the design and development of the FAST. It is an open-domain tool, free for anyone to use; see: http://www.praed foundation.org/Family%20Assessment%20and%20Support%20Tool%20Manual.pdf

A compendium of relationship/marital conflict measures to assess marital functioning can be downloaded from: http://www.childtrends.org/Files/04_Relationship&Marital ConflictMeasures_web.pdf

- Victim impact: Activities aimed at getting offenders to consider the impact of their behavior on their victims.
- Substance abuse: Application of any of the typical CBT techniques specifically to the issue of substance use and abuse.
- Behavior modification: Behavioral contracts and/or reward and penalty schemes designed to shape and reinforce prosocial behavior.
- Relapse prevention: Training in strategies to recognize and cope with high-risk situations and halt the relapse cycle before lapses turn into full relapses.
- Individual attention: Any individualized one-on-one treatment element that supplements CBT group sessions such as individual counseling.

Delivering effective intervention programs

Important considerations in the effective delivery of CBT interventions for juveniles are the training and supervision of those who will be implementing the program.

The integrity with which a program is implemented significantly affects the success rates achieved. Often, contacting the researcher and having them involved in designing a treatment program ensures that staff will more strongly adhere to the plan and will seek assistance when problems arise. Carefully monitoring implementation and ensuring that staff receive ongoing support and necessary training, improve the likelihood that youths in the program will benefit

from the intended treatment. Clearly training and continued supervision of a program's implementation requires significant resources, planning, and organization from the facility or agency.

An additional consideration is the nature and degree of the involvement of the juvenile
offender's family in the treatment process. Family involvement in treatment is a characteristic
of the most successful programs. By including the family members in treatment, the clinicians
will understand the degree of motivation on the part of the caregiver and understand whether
the family is a source of support or further complications. Secondly, the caregivers and other
family members may learn tools and strategies from the treatment that may carry over into the
family environment. Thirdly, family involvement increases the likelihood that the youth will be
able to practice new skills in the home thereby increasing the generalizability and rehearsal of
new skills in multiple contexts. Unfortunately, not all families are able to participate and many
have significant family dysfunction that works against the youth's maintenance and generalization of new skills. If possible, at a minimum, parents or other caregivers should have some type
of parent training in order to help develop appropriate responses to the youth at home.

In addition to training and family involvement, the following treatment delivery characteristics appear to be associated with the strongest and most lasting positive effects:

- Programs should simultaneously address *multiple* risk factors across *different* contexts and
  settings for the individual adolescent.
- Highly structured programs produce better results.
- Programs should be individualized for particular offender needs.
- There should be well-specified targets of change in the program curriculum.
- Programs that are rehabilitative in nature, as opposed to being punitive, are more effective.
- Programs that include a cognitive component (not just behavioral) to shift antisocial,
  normative beliefs seem more effective.
- The program should teach multiple *new* skills, to replace less functional/adaptable skills,
  and be strength based, not just risk-focused.
- Real-life opportunities to practice new skills, allowing success in order for skills to generalize and be internalized, need to be included.
- If possible, the interventions are implemented within the context of the juvenile's home
  environment and when family members are engaged as partners allowing for generalization and rehearsal of new skills.
- Ideally, programs should be research-based and include periodic checks for adherence to
  the treatment protocols.

Overview of Evidence-Based Programs for Juvenile Offenders

What follows is a review of treatment approaches that are based on cognitive-behavioral theory
and are relevant to clinical work with juvenile offenders and of the empirical evidence for the
overall effectiveness of each program. Several promising programs, not yet supported by an
empirical base, are also included.

Multisystemic Therapy (MST)

MST is the most extensively researched treatment of serious antisocial behavior of juvenile
offenders. This intensive, home-based model of service delivery was developed for youths at

risk for incarceration or out-of-home placement due to serious behavior problems. An ecological model provides the foundation for intervention in the youth's interconnected systems of living: family, peers, school, neighborhood, and community contexts. Drawing on family and social learning theories, MST therapists target instrumental (i.e., supervision and discipline) and affective (warmth and conflict) aspects of family functioning and integrate cognitive-behavioral strategies to address individualized treatment goals. According to Henggeler (2011), the in-home treatment delivery removes barriers to service access and enhances the maintenance and generalization of treatment gains.

Therapists, intensively trained and monitored, have small caseloads and are available 24/7 to each family. According to the MST website (www.mstservices.com), the average length of treatment is 60 hours of contact over the course of a 4-month period. The detailed treatment manual delineates the process by which youth and family problems are prioritized and targeted for change based upon nine core principles that serve to operationalize MST. These core principles help to integrate evidenced-based treatments (i.e., behavioral parent training, family therapy, problem-solving skills) into each of the contexts included in the ecological formulation. For example, at the family level, MST is designed to improve family structure and cohesion and to provide parents with effective monitoring, communication, and discipline strategies. At the peer level, MST is focused on increasing connections with prosocial peers and on helping parents to disengage their adolescents from antisocial peers (Huey, Henggeler, Brondino, & Pickrel, 2000). Treatment teams provide each therapist with support, consultation, supervision, and booster training. Finally, multiple methods are used in data collection to monitor treatment adherence and fidelity and to facilitate treatment decisions based upon observed or reported changes in youth functioning. Outcome data are ideally collected in each of the youth's contexts.

In a comprehensive review of 35 years of clinical research on MST, Henggeler (2011) charts the course from early university-based efficacy studies to those examining large-scale transfer to community settings. Results from 21 outcome studies (19 randomized trials) have indicated extensive improvements in family relations, peer relations, and academic performance in addition to significant decreases in recidivism at follow-up (Borduin et al., 1995; Sawyer & Borduin, 2011; Schaeffer & Borduin, 2005). However, the degree of positive impact found in efficacy studies might have been possible only in the near ideal conditions of the university research sites where the studies were conducted. Effectiveness studies in the community were not as positive, but nonetheless suggest that MST is effective in reducing incarceration, and that therapist fidelity was directly linked to lower recidivism (Henggeler, 2011). Just recently, a qualitative analysis was conducted on 37 semi-structured interviews of parents and young offenders 2 months after completion of the standard MST program. Results indicated that both the personal commitment and emotional availability of the MST therapist and the ways that the treatment was built around parent needs, were the primary factors responsible for program satisfaction and treatment gains (Tighe, Pistrang, Casdagli, Baruch & Butler, 2012). Although outcome results were somewhat mixed, these data support the notion that a good therapeutic alliance goes a long way in counteracting a family's negative history with mental health professionals.

Multidimensional Treatment Foster Care Program (MTFC)

Another comprehensive program designed for the treatment of serious and chronic juvenile offenders in the community was developed by Patricia Chamberlain and colleagues and is based on social learning theory. The MTFC program is coordinated across multiple settings and includes behavioral parent training for foster parents, family therapy for biological parents, skills training and supportive therapy for adolescents, and school-based behavioral interventions for youths who require out-of-home placement. According to the MTFC website (www.mtfc.com) foster parents are recruited, trained (for 20 pre-service hours), and supervised as they then implement individualized behavioral plans for the youth placed into the family setting for 6 to 9 months. Foster parents put into place a specific contingency management system, closely supervise the youth, and maintain clear rules and limits while also providing appropriate consequences (Leve & Chamberlain, 2005). Youths participate in weekly individual therapy. School attendance, academic performance, and homework completion are closely monitored by treatment team members.

To monitor effectiveness, the treatment team maintains daily contact with the foster parents via the Parent Daily Report (PDR) and weekly parent meetings. Further, team members are available 24/7 to all adults involved in the youth's home and school environments. According to Chamberlain (2003) the four main components of MTFC (adult supervision, fair and consistent discipline, positive relationships with caretaking adults, and strategies to limit association with deviant peers) combine to reduce post-treatment criminal activity and the need for residential placement. These intensive services and support, provided in settings that mirror normative life, are desirable alternatives to treating juvenile offenders in congregate care settings (Leve & Chamberlain, 2005).

Beginning in 1991, and continuing to the present, there have been numerous randomized trials and other studies to provide evidence for the feasibility, efficacy, and effectiveness of MTFC. Results from the randomized trials show positive outcomes for boys referred from juvenile justice (Chamberlain & Reid, 1998; Eddy & Chamberlain, 2000; Eddy, Whaley, & Chamberlain, 2004), youths discharged from a psychiatric hospital setting (Chamberlain & Reid, 1991), and youths in state-supported foster care (Chamberlain, Moreland & Reid, 1992). Further, a middle school prevention model for at-risk girls and parents in foster care (including prosocial and parent management skills training) resulted in lower levels of substance use and increased stability in home placements at a 36-month follow-up (Kim & Leve, 2011). However, comparisons to the control group in this randomized design yielded no changes in reported delinquent behavior.

Brief Strategic Family Therapy (BSFT)

A research group has developed and evaluated the use of BSFT with Hispanic drug-using youths and their families (Santisteban, Suarez-Morales, Robbins, & Szapocznik, 2006). The primary premise of BSFT is that adolescent behavior problems are reflective of dysfunctional family dynamics (inappropriate alliances, overly rigid or permeable boundaries, and the "identified-patient" process). The key BSFT techniques of joining, diagnosing, and family restructuring are implemented to transform members' interactions. Unlike other family interventions, BSFT maintains a consistent focus on the "within family" work, which reflects the strong family orientation characteristic of Hispanic families (Santisteban et al., 2006). BSFT can be delivered in 4–20 weekly one-hour sessions. Of clear interest to these researchers and service providers in Miami was identifying the best ways to engage typically resistant families into treatment. In the early years, they sometimes used an enhancement called SSSE – Strategic Structural Systems Engagement (Santisteban, Szapocznik, Perez-Vidal et al., 1996) – which included home visits as well as strategies of joining and reframing. Santisteban et al. (1996) detail varying levels of effort needed by treatment personnel to successfully engage these families. Outcome research on BSFT indicates that this approach is efficacious in engaging reluctant families and in reducing drug usage and serious acting out (Santisteban et al., 2006) and may even have a preventative impact when implemented with families of younger children.

A more recent iteration is Culturally Informed and Flexible Family-Based Treatment for Adolescents (CIFFTA), which includes some additional components designed to enhance engagement and outcomes. Increased emphasis on parental monitoring, consultation with the school and legal systems, and greater flexibility in treatment delivery were changes made to BSFT based upon cultural and clinical considerations(Santisteban & Mena, 2009). CIFFTA can be delivered over 4 months, with two sessions occurring in multiple modalities (adolescents alone, parents alone, adolescent groups, and co-joint family sessions). Youths are provided with specific individualized treatments (i.e., motivational interviewing, relapse prevention, interpersonal effectiveness skills) and focused didactic sessions to complement the more free-flowing family sessions. Santisteban and Mena (2009) recommend 11 distinct educational modules selected in an individualized treatment plan according to the needs of the family. Thus, the entire protocol is tailored to the unique adolescent and his/her family and seems to incorporate the most widely accepted CBT strategies available.

Functional Family Therapy (FFT)

FFT is a multi-step structured family-based intervention (Alexander & Parsons, 1982) to address highly problematic family interactions for youths with behavior problems. The FFT website (www.fftinc.com) indicates that the outpatient program has evolved into a three-phase model. The *engagement/motivation phase* is focused on the attitudes, expectations, emotional reactions, and perceptions of family members. Therapists help to reframe problematic, blaming interactions using family therapy strategies. The second phase, *behavior change*, is focused on the development of communication and problem-solving skills and on parenting techniques such as contingency contracting and contingent reinforcement. Through the use of family tasks and homework assignments, family members practice newly acquired skills. Finally, in the *generalization phase*, more independence is fostered and the frequency of therapy sessions declines. Therapists support the maintenance of changes while consulting with involved school and court personnel. Trained FFT therapists have caseloads of 10–12 families, and the program involves about 12 sessions during a 90-day period.

The FFT website presents information about another program in which the treatment was delivered by graduate students at Ohio University and outcomes were compared with a no-treatment group. Recidivism and recommitment rates for those 16–17-year-olds receiving FFT were lower than comparison youths. Few details about the actual treatment protocol or the training and supervision of FFT therapists are provided, and the use of reoffending rates as sole outcome data indicates caution in the consideration of FFT as evidence-based. The website includes information about requirements for site certification as well as clinical training and supervision requirements thought to ensure effective program implementation and fidelity.

Aggression Replacement Training (ART)

ART is an evidenced-based treatment program with three components: *skillstreaming, anger control training*, and *moral reasoning training* (Goldstein, Glick, & Gibbs, 1998). Based on research findings and cognitive-behavioral conceptualizations of aggression problems in youths, ART aims to target the following deficits: A lack of prosocial skills such as negotiation, handling accusations, and responding to other troubling situations; an inability to manage the intense physiological arousal embedded in the experience of anger; and thought processes that support antisocial behaviors (Goldstein et al., 1998). Each module contains 10 sessions, designed to be administered three times per week over 10 weeks, for a total of 30 sessions (see Appendix 17.B for an outline of the curriculum).

Skillstreaming requires youths to learn prosocial skills via modeling and practice them through role-plays. In the anger control component, participants practice engaging in a series of steps designed to deintensify emotional reactions and reduce impulsive responses to provoking situations. For example, youths are taught to utilize "self-talk" and "reminders" to help reduce the impulse to act out aggressively. Moral reasoning is a discussion-based format designed to promote thinking about moral problems and advance moral maturity according to Kohlberg's stages of moral development. Within the moral reasoning component, cognitive distortions and maladaptive thinking patterns are conceptualized as characteristic of immature or delayed moral development (i.e., the inability to take another's perspective) and challenged by the trainers according to the curriculum. Maladaptive cognitions are addressed both within the anger control module and the moral reasoning module. Appendix 17.C includes an example of the self-monitoring assessment form, The Hassle Log, used through ART training. This weekly checklist allows the youth to record, and therefore better understand, conflict incidents and to chart change across the program.

ART sessions make use of modeling, discussions, role-plays, games, and other strategies to engage youths with the material in the ART curriculum. ART is one of the few intervention programs designed for youths in residential or congregate care environments. The program is designed to be administered by staff at these juvenile facilities, although trainers and supervisors most likely are mental health professionals.

ART research has progressed substantially since its creation by Goldstein and colleagues over two decades ago. The program has been implemented in at least 45 states, six Canadian provinces, and numerous foreign countries, and is used with a variety of juvenile populations (Glick, 2006). ART has gradually gained support as an evidence-based treatment, effective in increasing prosocial behavior and moral reasoning abilities, and reducing impulsivity and antisocial behavior (Goldstein, Nensen, Deleflod, & Kalt, 2004). Effectiveness research strongly suggests that ART is effective in teaching social skills, improving anger management skills, and reducing self-reported anger and recidivism rates among juvenile delinquents (Goldstein et al., 2004).

Dialectical Behavior Therapy (DBT)

DBT is a comprehensive and well-researched cognitive-behavioral program originally designed by Marsha Linehan and colleagues to address the needs of chronically suicidal women usually diagnosed with Borderline Personality Disorder (BPD). The approach combines the basic strategies of behavior therapy with Eastern mindfulness practices, and the dialectic involves a balance between acceptance of the client's struggles while at the same time helping them to change. The program includes skills training modules designed to increase various adaptive behaviors and cognitions, develop mindfulness practices, tolerate distress, improve emotion regulation, and foster interpersonal effectiveness. During the past several decades, DBT has been adapted to both forensic and adolescent populations.

Berzins and Trestman (2004) provide a comprehensive review of the research on the implementation of DBT in 12 forensic settings and eight criminal justice settings in three countries. This review indicates some success in this DBT adaptation; however, there is only one report of DBT for juvenile offenders. Trupin, Stewart, Beach, and Boesky (2002) describe their program, which grew from an increase in the female incarcerated population and the documented links between delinquency and emotion dysregulation. Research has long indicated the co-occurrence of affective and behavioral dysregulation and aggressive antisocial behaviors and, in the female juvenile justice population, there is certainly an increased awareness of early BPD symptoms. Thus, this seems to be a logical extension of DBT programs to female juvenile offenders.

What also seem promising are the results from a recent modification of DBT skills training for adolescents with a diagnosis of Oppositional Defiant Disorder (ODD). Nelson-Gray and colleagues (Nelson-Gray et al., 2006), working with a group of defiant community-based adolescents (mean age 12.6 years) enumerated the similarities between adult BPD and ODD adolescents: Emotional dysregulation, interpersonal difficulties, and a poor response to stress. After implementing only the skills training component of DBT (see Nelson-Gray et al., 2006 for a more thorough description) results indicated that participants self-reported significant reductions in depressive symptoms, and internalizing and externalizing behaviors. Further, caregiver reports also revealed significant reductions in ODD symptoms and externalizing behaviors.

In sum, there seems to be sufficient theoretical and clinical reasons to consider the adaptation of the highly developed and structured DBT approach to the juvenile offender population. Although the evidence gathered thus far does not meet the requirements for consideration as an evidenced-based program for this population, the results are promising. The similarities in presenting problems and developmental history between juvenile offenders and populations greatly helped by DBT are clear (Quinn & Schera, 2009) and the interpersonal and internal deficits are similar targets for change. Given the importance of the family context, it would seem that although DBT might be adapted for residential environments, the inclusion of family skills training is advisable in order eventually to integrate the youths back into their communities (Quinn & Shera, 2009). As yet, the cost-effectiveness of the DBT approach has not been determined and it obviously requires an intensive staff commitment and training, not something readily available in the correctional system.

Coping Course

Based on a skills deficiency model of problem development, Rhode and colleagues (Rhode, Jorgensen, Seely, & Mace, 2004) designed a 16-session program focused on training adolescents to better manage their negative emotions. This included social skills, relaxation, cognitive restructuring, communication, and problem-solving, and was modeled on the Adolescent Coping with Depression Course (www.kpchr.org/acwd/acwd.html) with modifications for incarcerated youth. (see http://www.kpchr.org/research/public/acwd/acwd.html for the complete manual). Sessions were shortened to 90 minutes, examples in the manual were changed to reflect life experiences for teens in residence, homework tasks were reduced, and an in-session behavior management system was added. A major change was to expand the focus from depression to negative emotions in general, including sadness, boredom, anger, frustration, and fear. In research spanning several years, juveniles from Oregon were randomly assigned to either the Coping Course ($n=46$) or the usual care ($n=30$) in a closed custody secure setting. Results were then compared to youths ($n=62$) in a second control correctional facility. There were significant reductions in self-reported externalizing problems and suicide proneness, and increases in self-esteem and social interaction with staff. Further, treatment participants evidenced substantial increases in knowledge about cognitive-behavioral concepts. These promising results from a comprehensive pre-post assessment indicate that methodologically rigorous research should be conducted in real word settings with a manualized protocol.

Structured Psychotherapy for Adolescents Responding to Chronic Stress (SPARCS)

Another curriculum that has been utilized with juvenile justice populations is SPARCS (DeRosa & Pelcovitz, 2008). Originally implemented in outpatient, residential, and school settings, this intervention has been increasingly applied in a variety of settings including youths in foster care, runaway and homeless shelters, and with teens involved with the correctional system (including gang-involved youths). SPARCS is strength-based and is appropriate for trauma-tized adolescents with or without current/lifetime PTSD. Delivered over 16 sessions, SPARCS is a group intervention specifically designed to meet the needs of chronically traumatized ado-lescents who may still be living in unstable environments and are exhibiting multiple functional impairments – see the SPARCS website (http://sparcstraining.com/index.php) for additional information. These impairments include affect dysregulation, impulsivity, problems with self-perception, poor relationships, somatic complaints, dissociation, numbing and avoidance, and struggles finding purpose and meaning in life, as well as worldviews that make it difficult to be optimistic about the future. SPARCS was specifically designed to address these sequelae of multiple traumatic exposures and/or ongoing victimization (chronic physical/sexual abuse, repeated exposure to community violence, etc.) in a way that capitalizes on developmental tasks unique to adolescents (e.g. their burgeoning sense of independence, increased impor-tance and influence of their peer group). In order to survive chaotic and often violent environ-ments, youths must necessarily adopt a hypervigilant and defensive approach in order to guard against (and react to) potential threat. This defensive stance, while adaptive in high-conflict families and violent communities, becomes problematic in settings where the expectations and rules of engagement for conduct are different from a worldview where violence and victimiza-tion are the norm. By highlighting the impact of complex traumatic exposure, SPARCS addresses these underlying factors that contribute to delinquent behavior.

The primary goals of the program are captured within the *four Cs* and include: helping teens Cope more effectively in the moment and enhancing their self-efficacy; helping them Connect with others and establish supportive relationships; Cultivating awareness of themselves and others; and assisting them in Creating meaning in their lives. Teens practice the core SPARCS skills throughout the intervention and frequently report generalization of the skills to real-life situations. Core components of this intervention include mindfulness skills, relationship building/communication skills, distress tolerance, problem-solving, and meaning making. Additional treatment components include psychoeducation regarding stress, trauma, and trig-gers. In addition, Appendix 17.A includes an inventory that can be used to assess adolescents' exposure to chronic stress and trauma. SPARCS has a structured training program oriented primarily toward masters and doctoral level clinicians. A five-session skills-training version of the curriculum is available in draft form and can be co-led by a clinician and non-masters level per-sonnel (e.g. correctional and probations staff). The training includes didactic presentations, demonstrations, role-plays, in vivo practice of skills (including mindfulness), and consultation on the following: clinical application of material, fidelity, flexibility, sustainability, and evaluation.

Teen Anger Management (TAME)

Lastly, a repackaged anger management program for teens has been reported by Feindler and Gerber (2011). This 10-session skills training manual expands on Feindler's earlier work (Feindler & Guttman, 1994) and adds sessions on bullying, relational aggression, and interpersonal effectiveness. A group approach is used to teach the basic anger management skills such as arousal management, cognitive restructuring of hostile attributions, assertiveness, problem-solving, and conflict negotiation. In addition to modeling, group trainers rely heavily on the use of role-plays, in session tasks, and between-session homework to help youths practice and hone these skills. The self-monitoring tool, The Hassle Log (see Appendix 17.C), helps youths to understand both the internal and external triggers for their aggressive thoughts and actions and also serves as a script for role-play scenarios. The concepts of choice, self-regulation, and personal responsibility in response to actual or perceived provocations are emphasized throughout. Appendix 17.D includes an overview of this protocol that has not yet been empirically validated but shows promise. An unpublished session-by-session manual is available from the authors.

Summary/Conclusions

Clinicians and researchers will be well served by being more involved in the process of translating and communicating the benefits and value of productive treatments for the public good for justice involved adolescents. The landscape is complex, and understanding the varied goals of stakeholders is essential to be effective with this population. Policymakers could make scarce prevention, intervention, and rehabilitation resources go further by defining which offenders are most amenable to treatment and which intervention programs are most cost-effective. There is sufficient evidence to support the implementation of multi-component CBT-based intervention protocols. However, what also seems necessary to ensure positive outcomes is the inclusion of a family and/or parent treatment component. Establishing a good working alliance with the family and remaining flexible in the implementation of a treatment program are key ingredients for success. Effective interventions will be time consuming and therefore expensive, at least at the onset. Staff will need comprehensive training, ongoing support and supervision, and access to youth and family members in order to deliver treatment programming that is effective in achieving the prosocial, interpersonal, and self-regulatory skills needed for healthy adolescent development.

References

Alexander, J., & Parsons, B. V. (1982). *Functional family therapy.* Monterey, CA: Brooks/Cole.

Berzins, L. G., & Trestman, R. L. (2004). The development and implementation of dialectic behavior therapy in forensic settings. *International Journal of Forensic Mental Health, 3,* 93–103.

Borduin, C. M., Mann, B. J., Cone, L. T., Henggeler, S. W., Fucci, B. R., Blaske, D. M., & Williams, R. A. (1995). Multisystemic treatment of serious juvenile offenders: Long-term prevention of criminality and violence. *Journal of Consulting and Clinical Psychology, 63,* 569–578.

Chamberlain, P. (2003). *Treating chronic juvenile offenders: Advances made through the Oregon Multidimensional Treatment Foster Care model.* Washington, DC: American Psychological Association.

Chamberlain, P., Moreland, S., & Reid, K. (1992). Enhanced services and stipends for foster parents: Effects on retention rates and outcomes for children. *Child Welfare, 5,* 387–401.

Chamberlain, P., & Reid, J. B. (1991). Using a specialized foster care treatment model for children and adolescents leaving the state mental hospital. *Journal of Community Psychology, 19,* 266–276.

Chamberlain, P., & Reid, J. (1998). Comparison of two community alternatives to incarceration for chronic juvenile offenders. *Journal of Consulting and Clinical Psychology, 66,* 624–633.

Cocozza, J., & Skowyra, K. (2000). Youth with mental health disorders: Issues and emerging responses. *Office of Juvenile Justice and Delinquency Prevention Journal, 7*(1), 3–13.

DeRosa, R., & Pelcovitz. D. (2008). Igniting SPARCS of change: Structured psychotherapy for adolescents responding to chronic stress. In J. Ford, R. Pat-Horenczyk, & D. Brom (Eds.), *Treating traumatized children: risk, resilience and recovery* (pp. 225–239). New York: Routledge.

Dishion, T. J., McCord, J., & Poulin, F. (1999). When interventions harm: Peer groups and problem behavior. *American Psychologist, 54,* 755–764.

Eddy, J. M., & Chamberlain, P. (2000). Family management and deviant peer association as mediators of the impact of treatment condition on youth antisocial behavior. *Journal of Consulting and Clinical Psychology, 5* (68), 857–863.

Eddy, M., Whaley, R., & Chamberlain, P. (2004). The prevention of violent behavior by chronic and serious male juvenile offenders: a two year follow-up of a randomized trial. *Journal of Emotional and Behavioral Disorders, 12,* 2–8.

Federal Bureau of Investigation. (2009). *Uniform Crime Reports for the United States, 2008.* Retrieved from http://www2.fbi.gov/ucr/cius2007/about/index.html

Feindler, E. L. & Gerber, M. (2011). Youth anger management treatment for school violence prevention. In S. Jimerson, A. Nickerson, M. Mayer, & M. Furlong (Eds.), *Handbook of school violence and school safety: International research and practice* (2nd ed., pp. 409–422). New York: Routledge.

Feindler, E. L., & Guttman, J. (1994). Cognitive-behavioral anger control training: A treatment manual. In C. W. LeCroy (Ed.), *Handbook of child and adolescent treatment manuals* (pp. 170–199). New York: Lexington Books.

Glick, B. (2006). G & G Consultants, LLC homepage. Retrieved July 16, 2008, from http://artgang0.tripod.com

Goldstein, A. P., Glick, B., & Gibbs, J. C. (1998). *Aggression replacement training: A comprehensive intervention for aggressive youth* (rev. ed.). Champaign, IL: Research Press.

Goldstein, A. P., Nensen, R., Deleflod, B., & Kalt, M. (Eds.). (2004). *New perspectives on Aggression Replacement Training: Practice, research, and application.* Chichester, UK: John Wiley & Sons, Ltd.

Greenwood, P. (2008). Prevention and intervention children programs for juvenile offenders. *The Future of Children, 18,* 185–210.

Habib, M., & Labruna, V. (2006). *The Adolescent Trauma History Checklist and Interview.* Unpublished measure.

Henggeler, S. W. (2011). Efficacy studies to large-scale transport: The development and validation of multisystemic therapy programs. *Annual Review of Clinical Psychology, 7,* 351–381.

Huey, S., Henggeler, S., Brondino, M., & Pickrel, S. (2000). Mechanisms of change in multisystemic therapy: Reducing delinquent behavior through therapist adherence and improved family and peer functioning. *Journal of Consulting and Clinical Psychology, 68,* 451–467.

Kim, H. K., & Leve, L. D. (2011). Substance use and delinquency among middle school girls in foster care: A three-year follow-up of a randomized controlled trial. *Journal of Consulting and Clinical Psychology, 79*(6), 740–750.

Leve, L., Chamberlain, P., & Reid, J. (2005). Intervention outcomes for girls referred from juvenile justice: Effects of delinquency. *Journal of Consulting and Clinical Psychology, 73,* 1181–1185.

Linehan, M. M. (1993a). *Cognitive-behavioral treatment of borderline personality disorder.* New York, NY: Guilford Press.

Linehan, M. M. (1993b). *Skills training manual for treating borderline personality disorder.* New York, NY: Guilford Press.

Nelson-Grey, R. O., Keane, S. P., Hurst, R. M., Mitchell, J. T., Warburton, J. B., Chok, J. T., et al. (2006). A modified DBT skills training program for oppositional defiant adolescents: promising preliminary findings. *Behavior Research and Therapy, 44,* 1811–1820.

Quinn, A., & Shera, W. (2009). Evidence-based practice in group work with incarcerated youth. *International Journal of Law and Psychiatry, 32*(5), 288–293.

Rhode, P., Jorgensen, J. S., Seeley, J. R., & Mace, D. E. (2004). Pilot evaluation of the Coping Course: A cognitive-behavioral intervention to enhance coping skills in incarcerated youth. *Journal of the American Academy of Child and Adolescent Psychiatry, 43*(6), 669–676.

Rose, D. J., & Church, J. R. (1998). Learning to teach: The acquisition and maintenance of teaching skills. *Journal of Behavioral Education, 8*(1), 5–35.

Santisteban, D.A., & Mena, M.P. (2009). Culturally informed family therapy for adolescents: A tailored and integrative treatment for Hispanic youth. *Family Process, 48*, 253–268.

Santisteban, D. A., Suarez-Morales, L., Robbins, M. S., & Szapocznik, J. (2006). Brief Strategic Family Therapy: Lessons learned in efficacy research and challenges to blending research and practice. *Family Process, 45*(2), 259–271.

Santisteban, D.A., Szapocznik, J., Perez-Vidal, A., Kurtines, W.M., Murray, E.J., & LaPerriere, A. (1996). Engaging behavior problem drug abusing youth and their families into treatment: An investigation of the efficacy of specialized engagement interventions and factors that contribute to differential effectiveness. *Journal of Family Psychology, 10*(1), 35–44.

Sawyer, A. M., & Bourdain, C. M. (2011). Effects of multisystemic therapy through midlife: A 21-year follow-up to a randomized clinical trial with serious and violent juvenile offenders. *Journal of Consulting and Clinical Psychology, 79*, 643–652.

Schaeffer, C. M., & Borduin, C. M. (2005). Long-term follow-up to a randomized clinical trial of multisystemic therapy with serious and violent criminal offenders. *Journal of Consulting and Clinical Psychology, 73*, 445–453.

Tighe, N., Pistrang, N., Casdagli, L., Baruch, G., & Butler, S. (2012). Multisystemic therapy for young offenders: Families' experiences of therapeutic processes and outcomes. *Journal of Family Psychology, 26*, 187–197.

Trupin, E. W., Stewart, D. G., Beach, B., & Boesky, L. (2002). Effectiveness of a dialectical behavior therapy program for incarcerated female juvenile offenders. *Child and Adolescent Mental Health, 7*, 121–127.

Suggestions for Further Learning

Books

Feindler, E.L., & Gerber, M. (2011). Youth anger management treatment for school violence prevention. In S. Jimerson, A. Nickerson, M. Mayer, & M. Furlong (Eds.), *Handbook of school violence and school safety: International research and practice* (2nd ed., pp. 409–422). Routledge.

Goldstein, A.P., Nensen, R., Daleflod, B., & Kalt, M. (Eds.) (2004). *New perspectives on Aggression Replacement Training: Practice, research and application*. Chichester, UK: John Wiley & Sons, Ltd.

Henggeler, S.W., Cunningham, P.B., Schoenwald, S.K., Borduin, C.M., & Rowland, M.D. (2009). *Multisystemic therapy for antisocial behavior in children and adolescents* (2nd ed.). New York, NY: Guilford Press.

Hoge, R.D., Guerra, N.G., & Boxer, P. (eds.) (2008). *Treating the juvenile offender*. New York, NY: Guilford Press.

Sexton, T. (2010) *Functional Family Therapy in clinical practice: An evidence-based treatment model for working with troubled adolescents*. New York, NY: Routledge.

Swenson, C., Henggeler, S., Taylor, I., Addison, O., & Chamberlain, P. (Eds.) (2009). *Multisystemic therapy and neighborhood partnerships: Reducing adolescent violence and substance abuse*. New York, NY: Guilford Press.

Journal article

Greenwood, P. (2008). Prevention and intervention programs for juvenile offenders. *The Future of Children, 18*, 185–210.

Appendix 17.A

Trauma History Checklist and Interview

Date: _____   Interviewer: _____

"Sometimes things happen to people that are extremely upsetting, things like being in a life-threatening situation. I'd like to ask if any of these kinds of things have happened to you at any time during your life. You don't need to give me a lot of details."

Place "Y" or "N" before each item. Write notes to the right and list the most significant trauma at the bottom of this sheet. Provide details only for A1. traumas as defined by the DSM-IV criterion for PTSD. Include information regarding age of onset and duration of trauma. It is not necessary to include detail about items endorsed if they were not traumatic. Include information that others may consider to be traumatic, even if the adolescent does not view it as such.

INCLUDE DETAILS HERE:
Please DESCRIBE any significant DETAILS for each A1 Trauma:
(include age of onset & duration)

1. _____ Have you ever been in a major natural disaster, like a hurricane, earthquake, or flood?
2. _____ Have you ever been directly affected by a terrorist attack like 9/11?
3. _____ Have you or anyone in your family been involved in or affected by a war?
4. _____ Have you ever been in a fire?
5. _____ Have you ever been in a serious car accident?
6. _____ Has there ever been a time when you were seriously hurt or injured?
7. _____ Have you ever been in the hospital or undergone treatment for any serious or life-threatening illness or injuries?
8. _____ Have your parents or sibling(s) ever been in the hospital or undergone treatment for any serious or life-threatening problems?
9a. _____ Has anyone ever hit you or beaten you up (physically assaulted you)?
9b. _____ Has anyone ever threatened to physically assault you?
10a. _____ Have you ever been hit or intentionally hurt by a family member?
10b. _____ If yes, did you have bruises, marks, or injuries?
11a. _____ Was there a time when adults who were supposed to be taking care of you didn't?
11b. _____ Have you lived with someone other than your parents while you were growing up?
11c. _____ Has there ever been a time when you did not have enough food to eat?
12. _____ Have you ever been homeless?
13a. _____ Have you ever *seen* or *heard* someone in your family/house being beaten up or
13b. _____ Have you ever *seen* or *heard* someone in your family/house get threatened with bodily harm?
14a. _____ Have you ever *seen or heard* someone being beaten, or seen someone who was badly hurt?
14b. _____ Have you ever seen someone who was dead or dying, or *watched or heard* them being killed? Was this person a stranger, acquaintance, close friend, or family member? _____ (specify)

15. _____ Has anyone ever told you details of how someone you were close to was injured or killed?

16. _____ Have you ever been threatened with a weapon?

17. _____ Has anyone ever stalked you?

18. _____ Did anyone ever try to kidnap you?

19a. _____ Has anyone ever made you do sexual things you didn't want to do, like touch you, make you touch them, or try to have any kind of sex with you?

19b. _____ Has anyone ever *tried* to make you do sexual things you didn't want to do?

19c. _____ Has anyone ever forced you to have intercourse?

19d. _____ Has anyone ever *tried* to force you to have intercourse?

20. Is there anything else really scary or very upsetting that has happened to you that I haven't asked you about? Sometimes people have something in mind but they're not comfortable talking about the details. Is that true for you?

Most Significant Traumatic Event(s)

Of the things we've talked about, which is the worst? Which still really bothers you?
Brief Description (include corresponding item number from the list above):
Date (Month/Yr)   Age   Duration

_____

_____

IF NO SUCH EVENTS, CHECK HERE ___

Appendix 17.B

Ten-Week ART Curriculum

Week	Skillstreaming	Moral Reasoning Training	Anger Control Training
1	*Making a Complaint* 1. Decide what your complaint is. 2. Decide who to complain to. 3. Tell that person your complaint. 4. Tell that person what you would like done about the problem. 5. Ask how he/she feels about what you've said.	*Jim's Problem Situation*	*Introduction* 1. Explain the goals of Anger Control Training and "sell it" to the youngsters. 2. Explain the rules for participating and the training procedures. 3. Give initial assessments of the A-B-Cs of aggressive behavior: A = What led up to it? B = What did you do? C = What were the consequences? 4. Review goals, procedures, and A-B-Cs.
2	*Understanding the Feelings of Others* 1. Watch the other person. 2. Listen to what the other person is saying. 3. Figure out what the person might be feeling. 4. Think about ways to show you understand what he/she is feeling. 5. Decide on the best way and do it.	*Jerry's Problem Situation*	*Triggers* 1. Review the first session. 2. Introduce the Hassle Log. 3. Discuss what makes you angry (triggers). 4. Role-play triggers. 5. Review the Hassle Log and triggers.
3	*Getting Ready for a Difficult Conversation* 1. Think about how you will feel during the conversation. 2. Think about how the other person will feel. 3. Think about different ways you could say what you want to say. 4. Think about what the other person might say back to you. 5. Think about any other things that might happen during the conversation. 6. Choose the best approach you can think of and try it.	*Mark's Problem Situation*	*Cues and Anger Reducers 1, 2, and 3* 1. Review the second session. 2. Discuss how to know when you are angry (cues). 3. Discuss what to do when you know you are angry. • Anger reducer 1: Deep breathing • Anger reducer 2: Backward counting • Anger reducer 3: Pleasant imagery 4. Role-play triggers + cues + anger reducer(s) 5. Review the Hassle Log; triggers; cues; and anger reducers 1, 2, and 3.

Appendix 17.B (*Continued*)

Week	Skillstreaming	Moral Reasoning Training	Anger Control Training
4	*Dealing with Someone Else's Anger* 1. Listen to the person who is angry. 2. Try to understand what the angry person is saying and feeling. 3. Decide if you can say or do something to deal with the situation. 4. If you can, deal with the other person's anger.	*George's Problem Situation*	*Reminders* 1. Review the third session. 2. Introduce reminders. 3. Model using reminders. 4. Role-play triggers + cues + anger reducer(s) + reminders. 5. Review reminders.

5	*Keeping Out of Fights*
	1. Stop and think about why you want to fight.
	2. Decide what you want to happen in the long run.
	3. Think about other ways to handle the situation besides fighting.
	4. Decide on the best way to handle the situation and do it.
		Leon's Problem Situation	*Self-Evaluation*
			1. Review the fourth session.
			2. Introduce self-evaluation.
			  • Self-rewarding
			  • Self-coaching
			3. Role-play triggers + cues + anger reducer(s) + reminders + self-evaluation.
			4. Review self-evaluation.

6	*Helping Others*
	1. Decide if the other person might need and want your help.
	2. Think of the ways you could be helpful.
	3. Ask the other person if he/she needs and wants your help.
	4. Help the other person.
		Sam's Problem Situation	*Thinking Ahead (Anger Reducer 4)*
			1. Review the fifth session.
			2. Introduce thinking ahead.
			  • Short- and long-term consequences
			  • Internal and external consequences
			3. Role-play "if-then" thinking ahead.
			4. Role-play triggers + cues + anger reducer(s) + reminders + self-evaluation.
			5. Review thinking ahead.

7	*Dealing with an Accusation*
	1. Think about what the other person has accused you of.
	2. Think about why the person might have accused you.
	3. Think about ways to answer the person's accusation.
	4. Choose the best way and do it.
		Reggie's Problem Situation	*Angry Behavior Cycle*
			1. Review the sixth session.
			2. Introduce the Angry Behavior Cycle.
			  • Identify your own anger-provoking behavior.
			  • Change your own anger-provoking behavior.
			3. Role-play triggers + cues + anger reducer(s) + reminders + self-evaluation.
			4. Review the Angry Behavior Cycle.

(*Continued*)

Appendix 17.B   (*Continued*)

Week	Skillstreaming	Moral Reasoning Training	Anger Control Training
8	*Dealing with Group Pressure* 1. Think about what the group wants you to do and why. 2. Decide what you want to do. 3. Decide how to tell the group what you want to do. 4. Tell the group what you have decided.	*Alonzo's Problem Situation*	*Rehearsal of Full Sequence* 1. Review the seventh session. 2. Introduce the use of Skillstreaming skills in place of aggression. 3. Role-play triggers + cues + anger reducer(s) + reminders + Skillstreaming skill + self-evaluation.
9	*Expressing Affection* 1. Decide if you have good feelings about the other person. 2. Decide if the other person would like to know about your feelings. 3. Choose the best way to express your feelings. 4. Choose the best time and place to express your feelings. 5. Express your feelings in a friendly way.	*Juan's Problem Situation*	*Rehearsal of Full Sequence* 1. Review the Hassle Logs. 2. Role-play triggers + cues + anger reducer(s) + reminders + Skillstreaming skill + self-evaluation.
10	*Responding to Failure* 1. Decide if you have failed at something. 2. Think about why you failed. 3. Think about what you could do to keep from failing another time. 4. Decide if you want to try again. 5. Try again using your new idea.	*Antonio's Problem Situation*	*Overall Review* 1. Review the Hassle Logs. 2. Recap anger control techniques. 3. Role-play triggers + cues + anger reducer(s) + reminders + Skillstreaming skill + self-evaluation.

Appendix 17.C

The ART Hassle Log

Facility: Trainer: Date:

ID Code: Module: Session of Module:

1. Where were you? _____

2. What was your **External Trigger?** (something that happened outside of your body that might make you mad, example – name calling, pushed, etc.)

_____

_____

_____

3. What was your **Internal Trigger?** (negative thoughts that might make you mad, example – everybody is also picking on me, etc.)

_____

_____

_____

4. What were your **Cues?** (things that happen inside your body to let you know that you are angry, example – fast heart rate, clenched fists, etc.)

_____

_____

5. How angry were you?

Not at all				Somewhat					Burning Mad
1	2	3	4	5	6	7	8	9	10

6. What **Anger Reducer** did you use?
Counting Backwards – Deep Breathing – If-Then Thinking – Pleasant Imagery

7. Which **Reminder** did you use? (positive thinking/instructions that help calm you down, example – Relax, Roll with the punches, It's their problem not mine, etc.)

_____

_____

8. What were the positive and/or negative **Consequences** of your behavior?

_____

_____

_____

9. Which **skill** from the Skillstreaming group were you able to use during this situation?

_____

10.　**Self-Evaluation**

Self-Rewarding: Which steps did you do well with? Check all that apply.

Identifying Triggers
Identifying Cues
Using an Anger Reducer
Using a Reminder
Coaching yourself
Rewarding yourself for a good job
Looking at the positive and negative consequences of your behavior

Self-Coaching: What could you improve upon?

_____

_____

Appendix 17.D

TAME (Teen Anger Management) Protocol

- *Intake and screening of youths referred for TAME*: Treatment readiness is examined; assessments conducted; introduction of TAME components, including self-monitoring tool known as the "hassle log."
- *Session 1*: Orientation to structure of TAME group and rationale for program. Understanding emotions with emphasis on anger. Practice identification of angry responses and deep-breathing relaxation exercise.
- *Session 2*: Sequential analysis of behavioral incidents (activating event or trigger, behavioral response, consequences). Youths practice identification of components using idiosyncratic angry and/or aggressive episodes.
- *Session 3*: Aggressive beliefs and interpretations. Group identification of various cognitive distortions; practice reattribution exercises.
- *Session 4*: Relationship strategies and interpersonal techniques. Introduction of interpersonal effectiveness skills adapted from dialectical behavior therapy (Linehan, 1993b).
- *Session 5*: Self-instruction training. Introduction of in-the-moment self-coaching techniques for non-aggressive behavioral responses.
- *Session 6*: Anticipation of consequences. Practice thinking ahead – prediction and evaluation of possible consequences of aggressive behaviors.
- *Session 7*: Problem-solving. Introduction of multi-step problem-solving process including self-evaluation, reinforcement, and feedback.
- *Session 8*: Relational aggression prevention. Build awareness of types of teasing, use of rumors, and methods to evaluate friendships. Practice confrontation, apologizing, and self-respect skills.
- *Session 9*: Program review. Exercises designed to utilize all skills and concepts introduced over previous eight sessions. Individualized feedback to students. Administration of final assessment instruments.
- *Session 10*: Follow-up booster session. Review of all skills, including definition, demonstrated examples, and discussion of appropriate situations in which skills can be used. Check in with students regarding changes and progress since completing the program, including successful and unsuccessful attempts to use skills. Provide feedback and reinforcement to encourage skill maintenance and generalization.

18

Culturally Responsive CBT in Forensic Settings

Andrew Day

Contemporary approaches to working with offenders typically locate the causes of offending within the individual; antisocial behavior is explained in terms of various socio-cognitive deficits that impair not only the capacity to reason, but also how the individual sees and understands the self, other people, and the wider world (e.g., Ross & Fabiano, 1985). Offenders are also seen as lacking the social problem-solving skills that are considered necessary to resolve problems that are often associated with everyday living (McMurran, Fyffe, McCarthy, Duggan, & Latham, 2001). When the causes of offending are understood in this way, it is easy to understand how the interventions that are typically offered in forensic settings focus on changing maladaptive cognitions[1] and on improving problem-solving and self-control. It is no surprise to learn that cognitive-behavioral methods of treatment are now widely regarded as the treatment of choice for forensic clients.

There is an accumulating, and rather robust, body of evidence to suggest that the cognitive-behavioral approach is likely to be particularly well suited to achieving the primary goal of most forensic services, to reduce the risk of further offending. A meta-analytic review by Lipsey, Landenberger, and Wilson (2007) (aggregating the findings of over 50 separate studies) reported that offenders who had received cognitive-behavioral treatment achieved a mean reduction of 25% in subsequent recidivism rates over those who had received other types of treatment. The vast majority of these studies, however, were either conducted with those who identified with dominant cultural groups or the cultural background of participants was not reported. Given that minority cultural groups are massively over-represented in forensic institutions around the world, the aim of this chapter is to consider how cultural issues might impact upon the delivery of cognitive-behavioral therapy that is offered to offenders.

---

[1] ...or what are commonly referred to as cognitive distortions. This is a term that has become widely used to refer to particular beliefs that are considered to be important causal antecedents to offending (i.e., criminogenic), and have been classified in terms of either primary (self-centered attitudes, thoughts, and beliefs), or secondary (blaming others, minimizing/mislabeling, and assuming the worst of others). The latter are commonly understood in terms of post hoc rationalizations and justifications of the offending behavior (see Gibbs, Potter, & Goldstein, 1995).

Forensic CBT: A Handbook for Clinical Practice, First Edition.
Edited by Raymond Chip Tafrate and Damon Mitchell.
© 2014 John Wiley & Sons, Ltd. Published 2014 by John Wiley & Sons, Ltd.

There is increasing awareness within psychological practice generally about the need to consider how cultural issues might impact on treatment. Professional organizations have, in recent years, made a strong commitment toward increasing the cultural competence of their members (e.g., the American Psychological Association, 2002), and a number of practitioner-oriented texts are now available that identify important differences in how treatment should be framed, how social and cultural issues are incorporated, and how the practitioner should relate to his or her clients (see Hays & Iwamasa, 2006; Oei, 1998). Competency in this area is often understood in relation to a personal process whereby the therapist first becomes more culturally aware and knowledgeable, and then learns how to establish a therapeutic relationship, conduct assessments, test, make diagnoses, and provide treatment. In the forensic setting, however, culturally relevant practice is more difficult to achieve given the need to deliver treatments that may be mandated or coerced, that have goals around community safety rather than personal distress, and that are typically directed at clients who have low levels of readiness for treatment (see Day, Casey, Ward, Howells, & Vess, 2010).

In this chapter these issues are considered in relation to the treatment of offenders who identify from indigenous cultural backgrounds in Australia. While it is clear that the circumstances facing indigenous clients and the communities in which they live are in many ways unique, the issues raised in this discussion highlight the extent to which cultural perspectives can impact on the way treatment is framed and how this might impact on the development of a strong therapeutic alliance. Much of the material discussed below will resonate with practitioners who work in other countries, such as the United States, Canada, and New Zealand, where indigenous peoples are also over-represented in the criminal justice system. It is also possible to draw parallels with the issues that arise in the treatment of other minority cultural groups, such as those who are refugees or recent migrants.

Indigenous Over-Representation in the Criminal Justice System

The term "indigenous" is used in this chapter to refer to both the Aboriginal and Torres Strait Islander peoples of Australia, and describes more than 600 different cultures and tribal groups representing the oldest continuous culture of people in the world today (Raphael, Swan, & Martinek, 2008). It is a group that is massively over-represented across all parts of the Australian criminal justice system. For example, an indigenous young person aged 10–17 years is 15 times more likely than a non-indigenous young person to be under supervision by a juvenile justice agency on an average day (Australian Institute of Health and Welfare, 2011).

A great deal has been written in the indigenous-focused literature to help make sense of these high rates of over-representation. Typically, these analyses identify social, rather than psychological, determinants of offending as the most significant. For example, following extensive community consultations, the Victorian Indigenous Family Violence Task Force (2003) identified five factors that contribute to family violence: inherited grief and trauma; dispossession of land and loss of traditional language and cultural practices; loss of traditional cultural roles and status; economic exclusion and entrenched poverty; and difficulties confronting the issues for both victims and perpetrators. There is an immediate contrast between this perspective and that of cognitive-behavioral treatment with its focus on socio-cognitive deficits, problem-solving skills, and improving emotional regulation.

Many of these factors pertain to the effects of the colonization of Australia and its aftermath. At the time of colonization, in 1788, Australia was regarded as *terra nullius* (translated literally as "land of no people"), and the indigenous inhabitants were dispossessed of their lands and denied basic human rights. The cultural, political, and economic inequities experienced by the indigenous population since that time have reinforced the view that colonization has continued up until the present day, albeit in other forms. For example, indigenous Australians were not given the right to vote until 1967, and it was 1992 before any land rights were recognized. There remains a gross disparity in the social, health, and mental health indicators between indigenous and non-indigenous Australians (Australian Institute of Health and Welfare, 2008), and it is in this social context that offending occurs.

Social Disadvantage

Berkman and Glass (2000), in seeking to understand how health might be influenced by social and structural factors, proposed that systemic factors shape social network factors, which, in turn, influence psychosocial mechanisms. The macro, or social structural conditions, that are identified as particularly influential are *culture* (see below – norms and values, social cohesion, racism, sexism, competition/cooperation, individualism/collectivism), *socioeconomic factors* (relations of production, inequality, discrimination, conflict, labor market structure, poverty), *politics* (laws, public policy, differential political enfranchisement/participation, political culture), and *social change* (urbanization, war/civil unrest, economic depression). These factors are thought to influence both the structure and size of social networks that are available to an individual, which, in turn, determine the level of social support, the extent to which social influence constrains or enables health behaviors, levels of social engagement, personal contact, and access to other resources such as healthcare or housing. It is easy to see how such models can be applied to understanding offending behavior, and how factors such as social support or access to services might moderate treatment outcomes. It is also possible to link the high levels of social disadvantage that are experienced by many indigenous offenders (and those from other cultural minority groups) to cultural issues, suggesting that in the case of indigenous Australians, the loss of culture has to be acknowledged before any therapeutic work can begin.

Cultural Determinants of Offending

From a social psychological perspective, culture can be defined as relational structures or groups that we engage with and that help to define who we are. In essence the groups we identify with contribute to our sense of self, "providing a source of personal security, social companionship, emotional bonding, intellectual stimulation, and collaborative learning" (Haslam, Jetten, Postmes, & Haslam, 2009, p. 2). Cultural identity thus provides us with a sense of place, purpose, and belonging.

Based on a series of interviews with violent offenders from different cultural groups, Seidler (2010) proposes that it is helpful to understand offending as a way of achieving social identity. Seidler argues that violent offending in cultural minority groups is particularly likely when other ways of achieving identity are limited and/or when individuals have a fragile sense of self. This may occur, for example, when individuals feel disadvantaged, discriminated against, or disempowered. Seidler's research suggests that offenders from individualist cultures act violently to pursue self-interest, whereas those from collectivist cultures offend for group-oriented reasons such as standing up for family, group, or race, fulfilling interpersonal obligations, or "saving face." Collectivist cultures, including indigenous and most Asian cultures, are those in which high levels of interdependence exist (Markus & Kitayama, 1991) and can be contrasted with individualistic cultures, such as those in most Western countries. In working with individuals who identify with collectivist cultural groups, for example, it would seem important to locate their experiences within those of the community from which they come. This may influence, for example, their attitudes to treatment and readiness to change (e.g., the extent to which the community identifies particular behaviors as problematic), views about the authority and legitimacy of the treatment provider (e.g., whether treatment is endorsed by the community), and the ways in which social networks can both constrain and enable change.

Two related psychological themes have been consistently identified as relevant to understanding offending in indigenous clients in a way that can inform their subsequent treatment and risk management. First is damage to the role and identity of indigenous men. Second is the significance of unresolved grief, loss, and trauma, with a particular emphasis on how this can translate into aggressive and violent behavior. These are each explored in turn.

Indigenous men's role and identity

Many researchers in this field contend that the offending behavior of some indigenous men is driven by a need to compensate for the sense of powerlessness that they experience in relation to the majority culture and their broader lives. For example, service providers to the indigenous population who delivered group-based cognitive-behavioral anger management programs to violent offenders reported that male offenders, especially younger men in urban areas, often experienced very low self-esteem and a pervasive sense of frustration, powerlessness, and anger (Mals, Howells, Day, & Hall, 1999). These men directed their anger and resentment not only toward mainstream society but also toward their parents, whom they saw as having failed them. They saw their emotional problems as arising directly from colonization, disconnection from the land, and a legacy of social and economic marginalization. Similarly, Blagg (2005) has suggested that the key narrative of loss in indigenous cultures relates to the "redundancy" of the indigenous male role and status, and argues that this is often compensated for by an aggressive assertion of male rights over women and children. In short, it is suggested that important aspects of indigenous men's lives have been damaged through colonial processes, including the loss of cultural knowledge, diminished education and employment prospects, the capacity to meaningfully support one's family members and kin, the ability to pass on a legacy in which one takes pride, and the sense of positive agency and empowerment that accompany these things. It is these aspects of identity that might become important areas of focus for culturally responsive treatment.

Intergenerational trauma, grief, and anger

Australian indigenous practitioners Koolmatrie and Williams (2000) suggest that grief is by far the most intense, enduring, and distressing psychological disturbance that is experienced by Indigenous peoples. They suggest that the grieving process can be expressed as both an individual and a group loss. In terms of intergenerational effects, they specifically identify anger as an important emotion: "I've spoken to people who say they've felt a real rage, going back in response to massacres and killings of their peoples. They've felt it inside of them and they say it has origins going back into the history of their families and peoples" (p. 161). Koolmatrie and Williams identify aspects of grief theory that may be relevant to understanding the indigenous experience – namely, of dependent grief, forbidden mourning, forbidden action, and inexpressible rage. Inexpressible rage may be a particularly significant grief reaction for indigenous men who engage in violence. Inexpressible rage is described as follows:

> Anger is a normal component of adjustment to loss. Irrational anger at the departed for abandoning those who remain, at medical staff for failing to save a life, at other survivors, at fate itself, is normal. If a child is murdered, the terrible, 'just anger' of the parents finds relief in the state's determined efforts to arrest and punish the culprit. But what happens when the state itself is the culprit? When 'just rage' is forbidden from any expression? (p. 163)

Such accounts draw attention to the relationship between life events, loss, and traumatic responses. Raphael et al. (2008) have argued that high levels of loss, premature mortality, and family break-up contribute to the present high levels of stress experienced by indigenous peoples. For example, in an Aboriginal Child Health Study undertaken in Western Australia, Zubrick and colleagues (2004) reported that 22% of Aboriginal children had experienced seven or more severe life events in the previous 12 months (i.e., on average one event every few weeks).[2] These experiences are described as often traumatic, leading to higher levels of mental health problems, in particular depression and symptoms of post-traumatic stress. The suggestion here, then, is that for some indigenous men at least, intergenerational grief and loss is experienced as pervasive, generalized anger that is passed on to each generation on the basis of collective memories and experiences and that, fundamentally, have no legitimate outlet. Combining this internal experience with alcohol abuse and/or a series of other stressors such as financial problems, interpersonal conflict, or feelings of jealousy (see below) may therefore create a direct pathway to violence that is often disproportionate to the triggering event.

There has been particular interest in how intergenerational and chronic personal experiences of trauma can lead to specific symptoms that fall outside the core post-traumatic stress disorder criteria. The concept of "complex trauma" (Herman, 1992, 1997) suggests that exposure to prolonged interpersonal trauma leads to a complex array of symptoms, including personality changes, depression, suicidality, and substance abuse, in addition to the core features of post-traumatic stress disorder (Golding, 1999). It has attracted the interest of those who research the effects of ongoing childhood abuse (e.g., Roth, Newman, Pelcovitz, van der Kolk, & Mandel, 1997) and may be particularly relevant to understanding the needs of indigenous offenders.

Our own research into indigenous men's perceptions of anger helps to articulate some of the connections between past experience (including historical) and present violent behavior in a way that can guide cognitive-behavioral treatment (Day, Nakata, & Howells, 2008). An analysis of interviews with indigenous men, both in prison and in the community, identified four general triggers to anger and violence: anger at their own situation; anger at family and others; anger at historical treatment; and anger at perceived injustice (see Table 18.1). These

---

[2] With the rates rising for children whose parent/s had been forcibly removed when they were children. In Australia significant numbers of indigenous children were removed from their families by the government in an attempt to assimilate them into the dominant Western culture. This practice was widespread up until the late 1970s (see Commonwealth of Australia, 1997).

Table 18.1   Triggers and functions of violent offending in indigenous male prisoners.

General triggers	Functions of violence	Statements indicative of underlying beliefs
Anger at own situation Anger at family and others Anger at historical treatment, both in terms of their personal childhood experiences and family histories and in terms of the treatment of the indigenous population as a whole Anger at perceived injustice *Specific or immediate triggers* Frustration: at the world; at racism; at others; at small things Provocation: the perceived actions of others that provoke or require some response Perceived wrongful treatment Perceived wrongful treatment of family members by others Thinking or not processing thoughts positively Inability to express oneself Memory Inability to handle others' anger and verbal abuse Tiredness (of being pushed down, of name-calling) Drug and alcohol intoxication	*Retaliation* (a) as a response to being threatened, to stop abuse, or became an option that made sense for purposes of self-defence (b) as a defensive or protective strategy after abuse in childhood when the client had been too small to do anything *Inviting violence* (a) Tired of being threatened (b) As a form of self-harm and/or of deliberately encouraging a situation where anger could be released *Being charged up with alcohol or drugs*	*"…I actually thought if I wasn't going to do anything I was going to get hurt. I suppose that's why I got so vicious. Don't know if you understand, but you start playing for keeps…"* *"When I was younger I was too frightened to do anything, to fight back…. Till I started filling out and getting bigger than them and then I started retaliating back and getting into trouble…"* *"… acted out with anger and rage and almost throttled him you know and stopped him from abusing…so he never abused me, or my foster mother again after that."* *"hit me, don't shit me." "…I'd go into a place I know where there would be a violent situation in pubs or something, and I'd go and pick that biggest, ugliest looking bloke in there and I'd want him to hurt me, that was one way of self-harm you know and self-hatred…"* *"I wanted them to hurt me type of thing, but I'd fight them 'cos I'd take all my anger out on them…".* *"Drink too much of course and I don't know what I'm doing, or what I've done. I know I done something silly…"* *"I found release when I finished with all my fitness and everything…I was a very violent alcoholic."*

Source: Adapted from Nakata et al. (2008); first published in Day, Nakata, & Howells (eds.) (2008). *Anger and Indigenous Men.* © Federation Press.

general conditions appeared to "wrap around" the more immediate or specific triggers for anger reported by men, such as specific family problems; alcohol and other drugs; direct experiences of loss; and direct experiences of perceived discrimination. Contextual triggers were also identified by the men, and consistently fell into four categories:

- Growing up with disrupted family lives, defined as at least one (and often more) of the following experiences: Removal from families; institutionalization; foster care; juvenile detention; moving back and forth between institutions, foster care, and/or families; living apart from siblings or one or both parents that resulted in intermittent, complicated, or unresolved or ambivalent relationships between family members.
- Growing up experiencing or witnessing anger and/or violence, and being exposed to pervasive and sustained historical and contemporary anger across individuals, families and communities.
- Drug and alcohol abuse to block out pain, cope with life, and socialize. Its disinhibiting effects were seen as providing an outlet or a form of release through violence, including deliberately inciting violence as a form of self-harm.
- Feelings of powerlessness experienced on a daily basis, and a range of associated emotions leading to anger and violence, including frustration, being overwhelmed, being trapped, feeling threatened, feeling intimidated, loss of control, and fear of loss of control.

Key Considerations in Making Forensic CBT More Culturally Responsive

So what might this mean for those who are interested in delivery of cognitive-behavioral treatment (CBT) in a culturally responsive manner? The cultural perspectives described above suggest that a number of modifications should be made to how forensic CBT is delivered if it is to be regarded as culturally responsive. These are described below in terms of the contradictions that exist between the ways in which psychologists have been trained to practice and the ways in which relationships are typically structured in indigenous communities as identified by McConnochie, Ranzijn, Hodgson, Nolan, and Sampson (2012) in a series of interviews with non-indigenous psychologists who work with indigenous clients. They are used below to discuss how non-indigenous practitioners might work in more culturally responsive, and effective, ways.

Engage with the community

An important prerequisite to working effectively with indigenous clients is to be accepted as a person who is able to demonstrate appropriate respect to other community members according to cultural protocols. In the indigenous context, there is little likelihood of people participating unless the wider community supports the treatment that is being offered. Jones, Masters, Griffiths, and Moulday (2002) have suggested a range of strategies that can help practitioners to engage with the communities and establish their credentials. These include regular, ongoing cultural awareness training, cultural oversight and advice (from indigenous reference groups, elders councils, or other indigenous bodies), and regular cultural supervision from cultural experts to assist with matters of everyday practice. Similar suggestions are made by Vicary and Bishop (2005), who suggest that before undertaking assessment and therapy with indigenous clients there is a need for the practitioner to reflect on his or her own motives for wanting to work with indigenous clients and to undertake formative preparation (e.g., cultural awareness training, build relationships with indigenous colleagues, organizations and communities, and establish professional and cultural supervision mechanisms).

Establish rapport

McDermott (2008) has highlighted the need for non-indigenous workers to develop a range of specific skills and strategies when delivering psychological interventions to indigenous clients. These include an understanding of local indigenous community issues, cultural protocols and histories (what he refers to as being "clued in"), demonstrating a commitment to developing long-term relationships with clients and the communities in which they live, and using self-disclosure. McDermott argues that people from indigenous cultures often need to find out who a person *is*, and where they're *from*, suggesting that an effective, culturally safe way of building trust is allowing yourself to become known for "*who* you are," not "*what* you are/what you know." He identifies reciprocity, or the *sharing* of information, as central to establishing rapport. This contrasts markedly with the debates in professional psychology about the value of therapist self-disclosure to clients (Tjeltveit, 1999).

Develop communication strategies

In a project to improve the cultural responsiveness of a mainstream psychological treatment, McDermott (2006) highlighted the importance of what he calls "deep listening." He notes that many health professionals work from models of "professional distance," or feel required to maintain prescribed therapeutic relationships, but argues that where a power imbalance exists this approach can be seen as one-dimensional, alienating, culturally unsafe, and ineffective. McConnochie et al. (2012), in their interviews with non-indigenous psychologists who work with indigenous clients, described how they might "do things differently," including when, where, and how long sessions lasted. For example, some described meeting with clients outside of formal sessions, allowing more time to develop the relationship, and seeing them for shorter sessions but over longer periods than would be normally associated with cognitive-behavioral practice.

Decide on assessment tools

Considerable concerns exist about the application of Western definitions of mental health and illness to indigenous peoples, and the validity, reliability, and cultural appropriateness of psychiatric diagnostic tools. Hunter (2004), for example, has argued that:

> Psychiatry has, of course, attracted long and sustained criticism for the assumptions underlying its processes of classification and diagnosis across cultures. In relation to indigenous Australians there are also many disagreements and conflicting constructions – for instance, naïve 'psychology' that pathologizes indigenous cultural expressions; similarly naïve 'anthropology' that relativizes pathology as 'cultural;' professional investments that reject the 'medical model frame of reference;' and political agendas (well-intentioned or not) that result either in the medicalization of social problems or the subordination of fundamental mental health needs to wider social agendas
>
> Hunter (2004, p. 128; references removed)

The assessment tools that are routinely used in mainstream practice are rarely validated for use with cultural minority groups, norms are not available, and they may not consider culture-specific forms of mental illness such as those relating to "spiritual sickness" or complex presentations involving trauma, grief, and intergenerational factors. In the forensic context, where it is important to provide data to support clinical opinion and where the results of an assessment can have a profound influence on an offender's future, norms for psychometric measures are rarely available for specific cultural groups.

Language, one of the central features of any culture, may also influence how problems are defined in the development of assessment tools. To illustrate, one of the most widely used anger inventories, the STAXI-2 (Spielberger, 1991), was developed from Lakoff's psycholinguistic analysis of English metaphors for anger as a conceptual basis for developing the "anger-in" control scale (Spielberger, Reheiser, & Sydeman, 1995). Spielberger (1991) uses Lakoff's distinction between "keeping it bottled up and not letting it escape" and "reducing the intensity of suppressed anger by cooling down inside" to develop separate scales to assess controlling the expression of anger in aggressive behavior and reducing the intensity of suppressed anger by calming down inside. These are clearly culturally defined terms that draw on traditional Freudian notions of strangulated affect (Freud, 1961), invoking a hydraulic metaphor whereby angry feelings are kept in check until the pressure exceeds the capacity of the person's psychological resources to resist. Anger is thus conceptualized as being expressed in conditions of extreme arousal when existing psychological defenses break down (Davey & Day, 2007), and this may be a cultural construction. It is not clear whether similar concepts exist in the many different traditional indigenous languages.

When conducting a cognitive-behavioral assessment it is particularly important to understand the specific triggers and beliefs that maintain the problem behavior. Based on a series of qualitative interviews with indigenous prisoners, Nakata et al. (2008) identified a range of different proximal and distal antecedents for angry aggression, and provided an analysis of the statements men made about their about anger (see Table 18.1). These are indicative of beliefs that underpin angry aggression and offer a concrete illustration of the kind of belief that might be subjected to scrutiny in treatment. What is striking about these accounts is the consistency with which participants referred to an accumulation of triggering events and how this had influenced the way in which they reacted. Consider the following quote, for example: "And also as an aboriginal person I, not in that instant, but when I'm confronted, I don't think in a straight way. Oh yeah all these different things that have happened, but when they are piled up on top of the other, I just feel anger because of that snide remark, or that look that happened down that street." For all of these men, anger was synonymous with verbal and threatening aggression and/or physical violence.

Implementing response (treatment)

Interviewees in the McConnochie et al. (2012) study talked about the need to provide practical help to their clients, rather than focused psychological interventions. Others spoke about non-directive listening; for example: "For some of them, they wanted to just have a yarn [talk]. So that in itself was like therapy for them, just to be listened to and just not be judged" (McConnochie et al., 2012, p. 6). This perhaps illustrates the possible danger of compromising the integrity of treatment in an attempt to be culturally responsive.

In our study of anger and violence in indigenous men in prison (Day et al., 2008), we concluded that it was important to ensure that cognitive-behavioral treatment strategies were delivered (given the evidence base supporting their efficacy), but that they needed to be located within a cultural context of personal and intergenerational trauma. The importance of this strategy becomes apparent when one seeks to develop a case formulation that captures the experience of indigenous offenders. Case formulation in the forensic context can be understood in terms of an understanding of the circumstances in which further offending is most likely to occur, and how risk might best be managed. Thus while the assessment essentially leads to a *description* of the presenting problem, the case formulation develops an *explanation* that can be used to inform subsequent intervention and management (Casey, Day, Vess, & Ward, 2012). Acknowledging the cultural context in which offending behavior occurs seems integral to developing any meaningful explanation of problematic behavior.

Locating individual problems within a cultural and social context is likely not only to make sense to individual participants, but also may help to enlist the wider support of the broader indigenous community. This is seen as essential if treatment is to be both effective and sustainable. For example, treatment methods that seek to address problems with emotional recognition and awareness can still be used in the early stages of treatment, before using exposure to current provocations as the therapeutic material of later sessions. However, in our work, we complemented this with a story-telling method in which participants were invited to tell their own stories about anger to encourage personal reflection and consider the identity issues that face indigenous men more generally. Listening to the stories of others in a group setting was regarded both as culturally appropriate and clinically important. It led to some therapeutically useful discussions about personal responsibility for behavior in the context of cultural loss.

An alternative, or perhaps complementary, approach is to adapt mainstream offender group program activities to make them more culturally responsive. Jones and Atkinson (2008) have described how they approached this task in a cognitive skills offending behavior program, which utilizes cognitive-behavioral methods (Table 18.2). These activities provide concrete examples of how group treatment sessions can be delivered in ways that are considered culturally safe and can facilitate the engagement of offenders with program content.

Conclusion

What emerges from this chapter is the idea that personal histories and broader socio-political circumstances cannot, and should not, be separated when delivering cognitive-behavioral interventions with forensic clients. Indeed, it is suggested that only by virtue of the interconnections between these two levels of experience can offending be appreciated and understood. In the indigenous context, cultural responsiveness affects not only the way in which forensic CBT might be practiced but also the way in which risk is conceptualized. This is illustrated in this chapter by considering discussion of the needs of a cultural group characterized as collectivist in orientation and which experiences significant social disadvantage and the loss of traditional culture. In short, it would seem difficult to deliver effective treatment without an appreciation of how these experiences shape the way an individual views him or herself, other people, and the world.

Notwithstanding these issues, recent years have seen significant progress in how cognitive-behavioral methods can be used to successfully treat forensic clients (Andrews & Bonta, 2010) and it is important that this knowledge is used to inform the development of culturally responsive approaches to assessment and intervention. The conclusion from this chapter is that it may not be necessary to change the way relevant thinking targets and core beliefs are identified, or to alter strategies for disputing problematic thoughts or beliefs and reinforce new thinking and behavior patterns in order to provide culturally responsive treatment to forensic clients. There are, however, some critically important differences in how treatment should be framed, how social and cultural issues are incorporated, and in how the practitioner should relate to his or her clients. Such suggestions are consistent with what is considered good practice in working with cultural minority groups generally (Hays & Iwamasa, 2006) and although there are additional challenges in working in forensic settings, there are grounds for some optimism that properly designed and culturally relevant programs for offenders can have a meaningful impact on the safety of both the individual clients and the communities in which they live.

Table 18.2   Cultural adaptations to group offending behavior programs.

Adaptation	Example
Different strategies are used to introduce the program and start each session	Display map showing Australia according to indigenous tribal boundaries of land and country Group members introduce themselves by showing and discussing where they come from, with the map being displayed in all sessions thereafter Each session begins with a "Talking Circle," which includes reflection of the week since the last session A "Talking Stick" may be used as a tool to assist communication, connection, and participation of all group members in discussions and debriefing
More time is allowed for the group to form, with self-disclosure and offense disclosure occurring later in the program	Inclusion of a cultural camp in which participants are invited to talk individually about their offending, and then discuss in a group Program sessions are based around discussion and reflection rather than psychoeducation Sessions are less formal and less structured than in other programs
Focus on identity and personal and community strengths and survival	The program is based around developing a commitment to personal change arising from an awareness of each individual's personal history and development and how this fits in with the history and development of the local indigenous community Community members are invited to contribute to sessions, and organize activities for the group in the afternoon session
Traditional craft activities are integrated into the program	Use of a mural Men inscribe a shield Women decorate ornamental boxes
Aboriginal colors are used wherever possible	Flags are displayed in each session (Torres Strait Islander and Aboriginal)
Content of role-play and discussion topics more closely reflects Aboriginal interests, concerns and community conditions	Situations involving racism, discrimination, police harassment Being tempted to commit crimes due to material need Conflicts with government agencies or indigenous community-controlled organizations Drawing attention to community factors as well as individual and family factors (e.g., in their decisions to offend/not offend) Resolving conflicts between individuals that are underpinned by a longstanding family or community issue Resisting peer pressure involving substance abuse and crime
Literacy-based activities are altered to incorporate other modes of learning where possible	In a "recognizing feelings" activity, group members take photographs of each other acting out different emotions Problem-solving steps can be presented as stepping stones across a river Future planning involved a timeline chart on the floor and participants walking to the 6-month, 1-year, and 5-year points and saying what they see for themselves at each point, rather than writing it down Use of the mural Videos reflecting indigenous content are shown

(Continued)

Table 18.2   (*Continued*)

Adaptation	Example
Elements of a "rite of passage" are built into the final session	The formal presentation of certificates for graduation Giving of gifts to the facilitator from the participants
Consideration of gender issues	When an issue arises in the group that cannot be discussed in front of a woman, participants drop a note about the issue in the box. Then a session is conducted by a male facilitator (elder or mentor) to address the men-only issues together

Source: Adapted from Jones & Atkinson (2008); first published in Day, Nakata, & Howells (eds.) (2008). *Anger and Indigenous Men.* © Federation Press.

A more intriguing possibility, perhaps, is that further consideration of how culture and social disadvantage impact individual psychopathology might lead to improvements in the way in which CBT is delivered to all offenders, including those who identify with dominant cultural groups. Not only do offenders typically come from highly disadvantaged backgrounds but also there is significant current interest in developing ways in which interventions might be framed around an exploration of social identity.

Acknowledgment

I would like to thank Robin Jones for her insight and contribution to the work described in this chapter.

References

American Psychological Association. (2002). *Guidelines on multicultural education, training, research, practice, and organizational change for psychologists.* Retrieved from http://www.apa.org/pi/oema/resources/policy/multicultural-guidelines.aspx

Andrews, D. A., & Bonta, J. (2010). Rehabilitating criminal justice policy and practice. *Psychology, Public Policy, and Law, 16*, 39–55.

Australian Institute of Health and Welfare. (2011). *Juvenile justice in Australia 2008–09* (Juvenile justice series No. 7). Canberra: Author. Retrieved from http://www.aihw.gov.au

Australian Institute of Health and Welfare. (2008). *The health and welfare of Australia's Aboriginal and Torres Strait Islander Peoples.* Canberra: Author.

Berkman, L., & Glass, T. (2000). Social integration, social networks, social support and health. In L. Berkman & I. Kawachi (Eds.), *Social epidemiology* (pp. 143–173). New York: Oxford University Press.

Blagg, H. (2005). *A new way of doing justice business? Community justice mechanisms and sustainable governance in Western Australia.* Background Paper No. 8. Law Reform Commission of Western Australia, State Solicitor's Office.

Casey, S., Day, A., Vess, J., & Ward, T. (2012). *Foundations of offender rehabilitation.* London: Routledge Publishing.

Commonwealth of Australia (1997). *Bringing Them Home: Report of the National Inquiry into the Separation of Aboriginal and Torres Strait Islander Children from Their Families.* Canberra: Australian Government.

Davey, L., & Day, A. (2007). The poetics of anger control: Metaphorical conceptualizations of anger expression in violent offenders. In J. P. Welty (Ed.), *Psychology of anger* (pp. 293–309). New York: Nova Science Publishers.

Day, A., Casey, S., Ward, T., Howells, K., & Vess, J. (2010). *Transitions to better lives: Offender readiness and rehabilitation.* Cullompton, UK: Willan Press.

Day, A., Nakata, M., & Howells, K. (2008). *Anger and indigenous men: Understanding and responding to violence.* Annandale, NSW: Federation Press.

Freud, S. (1961). *The ego and the id* (J. Stachey, Trans.). New York: W.W. Norton. (Original work published 1923)

Gibbs, J. C., Potter, G. B., & Goldstein, A. P. (1995). *The EQUIP Program: Teaching youth to think and act responsibly through a peer-helping approach.* Champaign, IL: Research Press.

Golding, J. M. (1999). Intimate partner violence as a risk factor for mental disorders: A meta-analysis. *Journal of Family Violence, 14* (2), 99–132. doi: 10.1023/a:1022079418229.

Haslam, S. A., Jetten, J., Postmes, T., & Haslam, C. (2009). Social identity, health and well-being: An emerging agenda for applied psychology, *Applied Psychology, 58,* 1–23.

Hays, P. A., & Iwamasa, G. Y. (Eds.). (2006). *Culturally responsive cognitive-behavioral therapy: Assessment, practice,and supervision.* Washington, DC: American Psychological Association.

Herman, J. L. (1992). Complex PTSD: A syndrome in survivors of prolonged and repeated trauma. *Journal of Traumatic Stress, 5* (3), 377–391. doi: 10.1002/jts.2490050305.

Herman, L. (1997). *Trauma and recovery* (2nd ed.). New York: Basic Books.

Hunter, E. (2004). Commonality, difference and confusion: Changing constructions of Indigenous mental health. *Australian e-journal for the Advancement of Mental Health, 3,* 1–4.

Jones, R. L., & Atkinson, G. (2008). The Koori cognitive skills program redevelopment project: Findings and implications for other Indigenous offender rehabilitation programs. In A. Day, M. Nakata, & K. Howells (Eds.), *Indigenous men and anger: Understanding and responding to violence* (pp. 160–177). Annandale, NSW: Federation Press.

Jones, R. L., Masters, M., Griffiths, A., & Moulday, N. (2002). Culturally relevant assessment of Indigenous offenders: A literature review. *Australian Psychologist, 37,* 187–197.

Koolmatrie, J., & Williams, R. (2000). Unresolved grief and the removal of Indigenous children. *Australian Psychologist, 35,* 158–166.

Lipsey, M. W., Landenberger, N. A., & Wilson, S. J. (2007). Effects of cognitive-behavioural programs for criminal offenders. *Campbell Systematic Reviews, 6,* 1–30.

Mals, P., Howells, K., Day, A., & Hall, G. (1999). Adapting violence programs for the Aboriginal offender. *Journal of Offender Rehabilitation, 30,* 121–135.

Markus, H. R., & Kitayama, S. (1991). Culture and the self: Implications for cognition, emotion, and motivation. *Psychological Review 98,* 224–253.

McConnochie, K., Ranzijn, R., Hodgson, L., Nolan, W., & Sampson, R. (2012). Working in Indigenous contexts: Self-reported experiences of non-Indigenous Australian psychologists. *Australian Psychologist, 47,* 204–212. doi: 10.111/j.1742-9544.2011.00042.x

McDermott, D. (2006, December). *Understanding indigenous mental distress.* Presentation for VAC-CHO at St Vincent's Hospital, Melbourne.

McDermott, D. (2008, September). *Deep listening: Working with Indigenous mental distress.* Workshop on Social and Cultural Transitions, Northern Territory.

McMurran, M., Fyffe, S., McCarthy, L., Duggan, C., & Latham, A. (2001). *"Stop & Think!": Prevention and offender rehabilitation.* Ottawa, Canada: Air Training & Publications.

Nakata, M., Day, A., Howells, K., Wanganeen, R., McCausland, R., De Santolo, J., Nakata, V., & Havini, T. (2008). Beneath the surface of anger: Understanding the context of Indigenous men's anger. In A. Day, M. Nakata, & K. Howells (Eds.), *Indigenous men and anger: Understanding and responding to violence* (pp. 103–131). Annandale, NSW: Federation Press.

Oei, T. (1998). *Behavior therapy and cognitive-behaviour therapy in Asia.* Glebe, NSW: Edumedia.

Raphael, B., Swan, P., & Martinek, N. (2008). Intergenerational aspects of trauma for Australian Aboriginal people. In Y. Danieli (Ed.), *International handbook of multigenerational legacies of trauma* (pp. 327–339). New York: Plenum.

Ross, R. R., & Fabiano, E. A. (1985). Time to Think: A cognitive model of delinquency social problem-solving therapy with personality-disordered offenders. *Criminal Behaviour and Mental Health, 11,* 273–285.

Roth, S., Newman, E., Pelcovitz, D., van der Kolk, B., & Mandel, F. S. (1997). Complex PTSD in victims exposed to sexual and physical abuse: Results from the DSM-IV field trial for Posttraumatic Stress Disorder. *Journal of Traumatic Stress, 10,* 539–555.

Seidler, K. (2010). *Crime, culture and violence: Understanding how masculinity and identity shapes offending.* Bowen Hills: Australian Academic Press.

Spielberger, C. D. (1991). *State-Trait Anger Expression Inventory: Revised Research Edition: Professional Manual.* Odessa, FL: Psychological Assessment Resources.

Spielberger, C. D., Reheiser, E. C., & Sydeman, S.J. (1995). Measuring the experience, expression and control of anger. In H. Kassinove (Ed.), *Anger disorders* (pp. 49–67). Philadelphia: Taylor & Francis.

Tjeltveit, A. C. (1999). *Ethics and values in psychotherapy.* Florence, KY: Taylor & Francis/Routledge.

Vicary D. A., & Bishop, B. J. (2005). Western psychotherapeutic practice: Engaging Aboriginal people in culturally appropriate and respectful ways. *Australian Psychologist, 40,* 8–19.

Victorian Indigenous Family Violence Task Force (2003). *Final report.* Aboriginal Affairs Victoria, Department for Victorian Communities.

Zubrick, S., Lawrence, D., Silburn, S., Blair, E., Milroy, H., Wilke, T., & Li, J. (2004). *The Western Australian Aboriginal Child Health Survey: The health of Aboriginal children and young people.* Perth: Telethon Institute for Child Health Research. Available at http://aboriginal.childhealthresearch.org.au

Suggestions for Further Learning

Books

Day, A., Nakata, M., & Howells, K. (2008). *Indigenous men and anger: Understanding and responding to violence.* Annandale, NSW, Federation Press.

Hays, P. A., & Iwamasa, G. Y. (Eds.). (2006). *Culturally responsive cognitive-behavioral therapy: Assessment, practice, and supervision.* Washington, DC: American Psychological Association.

Oei, T. (1998). *Behavior therapy and cognitive-behaviour therapy in Asia.* Glebe, NSW: Edumedia.

Website

American Psychological Association. (2002). *Guidelines on multicultural education, training, research, practice, and organizational change for psychologists.* Retrieved from http://www.apa.org/pi/oema/resources/policy/multicultural-guidelines.aspx

Part IV
Emerging Ideas for Practice

19

Session-by-Session Assessment of Client Participation and Progress

David J. Simourd

Clinicians working within a forensic context have a front row seat to the unique characteristics, mannerisms, and thought processes of their clients. Simple observation of clients during clinical interactions reveals a vast array of useful information such as their physical characteristics (e.g., grooming, tattoos, physical disabilities, energy level), personal attributes (e.g., intellectual abilities, response style), cognitive orientation (e.g., degree of insight, interest in self-improvement, degree of dissimulation), and interpersonal skills (e.g., politeness, cooperativeness, respectfulness). The richness of this data is extraordinarily valuable in the formulation of a clinical opinion. This may be particularly true within the context of conducting forensic evaluations regarding such issues as criminal responsibility, sentencing recommendations, custody and release decisions, and/or future criminal potential (Heilbrun, 2009). These data can also be of considerable value in the context of a forensic treatment performance evaluation in which the objective is to determine the degree to which clients have benefited from therapeutic intervention. Unfortunately, surveys of clinicians (Hatfield & Ogles, 2004) and casual observation of the curricula of many standardized offender treatment programs indicate that this information is under-utilized in the evaluation of forensic client treatment performance. The purpose of the present chapter is to describe a multi-method approach of measuring treatment performance that uses dynamic client information obtained during the treatment process. In keeping with the orientation of this book, discussion of these procedures will be weighted more toward practical application than on theoretical/empirical considerations.

One problem in the typical analysis of forensic treatment success (i.e., its impact on recidivism and other outcomes) is that clients with a similar outcome are treated as though they changed an identical amount. That is, typically comparisons are made between some type of treatment and control group on recidivism, and comments are then made on the "effectiveness" of the program. The drawback to this approach is that group data are used to infer individual performance, which can create an artificial assumption that a certain client has progressed more or less than they have in reality, or in relation to their peers. In any group, there is always variability in the amount of genuine client change – some change considerably, some

Forensic CBT: A Handbook for Clinical Practice, First Edition.
Edited by Raymond Chip Tafrate and Damon Mitchell.
© 2014 John Wiley & Sons, Ltd. Published 2014 by John Wiley & Sons, Ltd.

modestly, and some change very little, if at all. Simply looking at a broad outcome such as recidivism as the only marker for treatment effectiveness may not capture the degree of client change.

Another problem with the current approach to determining treatment effectiveness is that treatment attendance is considered to be synonymous with treatment performance (i.e., success) in most clinical applications. In actual practice, the two are quite different. Treatment attendance means the client was in the room during the treatment process, whereas treatment performance relates to integrating treatment material into one's behavioral repertoire. Attendance alone is insufficient to correct behavioral disturbances among forensic clients (Simourd & Olver, 2011; Wormith, 1984). Skill acquisition is the key to promoting behavior change, which is consistent with both the notions of CBT and the principles of effective forensic rehabilitation. The failure to adequately measure client treatment performance may be perilous in the estimation of client treatment success. Perhaps an analogy may serve to drive home the difference between attendance and performance: Question 1: What do you call a person who finishes last in law school? (Answer: a lawyer). Question 2: Would you want this person representing you in court? (Answer: probably not).

Measurement of Participation and Progress

In the course of their clinical dealings with clients, clinicians are exposed to a wide range of client information that helps form the basis of their opinions about client progress. Meir (2008) suggests that the use of clinical process and outcome data can assist in decision-making because it offers both clients and clinicians feedback on treatment performance. Combine this notion with research (Lambert, Hansen, & Finch, 2001) showing that clients have better treatment outcomes when their progress is monitored, and a strong case can be made for the routine collection of client treatment progress data.

Unfortunately, client information related to treatment performance is often overlooked or under-utilized in the process of determining how much clients benefited from treatment. Surveys of psychologists (Hatfield & Ogles, 2004; Phelps, Eisman, & Kohout, 1998) find that a relatively small proportion (37% and 29%, respectively) collect outcome assessment data. Of the psychologists collecting data, the majority (e.g., between 60% and 74%) use standardized assessment instruments, with the Beck Depression Inventory (Beck, Ward, Mendelson, Mock, & Erbaugh, 1961) being the most popular. It is noteworthy that the Hatfield and Ogles (2004) survey found that clinicians using cognitive-behavioral therapy (CBT) were more likely to use outcome measures than were insight-oriented clinicians.

If clinicians have ready access to relevant treatment performance information and the collection of such information aids in the treatment process, then why do so few clinicians attend to it? In the Hatfield and Ogles (2004) survey of psychologists, the top four reasons offered for not collecting performance information were: (i) involves too much paperwork; (ii) takes too much time; (iii) places an extra burden on clients; and (iv) believe it is not useful. Appreciating whether these reasons are legitimate or not may depend in part on the styles by which typical client treatment performance data are collected. If the collection of treatment performance data is complicated or labor intensive, then acceptance of the reasons for not collecting such data are reasonable. However, if the methods of collecting such data are not overly burdensome, then the reasons for omitting treatment performance data become unacceptable. What, then, are the available procedures for collecting data on a client's treatment performance? The forensic clinical literature is virtually silent on this question; however, information exists within the general psychotherapy literature.

There are essentially two main types of client treatment performance data:

1. narrative summaries that essentially relate to clinical record keeping; and
2. administration of standardized assessment instruments.

It is a professional ethical responsibility, at least among psychologists (American Psychological Association, 2010), to maintain client records. There are, however, no guidelines as to the type and quality of information to be included in clinical records due to the complexity of differing clinical settings and varying styles of clinicians. In short, no standardization exists. It is within the context of record-keeping that most treatment performance opinions are expressed by clinicians. These tend to be narrative and quite often subjective (e.g., "*Mr K. has participated in treatment and seems to be better now than when he first began*").

The other broad approach to client treatment performance evaluation is based on the administration of standardized self-report assessment instruments. Normally the instruments administered are related to a specific clinical issue that can also be linked to general clinical symptoms. For example, a depressed client will be administered some type of depression measure whereas a client with anger control difficulties will be administered some type of anger instrument. The timing of the administration of the instruments can range from every session (Persons, 2008) to clinically opportune times during the treatment process (Whipple & Lambert, 2011), or pre-treatment/post-treatment assessment (Wormith, 1984). In any of these situations, the difference between the initial administration and subsequent administrations is used to infer treatment change. In a typical anger management intervention, for example, the client is administered an anger measure at the outset of treatment and readministered the instrument at the end of treatment. If the post-treatment score is lower than that of the pre-treatment administration then the client is viewed as "less angry," generally speaking.

There are obvious strengths and limitations of the narrative and assessment instrument methods of client treatment performance measurement. The narrative style provides valuable qualitative information but can be prone to subjective bias, which calls its accuracy into question. The standardized assessment instrument style offers accurate quantitative information but may be time consuming for the client (completing questionnaires) and the clinician (scoring and interpreting the questionnaires). Also, reliable instruments may be unavailable for certain clinical issues due to the complexities of human behavior. Integrating the two styles may be the best compromise.

A Session-by-Session Assessment Approach

Clinicians must be mindful of professional responsibilities, guiding clinical practices, and the uniqueness of individuals when providing treatment to clients. The pressure to balance these issues may tempt clinicians to adopt a complex client evaluation protocol with the hope of covering all bases. Alternatively, clinicians may become overwhelmed and adopt either a very rudimentary client evaluation process or no process at all. Neither of these situations need occur. The approach described in this chapter is a multi-method way of measuring client treatment performance that is uncomplicated but informative to the clinician and client. It consists of two broad areas of client measurement: (i) in-session client data, and (ii) adjunctive data.

One notable aspect of the present approach is its simplicity – with all relevant clinical data contained within a single document. The Clinical Session Notes document (a version of which appears in Appendix 19.A) is used to record both quantitative and narrative information pertaining to the client's presentation and functioning during clinical sessions. The upper and lower sections are typical of most clinical note-taking procedures. The upper section includes basic information such as client name, start and end time of session, location of session, and date. This information is mainly used for record-keeping purposes. The middle section quantifies four clinical indicators related to the client's in-session functioning. The quantitative information is used to rate the client's treatment performance and progress on various criteria. The lower section, identified as "notes," allows for narrative comments of the session. The narrative information is used primarily as a log of clinical activities addressed during treatment.

In-session client data: Quantitative

As can be seen from the Clinical Session Notes document, the second section covers four clinical indicators related to the client's in-session functioning. Based on clinical experience and previous use of this type of approach (Simourd, 2000), these four indicators are useful in the overall treatment performance evaluation of clients. The *Mood* indicator concerns the general orientation of the client in terms of both emotion (e.g., happy/sad, energetic/flat) and cognition (e.g., open/closed minded, reflective, dismissive). Mood is important in the treatment process because a client's mindset can influence the receptiveness to treatment target information. Clients who are in positive moods are more likely to be involved in session material and responsive to clinical suggestions whereas clients in a negative mood state are more likely to be argumentative or dismissive of treatment information.

The *Participation* indicator relates to the activeness of the client during the clinical session. Measuring client participation in treatment relates directly to the adage – "you get out what you put in." The degree to which clients are involved in treatment reflects their motivation for change and provides the clinician with information as to genuine treatment-induced change. Clients differ greatly on their degree of engagement with session content – ranging from the very curious and active to grossly uninterested (i.e., barely awake) and uninvolved. It is important to note that participation level must be relevant to the clinical task at hand. Some clients may be active in the session, but address irrelevant clinical tasks (which relates to the distinction between criminogenic and non-criminogenic factors). The reason for this may be either accidental (i.e., simply getting off topic) or a deliberate strategy to avoid discussing clinically important issues.

The *Insight* indicator concerns the degree to which clients integrate treatment information into their behavior repertoire. In other words, how much do they apply the treatment to their day-to-day lives. Insight is an important factor in human functioning. The greater a person recognizes their own strengths and limitations and makes behavioral decisions with these considerations in mind, the better life functioning they are likely to have. The notion of insight in treatment relates to the adage – "he can talk the talk, but he must walk the walk."

The final quantitative indicator, *Overall*, conveys the practitioner's broad sense of the entire performance of the client during the session. This indicator is not designed to be a simple aggregate of the other three criteria but rather an independent judgment of the client's total performance. In other words, the clinician should view the forest and not individual trees.

The four clinical indicators are scored using a typical five-point Likert-type scale, with lower scores reflecting weaker clinical treatment progress. The rating labels and their respective scores are:

1 = Far Below Expectation
2 = Below Expectation
3 = Meets Expectation
4 = Above Expectation
5 = Far Above Expectation.

These labels deviate from the traditional term of "average" (e.g., far below average, below average, average, above average, and far above average) because the intent of the current approach is to use an idiographic rating perspective, which measures clients against themselves, rather than the traditional nomothetic method, which measures clients against others. The current method is consistent with the responsivity principle of the Risk-Need-Responsivity (RNR) forensic treatment model that essentially relates to the issue of individual differences in human behavior (Andrews, Bonta, & Hoge, 1990). Two different client types may serve to illustrate this point. Client A is a shy and introverted person who attends all sessions on time, is neutral in mood (i.e., never obviously happy nor sad), is attentive to discussion topics but typically answers any questions with a simple "yes" or "no" or a very abbreviated answer. Client A tries to apply the treatment content to his life. For this client, the ratings on Mood, Participation, Insight, and Overall, may be "Meets Expectation" across all criteria. Client B is your typical boisterous extroverted client who attends regularly, is excessively energetic, constantly talking (essentially dominating the conversation), and offers numerous examples of attempts to integrate material into his/her behavior repertoire but invariably with failure. The ratings on Mood, Participation, Insight, and Overall, may be "Meets Expectation" across all criteria. Clearly these are two clients who have different conversational styles and mannerisms and each has related to the session information in their own unique way. That is, Client A is naturally shy and has a relatively low level of talking. However, when he talks it is on task and relevant to treatment tasks. Client B, on the other hand, talks a great deal but proportionally very little is related to the treatments tasks. Thus, both clients are rated as "Meets Expectation" on the performance criteria but for different reasons.

The third section of the Clinical Session Notes document concerns two clinical criteria related specifically to client functioning – *Clinical Symptoms*, and *Skills Utilization*. As indicated previously, a main theme in general psychotherapy relates to the reduction of problematic symptoms. Depressed clients, for example, seek relief from their low mood. Forensic clients are humans, after all, and vulnerable to the typical life disturbances experienced by non-forensic clients. Sometimes significant symptoms exist and sometimes they don't. Sometimes they exist and are relevant to the treatment process and sometimes they exist and are unrelated to the treatment process. Measuring these can assist in judgments regarding the clinical status of the client on an ongoing basis. The Clinical Symptoms criterion measures the degree to which psychological symptoms affect client functioning. The Skills Utilization criterion concerns the degree to which clients use the skills learned in treatment to resolve any clinical symptoms or challenging life situations. The essence of CBT is to understand and modify dysfunctional thinking and behavior patterns, which relates directly to skills utilization.

The two client functioning criteria are scored using a three-point Likert-type scale, with lower scores reflecting poorer status. The rating labels and their respective scores are:

1 = Problematic
2 = Normal
3 = Improved.

For the Clinical Symptoms criterion, a "Problematic" rating would apply in those instances where a client has obvious disturbance to their current functioning. A "Normal" rating would apply when the client has no significant symptoms, or they are stable; and the "Improved" rating would apply when a client has noticeable reduction of previous problematic symptoms and his/her functioning is enhanced. Client B, in the above example, was receiving treatment for anger control. He reported during one session that he was excessively angry the past week. When asked what he had done to manage his anger, he stated "nothing." In this instance, his Clinical Symptoms rating was "Problematic" because his anger affected his functioning. The rating for Skills Utilization was "Problematic" because he had not used any of the techniques discussed in treatment. The next session, however, things changed with Client B. He reported being less angry and that he was actually using various CBT techniques following the last session. His ratings were then "Improved" on both criteria at the next session.

In-session client data: Narrative

The narrative component of the Clinical Session Notes is consistent with traditional treatment note-taking. Relevant clinical information related to the treatment period is entered in this section. Clinicians must aim to balance parsimony and comprehensiveness in their record-keeping of client progress. Lengthy notes often result in a loss of clinical vitality whereas excessively brief notes can omit potentially important clinical information. As noted above, there is no standardization with respect to the type of information to be included in narrative clinical notes. The American Psychological Association (APA, 2010) suggests three general classes of information be recorded: general file information (e.g., name, contact information, referral source, plan of service), substantive contact documentation (e.g., style of intervention, mental status), and other information (e.g., extraneous case information, materials provided by client such as journals). The clinical experience of the author confirms the information captured by the APA's recommendations is sufficient to effectively monitor client treatment progress, although a change in how that information is organized is easier for clinical practice. It is suggested that clinicians attend to four main themes in narrative descriptions of client progress.

The first theme relates to the context of the session and initial orientation of the client to the session. Relevant information in this area includes the type of session (e.g., individual vs group), the session number (e.g., initial vs a string of sessions), the client's arrival time (e.g., on time vs late), and initial mood state (e.g., typical/different from previous sessions, talkative, cooperative, happy, angry). This theme provides historical and contextual information helpful to understanding the context of the session and the degree to which the client may be responsive to clinical suggestions offered during the current session.

The second theme relates to any non-treatment target events. Productive clinical sessions rarely begin by immediately barging into the treatment targets – quite the opposite. Psychologically based treatments such as CBT require a human touch, and brief "warm-up" casual conversation can ease into the treatment process. This warm-up, however, should be linked to the treatment process. For example, brief inquiry as to any substantive non-treatment target events that may have occurred since the last session is a nice way to begin the session. This discussion can be informative because it can aid in determining whether the client is distracted from the treatment intentions of the session. There are many possible non-treatment target events such as those related to social connections (e.g., family, friends, co-workers), vocation (e.g., work/school, financial), or life stability (e.g., accommodation, substance use). One way of beginning the discussion is to make a gentle inquiry such as: "*Has anything significant happened since our last session that you feel is important before we discuss specific topics?*" Clinicians must be cautious that a brief inquiry does not become a dominant discussion during the session, as it can be easy for either the clinician or client to get distracted (intentionally or unintentionally) from the treatment targets.

The third theme relates to specific therapeutic topics. This may include the introduction of new treatment information or a review of experiences the client had where he/she employed skills linked to the treatment process or any homework assignments completed by the client. For example, a client receiving treatment for anger management difficulties may be introduced to one of the typical A-B-C (antecedents, behavior, consequences; activating events, beliefs, consequences) models of CBT. In a subsequent session, the client may be probed as to whether any anger-eliciting situations occurred since the last session and to what degree they employed the A-B-C model and/or how the situation was managed.

The fourth theme in the narrative description of client progress relates to future sessions (e.g., date and time) and anticipated clinical activities. This information is helpful to the ongoing management of the case.

Adjunctive client data

Adjunctive data comprise client treatment information additional to the session performance ratings. Two types of adjunctive data are considered in the current approach: standardized assessment instruments, and homework assignments. As noted above, the use of standardized assessment instruments can be very helpful to the treatment evaluation process because they offer ranking type information on clinical topics. This allows determinations for the degree of problem, which can be used to inform decisions regarding treatment intensity (i.e., the risk notion of the RNR model). Take criminal thinking, for example: A client is administered a standardized measure of criminal attitudes prior to treatment and found to be in the "average" range based on a comparison reference group. This information is used to formulate the treatment plan. The same instrument is administered at the completion of treatment and the scores are in the "low" range. The difference is interpreted to mean the client is improved with the implication that treatment produced the effect.

Clinical work conducted outside treatment sessions can be helpful to accelerate the treatment process. Homework assignments can be particularly useful in this regard. CBT is a thought-based treatment, with the primary goal being to better recognize and modify problematic thinking. Thought records (logs of thoughts related to certain events) are homework-based tools designed to achieve these goals (Wilding & Milne, 2010). Thought records are typically used for clinical purposes in CBT; however, they are also a valuable source of treatment performance data – see Chapter 10 (Eckhardt et al.) and Chapter 13 (Wanberg & Milkman) for examples of thought records. Clients who regularly and diligently complete homework are often viewed as more involved in the treatment process than those clients who rarely complete homework or do so in a haphazard manner.

The full value of homework in the treatment evaluation process is to grade it using a quantitative method. The current approach rates homework on two simple criteria, *Effort* and *Insight*, using a Likert-type rating scale. The ratings of Effort and Insight are based on the same labels as the clinical indicators (e.g., Far Below Expectation, Below Expectation, Meets Expectation, Above Expectation, Far Above Expectation) with higher scores reflecting greater performance. The Effort criterion relates to the amount of energy expended on the homework, which is mostly reflected in how comprehensively the client addressed the assignment. The Insight criterion relates to the degree to which the client related the homework to him or herself. A client who records only tangential comments about the treatment material would be rated as "Far Below Expectation" whereas a client whose homework was very reflective to their situation would be rated as "Far Above Expectation." For example, a client is asked to complete thought records for anger incidents during a 1-week period. The client completes only two and these are very limited in detail and not linked to any treatment considerations. In this instance, "Below Expectation" ratings on both Effort and Insight may be appropriate. On the other hand, a client who completes several thought records with considerable detail, and links them to specific aspects of his or her life, may be rated as "Far Above Expectation." Information regarding homework ratings can be placed in the body of the notes section.

Timing of client ratings

Having the tools to measure client treatment performance is one thing, but using these tools can be something quite different. The majority of time spent with clients relates to direct clinical service. The documentation portion of clinical work assumes relatively less time but serves an important function in the treatment process, as has been alluded to in the present chapter. Moreover, client record-keeping may be the least desirable aspect of clinical work and, as such, clinician motivation for client record-keeping may not be particularly strong. This is likely true in the context of individual treatment sessions where recording treatment progress notes on a single client is required, but may be exacerbated in the context of group treatment sessions where recording the treatment progress of several clients is required. In spite of the clinician's workload and motivational issues related to record-keeping, it is nonetheless a vital component of the treatment process. The current approach is regarded as a parsimonious method of client record-keeping. The present author completes a Clinical Session Notes document for each client after each clinical session; whether it is an individual or group treatment. The completion time is relatively small but the benefits for client treatment performance evaluation are considerable.

Case Examples

To illustrate the practical application of the session-by-session assessment approach, several examples of Clinical Session Notes and Summary Reports are provided for a fictitious client. Appendix 19.B presents Clinical Session Notes typical of an initial session with a client (Mr Kidd). As can be seen, Mr Kidd was rated quite low on the quantitative indicators. With respect to clinical symptoms and skills utilization, the client had no significant difficulties when the assessment was done (which is not unusual during initial sessions) and thus a "Normal" rating was applied. The "Notes" portion provides qualitative information in a narrative style related to the main themes (i.e., initial orientation, non-treatment events, therapeutic topics, and future sessions) described above. It provides brief information about the client and his initial orientation toward the session, and treatment more generally.

Appendix 19.C provides a Clinical Session Note for the same client at the 15th session. With respect to the quantitative rating section, the ratings of this session reveal that the client had relatively normal mood ("Meets Expectation" rating) but he was very active in discussion and related it well to himself ("Above Expectation" for the other criteria). In addition, the client had no significant anger issues, and hence a rating of "Normal" for clinical symptoms. However, the client used CBT skills as reflected in discussion and his homework assignments, and thus his rating for skills utilization was "Improved." The narrative note section follows the same themes as the initial clinical note and sheds light on the clinical status of the client. For example, the client improved his session attendance style by being prompt, having a positive mood, and being respectful by removing his hat. These indicators suggest a change in the client. The non-therapeutic events section indicates he had additional positive changes in that he obtained employment. The therapeutic topics theme in the narrative note reveals that the client has actively used CBT techniques, and the quantitative ratings of his homework assignments reflect his progress.

Appendix 19.D provides the client's Treatment Summary Report, which integrates quantitative and narrative data from the course of treatment. Forensic clinicians are often required to provide written reports regarding their clinical activities with clients. A document that summarizes the clinical progress of a client is important to the treatment process. The timing of these reports, however, can vary depending on any number of circumstances, but a report commonly follows the completion of some specific clinical activity. For example, a clinician treating a client with CBT techniques across a range of treatment targets (anger, substance abuse, etc.) may complete a treatment report after each target has been addressed to some degree. Alternatively, a report may follow a set number of sessions. The time at which treatment reports are prepared is less important than the type and quality of information included in the report. For maximum utility, Treatment Summary Reports should try to balance professional demands, technical details, and brevity.

The first section provides a criminal history and sociodemographic background of the client. The next section (Treatment Objectives and Progress) outlines the number of sessions attended, the types of treatment topics covered, and the client's performance. This section includes both narrative and quantitative information. The last section (Summary) provides an overview of the clinical status of the client. The report is brief, only two pages, and is informative.

Appendix 19.E presents a Treatment Summary Report of the same client, but in this example participating in a structured group treatment program. Group treatment programs are quite popular in forensic contexts. The majority of these tend to be very structured and follow a standardized curriculum. In many ways, greater attention to client treatment performance measurement should occur in group treatment contexts than individual contexts. The main reason is that it is much easier for clients to avoid close scrutiny in group formats because of the sheer number of clients. The typical group format consists of at least 10 clients and one or two facilitators. The clinicians are often focused on presenting program content and attending to group dynamics, making it easy to overlook the performance of individual clients. The approach outlined in this chapter can assist clinicians in properly attending to the performance of all clients in a group session.

As can be seen in the report, both in-session and adjunctive data were utilized in the evaluation of Mr Kidd. It includes a brief description of the program and then describes Mr Kidd's performance. It also adds a narrative comment that goes beyond simple numbers and proffers a clinical opinion about his performance. At two pages in length, it certainly is parsimonious.

Summary

Front-line clinicians working in forensic settings are exposed to a great deal of information regarding the clients they serve. Although this information may be valuable for developing clinical opinions about clients, it seems to be under-utilized in the treatment evaluation process. For years, debates have raged in the academic literature regarding the effectiveness of treatment (e.g., Smith & Glass, 1977), the methods by which treatment evaluations are conducted by clinicians (e.g., Whipple & Lambert, 2011), and even the abilities of clinicians to form clinical judgments (e.g., Garb, 1998). Casual observation of this literature suggests the failings of clinicians are emphasized more than the accomplishments. The simple fact of the matter is that clinicians are not perfect and researchers are not always right. And in spite of the debates, clinical work will continue in forensic settings. Several advances have occurred over the years in the manner in which forensic treatment is delivered. Unfortunately, the methods by which client treatment performance is measured have not progressed at the same pace. The present client treatment evaluation approach aims to find a balance between clinical expertise and quantitative data such that the therapeutic success of clients is maximized.

The present approach offers a template to record both clinical and quantitative information obtained within therapeutic sessions. The method is simple and efficient, but clinically informative. The combination of in-session treatment performance ratings, adjunctive data such as standardized assessment instruments, and homework performance, provides a comprehensive understanding of client treatment gain. The sample treatment summary reports presented offer some guidance as to how this can occur. The one drawback with the present approach may rest with its simplicity. That a single document can be used to record narrative and quantitative clinical data may seduce users into abandoning the care and commitment required. Clinicians are human and therefore subject to the same natural decision-making biases as others (Garb, 1998). Users of the present approach must be vigilant in monitoring their objectivity in rating clients such that clients who do not improve during treatment are recognized to the same degree as those who do improve.

Author's Note

The author is grateful to all the colleagues and clients who have assisted in the evolution of thinking about how to deliver and measure clinical intervention within forensic psychology. Gratitude is also extended to Damon Mitchell and Raymond Chip Tafrate for their patience and editorial suggestions. Address all correspondence concerning this chapter to David Simourd, 86 Braemar Rd., Kingston, Ontario, Canada K7M 4B6. Email: dave@acesink.com.

References

American Psychological Association (2010). 2010 Amendments to the 2002 ethical principles of psychologists and code of conduct. *American Psychologist, 65*, 493.

Andrews, D. A., Bonta, J., & Hoge, R. D. (1990). Classification for effective rehabilitation: Rediscovering psychology. *Criminal Justice and Behavior, 17*, 19–52.

Beck, A. T., Ward, C.H., Mendelson, M., Mock, J., & Erbaugh, J. (1961). An inventory for measuring depression. *Archives of General Psychiatry, 4*, 561–571.

Garb, H. N. (1998). *Studying the clinician: Judgment research and psychological assessment*. Washington, DC: APA.

Hatfield, D. R., & Ogles, B. M. (2004). The use of outcome measures by psychologists in clinical practice. *Professional Psychology: Research and Practice, 35*, 485–491.

Heilbrun, K. (2009). *Evaluation for risk of violence in adults*. New York, NY: Oxford University Press.

Lambert, M. J., Hansen, N. B., & Finch, A.E. (2001). Patient-focused research: Using patient outcome data to enhance treatment effects. *Journal of Consulting and Clinical Psychology, 69*, 159–172.

Meir, S. T. (2008). *Measuring change in counseling and psychotherapy*. New York: Guilford Press.

Persons, J. B. (2008). *The case formulation approach to cognitive-behavior therapy*. New York: Guilford Press.

Phelps, R., Eisman, E. J., & Kohout, J. (1998). Psychological practice and managed care: Results of the CAPP practitioner survey. *Professional Psychology: Research and Practice, 29*, 31–36.

Simourd, D. J. (2000). *Evaluation of the Cognitive Intervention Program: The first follow-up*. Research report submitted to the Maricopa County Adult Probation Department, Phoenix, Arizona.

Simourd, D. J., & Olver, M.E. (2011). Use of the Self-Improvement Orientation Scheme-Self Report (SOS-SR) among incarcerated offenders. *Psychological Services, 8*, 200–211.

Smith, M. L., & Glass, G. V. (1977). Meta-analysis of psychotherapy outcome studies. *American Psychologist, 32*, 752–760.

Wilding, C., & Milne, A. (2010). *Cognitive behavior therapy*. Hodder Education.

Whipple, J. L., & Lambert, M.J. (2011). Outcome measures for practice. *Annual Review of Clinical Psychology, 7*, 87–111.

Wormith, J. S., (1984). Attitude and behavior change of correctional clientele. *Criminology, 22*, 595–618.

Suggestions for Further Learning

Journal article

Andrews, D. A., Bonta, J., & Hoge, R. D. (1990). Classification for effective rehabilitation: Rediscovering psychology. *Criminal Justice and Behavior, 17*, 19–52.

Book

Garb, H. N. (1998). *Studying the clinician: Judgment research and psychological assessment*. Washington, DC: APA.

Appendix 19.A

A Blank Clinical Session Notes Document

CLINICAL SESSION NOTES

Name:		Time:	
Location:		Date:	

	Far Below Expectation	Below Expectation	Meets Expectation	Above Expectation	Far Above Expectation
Mood					
Participation					
Insight					
Overall					

	Problematic	Normal	Improved
Clinical Symptoms			
Skills Utilization			

Notes:

Appendix 19.B

Clinical Session Notes for William Kidd's Initial Treatment Session

CLINICAL SESSION NOTES

Name:	Kidd, William T.	Time: 12:00–1:00
Location:	Office	Date: April 1, 2012

	Far Below Expectation	Below Expectation	Meets Expectation	Above Expectation	Far Above Expectation
Mood		X			
Participation		X			
Insight		X			
Overall		X			

	Problematic	Normal	Improved
Clinical Symptoms		X	
Skills Utilization		X	

Notes:
- Mr Kidd attended his initial individual session.
- He arrived late for his scheduled appoint., and seemed in a grumpy mood.
- Mr K. is a 30-year-old Caucasian male of average height/weight, and had a moustache.
- He wore a bowler style hat throughout the session, in what seemed like a lack of awareness or respect for social convention of being polite.
- He was soft spoken but had an abruptness to his style of conversation.
- Mr K. has been in the community for 3 months after serving a 5-year prison term for several burglary type offences against government industry.
- He is now on parole and was referred for anger issues.
- Mr K. was suspicious and resentful for being referred for anger treatment. He disagreed with the idea that he had anger problems.
- Mr K. reported he planned to associate with several of his companions and determine ways to generate income. He felt that any treatment appointments would interfere with his plans
- Future treatment considerations were explained to Mr K. This included several sessions to complete pre-tx. assessments to determine the precise treatment plan.
- He begrudgingly agreed to attend other sessions but requested a later appointment time.
- Next: – conduct pre-tx. Assessments.
    – April 13/12 – just before sundown.

David J. Simourd

Appendix 19.C

Clinical Session Notes for William Kidd's Subsequent Treatment Session

CLINICAL SESSION NOTES

Name:	Kidd, William T.	Time: 5:30–6:30
Location:	Office	Date: July 4, 2012

	Far Below Expectation	Below Expectation	Meets Expectation	Above Expectation	Far Above Expectation
Mood			X		
Participation				X	
Insight				X	
Overall				X	

	Problematic	Normal	Improved
Clinical Symptoms		X	
Skills Utilization			X

Notes:
- Mr K. attended his 15th individual session to address anger issues.
- He arrived on time, was in a positive mood, and was talkative. This is typical of his treatment state during the past several sessions. He didn't wear his hat.
- Mr K. reported he has sought legitimate employment; a first for him. He recognizes the need for positive experience and a source of income and to avoid problems in his life.
- As for treatment targets, Mr K. completed five thought records of his anger experience since the last session. He had considerable detail and related them to personal change he has had in the past few sessions. His ratings were 4/5 for effort and insight.
- The session focused on specific anger situations related to his friends.
- Mr K's friends are of an unsavory nature and have a negative influence on him. He has been making efforts to distance himself from them but finds this creates anger: something he rates as 8/10 (1 being no anger and 10 being extreme).
- We reviewed the A-B-C model and applied it to the situations with his friends.
- Mr K. agreed to work on this for our next session.
- Mr K. continues to show steady and gradual improvements in his anger management. He used to be hostile and indignant most of the time to all people, and this has changed such that he is only angry in situations with his friends.
- Next: – Review A-B-C of anger with friends
    – Introduce relapse prevention and begin planning for treatment termination.
    – July 4/12 – just before sundown.

Appendix 19.D

Individual Treatment Summary Report for William Kidd

TREATMENT SUMMARY REPORT

Name: Kidd, William T.   **ID#:**   8675309

Date Report Completed: November 11, 2012   **Author:** David Simourd, PhD

Background Information

Mr Kidd is a 30-year-old male who served a 5-year prison term followed by parole. These were related to his criminal actions in the burglary of several government establishments. Mr Kidd has a long history of conflict with the law, beginning at age 17 with minor antisocial acts and then increased to his current offenses. He was reasonably cooperative with expectations during his incarceration although he had several noted incidents in which he had anger outbursts. These were mainly yelling and threatening type actions toward other inmates. There was no evidence that he was actually violent. Upon his release Mr Kidd resided in a halfway house. He had some initial adjustment problems, mainly because he believed he had served his time and placement in a halfway house was further "punishment." After a short period of time, however, Mr Kidd adjusted to expectations. Mr Kidd has never held legitimate employment and has supported himself mainly through criminal activity. It is noteworthy that he secured legitimate employment during the latter stages of our clinical contact and seems to be doing well in that endeavor. For the most part, Mr Kidd has had positive community functioning.

Treatment Objectives and Progress

Mr Kidd was referred by his parole officer for anger difficulties. The first clinical session occurred on April 1, 2012 and the last was on November 11, 2012. In total Mr Kidd attended 19 clinical sessions that generally occurred every other week for one hour. He had somewhat tardy attendance during the first few sessions in that he was frequently late with no credible explanation. His mood and overall attitude in the sessions were quite poor and he seemed very uninterested in treatment or personal change in general. This improved dramatically after the fifth session for some unknown reason. From that point forward Mr Kidd was prompt in his attendance and very active in discussion. He was open in discussing relevant clinical topics and seemed to apply treatment information to various aspects of his life.

Mr Kidd experienced several notable events during the time he was involved in treatment. He secured employment for the first time in his life and seemed to genuinely enjoy working. He is employed in automotive sales and apparently does well. The second notable event was that he developed an interest in positive leisure activities. Over the course of his life Mr Kidd has not used his spare time wisely, which likely contributed to his criminality. After a few months on parole he became interested in horse riding and now is regularly and actively involved in this activity. The final notable event was that he suffered a minor back injury from some unknown cause. This kept him from working or involved in leisure activities. Mr Kidd did not show any regression in his newly established positive behavior and has now fully recovered. He apparently used the CBT skills taught in our sessions as a method of dealing with all these events.

Mr Kidd's performance in treatment was measured in several ways. First, he was administered several standardized assessment measures at the beginning of the treatment process and at the end. This included an anger measure, a faking measure, and a motivation for change measure. These measures were repeated at the end of treatment. Mr. Kidd's pre-treatment standardized assessment measures indicated he had considerable anger difficulties – he scored at the 82nd percentile compared to a normative group. This seemed to be an accurate measure because his faking score was in the low range (e.g., 17th percentile). Surprisingly, Mr Kidd's pre-treatment motivation for change was in the moderate range (e.g., 63rd percentile), which suggested he was reasonably inspired for treatment. Mr Kidd's post-treatment measures revealed a positive treatment effect. His anger score decreased to the 40th percentile, which is a considerable drop from pre-treatment. This difference was regarded as valid because his score on the faking measure at post-treatment was similar to his pre-treatment score.

In addition to the administration of standardized measures, Mr Kidd's functioning in clinical sessions was examined on his mood, participation, insight, and overall performance during sessions and rated using a 5-point scale, from 1 = "far below expectations," through 3 = "meets expectations," to 5 "far exceeds expectations." Ratings occurred in each clinical session. Mr Kidd's scores were generally in the 2 range across the criteria during the early portion of treatment, but increased steadily and were consistently in the 4–5 range at the end of treatment. In addition, Mr Kidd was administered homework assignments as part of the treatment process, which were rated on effort and insight using the same 5-point scale. Similar to his session ratings, Mr Kidd had generally poor ratings during the early homework assignments (e.g., 2–3 range) but this improved dramatically as the sessions continued wherein he was consistently rated as in the 4–5 range at the conclusion of treatment.

Summary

Mr Kidd has made excellent clinical progress from the time he was first released to the community up to the present time. He presents with a more prosocial orientation now than when treatment first began. Mr Kidd shows improvement in his moral standards and decision-making skills. He is more pleasant interpersonally and has very few anger control difficulties. Mr Kidd seems to possess the necessary skills to continue to make improvements in his life and he has an established relapse prevention plan should he encounter challenges. Although there may be several reasons for Mr Kidd's changes, the ratings of his performance in treatment were strong and suggest this contributed to his current functioning.

David J. Simourd, PhD,
Psychologist

Appendix 19.E

Group Treatment Summary Report for William Kidd

CRIMINAL ATTITUDE PROGRAM (CAP): TREATMENT SUMMARY REPORT

Name: Kidd, William T.   ID#:   8675309

Date: April 1, 2012

Mr Kidd is a 32-year-old male parolee who has eight criminal convictions on his record, all for burglary type offenses against government institutions. He was referred by his parole officer to address his criminal thinking. The Criminal Attitudes Program (CAP) is a 44-hour psycho-educational program that specifically addresses criminal thinking. The program has a cognitive-behavioral orientation and is delivered within a relapse prevention context. The CAP incorporates a comprehensive framework for assessing participant performance including: pre-post evaluations on a variety of criminal risk type measures (e.g., risk/needs, criminal attitudes, criminal expectancy, response bias, etc.), graded homework assignments, content tests, and session performance ratings. The version of the CAP Mr Kidd attended was conducted in a group format that operated two evenings per week for approximately 2 hours per session. The program began with 12 participants and ended with six.

Several standardized assessment measures were completed at the beginning of the program and at the end, with comparisons between the two time periods used to determine treatment gain. Mr Kidd's pre-treatment measures (compared to a representative normative group) indicated his general risk for reoffending was in the moderate range (48th percentile on a risk/need measure). However, his scores on a composite measure of criminal attitudes were in the high range (71st percentile), suggesting he has strong criminal attitudes. The accuracy of these measures, however, was somewhat suspect because his scores on a measure of response bias (i.e., faking) was slightly elevated (65th percentile) suggesting some distortion (either higher or lower than his obtained scores) of his true scores. Finally, Mr Kidd scored in the moderate range (53rd percentile) on a measure of treatment amenability, suggesting he is reasonably motivated for self-improvement. The general picture that emerges from pre-treatment scores is that Mr Kidd is a person who is at moderate risk for future criminal behavior, has strong criminal attitudes, and is reasonably amenable to change.

Mr Kidd attended 21 of 22 treatment sessions (he was ill for one session). His performance in these sessions was assessed through objective facilitator ratings on four separate criteria: mood (general state of mind), participation (level of engagement in the program activities), insight (link between treatment content and personal situations), and overall (combination of all treatment-related considerations). These criteria were evaluated according to "far below expectations," "below expectations," "average," "above expectations," and "far above expectations." Numerically, these criteria range from 1 to 5, respectively, such that higher scores reflect stronger treatment performance. Mr Kidd was an active participant in the CAP sessions, frequently stimulating discussion about relevant issues. He had acceptable comprehension of the material and made an effort to integrate it into his thinking. On the session ratings, Mr Kidd had consistent performance across the 21 sessions, with five sessions rated as a 3 ("average" and 16 rated as a 4 ("above expectations"). In total, Mr Kidd had a 3.7 rating, which is essentially in the above average range. The group scores ranged from 1.9 to 4.2, with an average of 3.2. Thus, Mr Kidd had slightly better average performance than the group as a whole.

Content tests, graded homework assignments, and post-treatment standardized measures are used to assess the degree of change exhibited by participants undertaking treatment. For the three content tests, Mr Kidd averaged 68%, suggesting above average understanding of the material. Homework assignments were graded on two criteria, effort and insight, on a scale from 1 (poor) to 5 (excellent). Mr Kidd completed four of eight homework assignments and averaged 3.5 and 2.8 out of 5 on effort and insight, respectively. This suggests that he was not overly committed to doing homework, in that he completed only half of the required homework, had average effort, and did not put much thought into the assignments.

Positive changes occurred on comparisons between Mr Kidd's pre-treatment and post-treatment standardized measures. His scores on a composite measure of criminal attitudes fell to the 2nd percentile at post-treatment, a drop of 69 points from pre-treatment levels. However, his scores on the faking measure *increased* slightly (to the 89th percentile) and continued to be in the high range. This is a particularly noteworthy finding and suggests that the degree of pre-post change indicated by the standardized measures may not accurately denote treatment change.

In summary, definitive comments about the amount of treatment gain Mr Kidd had are difficult because of strong inclination toward faking. Certainly his performance measures (i.e., homework, session ratings, tests) and clinical observations suggest he benefited from the CAP; the question remains, however, to what degree has he genuinely changed? On a more optimistic note, he showed a positive inclination toward making improvements with respect to criminal attitudes and made an effort to apply some of the treatment principles into his life. He has begun to question his thinking in three ways: (a) challenging his criminal automatic thoughts/attitudes; (b) reducing his commitment to criminally oriented peers and the criminal subculture; and (c) increasing his prosocial cognitions. In the event that Mr Kidd is required to undertake future programming, attention should continue to focus on issues such as challenging antisocial beliefs and reducing the social support for criminal conduct within the context of relapse prevention.

David Simourd, PhD,
Program Facilitator

20

Integrating Motivational Interviewing with Forensic CBT

Promoting Treatment Engagement and Behavior Change with Justice-Involved Clients

Raymond Chip Tafrate and Jennifer D. Luther

From its inception, motivational interviewing (MI) has resonated with forensic practitioners who endeavor to help justice-involved clients make positive behavior change in traditionally punitive environments. In particular, the Motivational Interviewing Professional Training Videotape Series that emerged in the late 1990s included vignettes depicting typical criminal justice scenarios such as intimate partner violence, prostitution, and problematic alcohol and drug use (Miller, Rollnick, & Moyers, 1998). The training videos vividly modeled a way of working with individuals that diverged significantly from the more authoritarian, confrontational, and directive approaches that dominated traditional forensic practice. MI provided a different way of thinking about clients who were pressured, coerced, or mandated into treatment; and fully acknowledged the reality that the choice to change resides within the individual, even when working with justice-involved clients.

The strong connection between MI and forensic treatment is clearly in evidence throughout this volume. The majority of clinical chapters make reference to incorporating MI skills, or adaptations of MI, prior to implementing more active-directive cognitive-behavioral techniques (CBT) and strategies (see Chapters 2, 6, 8, 9, 10, 12, 14, 16, and 17). Although not specifically designed for criminal justice settings, MI appears to have established itself as an approach that is commonly integrated into contemporary forensic practice.

The present chapter provides an overview of the application of the four processes of the MI model (*engaging*, *focusing*, *evoking*, and *planning*) in a forensic context, as well as discussion of steps for integration with more active-directive interventions such as CBT. Since both authors have considerable experience working with criminal justice practitioners, examples from applications in various correctional settings are provided to illustrate many of the foundational concepts and skills. Several international forums exist to promote up-to-date information in the application, research, and training of MI. Thus, credit for many of the ideas presented in this chapter must go to our creative and generous colleagues from the Motivational Interviewing Network of Trainers (MINT) and the Criminal Justice Motivational Interviewing Network of Trainers (CJ-MINTs). See Appendix 20.A for descriptions of these organizations.

Forensic CBT: A Handbook for Clinical Practice, First Edition.
Edited by Raymond Chip Tafrate and Damon Mitchell.
© 2014 John Wiley & Sons, Ltd. Published 2014 by John Wiley & Sons, Ltd.

Countering the "Righting Reflex"

The vast majority of criminal justice practitioners come to their jobs with the intention of helping justice-involved clients. The "righting reflex" is the natural impulse to set things right when witnessing behaviors likely to lead to continued antisocial patterns or human suffering. This noble intention to "fix" frequently translates into practitioners adopting an expert stance and thus leading the charge for change. Such a stance often leaves justice-involved clients in the role of passive recipients of a practitioner's expert advice provided through treatment activities. If such a straightforward approach worked, then practitioners could simply tell justice-involved individuals how to think and act in order to stay out of trouble and cease supervision. Obviously, much more is required.

When working with someone who is ambivalent about whether or not they want to make a change, the practitioner "righting reflex" is generally ineffective because it triggers client counter-change arguments: justifications and minimizations related to continuing current behaviors (also known as *sustain talk*, which is discussed later). Imagine that a probation officer with a strong righting reflex (Mr Expert) meets with a probationer (Mr Unsure) who is ambivalent about changing his friendships with drug-involved peers. Mr Unsure explains his dilemma to Mr Expert. Mr Expert formulates an opinion as to the correct solution and begins to advise, persuade, or argue for his recommended course of action. Since Mr Unsure can see both sides of the issue, his natural response is to give voice to the side of the argument not being articulated by the officer and to point out the shortcomings of the proposed solution (e.g., "*It would be hard for me not to hang out with them because we grew up together and live in the same neighborhood*"). In this way, MI differs from CBT and many other approaches, in that practitioners refrain from proposing solutions, dispensing advice, or providing expertise – resisting the impulse to "set things right." Instead, practitioners collaborate, support, and guide justice-involved clients toward talking about their individual reasons and methods for behavior change (Malcom Berg-Smith, 2010).

Consider the following example where a single practitioner response sets the stage for two very different conversations. In Box 20.1, the practitioner responds from an expert position and is quick to provide information. Predictably, this type of response leads the client to highlight barriers to change.

In Box 20.2 the practitioner is more client-centered, listens carefully, and pulls from the client's pre-existing motivation. The resulting verbalization from the client includes some potential reasons for change.

It is surprising how quickly a practitioner's response style influences a conversational trajectory. In criminal justice settings, practitioners often believe that directly telling people what to do takes less time. However, in this example, setting the stage for intrinsic change took no more time than providing information, which resulted in a resistant response.

Box 20.1   The Expert Stance Elicits Counter Change Arguments

CLIENT: I want to get a job, but I don't have time to look.
PRACTITIONER: You realize that getting a job is a condition of your probation.
CLIENT: Yes, but I don't know what I'm going to do about childcare. I don't have anyone to watch my daughter…

> **Box 20.2** The Client-Centered Stance Elicits Potential
> Reasons for Change
>
> CLIENT: I want to get a job, but I don't have time to look.
> PRACTITIONER: Working is important to you. Tell me more about that?
> CLIENT: Well, I want to be self-sufficient and be able to support myself. Plus, it would be really nice to get out of the house and interact with other adults…

Obviously, the conversation developing in Box 20.2 would be more efficient and helpful than what would naturally flow from the dialogue in Box 20.1. MI provides the framework to counter the righting reflex through macro processes and micro skills.

The Four Processes of MI

MI has most recently been defined as a "…collaborative, goal-oriented style of communication with particular attention to the language of change. It is designed to strengthen personal motivation for and commitment to a specific goal by eliciting and exploring the person's own reasons for change within an atmosphere of acceptance and compassion" (Miller & Rollnick, 2013, p. 29). Most commonly practiced among mental health professionals during one-on-one sessions, components of the MI style have been adapted for a wide range of uses (e.g., short de-escalation exchanges, intake and information gathering, feedback on assessment results, group facilitation, and even supervision coaching and feedback with practitioners). Often such variations of MI are referred to as "adaptations of motivational interviewing." For MI, and its adaptations, the primary objective is to construct conversations where the person feels comfortable discussing problematic or risky behaviors and the underlying motivations for and against continuing such behaviors. The tone or *spirit* of MI conversations is non-judgmental, non-confrontational, respectful, inquisitive, supportive, and collaborative, with an emphasis on client autonomy and self-direction.

MI is a complex communication style comprised of four broad and dynamic processes with several subcomponents contained in each process. The first process is *engaging* in a helpful, working relationship with the client. Successful engagement is foundational to everything that follows (Miller & Rollnick, 2013). Once such a relationship is established, the next process is *focusing* on a strategic direction around one or more change goals. With a strong alliance and clear direction, the third process, *evoking* the client's own reasons for change, can effectively occur. In essence it is the client who gives voice to behavioral choices and changes. The focal point of the final process, *planning*, is on consolidating commitment and developing a realistic and concrete plan of action. It is at this phase that a natural integration of MI and CBT is most likely to occur. An overview of the MI model is illustrated in Figure 20.1 and each process is briefly described below. For more comprehensive discussions of the MI processes, readers are referred to Miller and Rollnick (2013).

Process 1: engaging

The foundation of MI is client engagement. Successful engagement has a number of characteristics such as a helpful and respectful connection, a shared focus on treatment goals, and agreed upon steps to reach those goals (Bordin, 1979). As described above, one of the biggest

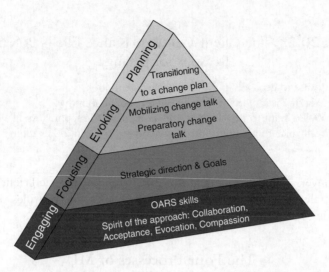

Figure 20.1   Processes of motivational interviewing. Based on Miller and Rollnick (2013).

obstacles to successful engagement, particularly in criminal justice settings, is when practitioners position themselves as experts, communicating the message "*I'm in charge and know what's best for you.*" In our experience, we occasionally meet custody-minded practitioners who see little value in putting energy toward engaging clients. This is particularly evident within the context of community corrections, where staff members lament the difficulties associated with program attrition, while missing opportunities to engage justice-involved clients in meaningful ways.

At the heart of the challenge to increase engagement skills among practitioners lies the belief that *supervision* and *monitoring* are the best way to ensure public safety rather than facilitating behavior change. Unfortunately, almost one-third of justice-involved clients in community-based programs drop out of treatment prematurely (Olver, Stockdale, & Wormith, 2011). More importantly, justice-involved clients who drop out of programs are more likely to reoffend compared to program completers: a meta-analysis by Olver and colleagues (2011) found that program non-completers had a 23% higher risk of recidivism than program completers. Similar findings have been reported in studies of institutional and community forensic programs (Berman, 2004; Beyko & Wong, 2005; Hiller, Knight, & Simpson, 1999; McMurran & Theodosi, 2007; Nunes & Cortoni, 2006). The consistency of these findings underscores the importance of engagement in working effectively with those involved in the criminal justice system.

OARS skills   The core counseling skills in MI are denoted by the acronym OARS, which stands for asking **o**pen questions, **a**ffirming, **r**eflecting, and **s**ummarizing. The good news, in terms of learning MI, is that the four skills are common to many models of counseling. Thus, the OARS skills may be familiar to many practitioners. However, within the context of MI, the levels of precision, fluency, relative emphasis, or frequency with which the skills are used are measurable and specific. In addition, there are a myriad of ways to use various types of open questions and reflective listening statements, elevating the skills to a more refined level.

Open questions   In the engagement phase, open questions are designed to promote insightful responses and broaden the conversation because the person has latitude to reveal what is most

Box 20.3 Sample Open Questions

Tell me about how you got involved with the criminal justice system?
What are you likely to lose if you do not make some changes?
Where do you see things headed if you violate your probation conditions?
What are some of the most important reasons to stay involved with your son?
What do you like about using drugs?
If you were to find a secure job, how might your life be different?

important. Open questions also encourage the individual answering the question to do more of the talking. Box 20.3 provides some examples of open questions.

In contrast, closed questions narrow the conversational focus and can be answered with minimal information (e.g., "*Did you use drugs this week?*" "*How old were you when you first got arrested?*" "*Did you make your restitution payment?*"). It is sometimes necessary to ask closed questions, yet these types of questions are kept to a bare minimum when using MI. Developing fluency with open questions can initially seem challenging, as it appears that control of the conversation is being given to the client. However, thoughtful open questions can be used to change the conversational direction and provide one method of steering (i.e., a practitioner who is curious about a client's marriage might ask: "*Tell me how your wife reacted to your recent arrest?*").

Most practitioners readily grasp the difference between open and closed questions. However, this knowledge, by itself, does not guarantee the use of open questions in real clinical interactions. Many practitioners mistakenly believe they are already asking open questions. More skillful practice can be fostered through observation activities, like recording and reviewing one-on-one sessions. The sessions can be coded using a validated instrument or informal count of specific utterances (see Appendix 20.A for a brief description of validated MI coding instruments).

Affirmations When introducing the concept of affirmations in criminal justice settings some practitioners bristle. The look on their faces communicates, "*Don't you know who I work with? How am I supposed to affirm gang members?*" Perhaps the term "affirmations" invokes images of fluffy positivity or phoniness. Further exploration reveals that such practitioners believe that because their clients are so difficult to engage, affirmations will have little or no effect. This notion turns out to be incorrect, as affirmations generally have a positive effect, especially with some of the most difficult cases. Chronic offenders routinely receive a constant stream of messages from others about what they are doing wrong. Keying into a few things that are going well and acknowledging strengths that a justice-involved client possesses will reduce defensiveness and enhance engagement. This idea is also consistent with the emerging trend in strength-based practice with challenging offender groups (Clark, 1998; see also Marshall & O'Brien (Chapter 14) and Fortune & Ward (Chapter 21)).

Affirmations are statements of appreciation for the client's accomplishments or strengths (Rosengren, 2009). Akin to behavioral reinforcers, affirming encourages specific behaviors, acknowledges difficulties, supports self-efficacy, and rewards successes. In addition, it enhances engagement and rapport by communicating an attitude of "*I am paying attention and recognizing your strengths along the way.*" Some guidelines for forming affirmations are offered by

Box 20.4 Sample Affirmations

It's so important for you to be a good father that you have sacrificed some things that used to be important to you.

Your focus on getting your general equivalency diploma is clear when you talk about how you stopped smoking pot and started attending the study group.

For someone who has been struggling with this issue for so long, you are showing great determination to improve your life.

Despite your reservations about this program, you have a lot of courage to come today.

Miller and Rollnick (2013) and Rosengren (2009) and include: (i) organizing the statement around the word "you" and resisting the temptation to start with the word "I"; (ii) focusing on specific behaviors and descriptions of those behaviors; and (iii) attending to strengths rather that deficits. In addition, genuine affirmations that identify a legitimate strength result in increased engagement and positive momentum. Several examples of affirmations are provided in Box 20.4.

Reflections The core skill in MI is reflective listening. Thoughtful use of reflections helps clarify the meaning of what clients are communicating and invites continued exploration. Sometimes, during training sessions, the notion of reflecting conjures up images of television sitcoms and bad psychotherapy, where the therapist mindlessly parrots back exactly what the client just said. Reflecting is not simply repeating a person's sentence. A reflection is a reasonable guess – delivered in the form of a statement – that emphasizes the meaning behind what a person communicated (Miller & Rollnick, 2013). Although there are many ways to reflect, the following sentence stems are commonly used to get practitioners started: *"It sounds like you…," "You're feeling…," "It seems that you…," "So, you…."*

There are two basic kinds of reflective listening statements: simple and complex. *Simple* reflections do not add much to what the client said and involve repeating back part of what was verbalized, sometimes with slight changes in wording. *Complex* reflections offer more of a guess in terms of unspoken meaning or emotion. In addition, complex reflections are placed slightly beyond what the client just said, but not too far, and convey a hypothesis as to what might come next. Furthermore, skillful use of complex reflections assists practitioners in steering the conversation toward possible strengths or positive change. This is sometimes referred to as *continuing the paragraph*, and is illustrated in Box 20.5.

Facilitating group sessions provides another platform for using reflections. Often group members verbalize differing perspectives on a particular topic. To them, it appears they disagree, and yet similarities may exist. An adept MI practitioner, listening closely for areas of agreement, uses reflective listening to create links between divergent opinions (e.g., *"It sounds like you guys have different perspectives on how to support a friend, and at the same time you're both saying that loyalty and support in friendship is important."*). For a complete discussion of adapting MI for group treatments, readers are referred to Wagner, Ingersoll, and Contributors (2013).

Reflective listening often feels clunky and artificial when practitioners first learn it. Learning to use reflections skillfully has been compared to learning a musical instrument. Certainly, individuals first learning to play an instrument often sound more like an animal in distress than

> **Box 20.5** Continuing the Paragraph – Sample Dialogue Using Just Reflections
>
> CLIENT: Yesterday I walked out of group when the facilitator started making fun of me.
> PRACTITIONER: You felt frustrated and wanted time to cool down.
> CLIENT: Yeah, and I was mad at him for embarrassing me in front of the whole group.
> PRACTITIONER: You really think what he did was unfair.
> CLIENT: Definitely, I had to get out of there.
> PRACTITIONER: And yet, you removed yourself from the situation before it escalated.
> CLIENT: Yes. I wanted to avoid what happened last time when we got into a shouting match.
> PRACTITIONER: So, you were more in control this time.
> CLIENT: I guess so, but I still got in trouble for leaving.
> PRACTITIONER: You can see that you're improving and would like to come up with a way to handle this situation in the future so that it doesn't blow up again and cause you problems.
> CLIENT: Yeah, instead of actually leaving, maybe I could close my eyes and try to imagine I'm outside until I cool down a bit.

a musical score. Becoming proficient at reflective listening takes time and practice. Often new trainees are asked to practice the skill in personal social situations, so they can improve and generalize the skill to professional settings. Feedback for improvement can be gleaned by paying attention to the other person's reaction to the reflective statement. When an accurate reflection is skillfully delivered, the other person usually nods, continues talking, or gets enthusiastic about being understood (e.g., "*Yes, that is exactly right! I often feel that way and…*").

Reflections that miss the mark provide valuable information as well. The client is likely to correct the statement and provide additional information (i.e., "*No, it's not that I feel angry, I just get depressed when it seems like I've lost control of the situation and that upsets me even more.*"). Over time, with coaching and feedback, competent MI practitioners favor reflections to questions and the skill becomes incredibly valuable once a level of fluency is developed.

Summarizations The essential difference between a summary and a reflection is that a summary encapsulates larger amounts of information. The most common place to put a summary is at the end of an interaction, although summaries may be strategically inserted at various points in a conversation. Summaries come in different forms and can serve several purposes such as highlighting what is most important for the client (*collecting summary*), contrasting divergent ideas and experiences (*linking summary*), and guiding the conversation in a new direction (*transitional summary*). The practitioner strategically decides what to include in a summary. Thus, the art of developing effective summaries is related to decisions about brevity and selectivity (Rosengren, 2009). Several examples of different types of summaries are presented in Box 20.6.

Exploring values and goals In the engagement phase of MI, practitioners also take time to explore justice-involved clients' core values and life priorities, as understanding what people value is critical to understanding what motivates them (Miller & Rollnick, 2013). Exploring values helps clients consider discrepancies between what they value and how they are living their lives, which can be a powerful motivator for change. In MI, practitioners maintain a

Box 20.6   Three Common Types of Summaries

Let's pull together everything you have said. Getting arrested has been really embarrassing. You see this whole situation as an argument that got out of hand and you do not like the idea of being labeled an abuser. It seems like you have decided that avoiding further criminal justice involvement is your most important priority and doing this program is the easiest way of putting this incident behind you. You are also hoping that your relationship will improve and couples counseling is something you are willing to consider. [Collecting summary]

You're not really sure if this substance abuse program will work for you. Your time is limited and the last program you tried was frustrating, so you dropped out. You also recognize that there are some helpful treatment programs because 7 years ago you had a counselor who you worked well with and you saw positive results. So, you're hoping for a good experience this time. [Linking summary]

You have really thought about this a lot. Your anger reactions have created problems in your relationships and career. Most recently you have become concerned about your reactions because you feel out of control with your kids and feel guilty after you yell at them. It seems like you are ready to make some changes. What do you see as the next step? [Transitional summary]

curious and exploratory stance when discussing the client's values and choices. Directly confronting or challenging value-behavior discrepancies can often lead to clients verbalizing sustain talk (discussed later) and thus reluctance to change. Instead, guiding clients to explore how specific behaviors may violate values encourages them to voice their own arguments for, or against, change in order to live a more harmonious life.

There are several structured activities, in the MI model, for eliciting and focusing on values. For example, clients self-select values from a provided list and/or translate them onto cards, and prioritize them by importance – see Moyers and Martino (2006) for a listing of 100 values and a more detailed description of the card sorting technique; see also Luther, Pitocco, and Lovins (2011) for an example of using this technique with substance-abusing justice-involved clients. Values can also be elicited in clinical discussions using open questions such as: "*Tell me what you care about most?*" "*How do you hope your life will be different a few years from now?*" Once values are elicited, either through structured activities or discussion, the practitioner follows up with reflections (e.g., "*So, taking care of your kids' well-being is really important to you.*") and open questions (*"How would your life be different if you began making decisions that are consistent with this value?*" "*How can you express this value while you are in prison?*" or "*Once you get out?*"). The use of open questions and reflections elicits deeper meaning around the chosen value, and encourages further client verbalizations for taking steps toward change.

In MI, values are explored to highlight the discrepancies between personal values and current behaviors as a means of increasing awareness and motivation for change. Of course, in criminal justice settings, concerns arise when justice-involved clients focus their values in antisocial ways (e.g., being successful in dealing drugs). In such cases, practitioners cannot support antisocial intentions. Thoughtful discussion usually reveals that justice-involved clients share common human aspirations (i.e., financial security, growth opportunities, positive interpersonal connections, etc.) and wish to improve their lives. In some cases, individuals do not possess the skills, resources, or supports to create a more prosocial life. In other cases, people have turned toward antisocial and self-defeating patterns to negotiate life's challenges. Despite a general belief that most justice-involved clients purposefully choose antisocial values, in practice antisocial behavior typically reflects more of a skills deficit and the effects of negative environmental influences. Even when practitioner-client values are discrepant, the use of MI provides a deeper and clearer exploration into the client's personal history, life factors, and desired outcomes.

Process 2: focusing

Focusing is about clarifying a general strategic direction and establishing change goals. In many cases the focus of services may be determined by clients' preferences (e.g., "*Getting a job is my highest priority.*" "*I need to get clean.*" "*I want to get through this program so I can get probation off my back and move on with my life.*"). The nature of the service setting may also dictate the focus in that many criminal justice programs are designed to address specific target areas or criminogenic needs (e.g., domestic violence, anger management, substance abuse). Focusing tends to be straightforward when clients articulate concrete and specific goals that are aligned with the mission of a particular program and practitioners' expectations as to what constitutes healthy change. When such alignment exists, practitioners need not spend too much time focusing and can move smoothly to the processes of evoking and planning (Miller & Rollnick, 2013). Focusing becomes increasingly complicated when the clinical picture is chaotic and muddled, there are important choices to be made in terms of which goals to pursue, or clients are uninterested in pursuing goals stipulated in court orders, community supervision conditions, or those outlined by a program's mission.

Chaotic and confused clinical picture In cases where justice-involved clients appear disorganized, emotionally volatile, or overwhelmed, practitioners will need to slow the process down – while continuing to utilize OARS skills – and remain patient until a clear focus emerges. Focusing prematurely on a goal not currently shared by the client is likely to result in disengagement.

Another potentially useful strategy for working with complex cases is to provide the client with a case formulation, or a guess, that might connect or unify what appear to be unrelated symptoms. When offering a case formulation in a manner consistent with MI, practitioners first ask permission to provide information and then follow up by eliciting the client's thoughts. Such formulations are offered tentatively with input from the client about what seems to fit and what does not. Box 20.7 provides an example of how to begin such a conversation.

Box 20.7   Offering a Case Formulation to Provide Focus

PRACTITIONER: When you look at the last few years, you see a lot of losses in your family relationships, difficulties maintaining steady employment, and ongoing legal problems. Sometimes you feel pretty overwhelmed and you're not sure what to do next to change your life or even where to start. For some people, working to improve one problem area helps other areas get better. Would it be OK if I shared with you what some people in your situation have focused on that helped them move forward?

CLIENT: Yeah.

PRACTITIONER: I'll give you some examples and you can tell me what fits for you and then we can decide together where to start.

Deciding among many goals   Justice-involved clients rarely have one problem. Since comorbidity is the norm, a common challenge is to sort out what problem area to focus on first. A useful first step, common across many models of counseling, is to create an inclusive list of client difficulties that might become the focus of discussions. A common CBT strategy is to have practitioners take the lead in synthesizing clinical history, test data, and information from clinical interviews to create (collaboratively and with buy-in from the client) what is known as the *problem list* (Persons, 2008). Miller and Rollnick (2013) have outlined a similar method called *agenda mapping*. Agenda mapping also begins with a list of possible topics or goals and has a strong collaborative emphasis (i.e., traveling companions consulting a map to decide where they might go and how best to get there). Box 20.8 presents an example of beginning an agenda-mapping conversation.

As noted above, some criminal justice programs, due to the nature of their funding and program missions, will be constrained to focus on a narrower range of clinical or criminogenic issues. Even in these types of situations some latitude and choice about where to go first usually exists. Box 20.9 provides a sample statement developed by juvenile probation officers to begin the process of focusing. In this example, adolescent clients are asked to pick from a range of common risk factors associated with future offending. We continue to be pleasantly surprised

---

Box 20.8   Agenda Mapping to Decide Focus

I really appreciate your honesty about the struggles you're facing. Let's take a step back for a moment and figure out together what is the most important issue to focus on first. Based on what you have said, I created a list of areas we might work on together. I also added a couple of my own ideas to the list. Let's review the list so you can tell me what jumps out as the most important issue to focus on first.

**Box 20.9   Juvenile Probation Officer Statement to Focus
on a Specific Risk Factor**

PRACTITIONER: As part of our meeting today, we will be working together to develop a plan for your period of probation. Kids get in trouble for different reasons. Some common reasons are problems with...

[The client is provided with a visual list of risk factors.]

- *Drugs and alcohol*
- *Family*
- *Companions and friends*
- *School*
- *Emotions (such as: anger, sadness, anxiety, or stress)*
- *Making decisions that often lead to trouble*
- *Difficulty following rules*

Which of these areas do you think is the most important to work on?

CLIENT: Following the rules.
PRACTITIONER: What made you pick that one?...

at how readily the majority of juvenile probationers will self-identify a risk factor when given the space to choose what is most important for them.

Lack of agreement on goals The most challenging scenario related to focusing is when a justice-involved client does not share the same change goals prescribed by forensic programs and practitioners. In many jurisdictions, dynamic, criminogenic risk factors, assessed using a validated risk-and-need assessment instrument, steer case management goals (Andrews, Bonta, & Wormith, 2006, 2008). In an attempt to obtain a collaborative focus on treatment goals, a practitioner might provide feedback on risk assessment results and move to the evoking process to elicit change talk (discussed below) and create some degree of ambivalence around a specific risk area. Another possibility is to explore the concerns that other people have voiced to the client in regard to specific risk areas, again with the goal of eliciting change talk. There may also be additional factors a justice-involved client wishes to discuss that are not part of formal assessment. Obviously, treatment goals identified collaboratively are most likely to hold intrinsic value to justice-involved clients.

Process 3: evoking

Evoking is the process of supporting and encouraging justice-involved clients in voicing their own motivations for change. It rests on the premise that what clients hear themselves say is more important than what practitioners say (Malcom Berg-Smith, 2010). Stated another way, "people talk themselves into changing…" (Miller & Rollnick, 2013, p. 28). Evoking builds on the foundational skills (OARS) previously described, but involves the ability to identify, elicit, and respond to specific forms of client language. The process of evoking lies at the strategic heart of the MI approach.

Two terms are relevant for understanding the evoking process: *change talk* and *sustain talk*. Change talk is any client speech that favors movement toward and commitment to change, whereas sustain talk involves client counter-change verbalizations that favor maintaining the status quo or not changing (Miller & Rollnick, 2013). Some examples of specific categories of change talk and sustain talk are provided in Table 20.1. There are two significant research conclusions relevant

Table 20.1 Examples of change talk and sustain talk.

Change talk	*Sustain talk*
Preparatory change talk	*Inverse of preparatory change talk*
D: Desire (*I want to leave the gang life.*)	**D:** Desire (*I don't want to leave the gang.*)
A: Ability (*I could leave the neighborhood and live with my sister across town.*)	**A:** Ability (*I don't know how to do anything except sell drugs.*)
R: Reasons (*My family wants me to get a job and stop selling drugs.*)	**R:** Reasons (*If I try to leave the gang, they will come after me.*)
N: Need (*I've got to find another way to support myself.*)	**N:** Need (*Being a member of the gang is the only way to avoid trouble in my neighborhood.*)
Mobilizing change talk	*Inverse of mobilizing change talk*
C: Commitment (*I'll talk to my sister on Monday and see if she's still open to having me room with her.*)	**C:** Commitment (*There is no way for me to avoid gang activity and have a regular job.*)
A: Activation (*I plan to make an appointment at the employment office.*)	**A:** Activation (*I am prepared to accept the risks of being a gang member.*)
T: Taking steps (*I've moved in with my sister and have two interviews lined up for next week.*)	**T:** Taking steps (*I started selling drugs again last week so I can pay my child support.*)

to the process of evoking. First, levels of client change talk and sustain talk in clinical interactions can be influenced by practitioners' response style (Glynn & Moyers, 2010; also previously illustrated in Boxes 20.1 and 20.2). Second, these two broad-spectrum client language patterns appear to be associated with subsequent outcomes. A predominance of change talk predicts actual behavior change, whereas a higher proportion of sustain talk – or equal levels of sustain talk and change talk – are predictive of not changing (Moyers, Martin, Houck, Christopher, & Tonigan, 2009). Skillful MI yields increasing levels of client change talk over time, and the ratio of change talk to sustain talk appears to be an important marker for consequent change.

Recognizing change talk   Two categories of change talk are important for practitioners to recognize. The first is known as *preparatory change talk*, which includes:

- Desire (*"I'd really like to be a better father"*)
- Ability (*"I could set aside time to see my son every week"*)
- Reasons (*"If I'm involved, maybe he won't make the same mistakes I made"*)
- Need (*"I've got to do whatever it takes to have a meaningful relationship with my son"*)

Preparatory change talk represents the pro-change side of ambivalence and signals that energy exists around change. The second category, known as *mobilizing change talk*, includes:

- Commitment (*"I give you my word that I will reach out to my son this week"*)
- Activation (*"I'm ready to set up a schedule so I can see him"*)
- Taking steps (*"I called my ex to let her know I can spend time with him on Friday"*)

Mobilizing change talk signals a potential resolution of ambivalence and is an indicator of possible behavioral movement toward change (Miller & Rollnick, 2013).

Learning to recognize change talk in real-life interactions can initially seem daunting to forensic practitioners who were taught to key into traditional CBT language constructs (demandingness, all-or-nothing thinking, justifying, etc.). Nonetheless, there are a number of everyday experiences that illustrate the distinction between preparatory change talk and mobilizing change talk, with which most practitioners can readily identify. The following example comes from training sessions:

> *Imagine you are at the mall one afternoon. You see someone you recognize walking toward you and smiling. It's Denise, a former co-worker who you really enjoyed working with. You have not seen her since she took a new job last year. Meeting in the hallway, you engage in small talk (e.g., "What's your new job like?" "What ever happened to Emily?" and so on…). After a few minutes, Denise checks her watch and says, "I have to get to an appointment, but let's try and do lunch sometime." You say, "Yeah, that'd be great." After saying goodbye, you go your separate ways.*

Practitioners are asked to analyze this interaction through the lens of the change talk model. What specific language categories emerged in the actual verbalizations? (Answer: *Only change talk around desire; nothing in the areas of ability, reasons, need, commitment, activation, taking steps.*) Is there some energy around getting together for lunch? (Answer: *Yes.*) Is lunch likely to happen? (Answer: *No.*) Most people intuitively understand that once people return to their busy lives the lunch date quickly drops off the radar and will probably not occur. What would have to happen in the mall interaction to make the lunch date more likely? (Answer: *Perhaps exchanging contact information, deciding where and when to meet for lunch.*) Such verbalizations would be indicators of mobilizing change talk (e.g., commitment, activation, taking steps). The change talk model becomes easier to grasp when analyzed in such an everyday context. A variety of additional training exercises have been developed by members of the Motivational Interviewing Network of Trainers (MINT) to hone practitioner identification of change talk. Several rounds of practice, using different exercises, are usually required to help practitioners tune their ears to change talk language.

Eliciting and responding to change talk The major task in the evoking phase is for practitioners to invite and explore change talk. Often, when justice-involved clients are fully engaged – in an MI consistent style – and given space to explore both sides of their ambivalence, change talk bubbles up naturally. When change talk spontaneously occurs, practitioners use OARS skills to elicit more change talk. Imagine a 24-year-old woman says:

> *I know I sometimes make poor decisions. I'm bothered by all of the things that have happened to me and that makes me feel depressed and angry. I get emotional just talking about it, but I don't think I'm crazy. Honestly, I'm just not sure about this program. Maybe talking about my problems will help me feel better, but it could make me feel worse, but I'm willing to give it a try.*

Several practitioner responses might encourage more change talk such as:

"*What is it about some of your recent decisions that bothers you?*" [Open question]
"*You have a lot of courage to come here and talk about your problems.*" [Affirmation]
"*Sounds like you would really like to feel proud of your decisions.*" [Reflection]
"*In the past, you mentioned that you really wanted your life to be different, and you weren't sure if you would even be able to talk about the things you've done that upset you, but today, I hear you saying that even though talking about all this is scary for you, you are willing to give it a try.*" [Summary]

Another strategy is to invite change talk using open questions constructed to elicit such verbalizations. Open questions such as those listed in Box 20.10 will likely initiate preparatory change talk.

Box 20.10   Open Questions Likely to Invite Change Talk

How would you like your life to be different?
What strengths do you have that might help you in changing _____?
What is at stake if you do not change _____?
What are the three most important reasons to change _____?
What is most urgent for you now?
If you did decide to change _____, why would that be a good thing?

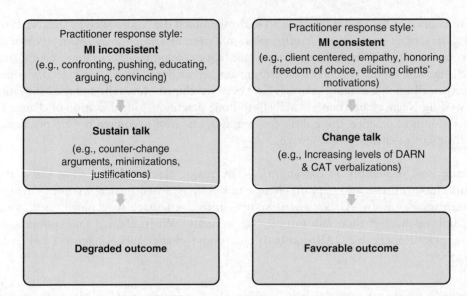

Figure 20.2 Practitioner response style, client language, and subsequent outcome. For explanation of "DARN" and "CAT" see Table 20.1. Based on Miller and Rose (2009).

Responding to sustain talk Change talk ebbs and flows, rarely remaining constant throughout a conversation. Skilled practitioners recognize that even when change talk appears, ambivalence indicates that unstated sustain talk lurks in the background and will surely re-emerge. Awareness and attunement are required when listening to client speech; the more clients verbalize sustain talk, the less likely a favorable outcome will follow. In responding to sustain talk, it is certainly necessary to acknowledge it to communicate an understanding of the larger picture. However, Miller and Rollnick (2013) generally caution against spending too much time exploring reasons against change. In the evoking process of MI, practitioners differentially attend to change talk (over sustain talk) because increasing the change-to-sustain-talk ratio is one of the hypothesized mechanisms for change (Miller & Rose, 2009; see Figure 20.2).

Process 4: planning

In the planning process, clients develop a concrete, specific, and realistic action plan. Once again, the use of OARS skills creates a collaborative environment and elicits from clients their own ideas about the steps they might take. Attentive listening and clinical judgment assist in the recognition of the most opportune time to transition to planning. Premature planning attempts halt momentum and increase sustain talk; at the same time, when client readiness occurs, missed opportunities result in client frustration and lost momentum. Perceptive practitioners use client language, such as increases in preparatory change talk, decreases in sustain talk, and the emergence of mobilizing change talk, as possible indicators of readiness to begin planning for change (Miller & Rollnick, 2013). Another straightforward strategy is to test the waters with a transitional summary and a *key question* (Rosengren, 2009). After a practitioner provides a summary of the dilemma, a brief mention of roadblocks, and highlights change talk, a key question can encourage clients to conceptualize and articulate possible next steps to consider. Box 20.11 provides some sample key questions.

> ## Box 20.11 Sample Summary Followed by Possible Key Questions
>
> You feel torn between wanting to make these changes and feeling stuck in old patterns. Most of your family members are still using and selling drugs and can't understand how you could have fun if you're sober. At the same time, you feel better than you have in years. You want to get a regular job while you finish your schooling. You think about a better life for yourself outside of the old neighborhood and want to make sure you're there for your kids while they're growing up.
>
> - *What's one thing you could do upon release to stay on track with your plan?*
> - *Given the situation, what option makes the most sense for you to pursue?*
> - *Where would you like to go from here?*
> - *What is the next step?*
> - *What do you think you can do to be successful?*

Clients who respond to a key question with a concrete, specific next step lay the foundation of a plan, and thereby demonstrate openness to change planning. Specific follow-up questions can be used to elicit mobilizing change talk to help consolidate the plan further: "*How would you start?*" "*When will the timing be right for you to take this step?*" "*What might get in the way? – And how would you deal with that?*"

In some cases, clients respond to key questions with the desire to move forward, but are unsure how. They may be considering several options or lack the knowledge of what might be a useful step forward. Practitioners can ask permission to brainstorm with the client regarding alternative paths to be considered (Rosengren, 2009). In the spirit of empowerment and collaboration, clients are then asked for input regarding which alternative might work best. If there is reluctance to discuss the specific next steps, then a return to the evoking phase may be required.

When clients are mandated into treatment, as in criminal justice settings, they may respond to a key question with committed sustain talk, like, "*I'm not going to do anything.*" In these cases, practitioners should keep personal frustration at bay, acknowledge the client's freedom of choice, and follow up with an open question (e.g., "*As you know, the court has sentenced you into this treatment program, but it's really up to you whether you attend or not. What are some reasons you may want to follow these terms and conditions?*"). Often, such a response will trigger change talk from the client that transitions the conversation back to focusing or evoking processes.

MI and Forensic CBT: Sequential and Stylistic Integration

Developed as a brief intervention for helping people resolve ambivalence and move toward change, MI was not originally intended as a stand-alone treatment (Miller & Rollnick, 2009). Nonetheless, for some clients, once a decision and commitment to change is reached, necessary steps are then taken to move forward with little or no further help from practitioners (Miller & Rollnick, 2013, p. 30). However, for other clients with limited problem-solving, decision-making, and social skills, a combination of MI and CBT is likely to produce the most effective long-term outcomes. Meta-analytic evidence to date suggests a synergistic effect when adding MI to other treatment approaches (Hettema, Steele, & Miller, 2005; Kertes, Westra, Angus, & Marcus, 2011; Miller & Rose, 2009), while other reviews have noted increased retention in offender programming (McMurran, 2009). Given that MI is unlikely to be delivered as a singular intervention in criminal justice settings, the question of compatibility and integration with other models becomes a central issue. In the remainder of this chapter, we explore critical differences between MI and CBT, and several ways in which MI can be successfully blended with forensic CBT programs.

Critical differences between MI and CBT

Since several components of MI are common to many counseling modalities, experienced CBT practitioners – when first exposed to MI – may be quick to dismiss the model as something they are already doing (Miller & Rollnick, 2009). At first glance, it may not appear that MI offers anything inherently different than the collaborative empiricism at the heart of traditional CBT (Beck, 2011). In fact, MI is quite distinct from CBT (see Table 20.2 for a summary of the points of divergence).

The focus of MI is eliciting the client's own motivations regarding change goals. These discussions typically focus on *why* and *how* one *might* change specific behavior. The crux of CBT is teaching skills to decrease negative symptoms and improve functioning, with a heavy emphasis on repeated skill practice in order to generalize new thoughts and actions to daily life. While MI has been described as more exploratory, broad, and focused on preparation for

Table 20.2   Contrasting MI and CBT.

Motivational interviewing	*Cognitive-behavioral therapy*
Primary focus is on increasing readiness and preparation for change	Primary focus is on using tools and practicing behavioral skills for how to successfully change
Reflective, exploratory, and client-centered	Directive, action oriented, and highly structured
Early sessions focused on allowing the client to elaborate on his or her broader concerns	Early sessions focused on assessment and information gathering
Arguments for changing beliefs and behavior patterns elicited from the client	Arguments for changing beliefs and behavior patterns provided by the practitioner
Client is the expert regarding what is most likely to be helpful	Practitioner is the expert regarding skills, techniques, and helpful solutions
Emphasis on clients' strengths, resources, and efforts	Emphasis on remediating problematic symptoms and skill deficits
Practitioner temporal focus and attention firmly rooted in present moment (e.g., verbalizations during the interaction; meeting the client where s/he is)	Practitioner temporal focus and attention is often several steps ahead of the client (e.g., case formulation, treatment targets, techniques, interventions and homework assignments that might be utilized)
Practitioner "keys into" verbalizations and client language related to change (e.g., change talk – verbalizations favoring change; DARN-CAT)	Practitioner "keys into" verbalizations and client language indicating problematic thinking (e.g., cognitive distortions, irrational beliefs, or criminal attitudes)

Note: for explanation of "DARN" and "CAT" see Table 20.1.

change (Kertes et al., 2011), CBT is viewed as a methodology for providing specific tools to help people make and sustain changes in distorted and exaggerated thinking patterns and self-defeating behaviors (O'Kelly, 2010).

Differences between MI and CBT exist in the degree to which they are client-centered. CBT practitioners, specializing in certain mental health problems, often come to the table as experts in particular disorders or syndromes. Competent CBT practitioners can communicate efficiently and empathically about the nature of behavior patterns that seem bewildering to clients; and provide options regarding what is likely to work in remediating symptoms. From the viewpoint of a competent MI practitioner, clients are experts on themselves, with a thorough understanding of the circumstances of their lives, and therefore know what is most effective to help them make long-term changes. With this in mind, clients take an active role in advocating and planning personal change (Kertes et al., 2011).

In contrasting MI and CBT interactions, there is also a distinction to be made in terms of the temporal focus of practitioners' energy and attention. Skilled CBT practitioners operate like chess players, thinking several moves ahead of their clients, conceptualizing how beliefs link to behaviors and reinforcement contingencies, and formulating strategies for altering established patterns. Due to the strong emphasis on active listening and client language, skilled practitioners using MI maintain a more moment-to-moment focus, not getting too far ahead of their clients (Simpson & Zuckoff, 2011). Like internet surfing, MI practitioners "click" on what seems most important in the moment, carefully following what is next communicated by the client, and then "clicking" again on what seems most useful.

Finally, across many models of counseling, practitioners are taught to pay attention to verbalizations reflecting certain theoretical constructs. Not everything justice-involved clients say is useful, and practitioners must continually make choices regarding how to respond. Thus, in CBT, practitioners pay attention to client statements representing certain belief constructs (e.g., all-or-nothing thinking, catastrophizing, victim stance, disregard for others) and respond accordingly. Those practicing MI look for different types of verbalizations, focusing their attention on language related to *change talk* – the person's own statements in favor of change (e.g., preparatory and mobilizing change talk). In working with practitioners who may have different educational backgrounds in MI or CBT, it quickly becomes apparent that each group is paying attention to the forms of client language related to their practice orientation. Therefore, teaching MI to CBT practitioners requires a shift in focus to naturally occurring language about change. For many CBT-trained practitioners, especially those in forensic settings, learning MI involves adding a new lens with which to view client language. In spite of the theoretical differences between MI and CBT, the two approaches can be complimentary (Burke, 2011), and several strategies for integration are presented below.

Sequential integration: MI as a pre-treatment

MI is often conceptualized as a prelude to other interventions (Burke, 2011; Lundahl, Kunz, Brownell, Tollefson, & Burke, 2010). For example, Kassinove and Tafrate (2011) propose MI be considered in the *preparation and engagement* phase of CBT anger treatment. Many clients with problematic anger reactions are coerced into programming and externalize blame (e.g., "*If my wife would just do her part, I wouldn't get so upset and strike out.*"). Initially approaching such clients with techniques for change often results in disinclination and subsequent treatment failure. Exploring potential reasons for changing anger reactions, prior to utilizing behavioral and cognitive strategies, is usually more productive. The goal of early sessions is for clients to provide their own arguments about whether or not they want to engage in the treatment intervention and therefore the change process.

For a variety of common criminal justice target areas, such as addictions, sexual aggression, and domestic violence, MI can be included in pre-treatment modules to increase engagement in CBT interventions. For example, a curriculum developed at the University of Cincinnati Corrections Institute (Cognitive-Behavioral Intervention for Substance Abuse) includes optional pre-treatment sessions focused on engagement. Such pre-treatment sessions can be delivered one-on-one or in a group format, and are recommended when client engagement in programming is lacking. Following the general pre-treatment sequence, the next set of sessions focuses on motivational engagement related specifically to a self-identified substance-abusing behavior, consistent with MI planning (Luther et al., 2011). The remaining sessions in the curriculum address cognitive restructuring, emotional regulation, social skills, and problem-solving, all components of traditional CBT. In these types of examples of sequential integration, both MI and CBT are delivered in a manner consistent with the spirit and skills embodied in each approach, and practitioners shift from one model to the other based on client need.

One advantage of formalizing MI as a prelude to CBT is to diminish the effects of two unproductive extremes: (i) lack of engagement in treatment, and (ii) failure to address important criminogenic needs (factors statistically related to offending; Andrews & Bonta, 2010a). Throughout our training and consulting work, we have encountered CBT-oriented practitioners who instruct justice-involved clients to engage in CBT activities, like cognitive restructuring, without identifying client motivation and perspective (e.g., "*Turn to page 14 of your workbook and complete the thought record.*"). Emphasis seems to be placed on completing structured lessons, delivered with fidelity to a specific manualized program. Of course this approach lacks the flexibility needed to successfully engage many justice-involved clients. On the other extreme lies the pitfall of using MI after client motivation is high, but skill deficits exists (e.g., "*So, you are at a loss for how to manage your life without substances and you're asking me what I think.*"). Well-meaning practitioners, who achieve a level of MI proficiency and then ask what comes after MI, highlight the importance of training in action-oriented interventions, as well.

With a sequential integration model, forensic programs can train practitioners to effectively engage justice-involved clients and then shift to action-oriented interventions focused on criminogenic need areas. Since motivation is dynamic, moments will still arise when a return to MI benefits a successful change process (Westra & Arkowitz, 2011). In this sense, MI can be conceptualized as both a pre-treatment sequence and a useful fallback position when barriers arise or ruptures in the therapeutic alliance emerge.

Stylistic integration: a more client-centered CBT delivery

Although not often discussed, CBT practitioners who develop a proficiency in MI are likely to see a "softening" of their CBT delivery style, especially those at the more active and directive end of the continuum. Learning MI may influence CBT practitioners to be more exploratory and to spend greater time eliciting client concerns around current behavior patterns prior to engaging in activities for restructuring beliefs. Practitioners who make this type of style shift may be influenced by the MI method, but are still operating from a CBT framework.

Consider the clinical discussion in Box 20.12 with a client who is on community supervision for problems related to anger regulation and fighting. In this example, the practitioner is utilizing a CBT conceptualization. The belief that "*I must always be treated with respect*" is targeted for change because available descriptive research suggests that such rigid and

Box 20.12 Stylistic Integration of MI and CBT

PRACTITIONER: *I know last time we talked about you feeling disrespected by one of your co-workers and how that led up to the argument last week. We also talked about the idea that not feeling respected often leads to situations that become confrontational. Would it be okay if we talked a bit more about this general idea of respect?* [Blend; Summary with the practitioner focusing on a clinical target but also asking permission]

CLIENT: *Yeah, sure. Respect is everything.*

PRACTITIONER: *Sounds like respect is really important to you.* [MI; Reflection]

CLIENT: *Yeah, people should always treat me with respect.*

PRACTITIONER: *Tell me how you developed that idea?* [Blend; Open question with a directional focus but also maintaining an exploratory stance]

[Practitioner listens as the client shares his history of growing up with a verbally abusive father and experiences of being bullied in high school. Both experiences appear to have contributed to his sensitivity around perceived disrespect.]

PRACTITIONER: *So, feeling disrespected in the past led you to a strong desire for respect now and you feel angry when you don't get it.* [MI; Reflection]

CLIENT: *Yeah. I guess I look for any signals that I'm not being respected. It could be what the person says or their tone of voice.*

PRACTITIONER: *How has this issue of respect affected other relationships?* [MI; Open question and exploratory stance]

CLIENT: *In my relationships with women and most recently with my baby's momma. We just couldn't get along, we'd argue, and I would feel disrespected, and things would erupt into a major fight. I really want that relationship to work out, so I can at least spend time with my son, and for things to be different.*

PRACTITIONER: *So, you are really hoping for a different outcome.* [MI; Reflection of change talk around desire for a different outcome]

CLIENT: *Yeah, I really wanted to be with her and my kid. My life is one big disappointment.*

PRACTITIONER: *Even though you really want relationships to work out, they keep falling apart.* [MI; Reflection of change talk around concern and a desire for change]

CLIENT: *Yeah. It just keeps happening.*

PRACTITIONER: *The results on your relationships are clear to you. How has this issue of being sensitive to disrespect affected your work life?* [MI; Open question maintaining an exploratory stance]

[Client reveals a long history of career instability due to disagreements with supervisors and co-workers. Practitioner listens and reflects back the desire for a different outcome in the future.]

PRACTITIONER: *So, this sensitivity to disrespect may be part of the reason why things are not working out the way you'd like at home and at work.* [MI; Reflection for clarification]

CLIENT: *Yeah, it's like I'm on high alert and then snap at the smallest thing.*

PRACTITIONER: *If you changed and didn't lash out when you felt disrespected, how might your life improve?* [MI; Open question to elicit change talk]

CLIENT: *Well, I'd probably get along with people better. I would be able to hold down a job. I also might be more relaxed.*

PRACTITIONER: *So, deciding to change this area is likely to improve your relationships, work situation, and overall mood.* [MI; Reflection of change talk]

CLIENT: *Definitely.*

PRACTITIONER: *In some ways this is a really important issue, because you would find life more fulfilling.* [MI; Reflection of change talk]

CLIENT: *Oh yeah. Big time.*

PRACTITIONER: *On a scale of 0–10 (where 0 is <u>not</u> at all important and 10 is the most important), how important is it for you to make a change how you react to disrespect?* [MI; Scaling question]

CLIENT: *It's like a 9.*

PRACTITIONER: *That seems really important. Why are you at a 9 and not a 6?* [MI; Reflection and open question to elicit change talk]

CLIENT: *I have to find a way to get along with my kid's mom, and I want to be a good dad, plus, I can't keep losing jobs.*

PRACTITIONER: *So it is important because you want to be more successful with family and work.* [MI; Reflection of change talk]

CLIENT: *Yes, I want to be more successful and I want less drama all the way around.*

PRACTITIONER: *On the same scale of 0–10, how confident are you that you could make a change in this area?* [MI; Scaling question]

CLIENT: *I'm probably at about a 3, because I've been this way my whole life. I get so angry with people. It seems like my anger just comes out of nowhere.* [Client verbalizes low self-efficacy regarding how to change]

PRACTITIONER: *What would it take for you to be at a 4 or 5?* [MI; Open question]

CLIENT: *I'm not really sure; maybe if I learned how to handle my anger better and had some success it would help me feel more confident.*

PRACTITIONER: *Okay, tell me about the last time you got angry because you felt disrespected?* [CBT; Open question to elicit a specific situation]

CLIENT: *That was the argument at work last week.*

PRACTITIONER: *Okay, what were you telling yourself right before things started to get heated and you told him off?* [CBT; Open question to elicit beliefs]

CLIENT: *I was thinking, "I'm not going to take orders from him. He is not my supervisor. He should treat me with more respect because I have more work experience than him."*

PRACTITIONER: *So, you thought he shouldn't be telling you what to do.* [Blend; Reflection to clarify belief]

CLIENT: *He's sort of arrogant and always thinks he's in charge.*

PRACTITIONER: *Ever since you've worked with him, he's acting this same way, and now you pretty much expect this kind of attitude from him.* [Blend; Reflection to clarify understanding]

CLIENT: *Yeah, that's right. The whole 6 months we've worked together he has acted like he's my boss or something.*

PRACTITIONER: *Since you're used to his style, I'm a bit confused as to why you would expect him to act differently than he usually does?* [CBT; Open question to challenge current thinking]

CLIENT: *Good point. I don't know. He probably isn't going to change.*

PRACTITIONER: *So this is really who he is. What feeling do you have when you expect him to act respectful and he acts the same as always?* [Blend; Reflection and closed question to help the client see the connection between thoughts and feelings]

CLIENT: *I get really pissed.*

PRACTITIONER:	*So, what do you think you could tell yourself in the future that might help you stay calm?* [CBT; Open question to elicit an alternative belief)]
CLIENT:	*Maybe something like "I don't like it, but I guess he is going to be who he is."*
PRACTITIONER:	*And what about respect?* [CBT; Open question continuing to elicit alternative thinking]
CLIENT:	*I guess some people are just going to "dis" me no matter what I do.*
PRACTITIONER:	*Tell me more about that?* [Blend; Open question both exploratory and designed to elicit alternative thinking]
CLIENT:	*Since expecting people to be respectful usually ends with me upset, it'd probably help a lot to realize not everyone is going to be respectful. I guess if I let go of this idea that I have to be respected, I'd be calmer and get into fewer arguments.*
PRACTITIONER:	*So letting stuff roll off your back, instead of taking it personally would get you closer to the goals you talked about, like keeping a job, getting along with others and being a good parent.* [Blend; Reflection of change talk related to new belief]
CLIENT:	*Yes. I think it would.*
PRACTITIONER:	*Imagine sometime in the future when being respected is less important than it is now. What will be different about how you react to other people that will tell you that you are starting to be successful?* [Blend; Open question to elicit change talk related to alternative belief]
CLIENT:	*I'll probably let stuff go, maybe walk away. I won't let other people affect me that much.*
PRACTITIONER:	*So you will be able to step back.* [Blend; Reflection of change talk related to new belief]
CLIENT:	*Yeah.*
PRACTITIONER:	*What do you think you can do to start practicing this new attitude?* [Blend; Open question to begin the planning process and setting up homework assignment]

[The client and practitioner collaboratively plan appropriate homework to reinforce and practice the new thinking in day-to-day life.]

demanding beliefs are among the most common during anger experiences (Tafrate, Kassinove, & Dundin, 2002). This example represents a stylistic integration because CBT is used to establish a focus on a clinical target, while the practitioner is also borrowing heavily from MI. Notations are made for each practitioner response, indicating the skills being used and if a response was informed by MI, CBT, or represents a blend that contains elements of both models.

The above clinical dialogue integrates elements of both MI and CBT to produce a harmonious interaction. In this example, the practitioner is keying into both an irrational belief target and also attempting to elicit and reinforce change talk around the possibility of changing a current way of thinking and developing a new outlook. A prerequisite for this type of integration is a fluency in both models, the ability to conceptualize from each framework, and a comfort in shifting from a client-centered to a more active-directive stance.

We recognize that this type of interaction is neither MI nor CBT in their pure individual forms; however, strong elements of both are present. As Miller and Rollnick (2009) noted, "At some point, such a reinvention no longer contains and may even violate the spirit and elements that defined the original approach" (p. 130). That is surely the case in this example, and adherents to MI, and to the traditional CBT models of Beck and Ellis, will be able to identify instances where the dialogue departs significantly from these original approaches.

Obviously, in the above example the practitioner has a clear direction and maintains a more expert stance. Yet, it can be done in a way that emphasizes collaboration, evocation from the client, accurate empathy, and compassion.

There is no evidence to suggest that stylistic integration of MI and CBT will produce better outcomes than either model alone. Also, such integration poses a research challenge in determining which active ingredients are central to treatment because fidelity to each model is obscured. We are simply suggesting that as more CBT practitioners become familiar with MI, it seems only natural that a blending is likely to occur, resulting in an eclectic style.

Final Comments: MI, CBT, and RNR

Since motivation is a key factor in justice-involved clients changing difficult and intractable antisocial patterns, MI has rapidly emerged as a core clinical practice across criminal justice agencies and programs. In this chapter, we have provided a brief overview of the MI approach as it is typically applied to justice-involved clients. We have also highlighted the major distinctions between MI and CBT, pointed out areas of conceptual overlap, and discussed several strategies for integrating the two models.

One more comment regarding integration is warranted. The current leading framework in offender rehabilitation is the Risk-Need-Responsivity (RNR; Andrews & Bonta, 2010a) model. Although RNR is well known in the correctional field, it remains less familiar to practitioners in clinical and counseling psychology. In brief, RNR proposes: (i) treatment dosage should be commensurate with risk level; (ii) interventions should target criminogenic need areas; and (iii) interventions should be based on cognitive social learning principles and specifically tailored to offenders' learning styles, abilities, and motivation (see Rugge & Bonta, Chapter 7). Proponents of RNR have voiced optimism about the increasing use of MI with correctional clientele in order to better address challenges related to specific responsivity to intervention (Andrews, Bonta, & Wormith, 2011). Within an RNR framework, there is a growing attentiveness to the development of strategies for fostering offender-client engagement and motivation (Simourd & Olver, 2011), which appear to be critical roadblocks to effective treatment (Olver et al., 2011). The incorporation of MI in discussions with clients about changing criminogenic need areas holds promise for enhancing the effectiveness of our most successful targeted interventions for reducing criminal behavior (Andrews & Bonta, 2010b).

Since issues of motivation and engagement were not, to a great extent, emphasized in the traditional Beck and Ellis formulations of CBT, or the criminal thinking models that emerged in the 1950s, perhaps MI offers a critical piece previously missing. Clearly, more discussion and research are needed on the most effective ways to integrate MI within existing CBT and RNR frameworks. In the meantime, CBT practitioners who develop a competency in MI will possess a powerful set of skills to more successfully meet justice-involved clients where they are, enhance meaningful participation in treatment activities, and potentially improve the lives of some of society's most marginalized members.

References

Andrews, D. A., & Bonta, J. (2010a). *The psychology of criminal conduct* (4th ed.). New Providence, NJ: Matthew Bard and Company.

Andrews, D. A., & Bonta, J. (2010b). Rehabilitating criminal justice policy and practice. *Psychology, Public Policy, and Law, 16*, 39–55.

Andrews, D. A., Bonta, J., & Wormith, S. J. (2006). The recent past and near future of risk and/or need assessment. *Crime & Delinquency, 52*, 7–27.

Andrews, D. A., Bonta, J., & Wormith, S. J. (2008). *Level of Service/Case Management Inventory (LS/CMI) supplement: A gender-informed risk/need/responsivity assessment.* Toronto: Multi-Health Systems.

Andrews, D. A., Bonta, J., & Wormith, S. J. (2011). The Risk-Need-Responsivity (RNR) model: does adding the Good Lives model contribute to effective crime prevention? *Criminal Justice and Behavior, 38*, 735–755.

Beck, J. S. (2011). *Cognitive therapy: Basics and beyond* (2nd ed.). New York, NY: Guilford Press.

Berman, A. H. (2004). The Reasoning and Rehabilitation program: Assessing short- and long-term outcomes among male Swedish prisoners. *Journal of Offender Rehabilitation, 40*, 85–103.

Beyko, M. J., & Wong, S. C. P. (2005). Predictors of treatment attrition as indicators for program improvement not offender shortcomings: A study of sex offender treatment attrition. *Sexual Abuse: A Journal of Research and Treatment, 17*, 375–389.

Bordin, E. S. (1979). The generalizability of the psychoanalytic concept of the working alliance. *Psychotherapy: Theory, Research, and Practice, 16*, 252–260.

Burke, B. L. (2011). What can motivational interviewing do for you? *Cognitive and Behavioral Practice, 18*, 74–81.

Clark, M. D. (1998). Strength based practice: The ABC's of working with adolescents who don't want to work with you. *Federal Probation Quarterly, June*, 46–53.

Glynn, L. H., & Moyers, T. B. (2010). Chasing change talk: The clinician's role in evoking client language about change. *Journal of Substance Abuse Treatment, 39*, 65–70.

Hettema, J., Steel, J., & Miller, W. R. (2005). Motivational interviewing. *Annual Review of Clinical Psychology, 1*, 91–111.

Hiller, M. L., Knight, K., & Simpson, D. D. (1999). Risk factors that predict dropout from corrections-based treatment for drug abuse. *The Prison Journal, 79*, 411–430.

Kassinove, K., & Tafrate, R. (2011). Application of a flexible, clinically driven approach for anger reduction in the case of Mr. P. *Cognitive and Behavioral Practice, 18*, 222–234.

Kertes, A., Westra, H. A., Angus, L., & Marcus, M. (2011). The impact of motivational interviewing on client experiences of cognitive behavioral therapy for generalized anxiety disorder. *Cognitive and Behavioral Practice, 18*, 55–69.

Lundahl, B. W., Kunz, C., Brownell, C., Tollefson, D., & Burke, B. L. (2010). Meta-analysis of motivational interviewing: Twenty-five years of empirical studies. *Research on Social Work Practice, 20*, 137–160.

Luther, J., Pitocco, K., & Lovins, L. (2011). *Cognitive behavioral interventions for substance abuse.* Curriculum, University of Cincinnati Corrections Institute, University of Cincinnati, Cincinnati, OH.

Malcom Berg-Smith, S. (2010). *Guiding the learning of Motivational Interviewing: A resource for trainers.* Available from: www.berg-smithtraining.com/dvd.html

McMurran, M. (2009). Motivational interviewing with offenders: A systematic review. *Legal and Criminological Psychology, 14*, 83–100.

McMurran, M., & Theodosi, E. (2007). Is treatment non-completion associated with increased reconviction over no treatment? *Psychology, Crime & Law, 13*, 333–343.

Miller, W., Moyers, T., Ernst, D., & Amrhein, P. (2008, January 8). *Manual for the Motivational Interviewing Skill Code version 2.1.* Retrieved from http://casaa.unm.edu/download/misc.pdf

Miller, W. R., & Rollnick, S. (2009). Ten things that Motivational Interviewing is not. *Behavioural and Cognitive Psychotherapy, 37*, 129–140.

Miller, W. R., & Rollnick, S. (2013). *Motivational interviewing: Helping people change* (3rd ed.). New York, NY: Guilford Press.

Miller, W. R., Rollnick, S., & Moyers, T. B. (1998). *Motivational Interviewing Professional Training VHS Videotape/DVD Series.* Albuquerque, NM: University of New Mexico Center on Alcoholism, Substance Abuse, and Addictions (UNM/CASAA).

Miller, W. R., & Rose, G. S. (2009). Toward a theory of Motivational Interviewing. *American Psychologist, 64*, 527–537.

Moyers, T. B., Martin, T., Houck, J. M., Christopher, P. J., & Tonigan, J. S. (2009). From in-session behaviors to drinking outcomes: A causal chain for motivational interviewing. *Journal of Consulting and Clinical Psychology, 77*, 1113–1124.

Moyers, T., Martin, T., Manuel, J., Miller, W., & Ernst, D. (2010, January 22). *Motivational interviewing treatment integrity instrument 3.1.1.* Retrieved from http://casaa.unm.edu/download/MITI3_1.pdf

Moyers, T., & Martino, S. (2006). *"What's important in my life?" The personal goals and values card sorting task for individuals with schizophrenia.* Retrieved from http://casaa.unm.edu/inst/Values Card Sorting Task for Individuals with Schizophrenia.pdf

Nunes, K. L., & Cortoni, F. (2006). *The heterogeneity of treatment noncompleters* (Research Report No. R-176). Ottawa, Ontario, Canada: Correctional Service of Canada.

O'Kelly, M. (2010). *CBT in action: A practitioner's tool kit.* Melbourne, Australia: CBT Australia.

Olver, M. E., Stockdale, K. C., & Wormith, J. S. (2011). A meta-analysis of predictors of offender treatment attrition and its relationship to recidivism. *Journal of Consulting and Clinical Psychology, 79*, 6–21.

Persons, J. B. (2008). *The Case Formulation Approach to cognitive-behavior therapy.* New York, NY: Guilford Press.

Rosengren, D. B. (2009). *Building motivational interviewing skills: A practitioner workbook.* New York, NY: Guilford Press.

Rosengren, D., Baer, J., Hartzler, B., Dunn, C., Wells, E., & Ogle, R. (2009, April). *Video assessment of simulated encounters.* Retrieved from http://adai.washington.edu/instruments/PDF/VASERScoringManual_145.pdf

Simourd, D. J., & Olver, M. E. (2011). Use of the Self-Improvement Orientation Scheme-Self Report (SOS-SR) among incarcerated offenders. *Psychological Services, 8*, 200–211.

Simpson, H.B., & Zuckoff, A. (2011). Using motivational interviewing to enhance treatment outcome in people with obsessive-compulsive disorder. *Cognitive and Behavioral Practice, 18*, 28–37.

Tafrate, R., Kassinove, H., & Dundin, L. (2002). Anger episodes in high and low trait anger community adults. *Journal of Clinical Psychology, 58*, 1573–1590.

Westra, H. A., & Arkowitz, H. (2011). Integrating motivational interviewing with cognitive behavioral therapy for a range of mental health problems. *Cognitive and Behavioral Practice, 18*, 1–4.

Wagner, C. C., Ingersoll, K. S., & Contributors (2013). *Motivational interviewing in groups.* New York, NY: Guilford Press.

Suggestions for Further Learning

Books

Miller, W.R., & Rollnick, S. (2013). *Motivational interviewing: Helping people change* (3rd ed.). New York: Guilford Press.

Narr-King, S., & Suarez, M. (2011). *Motivational interviewing with adolescents and young adults.* New York, NY: Guilford Press.

Rosengren, D. B. (2009). *Building motivational interviewing skills: A practitioner workbook.* New York: Guilford Press.

Wagner, C. C., Ingersoll, K. S., & contributors (2013). *Motivational interviewing in groups.* New York: Guilford Press.

Website

Motivational Interviewing Network of Trainers (MINT): http://www.motivationalinterviewing.org/

Appendix 20.A

MI-Related Materials and Resources

Motivational Interviewing Network of Trainers (MINT)

The international MINT represents a network of MI trainers from across the world who have successfully attended a Train-the-Trainer (TNT) workshop and been inducted into the group. Trainings have been provided in over 25 languages, continually expanding the practice of MI for diverse application. A network listserv provides a platform where members explore the current and future application, research, and training of MI. For more information, visit: www. motivationalinterviewing.org.

Criminal Justice Motivational Interviewing Network of Trainers (CJ-MINTs)

In addition to the MINT, a growing group of professionals share experiences and resources in applying MI for use with criminal justice populations. Inclusion requires attendance in a train-the-trainer event and request for admission sent to Ray Gingerich (rjgingerich@gmail.com).

Assessing MI proficiency: instruments for coding and counting

There are several validated instruments used to assess practitioner proficiency with MI.

- *Motivational Interviewing Treatment Integrity (MITI) Code* (Moyers, Martin, Manuel, Miller, & Ernst, 2010) – Assesses practitioner fidelity to MI adherent speech.
- *Motivational Interviewing Skills Code (MISC)* (Miller, Moyers, Ernst, & Amrhein, 2008) – Assesses practitioner fidelity to MI adherent speech as well as client change talk.
- *Video Assessment of Simulated Encounters – Revised (VASE-R)* (Rosengren et al., 2009) – Practitioners' written responses to video vignettes are scored.

21

Integrating Strength-Based Practice with Forensic CBT

The Good Lives Model of Offender Rehabilitation

Clare-Ann Fortune and Tony Ward

Introduction

Working with offenders presents a wide range of difficulties for practitioners mainly due to the overlap between the therapeutic, ethical, and legal domains. It is never a question of simply teaching offenders the skills to manage their specific array of risk factors. In addition to skill acquisition, consideration should also be given to the kind of lives offenders wish to live and what kind of resources are required to assist them in the process of transforming their frequently inchoate conceptions into realities. Of course, the ultimate goal for correctional practitioners is to reduce offending rates. How best to achieve this, in ethically acceptable ways, is not so easy to determine. The trick is to get the balance right between addressing the legitimate concerns of community safety while also offering offenders opportunities for living meaningful and better lives.

In our view, the key to developing effective correctional interventions is to grasp that rehabilitation is a *multifaceted* process that involves the re-entry and the reintegration of an offender into society. Rehabilitation offers offenders the opportunity to change aspects of their personal characteristics that are offence related. In order for rehabilitation to be successful the community will also need to provide adequate social support and resources to offenders' efforts to change. Therefore, there needs to be a focus on skill acquisition, capacity building, and the enhancement of well-being along with the reduction of risk (Ward & Maruna, 2007; Ward & Salmon, 2009). In working with individuals who have engaged in criminal behavior, practitioners must negotiate a range of theoretical, research, and practical challenges and problems.

Rehabilitation theories are comprehensive practice frameworks that provide practitioners with conceptual maps, which assist them in negotiating the various challenges associated with correctional and forensic therapeutic work (Ward & Maruna, 2007). Ideally, rehabilitation theories should provide guidance on such issues as the overall aims of intervention, what constitutes risk, the general causes of crime, how best to manage and

Forensic CBT: A Handbook for Clinical Practice, First Edition.
Edited by Raymond Chip Tafrate and Damon Mitchell.
© 2014 John Wiley & Sons, Ltd. Published 2014 by John Wiley & Sons, Ltd.

work with individuals who are often reluctant to change, and how to effectively balance offender needs with the interests of the community. There are a number of available rehabilitation theories to assist practitioners in negotiating these various challenges (Ward & Maruna, 2007).

In the recent past, offender rehabilitation models focused on risk management. The most eminent risk reduction approach is perhaps the Risk-Need-Responsivity (RNR) model, which proposes that: (i) higher-*risk* cases receive more services than lower-risk cases; (ii) interventions target *need* areas directly linked to criminal behavior; and (iii) interventions are tailored and *responsive* to learning styles, abilities, and motivational factors present in offender-clients (Andrews & Bonta, 2010; Andrews, Bonta, & Hoge, 1990). Despite being held as the gold standard, the strengths and limitations of the RNR approach, particularly due to its preoccupation with risk management, have been well highlighted (e.g., see Ward & Maruna, 2007; Ward, Yates, & Willis, 2012). Lösel (2010) has suggested that the RNR approach was an important step forward in the rehabilitation field but that it is time to broaden the scope of our intervention efforts. He recommends that effective intervention with offenders needs to move beyond the "technology" of the program to include factors such as personal and social resources and personal relationships. Lösel argues that crime is more than simply a criminal justice issue but is also a public health, education, welfare, and economic issue, and therefore programs should integrate a broader context and range of services than those that currently exist.

Alternative approaches to offender rehabilitation have been proposed in recent years, which allow for the inclusion of strengths-based perspectives. The main difference between these two approaches is that traditional risk management frameworks primarily concentrate on the detection and modification of dynamic risk factors or what have been termed "criminogenic needs," while strengths-based approaches primarily focus on creating or increasing an offender's knowledge, skills, opportunities (i.e., internal and external capabilities), and resources that reduce risk for recidivism (Laws & Ward, 2010; Ward & Maruna, 2007). A strengths-based assessment will seek to identify individuals' (i) aspirations and fundamental values, and (ii) specific areas of competence. The goal is to assist them in acquiring the psychological and social resources necessary to achieve outcomes that matter to them most, along with reducing their potential for committing further offences.

The Good Lives Model (GLM) has been proposed as an alternative approach to the RNR, with Ward (2010) stating that it has the ability to integrate components of treatment that may be inadequately addressed by the RNR model, such as the development of the therapeutic alliance, increased agency (e.g., self-direction) and motivation to commit to treatment, and to a future that includes desistance from criminal behavior. Thus, the RNR and GLM are not necessarily mutually exclusive models.

The GLM is consistent with the shift in emphasis that Lösel (2010) flagged as being the next necessary step in ensuring the ongoing development of effective rehabilitation approaches. The GLM provides a framework to guide practitioners in offender case management and is increasingly being applied internationally in a range of offender treatment programs (Purvis, Ward, & Willis, 2011). The GLM has demonstrated preliminary effectiveness in addressing some of the key limitations of the risk management approach to offender rehabilitation, through such factors as enhancing treatment engagement, promoting desistance, and increasing attention to environmental contexts (Ward, Yates, & Willis, 2012). A growing body of research has found positive results for sexual offending interventions that have incorporated the GLM principles (Gannon, King, Miles, Lockerbie,

& Willis, 2011; Lindsay, Ward, Morgan, & Wilson, 2007; Ware & Bright, 2008; Whitehead, Ward, & Collie, 2007). Other researchers have provided support for the underlying assumptions of the GLM (Barnett & Wood, 2008; Bouman, Schene, & de Ruiter, 2009; Willis & Grace, 2008; Willis & Ward, 2011) and with other populations such as forensic mental health clients (Barnao, Robertson, & Ward, 2010).

This chapter is not intended to replace training for practitioners wanting to utilize the GLM but it does provide those interested with an introduction to a more strengths-based or positive approach to offender rehabilitation. For those already familiar with the GLM, it provides an overview of how it might be applied alongside cognitive-behavior therapy (CBT)-based programs, and some additional resources that may complement their existing CBT-focused resources.

The Good Lives Model

The GLM is a strengths-based approach to offender rehabilitation that was first proposed by Ward and Stewart in 2003, and further developed by Ward and colleagues (e.g., see Laws & Ward, 2011; Ward & Gannon, 2006; Ward & Marshall, 2004; Ward & Maruna, 2007; Yates, Prescott, & Ward, 2010). The model is responsive to offenders' particular interests, abilities, and aspirations. Using the GLM, practitioners develop intervention plans that will assist offenders in acquiring the capabilities and accessing the relevant internal and external resources to achieve personally meaningful goals. At the same time, intervention plans are also concerned with addressing public safety and risk reduction (Purvis et al., 2011).

One of the underlying assumptions of the GLM is that all individuals have similar basic aspirations and needs, and that one of the primary responsibilities of parents, teachers, and the broader community is to help each individual acquire the necessary tools to make their way in the world and live their good life. The GLM emphasizes offender agency as an inherent part of its focus on an offender's life values. According to the GLM, criminal behavior is seen as representing an individual's maladaptive attempts to acquire life values or "primary human goods" (Ward & Stewart, 2003) and results from an individual lacking adequate internal and external resources to attain desired values in a prosocial manner. This means that offenders, like the rest of us, are seen as actively seeking to satisfy their life values through whatever means are available to them; the problem being that sometimes their approaches are counterproductive, ineffective, and/or socially unacceptable.

From the GLM perspective, rehabilitation should: (i) provide offenders with the necessary knowledge, skills, opportunities, and resources to achieve their life goals in ways that do not cause harm to others; and (ii) recognize that offenders may require different levels of scaffolding in order to develop the skills they require in order to construct and implement a prosocial life plan that is meaningful to them (Ward, 2010). The GLM has practical utility for desistance-oriented interventions due to the fact that it draws practitioner attention to an offender's internal values and life priorities, as well as external factors they may require such as access to the necessary resources and opportunities.

The GLM contains three hierarchical sets of assumptions: general assumptions or concepts in relation to the aims of rehabilitation; etiological assumptions that account for the onset and maintenance of offending; and practical implications arising from the first and second sets of assumptions. These three sets of assumptions are outlined in more detail below.

Box 21.1 Eleven Primary Goods

1. Life (including healthy living and functioning)
2. Knowledge
3. Excellence in play
4. Excellence in work (including mastery experiences)
5. Excellence in agency (i.e., autonomy and self-directedness)
6. Inner peace (i.e., freedom from emotional turmoil and stress)
7. Relatedness (including intimate, romantic, and family relationships)
8. Community
9. Spirituality (in the broad sense of finding meaning and purpose in life)
10. Pleasure
11. Creativity

Adapted from Ward and Gannon, 2006, p. 79.

General concepts of the GLM

The GLM emphasizes the concept of human agency due to its grounding in the ethical concept of human dignity (see Ward & Syversen, 2009) and universal human rights. The GLM seeks to promote an individual's ability to select goals, and to develop and implement plans to achieve those goals. The GLM distinguishes between *primary* and *secondary goods*. Based on their review of psychological, social, biological, and anthropological research, Ward and colleagues (e.g., Ward & Brown, 2004; Ward & Marshall, 2004) initially proposed 10 classes of primary goods. More recently (e.g., Ward & Gannon, 2006; Ward, Mann, & Gannon, 2007), based on research by Purvis (2010), the goods of friendship and community have been divided to produce 11 classes of primary goods, as listed in Box 21.1.

A key assumption of the GLM is that all humans seek each of these 11 primary goods to some extent. There will be individual differences in the level of importance placed on a specific primary good due to differences in values and life priorities. This becomes an important consideration for practitioners working with offenders as care must be taken to identify an individual's motivations and the order in which each individual prioritizes pursuing the 11 primary goods (Ward, 2010). Part of this process involves exploring the *practical identities* an individual has. A client may have a number of practical identities they draw on in different contexts, for example, within family (e.g., roles of parent and spouse), work (e.g., psychologist or builder), and leisure (e.g., rugby player or darts player). According to Korsgaard (1996), conceptions of practical identity provide "a description under which you value yourself and find your life worth living and your actions to be worth undertaking" (p. 101). Thus individuals' sense of identity emerges from their basic value commitments, the goods they pursue in search of better lives. People have a number of practical identities, which all exert normative pressure on their decision-making and subsequent actions.

The GLM also takes into account instrumental goods, or *secondary goods*, which provide the means for obtaining the desired primary goods (Ward, Vess, Collie, & Gannon, 2006). For example, an individual completing a building apprenticeship (secondary good) might satisfy the primary goods of knowledge and excellence in work, whereas joining a sports team or cultural group (both secondary goods) might satisfy the primary goods of friendship. These prosocial activities are seen as being incompatible with dynamic risk (criminogenic) factors. This notion of instrumental or secondary goods is an important component of the GLM when considering offending as it is assumed that an individual's offending behavior occurred as a maladaptive or inappropriate attempt to secure primary goods (Ward, 2010). Therefore, interventions are designed to incorporate the primary goods and ways of achieving these in a manner that does not cause harm to others.

The distinction between avoidance and approach goals is also important to consider. Essentially, avoidance goals are associated with negative reinforcement (i.e., avoidance of criticism or punishment – aversive states – is reinforcing) and approach goals with positive reinforcement (i.e., their attainment is reinforcing). Historically those involved in the case management of, and interventions with, offenders have focused on avoidance goals. Avoidance goals represent undesirable states or situations. For example, a common avoidance goal for sexual offenders is not sexually reoffending. On the other hand, approach goals represent desired states or situations, such as obtaining a job. The GLM directly targets approach goals while indirectly targeting avoidance goals. For example, a sexual offender may have a goal of living a positive and prosocial life with appropriate social and intimate relationships. By striving for this approach goal he would also achieve the goal of not sexually reoffending. The approach goal provides an individual with a clearer guideline on how the avoidance goal will be achieved because it specifies an outcome a person needs to achieve in order to reduce the chances of experiencing an aversive state such as punishment or social criticism. For example, by establishing a relationship with an adult, a child sex offender reduces his chances of feeling lonely and thus should be less likely to seek sex with a child.

Etiological aspects of the GLM

According to the GLM there are two primary routes to the onset of offending: direct and indirect (Ward & Gannon, 2006; Ward & Maruna, 2007). The direct pathway refers to instances when an offender actively attempts (often implicitly) to directly attain primary goods through their criminal behavior. For example, an individual who lacks the skills and opportunities in their environment to realize the good of intimacy with an adult might instead attempt to achieve this good through sexual offending. The indirect pathway is implicated when the pursuit of one or more goods (particularly if there is conflict between them), creates a ripple or cascading effect, which may be unexpected and lead to an individual engaging in criminal activity. For example, conflict between the goods of intimacy and autonomy might lead to the break-up of a relationship, and subsequent feelings of loneliness and distress. Maladaptive coping strategies such as the use of alcohol to alleviate distress might, in specific circumstances, lead to a loss of control and culminate in offending (Ward, 2010).

Within the GLM framework, empirically identified criminogenic needs are conceptualized as internal (e.g., psychological) or external (e.g., social, economic) obstacles that interfere with an individual's capacity to attain their desired primary goods. For example, impulsivity might obstruct good fulfilment, while poor emotional regulation might prevent the achievement of inner peace. Each of the primary goods can be linked with one or more criminogenic needs (Ward & Maruna, 2007). Possible linkages between primary goods and criminogenic needs are presented in Table 21.1.

The GLM proposes four types of difficulties that offenders experience in their efforts to obtain primary goods. The difficulty is not with the primary goods themselves but resides in the

Table 21.1   Primary goods sand criminogenic needs.

Primary goods	*Criminogenic needs*
Agency	Impulsivity
Inner peace	Emotional dysregulation
Happiness	Deviant sexual preferences (pleasure)
Knowledge	Offense-supportive beliefs and attitudes
Excellence in play	Deviant sexual preferences
Excellence in work	Unemployment
Spirituality	Offense-supportive beliefs and attitudes
Community	Antisocial associates
Relatedness	Intimacy deficits
Creativity	Possibly unemployment/offense-supportive beliefs and attitudes
Life	Drug and alcohol abuse

problematic strategies offenders use to obtain the primary goods (Ward, 2010). The most common strategy, with a direct route to offending, is the use of *inappropriate secondary goods* to achieve primary goods. For example, as mentioned above, sexual offending may represent an inappropriate attempt to achieve the primary good of intimacy. Second, an individual's good life plan may have a *lack of scope* when a number of important goods are not included. A lack of scope occurs when individuals' implicit good lives plans do not include all the primary goods, for example, one characterized by a lack of attention to health or relatedness. This could contribute to an imbalance in which one or more components of their life (e.g., employment, social life) are undeveloped. Third, acute psychological stress and/or unhappiness may occur due to *conflict* arising in the pursuit of goods, particularly when there is a lack of coherence in the goods sought. When the goods sought by an individual are not ordered or coherently related to each other, this can contribute to feelings of frustration and/or cause harm to an individual and may also result in a life that seems to lack purpose or meaning (Ward & Stewart, 2003). The GLM refers to two different types of coherence – horizontal and vertical coherence. *Horizontal coherence* refers to the extent to which goods are related to each other in a logical manner and are not in conflict with each other. *Vertical coherence* refers to the extent to which goods are ranked hierarchically in a sensible manner by an individual. Finally, an individual may lack the *internal* (e.g., skills or knowledge) and *external* (e.g., supports, resources, employment opportunities) *capacities* to implement or adapt their life plan and may, therefore, fail to achieve their desired primary goods in a prosocial manner within their current environment.

How Can a Strengths-Based Approach Complement Forensic CBT?

The GLM is intended to supply practitioners with a more comprehensive rehabilitation framework for working with offenders than currently exists. As stated above, it functions as a broad "map" that needs to be supplemented by specific theories concerning concrete interventions such as CBT techniques (Ward & Maruna, 2007). Programs can, and have been, developed that reflect GLM assumptions and are best understood as GLM-consistent programs, not the GLM itself (Laws & Ward, 2011; Ward & Maruna, 2007). There are a number of practical advantages in integrating the GLM into forensic practice.

One advantage of strengths-based correctional frameworks is that they resonate with long-standing criminological research into the desistance process. Desistance theory and research seek to identify factors that are associated with the cessation of criminal behavior. Research has found that offenders respond well to practitioners who demonstrate an interest in them and believe in their capacity to make positive changes in their lives (McNeill, Batchelor, Burnett, & Knox, 2005). Reminding ourselves that offenders are human beings like us may assist us, as practitioners, in relating to them more constructively and improve correctional outcomes.

Another positive feature of strengths-based interventions are that they are responsive to offenders' commitments and interests, and thus are, arguably, likely to result in strong working alliances that facilitate the changes required for individuals to live more fulfilling and prosocial lives. Therefore, working from a GLM framework is likely to assist offenders' level of therapeutic engagement (Gannon et al., 2011).

Many components of CBT can fit within a GLM framework. For example, understanding a client's offending behavior within a CBT framework will also provide information to increase a practitioner's understanding of the individual within a GLM framework and assist the client in understanding their offending, thus contributing to the primary good of knowledge. The GLM also encourages practitioners to actively explore strengths the individual possesses (e.g., past successes and opportunities) and uncover what motivates the individual in terms of life goals, priorities, and desires. If this analysis reveals deficits that will impact an offender's ability to attain desired primary goods as such as friendship and happiness, then the social skills component of CBT would be appropriate to include in the therapeutic plan. Aspects such as social skills training, which are commonly part of a CBT intervention, fit within a GLM framework in that they allow a basis for providing an individual with knowledge and skills that may assist them in achieving the primary goods (e.g., friendship and happiness) through prosocial means. Standard CBT techniques are used in the acquisition and enhancement of these skills.

The GLM can be viewed as the overarching conceptual structure within which specific CBT techniques are embedded. In essence, within the GLM framework, CBT techniques are "wrapped around" individuals' life priorities or overarching goods. They provide concrete strategies for assisting individuals in formulating a good lives plan and translating that plan into action. For example, in order to pursue his dream of going to university and studying indigenous culture an offender will need to acquire the skills to dress and wash appropriately, communicate effectively to other students and teachers, resolve conflicts verbally, accept academic criticism, reduce substance intake, and so on.

Clinical Application: Suggestions for Integrating Strengths-Based Work into Forensic CBT

Within a GLM framework, the aim of intervention is to encourage the attainment of primary goods, or human needs that, once met, will enhance an individual's psychological well-being (Ward & Brown, 2004). To achieve this, the GLM supports the development of skills, knowledge, and resources for capacity building. When applying the GLM, the process begins with an assessment that maps out an offender's good lives conceptualization by identifying the value the individual places on various primary goods. There are two approaches used in achieving this: the first involves asking increasingly detailed questions about an offender's core commitments in life and what they value most in their daily activities and experiences, while the second involves identifying the underlying goals and values that are apparent in an offender's criminal behavior.

Ward (2010) provides a summary of the five phases of the GLM rehabilitation approach (e.g., see Laws & Ward, 2010; Ward & Maruna, 2007; Ward et al., 2007, for a more detailed description). Phase one of interventions with offenders using the GLM framework involves identifying the social, psychological, and material aspects of their offending including their level of risk and their social, physical, and psychological resources (e.g., substance use, housing and financial situation, personality patterns such as impulsivity) at the time of their offending and in the past. The second phase identifies the function of offending through exploration of the primary goods directly and indirectly associated with the criminal activity. The third phase involves identifying core practical identities and their associated primary goods or values to assist with the development of a life plan. Once an offender's conceptualization of what constitutes a good life is understood, future-oriented secondary goods can be identified collaboratively, which will assist individuals in achieving their desired primary goods in socially acceptable ways. Phase four therefore involves fleshing out the details from the previous phase including the secondary goods that will help with translating primary goods/values into a way of functioning and living the offender's good life. This information is used subsequently to develop a good lives plan (GLP). As part of understanding offenders' behavior it is important also to take into account the context within which the behavior occurred and the environment within which the individual is likely to function in the future, including considering the social, psychological, and material resources that will be available to assist them in attaining their primary goals (Ward, 2010). The fifth and final stage involves developing a detailed intervention plan that is holistic and incorporates both the internal and external conditions that are required in order to accomplish the offender's plan, which revolves around their core goals/values and practical identities. Practical steps are then identified to put the plan into action including the required resources/supports to achieve it. The plan is driven by the values, goals, and identities of the offender while the practitioner assists with forming the plan and balancing other considerations such as ethical entitlements of victims and the wider community.

Within the GLM framework, interventions are personalized around an offender's core values and identities (e.g., that of employee, partner, father), to assist them in attaining primary goods, in socially acceptable ways, and are designed to assist them in implementing their good lives intervention plan while simultaneously addressing criminogenic needs/risks that might be preventing them from attaining primary goods. The GLM, therefore, addresses criminogenic needs/dynamic risk factors indirectly through cognitive-behavioral techniques and social interventions, which are used to assist the offender in acquiring the required competencies to achieve their plan. Interventions may involve a range of aspects including building an individual's internal capacity, skills, and knowledge, and maximizing social supports and external resources. The focus therefore is on increasing agency, individual psychological well-being, and maximizing opportunities that will assist offenders in living a more prosocial life (Ward & Gannon, 2006).

The GLM can be incorporated into existing offender treatment programs. Ward et al. (2007) outlined a group-based application of the GLM based on seven modules typically incorporated into current best-practice cognitive-behavioral sexual offender treatment programs:

1. establishing therapy norms;
2. understanding offending and cognitive restructuring;

3. dealing with deviant arousal;
4. victim impact and empathy training;
5. affect regulation;
6. social skills training; and
7. relapse prevention.

For example, consistent with the GLM notion that dynamic risk factors can be viewed as maladaptive mechanisms for acquiring primary goods, the links between various modules and the associated primary goods were highlighted. The overarching good of knowledge can be gained when offenders understand how their thoughts, feelings, and actions contribute to their offending as part of the understanding offending and cognitive restructuring module. The overarching goods of friendship, community, and agency can be addressed through a social skills training module where the individual offender's good lives plan informs the nature of the interventions provided. For some offenders, who place high value on intimate relationships, intensive therapeutic work is likely to focus on intimacy and relationships, while for those who value other primary goods such as excellence in play and work over the good of friendship, basic social skills training will likely suffice.

Worksheets and Exercises

There are two worksheets (see Appendices 21.A and 21.B) which are taken from Purvis et al. (2011). These provide practitioners with the tools to record the information described above. The use of the worksheets also fosters a collaborative therapeutic approach and provides a record of what is discussed in a coherent and visual manner. The GLM Mapping Table (see Appendix 21.A) documents the client's internal and external *capacities* for achieving their desired primary goods. It also details whether the client has the required *means* to achieve their primary goods and what, if any, relationship those means might have with their prior criminal behavior. This process can also help clients identify what will assist them in achieving their "good life" as they move forward.

Appendix 21.B is the GLM Analysis Table, which was developed by Purvis et al. (2011) for use by case managers but could be used by other practitioners working with offenders. The GLM Analysis Table provides analysis of an individual offender's capacity for change, consideration of the range of appropriate and inappropriate means they have at their disposal to achieve their desired goods, and whether there is vertical and/or horizontal coherence to their life goals. It also helps highlight gaps in the scope of their desired goods, lack of means to achieve their desired goods or poor coherence. These gaps, along with identified strengths (e.g., appropriate means previously used), help in the development of the individualized intervention plan – their personally meaningful and prosocial Good Lives Plan (GLP).

Case Study: Sam the Gang Member

This case is essentially a fictional one drawn from characteristics of a number of offenders. The two worksheets (GLM Mapping and GLM Analysis) have been completed using the case study of Sam as an example to help illustrate their use in clinical practice (see Tables 21.2 and 21.3).

Table 21.2   The GLM mapping table for Sam.

Name: *Sam*
Person ID:

Table Number: _____
Date table commenced: ___/___/___

GOODS	WEIGHTING (preferences/ most valued good/s)	CAPACITY				MEANS Appropriate vs Inappropriate	RELATIONSHIP TO OFFENDING Direct or Indirect Pathway Protective or No Relationship
		Internal Capabilities (strengths)	Internal Obstacles (deficits)	External Capabilities	External Obstacles		
Relatedness	✓	Capacity for caring & empathy	Impulsivity, substance use, distrustful	Supportive tribal network, university support	Antisocial peers & environment, estrangement from family	Inappropriate	Indirect
Community	✓	Cultural identity & interest	Impulsivity, substance use, distrustful	Tribal affiliation	Gang membership, estrangement from tribal links	Inappropriate	Direct
Excellence in Work							
Pleasure							
Inner Peace							
Excellence in Agency							
Creativity							
Knowledge	✓	Superior intelligence, reads widely & cultural research	Impulsivity, substance use, lack of study skills	Local university opportunities, tribal support	Criminal associates, lack of formal education	Inappropriate – e.g., "intelligence officer"	Direct
Spirituality							
Life							
Excellence in Play							

Source: From Purvis, Ward, & Willis, 2011.

Brief description

Sam is a 35-year-old member of a Māori gang (Māori are New Zealand's indigenous people); he has a long criminal history and has been imprisoned in the past for serious sexual, drug, property, and violent crimes. His most recent sentence was for the rape of a young woman and

Table 21.3 The GLM analysis table for Sam.

Name: *Sam* Person ID:			Table Number: _____ Date table commenced: ___/___/_____		
LIFE PLAN – PAST/TIME OF OFFENDING			**LIFE PLAN – PRESENT TIME/FUTURE**		
TYPE OF LIFE PLAN:	PATHWAY TO OFFENDING:		TYPE OF LIFE PLAN:	PATHWAY TO OFFENDING:	
☐ Explicit – Overt	☐ Direct ☐ Indirect ☐ Undetected		☐ Explicit	✓Direct ☐ Indirect ☐ Undetected	
☐ Explicit – Covert	☐ Direct ☐ Indirect ☐ Undetected		✓ **Implicit**: *Unaware of somewhat disorganized & chaotic lifestyle; antisocial activities*	☐ Indirect ☐ Undetected	
☐ Implicit	☐ Indirect ☐ Undetected			☐ Indirect ☐ Undetected	
LIFE PLAN DESCRIPTION AND ANALYSIS:			LIFE PLAN DESCRIPTION AND ANALYSIS		

SCOPE and MEANS					
Goods Sought and Secured via Appropriate means		Goods Sought and Secured via Inappropriate means		Non-secured Goods	
Knowledge	*Through self-study*	*Knowledge*	*"Intelligence officer"*	*Spirituality*	*Disconnected from cultural beliefs*
Leisure	*Plays touch football*	*Relatedness*	*Gang membership, impersonal sexual relationships*	*Creativity*	*Criminal planning*
		Community	*Gang associates*	*Life/Health*	*Substance use, poor diet*
		Pleasure	*Sexual assault*	*Leisure*	*Lacks scope*
		Inner peace	*Substance use*	*Work mastery*	*Criminal activities*
				Agency	*Impulsivity, intimidation & violence*

Analysis:
Primary goods are community, relatedness & knowledge which are sought through gang membership. The primary flaws in his offense-related GLP are those of conflict between his pleasure in knowledge & the narrowness of his role, & a lack of formal opportunities to explore his cultural heritage. Furthermore, Sam still has problems controlling his anger & finds it difficult to control his drug taking (capacity problems).

Table 21.3 (*Continued*)

CAPACITY					
Key Strengths: (will be largely presented in goods with appropriate means)		**Key Obstacles**: (will be largely presented in goods with inappropriate means)			New strengths being developed/ focused on:
Internal	External	Internal	State of change	External	
Intelligence & learning	*Supportive university*				
Capacity for caring & empathy	*Good therapeutic relationship*				
Cultural identity	*Supportive tribe*				
Persistence	*Educational supports & Supportive tribe*				

COHERENCE		
Horizontal Coherence	Vertical Coherence	
Limited scope although many goods are "met" through gang membership & criminal activity	HIGHEST WEIGHTED GOODS	PATHWAY TO OFFENDING
Problems of coherence associated with relationships characterized by distrust & violence	*Knowledge – Ineffective strategies for obtaining cultural training & expertise*	☐ **Direct** ☐ Protective ☐ Indirect ☐ Unrelated
	Relatedness – relationships characterized by intimidation & violence	☐ Direct ☐ Protective ☐ **indirect** ☐ Unrelated
	Community – lack of link between cultural interest & level of tribal connection & knowledge	☐ **Direct** ☐ Protective ☐ Indirect ☐ Unrelated
	ANALYSIS: *Need to formulate a good lives plan (GLP) that explicitly links the goods of knowledge, community, & relatedness to Sam's practical identities (secondary goods & contexts) of being a university student & member of the university & Māori support & cultural groups.*	

Source: From Purvis, Ward, & Willis, 2011.

a serious assault on her boyfriend. Sam was recently released on parole but is still associating with gang members. He has spent most of his adult life in prison and has never managed to complete a period of parole without committing another offense. His role in the gang appears to be that of an "intelligence officer" – essentially the gang thinker and planner. Sam had attended several RNR-type programs in the past, without much success. He is estranged from his family (father, mother, four siblings) and has several children with a partner, from whom he is now separated.

Detection of offending-related phenomena

Sam underwent a comprehensive psychological and social assessment, which revealed a significant number of dynamic risk factors (criminogenic needs) and general problems, and also determined that he was at high risk for further offending. The specific problems identified were substance abuse, attitudes and beliefs that were supportive of both sexual and non-sexual offending, high levels of aggression and anger, gang membership (with known criminal associates), alienation from his Māori tribe and culture, and lack of intimacy. Sam is a highly intelligent individual (assessed as possessing superior intelligence) who has had little formal education but who is self-educated; he reads widely on politics, popular science, and Māori history and culture. He expressed dissatisfaction over his current lifestyle but believes that he has few realistic options for change.

Practical identities: identification of offense-related primary goods

Sam's central primary goods are those of knowledge and community. He enjoys the planning aspect of his role in the gang, and is always meticulous in gathering and analyzing information relating to planning future crimes. Furthermore, he reads widely on history and researches his cultural heritage. From Sam's perspective, he is a thinker and planner, something he enjoys for its own sake although there are also elements of mastery evident as well. In addition, he obtains a sense of belonging through being a member of the gang, which he describes as a brotherhood that allows him to be *"part of a community."* Identifying as Māori is a source of immense pride for Sam although he is unable to speak the language and lacks formal ties with his tribe. Thus, Sam's two primary practical identities were assessed as being an intellectual, a strategic thinker, and being part of a Māori (gang) fellowship. It is evident that Sam is at a turning point as he is starting to feel frustrated over the narrowness of his gang role and distressed at the violent nature of his community. The primary flaws in his offense-related GLP are those of conflict between his pleasure in knowledge and the narrowness of his role, and a lack of formal opportunities to explore his cultural heritage. Furthermore, he still has problems controlling his anger at times and finds it difficult to control his drug taking (capacity problems).

Selection of practical identities: looking to the future

When asked about his future aspirations, Sam replied that he had always wanted to attend a university to study Māori culture and history, and also wished that he was in a stable and loving relationship with a woman. It is clear that continued membership in the gang is a significant constraint in advancing his endorsed primary goods of community, knowledge, and relatedness. Sam is desperate to turn his life around and is discouraged by his history of being in and out of prison and of having relationships undermined by his fear and lack of commitment.

Social ecologies and practical identities: taking context into account

The Dean of Arts at the local university, which has a strong interest in Māori culture and scholarship, was willing to enroll Sam in a preparatory university course and, if he was successful, allow him subsequently to enroll full time. A condition of this enrollment was that Sam did not wear his gang patch on campus, did not attend classes under the influence of substances, and did not behave in a threatening or violent manner. Furthermore, Sam was introduced to a Māori support group that contained a number of mature students like himself. Around this time he decided to leave the gang and after some initial problems was allowed to do so. Sam was also given the opportunity to renew contact with his tribe through a fellow student at the university.

Formulation of detailed good lives plan

The practitioner working with Sam formulated a good lives plan (GLP) that explicitly linked the goods of knowledge, community, and relatedness to his practical identities (secondary goods and contexts) of being a university student and member of the university and Māori support and cultural groups. Using a variety of empirically validated CBT techniques, Sam learned in therapy how to manage his anger, and alcohol and drug use, and to apply more adaptive norms and beliefs when dealing with people. This work was able fruitfully to build upon his past participation in RNR violence programs and, because the techniques he was learning were recruited in the service of goals he was totally committed to, Sam was more motivated to learn how to master them. It was anticipated that he would cultivate social and even romantic relationships with the non-gang people he mixed with in the various support groups he attended, possibly taking up the numerous opportunities to join in prosocial recreational and sporting activities. The whole range of primary goods were built into Sam's GLP with an emphasis being on the two primary practical identities of a Māori history and culture student and being a member of a Māori community and tribe; and their respective goods of knowledge and community.

Comments

For the first time Sam was able to complete his parole and is not known to have committed any additional offenses. He is completing a degree in Māori studies and is in a significant relationship with a Māori woman (non-gang member) who is also studying at the university. Sam has formed good supportive relationships with other non-offending Māori men and has been in touch with the elders from his tribe. In our view, the turning point in his desistance journey began when a psychologist asked Sam about what he had always wanted to do. This question gave him space to reflect more critically on his life and to identify personal aspirations that had been hovering just below the surface of his mind. The formulation of a plan that he personally endorsed, that he could see was going to give him a chance at a better, more meaningful life, was pivotal. We cannot expect men and woman to commit themselves to years of sustained hard work and anxiety with a vague promise that they will be less likely to reoffend. Rather, helping them to fashion good lives plans that resonate with their values and hopes, and that actively recruit and build internal and external resources, is much more likely to persuade someone to make the effort.

In this example, effective intervention involved the reintegration of Sam into the community and the acquisition of various skills through the process of therapy. Social intimacy, self-regulation, problem-solving, sexual regulation, and emotional management skills programs work by enhancing individuals' agency capacity and therefore allowing them to build lives that align with their needs and core commitments. As we saw in the case of Sam, arguably most of the decisive rehabilitation work was done outside the therapy room and in the community with the assistance of friends, community agencies, and educational personnel. Essentially this rehabilitation work involved the utilization of social and cultural resources, and social capital. A notable feature of a comprehensive or "holistic" rehabilitation theory like the GLM is that it can seamlessly integrate psychological and social resources in ways that promote well-being while simultaneously reducing risk for further offending. It does this, in part, by assisting people in capitalizing on natural desistance moments such as a job offer, an opportunity to study, or someone extending a hand of friendship.

Conclusion

There has been increasing interest in positive psychology or strengths-based approaches, of which the GLM is an example. It provides practitioners with an approach to offender rehabil-itation that focuses on working collaboratively with the individual to achieve their life goals through prosocial means while not ignoring the importance of reducing their risk of further offending. As a rehabilitation framework, the strengths-based approach can be combined with (or more accurately incorporate) other specific theories, such as CBT, in an effort to increase the individual's capacity (i.e., internal and external resources, skills, and knowledge) for achiev-ing their good lives goals. The benefits of utilizing a strengths-based approach, such as the GLM, can include improved therapeutic alliances, and increases in an individual's sense of agency (e.g., self-direction) and motivation to commit to treatment, and a future that includes desistance from further criminal behavior.

References

Andrews, D. A., & Bonta, J. (2010). *The psychology of criminal conduct* (5th ed.). New Providence, NJ: Matthew Bender & Company Inc.

Andrews, D. A., Bonta, J., & Hoge, R. D. (1990). Classification for effective rehabilitation: Rediscovering psychology. *Criminal Justice and Behavior, 17* (1), 19–52. doi: 10.1177/0093854890017001004

Barnao, M., Robertson, P., & Ward, T. (2010). The Good Lives Model applied to a forensic population. *Psychiatry, Psycholog, & Law, 17,* 202–217.

Barnett, G., & Wood, J. L. (2008). Agency, relatedness, inner peace, and problem solving in sexual of-fending: How sexual offenders prioritize and operationalize their good lives conceptions. *Sexual Abuse: Journal of Research and Treatment 20* (4), 444–465. doi: 10.1177/1079063208325202

Bouman, Y. H. A., Schene, A. H., & de Ruiter, C. (2009). Subjective well-being and recidivism in foren-sic psychiatric outpatients. *International Journal of Forensic Mental Health, 8* (3), 225–234. doi: 10.1080/14999011003635647

Gannon, T. A., King, T., Miles, H., Lockerbie, L., & Willis, G. M. (2011). Good lives sexual offender treatment for mentally disordered offenders. *British Journal of Forensic Practice, 13* (3), 153–168. doi: 10.1108/14636641111157805

Korsgaard, C. M. (1996). *The sources of normativity.* Cambridge: Cambridge University Press.

Laws, D. R., & Ward, T. (2010). Desistance from sex offending: Motivating change, enriching practice. *International Journal of Forensic Mental Health, 9,* 11–23. doi: 10.1080/14999011003791598

Laws, D. R., & Ward, T. (2011). *Desistance from sex offending: Alternatives to throwing away the keys.* New York, NY: Guilford Press.

Lindsay, W. R., Ward, T., Morgan, T., & Wilson, I. (2007). Self-regulation of sex offending, future pathways and the Good Lives Model: Applications and problems. *Journal of Sexual Aggression, 13* (1), 37–50. doi:10.1080/13552600701365613

Lösel, F. (2010). *What works in offender rehabilitation: A global perspective.* Paper presented at the 12th Annual Conference of the International Corrections and Prisons Association.

McNeill, F., Batchelor, S., Burnett, R., & Knox, J. (2005). *21st century social work. Reducing Reoffending: Key practice skills.* Edinburgh: Scottish Executive.

Purvis, M. (2010). *Seeking a Good Life: Human goods and sexual offending.* Lambert Academic Press, Germany.

Purvis, M., Ward, T., & Willis, G. M. (2011). The Good Lives Model in practice: Offence pathways and case management. *European Journal of Probation, 3* (2), 4–28.

Ward, T. (2010). The Good Lives Model of offender rehabiliation: Basic assumptions, aetiological commitments, and practice implications. In F. McNeill, P. Raynor, & C. Trotter (Eds.), *Offender supervision: New directions in theory, research and practice* (pp. 41–64). Oxon, UK: Willan Publishing.

Ward, T., & Brown, M. (2004). The Good Lives Model and conceptual issues in offender rehabilitation. *Psychology, Crime & Law 10* (3), 243–257. doi: 10.1080/10683160410001662744

Ward, T., & Gannon, T. A. (2006). Rehabilitation, etiology, and self-regulation: The comprehensive good lives model of treatment for sexual offenders. *Aggression and Violent Behavior, 11* (1), 77–94. doi: 10.1016/j.avb.2005.06.001

Ward, T., Mann, R. E., & Gannon, T. A. (2007). The Good Lives Model of offender rehabilitation: Clinical implications. *Aggression and Violent Behavior, 12* (1), 87–107. doi: 10.1016/j.avb.2006.03.004

Ward, T., & Marshall, W. L. (2004). Good lives, aetiology and the rehabilitation of sex offenders: A bridging theory. *Journal of Sexual Aggression, Special Issue: Treatment & Treatability, 10* (2), 153–169. doi: 10.1080/13552600412331290102

Ward, T., & Maruna, S. (2007). *Rehabilitation: Beyond the risk assessment paradigm.* London, UK: Routledge.

Ward, T., & Salmon, K. (2009). The ethics of punishment: Correctional practice implications. *Aggression and Violent Behavior, 13* (4), 239–247. doi: 10.1016/j.avb.2009.03.009

Ward, T., & Stewart, C. A. (2003). The treatment of sex offenders: Risk management and good lives. *Professional Psychology: Research and Practice, 34* (4), 353–360. doi: 10.1037/0735-7028.34.4.353

Ward, T., & Syversen, K. (2009). Human dignity and vulnerable agency: An ethical framework for forensic practice. *Aggression and Violent Behavior, 14* (2), 94–105. doi: 10.1016/j.avb.2008.12.002

Ward, T., Vess, J., Collie, R. M., & Gannon, T. A. (2006). Risk management or goods promotion: The relationship between approach and avoidance goals in treatment for sex offenders. *Aggression and Violent Behavior, 11* (4), 378–393. doi: 10.1016/j.avb.2006.01.001

Ward T., Yates, P., & Willis, G. (2012). The Good Lives Model and the Risk Need Responsivity model: A critical response. *Criminal Justice and Behavior, 39*, 94–110.

Ware, J., & Bright, D. A. (2008). Evolution of a treatment programme for sex offenders: Changes to the NSW Custody-Based Intensive Treatment (CUBIT). *Psychiatry, Psychology and Law, 15* (2), 340–349.

Whitehead, P. R., Ward, T., & Collie, R. M. (2007). Time for a change: Applying the Good Lives Model of rehabilitation to a high-risk violent offender. *International Journal of Offender Therapy and Comparative Criminology, 51* (5), 578–598. doi: 10.1177/0306624X06296236

Willis, G. M., & Grace, R. C. (2008). The quality of community reintegration planning for child molesters: effects on sexual recidivism. *Sexual Abuse: A Journal of Research and Treatment 20* (2), 218–240. doi: 10.1177/1079063208318005

Willis, G. M., & Ward, T. (2011). Striving for a good life: The Good Lives Model applied to released child molesters. *Journal of Sexual Aggression, 17*, 290–303. doi: 10.1080/13552600.2010.505349

Yates, P. M., Prescott, D., & Ward, T. (2010). *Applying the Good Lives and Self-Regulation Models to sex offender treatment: A practical guide for clinicians.* Brandon, VT: Safer Society Press.

Suggestions for Further Learning

Book

Yates, P. M., & Prescott, D. S. (2011). *Building a better life: A good lives and self-regulation workbook.* Brandon, VT: Safer Society Press.

Website

Good Lives Model website (www.goodlivesmodel.com) provides a range of resources including a list of publications on the GLM and profiles on some of the researchers and scholars who have contributed to the development and evaluation of GLM-consistent programs.

Appendix 21.A

The GLM Mapping Table

Name: _____

Person ID: _____

Table Number: _____

Date table commenced: ___ / ___ / ___

GOODS	WEIGHTING (preferences/ most valued good/s)	CAPACITY				MEANS	RELATIONSHIP TO OFFENDING
		Internal Capabilities (strengths)	Internal Obstacles (deficits)	External Capabilities	External Obstacles	Appropriate vs Inappropriate	Direct or Indirect Pathway Protective or No Relationship
Relatedness							
Community							
Excellence in Work							
Pleasure							
Inner Peace							
Excellence in Agency							
Creativity							
Knowledge							
Spirituality							
Life							
Excellence in Play							

Source: From Purvis, Ward, & Willis, 2011.

Appendix 21.B

The GLM Analysis Table

Name: Table Number: _____
Person ID: Date table commenced: ___/___/_____

LIFE PLAN – PAST/TIME OF OFFENDING		LIFE PLAN – PRESENT TIME/FUTURE	
TYPE OF LIFE PLAN:	PATHWAY TO OFFENDING:	TYPE OF LIFE PLAN:	PATHWAY TO OFFENDING:
☐ Explicit – Overt	☐ Direct ☐ Indirect ☐ Undetected	☐ Explicit	☐ Direct ☐ Indirect ☐ Undetected
☐ Explicit – Covert	☐ Direct ☐ Indirect ☐ Undetected	☐ Implicit	☐ Indirect ☐ Undetected
☐ Implicit	☐ Indirect ☐ Undetected		☐ Indirect ☐ Undetected
LIFE PLAN DESCRIPTION AND ANALYSIS:		LIFE PLAN DESCRIPTION AND ANALYSIS	

SCOPE and MEANS		
Goods Sought and Secured via Appropriate means	Goods Sought and Secured via Inappropriate means	Non-secured Goods
Analysis:		

CAPACITY					
Key Strengths: (will be largely presented in goods with appropriate means)		Key Obstacles: (will be largely presented in goods with inappropriate means)			New strengths being developed/ focused on:
Internal	External	Internal	State of change	External	

COHERENCE			
Horizontal Coherence	Vertical Coherence		
	HIGHEST WEIGHTED GOODS	PATHWAY TO OFFENDING	
		☐ Direct ☐ Indirect	☐ Protective ☐ Unrelated
		☐ Direct ☐ Indirect	☐ Protective ☐ Unrelated
		☐ Direct ☐ Indirect	☐ Protective ☐ Unrelated
	ANALYSIS:		

Source: From Purvis, Ward, & Willis, 2011.

22

Treating Depression and PTSD Behind Bars

An Interaction Schemas Approach

Key Sun

The Need for Treating Depression and PTSD in Incarcerated Clients

Among the growing population of mentally disordered offenders in the prisons and jails across the correctional system, a large proportion suffer from depression and/or post-traumatic stress disorder (PTSD) (Bureau of Justice Statistics [BJS], 2006; Heckman, Cropsey, & Olds-Davis, 2007). For example, a BJS report (2006) indicated that about 23% of state prisoners and 30% of jail inmates reported symptoms of major depression. A review by Heckman et al. (2007) showed that PTSD rates among prisoners were also very high, reaching approximately 21% among male inmates, 48% among female prisoners, and 24–65% among male juvenile offenders. These rates were much higher than the 5–12% PTSD rates observed in community samples.

In spite of the critical need to treat the depressive and PTSD symptoms of incarcerated clients, the majority of cognitive-behavioral treatments (CBT) in facilities of confinement appear mainly focused on issues related to reducing recidivism (e.g., antisocial values, criminal peers, low self-control, dysfunctional family ties, substance abuse, and criminal personality; see Hansen, 2008), rather than on treating mental disorders. Although some research shows that a CBT-based approach can successfully reduce depressive and PTSD symptoms in incarcerated offenders by increasing coping and problem-solving skills, improving anger management, and reducing stress (e.g., Heckman et al., 2007; Smedley, 2010; Spiropoulos, Spruance, Van Voorhis, & Schmitt, 2005), a number of issues, including how different schemas regulate cognitive processes (e.g., appraisals, interpretations, explanations, adjustments), remain to be examined.

The Intrinsic Association Between Depression and PTSD

Depression and PTSD are best treated as a combined problem in cognitive therapy for incarcerated clients because research has demonstrated that there is an intrinsic connection between depression and PTSD symptoms for offenders. Although the *Diagnostic and Statistical*

Forensic CBT: A Handbook for Clinical Practice, First Edition.
Edited by Raymond Chip Tafrate and Damon Mitchell.
© 2014 John Wiley & Sons, Ltd. Published 2014 by John Wiley & Sons, Ltd.

Manual (4th edn., text revision) (DSM-IV-TR; American Psychiatric Association, 2000) classifies depression as a mood disorder and PTSD as an anxiety disorder, both share similar symptoms, such as: feelings of ineffectiveness, shame, despair, or hopelessness; feelings of worthlessness or excessive guilt; insomnia or hypersomnia, feeling permanently damaged; a significant change in previously sustained beliefs; hostility; social withdrawal; feeling constantly threatened; impaired relationships with others; or a change in previous personality character-istics. The correlation between depression and PTSD is also demonstrated by the high fre-quency that they precede, follow, or emerge concurrently with one another.

Foa, Ehlers, Clark, Tolin, and Orsillo (1999) found that the most typical PTSD symptoms include negative cognitions about self, negative cognitions about the world (e.g., the world is entirely dangerous; distrust of others), and self-blame, which were correlated moderately or strongly with depression and general anxiety symptoms. In addition, clinical observations (e.g., Sun, 2008; Wolff & Shi, 2010) suggest that the overwhelming majority of offenders with mental disorders have been the victims of interpersonal violence (e.g., childhood sexual or physical abuse, domestic battering). Nevertheless, it is important for therapists to pay attention to the unique symptoms of PTSD, which include: (i) exposure to a severe stressor resulting in intense fear, helplessness, or horror; (ii) re-experiencing the trauma; (iii) avoid-ance/numbing; and (iv) increased arousal (Heckman et al., 2007), as well as the fear to express emotions, and intrusive recollections, thoughts, and flashbacks (Clark & Beck, 2010).

Treating Incarcerated Clients Poses Unique Challenges

Counselors/therapists working with offenders in a facility of confinement would be wise to take into consideration three factors: (i) the setting, (ii) client characteristics, and (iii) the unique counseling/treatment process. Each of these factors may influence the effectiveness of counseling practice with correctional clients.

First, correctional centers (e.g., federal and state prisons, jails, and juvenile detention cen-ters) do not represent a very salubrious environment for therapy. Not only is the architectural design of the physical environment (particularly if the prison is fortress-like) not conducive to counseling and treatment, but also the punitive atmosphere and unavoidable interpersonal conflicts (e.g., dysfunctional interactions with inmates and custody staff) can undermine the best treatment efforts and aggravate existing mental disorders. Another disadvantage of cor-rectional environments includes the clients' isolation stemming from a lack of support from their families and communities. Thus, treatment personnel would be wise to take into account the physical and interpersonal aspects of a correctional settings and how these factors might influence the effectiveness of interventions (see Sun, 2008).

Second, not all correctional clients have the same degree of responsivity to correctional interventions. Responsivity factors can include the offender's verbal ability, motivation, per-sonality factors, interpersonal competence, and/or learning style (Andrews & Bonta, 2006, 2010). Some inmates have resistant attitudes toward counseling and treatment characterized as uncommunicative, hostile, detached, mistrustful, avoidant of self-disclosure (e.g., refusing to share personal problems with his/her therapist/counselor or treatment group), cynical (e.g., the belief that prison counseling is useless "bull" sessions), as well as a tendency to min-imize and deny problems. Developing a therapeutic alliance, which has been found to be strongly associated with better client outcomes, can pose a significant challenge with correc-tional clients. The therapeutic alliance is defined as the collaborative relationship between therapist and client that is characterized by agreement between the counselor and the client on the goals of intervention, a joint effort in developing and completing treatment goals, and therapeutic values (e.g., trust, respect, acceptance, empathy, and support) (see Matthews & Hubbard, 2007).

For female offenders with depression and PTSD, therapists may need to consider the potential impact of what have been referred to as *gender-responsive factors* on treatment. An accumulating body of literature suggests that risks and needs are somewhat different for male and female offenders, with female offenders more likely to be impacted by trauma and abuse, unhealthy relationships, parental stress, depression, substance abuse, anger/hostility, poverty, and concerns for personal safety (Salisbury, Van Voorhis, & Spiropoulos, 2009; Van Voorhis, Wright, Salisbury, & Bauman, 2010). For more comprehensive discussion of working with female offenders see Van Dieten and King (Chapter 16).

Third, for incarcerated clients, the counseling process (assessment, intervention, and termination/follow-up) also poses some unique challenges not commonly encountered in outpatient therapy. For example, the concept of termination carries a different meaning in a correctional counseling setting. More often than not, the counseling process for a correctional client is terminated not because treatment goals have been reached, but because the client must be transferred to another correctional institution or unit. Further complicating treatment, for security reasons, the counselor may not be allowed to inform the client about the transfer until the day before. Correctional counselors in prison settings will seldom complete treatments as planned.

Furthermore, the unprepared treatment termination tends to produce a wide variety of negative feelings and behaviors from the clients. According to Baum (2005), clients are inclined to show great resistance, anger, rage, anxiety, and frustration regarding treatment termination when it is abrupt and outside their control and desire. On the other hand the more clients believe that they have attained their therapeutic goals and have some degree of choice in ending treatment, the more positive feelings and reactions they have toward the termination. This problem may, to some extent, aggravate the client's depression because it generates a sense of unpredictability and instability. One way to prevent or alleviate the client's anger and negative behavior in response to an unwanted termination is to inform him or her early on in treatment about the possibility of an unanticipated counseling termination and to develop a plan to handle the negative reactions when they occur.

The Interaction Schemas Approach

The interaction schemas approach is a cognitive model to explain mental and interpersonal experiences (Sun, 2008, 2013). This perspective is similar to other cognitive schema models (e.g., Beck, 1991; Martin & Young, 2010) emphasizing that distorted cognition leads to conflict in the mental and interpersonal domains; while successfully modifying distorted cognition creates and maintains emotional well-being and interpersonal harmony. However, the interaction schemas approach differs from other schema models in its definition of cognitive schemas, cognitive distortions, and in the underlying treatment rationale. For example, the interaction schemas approach views self-appraisals as determined by accurate or inaccurate cognitive structures (pattern and interpersonal schemas) representing interpersonal reality and its patterns. In contrast, other cognitive models regard self-appraisals (self-schemas) as primary, in that self-schemas serve as both the main source of mental conflict and the solution. The term "interaction schemas" is used to emphasize that self-appraisals are derived from cognitive (knowledge) structures regulating interactions with actual or imagined others and environments. There are at least three important differences that separate the interaction schemas approach from the other popular cognitive models. For detailed discussions of the application of other schema models to offenders, see Seeler et al. (Chapter 2) and Keulen-de Vos et al. (Chapter 4).

First, in contrast to traditional cognitive therapy (e.g., Beck, 1991), which sees the self-concept as the essential content of schemas, the interaction schemas approach posits that our cognitions (schemas) comprise three interrelated mental representations: *self-schema*, *pattern schemas* (perceived patterns or rules governing human behavior and interactions), and *interpersonal schemas* (cognitions about others and situations in interaction with the self). Self-appraisals result from applying the pattern and interpersonal schemas to the evaluation of the self's attributes and experiences in terms of perceived validation and invalidation from the others and situations. Although there is some overlap between the notion of "invalidation" in the current interpersonal schemas approach and the conceptions of "disconnection" and "rejection" in Young's (Martin & Young, 2010) schema therapy, the other theoretical premises are different.

Second, traditional cognitive therapy (e.g., Beck, 1991; Clark & Beck, 2010) seems to view a negative or maladaptive self-schema as the locus of distorted cognitions that serve as a main source of mental conflict. The current model, however, regards distorted cognition as including distorted pattern schemas and interpersonal schemas, which engender maladaptive self-appraisals and interpersonal behavior.

Third, in terms of treatment, rather than emphasizing modifying the negative beliefs about the self, the interaction schemas approach suggests focusing on identifying and modifying the client's distorted pattern schemas (cognitions about what regulates human interactions and psychological experiences) and interpersonal schemas.

The following sections of this chapter will highlight the characteristics of the interaction schemas approach and its application to correctional clients.

Self-appraisals are regulated by the interaction schemas

It is necessary to first specify the meaning of schemas in the human domain. They refer to cognitive (knowledge) structures or organized mental representations of social entities (e.g., self, others, human interaction, and/or events). In this chapter, the terms such as schemas, cognition, perception, and belief are used interchangeably to designate the same structured cognitive system.

As noted above, instead of viewing the self-concept as the essence of schemas, the current approach maintains that people's schemas about human reality consist of three interrelated mental components, including: (i) self-schema (e.g., cognition related to self's attributes, actions, and experiences); (ii) pattern schemas (e.g., cognitions about why people act the way they do; or standards, rules, and criteria that are assumed to explain and control human behavior and interpersonal reality); and (iii) interpersonal schemas (e.g., cognitions about how actual or perceived others validate or invalidate the self). The three related schemas can be simplified as our mental representations of "how" and "why" regarding human reality. The mental representations of "how" include interactions of self and interpersonal schemas. The cognition of "why" contains pattern schemas that underline perceived reasons or causations related to the interactions between self and other entities.

For instance, correctional clients may have several (distorted) pattern schemas (e.g., violence, intimidation, wealth, beauty, physical or other types of perfection) that are believed to regulate and explain their experiences in interacting with others. Take the belief in physical perfection or beauty as an example. Many depressed offender-clients are inclined to explain their interpersonal frustrations and rejections as caused by their defective or inferior physical appearance. This self-appraisal is based on the cognition that physical perfection has a transcending power over others, and, if they are deviant from the pattern schema (i.e., an inconsistency between the self's attributes and the pattern), they will not be able to meet their needs or expectations in interpersonal situations. It should be noted that although the pattern schemas are subjectively conceived and vary with individuals, the content of the patterns is independent from the self-schema. For instance, a correctional client may feel excessive guilt over a minor mistake, because she considers her error to be a serious violation of a moral code. The moral code is not a part of her self-schema, but is a part of her pattern schema and serves as an important criterion for self-appraisal.

Pattern schemas are a dominant part of cognitive structures about human reality because people are implicitly or explicitly aware that patterns or laws regulate psychological experiences (e.g., emotions, motivations, cognitions, perceptions, attitudes), and human behavior and interactions, similar to those patterns or laws administering the operations of physical phenomena in the natural world. They also have the awareness that the subjective experience of success or frustration is related to their relations (i.e., consistency or inconsistency) with the patterns. However, individuals are often unaware that their schemas are inaccurate or distorted, blindly assuming that their pattern schemas represent "what is" about the patterns governing human reality.

In addition, interpersonal schemas are an integral part of cognition (e.g., Cloitre, Cohen, & Scarvalone, 2002). Examples of correctional clients' interpersonal schemas include representations of other people who are (as perceived by the offenders) interacting with them – from family members such as father, mother, spouse, brothers, and sisters, to peers, teachers, children, friends, enemies, law enforcement officers, prosecutors, judges, correctional officers and counselors, and other staff. The most essential elements of interpersonal schemas involve perceived validation and invalidation from the others. Validation in interaction can be defined as the processes in which a person's communications and messages (including intentions, desires, evaluations, judgments, and emotions) are recognized, accepted, encouraged, and confirmed by others. Invalidation refers to the process in which a person's communication, intentions, emotions, and judgments are denied, dismissed, or nullified by the others. Both the validation and invalidation in interaction are perceived, therefore an individual's cognition of the two processes may be accurate or distorted.

Pattern schemas and interpersonal schemas regulate self-appraisals in several ways. To begin with, self-appraisals depend upon evaluating the self according to the pattern schemas. For example, correctional clients' self-appraisals are influenced through the process of discerning consistency and inconsistency between the self's attributes or experiences and existing pattern schemas. A perceived consistency between a client's attributes and the pattern schemas s/he subscribes to generates positive assessments of the self (e.g., self-confidence, jubilation, and tranquillity). Perceived deviation or inconsistency from the pattern schemas results in negative self-evaluations and related emotional suffering (low self-esteem, diffidence, guilt, unworthiness, fear, depression/anxiety, self-blame, and anger). Interpersonal schemas (perceived invalidation, frustrations, rejections, acceptance, or validation, rewards from the interacting others or situations) also contribute to the process of self-appraisals by serving as the stimuli that promote the person to evaluate his/her consistency/inconsistency with the pattern schemas. In other words, a positive or negative self-appraisal regarding interactions with others is mediated through the perceived alignment with the pattern schemas. For example, an inmate has developed depressive symptoms after being rejected by a woman with whom he has been corresponding. The negative stimulus (e.g., social rejection) initiates and aggravates his negative self-concept only when he explains the rejection by seeing his attributes (e.g., being older) as having violated his pattern schemas (e.g., desirability of youthfulness). In addition, the experience of validation or invalidation in interpersonal situations can also change people's cognitions about what constitute the true patterns that regulate human behavior. For example, a client who has suffered chronic abuse and experienced a long history of frustrations in finding love may change his previous pattern schemas (e.g., being nice represents the transcending power over interacting others) to a new pattern schema that emphasizes dominance and manipulation in close relationships.

Individuals use their pattern and interpersonal schemas to appraise and explain the self's (and others') attributes and to understand experiences of validation and invalidation in the social world. Individuals, including correctional clients, who are aware that human behaviors and the world are governed by patterns or rules, typically try to make sense of their experiences of validation or invalidation by discerning the type of patterns or rules regulating human behavior and interactions and determining whether their own attributes or actions have violated or followed the patterns or rules. Negative self-appraisals result from the perceived infringements.

In addition, although self-appraisals may influence how the mind processes (e.g., attending, encoding, perceiving, evaluating, and attributing) self-related information, the valence (being either positive or negative) of self-appraisals does not provide people with accurate understanding of their experiences. For example, possessing a positive self-concept has little to do with the ability either to avoid or understand and overcome frustrations or invalidations.

The meaning of distorted cognitions

In contrast to the view that regards negative self-schemas as a main cognitive source of mental conflict, the interaction schemas approach considers distorted pattern schemas and interpersonal schemas as the primary cognitive constructs responsible for generating maladaptive self-appraisals. Thus, inaccurate self-evaluations (e.g., erroneous interpretations of experiences, selective abstraction, overgeneralization or exaggeration of negative experiences) are seen as symptoms, but not the root of cognitive distortions, because they are not the psychological reason *why* clients hold these beliefs.

The interaction schemas approach maintains that therapists who treat correctional clients suffering from depression and/or PTSD need not only to recognize the symptoms but also to discern and modify distorted pattern schemas and interpersonal schemas, which cause and sustain negative or inaccurate self-schemas, mental conflicts, and dysfunctional emotions (e.g., excessive sadness, guilt, shame, hopelessness), and problematic interpersonal behaviors (e.g., distrust, manipulation, lack of empathy).

Correctional clients' distorted pattern schemas may include cognitions that violence, intimidation, wealth, beauty, adherence to certain moral codes, and physical or other types of perfection epitomize the patterns that explain their interpersonal success or failure. Those cognitions are distorted, not because some of them are not useful values but because those ostensible rules represent misunderstandings about human behavior and interactions. Such rules often do not adequately explain the experiences of invalidation and frustration in interpersonal situations even though they are used as guidelines in human interaction.

Additionally, distorted interpersonal schemas include the misunderstandings of intentions, feelings, needs, motivations, cognitions, and evaluations of the interacting others, such as mistaking others' goodwill as a sign of hostility or misidentifying others' disdain as an indication of admiration. The following examples illustrate how negative self-concepts and dysfunctional behaviors are influenced by distorted pattern and interpersonal schemas.

Correctional clients with depressive or other mental health symptoms tend to appraise and explain the experience of frustration or failure in various domains by assessing the self's attributes (e.g., their inmate status or other categorical memberships such as physical imperfection, chronic disease, learning disabilities, and childhood victimization) according to some distorted pattern schemas such as elevated standards of perfection or social desirability, which are viewed as laws governing human interactions. When clients regard their shortcomings (e.g., physical defects, undesirable category memberships, and/or childhood victimization) from the pattern schemas as the explanation for their experience of interpersonal frustrations, rejections, and invalidations, they will maintain a sense of vulnerability, negative self-perceptions, and a pessimistic view of their future.

Interpersonally, distorted interpersonal and pattern schemas serve as the cognitive cause for dysfunctional actions. For example, many offenders' distorted interpersonal schemas include misconstruing neutral, or even positive, gestures of others as actions with hostile intention. Further, it is also believed that aggression and violence are the universal standards that control and regulate human behavior. As the result, such clients are inclined to use violence or aggression to get what they want in interpersonal situations (e.g., others obeying their orders or satisfying their needs).

Similarly, some correctional clients' lack of assertiveness stems from their misunderstanding of how to reach validation and overcome invalidation in situations of power disparity. A repeated theme in correctional counseling involves childhood trauma such as being sexually or physically abused. In situations in which the abuser (the powerful adult) had power over the child, victims experience fear in communicating feelings because they believed that the powerful adult, who generally dislikes unpleasant stimuli, will treat any negative communication as a sign of provocation, triggering more abuse. The same issue can persist for many correctional clients throughout their lives as they continue to misunderstand how to overcome the interpersonal abyss or disconnection between the self and others. For instance, some correctional clients told this author that they are afraid to make friends with fellow inmates by initiating conversations, or in communicating their authentic feelings to an authority figure because they fear their efforts will be invalidated. The nature of the issue of predicting failure, however, involves the victims' use of their distorted pattern and interpersonal schemas as the guideline to assess their alleged undesirable attributes and actions.

Modifying distorted cognitions

Differing from cognitive therapies that modify negative self-schemas by challenging and restructuring present automatic thoughts, the interaction schemas approach suggests that cognitive interventions need to discern and modify distorted pattern and interpersonal schemas that serve as the guideline for self-appraisals and interpersonal actions.

In this approach the therapist investigates how the clients' past experiences of invalidation have produced and maintained their misunderstanding of others and the patterns governing interpersonal reality and human behavior. It has been well documented (e.g., Krause, Mendelson, & Lynch, 2003) that early childhood traumas and a history of childhood emotional invalidation (i.e., psychological abuse and parental punishment, minimization, and distress in response to negative emotion) are strongly associated with chronic emotional inhibition and psychological distress in adulthood (i.e., ambivalence over emotional expression, thought suppression, and avoidant stress responses, as well as depression and anxiety symptoms). Clinical observations also suggest that many offenders have experienced severe frustrations in meeting their basic human needs and have an inability to accurately understand and handle conflict. They have suffered interpersonal conflicts, family tensions, and/or other human tragedies, had experience with trauma and abuse (sexual, emotional, and/or physical), and domestic violence in the home, with few opportunities for legitimate employment (e.g., Sun, 2013; Wolff & Shi, 2010). Juvenile offenders may have school difficulties, delinquent peer associations, and socio-economic disadvantage (Howell & Egley, 2005; Tarolla, Wagner, Rabinowitz, & Tubman, 2002). However, the interaction schema model provides a unique take on how people learn from negative experiences. It argues that negative experiences do not impact the negative self-schema (e.g., self-blame and other depressive or PTSD symptoms) directly, but develop and exacerbate the perceiver's misunderstandings of interpersonal reality and the governing patterns, resulting in his or her distorted interpersonal and pattern schemas by which the self is appraised. For correctional clients, these frustrations and invalidations in life have created strong pressures to organize and explain their experiences of invalidation by discerning how the self's attributes and actions are deviant from conveniently available, yet unrealistic, models such as physical perfection and/or social desirability (see Sun, 2008).

This current approach views treatments that repress or change negative beliefs about the self as insufficient in healing mental or emotional injuries. Focusing on the positive aspects of the self may temporarily insulate individuals from their emotional anguish but doing so is not a panacea for understanding mental conflict and interpersonal experiences of invalidation. Rather, the interaction schemas approach helps correctional clients comprehend that negative self-concepts are the symptoms rather than the cognitive source of conflicts. They need to be made aware that their distorted pattern and interpersonal schemas are responsible for their maladaptive self-appraisals, distorted explanations for their past frustrations in meeting important needs, and their inaccurate anticipations about the future. To modify distorted interpersonal schemas, clients should be provided with opportunities to share their interpersonal perceptions with one another in a safe and secure environment; thus they each can recognize the discrepancy between their interpersonal schemas and interpersonal reality through honest interpersonal communications with others. It is also helpful to recognize that others' dysfunctional interpersonal behaviors toward them are likely influenced by the others' distorted pattern and interpersonal schemas. Furthermore, although it is not easy to tell correctional clients what represents exactly accurate pattern schemas, practitioners can teach clients that accurate pattern schemas have at least the following characteristics.

First, because they accurately represent human reality, accurate pattern schemas can generate mental peace and more harmonious interactions with others than distorted pattern schemas. Second, a person's individual identity is defined by his/her cognition of human reality, rather than by fixed categories (e.g., physical looks, inmate status, or perfection in a range of areas). Third, accurate pattern schemas give individuals more choices or alternatives in perceiving, interpreting, evaluating, and reacting to others or events. In other words, increased alternatives and flexibility indicate more accurate and less distorted pattern schemas. These intervention strategies are based on the consideration that offenders are not just criminals or patients who need to be corrected or treated but are individuals who use their cognitions to understand and explain their crimes, mental disorders, interpersonal experiences, and/

or need areas. People are motivated to minimize the disparity between their belief of "what is true" and the actual truth about human reality and patterns. Of course, cognition can be modified and become increasingly more accurate as a result of encountering new information, social stimuli, and successfully adapting to new situations.

The Treatment Plan

The treatment plan based on the interaction schemas approach shares the fundamental cognitive propositions that cognitive activity affects emotions and behavior. Developing positive psychological and emotional experiences may be produced through cognitive change. The interaction schemas approach suggests that treatment should modify inaccurate pattern and interpersonal schemas that sustain mental conflicts, distorted appraisals and explanations, and maladaptive actions.

When treating depression and PTSD, it is best for practitioners to keep in mind that correctional counseling is intended to help clients balance their important relationships, and understand and overcome their internal and external conflicts through developing more accurate social cognitions about themselves and others as well as the patterns governing their interactions. Like the general public, incarcerated clients have two basic psychological needs: mental peace and interpersonal harmony. It is important to see offenders as individuals who seek to understand and solve their problems and to balance their mental and interpersonal relationships. The issue of mental peace includes such topics as how to create and maintain inner tranquility, how to experience healing and joy, and how to unlearn past emotional hurts and extricate oneself from fear, anxiety, and depression. The issue of interpersonal harmony covers such areas as how to obtain and maintain love and good relationships, improve communication, increase cooperation, create a better future, achieve success, and avoid or overcome human discord, tribulation, and calamity. In addition to understanding and ameliorating negative symptoms, practitioners help clients master the cognitive principles of interaction schemas that can provide them with the ability to appraise and react to experiences of invalidation in an accurate and adaptive way, and thus, develop a sense of cognitive control and emotional freedom.

Treatment goals are achieved by employing the following strategies: (i) psychoeducation; (ii) using the client's narratives of victimization and trauma (which also serve as imaginal exposure stimuli); and (iii) fostering cognitive growth and understanding about mental and interpersonal experiences. Psychoeducation involves teaching the client about the symptoms of his/her mental disorders, psychological theories or explanations for the disorders, and the treatment processes. The narratives refer to the client's written or oral descriptions or recollections of past trauma and victimization. Cognitive growth and understanding represents the intervention strategy that develops the client's more accurate cognitions about the self, others, interpersonal reality, and patterns.

The treatment also addresses the issue of recidivism in addition to treating the client's mental disorders. Offenders' crimes and criminal behavior are often just symptoms of dysfunctions that are rooted in their distorted cognitions about themselves, others, the environment, and the patterns that regulate their conflict-ridden interactions. Although a criminal conviction is the official reason a person enters the correctional system, counseling efforts that focus only on their crimes miss causal factors that led to the violation of the law. The most important causal factor, among those variables that can be addressed by correctional counseling, involves the client's distorted cognitions for evaluating, explaining, and adjusting personal experiences and actions. It is offenders' cognitions that mediate how they understand and explain conflicts and whether they react in a prosocial or criminal way (Sun, 2008).

Assessment and Intervention: A Case Vignette

This section describes a case vignette and illustrates how to use the interaction schemas approach to perform assessment and intervention for incarcerated clients with both depression and PTSD.

A.L. is a 43-year-old male offender residing in the mental health unit of a state prison. When meeting with his therapist, he reports being depressed for as long as he can remember, and that both he and his younger brother were sexually and physically abused by their father, who was an alcoholic. A.L. also reports that he suffers from regular nightmares and frequent flashbacks of his abuse. He has been afraid to share information about his childhood trauma because a previous therapist told him to forget it and not to ruminate about a past that he could not change. With a sign of irritability, he also tells his current therapist that he plans to physically fight with a correctional officer who tries to get on his nerves. Another source of his frustration comes from his difficulty and struggle in completing the adult basic education program in prison. His current symptoms meet diagnostic criteria for both PTSD and major depressive disorder.

The assessment concentrates on the following:

1. Assess A.L.'s symptoms of depression and PTSD through a clinical interview and careful attention to the client's narratives.
2. Let the client recount his frustrations and past hurts (e.g., being sexually and physically abused). His narratives about his trauma not only help the counselor gather information and obtain a basic understanding of his trauma history, but also serve as an effective means of imaginal exposure (i.e., exposure to trauma memories), which is likely to lead to less emotional reactivity in the future. He is also encouraged to talk about his current issues, including his struggle in the adult education program and his conflict with the correctional officer.
3. Assess how A.L. explains and copes with frustrations and depression, including how he evaluates and interprets the others' (the abuser– his father – and the officer) actions and their mental states (emotions, motivations, perceptions).
4. Identify A.L.'s distorted pattern schemas and interpersonal schemas, which serve as the maladaptive guidelines for evaluating and interpreting his mental and interpersonal experiences. These appraisals are performed by analyzing the information revealed in the clinical interviews, conversations, and his narratives. The results of these discussions reveal that A.L. possesses several distorted pattern and interpersonal schemas. For example, A.L regards his membership in some unchangeable categories (e.g., inmate status; physical imperfection) as deviant from his pattern schemas (e.g., social desirability and perfection in a range of areas). Specifically, he sees his inmate status as unchangeable and as being attached to him throughout his life. He also believes that his physical imperfection (a visible and permanent scar on his head) makes him unattractive to others and causes him to never be able to find love in life. Interpersonally, his pattern schemas manifest in two behavioral tendencies: the use of violence and being submissive (see Box 22.1 for a list of distorted schemas that are

Box 22.1 Typical Distorted Interaction Schemas for Correctional Clients with Depression/PTSD

Pattern schemas

1. Social desirability (e.g., youthfulness, good health, wealth) governs interpersonal relations.
2. Perfection (in physical looks or other categories) governs interpersonal relations.
3. Violence can get you what you want.

Self schemas

4. I feel guilty constantly because I have violated some moral standards and must be punished.
5. I will always get rejected because I am physically imperfect (deviant from the perfection standard).
6. I am vulnerable to rejection because I really look ugly.
7. I deserve rejections from others because I am too old.
8. I deserved being abused because that was my fate.

Interpersonal schemas

9. Others respect threat and violence because they are afraid of punishment and pain.
10. I must always be agreeable with others because being nice is a universal rule.
11. What I know about the others (e.g., correctional officers, fellow inmates, and therapist) is what I have observed (unaware of the self's distorted cognitions about the others' mental states).

typical for correctional clients with depression and PTSD). These cognitive distortions are the product of his maladaptive learning experiences. His belief in violence comes from his exposure to interpersonal violence from childhood. He indicates that his submissiveness or lack of assertiveness comes from being a victim of abuse. He reports that he could take the abuser's perspective and understand what he wanted, but he was unable to make the abuser understand his viewpoint without eliciting retaliation in a situation of power disparity. He was also too young to physically defend himself.

In terms of treatment and intervention, the practitioner focuses on the following strategies:

1. Validating, rather than disputing or challenging, A.L's narratives about his past hurts and experiences is crucial in motivating him to work on his depression and PTSD. Like other people, he possesses the need for developing cognitive control through understanding social reality by seeking meaning in his social and mental experiences. In fact, his flash-backs and ruminations on the negative experiences indicate, at least in part, an involuntary effort to understand and make sense of his experiences so that he will know how to avoid or deal with similar events in the future.

    Because of his impulsivity in dealing with interpersonally challenging situations, he is encouraged to practice small steps toward the treatment goals (i.e., *"A journey of a thousand miles begins with a single step."*).

2. The treatment starts with psychoeducation about understanding depressive and PTSD symptoms from the perspective of interaction schemas. The psychoeducation activities include the counselor's explanation of relevant psychological principles, such as emotions, cognition, schemas, and distorted cognitions; and the principle that mental and interpersonal conflict result from a failure to correct distorted pattern and interpersonal schemas. In addition, the client is informed that the focus of the treatment involves helping him develop more accurate cognitions about the self, others, and patterns.

   The client is also made aware that, in the counseling process, the therapist/counselor may challenge his false schemas by communicating information about a new reality. For example, A.L. has core cognition that his physical imperfection is responsible for his experience of rejection and frustration in interpersonal relationships. The therapist challenges the belief by pointing out that it was his distorted cognitions about what regulates human interactions – about a woman he previously met and his subsequent failure to respond to her goodwill communications, prior to his incarceration – that actually ruined the relationship. It had nothing to do with his alleged physical defect. This type of challenging is intended to help A.L. modify and adjust his cognitive system by seeing the discrepancy between his perception and the reality of what actually guided the interaction.

3. The counselor helps A.L. view his negative self-appraisals (e.g., self-blame) and his dysfunctional interpersonal behavior as produced by his use of distorted pattern (e.g., his category-based belief systems, including comparing his inmate status and physical imperfection with the standard of social desirability) and interpersonal schemas. His cognitive distortions generate and sustain his depressive and PTSD symptoms, and other problems in several ways. His distorted cognitions, related to frustration and invalidation, mislead his perceptions of interpersonal reality and generate dysfunctional and self-defeating actions toward others. The therapist helps A.L. modify his pattern and interpersonal schemas by re-evaluating experiences of frustration and invalidation. He also learns to attribute his victimization to the abuser's distorted cognitions about him. That is, this intervention requires the client not only recount what the abuser did to him, but also recognize how the abuser's distorted cognitions about his emotional pains, reactions, and cognitions contributed to the abuse against him. In addition, homework assignments include identifying and practicing how to use the newly learned principles to reinterpret his frustrations in the past and at present.

   The solution to mental conflict and the strategy for creating peace (e.g., high self-confidence and esteem, psychological well-being and/or joy) is based on revising misperceptions about the reality and on discerning the true patterns governing human interactions (see Box 22.2 for a list of common homework assignments used in correctional settings).

4. Assisting A.L. in responding more effectively to interpersonal conflicts is the last component of treatment. This intervention consists of developing or expanding his alternative (more accurate) cognitions about interpersonal relationships, including helping him to evaluate, perceive, interpret, and react to frustrations in an alternative or more accurate way. This approach includes helping the client understand how to interact with others whose mental cognitions better match human reality; and also how not to validate others' distorted pattern and interpersonal schemas by using strategies emphasizing fear, coercion, intimidation, or violence. Belligerence in dealing with human conflicts is counterproductive because violence only corroborates the interacting partners' cognitive distortions about the validity of violence. The client also practices how to differentiate between blockages and opportunities in interpersonal situations. For example, he learns

Box 22.2   Common Homework Assignments for Correctional Clients

1. Write and rewrite narratives about trauma and victimization.
2. Rehearse the principle that cognitive distortions (misunderstanding about interpersonal reality and patterns) are responsible for mental conflicts and dysfunctional interactions; use personal examples to validate the principle.
3. Reaffirm the belief that the client can overcome mental conflicts once a new cognitive understanding about patterns regulating human interactions is developed.
4. Reattribution of the victimization experience to the abuser's cognitive distortions of social reality.
5. Understand and make sense of experiences of frustration from the cognitive perspective; seeing rumination related to trauma and negative emotion as an effort to learn from the negativity.
6. Develop the cognition that for every problem, there are always multiple and more constructive solutions; and for every goal or need, there are always multiple ways to achieve it. Learn to use alternative ways to evaluate, interpret, and react to situations.
7. Encourage the client to practice small steps toward treatment goals and to keep in mind that "A journey of a thousand miles begins with a single step."
8. View negative self-appraisals (e.g., self-blame) as produced by distorted pattern schemas (e.g., category-based belief systems, including inmate status and physical imperfection).
9. Reaffirm the principle that in conflict situations violence will likely validate the cognitive distortions of the interacting others.
10. Practice assertiveness with fellow inmates and recognize the rationale for doing so from the interaction schemas perspective.

how to detach from blockages (e.g., conflict situations, such as the one where an inmate tries to provoke a fight); and how to grab opportunities, including registering for prison programs (e.g., horticulture, computer repair classes) that develop skills for employment, and pursuing communications with fellow inmates who have a sincere intention for connecting socially.

The practitioner also suggests that A.L.'s plan to resort to aggression against the officer does not help solve the conflict. After learning and rehearsing new social skills (e.g., peaceful conversations and non-violent communications), A.L. talked directly with the officer. Following the honest exchange of opinions, the officer stopped his former aggravating practices and the client's anger was greatly reduced. In this case A.L. learned not only to practice assertiveness as a way to deal with conflict, but also to understand the rationale for doing so from the interaction schemas perspective.

Suggested Modified Methods in Group Sessions

In group treatment the basic principles, assessment, and intervention issues will remain the same; however, the practitioner can take full advantage of the group as a social microcosm. In the group, clients can be taught to practice assertiveness and other communications skills in interpersonal situations, and work on a common task (e.g., a math problem) by generating multiple solutions. Group settings also encourage members to share their feelings, learning to trust and gain support from others in the group, learning to accept their own painful feelings about past traumas, and promoting the sense of belonging. Additionally, when members confront one another directly and immediately in an authentic manner, the social interaction helps to rectify members' distorted cognitions of interpersonal reality and develop new and accurate cognitions and constructive interpersonal behavior.

Conclusions

This chapter provides an overview of the interaction schemas approach to the treatment of depression and PTSD in incarcerated clients. This approach emphasizes that evaluations, explanations, perceptions, and emotional and behavioral reactions represent an interconnected mental system. Namely, the schemas comprise three interrelated mental representations of human reality: self-schemas, interpersonal schemas (cognitions about others in interaction with the self), and pattern schemas (perceived patterns or rules governing human behavior and interactions). Self-appraisals result from applying the pattern schemas to evaluate the self's attributes and experiences in responding to perceived validation or frustration and invalidation from others. Therefore, revising distorted pattern and interpersonal schemas is central to modifying negative and maladaptive self-appraisals. Treatment is focused on psychoeducation about the model, eliciting the client's narratives of victimization and trauma, and modifying distorted schemas in connection with past and present social interactions.

References

American Psychiatric Association. (2000). *Diagnostic and statistical manual of mental disorders* (4th ed., text revision). Washington, DC: Author.

Andrews, D. A., & Bonta, J. (2006). *The psychology of criminal conduct* (4th ed.). Newark, NJ: LexisNexis/ Matthew Bender.

Andrews, D. A., & Bonta, J. (2010). Rehabilitating criminal justice policy and practice. *Psychology, Public Policy, and Law, 16,* 39–55.

Baum, N. (2005). Correlates of clients' emotional and behavioral responses to treatment termination. *Clinical Social Work Journal, 33,* 309–326.

Beck, A. T. (1991). Cognitive therapy: A 30-year retrospective. *American Psychologist, 46,* 368–375.

Bureau of Justice Statistics. (2006). *Mental health problems of prison and jail inmates.* Retrieved from http://bjs.ojp.usdoj.gov/index.cfm?ty=pbdetail&iid=789

Clark, D. A., & Beck, A. T. (2010). *Cognitive therapy of anxiety disorders: Science and practice.* New York, NY: Guilford Press.

Cloitre, M., Cohen, L. R., & Scarvalone, P. (2002). Understanding revictimization among childhood sexual abuse survivors: An interpersonal schema approach. *Journal of Cognitive Psychotherapy, 16* (1), 91–112.

Foa, E. B., Ehlers, A., Clark, D. M., Tolin, D. F., & Orsillo, S. M. (1999). The Posttraumatic Cognitions Inventory (PTCI): Development and validation *Psychological Assessment, 11,* 303–314.

Hansen, C. (2008). Cognitive-behavioral interventions: Where they come from and what they do. *Federal Probation, 72* (2), 43–49.

Heckman, C. J., Cropsey, K. L., & Olds-Davis, T. (2007). Posttraumatic stress disorder treatment in correctional settings: A brief review of the empirical literature and suggestions for future research. *Psychotherapy: Theory, Research, Practice, Training, 44,* 46–53.

Howell, J. C., & Egley, A. (2005). Moving risk factors into developmental theories of gang membership. *Youth Violence and Juvenile Justice, 3,* 334–354.

Krause, E. D., Mendelson, T., & Lynch, T. R. (2003). Childhood emotional invalidation and adult psychological distress: The mediating role of emotional inhibition. *Child Abuse & Neglect, 27,* 199–213.

Martin, R., & Young, J. (2010). Schema therapy. In K. S. Dobson (Ed.), *Handbook of cognitive-behavioral therapies* (3rd ed., pp. 317–346). New York, NY: Guilford Press.

Matthews, B., & Hubbard, D. (2007). The helping alliance in juvenile probation: The missing element in the "what works" literature. *Journal of Offender Rehabilitation, 45,* 105–122.

Salisbury, E. J., Van Voorhis, P., & Spiropoulos, G. V. (2009). The predictive validity of a gender-responsive needs assessment: An exploratory study. *Crime & Delinquency, 55,* 550–585.

Smedley, K. (2010). Cognitive behavior therapy with adolescents in secure settings. In J. Harvey & K. Smedley (Eds.), *Psychological therapy in prisons and other secure settings* (pp. 71–101). Devon, UK: Willan Publishing.

Spiropoulos, G. V., Spruance, L., Van Voorhis, P., & Schmitt, M. M. (2005). Pathfinders and problem solving: Comparative effects of two cognitive-behavioral programs among men and women offenders in community and prison. *Journal of Offender Rehabilitation, 42,* 69–94.

Sun. K. (2008). *Correctional counseling: A cognitive growth perspective.* Sudbury, MA: Jones & Bartlett Publishers.

Sun, K. (2013). *Correctional counseling: A cognitive growth perspective* (2nd ed.). Burlington, MA: Jones & Bartlett Learning.

Tarolla, S. M., Wagner, E. F., Rabinowitz, J., & Tubman, J. G. (2002). Understanding and treating juvenile offenders: A review of current knowledge and future directions. *Aggression and Violent Behavior, 7,* 125–144.

Van Voorhis, P., Wright, E. M., Salisbury, E., & Bauman, A. (2010). Women's risk factors and their contributions to existing risk/needs assessment: The current status of a gender-responsive supplement. *Criminal Justice and Behavior, 37,* 261–288.

Wolff, N. L., & Shi, J. (2010). Trauma and incarcerated persons. In C. L. Scott (Ed.), *Handbook of correctional mental health* (2nd ed., pp. 277–320). Arlington, VA: American Psychiatric Publishing, Inc.

Suggestions for Further Learning

Book

Sun, K. (2013). *Correctional counseling: A cognitive growth perspective* (2nd ed.). Burlington, MA: Jones & Bartlett Learning.

Journal article

Cloitre, M., Cohen, L. R., & Scarvalone, P. (2002). Understanding revictimization among childhood sexual abuse survivors: An interpersonal schema approach. *Journal of Cognitive Psychotherapy, 16* (1), 91–112. doi: 10.1891/jcop.16.1.91.63698

Part V
Conclusions

23

Forensic CBT

Five Recommendations for Clinical Practice and Five Topics in Need of More Attention

Raymond Chip Tafrate, Damon Mitchell, and Raymond W. Novaco

In conveying some of the frustrations of working with clients alternately described as antisocial, psychopathic, dissocial, justice-involved, or criminal (among other labels), Hervey Cleckley noted in the preface of *The Mask of Sanity* (1941): "The diversity of opinion among different psychiatrists concerning the status of these patients never grew less. Little agreement was found as to what was actually the matter with them. No satisfactory means of dealing with them was presented by any psychiatric authority, and meanwhile their status in the eyes of the law usually made it impossible to treat them at all. They continued, however, to constitute a most grave and a constant problem to the hospital and to the community" (p. xi). Over 70 years since the publication of that classic text, Cleckley's comments regarding the difficulties of clinical problem conceptualization and the importance to effect change with the justice-involved population continue to reflect areas of ongoing concern, rather than historical interest. Treatment of antisocial patterns remains a highly challenging and emerging, rather than an established, area of practice (Duggan, 2009; Trestman & Lazrove, 2010). Yet, there have been meaningful improvements in forensic treatment (D. A. Andrews et al., 1990b; Landenberger & Lipsey, 2005; Smith, Gendreau, & Swartz, 2009), and we hope the preceding chapters have provided a practitioner-friendly resource that furthers the development of effective forensic clinical work.

In this chapter we summarize common themes that emerged across different models, clinical problem areas, or subpopulations, and distill five broad recommendations for working with justice-involved clients. In some cases, areas of divergence among the various chapter authors are identified to highlight evolving issues in need of further investigation and discussion. Although readers may draw different conclusions, this closing chapter pulls together our own thoughts and observations from the rich clinical knowledge base contained within this volume.

Forensic CBT: A Handbook for Clinical Practice, First Edition.
Edited by Raymond Chip Tafrate and Damon Mitchell.
© 2014 John Wiley & Sons, Ltd. Published 2014 by John Wiley & Sons, Ltd.

Five Recommendations for Treating Justice-Involved Clients

Recommendation 1: Minimize confrontation, build motivation

There is unanimous consensus among the chapter contributors about what *not* to do with justice-involved clients. A "get tough," "get real," or "confrontational" approach is not advocated by *any* of the authors in this volume. In particular, the eschewing of confrontation in treatment is notable in the chapters on interpersonal violence (IPV; see Eckhardt et al., Chapter 10; Ronan et al., Chapter 11) and sexual aggression (see Marshall & O'Brien, Chapter 14). In addition, with regard to the treatment of addictions, contrary to what is portrayed on popular reality television shows, confrontation is not advocated (see Bishop, Chapter 12; Wanberg & Milkman, Chapter 13). The authors in the present volume are instead proposing that practitioners develop a sophisticated set of engagement skills and allocate time to establish a good working relationship, prior to utilizing more structured and directive interventions. Confrontation about personal responsibility is replaced with challenges to distorted or irrational thoughts, and such challenges are undertaken in a collaborative spirit.

Perhaps confrontational styles persist in some forensic settings because practitioners have not developed fluency with a range of behavior change skills. The chapters in this book provide alternative options. We have met many practitioners whose hearts are in the right place in wanting healthy change for their clients, but, in the absence of clinical knowledge and skills, correctionally minded confrontation becomes the default approach.

Confrontation can instead be done empathically. While the idea of working in a collaborative spirit with offenders may activate alarm about being co-opted or manipulated by the client, collaboration should mean that clients assume greater responsibility and ownership of the behavioral change process and goal-setting that nurtures hope and bolsters self-efficacy. Further, CBT approaches are not devoid of limit-setting. In fact, the limit-setting inherent in some CBT approaches may be of particular benefit for personality disordered clients (see Keulen-de Vos et al., Chapter 4).

Because the overwhelming majority of justice-involved clients are coerced into programs, their interest in participating in treatment and making changes in their behavior cannot be assumed. Unfortunately, a recent meta-analysis reached the stark conclusion that mandated offender treatment was generally ineffective, whereas voluntary treatment in both institutional and community forensic settings was associated with positive effects (Parhar, Wormith, Derkzen, & Beauregard, 2008). One implication of this finding is that in order for mandated treatment to be effective, clients must develop an interest in change akin to that of their voluntary counterparts. In essence, we should strive to create an environment where clients, who tell us they are *"forced to be here,"* come to say they *"want to make changes anyway."*

If the clinical reality is that clients' decision-making about whether or not to make a change is of primary importance, then early in the treatment process motivation must be gauged, and if necessary, enhanced. One of the strongest areas of agreement among the chapter contributors is the recommendation to incorporate motivational interviewing (MI), or adaptations of MI, into forensic practice. This suggestion is made in 10 chapters. MI has immediate practical advantages in the early stages of treatment, moving clients toward greater engagement and collaboration and moving practitioners away from confrontation, advice-giving, and interventions for which the client is not yet ready. MI skills are useful throughout the course of treatment and programming. As Tafrate and Luther (Chapter 20) point out, MI is a complex therapeutic style that, once learned, can be practically integrated with more action-oriented CBT interventions. MI becomes a style that supports and increases the client's responsivity to a specific intervention.

We recommend that forensic CBT practitioners take the time to receive sufficient training in MI to develop its practical engagement, focusing, evoking, and planning skills (Miller & Rollnick, 2013). We also recommend that programs that invest in MI training for their staff implement some degree of ongoing follow-up and support. A one- or two-day training may introduce the principles of MI, but follow-up supervision or booster sessions are important in transitioning the skills from the training session into everyday practice in delivering interventions.

Recommendation 2: Discuss the impact of antisocial patterns

Several chapter authors recommend reviewing the symptoms associated with antisocial personality disorder (ASPD) or psychopathy with justice-involved clients. For example, in discussing traditional CBT approaches, Seeler and colleagues (Chapter 2) suggest framing antisocial patterns as a "lifestyle disorder" that develops over time: Individuals usually remain unaware of their symptoms, and if not addressed the lifestyle disorder will result in serious negative long-term consequences (e.g., damaged relationships, vocational maladjustment, financial instability, and incarceration). A similar set of recommendations was made in earlier work discussing cognitive therapy for antisocial personality disorder (Beck, Freeman, & Associates, 1990; Beck, Freeman, Davis, and Associates, 2004). Wanberg and Milkman (Chapter 13) recommend providing clients with a list of common antisocial characteristics. Their list includes symptoms from both the *Diagnostic and Statistical Manual of Mental Disorders* (DSM) criteria for ASPD as well as features of psychopathy. Clients are then asked to review the list and note the ones that fit and don't fit with their own history and patterns. This can be done in a group or individual session.

Both sets of authors recommend providing feedback on antisocial patterns as a way of raising client awareness about important symptom clusters that may not have been previously viewed as part of a unified problem. One benefit for clients is that seemingly disparate behavior patterns become connected and seen as part of an overarching theme, helping to make sense of problems in multiple areas of the client's life. It is important to keep in mind that the purpose of reviewing diagnostic category symptoms and behavior patterns is not to label the client. In fact, we recommend in such discussions with clients avoiding the use of labels such as "antisocial," "sociopath," or "psychopath," not only because these labels may trigger reactance and argumentativeness, but also because these labels signify "badness" and evoke distressed emotions that undermine treatment engagement. The objective is to raise clients' awareness of the negative consequences associated with their longstanding and pervasive behavior patterns.

Other chapter authors who did not explicitly recommend reviewing formal diagnostic criteria, do recommend identifying and reviewing the nature and impact of antisocial beliefs and behavior patterns with clients, including forensic schemas (Keulen-de Vos and colleagues, Chapter 4) and criminal thinking patterns (Kroner & Morgan, Chapter 5; Walters, Chapter 6). Discussions of diagnostic criteria related to ongoing belief or behavior patterns can be used as a platform to explore core values and set the treatment agenda. Clients can be asked, "*Which of these patterns have you noticed in your life?*" Once a pattern or symptom is identified, further exploration using MI skills can commence (e.g., "*When did the pattern first emerge?*" "*How has this pattern negatively affected your life?*" "*What is at stake if you do not change it?*" "*How might you take steps to correct this pattern?*" etc.). What is most important is that practitioners have the ability to identify and bring into focus the specific patterns that are most associated with a client's antisocial and self-destructive behaviors.

The vast majority of chapters in this volume make no reference to the DSM, raising the question: Is the DSM, and diagnosis in general, important in the treatment of antisocial patterns? The answer seems to be no. The criteria for antisocial personality have changed considerably across the various editions of the DSM. One unfortunate outcome of the shifting criteria is that a robust research base on the nature and course of ASPD has not developed. Further complicating the picture is the presence of different conceptualizations of antisocial patterns (e.g., ASPD in the DSM, dissocial personality in the *International Classification of Diseases*, and psychopathy). As noted by Ogloff (2006), the distinctions between the varying conceptualizations are such that findings based on one diagnostic group are not necessarily applicable to the others. Assessment criteria for ASPD are behaviorally rooted, while those for psychopathy are characterological (traits) and behavioral. Yet, as can be found in the early conceptualization of psychopathy by Karpman (1941) and shown empirically by Skeem, Johansson, Andershed, Kerr, and Eno Louden (2007), there are important distinctions between subtypes of psychopathy (primary and secondary), which bear substantially on the treatment approach. Secondary psychopaths, who are more anxiety-driven, emotionally reactive (e.g., anger), withdrawn, and unassertive, can be expected to be more responsive to CBT interventions. We recommend that forensic CBT practitioners become familiar with the emerging literature on psychopathy subtypes and its implications for treatment.

Recommendation 3: Focus on belief targets and risk factors relevant to criminality

Thinking patterns empirically demonstrated to exist in offender groups should establish the foundation of cognitive targets to be modified in forensic CBT programs. As noted by Mitchell and colleagues (Chapter 1), the belief targets around which traditional CBT was developed may be limited in their usefulness for justice-involved clients. We believe the identification and conceptualization of offender-relevant thinking patterns is critical if CBT interventions provided to justice-involved clients are to match the effectiveness achieved in programs delivered to those with traditional mental health disorders. We recommend that forensic CBT practitioners become familiar with the range of relevant thinking patterns presented throughout this volume (see Kassinove & Toohey, Chapter 8; Keulen-de Vos et al., Chapter 4; Kroner & Morgan, Chapter 5; Seeler et al., Chapter 2; Sun, Chapter 22; Walters, Chapter 6). Additionally, we recommend that practitioners consider using a validated criminal thinking assessment instrument as part of their intake procedures (see Kroner & Morgan, Chapter 5; Walters, Chapter 6).

There is convergence among the chapter contributors that an assortment of thinking patterns be considered in treatment formulations of justice-involved clients. This theme runs contrary to many offender intervention programs where emphasis is placed on challenging thinking patterns that minimize accountability – with the goal of having justice-involved clients take personal responsibility for their actions (Maruna & Mann, 2006). Although justification and minimization are central foci for many practitioners, there is growing recognition that thinking patterns such as disregard for others and for authority, overgeneralization, and extreme judging may be just as, or more, important to address in intervention (Kroner & Morgan, Chapter 5; Mitchell, Tafrate, Hogan, & Olver, 2013). Some authors have made the observation that making excuses and external attributions for one's shortcomings is normative (and often psychologically healthy) in everyday life, although condemned when verbalized by offenders (Henning & Holdford, 2006; Maruna & Mann, 2006). Accepting responsibility for overcoming one's obstacles, while avoiding responsibility for the origins of those problems may, in fact, be a natural part of the desistance process for offenders (Maruna,

2004). While justifications and minimizations are certainly a piece of the criminal justice landscape, a singular focus on these thinking patterns will mean that practitioners will pay too little attention to other, perhaps more important, cognitive patterns contributing to offending behavior (Henning & Holdford, 2006; Maruna & Copes, 2005; Maruna & Mann, 2006). In addition, identifying specific thinking patterns (e.g., cognitive profiles) for particular offender groups has the potential to lead to more focused CBT interventions and is an exciting avenue of future research.

While agreement exists across chapters that criminal thinking is multifaceted and not adequately represented by a single pattern, there is divergence among the contributors regarding the level of belief constructs (i.e., surface automatic thoughts, intermediate beliefs, schemas) most important to address in forensic CBT. In discussing traditional CBT, Seeler et al. (Chapter 2) cover a range of belief levels and suggest that practitioners conceptualize, build client awareness, and develop alternative thinking schemes to guide behavior at the intermediate level at a minimum. Similarly, from a rational emotive behavioral therapy (REBT) framework, "demands" for comfort and control are emphasized as being central to the development and maintenance of criminality (see Bishop, Chapter 12; Kassinove & Toohey, Chapter 8; Seeler et al., Chapter 2).

The chapters covering criminal thinking models also discuss belief targets that exist at the intermediate level (see Kroner & Morgan, Chapter 5; Walters, Chapter 6). There are several contributors who recommend focusing interventions on schemas. Keulen-de Vos et al. (Chapter 4) suggest targeting forensic schema modes, while Sun (Chapter 22) advises that schemas related to interactions with others are most important to address when working with justice-involved clients. We recommend that forensic CBT practitioners be prepared to conceptualize and target levels of belief beyond automatic thoughts. Targeting intermediate level beliefs may be best suited for the time-limited and group modalities common to forensic settings, while opportunities to address schemas are better suited to those environments where longer-term individual treatment is an option.

We offer a caution about how language is used in describing offender-relevant thinking patterns. The term *criminal thinking*, which commonly appears in the literature, may reinforce the idea that the thinking of justice-involved clients is somehow qualitatively different from that of other people and therefore inherently resistant to change. In contrast to this view, criminal thinking patterns may simply represent a normative, but maladaptive, cognitive coping style that develops over time with repetition. In the face of life's challenges and struggles, everyone has the potential to crave excitement or to fail to sufficiently consider the impact of one's actions on the suffering of others. For certain people, such patterns may become more prevalent and automatic, setting the stage for choices, some of which are more likely to lead to criminal behavior. In that sense, we see criminal thinking patterns, such as those proposed in the present volume, as a set of beliefs that affect choices and behaviors, which if unaltered, ultimately influence one's life trajectory.

Finally, the development and maintenance of criminal behavior is certainly complex and multi-determined. Although thinking patterns may direct behavior, they also emerge from individual experiences, environmental circumstances, and reinforcement histories. Thus, we do not believe that criminal thinking should be the sole focus of offender assessment and rehabilitation. Instead, criminal thinking is one of a host of criminal risk factors (e.g., criminal peers groups, substance abuse) to be considered in the treatment of offenders (Simourd & Olver, 2002). Similarly, a focus on context and environment related to criminal behavior seem to be particularly important in working with justice-involved women (Van Dieten & King, Chapter 16) and indigenous offender populations (Day, Chapter 18). Another very strong area of agreement among the chapter contributors is to focus treatment on empirically established criminal risk variables. Specifically, the Risk-Need-Responsivity (RNR: D. A. Andrews, 2012; D. A. Andrews, Bonta, & Hoge, 1990a; D. A. Andrews & Bonta, 2010a) model is noted as a core competency for forensic practice in 10 chapters.

Recommendation 4: Discuss strengths and core values

Practitioners may have been surprised by the degree to which the influence of positive psychology (Seligman, 2002) is evident in the preceding chapters. A number of authors recommend having discussions with justice-involved clients about their core values and adopting a more strengths-based perspective than has traditionally been associated with forensic treatment. These suggestions are not presented as an alternative to CBT, but as pieces to be integrated into CBT practices.

Building on clients' strengths is a fundamental therapeutic principle. The tag "treatment resistant" is often applied to clients in forensic settings, as they commonly have histories of attempted interventions that produced few positive results. Having taken on the identity of being "incorrigible" and "bad," and having seen many helpers give up on them, they are suspicious of change efforts and are skeptical of those who offer treatment. Howells and Day (2003), in discussing interventions for anger, argued that "treatment resistance" is better understood as a matter of client "readiness." Acknowledging a client's strengths helps to bring the client on board with our change efforts, and that is congruent with the MI style that we have advocated.

In addition to Fortune and Ward's (Chapter 21) overview of the integration of the strengths-based Good Lives Model (GLM) into CBT, chapters on sexual aggression (Marshall & O'Brien, Chapter 14; Wheeler & Covell, Chapter 15), substance abuse (Wanberg & Milkman, Chapter 13), working with justice-involved women (Van Dieten & King, Chapter 16), adolescents (Feindler & Byers, Chapter 17), and culturally diverse groups (Day, Chapter 18) recommend an assessment of client strengths. Across these varied chapters there is a solution-focused rationale: discover the client's competencies, enhance them, and utilize them in order to work on the presenting problem.

Similarly, recommendations for assessing client values are advocated in chapters on acceptance-based CBT (Amrod & Hayes, Chapter 3; Gardner & Moore, Chapter 9), the GLM (Fortune & Ward, Chapter 21), and MI (Tafrate & Luther, Chapter 20), although with slightly differing conceptualizations and purposes. Amrod and Hayes (Chapter 3) and Gardner and Moore (Chapter 9) make the argument that values are like psychological anchoring points rather than outcomes. Therefore, in acceptance and commitment therapy (ACT) a distinction is made between goals (things that can be achieved or not achieved) and values (a series of intentional present moment choices likely to lead to a life worth living). For example, a parent might have the goal of attending their children's soccer games and dance recitals. The goal might end once their children outgrows these activities, while the underlying value of "being an involved parent" will manifest itself in a variety of ways throughout different phases of the children's lives.

In the GLM (Fortune & Ward, Chapter 21), values are referred to as "primary goods," broad sources of satisfaction common across many individuals (e.g., having a sense of belonging in the community; achieving excellence in one's work). Criminal behavior is seen as an attempt to fulfill one's values, but in a manner that is antisocial or self-destructive. For example, someone who values belonging to a community may attempt to fulfill that value by becoming part of a gang because they lack the resources to fulfill that goal in a more prosocial manner.

An emphasis on values is also evident in Tafrate and Luther's (Chapter 20) presentation of MI. In assessing their clients' values, practitioners discover a potentially powerful motivator for behavior change. Once broad life values are articulated, practitioners can explore discrepancies between clients' antisocial behavior and stated values. Through MI, clients can build awareness of how specific behaviors may violate values and develop their own arguments for, or against, changing such behaviors in order to live a more harmonious life. Once illuminated, reducing this discrepancy can be a powerful motivator for making changes to antisocial patterns.

While ACT, the GLM, and MI recommend assessing and understanding what is most important to clients, a subtle difference exists regarding the purpose of values exploration. In ACT, the exploration of values is used to establish anchor points to guide future behavioral choices; aiding in minimizing behaviors that will interfere with core values and instead developing behavioral activation plans likely to lead to a more meaningful life. In the GLM, the exploration of values helps the practitioner identify the types of resources the client will need to live according to their values in a constructive rather than an antisocial manner. In MI, values exploration is done to highlight the discrepancies between values and current behaviors as a means of increasing awareness and motivation for personal change.

We have noticed in our consulting work a degree of concern among criminal justice practitioners that discussions around core values will be counterproductive, because clients may hold values and goals that are at odds with prosocial and healthy change. Because of this concern, chapter authors who advocated discussions around core values were asked to provide comments about how to work with clients who seem to possess inherently antisocial values (e.g., being the most respected drug dealer in the neighborhood). Their responses indicate that discussions with justice-involved clients around values and goals invariably revealed commonalties with traditional clients: desires for opportunities to provide for family, connect with others, to have meaningful work, etc. In the majority of instances, antisocial patterns were typically inconsistent with client values, and a reflection of unskilled attempts to meet one's values and cope (albeit unproductively) with the challenges of life.

This is not to say that practitioners will never encounter clients possessing antisocial values. In their responses, the authors of these chapters also made the observation that practitioners, even with the highest skill levels, cannot expect to be effective with all clients. Given the reality of limited time and resources across criminal justice programs, it may be best to focus on those clients who have a willingness to consider making changes to live in a way more consistent with healthy values. It is recommended that forensic CBT practitioners take the time to attempt a deeper and clearer exploration into their client's values and the personal history and life factors that have influenced them. Prematurely assuming that the majority of justice-involved clients have inherently antisocial values shuts the door for powerful discussions about what matters most.

Recommendation 5: Enhance prosocial relationships and networks

Our training in clinical psychology has ingrained in us a tendency to attend to intrapersonal factors when conceptualizing the causes and maintenance of antisocial patterns. Yet two of the

Central Eight risk factors for recidivism concern the potential influence of others on a justice-involved client's behavior: dysfunctional family/marital relationships and criminally oriented peers (D. A. Andrews & Bonta, 2010a). Additionally, a rich literature in social psychology has consistently demonstrated the important influence of situational factors in shaping antisocial behavior (for a detailed review see Zimbardo, 2007). In the present volume, the importance of modifying the social context of justice-involved clients emerges in different forms as a crucial theme across several chapters.

Wanberg and Milkman (Chapter 13), in what they refer to as a sociocentric approach to CBT, consider the fostering of prosocial relationships and networks as foundational to effective treatment. In their approach, cognitive restructuring becomes a means to achieve prosocial outcomes, not just personal growth. Social skills training becomes a means to help clients explore and achieve mutually beneficial outcomes in relationships. The justice-involved client's relationship with the community in which they live becomes restructured along a prosocial dimension through a focus on social and community responsibility.

One of the distinguishing features of the sex offender treatment described by Wheeler and Covell (Chapter 15) is its emphasis on approach goals in addition to the traditional avoidance goals. Sex offenders do not just work on avoiding antisocial or high-risk behaviors, they work toward prosocial goals such as developing long-term, healthy relationships with adults. A similar goal is echoed in Marshall and O'Brien's chapter on the treatment of sexual aggression (Chapter 14), both chapters on the treatment of IPV (Eckhardt et al., Chapter 10; Ronan et al., Chapter 11), as well as the chapters on the treatment of justice-involved adolescents (Feindler & Byers, Chapter 17) and women (Van Dieten & King, Chapter 16).

Encouraging clients to work toward prosocial interpersonal goals is consistent with both the GLM and RNR models. Within the GLM, working with justice-involved clients to desist from high-risk behaviors (avoidance goals) is conceptualized as only part of the change process: helping justice-involved clients develop behavioral paths to a life worth living (approach goals) is an equally important component (Fortune & Ward, Chapter 21). In the RNR model, it is noted that the development of prosocial relationships reduces the client's risk for recidivism because such relationships reduce the opportunity for the influence of the criminal companions (D.A. Andrews & Bonta, 2010a). To this end, we recommend that forensic CBT practitioners consider how their clients can establish and strengthen interpersonal and community relationships in ways that are likely to support a prosocial lifestyle.

Five Topics in Need of More Attention

Beyond the wide-ranging clinical themes covered in the preceding chapters there remain many topical areas that we were unable to address in this volume. In this final section we highlight two under-researched and underappreciated forensic client characteristics that impact treatment need and responsivity: trauma history and intellectual disability. We also highlight three facets of treatment context that require further consideration in adapting CBT to justice-involved populations that were not comprehensively presented in the present volume. In hindsight, we would have wanted to devote a chapter to each of the following topics.

Topic 1: Trauma history

It is widely acknowledged that justice-involved men and women often have traumatic backgrounds. The landmark article by Widom (1989) established that physical abuse in childhood (records-based) was prospectively associated with arrests for violence through young adulthood, controlling for gender, race, and age. In the Pittsburgh longitudinal study of young men from primary school to young adulthood by Loeber et al. (2005), child abuse significantly differentiated violent offenders from non-violent offenders and non-offenders. Spitzer et al. (2001) reported a 56% lifetime rate of trauma exposure in a predominantly male sample of forensic inpatients. A recent review by Ford, Chapman, Conner, and Cruise (2012) estimates that complex trauma has a 35% prevalence among youths in juvenile justice settings, and they argue that aggressive behavior and criminal offending are its sequelae. Novaco and Taylor (2008) found that for male forensic patients with intellectual disabilities, physical abuse during childhood was significantly associated with patient self-reported anger, staff-rated anger and aggressive behavior, and records of physical assaults in a hospital.

Violence-induced trauma is also known to be highly prevalent among females in prisons (e.g., DeHart, 2008; Messina & Grella, 2006; see also Van Dieten & King, Chapter 16). In a population-based study by Pollock, Mullings, and Crouch (2006), 44% of Texas female prisoners had childhood victimization of physical or sexual abuse, and those incarcerated for violent offenses were more likely to have been physically or sexually abused as a child. In adulthood, 61% of women reported physical abuse victimization. Cauffman, Feldman, Waterman, and Steiner (1998) found a 49% prevalence of posttraumatic stress disorder (PTSD) among incarcerated female juvenile delinquents. It is well established that violent victimization is strongly associated post-traumatic stress disorder and anger (e.g., B. Andrews, Brewin, Rose, & Kirk, 2000; Feeney, Zoellner, & Foa, 2000).

Given the high prevalence of traumatic experiences in the histories of both men and women in forensic settings, as well as its clinical and criminological relevance, it is imperative that CBT practitioners develop expertise in assessing and treating trauma symptoms and memories (see Sun, Chapter 22). Unfortunately, there is a paucity of research on the effectiveness of treating PTSD in justice-involved clients. A review of PTSD treatment in correctional settings by Heckman, Cropsey, and Olds-Davis (2007) uncovered a total of eight studies, only three of which had CBT features. All treatments were brief, varying from 3 to 18 sessions. The time is ripe for developing a systematic CBT protocol for the treatment of PTSD for forensic clients. The imagery rescripting described and illustrated by Keulen-de Vos et al. in Chapter 4 is one valuable tool, which could serve as a module within a more comprehensive treatment program.

Topic 2: Intellectual disabilities (ID)

The implementation of CBT to persons with ID, in both research and practice, is predominantly found in the United Kingdom, where it has seen a burgeoning development over the past decade. Curiously, this disparity between the US and UK practice of CBT is also found in the treatment of psychosis, a domain in which British clinical scientists have done extensive research (Birchwood & Trower, 2006; Mueser & Noordsy, 2005; Tarrier et al., 1998), including studies incorporating MI into a CBT protocol for forensic patients with schizophrenia (see Haddock et al., 2003, 2009).

That there are often deficiencies in intellectual functioning among those incarcerated in prisons and jails is well established. For example, Guy, Platt, Zwerling, and Bullock (1985) reported an average IQ in the high borderline range and an average reading level of 6.6 years of education among admissions to the prison system in Philadelphia. Similarly, the California Department of Corrections and Rehabilitation, the largest prison system in the United States, reports annually that the average reading age is seventh grade. Although reports of intellectual functioning among prisoners vary widely, Herrington's (2009) study of men incarcerated in the United Kingdom revealed that 11% had borderline intellectual functioning. A study of Texas prisoners found the average IQ was 90 (SD = 13) and that IQ was predictive of violent prison misconduct, even after controlling for a host of inmate background and prison context variables (Diamond, Morris, & Barnes, 2012).

Intellectual disabilities are relevant to the specific responsivity principle outlined by D. A. Andrews (2012): the style and mode of intervention should be adapted to fit the characteristics of the individual. Therefore, CBT practitioners working in forensic services should become familiar with emerging resources in the application of CBT to people with ID. Taylor, Lindsay, Hastings, and Hatton (2013) present psychological therapies for ID clients in conjunction with a range of disorders (e.g., anxiety, mood, psychosis, anger, sexual offending), as well as guidance for adapting assessment and treatment procedures, including mindfulness and acceptance-based approaches. Lindsay's (2009) review presents ID adaptations for offenders with regard to psychiatric symptoms, anger and aggression, sexual offending, and criminal thinking. An entire CBT protocol for the treatment of anger and aggression with ID forensic patients is contained in two chapters of Taylor and Novaco (2005). As can be seen in Lindsay's review, sex offender and anger CBT programs have produced sustained treatment gains. Whatever reasons have curtailed the use of CBT interventions in forensic services with ID clients, there is no clinical or empirical justification for their omission. Given that rehabilitation remains a broadly accepted tenet of the criminal justice system, we have a prevailing duty to deliver programs that are congruent with the cognitive and social skill levels of the recipients.

Topic 3: Consideration of forensic setting on CBT delivery

Only touched on in the present volume is the influence the forensic setting is likely to have on treatment delivery. More discussion around the characteristics of the setting in which treatment is delivered is required to better adapt CBT to justice-involved populations. The therapeutic context is substantially different between forensic hospitals, prisons, probation offices, community clinics, residential group homes, and private practice. Each setting carries with it its own unique characteristics and challenges. For example, forensic hospitals house patients with serious mental disorders, many of whom have been transferred from prisons whose psychiatric units could not manage their clinical problems or their assaultive behavior. Even in a community context, one can see, for example, considerable differences in scope in the programs described by Feindler and Byers (Chapter 17), ranging from coping skills courses to dialectical behavior therapy to the Multisystemic Therapy for adolescents with serious antisocial behavior problems. The treatment targets and the scope of intervention programs must then vary accordingly. As the field develops we will hopefully see forensic programs more specifically tailored to the unique features of the settings in which they will be delivered.

Topic 4: Consideration of treatment scope

Another area requiring further exploration is the question: *How comprehensive must interventions be in order to be effective?* If the objective is to reduce violent recidivism, then the intervention must be sufficiently comprehensive to affect a multifactorial problem. For example, whatever the value of CBT anger treatment with justice-involved clients (Novaco, 2013), it is best understood as an auxiliary intervention that cannot be expected to reach many of the treatment needs of prisoners or forensic inpatients, nor be expected to substantially reduce violent recidivism. In contrast, one can compare it with the complexity and range of the CBT intervention for high-risk violent offenders by Polaschek, Wilson, Townsend, and Daly (2005) at the Violence Prevention Unit attached to a New Zealand prison, which succeeded in lowering violent recidivism. Their program involved understanding the offense chain, understanding support systems, restructuring offense-supported thinking, emotion management, victim empathy, moral reasoning enhancement, problem-solving skills, relationship skills, relapse prevention, and meeting with family members to facilitate release planning. As noted earlier, forensic CBT programs should seek to provide community-based social supports with family and prosocial peers to help offenders redefine their self-image, establish a prosocial lifestyle, find appropriate jobs, and avoid high-risk people and places. A comprehensive perspective on what is known about effectiveness in reducing violent offending and the challenges that prevail in correctional systems can be found in Dvoskin, Skeem, Novaco, and Douglas (2012).

Topic 5: Multidisciplinary collaboration

Finally, more discussion on collaborating effectively with professionals in other disciplines, a requirement for successful forensic practice in both institutional and community settings, seems warranted. Practitioners working in institutions often have access to auxiliary resources through ancillary professionals and facilities (medical/nursing, social work, security, educational, occupational therapy, and recreation). Level of care staff are easily put off by psychotherapeutic staff who appear insular and disconnected from the practical realities of managing the behavior of high-risk patients. It is in the interest of CBT practitioners to learn about the practices of other professionals serving their clients and to forge alliances with multidisciplinary sectors. Within institutional settings, expertise and evaluative input is easily drawn from affiliated staff and can enhance CBT interventions. Another important asset when implementing programs in forensic institutions is the opportunity to work in a team. Treatment teams provide forums for the incubation of ideas, as well as ongoing support and peer supervision, which are needed when working with high-risk clients.

Concluding Remarks

Looking back on the preceding chapters, we distill five recommendations to enhance CBT with justice-involved clients, and have ordered them not by importance, but by the approximate order in which they present themselves. First, practitioners cannot assume that justice-involved clients are interested in changing the behaviors that led them into treatment in the first place, particularly if treatment was initiated by the court rather than the client. The use of MI skills can help work through this first potential roadblock and help to build the therapeutic alliance and readiness to change. Second, once a relationship with the client is established, a discussion of the antisocial patterns that led to the referral can be helpful in building awareness of a need for change and in focusing attention on larger problematic behavioral patterns than simply the incident that led the client to be involved with the criminal justice system. Third, antisocial patterns are facilitated by antisocial or criminal thinking patterns, and these should be assessed and addressed in treatment. Fourth, successful rehabilitation is not just about what not to do. Instead, antisocial patterns must be replaced with those that are prosocial. Discussions with clients around strengths and core values can identify prosocial goals, potential assets to overcome antisocial patterns, and further enhance motivation to change. Fifth, the influence of dysfunctional relationships and criminal companions on risk for recidivism also means that reducing risk can be aided by the establishment of prosocial relationships and social networks.

We wish to thank readers for spending time with this book. As we conclude, we are mindful of the many clinical concerns and complexities we were unable to address and are optimistic that future scholarship around forensic CBT will fill in those gaps. We hope CBT researchers and practitioners will be an increasingly important voice in the future development of effective interventions for the justice-involved population. We hope this volume serves as a resource in guiding the clinical work that reduces the harm caused by antisocial patterns, and offers justice-involved clients an opportunity to avoid the cycle of recidivism prevalent in today's criminal justice system.

References

Andrews, B., Brewin, C. R., Rose, S., & Kirk, M. (2000). Predicting PTSD symptoms in victims of violent crime: The role of shame, anger, and childhood abuse. *Journal of Abnormal Psychology, 109*, 69–73.

Andrews, D. A. (2012). The risk-need-responsivity (RNR) model of correctional assessment and treatment. In J. Dvoskin, J. Skeem, R. Novaco, & K. Douglas (Eds.), *Applying social science to reduce violent offending* (pp. 127–156). New York: Oxford University Press.

Andrews, D. A., & Bonta, J. (2010a). *The psychology of criminal conduct* (4th ed.). New Providence, NJ: Matthew Bard and Company.

Andrews, D. A., & Bonta, J. (2010b). Rehabilitating criminal justice policy and practice. *Psychology, Public Policy, and Law, 16*, 39–55.

Andrews, D. A., Bonta, J., & Hoge, R. D. (1990a). Classification for effective rehabilitation: Rediscovering psychology. *Criminal Justice and Behavior, 17*, 19–52.

Andrews, D. A., Zinger, I., Hoge, R. D., Bonta, J., Gendreau, P., & Cullen, F. T. (1990b). Does correctional treatment work? A clinically relevant and psychologically informed meta-analysis. *Criminology, 28*, 369–404.

Beck, A. T., Freeman, A., & Associates. (1990). *Cognitive therapy of personality disorders*. New York, NY: Guilford Press.

Beck, A. T., Freeman, A., Davis, D. D., & Associates. (2004). *Cognitive therapy of personality disorders* (2nd ed.). New York, NY: Guilford Press.

Birchwood, M., & Trower, P. (2006). The future of cognitive behavioural therapy for psychosis: not a quasi-neuroleptic. *British Journal of Psychiatry, 188*, 107–108.

Cauffman, E., Feldman, S. S., Waterman, J., & Steiner, H. (1998). Posttraumatic stress disorder among female juvenile offenders. *Journal of the American Academy of Child and Adolescent Psychiatry, 37*, 1209–1216.

Cleckley, H. (1941). *The mask of sanity*. St Louis, MO: Mosby.

DeHart, D. D. (2008). Pathways to prison: Impact of victimization in the lives of incarcerated women. *Violence Against Women, 14*, 1362–1381.

Diamond, B., Morris, R. G., & Barnes, J. C. (2012). Individual and group IQ predict inmate violence. *Intelligence, 40*, 115–122.

Duggan, C. (2009). A treatment guideline for people with antisocial personality disorder: Overcoming attitudinal barriers and evidential limitations. *Criminal Behaviour and Mental Health, 19*, 219–223.

Dvoskin, J., Skeem, J. L., Novaco, R. W., & Douglas, K. S. (2012). *Applying social science to reduce violent offending.* New York: Oxford University Press.

Feeney, N. C., Zoellner, L. A., & Foa, E. B. (2000). Anger, dissociation, and posttraumatic stress disorder among female assault victims. *Journal of Traumatic Stress, 13,* 89–100.

Ford, J. D., Chapman, J., Conner, D. F., & Cruise, K. R. (2012). Complex trauma and aggression in secure juvenile justice settings. *Criminal Justice and Behavior, 39,* 694–724.

Guy, E., Platt, J. J., Zwerling, I., & Bullock, S. (1985). Mental health status in an urban jail. *Criminal Justice and Behavior, 12,* 29–53.

Haddock, G., Barrowclough, C., Shaw, J., Dunn, G., Novaco, R., & Tarrier, N. (2009). Randomised control trial of CBT for psychosis and anger in people with schizophrenia at risk for violence. *British Journal of Psychiatry, 194,* 152–157.

Haddock, G., Barrowclough, C., Tarrier, N., Moring, J., O'Brien, R., Schofield, N., Quinn, J., Palmer, S., Davies, L., Lowens, I., McGovern, J., & Lewis, S. (2003). Cognitive-behavioural therapy and motivational intervention for schizophrenia and substance misuse. *British Journal of Psychiatry, 183,* 418–426.

Heckman, C., Cropsey, K. L., & Olds-Davis, T. (2007). Posttraumatic stress disorder treatment in correctional settings: A brief review of the empirical literature and suggestions for future research. *Psychotherapy: Theory, Research, Practice, and Training, 44,* 46–53.

Henning, K., & Holdford, R. (2006). Minimization, denial, and victim blaming by batterers: How much does the truth matter? *Criminal Justice and Behavior, 33,* 110–130.

Herrington, V. (2009). Assessing the prevalence of intellectual disability among young male prisoners. *Journal of Intellectual Disability Research, 53,* 397–410.

Howells, K., & Day, A. (2003). Readiness for anger management: Clinical and theoretical issues. *Clinical Psychology Review, 23,* 319–337.

Karpman, B. (1941). On the need of separating psychopathy into two distinct clinical types: the symptomatic and the diagnostic. *Journal of Criminal Psychopathology, 3,* 112–137.

Landenberger, N. A., & Lipsey, M. W. (2005). The positive effects of cognitive-behavioral programs for offenders: A meta-analysis of factors associated with effective treatment. *Journal of Experimental Criminology, 1,* 451–476.

Lindsay, W. R. (2009). Adaptations and developments in treatment programmes for offenders with developmental disabilities. *Psychiatry, Psychology, and Law, 16,* S18–S35.

Loeber, R., Pardini, D., Homish, D. L., Wei, E. H., Crawford, A. M., Farrington, D. P., Stouthamer-Loeber, M., Creemers, J., Koehler, S. A., & Rosenfeld, R. (2005). The prediction of violence and homicide in young men. *Journal of Consulting and Clinical Psychology, 73,* 1074–1088.

Maruna, S. (2004). Desistance from crime and explanatory style: A new direction in the psychology of reform. *Journal of Contemporary Criminal Justice, 20,* 184–200.

Maruna, S., & Copes, H. (2005). What have we learned in five decades of neutralization research? *Crime and Justice, 32,* 221–320.

Maruna, S., & Mann, R. E. (2006). A fundamental attribution error? Rethinking cognitive distortions. *Legal and Criminological Psychology, 11,* 155–177.

Messina, N., & Grella, C. (2006). Childhood trauma and women's health outcomes in a California prison population. *American Journal of Public Health, 96,* 1842–1848.

Miller, W. R., & Rollnick, S. (2013). *Motivational interviewing: Helping people change* (3rd ed.). New York, NY: Guilford Press.

Mitchell, D., Tafrate, R. C., Hogan, T., & Olver, M. E. (2013). An exploration of the association between criminal thinking styles and community program attrition. *Journal of Criminal Justice, 41,* 81–89.

Mueser, K. T., & Noordsy, D. L. (2005). Cognitive behavior therapy for psychosis: A call to action. *Clinical Psychology: Science and Practice, 12,* 68–71.

Novaco, R. W. (2013). Reducing anger-related offending: What works. In L. A. Craig, L. Dixon, & T. A. Gannon (Eds.), *What works in offender rehabilitation: An evidence-based approach to assessment and treatment* (pp. 211–236). Chicester, UK: John Wiley & Sons, Ltd.

Novaco, R. W., & Taylor, J. L. (2008). Anger and assaultiveness of male forensic patients with developmental disabilities: Links to volatile parents. *Aggressive Behavior, 34*, 380–393.

Ogloff, J.R.P. (2006). Psychopathy/antisocial personality disorder conundrum. *Australian and New Zealand Journal of Psychiatry, 40*, 519–528.

Parhar, K.K., Wormith, S., Derkzen, D.M., & Beauregard, A.M. (2008). Offender coercion in treatment: A meta-analysis of effectiveness. *Criminal Justice and Behavior, 35*, 1109–1135.

Polaschek, D. L. L., Wilson, N. J., Townsend, M. R., & Daly, L. R., (2005). Cognitive-behavioral rehabilitation for high-risk violent offenders. *Journal of Interpersonal Violence, 20*, 1611–1627.

Pollock, J., Mullings, J., & Crouch, B. (2006). Violent women: Findings from the Texas Women Inmates Study. *Journal of Interpersonal Violence, 21*, 485–502.

Seligman, M. E. (2002). *Handbook of positive psychology.* New York, NY: Oxford University Press.

Simourd, D. J., & Olver, M. E. (2002). The future of criminal attitudes research and practice. *Criminal Justice and Behavior, 29*, 427–446.

Skeem, J., Johansson, P., Andershed, H., Kerr, M., & Eno Louden, J. (2007). Two subtypes of psychopathic violent offenders that parallel primary and secondary variants. *Journal of Abnormal Psychology, 116*, 395–409.

Smith, P., Gendreau, P., & Swartz, K. (2009). Validating the principles of effective intervention: A systematic review of the contributions of meta-analysis in the field of corrections. *Victims and Offenders, 2*, 148–169.

Spitzer, C., Dudeck, M., Liss, H., Orlob, S., Gillner, M., & Freyberger, H. J. (2001). Post-traumatic stress disorder in forensic inpatients. *Journal of Forensic Psychiatry, 12*, 63–77.

Tarrier, N., Yusupoff, L., Kinney, C., McCarthy, E., Gledhill, A., Haddock, G., & Morris, J. (1998). Randomized controlled trial of intensive cognitive behaviour therapy for patients with chronic schizophrenia. *British Medical Journal, 317*, 303–307.

Taylor, J. L., Lindsay, W. R., Hastings, R. P., & Hatton, C. (2013). *Psychological therapies for adults with intellectual disabilities.* Chicester, UK: Wiley-Blackwell.

Taylor, J. L., & Novaco, R. W. (2005). *Anger treatment for people with developmental disabilities.* Chichester, UK: John Wiley & Sons, Ltd.

Trestman, R. L., & Lazrove, S. (2010). On the coming of age of antisocial personality disorder: A commentary on the NICE treatment guidelines for antisocial personality disorder. *Personality and Mental Health, 2*, 12–15.

Widom, C. S., (1989). The cycle of violence. *Science, 244*, 160–166.

Zimbardo, P. G. (2007). *The Lucifer Effect: Understanding how good people turn evil.* New York: Random House.

Index

Forensic CBT: A Handbook for Clinical Practice, First Edition.
Edited by Raymond Chip Tafrate and Damon Mitchell.
© 2014 John Wiley & Sons, Ltd. Published 2014 by John Wiley & Sons, Ltd.